THE UK VINEYARDS GUIDE

Stephen Skelton has been growing grapes, making wine and advising growers on matters viticultural in the United Kingdom since 1975. He is an expert on the wines and vineyards of the United Kingdom and has several books on the subject. He is also a Master of Wine. Further biographical details await you at the end of this book.

THE UK VINEYARDS GUIDE

A GUIDE TO THE VINEYARDS
AND WINES OF THE UNITED KINGDOM
AND THE CHANNEL ISLANDS

STEPHEN SKELTON MW

Published by the Author
December 2009

This edition published by Stephen Skelton
Copyright © Stephen Skelton 2010
1B Lettice Street, London
SW6 4EH
E-mail: spskelton@btinternet.com
Telephone: 07768 583700
www.englishwine.com

ISBN: 978-0-9514703-4-3
Ed: 10-008a

This book, together with "Viticulture – An introduction to commercial grape growing
for wine production",
are available from **www.lulu.com** under the following reference numbers:
UK Vineyards Guide 2010 – Ref: 7848482
Viticulture – Ref: 688007

Acknowledgements

My thanks go to the many friends and colleagues in the wine-producing community in the UK who have provided – sometimes after considerable cajoling – information for the vineyards section of this guide. I would also like to thank Geoff Green for his book designing skills, Nyetimber Vineyard for the provision of the photograph of their Netherlands vineyard for the front cover and for the Freedom of Information Act and the Information Commissioner who together persuaded the Wine Standards Branch to release the Vineyard Register to me.

Introduction to 2010 edition

Since the last edition of this guide was published (in 2008), the rate of planting in the UK has shown little sign of slowing down. This edition contains 439 vineyards, ninety-one more than last time, which cover 1,270-hectares – up by 170-hectares. Although the increase in the number of vineyards is partly explainable by my successful application under the Freedom of Information Act for access to the Vineyard Register (see below), the extra amount of land down to vines in the UK is due to optimism on the part of vineyard owners. Some planting is down to the 'big three' – Nyetimber, RidgeView and Chapel Down – either buying land themselves, or giving out grape-supply contracts to growers, whilst other new vineyards are pure speculation, buoyed up by the good prices that both grapes and wine are achieving and by the many reports of shortages of wine and existing growers saying that 'we can sell all we produce'.

As I said in the introduction to the 2008 edition, this time I really do think the English Wine industry is onto something different and it is my hope that the huge increase in supply – which must eventually come, especially with the large 2009 crop that everyone has just enjoyed – will not lead to massive price cuts and any dumping.

The 2009 harvest remains a miracle to most and after two horrible vintages, a welcome relief. Perfect early spring and flowering weather was followed by an extra-damp July, an indifferent August, but a warm and dry September and October. Sugars rose quite quickly and picking started in late September with early varieties and finished with Chardonnay in the last week of October. The sugar levels on even difficult varieties were outstanding. Reports of 11% natural alcohol and even higher have been commonplace. Truly a vintage of the century.

The access to the Vineyard Register was not an overnight occurrence. I applied under the Freedom of Information Act in 2005, but was rebuffed. In May 2009 I asked again and after 6 months of stalling, the Wine Standards Branch decided that Regulation 436/2009 of August 2009 absolved them from the need to keep the register secret and sent me the full list of 417 vineyard names with declared hectarage, postal town and postcode – full addresses would take a little longer! Having cross-referenced this with my vineyards database, I discovered several things: the WSB's list is somewhat out of date and inaccurate and contains vineyards on it that have been dormant for years and some that have even been grubbed up! However, I now have a list of 130 additional vineyard names to add to the 439 in this book, a total of 569, although I know some of them will undoubtedly turn out to have been grubbed.

Stephen Skelton, Fulham, November 2009

Introduction to 2008 edition

Each time I have written a guide to UK vineyards – and this is number three – we seem to be just about to enter a new phase in our tiny industry's development. In 1989, when I wrote *The Vineyards of England*, English (and Welsh) wines were just becoming recognised by the wider wine world and the prospect of commercial respectability seemed possible. In 2001 when Faber & Faber published *The Wines of Britain and Ireland*, English Wines were well into the commercial mainstream (albeit in very small volumes) and there was a prospect that maybe sparkling wines offered a way out of the seemingly impossible task of making money out of a UK vineyard. In 2008, as I put this version together, the speed of change from a still wine landscape to a sparkling wine one is frightening.

Since 2003, the very hot year which saw Champagne's vineyards wilt in summer temperatures never before seen, UK vineyard owners, many of them completely new to the industry, have planted somewhere around 375-hectares of Champagne varieties, maybe more (the uncertainty is because the collection of official figures lags woefully behind reality). Many of these new vineyards (but by no means all) are either owned by or tied into the big three in sparkling wine – Chapel Down, Nyetimber and RidgeView – who will use the grapes to expand their production. Others have planted sparkling wine vineyards seemingly on spec with little idea of where they will sell their wines. The bold question to ask is: are things different this time?

A rapid expansion of the UK vineyard area is something we have seen before. In the late 1980s, a combination of seemingly buoyant sales of English wines, a general feeling of expansion in the economy and the fear of a possible planting ban saw an unprecedented enthusiasm for vineyards. The official figures show that by 1992 the area under vine, but too young to be in production, had risen to 353-hectares or 33 per cent of the total planted area and the following year, 1993, the total area planted had risen to 1,065-hectares, the highest figure ever (officially) reached and still 73 hectares short of today's planted total of 992-hectares. The result of this rapid expansion was that when the vines started cropping, vineyards and wineries were unable to find a market for their wines in the time scale of still-wine production and the inevitable happened. Many vineyards, large and small, gave up the struggle and went under. By 2003/4, the planted area had fallen to 761-hectares, the lowest since accurate records have been kept. Growers lost many hundreds of thousands of pounds and the number of individual vineyards fell from 479 to 333 and wineries from 157 to 90.

My answer to the 'are things different this time' question is (for me) fairly positive: maybe. The grounds for this guarded optimism are severalfold. The product that will come to anchor the industry is different: sparkling wine rather than still wine. Sparkling wines occupy a much higher price niche than still wines (although of course there are greater costs) and the potential for profits is therefore greater. The best English and Welsh wines, still and sparkling, are genuinely better than they have ever been and more importantly, both the wine trade and the wine buying public believe them to be better. This confidence in the product has come about because the quite significant changes to our climate have meant we can now grow 'classic' varieties and ripeness levels (and therefore quality levels) are improving. For growers there is an additional benefit that has come with climate change: higher yields which can only help increase incomes. For sparkling wines, the time taken from planting to sale is much longer than still wine – at least six years and often much longer – which although adding to the costs of production, is in fact a great advantage. Sparkling wines can be released slowly with stock gaining in maturity and quality: the perceived wisdom is that a sparkling wine with four years bottle age is better than one with two years, the complete opposite of the attitude towards most still English wines. A final factor is one of scale. Although Lamberhurst was, at its peak, as big as Chapel Down is today, the projected sizes of today's big three producers eclipse by a significant margin anything yet seen: Chapel Down, Nyetimber and RidgeView are all talking of 1,000 tonne plus harvests. These sizes give them economies in production and marketing and mean that they can deal with today's major retailers, the high-street supermarkets and off-licence chains. Taken together, I believe these factors make a significant difference to the outlook for UK grown wines – hence my optimism.

However, a market for all the wine from the new vineyards still has to be found and this will, for some growers, be a struggle. As an industry, quality must be at the top of the agenda and as the March 2008 *Decanter Magazine* mega-tasting of sparkling wines showed, at least 50 per cent of the sparkling wines being marketed today are nowhere near the quality of the opposition they face. If you sell a sparkling wine in the £10 to £20 range, it *has* to be of good quality. Only if the industry can collectively face this challenge will it be able to tackle this problem and, in my opinion, a quality scheme for sparkling wines must be introduced as soon as possible. The Quality Wine and Regional Wine Schemes have worked wonders for still wines and a similar scheme can surely do the same for sparkling wines?

As I look back on my 34-year involvement with English and Welsh wines, I still marvel that despite the vagaries of the British weather, the British wine trade and the British wine buying public, there are still hundreds of vineyards, with more hectares of vines than ever and that a new golden age appears to be on the horizon. I hope that this time things really *are* different and that we can make the change from what was once considered a joke into a sustainable industry.

Stephen Skelton,
Fulham, June 2008

Introduction to 2001 edition

The level of production of wine in Britain, Ireland and the Channel Isles is minute. For every one bottle of wine made from grapes grown in our vineyards, there are over 18,000 bottles of wine from other countries and it is therefore hardly surprising that English and Welsh wines – to say nothing of wines from Ireland and the Channel Islands – are sometimes hard to track down. This book is both an introduction to the subject – its past and recent history, present day viticultural and winemaking practices including the major vine varieties being grown today – as well as a guide to some 260 vineyards. As with any book of this nature, there are some omissions. It has not been possible to track down every vineyard and indeed, some vineyards, even though their details were known to me, specifically asked to be left out for privacy reasons. It does, however, contain details of all the major estates both in terms of size and importance and of wine quality.

English wine has been dear to my heart for over 25 years. My career in wine started with a conviction that it was possible to produce good wines in this climate. It had been done in the past – there was a history of viticulture in these islands stretching back to before the Roman invasion – and others around me in Kent were doing it again; why shouldn't I have a go? Of course, the lure of owing a vineyard, of having a bottle of wine with one's name on it is a seductive one and hides the sheer hard work it takes to plant and look after a vineyard, to say nothing of the heartaches over the years.

To pretend that growing grapes and making wine in our climate is always easy would be crazy. Many are the times over the past 22 vintages when I have wished for a slightly better climate, one more naturally suited to growing a species which has its origins in the Middle East. However, my answer to those who have constantly asked me 'why England' is always the same: I say that ripening the grapes is not actually the problem and that in all the time I have made wine in the UK I have never had grapes so unripe that I could not make them into palatable wine. My career in wine has been as fulfilling and rewarding as I had ever hoped and I have enjoyed the 'big fish, little pond' reputation that surrounds English winegrowers wherever they go.

In the introduction to the first edition of this guide, published in 1989, I wrote: *the future of the industry is unpredictable and who knows what developments lie ahead.* I also wrote about the few producers who had started to move away from the Germanic style of wines then being produced and were experimenting with oak-ageing and bottle-fermented sparkling wines. Today, that move has accelerated into a rush. The leaders of the industry are producing still wines with a distinctly New World slant and sparkling wines that are as good (yes, really) as those from Champagne. In addition, there are red wines of genuine interest and sweet wines of an extremely high standard.

These changes have been brought about by the need, in the face of today's competitive wine environment, to sink or swim: there are no half-measures. The UK has a very sophisticated retail wine market and one which does not accept poor-quality, over-priced products. If English and Welsh wines are to stand on the shelves alongside those from the rest of the world they have to be the right quality and the right price. It is a testament to today's growers and winemakers that every major supermarket chain and every major high-street wine merchant (at least in their branches in the southern half of the country) stock at least one home-grown wine.

I do not believe that global warming is having any practical effect upon growing grapes in these islands (if it was, surely we would be enjoying early harvests and higher natural sugar levels?) but growers do seem to be able to ripen grapes more fully and wine quality rises year on year. This is probably due to a better understanding of the correct way to trellis and prune vines and a greater degree of control over diseases. It is also certainly due to more experienced winemakers and better equipped wineries – while stainless steel tanks were only just appearing in UK wineries in the late 1980s, today they are everywhere.

The one really bright star on the horizon is that of bottle-fermented sparkling wines. While I have never been a fan of the classic Champagne varieties, I have to admit that the few specialist producers who have had the courage (and the wallets) to invest heavily in all aspects of the job have pulled off some remarkable coups and proved – at least to themselves and to some of the nation's wine writers – that we really can make sparkling wines of real quality. The only (only!) task now facing them is to convince the public that these wines are worth paying the right price for. Everyone in the industry wishes them good luck.

So what of the future? Most of the early pioneers are no longer alive and, sadly, many of their vineyards have been grubbed-up. Although the number of growers in England and Wales fell from 442 (owning vineyards of one tenth of a hectare or over) to around 370 – a fall of 16 per cent – the productive area of vines has risen from 652 to 835-hectares – a rise of 28 per cent! Clearly there is some consolidation in the industry as the smaller 'hobby' growers get out and the larger, more commercial growers find their feet. This can only be welcomed by those both within and without the industry. Many of these small growers had neither the resources for, nor really the interest in, the production of good wine and their vineyards were often planted on poor sites and with the wrong varieties. Sad though I am to see any vineyard fail, it has to be said that some did the general reputation of our wines no good at all. The next decade will undoubtedly see this consolidation continue. The bigger wineries will get bigger and small producers, unless they can successfully sell their wines direct to the public over the farm-gate, will find life increasingly more difficult. The Internet may well become a valuable way of selling wine and sites like my own (www.englishwine.com) will help spread the word about the subject.

The greatest challenge facing the industry today is that of persuading more buyers – both trade and retail – to buy our wines. The best of our wines are now genuinely world-class and deserve a place on the nation's tables. The recent MAFF grant given to the United Kingdom Vineyards Association (UKVA) and English Wine Producers (EWP) to aid the marketing of English Wine (the Welsh have their own scheme) has given the industry a one-off chance to try and inform the public of its wines. The development of the English Wine Marque is a step in the right direction.

Stephen Skelton
Southwark, August 2001

Introduction to the 1989 edition

English vineyards and English wines were for years a sort of music hall joke: something that only retired people of a military bearing or the odd farmer were involved with. I suppose it was in about the mid-1970s that this attitude started to alter – it may have been the long hot summer of 1976 that had something to do with it, for after that the volume of English Wine available rose dramatically.

Today, with over 2,000 acres of vines planted, the industry is well established. A third of that acreage is too young to be fully cropping, so the true impact on wine supplies has still to be felt. (Compare this, however, to France's 2.6 million acres, and it doesn't seem quite so much!) The quality of English Wines has improved greatly since the early years. Better site and variety selection and better trained and more experienced winemakers have all played their part. Yields per acre still swing violently with the years. Over the past ten we have had about five good years and five bad years, although individual vineyards vary enormously. The past two years have been poor and the whole industry is praying for a run of good ones as stocks are getting low.

I have often been asked why it was that I became involved with growing vines and I really wish I knew the reason. In 1972 we were house-hunting around the villages of Sutton Valence and Ulcombe, right in the middle of the Kentish fruit and hop growing region. I suppose we thought that some of the slopes around there looked ideal for vines and that the idea was worth pursuing. I recall our first visit to an English vineyard, Kentish Vineyards at Nettlestead near Maidstone. At the time it was for sale, and we went along to see if we might buy it. We rapidly realised that we didn't know the first thing about the job and that if we were serious about it we had better get some training.

Two years later, having spent a year in the vineyards and winery at Schloss Schönborn and another year as a guest student at the world famous Geisenheim school of viticulture and winemaking, I felt a little better prepared and in 1977 we established Tenterden Vineyards.

Twelve years on, I am still wondering at the whole business. It seems that there is no slackening of interest. More new vineyards than ever are being planted and established ones are being expanded. The public are as willing as ever to buy our wines, despite prices that some think are high. More and more English Wine is sold directly from the 'farm-gate' to people who come to the vineyard to taste and if they are prepared to buy at £3.50–£4.00 a bottle having tasted the product, who can say that our prices are too high?

The vineyards in this guide range from the minute amateur vineyard with only a few vines, up to the country's largest with over 200 acres. In between are all kinds. Some 75 per cent of the vineyards in this guide are of 5 acres or less, many of them run as part-time enterprises. At the other end, there are some 25 vineyards of 15 acres or more, who between them account for over 50 per cent of the total national acreage. These are vineyards who employ a significant number of people and whose wines are (or will be when their vineyards are fully cropping) widely available.

The future of the industry is unpredictable. With the total UK area now over 500-hectares, the Common Market has now started taking notice of us and a 'Vineyard Register', officially detailing every vine in the country, is in the course of preparation. The quality of English Wines will continue to improve and the styles continue to develop. In the past few years, both bottle-fermented sparkling wines and oak-aged white wines have appeared and been well received. Who knows what developments lie in the future?

Stephen Skelton
Scotts Hall, Ashford, Kent, April 1989

Contents

PART I

CHAPTER 1

Viticulture in the British Isles, Pre-Roman to 1939

Pre-Roman Britain

Whether or not vines were grown, grapes harvested and wine made in Britain before the arrival of the Romans is open to debate and as there are no reliable records pointing one way or the other, it is anyone's guess. The native Celts, heavy drinkers though they were, seem to have preferred beer and mead which they could make from local indigenous ingredients. The Belgae, who had established themselves in the east and south of Britain prior to the Roman invasion, did have a liking for wine, and amphorae[1] dating from before the Roman conquest have been discovered on sites in southern England. Edward Hyams,[2] in his book *Dionysus – A Social History of the Wine Vine,* shows a picture of a fine, 1.25-metre high Roman amphora, together with a silver wine cup, both recovered from the British tombs of Belgic Chieftains of the first century BC. Their strong trading links with France and Italy allowed them to import wine relatively easily and it would therefore seem unlikely that they had any need to establish vineyards in this country. Peter Salway, in his *Oxford History of Roman Britain* (p. 653-4) writes that before the Romans arrived, both Spanish and Italian wines were imported into Britain and that wine also came up the Mosel and the Rhine to Holland and across the Channel, a shorter (and safer) distance than from Mediterranean or Atlantic ports.

Roman viticulture – fact or fiction?

Most books with anything to say about the origins of British viticulture state with absolute certainty that 'the Romans introduced the vine' to these shores and then usually go on to give the impression that swathes of vines covered most of the slopes in southern England. Fields that look like they have been terraced by human hand – which in all probability have naturally evolved or have been created by nothing more than hundreds of years of sheep tramping up and down on them – are especially prone to be said to have been 'a Roman vineyard' when absolutely no evidence for one exists. Place names, such as housing estates called 'The Vines' and roads called

---

1 Amphorae were used for transporting all manner of liquids (wine, olive oil and fish sauce were the most usual) over long distances and their presence therefore does not necessarily confirm a connection with wine.
2 Edward Hyams played a not inconsiderable part in the twentieth-century revival of viticulture in the UK and his story is told in Chapter 2.

'Vinegar Lane', are often trotted out as 'evidence' of viticultural activity in former times, but this is hardly conclusive. In 1893/4 at Tolsey, near Tewkesbury in Gloucestershire, grape seeds and skins (but no stalks) were found, which excited the pro-Roman vineyard enthusiasts as it was known that a group of ex-Roman legionnaires established a colony in the area in the post-Domitian era. However, these seeds could just as easily have come from imported raisins as fresh grapes.

Dr Tim Unwin, in his scholarly book *Wine and the Vine, a historical geography of viticulture and the wine trade*, writes that: *the northern limit of viticulture in the Roman era is widely considered to have been just north of Paris and that much of the evidence adduced in support of the cultivation of vines in Roman Britain has been shown ... to be of dubious validity.* Hyams conjectures that: *vines were introduced by the Romans more by way of an ornamental re-creation of the Mediterranean atmosphere, than for the grapes they yielded.* The Roman historian Tacitus, writing at the end of the first century AD in Vita Agricolae declared that: *our climate was objectionable and not at all suitable for growing vines or olives.* This could suggest that someone had at least tried to establish vines, even if they had been unsuccessful. Archaeological digs of Roman sites in Britain have also failed to uncover any implements specific to viticulture such as the double-sided vine billhook – the *falx vinitoria* – which are a feature of sites on the continent where the Romans grew vines. These are small, easily lost tools and one might have thought that at least a single example would have been found. (Plenty of the usual harvesting and cutting single-sided billhooks used in general agriculture have been found however.) In addition, no winemaking equipment such as the bases of presses or treading troughs,[3] again a feature of overseas sites where winemaking was carried out, has ever been uncovered. The absence of these is perhaps more understandable, as being floor-level constructions they would have normally been removed once they fell into disuse. Of course, the absence of these items neither proves nor disproves anything but it is generally recognised that there is considerable uncertainty about the scope and scale of Roman viticulture. There is plenty of evidence that wine was imported into Britain during the Roman era and it is said that there are streets in St. Emilion paved with stones which came from Britain as ballast. The official Bordeaux wine museum, run by the CIVB *(Conseil Interprofessional de Vins de Bordeaux),* shows a picture of the Silchester wine barrel to illustrate their Roman wine industry! This barrel, made from a silver fir only found in the Alps, was discovered lining the walls of a Roman-era well in the town of Silchester, near Basingstoke.

According to the Roman writer Suetonius, in AD 90 the Emperor Domitian issued an edict forbidding native inhabitants of countries conquered by the Romans from planting vines on their own lands. Of course, this edict – about whose accuracy Hugh

---

3   Although stone treading troughs and press bases have been found on the continent, there is plenty of evidence to show that the Romans preferred to press grapes in large, shallow wooden troughs which would naturally not have survived for over 2,000 years.

Barty-King in his book *A Tradition of English Wine* has expressed some doubts – did not specifically relate to Britain and therefore neither proves nor disproves the existence of vineyards in these islands. The Roman writer Tacitus wrote a biography of Julius Agricola, Governor of Britain from AD 78-85, and in it said of the country that: *with the exception of the olive and vine, and plants which usually grow in warmer climates, the soil will yield, and even abundantly, all ordinary produce. It ripens indeed slowly, but is of rapid growth, the cause in each case being the same, namely, the excessive moisture of the soil and of the atmosphere.* (I could have written much the same thing almost 2,000 years later). The Roman Emperor at this time was Trajan, a Spaniard and an expert in viticulture. During his reign, and that of his successor, Hadrian (who was related by marriage), viticulture was promoted throughout the empire. It seems to me impossible that had Britain been suitable for vines at this time, when the Roman Empire was at its zenith, they would have been planted here.

What does not appear to be in doubt is the Romans' liking for wine, whether home-grown or imported. After Claudius's army invaded Britain in AD 43, wine drinking became more commonplace and whenever Roman villas, houses and garrisons have been excavated, archaeologists have nearly always found remains of wine amphorae and drinking cups. In addition, grape pips and stalks of bunches of grapes are occasionally found, although whether these are from imported or home-grown fruit it is not possible to say. What has never been found is remains of grapes – pips, skins and stems – in a considerable quantity in one place, which, had they been, might well have been evidence of grape pressing and therefore winemaking.

The much-mentioned 'Roman vineyard' at North Thoresby, just south of Grimsby in Lincolnshire is an interesting example of the wish for the existence of Roman viticultural activity taking second place to the evidence. In 1955 a landowner found large amounts of pottery sherds (fragments of pots) on a 4.50-hectare field he owned and had ploughed. Upon investigation, these turned out to be of Romano-British origin dating from the third century with AD 277 being pinpointed as the nearest date for a substantial proportion of the sherds. It was also discovered, by aerial photography and by digging trenches across the site, that the land was covered with an irregular pattern of trenches (wide enough to perhaps be called ditches), about 5 to 6 feet wide, 3 feet to 4 feet 6 inches deep and 25 feet apart (1.52–1.83-metres wide, 0.91–1.48-metres deep and 7.62-metres apart). These trenches contained layers of old pottery and stones (many more than in the adjacent untrenched land) which would appear to indicate an attempt at draining what was (and of course still is) a fairly heavy clay soil. Phosphate levels in the lower levels of the trenches were also tested and found to be eight times higher than in the adjacent land. High phosphate levels are indicative of well-manured land, such as might be found on productive arable or horticultural land. In addition, the humus content of the trenched land was twice as high as untrenched land, again indicating both manuring and residues from plants that grew in the trenches. A report entitled: *A possible Vineyard of the Romano-British period at North Thoresby, Lincolnshire* was written by the archaeologists who carried out the investigations, D. and H. Webster and D. F. Petch, and published in *Lincolnshire History and Archaeology No.2* in 1967. The evidence, the authors suggested, showed that because of the amount of work that went into digging the ditches and importing the stone and pottery to aid drainage, the crop would have had to have been a high-value one. Since olives can be discounted as a commercial crop at these latitudes and other fruits such as apples would not have been of high enough value, it was suggested that grapes were the most likely crop. This was despite the fact that the site was so far north, despite the heavy clay and despite the very wide rows – far wider than vineyards usually planted by Roman vinegrowers. Ray Brock (whose part in the revival of viticulture in Great Britain is fully detailed in Chapter 2), was consulted at the time and he too thought the evidence too flimsy to confirm that this site had been a vineyard. The authors of the report were also somewhat hesitant in declaring the site to have definitely been a Roman vineyard and concluded by saying: *it is tentatively proposed, therefore, that the site at North Thoresby was an unsuccessful experimental vineyard* – hardly a ringing endorsement! Yet, if you Google 'Vineyard North Thoresby', the BBC Gardening website appears, which states: *AD 280 to 285 Evidence suggests a 12-acre vineyard is set up at North Thoresby in Lincolnshire*, which is a lot more positive than 'tentatively proposed'. The evidence actually suggests nothing of the sort. The presence of drained trenches on clay land can be seen as prudent agriculture of the time and when indented (i.e. virtually slave) labour was available, was the cost that relevant? The spacing of 25 feet (7.62-metres) apart would instantly suggest a crop that needed this space – vines do not and would never have done. Apples, pears, plums, walnuts, even mulberries (for silkworms) – all of which the Romans grew in Britain – are just as likely, or even *more* likely, a candidate as vines.

A Roman vineyard discovered

There is however one Roman site in Britain where archaeological investigations have taken place that does lead me to believe that vineyards might have been established during the Roman occupation *on this site*. On a 35-hectare Romano-British site at Wollaston in the Nene Valley (near Wellingborough in Northamptonshire), Ian Meadows, an archaeologist with Northamptonshire County Council, has excavated an area of ground which has revealed a series of parallel trenches covering 7.5-hectares, a substantial area of ground. These trenches, measuring 0.85-metres wide by 0.30 metres deep and spaced 5-metres apart, were excavated to see what they might have been used for. Early theories about irrigation channels or deep cultivation beds were discounted when what appeared to be regular holes along the trenches were uncovered. The formation of deposits within these holes suggested that each hole had contained either a post or the roots of a plant, suggesting a crop that had been grown up some form of trelliswork. These holes, each measuring about 150 mm in diameter and the same distance in depth, were spaced at more-or-less regular intervals of 1.50 metres – the sort of spacing within the row that one would adopt for vines. A Roman writer called Columella, writing in *De Re Rustica* in the first century AD, described growing vines in just such a manner, calling it *pastinatio*.

Soil samples were taken from across the 7.5-hectare site containing the trenches. Simple washing and sieving failed to reveal any plant matter that might give a clue as to what species of plant had been grown in the trenches and therefore Dr Tony Brown from Exeter University, an expert in this type of investigative work, was asked to inspect the samples and see what conclusions he came to. To his surprise, in the samples, he discovered significant numbers of grape vine pollen grains, much larger than could be explained by the grains having been carried there by the wind or by insects. The pollen grains, he suggested, had become washed down the stem of the vines and survived in the soil which had surrounded the roots. In addition, the soil samples revealed that few other plants, such as grasses (whose pollen is very persistent), weeds or other agricultural crops, had been grown on the site at the time. This absence of other pollens would indicate that if there were grasses and weeds they were kept short by mowing so that they did not flower (and produce pollen) or that the soil was kept bare – a common practice in vineyards on the continent both then and now – as a way of improving the microclimate in the vineyard.

Since this initial site was excavated, further sites in this area have been looked at – one of between 4 and 5-hectares and several smaller ones. As at Wollaston, the same pattern of trenches and post holes has been discovered, as well as the conclusive grapevine pollen. Of course, growing vines is one thing, getting them to fruit and grapes to ripen so that wine can be made from them another. The discovery of artefacts associated with winegrowing and winemaking – viticultural implements, amphorae and pressing equipment – would be a huge breakthrough and further strengthen the claims that the Romans introduced vinegrowing and winemaking to our islands.

In AD 277 (some references say AD 280), the Emperor Probus repealed Domitian's earlier edict which prevented native inhabitants from planting vines in countries under the Roman yoke (specifically 'Gauls, Spaniards and Britons'). This may have provided the impetus needed for Britons to start growing vines and supplying both their rulers, and perhaps some of the very early Christians, with home-produced wines.

Salway, in *Roman Britain* states at the end of his section on the Roman-era wine trade that: *The evidence for British vine-growing is so far exceedingly thin, though there is some reason to think this may be partly due to inadequate recording in past excavations. Only at Gloucestershire* [at Tolsey, Tewkesbury, already referred to] *is there anything remotely satisfactory, and that is from the report of a nineteenth-century find and has little detail. If there were British vineyards, we do not know if their production went beyond the small-scale operation that has revived in this country in recent years* [this was written in 1991], *nor whether it extended beyond domestic consumption to the commercial market.*

My considered views on the likelihood of Roman vineyards is that there appear to have been some attempts at viticulture – the pollen grain discovery at Wollaston seems to confirm this – but that the absence of other hard evidence tends to suggest that *successful* vinegrowing and winemaking was, if it existed at all, very limited. Without chemical protection and without modern clones and varieties, growing vines and producing viable crops of grapes must have been a risky enough business even in the much more climatically favourable countries that the Romans occupied. Why on earth would they have wanted to establish vineyards in the climatically hostile British Isles, especially as they could bring all the wine they wanted from overseas? I am still very sceptical about the scope and scale of Roman vineyards and feel the evidence very much suggests that if they did exist, they were very rare and probably unsuccessful. I can easily imagine that over the 300+ years of Roman occupation and influence, some individuals did at least try and grow grapes (vines growing up walls and over pergolas probably being quite common), but their efforts at growing vines on a large scale in the open were not well rewarded and their vineyards were never long-lived. There are, to my knowledge at least (and I would welcome evidence to the contrary), no mentions of wine of UK origin in Roman writings of the time of their occupation of the British Isles. Again, this is another fact that mitigates against anything other than very limited attempts at viticulture by the Romans.

Vineyards after the Romans

When the Romans began to leave at the end of the fourth century, Christianity, which had been made the official religion in the empire by Constantine in AD 312, became more widespread and wine drinking, playing as it did an important part in Christian ceremonies, became more accepted. Whether this was of local or imported wine, it is hard to say. If there were vineyards, then they were undoubtedly attached to religious institutions such as abbeys and monasteries. As the Romans finally left Britain, the country was plunged into what we call the Dark Ages and invasions by the Jutes, the Angles and the Saxons destroyed much of the limited civilisation that the Romans had established during their 300 years of occupation. These warring tribes had neither the time nor the inclination to settle down and become farmers and whatever vineyards there had been at this time undoubtedly became neglected. The early Christians, fleeing from these tribal disturbances, retreated to the corners of these islands – mainly to Wales and Cornwall – taking with them their skills as winegrowers. Whether they set up vineyards is not recorded. Apart from any other reason, many of these early Christian settlements (such as on Lindisfarne and Iona) were in areas not suitable, either then or now, for vines.

When Augustine (the first Archbishop of Canterbury) landed on the Kentish Isle of

Thanet in AD 596, sent to Britain by Pope Gregory to convert the early Celtic Christians to a Roman way of Christian worship, he probably brought wine with him and would have obtained further supplies from continental traders. Whether he planted vineyards in England or not is unknown. It would be nice to think that he did and as Canterbury was (and still is) a favourable area for fruit growing, it is not an impossible thought. As Christianity spread into the climatically more favourable areas of Britain, old skills were revived and there is some evidence that vineyards were re-established. However, given that growing conditions on the continent were more suitable for commercial viticulture and that wine travelled, why would anyone want to establish a vineyard with all its attendant costs, unless they were perhaps members of an enclosed religious order? The fact is that trade with mainland Europe was increasing and it is well recorded that wine played an important part in that trade, thus lessening the need for the home-grown product.

The Venerable Bede, writing in his *Ecclesiastical History of the English People*, completed in AD 731, stated that: *vines are cultivated in various localities* (which Hyams renders as: *it* [Britain] *also produces wines in some places*, a slightly more positive statement than Bede's actual words). Whichever translation is more accurate, Bede's words seem to have been taken by many as proof-positive that vineyards flourished all over these islands. However, Dr Unwin notes that there is doubt about its accuracy and Bede's later assertion that: *Ireland abounds in milk and honey, nor is there any want of vines* was challenged by a twelfth-century writer, Giraldus Cambrensis, who stated that Bede was wrong and that Ireland has not, and never had, vines. In any event, the Vikings, who raped and pillaged their way around much of the country during this period, destroyed many monasteries and once again skills such as vinegrowing and winemaking – had they existed – would have become lost.

King Alfred, the Anglo-Saxon ruler of Wessex from AD 871 to 899, who defeated the Danes at Edington in Wiltshire and saved the country from becoming ruled by Scandinavians, helped re-establish the Christian religion, and in doing so, undoubtedly encouraged a revival of viticulture (although perhaps not of cake-baking). It is often stated that he approved a law giving owners of vineyards compensation in the event of damage by trespassers and this is often taken – once again – as proof-positive that vineyards were definitely being cultivated. Dr Unwin questions this and states that in fact this reference to vineyards occurs in the preamble to Alfred's laws where he is quoting from the Bible (Exodus 20) and that there is *no* mention of vineyards in his own new laws. However, whether or not winegrowing was a feature of ninth-century Britain, there is far less doubt that by the tenth century, vineyards existed and wine was made.

In AD 956 King Eadwig (sometimes called Edwy), Alfred's great grandson, granted Dunstan, the Abbot of St Mary's Abbey, Glastonbury, a vineyard at Panborough in Somerset, and although the original document stating this is lost, it survives in a fourteenth-century copy in the Bodleian Library. Panborough, which has south-facing slopes, is only four miles from Glastonbury where the Benedictine monastery was re-established in AD 940. Somerset appears to have been something of a centre of winegrowing and several vineyards were recorded there, including one at Watchet, overlooking the Bristol Channel, which King Edgar (the Peaceful) granted to Abingdon Abbey in AD 962 (Hooke 1990).

Norman Conquest to the Black Death (1066–1350)

By the time William the Conqueror set foot on British soil in 1066 and defeated King Harold at Hastings, monastic viticulture was at a fairly low ebb. Desmond Seward in his *Monks and Wine* says that there were probably no more than 850 monks in the whole of England at the time of the Norman invasion (although out of a population of just under 3 million this is quite a large number), so it is unlikely that monastic vineyards were widespread. However, not only did King William bring with him French soldiers and courtiers for whom wine was a daily requirement, he also brought French Abbots and their monks who were experienced in winegrowing. The year 1066 marked the start of an era of viticultural activity that would not be matched until the current revival, which began almost 900 years later.

King William's Domesday Surveys,[4] which started in 1086 (and were completed by his son William Rufus after William's death in 1087), covered much of the southern half of Britain and record vineyards in 42 definite locations, with references to vines and wines in another three. Ten of the vineyards had been recently planted, suggesting that the Normans were instrumental in supporting viticulture in their newly conquered country. In a few instances the sizes of vineyards are given in acres, while they are mostly given in arpents (also spelt arpends) – a measure of area about whose exact size there is uncertainty, but believed to be slightly less than an acre. Most of the vineyards recorded were in two main regions: around London and up into Essex, Suffolk and Norfolk (the area covered by the more detailed Little Domesday survey); and in the western counties of Somerset and Dorset. Apart from three in Kent, at Leeds Castle (*two arpents of vineyard*), Chart Sutton, near Maidstone (*three arpents of vineyard, and a park of beasts of the forest*) and at Chislet near Canterbury, and one in Surrey at Staines, there were none recorded in the southern counties of Kent, Surrey, East and West Sussex or Hampshire, the home of a large number of today's vineyards. Was this to do with land ownership, with land use or for some other reason? The probable reason is that these were very heavily wooded regions (timber and charcoal production were extremely important at this time) and the large-scale clearances of land for agriculture had not yet begun. The vineyard listed at Leeds Castle was on land that King William gave to his half-brother Bishop Odo of Bayeux and was given

---

4   The two surveys, Little Domesday and Great Domesday, were by no means a complete survey of the whole of Britain and they excluded Scotland, Wales, much of northern England, as well as the cities of London and Winchester. In some of these places there may well have been vineyards.

together with 8 acres of meadow. Whether today's vineyard at Leeds Castle, planted almost 900 years later, occupies the same site is not known, but the direct connection with the past cannot be denied.

It is also interesting to note that only 12 of the Domesday vineyards were attached to monasteries. The majority of vineyards belonged to nobles and they were undoubtedly cultivated to provide them with wine for their dining tables and altars, rather than with wine for commercial sale. On almost all of the manors where Domesday vineyards were recorded, there were higher-than-average numbers of both slaves and plough teams, and Unwin suggests that these indicate that vineyards were situated on large and prosperous manors. Even King William himself was recorded as owning one at North Curry in Somerset (which had previously been owned by King Harold) and was, at 7 acres, the largest vineyard recorded in Great Domesday. In only one instance do the Domesday Surveys record a yield, that of a vineyard at Rayleigh in Essex. Here, six arpents (about 2-hectares) yielded 20 *modii*, each *modius* being a measure of liquid volume that Barty-King gives as equal to 36 gallons or 164 litres. This gives a yield of about 16 hl/ha which compares not unfavourably to yields in pre-*phylloxera* vineyards in France of the 1860s of 15–20 hl/ha.

The conquest of the country by the Normans led to a large influx of different religious orders. The pre-conquest Benedictine monks were soon joined by Cistercians, Carthusians and Augustinians, all of whom needed wine for their religious observances and the number of vineyards known to be in existence expanded to new levels. There were two main areas of post-invasion monastic viticulture: the southern coastal areas of Kent, East and West Sussex and Hampshire; and Somerset, Gloucestershire and Hereford and Worcester. William of Malmesbury (a historian who, among other things, updated Bede's *Ecclesiastical History of the English People* and who died in 1143) claimed that Gloucestershire was: *more thickly planted with vineyards* than any other part of England. Henry II (1154–1189) had vineyards and the Pipe Rolls[5] of 1155 stated that: *it moreover appearethe that tythe hathe bene payed of wyne pressed out of grapes that grewe in the Little Parke theare, to the Abbot of Waltham, which was parson bothe of the Old and New Wyndsore, and that accompts have bene made of the charges of planting the vines that grewe in the saide parke, as also of making the wynes, whearof somme partes weare spent in the householde, and somme solde for the kinges profit.*

The Diocese of Canterbury had vineyards at Teynham and Northfleet, both near the north Kent coast, on which the Archbishop spent considerable sums of money. His accounts of 1235 show that the expenses of the vineyard were somewhat greater than the income from it, another reminder that England was then (as it still is today) on the margins for successful commercial viticulture. Kent seemed to be quite well endowed with vineyards. Apart from those already mentioned, vineyards were recorded at Great

---

5   Pipe rolls were the Exchequer's 'books' which recorded financial transactions and taxes.

Chart, Leeds Castle, Chart Sutton, Halling, Snodland, Hythe, Folkestone, Barming, Tonbridge, Wingham and Sevenoaks. In Gloucestershire over 20 vineyards are known to have been cultivated in the 1200s, all of them attached to monasteries. Many sources point out that the climate improved for a period of 300 years starting from about the time of the Norman invasion and citing this as the reason why so many vineyards were planted. However, not everyone found this to be the case.

In 1230 the Abbot of Glastonbury, Michael of Amesbury, who had a summer palace at Pilton, Somerset, had a vineyard planted on a sloping site there and in 1235 appointed William the Goldsmith to manage it and make the wine. Although the Abbot liked Pilton – he had a new house built there in about 1240 – his vineyard was relatively short-lived and after 30 years the vines were taken out and the hillside converted into a park for game. It is recorded that the summers between 1220 and 1260 were particularly poor and several other vineyards in the country at that time were grubbed-up. (What makes this tale doubly interesting is that Pilton Manor was the site for one of the first major commercial vineyards to be planted in the twentieth century. Nigel Godden started planting in 1966 and at one time there were almost 8-hectares of vines planted. The wines produced were among the best in the country, winning the Gore-Browne Trophy[6] three times: in 1975, 1976 and 1992. After at least two changes of ownership the vineyard was grubbed-up in about 2001.) By 1270, there were some 14,000 monks in the country (Seward 1979), still out of a total population of less than 3 million. Many of these, especially from the Benedictine and Cistercian orders, lived in enclosed communities dependent on what they could grow and produce to survive. Under these circumstances vineyards would have been a necessity rather than a luxury. Vineyards were also cultivated by the nobles of the period, and many mansions and castles had vineyards attached. The many references to vineyards in the records of the day show that they were far from rare.

Of course, what the wines were like during this era, no one can tell. The wine would have been made in wooden casks and kept in them until consumed. Glass was in use by the nobility for serving wine in and drinking wine from, but bottles and corks were not in use for storing wine in the way we do today. The process of sweetening the juice before fermentation to increase the final alcoholic content was understood and the wines of that period would probably have been high in alcohol as a result. This would have aided their keeping properties and made them more palatable. They would also quite possibly have been sweetened after fermentation with honey and perhaps flavoured with herbs and spices – there were after all no *appellation* regulations or trading standards officers around to enforce labelling laws!

At this time, wines were often made using raisins, either in conjunction with fresh grapes or, when they were not available, on their own. This enabled a 'wine' to be made at any time of the year. The idea that wine is only made from 'the freshly

---

6   The Gore-Browne Trophy is awarded annually to the best wine produced in the UK.

fermented juice of fresh grapes'[7] is relatively recent. Winemakers in the Middle Ages (and indeed up until more modern times) thought nothing of 'improving' wine by adding whatever they felt was required. Apart from water to increase volumes, the marc (the residue left over after the pressing of white grapes or the fermentation of reds) would often be soaked in water to extract some flavour and, with enough sugar added, could be turned into something that vaguely resembled wine (and which could be blended with proper wine). Sometimes pine resin was added to wine, a practice the Romans learnt from the Greeks, and which of course is still practised today in the making of Retsina. The resin helped preserve the wine and cover up any 'off' flavours that might have developed. Grapes were looked upon in those times as just one of the ingredients that went into making wine and without today's rules and regulations, almost anything could be added to help improve the wine or aid its keeping qualities, including brandy. Unripe grapes could also be used to make *verjuice*,[8] which was used in place of vinegar or lemon juice in salad dressings and in cooking.

The wines made at this time were best drunk during the cooler weather of the winter and the spring following the harvest and were probably finished well before the weather warmed up. The principle of conserving wine with sulphur dioxide was not at this stage known about[9] and wines kept for any length of time, unless they were high in alcohol or sugar – both of which can act as preservatives – would have deteriorated quite quickly. Warmer weather would have caused wines to oxidise, spoil and turn to vinegar. Imported wines, of which there appeared to be no shortage, also suffered from the same problems and 'sour' wine (i.e. wine affected by acetic bacteria and turning to vinegar) appears to have been a constant complaint judging by the literature of the time. At least home-produced wine did not have to travel far and probably suffered less than imported wines from oxidation, thus partially explaining its apparent popularity.

Middle Ages to the end of the Great War (1350–1918)

The story of vinegrowing and winemaking during this long, almost 600-year period is one of change and gradual decline. Why viticulture did not really become a viable alternative for farmers and growers, as it did in other countries where monastic

---

7   This is the EU's definition of wine and one accepted worldwide.

8   Verjuice (from the French *vert jus* or green juice) was a sour juice (sometimes also a partially fermented wine), made from soaking unripe grapes (as well as other sour fruit such as crab-apples) in water. Some reports say that verjuice, once kept for several years, turns into an acceptable, wine-like, product. The truth of this last statement probably depends on what else in the larder there is to drink!

9   The Romans knew about the use of sulphur in winemaking and burnt sulphur candles in their barrels to keep them sweet, a practice that English and Dutch wine traders also followed. Sulphur dioxide appears to have been first used in wine in the fifteenth century and a Prussian royal decree of 1487 is apparently the first reference to it as an officially permitted additive to wine.

viticulture was common, is open to debate, but probable changes in the climate, together with commercial and practical considerations, have to be important.

While vineyards were tended by monks and friars and by serfs and slaves who in truth had little option but to do but what their masters required of them, the question of whether growing grapes and making wine was profitable was probably of little consequence. However, when workers required reward for their hire, the question of whether it was more economical to drink home-grown or imported wine became important. Before the Black Death arrived the religious orders had prospered, benefiting from a pliable and available workforce. However, finding their manpower depleted by the plague, they took to leasing their land rather than working it themselves, and their new tenants, dependent upon short-term cash-crops to pay the rent, did not want to grow vines, which then, as now, are expensive to establish and can really only be grown on a long-term basis. This was the time when rural populations declined, when sheep, and perhaps more importantly their wool, became the mainstay of British agriculture. The populations of towns and cities started to expand rapidly and the production of beer and ale[10] became important. Brewing, whose main ingredient, barley, can be stored year-round, can take place week-in and week-out subject to demand and as the water for the brewing process has to be boiled, beer and ale were safer to drink than most of the water then available, as well as being both alcoholic and thirst quenching. The rise of beer as the drink of the masses was probably another contributory factor in the decline of vineyards.

The last vineyard owned by the Archbishop of Canterbury was pulled up in 1350, the year the plague arrived in Kent. By 1370, the number of monks and friars had dropped to 8,000 compared to a high point of 14,000 one hundred years earlier. Although the Dissolution of the Monasteries in 1536, which came about after the break-up of Henry VIII's marriage to Anne Boleyn in 1533, is often cited as being the single event that destroyed medieval winegrowing and winemaking in England, it would appear that by this time many monasteries had already given up viticulture from either lack of manpower, indolence or a combination of both. After the split with Rome and the taking over of the Church's properties by the king, fewer vineyards remained to be cultivated. The new barons and earls who had been handed these religious assets, like their monastic predecessors, wanted rents in cash, not in kind, and there was no place for viticulture.

Climate change can also be introduced as a possible reason why the tending of vineyards started to decline. It is known from a wide number of sources that northern Europe warmed up from about 550 BC until the end of the thirteenth century (known

---

10   At this time the difference between beer and ale was that beer was flavoured with hops, whereas ale was 'un-hopped' i.e. made without hops. Today, ale is made with top-fermenting yeast and matures more quickly than beer which is made with bottom-fermenting yeast and requires more ageing. Both will usually be made using hops (or hop extract) to add flavour.

as the 'Medieval Warm Period'). This meant that in the period between 1100 and 1300, summers were warmer with average temperatures about 1–1.5 °C higher than today's long-term average (although probably about the same as the average over the past ten years), but with colder winters. This equates to today's climate on the Mosel or in Champagne and Chablis. After the mid-1300s, it is said that the British climate generally became wetter, with cooler summers and milder winters, leading to less ripe grapes and more fungal diseases, both of which would have been disincentives to profitable grapegrowing and winemaking. Wine had been coming into the country from Bordeaux since Henry II (who had married Eleanor of Aquitaine in 1152) became king of England. As more and more wine (and other goods) came into the country from overseas, both transport conditions and speeds improved and the transport of wine became cheaper. Also, as techniques of preserving wine for long journeys improved, imported wines arrived in better condition. Thus poorer quality, lower alcohol (and mainly white) home-produced wine stood little chance against the competition. The love by the British of *Bordeaux Clairete*, the light red wines of Bordeaux, stems from this day. England signed trading treaties with Portugal from as early as 1353 and whenever we were at war with France, we were at peace with Portugal, which helped secure a supply of good wine (Fielden 1989). According to Seward, 3 million gallons (136,363 hl) came into the country from Bordeaux in 1448–1449, which on a per capita basis is higher than today's imports from the same region!

Other factors also played their part in viticulture's problems. The Black Death, which lasted from 1348 until the 1370s, not only cut the population dramatically, but forced changes in agriculture which had far-reaching social and demographic effects. Our fields, until then tended on the feudal strip system, became divided up into larger fenced and hedged enclosures. Livestock – in particular sheep – required far less manpower than arable crops, and they became commonplace. The resultant drop in the production of grain was compensated for by a rise in imports from the mainland of Europe, where growing conditions were generally better and supplies could be obtained more easily. This led to an increase in trade of many other goods from overseas, including wine.

During the almost 400 years between the Dissolution of the Monasteries and the end of the First World War, viticulture became very much an occupation for the enthusiast, the eccentric and the adventurous, rather than for the farmer seeking income from his land and although there may have been vineyards cultivated for profit, the best known were cultivated more for pleasure. The reasons why the growing of grapes for the production of wine declined in this period are clear: the climate and the competition. The weather during this later period was, as far as one can ever tell, broadly similar to the weather enjoyed during the first 30–40 years of the current revival of viticulture in the UK, before the recent upturn in temperatures we are now experiencing. Growers faced the same hazards that we now sometimes face (although hopefully not all in the same year): spring frosts, poor weather at flowering, wet summers that bring on mould and rot (although *Oidium Tuckerii* – powdery mildew – was unknown in Europe until 1847 when it was first discovered in Margate in a greenhouse under Mr Tucker's control) and cool autumns that fail to ripen grapes sufficiently. Remember also that growers then did not have today's modern varieties and clones of varieties which have been developed both to fruit and ripen in cooler climates and to resist disease. They also did not have the armoury of modern fungicides which make viticulture a commercial reality for most of today's growers.

Home-produced wines also faced, as they do today, considerable competition from imported wines. From the mid-1300s, the trade in wine from overseas became more and more sophisticated and England (and for that matter Scotland and Ireland) were substantial importers of wine from all over the world. In 1363, Sir Henry Picard, a member of the 'Mystery of Vintners' (the forerunners of the Worshipful Company of Vintners which was incorporated in 1437), gave a celebrated banquet for the kings of England, Scotland, France, Denmark and Cyprus (which is why today the London address of Vintner's Hall is Five Kings' House) and secured for his members the exclusive right to buy and sell wine from Gascony, a region which then supplied much of our wine requirements. Great Britain became renowned for its expertise in selecting, importing, bottling and cellaring wine and much of the finest wine came into ports such as London, Bristol and Leith. Indeed, wines such as Claret, Port, Madeira, Sherry, Hock and Moselle were, if not invented, then refined, nurtured and made more famous by their association with Britain. The taste of wine drinkers of the day was for red wines, for sweet wines and for fortified wines – wines which today's UK winegrowers have difficulty producing regularly and which certainly winegrowers centuries ago would have found even more difficult to produce, given the vine varieties and technology available, as well as the prevailing climate.

With these disadvantages, it is perhaps not surprising that commercial viticulture suffered and vineyard owners, unless they were prepared to support their efforts out of funds from other sources, found more profitable uses for their land. However, despite these problems, vineyards *were* planted and wines *were* made and there are many references to vineyards throughout the literature of the era. Barty-King's book *A Tradition of English Wine* is the most complete history of viticulture in the British Isles yet published and I therefore mention only a few that are of special interest.

James I, who ruled England from 1603 to 1625, had vineyards at Oatlands Park in Surrey, together with a 'vine garden' at St James's Palace, although it is not recorded whether they cropped well (or cropped at all) or whether the grapes were for the table or for winemaking. In 1610, Robert Cecil, the first Earl of Salisbury, asked the great botanist John Tradescant to go to Flanders to search for some suitable vines for his estate. The next year 20,000 vines (at '8 crowns the thousand') were sent from France, with more following in later years. Lord Salisbury's vineyard at Hatfield House, planted on the banks of the river Lee, was well known throughout the seventeenth century. The great diarist Samuel Pepys visited it on 22 July 1661 and commented that he: *walked all alone to the Vineyard which is now a very beautiful place again* (which seems to suggest that it had been neglected previously). He visited it again in 1667. In between these two dates he visited another vineyard owned by Colonell [sic] Blunt near Blackheath. On 1 May 1665 Pepys writes that he went to Greenwich (by boat from Tower Wharf) and then: *to his house, a very stately sight for the situation and brave plantations; and among others, a vineyard, the first I ever did see!* Unless his previous diary entry was incorrect, it would appear that the Hatfield vineyard failed to make much of an impression on him. Blunt's vineyard was obviously famous (and rare?), as several writers of the day visited and commented upon it. Pepys went again to Lord Salisbury's Hatfield vineyard and writes that on 11 August 1667: *the church being done* [it was a Sunday] *we to our inn, and there dined very well, and mighty merry; and as soon as we had dined we walked out into the Park through the fine walk of trees, and to the Vineyard, and there shewed them that, which is good order, and indeed a place of great delight.*

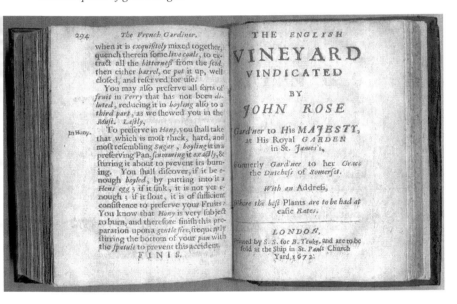

John Evelyn, the writer and diarist, visited Blunt's house and gardens a few years before Pepys in 1655 and wrote that he: *had drunk of the wine of his* [Blunt's] *vineyard which was good for little!* Sir Thomas Hamner (a well-connected Welsh Royalist and gardening authority) also visited it (in 1656). In 1659 Hamner wrote in his *Garden Book* – one of the first and most important books on gardening in English – that: *the vineyard was betwixt one and two acres and was on a hill which lyes full facing on the south.* Hamner describes the system of growing in full and comments that: *the Colonell sayth hee uses no dung or compost to this barren earth of his vineyard, which is very strange.* Evidently, 'the Colonell' had discovered what modern growers know only too well: vines in our climate are often too vigorous and benefit from a lack of nitrogenous fertiliser! Hamner makes no comments on the produce of the vineyard, so perhaps Blunt had stopped offering it to visitors, however grand. Samuel Hartlib, also writing in 1659, said: *I dare say it's probable that vineyards have formerly flourished in England, and we are to blame that so little is attempted to revive them again* (Barty-King 1977).

In 1666 John Rose, *Gard'ner to his Majesty* [Charles II] *at His Royal Garden in St James's*, wrote a treatise (a bare 48 small pages long) on the cultivation of vines in this country called *The English Vineyard Vindicated*. It was republished three times: in 1672, 1675 and 1691. It was also published, bound together with a translation by John Evelyn of *The French Gardiner* [sic] – an important work in its time – in 1669 and 1672 (the date of my copy shown on the previous page). In his opening 'Epistle Dedicatory' Rose states: *I know your Majesty can have no great opinion of our English Wines as hitherto they have been order'd*. He then goes on to say that: *he hopes that by his instructions and recommendations that precious Liquor may haply once again recover its just estimation*. In the preface, written by Philocepos (John Evelyn's pseudonym) it is stated that he (Evelyn): *discussed with Mr Rose the Cause of the neglect of Vineyards of late in England and questioned why they had declined when one considered how frequently they were heretofore planted in this Country of ours*.

In his treatise, Rose discusses the question of site selection, vine varieties, pruning and training (with illustrations) and care of the vines up to the harvest. He was also a commercial nurseryman as on the front page of the treatise he states that it contains: *an Address where the best Plants are to be had at easie rates* and ends it by advertising that he has: *a plentiful stock of sets and plants for sale and that readers may receive them of me at very reasonable Rates*. Rose, obviously a talented gardener, is generally regarded as the first person to grow an *Ananas* (pineapple) in England which he presented to King Charles II in 1671. A picture, painted in 1675 by Hendrik Danckerts, shown here, depicts the occasion.

In 1670, one Will Hughes, a servant to the Right Honourable Edward, Lord Viscount Conway and Kilulta wrote a book entitled *The Compleat Vineyard: or An Excellent Way for the Planting of Vines According to the French and German Manner and Long Practised in England*. In the introduction he states that: *there have been plenty of vineyards in England heretofore; and it is very well known that there are now in Kent, and other places of this Nation, such Vineyards and Wall-vines as produce great store of excellent good wine.* In his book he gives explicit instructions on all aspects of growing vines: site selection and preparation, choice of varieties – *the lesser and greater white Muscadine, the red Muscadine, the Frantinick, the Parsley-grape (more for show and rarity than profit) and the Rhenishwine vine* – how to stake and grow them, when to pick (*when they are ripe by their sweet and pleasant taste*) and finally how to make the most of them in the winery.

Despite these exhortations from the good and the great of the time, vineyards do not appear to have been widely planted. However, a few vineyards were. Richard Selley in his book *The Winelands of Britain: Past, Present and Prospective* tells of a substantial vineyard at Deepdene, near Dorking. Here, Charles Howard, the fourth son of the Duke of Norfolk (whose descendent was to plant one a century later at the family seat, Arundel Castle) planted a vineyard which seems to have been popular with writers. John Evelyn made several visits to Deepdene between 1655 and 1670 but did not mention the vineyard, so perhaps it had not been planted by then. John Aubrey visited in 1673, by which time it had been planted as he produced a plan showing it to cover 7 acres, 1 rood and 1 pole[11] (2.94-hectares). In 1724 Daniel Defoe wrote in his book *A Tour through the Whole of Great Britain* that the vineyard has produced: *most excellent good wines and a very great quantity of them.* By 1762, however, the vineyard appears to have been abandoned.

In 1690 or thereabouts, one 'D. S.' wrote a book called *Vinetum Angliae: or A new and easy way to make Wine of English Grapes, and other fruit, equal to that of France, Spain etc, with their Physical Virtues*, which was published by G. Conyers, at the Gold Ring in Little Britain (price 1 shilling). Chapter 1 of this little book, charmingly entitled *England's Happiness Improved: or, an Infallible Way to get Riches, Encrease* [sic] *Plenty, and promote Pleasure* the author states: *That Vineyards have been frequent in England is apparent, upon the account of the many places now bearing Corn and Pasture retaining that Name* and continues by saying that: *it is the Opinion of the most experienced in this way, that the Southern parts of this Island, with the Industry of the Natives, might produce Vines* [sic] *equal to those of France, either Claret or White-Wines.* D. S. then sets out the precise way in which vines should be planted and manured (although surprisingly does not mention which varieties of grape would be best), then continues with a section entitled: *To make Wine of the Grapes of the Growth of England* in which he details the complete winemaking process finishing with the advice that: *the white grapes not too ripe give a good Rhenish-Tast,* [sic] *and are wonderful cooling.*

Between 1720 and 1732, the young MP for Haslemere, James Oglethorpe, who lived in some splendour at Westbrook Place, Godalming, Surrey, had a 400-yard (366-

---

11   A rood is an area of 1 furlong (660') long by one rod (16'5") wide. There are 4 roods to the acre. A pole is 1/160th of an acre.

metre) wall built in his garden and constructed two broad south-facing terraces on which he planted vines. His wine, which he served at the many soirées and political gatherings that were held there, became well known, as did the French snails which he apparently bred upon the vine leaves. His vineyard and press-house appeared to survive for many years. When Oglethorpe died and his estate was put up for sale in 1785, part of the property was described as: *a Vineyard of considerable extent.* However, 38 years later (1823) when the estate was again sold, no mention was made of a vineyard.

In 1727, a 'Gentleman', known only by his initials S. J. published a relatively large handbook (192 pages) on growing vines (as well as a wide variety of other fruits).[12] It was called *The Vineyard* and in it S. J. writes: *Tis not above a century or two of years since the planting of the Peach, the Nectrine, the Apricot, the Cherry and the Hop, were treated in as ridiculous a manner, as the Vine-yards at present are, in this Country* and goes on to demonstrate in careful detail how vines would grow and fruit in our climate. He continued that: *the Want of Wine in England is not owing to the Unkindness of our Soil, or the Want of a benign Climate, but to the Inexperience of our Natives.* How experienced S. J. was is open to conjecture as he also advocated the growing of almonds and olives, fruits which even the most optimistic of growers would find difficult to grow today in the open air.

Painshill Place

One of the most famous vineyards of this era was that at Painshill Place, Cobham, Surrey (the Painshill junction on the A3 is named after it) which was planted by the Honourable Charles Hamilton in 1740. Hamilton, the ninth and youngest son of the Earl of Abercorn, was an extraordinary character, as so many in this saga seem to be. In 1738, aged 34, he took a long lease on a 300-acre (121-hectare) property and started to construct one of the most fabulous gardens of its time. He landscaped it and filled it with follies including a ruined abbey, a Roman temple, a Turkish tent, a Temple of Bacchus, a fantastic shell-filled grotto, a hermitage complete with hermit,[13]

---

12   Blanche Henrey in *British Botanical and Horticultural Literature before 1800* suggests that the author of this book was in fact Richard Bradley, Professor of Botany at Cambridge. Bradley's publisher, Mears (who also published *The Vineyard*) did publish a number of his works and included a similar title in a list of his publications. However, this is only an assumption based on circumstantial evidence as there is no obvious reason why Bradley would publish this anonymously as he was (apparently) a self-seeking, ambitious man, and no evidence of his travelling in France (the book makes frequent reference to French vineyards). Also, as Bradley was a well-known writer at the time, it is hard to believe that his publisher would fail to use his name in this work and lose potential sales. S. J. was most probably someone else entirely.

13   The hermit was to be paid 700 guineas (for a seven year contract) and had to agree to the following conditions: He must remain for seven years with a Bible, optical glasses, a mat for his feet, a hassock for his pillow, an hourglass for his timepiece, water for his beverage, and food from the house. He must wear a camel robe, and never, under any circumstances, must

and some Roman steps. The gardens also featured a vineyard.

Planted between 1741 and 1743 on a steep 45-degree slope, it overlooked a magnificent lake constructed so that it was 12 feet (3.66 metres) above the level of the nearby river Mole – to stop it becoming flooded – and kept at exactly the same level, summer and winter by being constantly topped up by a 35-foot (10.67-metre) water wheel which brought water up from the adjacent river.

The 'ruined abbey', vineyard and lake at Painshill Place in 2007

Hamilton employed David Geneste, a Huguenot refugee from a winegrowing family from Clairac, a town near Agen in south-west France, to tend his vines and make his wine. Geneste appears to have started working for Hamilton by 1748 as according to letters he wrote to a friend in the October of that year, the vineyard then extended to fifteen *cartonnats* (about 5-acres or 2-hectares) and Hamilton wanted to plant a further 10-acres (4.05-hectares) in the next year. Geneste commented that the vineyard was in a very poor state when he arrived but he soon set-to and by 1750 the vineyard contained six different varieties.Geneste was earning a *louis d'or* (a guinea)

he cut his hair, beard, or nails, stray beyond the limits of Mr Hamilton's grounds, or exchange one word with the servants. Perhaps, not surprisingly, he found it difficult to adhere to these conditions and legend has it that after three weeks he was found in a drunken state in the local inn and was dismissed.

a week, but received gifts from the many visitors to the vineyard. He says that he had already amassed £50 – almost a year's wages – in tips, so presumably must have already been there for a while. Geneste apparently did not know a lot about cultivating vines and in a letter written in December 1750 to his sister Marie, who lived in Bordeaux, he asked when the best time to plant vines was and asked for tips on cultivation. He said that the vineyard was in a very poor state, that there was a lot of work for him to do and no one in the country who knew how to cultivate vines. He also asked for some examples of pruning knives to be sent (via a Mr Thomas Minet in London) so that he could have copies made. He also asked for some wallflower seeds to be sent! He told her that the varieties of vines in the vineyard were *Pied rouge, Muscat blanc, Muscat rouge, Guillan blanc, and Sauviot together with a few other hatifs* (early ripening varieties) whose names he did not know. Almost a year later, on 11 November 1751, he wrote again to say that although they had hoped to harvest eight to ten barrels of wine, continuous rain during flowering had caused most of the flowers to drop and an early frost had prevented what grapes there were from ripening (shades of the 2007 vintage!). The net result was that only two barrels were made, of which half was more like verjuice. He went on to say that this had happened in all the vineyards in England. He ends his letter by asking for recipes for sausages and *boudins* as he had bought a pig which he intended to kill for Christmas and no one locally knew how to prepare these.

In September 1752, the letters show that Geneste was looking for labourers from Bordeaux to come to England to help him and asked that they bring pruning hooks, sharpening stones and *becats*[14] with them. From later letters it appears that two labourers, Matthieu Potevin (a good name for a vineyard worker) and Paul Ducos (the two were in fact cousins), did come over and were followed by two more. In December 1754 Geneste again wrote to his sister to say that four barrels of wine had been made, two of which were sold as *vin de Champaign at 50 pièces* [7 guineas] a barrel.[15] According to further letters between Geneste and his sister, his relationship with Hamilton was not always a smooth one. In a letter dated 30 March 1755, Geneste said that after the white wine from the 1753 vintage had been sold after eight months for 60 guineas a barrel (about £7,500 in today's money), he had asked for a pay rise. Hamilton had responded by saying that he would not pay him a *liard*[16] more and Geneste said he would leave. However, a month before Geneste was due to pack his bags, after a tasting of the 1754 wines (five barrels of white and five barrels of red all made from red grapes) peace broke out between the two and with an offer of an extra £15 a year and free rent, Geneste decided to stay. Geneste also wrote in his letter that there were several gentlemen who are *considering planting* [vines] *and I am the only*

---

14   *Becats* were a type of hoe used for digging and weeding around the roots of vines.
15   See Appendix I on Champagne and the part that the British played in its development into the product we know today.
16   A liard was a French copper coin worth about a halfpenny.

one who can supply stock. He estimated he would be able to sell between 30,000 and 35,000 plants and make a lot of money. He also said that the winter had been very bad and that there were still three *cartonnats* (about an acre) still to prune, but that they hoped to finish that week. Geneste also says that the vines grow extremely strongly with canes 10–15 feet long and as thick as your thumb and asks what he can do about it. The soil he says is as poor as soil can be. He also says that the tools he asked for have been seized by the Customs in London and asks for clogs and sharpening stones. These are to be sent via his nephew in Rotterdam – presumably in an attempt to circumvent the Customs officers. What became of Geneste in the end is unclear. His first wife had died in about 1748 and he later remarried a woman called Elisabeth. They had at least three children, born in 1754, 1757 and 1761. The first two, both called David (the first child died in infancy), were baptised in Cobham (the nearest village to the vineyard). The third child, Benjamin, was baptised in Bermondsey, so perhaps by then they had moved away? [17]

In 1775, after Hamilton had given up the lease to the estate (see below), he wrote to a friend that the vineyard:

was planted with two sorts of Burgundy grapes, the Auvernat, which is the most delicate, but the tenderest, and the Miller grape, commonly called the black cluster, which is more hardy. The vineyard at Painshill is situated on the south-side of a gentle hill, the soil gravelly sand. The first year, I attempted to make red Wine, in the usual way, by treading the grapes, then letting them ferment in a vat, till all the husks and impurities formed a thick crust at the top, the boiling ceased, and the clear Wine was drawn off from the bottom. It was so very harsh and austere, that I despaired of ever making red Wine fit to drink; but through that harshness I perceived a flavour something like that of some small French white Wines, which made me hope I should succeed better with white Wine. That experiment succeeded far beyond my most sanguine expectations; for the very first year I made white Wine, it nearly resembled the flavour of Champaign; and in two or three years more, as the Vines grew stronger, to my great amazement, my Wine had a finer flavour than the best Champaign I ever tasted; but such is the prejudice of most people against any thing of English growth, I generally found it most prudent not to declare where it grew, till after they had passed their verdict upon [This advice, unfortunately, is probably just as true today as it was in 1775!]. *The surest proof I can give of its excellence is, that I have sold it to Wine-merchants for fifty guineas a hogshead; and one Wine-merchant, to whom I sold five hundred pounds worth at one time, assured me, he sold some of the best of it from 7s.6d*

---

17 I am indebted to a small booklet *David Geneste – A Huguenot Vine Grower at Cobham* written by a Mr Claude Martin and republished in the Surrey Archaeological Collections Volume LXVIII, 1971 for much of the detail about Geneste.

to 10s.6d per bottle.

Painshill's vineyard seems to have survived for some years after Geneste left until, in 1773, Hamilton fell on hard times and was forced to give up the lease.

1779 *Vendange at Painshill*, attributed to William Hannan

The new owner (or perhaps tenant) of Painshill was called Benjamin Bond Hopkins. Hopkins kept the park and vineyard as it had been in Hamilton's time (although he tore down Hamilton's 'modest' residence and built a far grander one) and had a picture painted by George Barrett and Sawrey Gilpin of the vineyard, the lake and the Ruined Abbey. This picture, and a painting of the 1779 *vendange* attributed to William Hannan, remain the only known pictures of an eighteenth-century English vineyard. How long the vineyard lasted no one is sure. Hopkins died in 1794 and the estate remained untended until 1804 when it was bought by the Earl of Carhampton. He had no time for vineyards, saying that they were: *fine for eccentric romantics* (Barty-King 1977) and one must assume that whatever remains were still there, were then removed.

What makes the Painshill vineyard doubly interesting is that in 1989 the vineyard site was restored and the vines replanted. Since 1980 the estate has been in the hands of the Painshill Park Trust, a charity dedicated to the restoration of the park in all its glory. As part of this restoration, I was asked to advise on the replanting of the vineyard and in the winter of 1988 the task of clearing the original site, by then covered with 200-year-old Scot's Pines, was started with the help of men and machinery loaned by Sir Robert McAlpine and Sons.[18] After the site was cleared and stabilised, the first vines, Chardonnay and Pinot noir – varieties which we hoped were as near to the originals as possible – were planted, as well as Seyval blanc (in order to guarantee a harvest).[19] Today, the 0.73-hectare vineyard is back in production and attempting to re-create a wine in the style of Hamilton's best *Champaign*!

In 1747, Philip Miller, writing in his *Gardener's Dictionary* (the first edition of which was published in 1731) said: *that there have of late years been but very few vineyards in England though they were formerly very common and that at this day very few Persons will believe it* [wine production] *possible to be effected*. In the sixth edition, published in 1771, Miller recommends planting *the Black Cluster or Munier* [sic] *Grape, as it is called by the French, from the hoary down of the leaves*. (Barty-King surmises that the 'Dusty Miller', a synonym for Pinot Meunier, was named after Philip Miller himself. I find this less than probable and am sure that the name derives from the floury look that the leaves of this vine have.) Miller's *Gardener's Dictionary* became a standard work on all things horticultural and went to nine editions, the last being published in 1835 with the inscription '*Ebenus Cretica*' (no more published) (Gabler 1985). The sixth edition, although it has a large section on wine and winemaking (not only from grapes), has more on growing table grapes than on wine grapes under the entry for *Vitis*.

In 1786, Francis Xavier Vispré (quite a well-known painter at the time) who had owned a small vineyard in Wimbledon (and was later to have another one in Chelsea) and who had given a talk at the Society of Arts two years earlier called *A Plan for Cultivating Vineyards Adapted to this Climate*, wrote a small book on the subject – *A Dissertation on the Growth of Wine in England* – which gained some popularity, even notoriety. This was possibly because he challenged a Revd M. Le Brocq over a system of growing vines that he (Vispré) had been using for some years and which Le Brocq had patented. Vispré writes (with little modesty) that he was: *sufficiently satisfied with the prospect of being the restorer of Vineyards in this country* and was obviously peeved that Le Brocq had stolen both his thunder and apparently his methods.

The Duke of Norfolk had a vineyard at Arundel Castle which appears on maps of the estate dated 1772 and 1804 (Barty-King 1977). H. M. Tod in his book *Vine-Growing in England* states that, in 1763, 60 pipes of Burgundy were made *not as equal to the best of Beaune, but better than ordinary* from the Arundel vines. Quite how long this vineyard was kept going no one appears to be able to say. Even the Duke of Norfolk's archives give no clues.

---

18   At this time I was winemaker and general manager at Lamberhurst Vineyards, owned by Kenneth McAlpine, a partner in Sir Robert McAlpine and Sons.

19   Planting these first vines, which I personally did with the help of Lamberhurst's then vineyard manager, was, as I recall, a fairly strenuous task. The soil was very stony and, on the 45-degree slope, prone to sliding down the hill as the planting holes were dug. However, they mostly established well and are still thriving.

It was in the latter half of the eighteenth century that the cultivation of table grapes became widespread and one of the most important books on British viticulture (British because Ireland, Scotland and Wales had their share of table grapes as well) came to be written. *Speechly on the Vine* as it is known among aficionados – *A Treatise on the Culture of the Vine, Exhibiting New and Advantageous Methods of Propagating, Cultivating, and Training that Plant so as to Render it Abundantly Fruitful. Together with New Hints on the Formation of Vineyards in England by William Speechly, Gardener to the Duke of Portland* – to give it is full title, was written in 1789 and privately published in 1790 by the author for a list of subscribers whose names appear in the front. They comprise a glorious roll-call of the good and the great of the late eighteenth century. In the year that their compatriots in France were suffering a little pruning by the guillotine, Dukes and Earls, Marquesses and Viscounts (and their gardeners) were subscribing to this book on the mysteries of the vine. Speechly's greatest triumph as a gardener seems to have been a bunch of grapes that he produced while employed by the Duke of Portland at Welbeck Abbey, the Duke's mansion near Sheffield, in 1781. The bunch, from a vine of the variety Syrian, weighed 19½ lb, had a diameter of 19 inches, a length of 21¼ inches and was presented by the Duke to the Marquess of Rockingham. Four 'labourers' carried it suspended on a staff, in pairs, by turns to Wentworth House, Rockingham's home, which is near Corby, a distance of almost 75 miles!

The use of glass as a means of cultivating what we might today call 'exotics' came about quite slowly, although it was known about from about the middle of the sixteenth century (at the same time as glass was first used for domestic windows). Early greenhouses were just simple cloches,[20] free standing or leaning against walls. Sheets of glass were at first small and very expensive and the technique of making larger sheets of glass which could then be placed into frames and used to build 'houses' was not learnt until towards the end of the 1500s when French glassmakers settled in Britain. Once secure structures, walled and roofed with glass, could be built which would keep out the elements and could be heated if necessary with stoves or heating pipes, the production of table grapes became commonplace. The literature on growing table grapes in greenhouses in this country published between 1600 and the early 1900s is prodigious. Almost every palace, mansion and large house had its 'vinery' (as well as in many cases a separate greenhouse for growing pineapples, figs, peaches, nectarines and even oranges) and there was tremendous interest in growing vines and Speechly was the expert.

On the subject of vines out of doors for the production of wine, Speechly is not so certain. In the preface to his book he writes:

of all the numerous sorts of fruits indulgent nature produces for the use of

---

20   A cloche is a small tent made (usually) of two panes of glass which, clipped together at the top, sit over the plant providing shelter and additional heat.

man, that of the grape must be esteemed her noblest gift. He then writes that: *the vine's most important and most transcendant* [sic] *article wine, may justly be esteemed as one of our choicest blessings,* but continues: *that from the situation of this island, and from the nature of the Vine, it may seem doubtful whether wine can be made in this country to any considerable advantage.*

In the back of Speechly's book is a chapter titled *On Vineyards* which is largely taken up with an account of the Painshill vineyard that Sir Edward Barry reproduced in his 1775 book *Observations on the Wines of the Ancients.* In it, Speechly says that: *It has much been disputed of late whether the various places in the different counties of England, which still retain the name of Vineyards, were plantations for the purpose of making wine.* He refrains from entering into the debate as he has: *not the least pretension to antiquarian knowledge* but goes on to say that: *good wines are constantly made in a part of Germany which is under the same parallel of latitude with many counties in the Southern part of England* (vineyards in Germany at this period were planted further north than the Ahr region which is today their most northerly growing region), and continues: *that where the situation and soil are proper for Vines, the lands cannot possibly be more beneficially employed than by being converted into Vineyards.*

Speechly cited several other commentators of the day on outdoor viticulture – Vispré, Bradley, Switzer and Barry – and ends by saying: *From the foregoing accounts, it is evident that good wine may be made in this country in a propitious season.* He ends up by saying about the disappearance of vineyards that: *Antiquaries are silent as to the reasons of their being rooted up and neglected.* One cannot help but get the impression from this articulate and seasoned gardener that he felt that outdoor vineyards for wine production were fairly speculative. Speechly, who lived until 1819 (having been born in 1733), went on to write two more editions of his book, the last at 363 pages over half again as long as the first edition and containing much more information about growing *the Ananas or Pine-Apple* – a fruit then all the rage.

Despite all this writing and proselytising about outdoor vineyards, they did not really become widespread or commercially successful. Painshill died out at the end of the 1800s and although there were others, the story was much the same. After the initial enthusiasm of the owners (mainly gentlemen of property and considerable income), the uncertainty of the climate and the variability of the crops in terms of both quality and quantity took their toll and the vineyards were abandoned. Tastes and fashions in wines also changed. Sweet, heavy, fortified wines from 'the colonies' (Australia and South Africa) were popular and home-grown wines could never match these. During the shortages of wine from the mainland of Europe in the latter part of the nineteenth century due to the damage done to vineyards by *Phylloxera*, British companies, as did firms on the continent, started to make wines from both raisins and grape concentrate and the 'British Wine' industry was born. (These so-called wines – under EU law they are not wines as defined, nor for that matter are they very British –

achieved a significant share of the bottom end of the market. This was partly because the raw ingredients were cheap, but also because these wines bore a preferential rate of excise duty. Until the excise duty on these wines was aligned with that of proper wines, British wines, especially fortified examples, were one of the cheapest ways of buying alcohol.)

The Bute family and Castle Coch

The last great experiment into commercial viticulture – that is before the start of the modern revival – was that of Lord Bute's at Castel Coch, to give it its Welsh name, although it is more usually called Castle Coch (sometimes also called in literature of the time Castle Cock). The third Marquess of Bute, John Patrick Crichton-Stuart, was a landowner and industrialist who had the wherewithal to indulge his visions and fantasies. His father, sometimes known as 'the creator of modern Cardiff', had died in 1848, leaving him not only vast properties all over the country, but also the ruins of Castle Coch some 5 miles outside Cardiff.[21] In 1871, the 24-year-old Marquess, who was intrigued by the Middle Ages, commissioned the architect William Burges to restore the castle to its medieval glory. In 1873 he summoned Andrew Pettigrew, his head gardener at his main residence, Mount Stuart on the Isle of Bute in Scotland, and told him of his plan to complete his vision of the past at Castle Coch by surrounding it with a vineyard. He sent Pettigrew to Castle Coch to survey the site and report back.

Not one to do anything by half, the enthusiastic Marquess dispatched Pettigrew to France to see how vines should be grown. Pettigrew appears to have been well looked after especially by a Champagne grower called Jacquesson who arranged for him to travel to Bordeaux in the company of one of his clerks, Scottish by birth but a fluent French speaker, who showed Pettigrew the 1873 *vendange* at Châteaux Latour, Lafite and Margaux. Following his visit, vines were ordered and in the spring of 1875 they

---

21   The Butes' fortunes were founded on their enterprise in building Cardiff Docks, together with the railways that brought coal and iron ore in from the mines. At one point Cardiff Docks handled a third of the world's exports (by weight) of all products.

were delivered, the varieties chosen being Gamay noir and Millie Blanche (also sometimes called Miel Blanc). According to a report by Pettigrew in the Royal Horticultural Society's (RHS) Journal of 1895, only enough vines were procured to cover one eighth of the 3 acres selected to be planted, so Pettigrew took cuttings and had soon propagated enough to cover the full area. The land chosen was the southern slope below the castle, just 4 miles from the Bristol Channel. It had previously been cleared of weeds by taking a crop of potatoes and had then been trenched to help with the drainage. The vines were planted on a 3-foot (0.91-metre) square system, low trained to the ground on a 4-foot (1.22-metre) high trellis, in the manner suggested by Miller in his *Gardener's Dictionary*. (Millie Blanche did not prove to be a successful variety and it was eventually replaced with Gamay noir.)

The years between 1875 and 1877 were good ones – warm and dry – and the vines were able to establish themselves well, while disease, especially *Oidium Tuckerii* was kept to a minimum. In 1877, the first small crop was harvested and made into wine at a winery established in Cardiff Castle (where the original press can still be seen). The grapes were crushed and a little water and 3 lb of cane sugar to every gallon were added and the wine allowed to ferment for 20 days. In that first vintage only 240 bottles were made. Despite *Punch* magazine's assertion that if ever a bottle of wine was produced it would take four men to drink it – two to hold the victim and one to pour it down his throat – the wine was well received and likened to a still Champagne (as the wine from Painshill had been).

Lord Bute was pleased with the success of the original vineyard and asked Pettigrew to look for further sites on his estate. Over the next 35 years, the original site below Castle Coch was expanded and a further two sites were planted. One was at nearby Swanbridge, between Penarth and Barry, where, in 1886, 5 acres of vines were established. Another, a smaller one, was planted at St Quentins near Cowbridge, overlooking the Bristol Channel, but was abandoned owing to it being much too windswept. These two later sites were planted with Gamay noir cuttings from the original Castle Coch vineyard.

Throughout the life of Bute's vineyards there were tremendous variations in cropping levels. In 1879 poor flowering weather caused all the flowers to drop off and no crop was taken at all, Pettigrew reporting that a total of 44.4 inches (1,128 mm) of rain fell on 196 days in the year. Likewise, cold weather caused total crop losses in 1880, 1882, 1883 and 1886. However, 1,500 bottles were made in both 1884 and 1885 and in 1887 3,600 bottles were made, the largest ever crop from the Castle site. Between 1878 and 1892 only white wines were made, but in 1893 the harvest was huge and a good red wine was made. In total, from all the vineyards,[22] 40 hogsheads were made (around 9,560 litres), yielding a total of 1,000 cases of a dozen bottles each

---

22   The actual size of the Bute vineyards is open to question and various publications – contemporary and modern – give different acreages. My best guess is 13-acres (5.26-hectares) in total, not including the unsuccessful site at St Quentins.

(a yield of about 1 tonne/acre or 17 hl/ha). It was calculated that at 60 shillings (£3) a dozen the potential income from the 1893 harvest alone was sufficient to repay all the expenses of the vineyards to date. However, as the usual practice was to leave the wine in barrel for three years and four in bottle before it was sold, there was no prospect of instant income. The wine from the 1893 vintage however, was not a great success. Pettigrew's son, also called Andrew who succeeded him as Bute's gardener, said that although: *a deficiency of three degrees of saccharinity was recorded ... Lord Bute refused to allow the addition of sugar, with the result that only a vinegary liquor was produced.*

Contemporary accounts vary as to the quality of the wine. At an RHS meeting in September 1894, at which Pettigrew (a Fellow of the RHS) gave a talk, samples of the wines were available. Mr Lance, a fellow Fellow and a chemist to boot, said that: *the samples of wine on the table were most excellent as a British production; not only full of alcoholic strength, but containing an agreeable amount of natural acid tartrate, as well as aroma, being far in advance of Grape wines generally manufactured in this country.* However, a Mr W. Roupell, present at the talk, said that: *experiments should be conducted with a view to producing a wine with a character of hock not sherry* indicating that the some of the wines tasted were both high in alcohol and quite sweet (dry sherry being a relatively modern invention). Pettigrew said that the standard winemaking practice was: *to bring the must up to 30° proof* [approximately 15 per cent alcohol] *before putting it in the barrel.* However, Tod, writing in 1911, says that he was a regular visitor to the vineyards and had drunk several vintages. He drank the 1881, listed as a 'still Champagne' in the Angel Hotel, Cardiff (a Bute-owned establishment), so it would appear that there were at least two different styles produced. Tod was not really impressed with the Bute wines and later wrote that there: *was a want of definiteness of style and character in the wines and that they remind one of a mixture of incompatible sorts.* Hardly a ringing endorsement!

Tod continued to keep in contact with Pettigrew and in 1905 was sent some vines of the variety Noir Hâtif de Saumur which he planted in his vineyard at Wisley in 1906. Tod's vineyard, for which he had great plans, seems to have disappeared into the ether and it is unknown whether it produced wine. Tod claimed the (fairly dubious) distinction of having been the person to introduce the French-American hybrid Brandt (often incorrectly spelt as Brant) into the country in 1886 which, being resistant to *Oidium* – then causing very bad damage to vines – he felt was the ideal vine for England. Tod supplied cuttings of both Brandt and Gamay – presumably obtained from Castle Coch – to a Mr James Wingfield who lived in Middlesex, *on a town on the Thames* and who grew vines outside without shelter up until at least 1943. Wingfield moved from the un-named Thames-side town and, as reported in the RHS Journal of December 1943, ended up in Kent where he successfully grew Brandt outside, but only used the grapes for the table or to produce *some very good jelly.* It appears that he did not make wine with them.

Pettigrew continued to look after the vines for Lord Bute and despite a run of dreadful years, continued to be optimistic. The wines were sold locally and the 1881 was sold at the usual price of 60 shillings per dozen and some even higher. A price of 115 shillings (£5.75) a dozen was achieved at auction when the contents of a local doctor's cellar was sold! The wines were also stocked by the London firm of Hatch, Mansfield & Co. and listed as 'Canary Brand, Welsh Wines' with the 1887 vintage available in four different styles all priced: *at 44/- (£2.20) the dozen ... payment of carriage to any railway station in Great Britain or Port in Ireland* included. Interestingly, the styles of wine described mainly appear to be sweet; the four 1887 wines are described as: *Full Golden Rather Sweet, Dark Golden Medium Sweet, A Luscious Golden Wine and Light Golden Mellow.* Considering that Gamay would be considered a difficult variety to ripen today and knowing the usual natural sugar levels of suitable varieties of grapes grown in South Wales today, it is not surprising that considerable amounts of sugar had to be added to the juice before fermentation. Whatever these tasted like, it is fairly certain that they can have borne little relation to the light fruity wines that are produced in South Wales now.

The third Marquess of Bute died in 1900 and was succeeded by his 19-year-old son, who was equally as enthusiastic about the vineyards. Poor vintages, however, coupled with bad attacks of *Oidium*, put the whole venture at risk. Even so, Tod visited the vineyard in 1905 and noted that he found 63,000 vines in fruit which at 3 square feet meant there were some 13-acres (5.25-hectares) cropping. The summer of 1911 was apparently good and wines were made, but even so (according to Barty-King), 3½ lb of sugar to every gallon was required which by my calculations would have raised the potential alcohol by 20 per cent over its natural level. This would indeed have given a very sweet, high-alcohol wine!

The 1911 appears to have been the last successful vintage at Castle Coch. The Great War brought many shortages, and sugar, which then as now, was required to bring the alcohol up to acceptable levels, could not be spared. No wine was made during the war and in 1920 the vines were grubbed-up. Pettigrew junior, speaking to the Cardiff Naturalists' Society in 1926, was fairly clear as to why the vineyards previously under his and his father's care had not survived:

> *here* [in Glamorgan] *viticulture holds out no promise of success. There is obviously something wrong with the climate when even in the most favourable of seasons it has been found necessary to resort to the artificial addition of sugar or (as in some cases) of alcohol.*

He also added that in only seven out of the 45 years did the grapes fully ripen.

The Bute vineyards at Castle Coch and Swanbridge were the last vineyards of anything approaching a commercial size to be planted in Great Britain expressly for the production of wine before the modern revival began in the 1950s. In between 1911 and 1952 (when the first 'revival' vineyard was planted at Hambledon) there were two world wars and the economic upheaval of the depression of the 1930s. It is perhaps not surprising that planting vineyards and making wine did not occur on a commercial scale during this 40-year period.

Table grape production

The cultivation of table grapes, on the other hand, was another matter. Archibald Barron, Superintendent of the RHS Gardens at Chiswick, wrote the first edition of the standard work on table grape production in English *Vines and Vine Culture* in 1883. This book, which ran to five editions, the last being updated by his widow in 1912, gives a fascinating glimpse into the late Victorian and Edwardian era where even people of modest means had servants and those with larger incomes could afford teams of gardeners to grow every type fruit, flower and vegetable. Without the transport systems and refrigeration that we accept today as normal, the only way then to have fresh fruit and vegetables on the table on a regular basis was to grow them yourself. Barron goes into every conceivable detail on growing table grapes, ending up with a list of over 100 varieties, including speciality varieties: producing the largest bunch, for early forcing, for late keeping, for pot culture and so on. He shows how, by using a selection of varieties, it was possible to produce grapes for the table all year round. Black Hamburg, then as now, one of the standard greenhouse varieties, if forced into growth in November, would have ripe fruit by April. For late grapes, a variety such as Gros Colman (or Colmar) could be left hanging on the vine until March or April or, if a proper 'grape house' was available, the bunches could be cut after Christmas and inserted into bottles filled with water on a special angled rack that left the bunches hanging freely. Barron also mentions 'famous vines'. The largest in the country was at Manresa House in Roehampton (once home to the poet Lord Byron's lover, Lady Caroline Lamb) where a single Black Hamburg (planted interestingly to supply *leaves for garnishing*) filled a vinery which was 424 feet (129 metres) long. The most productive vine was at Cumberland Lodge, Windsor Park where another Black Hamburg in a greenhouse measuring 138 feet by 20 feet, produced, in 1879, 2,500 lb (1,134 kg) of fruit. The largest single bunch then recorded was one from a Trebbiano vine which Mr Curror of Eskbank exhibited in Edinburgh in 1875 which weighed 26 lb 4 oz (approximately 12 kg)!

In a short chapter in the 1912 (fifth) edition called *Commercial Grape Culture, or the Growing of Grapes for the Market* Barron writes about the extraordinary increase in the cultivation of *Grapes for sale or market purposes* over the past few years. He says that the popularity of grapes is due to the public's sudden demand for tomatoes, which were then becoming very popular. Growers were able to erect glasshouses, plant them with vines and during the first four or five years while the vine was making wood and not producing fruit, crop the glasshouse with tomatoes. Once the vines were established and fruiting, tomato growing would stop.

Part of the Vinery at Cumberland Lodge, Windsor

Barron says that the centres of table grape production were the Channel Islands, Hertfordshire, Worthing, Finchley and Galashiels in Scotland and that: *several of the Vineyards or Grape-growing establishments are of a leviathan character.* One grower, Rochfords at Cheshunt in Hertfordshire, had over 50-acres (20-hectares) of glass in total, with half of it devoted to vines and expected to send between 300 and 400-tons of grapes annually to Covent Garden. At 2 shillings a pound, this equated to a return of £224 an acre – worth around £15,600 per acre at today's values. Grapes were also sent by *fast steamer* to New York and arrived about ten days after cutting in good condition. Sadly, many of these enterprises ended during the First World War when both manpower and fuel became short and expensive, although a few growers in Worthing did keep their greenhouses producing grapes until the 1930s. The chapter in Barron ends with a paragraph on *Grape Growing in Belgium and France* and reports on similar vine and tomato establishments to those found in England that send large quantities to the markets. It ends by saying that the French had put a tax of *five francs a kilo* on non-French grapes coming onto the Paris markets, the result of which was that the Belgians sent all theirs *to the English markets.*

Two thousand years of grape growing

Anyone looking back over the almost two thousand years from the Roman occupation to the end of the Bute vineyards, would have to admit that outdoor viticulture for the production of wine grapes had been tried and had not proved itself commercially viable in these islands. The historical evidence is of brave attempts – some might even say foolishly brave attempts – at establishing vineyards, only to have them, ultimately, fail. Whatever successes growers did have at growing and ripening grapes, the quality of the wine was never good enough to sustain the vineyard longer than the enthusiasm of the man (and in all this history I can find no record of a female *vigneron*) who initially planted and supported it.

The revival,[23] if that is what it is, had to wait for the arrival of some brave – again, some would call them foolhardy – pioneers who wanted to disprove the theory then abroad that wine could not be made from grapes grown outside in our climate. A combination of new varieties, more suitable growing techniques, better disease control and an acceptance by the public of the style of wines that those varieties produced, were the key elements in that revival.

---

23   I have never been totally comfortable with referring to the twentieth-century recurrence of grape growing as a 'revival', as the wine produced in earlier times was usually not intended for sale and the vineyards were very non-commercial. However, everyone likes to hark back to golden eras (that were often never that golden and usually fairly tarnished), so I will go with the flow on this one and keep referring to it as a 'revival'.

CHAPTER 2

The revival 1939–1951

To say that vinegrowing in the British Isles totally disappeared after the end of the Marquess of Bute's efforts in South Wales would be incorrect. Yes, it would appear that the growing of vines for commercial wine production ceased, but this did not stop there being a lively interest in the growing of grapes for both home-made wines and for the table. No doubt because of the state of the economy after the First World War and during the recession of the late 1920s and 1930s, many more people had vegetable gardens, allotments and smallholdings in which they raised a wide variety of fruits, vines included. In addition, there was a very wide use of glass cloches to protect tender plants and two manufacturers, Horticultural Utilities Ltd of Liverpool and Chase Protected Cultivation Ltd of Shepperton, did much to promote the cultivation of vines under glass, both before and after the Second World War. There were also commercial growers in several places, Worthing in West Sussex and in the Channel Islands to name but two, who still grew grapes for the table under glass (Black Hamburg, Muscat of Alexandria and Gros Colmar were the standard dessert varieties) and who sent the fruit, carefully packed in baskets, up to Covent Garden for sale.

Roland Lee and the Cheshire vineyards

A small booklet called *Growing Grapes in the Open* by Roland Lee, published in 1938, throws some interesting light on the situation before the experimental vineyards at Oxted were planted by Ray Brock (of whom more later). In this booklet (which Brock gave me when I visited him shortly before he died), Lee states that: *the urge to cultivate the grapevine was handed down by my forebears* and said that he came from a long line of vinegrowers, claiming that as long ago as 1249 an ancestor, one Robert Dacre, was *Keeper of Vineyards by Letters Patent*. He also stated that the first vineyard owned by the Lee family was: *established by James Lee in about 1720 ... at Hammersmith* although his business logo clearly states *First Established in 1770*. Barty-King (1977) throws some light on the Lee family and says that they co-owned London's famous 'Vineyard Nursery'. This was started in about 1745 on the site of what had been a vineyard and which is today where Olympia stands. This continued to be owned and operated by the Lees and their descendants until the 1890s. J. C. Loudon's *Encyclopaedia of Gardening* of 1834 says that there had been a vineyard on the site, owned by Lee and Kennedy, and that: *a considerable quantity of burgundy wine was made year by year.*

It is obvious from both the text and the photographs in Lee's booklet that he was serious when it came to growing vines out of doors. At Oxton (near Birkenhead) in Cheshire, he had a 2½-acre (1 hectare) vineyard (said on the back of the booklet to be the *only Outdoor Vineyard Nursery in Great Britain*) of 12,500 grafted vines of three to four years old of the varieties Alicante and Black Campanella (the latter being a black variety which he claimed as his own crossing), together with a vine nursery containing over 90,000 young grafted vines *ready for lifting and sale*. Apart from Alicante and Black Campanella, Lee recommended two other black varieties, Black Hamburg and Reine Olga; and three whites, Roland's Muscatel (another exclusive variety), Royal Muscadine (also known as Chasselas Doré) and Queen of Vineyards. On the inside of the back of the booklet Lee quotes many newspaper and magazine articles (*Daily Mail, The Times, Daily Herald, Ideal Home, Popular Gardening* and several more) all of which take the same line: that they were surprised, but pleased, that someone was showing that table grapes (and nowhere in the booklet are wine varieties mentioned) could be successfully grown outside and ripened without glass. The booklet also contains a report of a radio broadcast (BBC National Service, at 2 pm on Sunday 23 October 1938) in which Mr Middleton (C. H. Middleton, a popular radio broadcaster of the time) and a Mr F. Jordan gave a talk on *Outdoor Vines, Peaches and suitable Fruits for Walls* which: *has done much to popularise outdoor Vines*. This twenty minute talk, sandwiched between 'Troise and his Banjoliers' and 'Charles Ernesco and his Quintet' (how times have changed!) was reported in *The Listener* (a weekly magazine published by the BBC). It made no mention, however, of vines for winemaking.

What happened to Roland Lee and his vineyards remains something of a mystery. In 1939 his company appears to have been taken over by Cheshire Vineyards Ltd, who also claimed the only *Outdoor Vineyard Nursery in Great Britain* (presumably the same one). It is known from a letter dated 1949, sent to Ray Brock by the well-known vine nursery owned by the Teleki family in Austria, that they sent *important quantities of grafted vines* to Liverpool in 1939 and Cheshire Vineyards may well have been the destination. (Unfortunately, all Teleki's records were destroyed through bombing so they could not be certain where the vines had actually been sent.)

After 1939 the trail more or less goes cold. Hyams, in a note after the preface to his book *The Grape Vine in England*, published in 1949, apologises for: *having failed to mention, among recent British vineyards, the Cheshire vineyard of hardy hybrids which was established successfully before the late war,* but gives no further details. Brock mentions neither Lee nor his proprietary varieties in any of his (Brock's) publications even though Lee's booklet was in his possession. Both Hyams and Brock mention Horticultural Utilities Ltd of Rigby Street, Liverpool who, in catalogues from 1951, claimed that at Formby they had *The Principal Vine Nursery of England* (which might imply that there was at least one other). Since Birkenhead and Formby are but 12 miles away (as the crow flies) one has to assume that by then Lee's vineyard had, if not totally disappeared, significantly diminished. Horticultural Utilities published two small pamphlets *Vines under glass and in the open* (ca 1951) and *Successful growing of grape vines* (ca 1954) both written by S. E. Lytle. In the 1951 booklet virtually all of the varieties offered for sale were for table grape production, whereas by 1954, both *viniferas* and hybrids (including Seyve Villard 5/276) are offered, reflecting the early trials work being carried out by Brock at Oxted.

Raymond Bush, a noted writer in the 1930s and 1940s on matters both agricultural and horticultural, has a few brief pages on *Grapes out of Doors* in his book *Fruit Growing Outdoors*, first published in 1935, with subsequent editions in 1942 and 1946. He states that: *Excellent wine has been made from English grapes in the past, and there is no reason why it should not be made today if we cared to grow the grapes.* His varietal selection though, leaves much to be desired. The 1935 edition gives Black Hamburg and Royal Muscadine as the only two varieties worth considering. In the 1946 edition, Bush quotes James Wingfield (the grower who had obtained cuttings of the Castle Coch vines from H. M. Tod) who said that the best reds were *Brandt, Gamay Frew* [sic] *and Black Hamburg* and the best whites *Royal Muscadine and Muscatel.* With hindsight one can now say that the level of knowledge at this time of what vine varieties might be grown to full ripeness and successfully turned into palatable wine without recourse to the shelter of south-facing walls or glass protection was pretty low.

By the mid-1940s, with the country at war, growing grapes commercially to make wine must have seemed a fairly remote prospect. If English and Welsh viticulturalists were ever to succeed, they were certainly by now in need of a Moses to lead them to the promised vineyard. In fact, three people appeared who, in their own ways, brought about the start of the revival which resulted in the planting, in 1952, of the first commercial vineyard of modern times at Hambledon in Hampshire. These three were Ray Brock, Edward Hyams and George Ordish.

Raymond Barrington Brock 1908–1999

Ray Brock must be considered as one of the founding fathers – if not THE founding father – of the revival in wine production in the British Isles. At the start of the war he was in a reserved occupation – he was managing director of Townson and Mercer Ltd, a well known firm of scientific instrument makers – and wished to move away from Croydon where he and his wife lived and which at the time was being heavily bombed.[1] In 1941, they moved to a house called Summerfield which had been built in 1938 by a lady called Doris Foster who, on account of the bombing, wanted to move to Cornwall. Summerfield, at Rockfield Road, Oxted, Surrey, is situated at an altitude

1   In fact, their house in Croydon never suffered damage while the Brocks lived there, but soon after moving to Oxted, a Heinkel dropped a stick of bombs in the garden and blew quite a few tiles off their roof. Always one to see an advantage where others might see a misfortune, Brock excavated the hole and built himself a swimming pool.

of 400–450-feet (122–137-metres) on the South Downs, overlooking the Weald. With considerable enthusiasm and dedication – and aged only 33 – he took to gardening and, as recorded in his meticulously kept garden notebooks, planned and set out a substantial garden, including a large area devoted to fruit trees of all types. In March 1943, on one wall of the house, he planted the first of what was to be many vines – a Brandt which came from Hilliers of Winchester. He noted when it arrived that it was *very badly pruned*!

Among his fruit collection were several peach trees which, he recorded, even at that altitude, ripened their fruit well. As the received horticultural wisdom of the time was that peaches needed at least a south-facing wall, if not a proper peach house, to ripen them, Brock started to consider what other 'exotic' fruits he might grow. His thoughts turned to grapes. In the preface to his book *Outdoor Grapes in Cool Climates* (1949) he writes that:

> *it is now difficult to remember just why we originally decided to start a Vineyard, although we are now very frequently asked this question. We think that primarily we were so interested to discover the ease with which Peaches could be ripened on bush trees out-of-doors, despite all the old gardening literature on the subject* [which said it was impossible to ripen them] *that we felt equally sceptical about the comments on Grapes.*

Brock was an avid user of cloches to advance the maturity of a wide range of different fruits and vegetables and maybe one of the cloche manufacturers had also sparked his enthusiasm. As can be seen from the Roland Lee booklet, there seems to have been considerable press interest in the subject before (and possibly during) the war and perhaps Brock saw grapes as just the challenge he needed. Maybe he had also heard Middleton and Jordan's radio talk? Whatever it was that really started him off down this road, he was determined from the outset to undertake the task in a thoroughly professional manner. Brock had managed to obtain a copy of a book called the *Handbook on Viticulture for Victoria*, written in 1891 by François de Castella and published by the (Australian) Royal Commission on Vegetable Products, which contained some interesting observations on growing vines in cool regions. This book, which Brock considered a masterpiece of compression and lucidity and which gave an extremely clear résumé of grape-growing methods in use in Europe, convinced him that close planting was the key to achieving full ripeness and it did much to determine the layout of the vineyards at Oxted. (In 1946 Brock was amazed to discover that de Castella was still very much alive and well and living in Ivanhoe-East near Melbourne, aged 80 – he was only 24 when the handbook had been written – and conducted a correspondence with him about the Research Station. De Castella recommended planting the Pinots, Riesling, Gamay and Chasselas *very close, so that each will be quite small.* The correspondence went on for a few years.)

The Oxted Viticultural Research Station

Brock's vineyard, initially called the Beebrock Vineyard, but later renamed (with typical Brock confidence) The Oxted Viticultural Research Station, was conceived with great care and a 'grand plan' was drawn up. There would be a number of trial plots with vines planted in accordance with their assumed ripening period (first epoch, second epoch, etc.) and as many varieties as possible would be tried. The accent would be on table grape vine varieties, although some wine grape vine varieties were to be included. The standard spacing was 2-feet (0.60-metres) between the rows and 2-feet-6-inches (0.76-metres) between the vines (impossibly close by today's standards) although some plots were laid out with twin rows 18-inches (0.46-metres) apart with a 2-foot-6-inch (0.76-metre) gangway between the pairs. The lower half of each vine, where the grapes could be expected to appear, would be protected with glass cloches although one plot was to be devoted to closely spaced table grapes without cloche protection. The rows would all run north–south and the borders would be planted with bush peaches and pyramid apples and pears (that is, apple and pear trees trained to a pyramid shape).

The vineyard was located on two separate plots. A small part was in his existing garden and this he prepared in July 1945. The larger part was established on an additional acre (0.40-hectares) of land that adjoined his garden and which his accounts for 1944/5 show he purchased for £980.[2] Brock noted in his garden diary that he: *Spent two whole days (four in all) clearing Vineyard site. Managed to burn everything and got up a lot of Brambles.* On 28 November 1945, Ernie Walker, a man he had taken on to help with the work (and who had been offered the job while still a serving soldier building Bailey bridges in Germany), ploughed the land.[3]

The scientist in Brock could not be suppressed and a long, low wall was built to conduct an experiment into whether different wall surfaces would advance maturity. The wall was constructed in the following sections:

- plain brick left dark red
- plain brick whitewashed
- plain brick blackened
- breeze block whitewashed
- breeze block blackened
- sheet metal whitewashed
- sheet metal blackened.

Two Black Hamburg vines were planted in each section, raised from cuttings obtained from the RHS, and the results eagerly awaited. The experiment was a failure, however. In his Ph.D. thesis of 1951 Brock states that: *this grape* [Black Hamburg]

---

2   At a later stage, Brock decided that he needed more land for the vineyard and was able to buy an additional 2-hectares (5-acres) of land adjacent to the house.

3   Brock always referred to Walker as his 'vinearon'. See section on Hyams for the origin of this term.

appears to be one of the most unsuccessful for outdoor cultivation of all those which have been tested ... and it has completely ruined this experiment.

The major task facing Brock in 1945 was that of locating and obtaining different vine varieties to plant. The effort and diligence – as well as time and money – which he put into this task was formidable and with the benefit of hindsight one can safely say that the real achievement of Brock's vine growing was the assembling and trialing of some 600 different vine varieties over the 25 years of the research station's life. Brock mounted what can only be described as a one-man crusade to collect as many different vine varieties as he could. He already had a few vines on various walls around the house and garden and cuttings were taken (his garden notebook records that he bought a new pair of 'Rolcut' secateurs at a cost of 11/6d for the purpose). He was a member of the RHS – he was invited to serve on their Fruit Group Committee in 1946 – and through their magazine, *The Garden*, he asked members to send hardwood cuttings of vines in their gardens and greenhouses to Wisley (RHS headquarters), which, when they had been rooted, were sent on to Oxted. Hundreds of cuttings arrived, many of them misnamed, many of them duplicates. They were all heeled in and, on 25 March 1946, the first were planted out. Brock, assisted by Walker and another gardener called Poynter, did all the work and Brock noted: *home for 1½ days to plant Vineyard. Weather perfect and up to 56 °F in shade. Frost at night.* Initially, the varieties selected were all standard greenhouse table grape vine varieties: Black Hamburg, Muscat Hamburg, Ascot Citronelle and White Frontignon. These, together with another eight varieties, were set out in rows. He also obtained rooted cuttings from Mr Lytle of Horticultural Utilities. These were, however, but the beginning. By 1947, Brock had 1,400 vines of 29 varieties and by 1950 this had expanded to over 7,000 vines of 60 different varieties.

Brock knew that to find the most suitable varieties, he would have to search far and wide. He therefore set about writing to as many overseas sources as possible and, starting in 1946, he wrote to all the colleges, universities and viticultural research stations in the major winegrowing countries of Europe (including Hungary) as well as to Russia and various parts of the United States. He visited Switzerland in 1946 (and again in 1947) and made good contact with Mr Leyvraz at the Swiss Federal Vine Testing Station at Caudoz-sur-Pully. For several years they sent him (free of charge) cuttings of a large number of varieties from their collection including the two which would, in future years, become the backbone of the early English and Welsh wine industry: Müller-Thurgau (then called Riesling Sylvaner) and Seyve Villard 5/276 (Seyval blanc). Others included Chasselas doré 1921, Perle de Czaba, Pirovano 14 (Bellino x Madeleine Angevine), Seibel 13.053, all of which Brock trialled and thought highly of. Perle de Czaba and Seibel 13.053 (now renamed Cascade) are still to be found in UK vineyards, albeit in tiny amounts. The relationship with Mr Leyraz at Pully continued until at least 1956 and the trade in vines became a two-way affair with Brock offering interesting vines that he had obtained from Germany and Russia back to the Swiss. Leyraz did, however, refuse the offer of Wrotham Pinot cuttings (see Appendix IV for the full Wrotham Pinot story), saying that: *the Swiss did not like this variety.*

Mrs Raymond Brock tending vines at Oxted in 1950

Import licences were obtained from the Ministry of Agriculture, Fisheries and Food (MAFF) and in the spring of 1947, the first vines arrived and were inspected by a Mr Rhodes, the local MAFF plant health inspector and pronounced 'healthy'. The Director of the French vine research station in Colmar, Alsace offered 50 each of Riesling, Portugieser Blau, Chasselas Rosé and Madeleine Royale and these were gladly accepted. Contact with Herr Kessler, Director of the Swiss research station at Wädenswil in Thurgau (which in the 1890s had been where Dr Müller had carried out development work on his eponymous crossing) was made and both valuable advice and varieties were obtained. In 1947 he received a copy of a letter originally sent to East Malling Research Station by a Mr Ed Graville of Junction City, Oregon, who suggested that the genuine American grape (by which he meant *Vitis labrusca* varieties) ought to be grown in Great Britain. Graville wrote that: *they made grand juices, jams and jellies which would add something to the average diet of the Britisher.* Brock wrote back saying that he already grew one – Brandt – and that the flavour was considered: *a little foxy, but not impossibly so for British palates.* A correspondence ensued and yet more varieties arrived.

In 1949 Brock received a letter (complete with a purple censor's stamp) from Andor Teleki, Director of the Österreichen Rebschulen Teleki (renamed Pépinières Teleki S.A. in the 1950s) in Vienna. (The family were responsible for the rootstocks

5BB and 5C, had huge mother-vine nurseries in Austria, Hungary and Israel and were major suppliers of vines for both wine and table grapes.) Teleki said that he had read articles in both the *Bulletin International du Vin* and the *Swiss Wine Journal* about the Oxted Viticultural Research Station and was intrigued to know more. He pointed out that his firm had supplied vines to nurseries in Liverpool and Kent before the war and that he knew of a vineyard near Dartford in Kent (did this belong to Mr James Wingfield who had obtained vines from Castle Coch via Mr Tod?) which had been planted with his vines. Teleki made suggestions for varieties that Brock ought to try and put him in touch with a good friend who was Director of the Luxembourg Experimental Vineyard at Remich. Brock and Teleki corresponded and Teleki suggested a visit to Austria in September 1951. Whether he went or not is not known.

In 1950 Brock made contact with the *Selskabet Til Vinavlens Fremme I Norden* (translated on their headed notepaper as *The society for the promotion of Vine-Grapes in Scandinavia*) based at Hillerød in Denmark. This unlikely sounding organisation put him in touch with growers in Denmark, Sweden and Finland, who in turn passed on varieties obtained from Russia, Hungary and East Germany. He was in correspondence with a grower in Sweden, Nils Endlandsson, who sent him cuttings of a variety called Schmidtmann that had been growing in Sweden since it was sent from Germany in 1860 and which he hoped would do well in English conditions. Endlandsson, who knew other growers in both Denmark and Finland (where it was reported – but not really believed – that a good "Burgundy" had been made from American varieties), also had contact with Hyams and together, the three of them seemed to have operated a vine-swapping service.

Requests for varieties were sent to the University of California, the University of Florida's Watermelon and Grape Investigations Laboratory, Cornell University's New York State Agricultural Experiment Station in Geneva, Professor Duruz at the Oregon State College and the Canadian vine research station at Summerland in British Columbia. Although quarantine regulations made importations of vines difficult from some of these, a few varieties were obtained and eventually planted out at Oxted. Trade with some of these again was a two-way affair, with vines going back to Oregon and Florida in later years.

Surprising as it may seem from today's perspective, there was once a small but vocal body of opinion in some parts of winegrowing Europe (especially the less climatically favoured parts) that supported the use of hybrids for both wine and table grape production. In France there was an organisation called the *Fédération Nationale d'Etudes de la Défense des Hybrides et Métis* (FENAVINO), founded in 1948 in Poitiers, to promote *les cépage Français issus de l'hybridation et metissage* (French vine varieties produced by hybridisation and cross breeding). The growers of non-*vinifera* varieties had a real fight on their hands and were up against the combined forces of the chemical and rootstock industries who did not want to see pest and disease-resistant varieties grown on their own roots, as well as those *vignerons* in the classic areas who saw their livelihoods under pressure from hybrid growers whose costs of production were lower than theirs. Brock subscribed to *La Viticulture Nouvelle*, the magazine of FENAVINO, described in an editorial as *a medium of battle and friendship* (sounds a bit like the early editions of the *Grape Press*[4]) which contained all the latest information and advice for those wishing to grow and make wine without having to resort to grafting or fungicides and pesticides.

Through this magazine Brock was put in contact with nurserymen such as Bertille and Joannès Seyve, Jean Tissier-Ravat, Seibel, Couderc and Landot, all of whom offered advice and vines. He corresponded with other vine-growing members of FENAVINO in the Pas-de-Calais and Finistère in France and in Belgium and Holland, searching for information, advice and varieties. The magazine's editor, Gerard Marot, later contributed a chapter on *Hybrid Vines and the New Viticulture* in the book edited by Edward Hyams (*Vineyards in England* published in 1953) which did so much to promote the revival of interest in viticulture in the UK.

Brock also had close contact with growers in other marginal parts of Europe including Belgium where he got to know Georges Mariman who had a small vineyard at Boitsfort outside Brussels. Here the best varieties were Oberlin 595, Maréchal Foch, Triomphe d'Alsace, Seibel 13/053 and Seyve Villard 5/276 – all hardy hybrids. There appear to have been quite a number of small vineyards in the north-east of France, Belgium and Holland mostly planted just after the war, although a few were much older. Most of these growers seemed to be subscribers of *La Viticulture Nouvelle* and mainly grew French–American hybrids, with a sprinkling of American crosses, although Riesling Sylvaner (Müller-Thurgau) was starting to make its mark.

Belgium has a history of viticulture at least as old as Great Britain's and the earliest recorded vineyard – at Dinant – dates from 854. The Prince-Bishops of Liége owned vineyards situated along the rivers Ourthe and Meuse, and at Huy, where they had their main summer residence, they had vineyards producing wine throughout the period from 900 to 1200. Belgium's viticultural history is in many respects similar to that of Great Britain with vineyards being mainly owned and supported by Royalty and the Church and records show that vines were grown and wines were made up until the end of the 1900s. The vintages of 1836, 1875 and 1882 were noted for their quality and abundance. The varieties being grown for wine production were the Gros and Petit Morillon noir (both clones of Pinot noir), Chasselas blanc and Chasselas-de-Bar-sur-Aube. With the advent of better communications, Belgium became a centre of hot-house grape production with large areas of Black Hamburg – or Hammelshoden as it

---

4   The *Grape Press* is the UK Vineyards Association's (UKVA) magazine. It first appeared as the English Vineyards Association's (EVA) annual newsletter which printed vintage reports, news, views and correspondence. In 1978, under the editorship of the late Ian Paget from Chilsdown Vineyard, it became the bi-monthly *Grape Press*. It continued to be published at this frequency until 2006 when the advent of a monthly e-mail report, the UKVA Bulletin, made this unnecessary. The *Grape Press* is now published twice a year.

was known locally – and Foster's White Seedling being grown for the table. The Comte de Flandres, brother of King Leopold II, was a major glasshouse owner (Basserman-Jordan 1955).

Mariman wrote several articles for a French magazine called *Arbres et Fruits* and a Belgian magazine called the *Courier Horticole* on the subject of *La viticulture septentrionale* (cool-climate viticulture). Two articles in the French magazine of April and May 1948, which Brock obtained, gave the history of vinegrowing in Belgium and north-eastern France (around Lille) and discussed in some detail the varieties that were best suited for a cooler climate. Brock sent Mariman the first tentative results of his Oxted experiments and an article on these appeared in the *Courier Horticole* of May 1950. (It also mentioned Hyams who likewise corresponded with Mariman). In a letter to Brock dated November 1951, Mariman thanks Brock for sending him a copy of his Ph.D. thesis and gives him copious information about the situation in the Belgian and Dutch vineyards, including the one at the Vilvorde Horticultural School near Brussels. He enclosed data covering the 51 varieties grown in the experimental vineyard at the School and gave him the names of 19 varieties that Brock was not growing at Oxted, saying that he must try them and that *success is nearly certain with these varieties*! (Of the 19 recommended, only Maréchal Foch, Léon Millot and Triomphe remain in fairly minor use in the UK today.) He also gave Brock the names of some useful contacts in France and Italy – nurserymen and vine breeders – and it is known that Brock obtained stock from them. Mariman seems to have been something of a guru for cool climate winegrowers and it would be interesting to know how much influence he had over Brock's (and Hyams') choice of varieties. Mariman invited Brock to go and see the vineyards of the Vilvorde Horticultural School, which had substantial variety trials, together with a number of other vineyards in the area. Whether Brock went or not is unknown.[5]

Some of the most interesting and fruitful contacts Brock made were with the German vine breeding stations at Geilweilerhof and Alzey. Geilweilerhof, which was (and still is) at Siebeldingen near Landau in the Pfalz, was established at the end of the war by staff that had fled from the Kaiser Wilhelm Institute (KWI) near Berlin weeks before it was 'liberated' by the Russian Army in 1945. Many of the varieties available immediately after the war in Germany had been developed at the KWI. Geilweilerhof was at that time run by Professor Husfeld (who remained there until 1970) and also employed Peter Morio, a well-known vine breeder, who developed Bacchus, Optima and Morio-Muskat. Apart from breeding new *vinifera* crosses, the station also concentrated on disease resistant hybrids using Seyve Villard 12/375 (Villard blanc) as a crossing partner and was therefore a source of great interest to Brock. Geilweilerhof is today state – as opposed to *Lande* – owned and staffed and concentrates entirely on producing disease-resistant clones and crosses. It is

---

5   For French speakers there is a complete history of Belgian winegrowing on www.vignes.be together with information on the current winegrowing situation there.

responsible for Orion, Phoenix and Regent, all today in use in UK vineyards, as well as Pollux, Sirius, Stauffer and Domina.

In 1949 Hyams got in touch with Husfeld and in 1950 was sent three new crosses: Madeleine Angevine x Gutedal No.3 28/28, Madeleine Angevine x Sylvaner F2 31/16/52 and Madeleine Angevine x Sylvaner III 28/51. Hyams then sent two cuttings of each to Brock to put in his collection at Oxted. In 1955, Brock sent a report on these three varieties to Husfeld which set out how each had fared and ended by saying that only the Madeleine Angevine x Sylvaner III 28/51 was really worth continuing with and the other two crosses had been abandoned. Brock kept in touch with Husfeld, sending him reports from time to time. So fascinated was Husfeld by the apparent success of the Madeleine Angevine x Sylvaner III 28/51, and finding that his own institute had abandoned it some years previously, in 1961 he asked Brock to send him back cuttings so he could evaluate them. This Brock naturally agreed to do and six cuttings were sent the next March. (Husfeld and Morio developed several Madeleine Angevine x Sylvaner F2 crossings including Forta and Noblessa which are still in the Geilweilerhof research vineyard.) Brock also made some suggestions about varieties he thought Husfeld should be using as crossing partners (Gamay Hâtif des Vosges and Précoce de Malingre) and suggested various combinations that he thought might be interesting. Again, Husfeld asked Brock: *to send him the special clonal selections of Gamay Hâtif des Vosges* that he had at Oxted, *as the ones at Geilweilerhof did not show any real promise.*

Brock's Alzey connection was even more fruitful. This research station in the Rheinland-Pfalz had its origins in the Hessiche Rebenzuchtstation which had been located at Pfeddersheim near Worms and whose Director was Georg Scheu. It was moved to Alzey before the Second World War and there Scheu was responsible for developing, through clonal selection, many of the varieties he had raised at Pfeddersheim, as well as breeding new varieties. The roll-call of his crossings is impressive: Scheurebe (1916), Huxelrebe, Kanzler and Septimer (all 1927), Faberrebe, Siegerrebe and Regner (all 1929) and Würzer (1932). He was also responsible for doing much of the clonal selection work on Müller-Thurgau after it had been released by the Swiss in the 1920s and was principally responsible for introducing it into the Rheinland-Pfalz where it became the dominant variety and very widely planted during the post-war reconstruction and replanting of vineyards in this region. He was very interested in breeding aromatic varieties and all of his show good fruit characters. He used Gewürztraminer in many of his crossings as well as table grape vine varieties such as Madeleine Angevine, Courtillier musqué, Chasselas and Luglienca bianca. He smoked a pipe and was (so I am told) always to be seen in his trial plots, pipe in one hand, grape in the other. It is said that he knew when he had a grape worth persevering with when he could detect the fruit flavour through the taste of the tobacco!

In 1957, Brock was sent hardwood cuttings from Alzey of three named varieties,

Müller-Thurgau, Siegerrebe and Scheurebe, and two un-named varieties known only by their breeding titles *Sämling* [seedling] 7672 and *Sämling* 23469. These five varieties were rooted and set out in the vineyard. By 1960, Brock was able to report the following:

Müller-Thurgau *Appears to be identical to Riesling Sylvaner received from the Swiss* [it was] *and giving excellent flavour and bouquet.*

Siegerrebe *Exceptionally early and the grapes have a strong bouquet.*

Scheurebe *Giving big crops, but appears to be very late ripening. Even in 1959* [which was a very hot year] *it only ripened after the late varieties.*

Sämling 7672 *Giving large crops which ripen with Riesling Sylvaner. Considered to be a promising variety.*

Sämling 23469 *Has not produced any flowers and cannot be recommended at all.*

To start with, the parentage of the two un-named seedling varieties was unknown, but a letter to Dr Zimmerman (who later became Director of the Alzey station) produced the information that *Sämling* 7672 was a freely pollinated seedling of Madeleine Angevine and that *Sämling* 23469 was Lubeck x Triomphe. (Interestingly Siegerrebe, which at one time was credited with being a Madeleine Angevine x Gewürztraminer crossing, was unmasked by Heinz Scheu, Georg's son, as also being a freely pollinated Madeleine Angevine seedling). The naming of *Sämling* 23469 never became an issue as it performed badly and Brock soon abandoned it. However, as *Sämling* 7672 was showing promise, Brock started calling it Madeleine Angevine 7672 for the sake of convenience. Unfortunately, as vineyards started to be planted with this variety and wine was made, the 7672 was left off labels and it soon became referred to simply as 'Madeleine Angevine'.

When the UK joined the Common Market in 1973 and had to register varieties with the Commission, this was the name used. Why this was allowed is another matter as Madeleine Angevine is a perfectly well-known table grape variety (a crossing of Précoce de Malingre and Madeleine Royale carried out in Angers in 1859) which only has female flowers and needs to be grown alongside a pollinator. Confusion was bound to arise. When vineyard owners started ordering 'Madeleine Angevine' vines directly from nurseries in France and Germany, that was exactly what they received: the table grape, rather than *Sämling* 7672. This led to growers being less than satisfied with what they thought was Brock's selection and in part gave rise to its reputation as being a poor flowering variety. Brock did sell rooted cuttings of *Sämling* 7672 and even today some vineyards survive from his original cuttings.[6]

---

6   In 1988 I took wood from MA 7672 vines growing in Robin Don's Elmham Park vineyard in Norfolk which had been planted with genuine Brock-grown cuttings. Single buds from this wood was then grafted onto resistant rootstock and the resultant grafted vines sold to various growers around the country. Sharpham Vineyard in Devon is probably the best known and the wine regularly wins prizes with its 'Barrel Select' Madeleine Angevine.

As information about the work Brock was doing at Oxted spread, so did his circle of contacts. In June 1961, he heard from Nelson Shaulis, Professor of Pomology (inventor of the Geneva Double Curtain – GDC – training system and Dr Richard Smart's mentor) at Cornell University, Geneva, New York, who said that he would be coming to the UK in September and wished to visit Oxted. Shaulis paid a visit and in a letter sent in November that year, thanked Brock for his hospitality, saying that the noon meal: *was very delightful, especially the ginger beer shandy* (home-made no doubt). Shaulis also said that he was just concluding the harvest at Geneva and yields had been between 3 and 9 tons per acre! What Brock must have made of Shaulis' views on trellising is not recorded, but it would be interesting to know. Brock's standard planting distances for wine grapes were by that time 3-feet (0.91 metres) between the rows and 4-feet (1.22 metres) between the vines – 3,620 per acre or 8,941 per hectare – with vines Guyot trained low to the ground. The standard GDC is based on 12-feet by 8-feet (3.66-metres by 2.44-metres) spacings – 454 vines per acre or 1,121 per hectare – and is a high-wire cordon system. Brock remained convinced throughout the life of the Oxted Station that close planting encouraged root competition and that vines close to the ground ripened their fruit better as they absorbed heat from the soil. He was certainly not a GDC-man.

Brock also had correspondence with Pierre Galet, long term Director of the Montpellier School of Viticulture and author of several massive works on vine varieties and the science of ampelography (vine identification). In a letter dated May 1961, Galet thanked him for his *Report No.3* and hoped that Brock would get in touch if he needed help, partly because he was always interested in other people's researches into vines, but also because *je suis Anglais par la famille de ma Mère* (I am English from my mother's family) – what better reason?

Brock also had quite extensive contacts with a variety of Russian institutions and, as ever, vines were both received and sent. In 1961, Brock was sent some cuttings by a Mr G. G. Yearsley of Grantham, Lincolnshire who had received some new varieties from a friend at the Moscow Botanical Gardens. One of these was Saperavi Severnyi, a crossing of Saperavi (a native variety from Georgia) and Severnyi (a crossing of Seyanets Malengra and *Amurensis)* which had been bred at the All-Russia Research Institiute of Viticulture and Winemaking at Novocherkassk in Rostov Province . Yearsley thought highly of it, mainly because it was very early (which it would have to have been to ripen in Grantham!). Brock, however, never thought much of it. It is interesting to note that Seyanets Malengra was one of the varieties that went into Rondo which Professor Helmut Becker developed at Geisenheim Research Station in Germany and is one of the major red varieties grown in the UK today.

In 1965, Brock received a letter from Mr Ibrahim Aitov, a 75-year-old scientist who worked at the All-Russia Research Institute He had been sent an extract from Brock's *Report No.4* which gave details of two *Amurensis* crosses which were on trial at Oxted and of which Brock thought quite highly. They had come to Oxted via

Yearsley and were named Fioletovyi Rannii (Early Violet) – Saperavi Severnyi x Muscat Hamburg – and Early Ripening (of unknown parentage). Brock, not knowing anything about their parentage at the time he received them, had taken it upon himself to rename them and had called them Gagarin Blue and Terseshkova (in honour of the first astronauts). In a reply to Aitov he sent copies of *Reports Nos. 3 and 4* and asked for more details about the vines that he had and asked him to send some wine from these two varieties (which Aitov had offered to do). In due course the wine arrived and Brock, in reply, sent him two pairs of secateurs and eight pencils (both probably being in short supply in Russia at the time and therefore highly prized). Aitov wrote that he had given one pair of secateurs and four pencils to his Director, Yakov Potapenko, who was very grateful for the gift and asked Brock to send two more pairs of the Lion brand secateurs, one of them required by the Institute for their collection. (It would be fascinating to know if this collection, complete with Lion brand secateurs, still exists.) Aitov said that Potapenko had been to Moscow to try and get an export permit to send cuttings to the UK (and Canada) but without success as the registration of the varieties had not yet been completed. He added: *if you should arrive in the USSR in the autumn you could take the cuttings yourself*! Brock never went there.

In 1965, Brock conducted a correspondence with a Professeur Henri Brécot who had recently retired after 40 years working with vines, 30 of them at the Centre for Viticultural Research at the School of Agriculture in La Mothe-Achard, a town near the coast between Nantes and La Rochelle. Brécot had been President of FENAVINO in the Vendée and had, in his time at the School, been a great proponent of disease resistant hybrids. Brécot, who was now a brother at St Gabriel's College in Putney, had written an article for *La Viticulture Nouvelle* on grapegrowing in England and needed it proof-read by Brock. Brécot also arranged for cuttings of Seibel 11701, Joannès Seyve 24.651 and Castel 19.637 to be sent to Oxted from the School, as well as some wines from the Vendeé region. Brock was very pleased that Brécot had made contact, took him out to lunch on several occasions and took delight in showing him the vines at Oxted.

A grower in New Zealand, E. D. Forester, who grew vines at Rotorua in the centre of the North Island, visited Oxted in 1965 (Brock was unfortunately away at the time and Forester had to make do with Ernie Walker) and, on returning home, wrote to Brock suggesting that the only vines that would thrive in our climate were American hybrids. Despite Brock's scepticism that these would be any good, Forester sent him cuttings of Iona, Gaillard Gerrard 157 and Pontac. As these never appeared in any of Brock's recommendations, one has to assume that they were not a success. He corresponded with Forester and exchanged winemaking tips. Brock was especially interested in learning how to retain a small amount of residual sugar in his wines without them re-fermenting. He obviously had not learnt the secret of sterile filtration and bottling.

As a result of this world-wide search for suitable varieties, the scope and nature of the Viticulture Research Station changed and expanded. Once the initial plantings of mainly table grape vine varieties started cropping and ripeness levels and cultural suitabilties were assessed, it soon became obvious that the size of the vineyards (and the costs of running them) would expand beyond all reason and as early as the winter of 1948, the culling of less suitable varieties started. A common problem with many of the first vines which came via the RHS appeal was that they were in fact the same varieties, masquerading under different (and often incorrect) names, and Brock quickly had to become skilled in ampelography (the science of grapevine identification) in order to distinguish the different varieties. He admitted that this task remained one of the hardest. He was also constantly being offered from overseas sources, varieties sure to succeed which ultimately, after years of trialling, proved worthless in our climate. As late as 1970, Brock laments in his vine price list that 27 new French hybrids recommended recently by some of the French research stations have all proved hopeless after five years of testing. When one looks back at the remarkable amount of effort and energy that Brock put into his search for vine varieties, all undertaken in the days before the advent of the Internet and e-mail, even before many people had access to a telephone and when communication was mostly conducted by letter, it seems an almost impossible task. Yet, one can see the results and one has to be in awe of his achievements.

Much of the early work at Oxted was concentrated on growing vines – mainly table-grape vine varieties – under cloches. Chase Protected Cultivation Ltd of Shepperton, a company that specialised in glass cloches, did much to help and encourage the work and undoubtedly helped spread the news that vines could be grown in Great Britain. The company ran a club for its customers known as the Chase Guild and through its publication Chase News helped promote both viticulture and of course, the company's cloches. At the first of the Station's open days in 1948, 140 members of the Chase Guild arrived eager to learn more about the subject. Mr J. L. H. Chase, the company's owner, was personally very interested in the work at Oxted and gave much helpful advice, as well as practical assistance in the shape of redesigned cloches, more suited to grape cultivation, which were supplied free-of-charge. The standard cloche used at Oxted was the Tomato Cloche made of three pieces of glass; two 24" x 24" pieces for the walls and a single 24" x 12" piece for the roof. Chase made a modification to the spring wire clip that held the glass together so that the abundant shoots and foliage of the vines could continue to grow upwards, outside the cloche, just leaving the fruit protected beneath.

Until 1954, the work at Oxted concentrated on table grapes. Although a few wine-grape vine varieties had been planted in the first years, it was not until 1950 that it was decided that this might in the long term prove a more interesting and successful avenue to go down. There were a number of reasons why this change took place. The knowledge that table grapes could be successfully grown in an open vineyard, but under cloches, was perhaps not too surprising. The cultivation of table grapes in greenhouses – which is after all essentially what a cloche is – was a pursuit that the British had long excelled at. Indeed, it is surprising how many table-grape vine varieties used throughout the world today, grown in both greenhouses and outside, have their origins in the British Isles.

First harvest at Oxted

Brock first picked grapes from the Brandt on the house wall in November 1946: *gathered the vintage* [he noted] *about 50 grapes!!!* (Brock's exclamation marks). The next year he was more successful. In October 1947 he exhibited five bunches of Brandt (*small but good*) at the RHS Fruit Show on 11 October 1947. The first harvest from the 1946 planted vines in the trial plots did not come until 1948 and owing to tremendous problems with diseases – powdery and downy mildew and *Botrytis* – as well as birds and rabbits, yields were small and the grapes were either eaten, sold or given away. The situation in 1949 was different. More timely use of Bordeaux Mixture to control downy mildew and sulphur dusting against powdery mildew, together with better bird control (using both netting and a new shotgun – a Webley and Scott .410 – bought from the Army and Navy Stores in December 1948 for £14.10.0) meant that on 9 October 1949 Brock picked about 100 lb of grapes. These were taken over to Hyams' cottage at Molash in East Kent and together with others from Hyams' own vineyard, were crushed, pressed and eventually fermented, using a yeast culture – Johannisberg 43 – sent to Hyams by the Wädenswil Research Station in Switzerland. (Hyams had offered his winemaking skills as he had been making home-made wines for some years). However, when Brock arrived with his grapes, the press was not ready and much of the juice was lost! When Brock tasted the Shottenden Rosé (as they called the wine, Hyams' cottage being on the Shottenden Road) shortly after it had finished fermenting, he commented: *flavour very poor and yeasty*. After some of it had been bottled and kept for almost a year, it was tasted again and the comments were no more favourable: *distinctly sedimented, yeasty and decidedly off-flavour. Rejected as of no promise. Used both bottles for Fire Water* (which meant it was distilled). Hyams' prowess as a winemaker did not impress Brock!

Brock harvested the remainder of his 1949 grapes a week later and had a go at turning them into wine himself at Oxted. He seems to have all kinds of problems with the wine which was fermented on the skins as many of the grapes were red. He also used the same Johannisberg 43 yeast which was so active that the fermentation was finished before Brock thought it had even started. He tried heating it twice to get it to start, but merely destroyed what character it originally had. He wrote that: *he left the skins in contact with the wine for far too long.* The wine was over acidic and some calcium carbonate was added to reduce the acidity. This helped soften the wine, but it still tasted harsh and tannic (due Brock thought to the heating he had given it) and the end results were not spectacular. Some was bottled, but the remainder used for a trial into vinegar production (which appears to have been as unsuccessful as the winemaking) or for distillation.

In 1950, Brock seems to have got himself better organised for winemaking and the results were more promising. He also sent grapes over to Hyams and this year the wine was described as: *definitely a good normal light wine. One of the best with real character.* Brock's remarks, made in his fermentations book, are heavily underlined and one can almost sense the relief that at last something drinkable had at last come from his years of hard work, to say nothing of the expense. Brock seems to have had the services of a Mr Rivollier who acted as his winetaster and came by from time to time to pass judgement on various wines. Perhaps he had good reason, but some of his

comments seem very harsh! Over the next three years, Brock seems to have had his fair share of problems in the winery. Much wine seems to have been destroyed because of oxidation or films of mould and fungus forming on top of the wines, or just because they tasted terrible, usually far too acidic. For many, distillation was the only course. In 1954 the new winery was under construction and no wine was made at all. By the 1955 harvest, the new winery was complete and Brock at last started to make some batches of trial wines that could be bottled and put away to see how they matured.

This picture of a home-made press, which uses a car-jack as the motive power, was the one that Brock copied for his own winery. This photograph was sent to Brock by Carl Pederson from the New York State Agricultural Experimental Station in Geneva on the Finger Lakes, New York

With a total lack of winemaking experience, it is perhaps not surprising that Brock's early efforts were less than perfect. Whether he was helped or hindered by Hyams' involvement – who can say – the wines produced by Hyams seem to have been no better than those Brock initially made himself. Hyams' section on winemaking in his 1949 book *The Grape Vine in England* is fairly rudimentary and it is obvious from his instructions that winemaking was not his first discipline! In the

1953 book *Vineyards in England* which Hyams edited, the winemaking chapter was written by Dr Alfred Pollard of the Cider Department at Long Ashton Research Station, then part of Bristol University where in 1965 a half-acre of vines was established. This chapter gives far more technical (and accurate) information than in Hyams' own 1949 book and while today some of the instructions look very old-fashioned, no doubt at the time they were current industry practice. Bottling wines with residual sugar was obviously something that winemakers of the day had not cracked and the art of sterile bottling using very fine filters (developed in about 1947 by the Seitz Filter Company in Germany) had obviously not been heard of in the UK. This meant that wines that were bottled with residual sugar either had to be so heavily dosed with free sulphur as to render them objectionable or were subject to chance re-fermentation which inevitably led to spoilage or explosion (or both). One of the most useful tools in the English or Welsh winemaker's locker today is the ability to soften fresh, fruity wines which have what one might call a 'crisp' (i.e. high) acidity with a few grams per litre of residual sugar. This can only really be achieved through sterile bottling. Brock also made bottle-fermented sparkling wines, a few bottles of which survived until the 1980s.

To improve his winemaking skills, Brock made contact with various institutions and organisations. Dr Pollard and his colleague at Long Ashton, Fred Beech, were keen to help and offered advice and yeast cultures. (Beech continued to help both Brock and others in the industry for many years and as late as 1980 was putting on seminars for English and Welsh winemakers.) Another organisation that helped out with yeasts was the Brewing Industry Research Foundation which maintained the National Yeast Collection. Brock also received yeasts from various other sources, including Beecham's Food and Drink Division Ltd. In the first few years he sent batches of grapes to the Moussec Company who were part of the British Wine industry (i.e. wine made from imported grape concentrates) and they made several trial batches. He also received yeasts from them with which he made starter cultures. There was no doubt that his enterprise created a lot of good will and people were intrigued to see how English and Welsh viticulture would develop.

Distillation was something that Brock was particularly keen on. It was a subject that fascinated him and he had access to simple laboratory distillation equipment from the company that he ran. Distillation was also a way of turning relatively small quantities of not very good quality (usually quite acidic) wine made from the wide variety of grapes grown, into something that might be of interest. On 25 October 1949 Brock wrote to the Customs and Excise in Croydon requesting permission to keep and use an experimental laboratory still. On 23 March 1950 he received a letter granting him an *indulgence for experimental brandy distillation*. In September of the same year Customs and Excise wrote to him, asking when the experiments would begin and reminding him that he needed to take out a licence for the still at a cost of 10 shillings for a full year or 7/6 if taken out after 11 October. Brock wrote at once and sent a cheque for 10 shillings requesting a licence for a full year. As ever, he took the subject seriously and made enquiries wherever he could about the best methods and techniques and (apart from 1954 when no wine was produced because the new winery was under construction) distillation of what Brock called Fire Water or Grappa took place. The quantities were necessarily small and once he had refined his techniques, the quality good. He sent samples of the 1952 distillations to his friends in Switzerland where they were adjudged to be *equal to best Italian and superior to Swiss normal.* Brock's last distillations were in 1960, after which he appeared to lose interest in brandy production, although he kept a distillation licence and record book until 1973.

Throughout the 27 years of its existence, the only income that Brock derived from his activities with vines was through sales of books and vine cuttings and the occasional lecture and writing fee. No entry fees were ever charged for the annual open days and in reality, the income amounted to far less than the outgoings. The first sales he made were of books following the publication in 1949 of *Report No.1 – Outdoor Grapes in Cold Climates.* He had this privately printed and paid Tonbridge Printers £73.19.6 to print 2,000 copies with a cover price of 6 shillings each – an income of some £600 if all were sold at the full price. Three subsequent publications followed – *Report No.2 – More Outdoor Grapes* in 1950, *Report No.3 – Progress with Vines and Wines* in 1961 and *Report No.4 – Starting a Vineyard* in 1964 – all privately financed by Brock. These masterly booklets contained a mass of information to anyone contemplating planting a vineyard and are, in many respects, still relevant, although his varietal recommendations even then left something to be desired. In his first book he gave a fairly unexciting list of varieties for open air (as opposed to cloched) wine production and suggested several varieties: Blue Portuguese, Chasselas 1921, Gamay Hâtif des Vosges, Golden Chasselas, Madeleine Royale and Meslier Précoce. These were early days in his researches. He adds that Riesling Sylvaner (Müller-Thurgau) had just been imported and it may be possible over here but needed another vintage to assess it. The next year – 1950 – when the second report was published, Madeleine Royale and Gamay Hâtif des Vosges took pride of place for wine grapes, with a suggestion that Seyve-Villard 5/276 (Seyval blanc) and Seibel 13/053 (Cascade) might be suitable. He added though that there is far too much partisanship among the sponsors of these various varieties to believe anything they told him and he was waiting until he had tried them under our own conditions before recommending them. The propaganda war between the pro- and anti-hybrid forces was then raging in France.

Brock did contemplate writing a much longer book on the whole subject to be called *Vine Growing and Wine Making* and wrote a 50,000 word draft of the winemaking section. A synopsis of the book was sent to Edward Hyams in January 1961, asking for his advice on the best way to publish it. Hyams replied in February saying that he thought that a joint venture with a publisher such as Faber and Faber (who had published two of Hyams' viticulture books) or Collingridge, well known for publishing books on gardening and horticulture, would be best, with Brock, who reckoned he could sell 3,000 copies himself, putting up £1,000 to fund printing and publication. In the end, the venture came to nought.

The Oxted open days became something of an institution and they were the ideal opportunity for him to demonstrate what he was achieving, sell books, take orders for vines and engender enthusiasm for his cause. He encouraged people to bring samples of leaves and grapes for him to identify and very often found that varieties sold with one name, turned out to be something completely different. The first open day was on 23 October 1948, when about 150 people turned up, most of them members of the Chase Guild. 1949's open day was held on 8 October when 200 people arrived and Brock and his wife entertained Chase Protected Cultivation Ltd's staff to tea. Brock records that he sold some grapes and 29 books and the television cameras took pictures. It would be fascinating to know where that camera footage is now! By 1950 the number of open days had expanded to three per season: one for RHS members (150 arrived including large parties from East Malling and Wye College); another for Chase Guild members; and a third for general members of the public. 1951 saw four open days, but perhaps by then some of the novelty had worn off, as, on the first day, there were no visitors at all (it also rained hard all day), and the subsequent ones were poorly attended. Despite this setback, Brock continued to open the vineyard to the public on two to three days a year and although numbers never reached those achieved in the first three years, a regular 30 to 40 people would turn up on each occasion and the open days continued right up until at least 1971, by which time most of the vines had been grubbed-up.

The income from vine sales started in 1950 following the establishment of a nursery bed the previous year and continued throughout the life of the Research Station. Many of the varieties that Brock received from his contacts were unique and he was in reality the only source of varieties such as Madeleine x Angevine 7672, Madeleine Angevine x Sylvaner III 28/51 and Seibel 13/053 (later renamed Cascade), all of which, in the early years, were much sought after. He only ever sold either bare wood cuttings for prospective vineyard owners to root themselves or one-year-old rooted cuttings for immediate planting. Many of the earliest vineyards to be planted (Beaulieu, Horam Manor, Elmham Park, Felsted and Yearlstone) obtained vines from Oxted. However, as the new commercially orientated vineyards needed larger quantities than Brock could reasonably supply, and additionally most wanted them grafted on to *Phylloxera* resistant rootstock, vines were imported directly from French and German nurseries. Looking through the sales lists for the early years, the names of a few of Brock's customers give something of the flavour of the time: Lt. Col. A. J. Odling-Smee, Lady Stubb, Hon. T. Brand, Dr G. Loxton – a very regular customer – and Col. Sir E. le Breton. The first year that any income was earned was 1948/9 when £52 was gathered in; the next year a much more acceptable £416 was taken and in subsequent years (at least up until 1960) an average of £300 a year was taken. (In 2008 terms, £300 in 1950 is now worth about £7,000.)

The costs, however, of establishing and running the Research Station were considerable. Apart from the purchase of the extra land Brock erected a 'store' as it is called in his accounts (at a cost of £95.10.0), which was subsequently taken down and replaced in September 1954 with a purpose built winery containing a small laboratory, a room for his still, and a refrigerated underground cellar. This cost a total of £770 – around £18,500 in 2008 prices. Apart from land and buildings, the Research Station required a considerable amount of plant and equipment to operate it. Tractors, rotovators, mowers and a myriad of handtools had to be bought for the agricultural side of the business and the winery, although not lavishly equipped as it was never the intention to produce wine for sale, had the usual small crusher, press and fermentation equipment.

Throughout the life of the enterprise, Brock continued to support it from his other income (he remained in full-time employment throughout the life of the Research Station). He established it as a separate venture which had its own accounts and initially was able to offset losses against his other income. In 1960 a struggle started with the Inspector of Taxes who, realising that it would never make a profit, decided to end this arrangement, although allowing him to set off depreciation on plant and equipment already bought until such time as it was down to a nil balance. Ray battled against this decision, but, as is the way of these things, eventually lost. It was at that stage that the separate accounting ended and although a Research Station bank account was maintained, no detailed account books were kept after this time. In *Report No.3* (1961) Brock wrote that: *up until he lost his battle with the Inland Revenue, the total loss on the vineyard was the sort of amount which ... could reasonably be spent on my hobby*.

Brock employed Ernie Walker on a full time basis, paying him £3.10.0 a week to start with (in 1946) plus a bonus of a week's pay at Christmas. Walker's weekly pay had risen to £8.5.0 by 1960. He also employed additional help when and as required. The accounts books also show that Brock paid himself a weekly wage out of the enterprise, amounting to half Walker's earnings and in addition, charged considerable travelling expenses (undoubtedly fact and vine-finding trips to France and Switzerland were included) as well as entertaining expenses, quite a large annual sum for 'sample wines', various gardening publications and memberships to clubs and societies. At one stage the Inspector wished to know whether the purchase of a Bond Minicar (for £368.15.10) was necessary for the running of the Research Station and Brock convinced him that it was, estimating that he did 7,000 miles a year in it on behalf of the business! The accounts would also suggest that some of Brock's other living expenses were probably met out of the Research Station, so perhaps after 15 years of continuous losses and mounting expenses, the Inspector's view that Brock had had a good run for his money was understandable.

In the early years, Brock had looked for financial support from various organisations. On 27 September 1951, he wrote to Sir William Slater at the Agricultural Research Council asking for financial assistance. Slater replied on 5 December saying that until such time as there is evidence of the economic possibilities of the grape crop they could not support him. They also added that: *with France prepared to sell us more wine than we can buy, it is clear that the market would be highly competitive, and this country must start with an ecological handicap in raising the crop.* Ray found this response something of an affront to his five or six years of work and said that unless the work was carried out, it would never be possible to prove one way or the other whether growing grapes was viable or not. Brock felt it was very much a 'heads you lose, tails I win' situation. In February 1952, he applied to The Royal Society for a grant, but D. C. Martin, the Assistant Secretary, wrote saying that Sir Edward Salisbury (Physical Sciences Secretary of the Royal Society, Director of Kew Gardens and author of *Weeds and Aliens*) had commented that: *the work is essentially of an applied nature and I doubt if the demonstration that vines can be grown successfully in England is of great practical importance.* Brock was once again turned down.

Ernie Walker, Brock's "vinearon" tending vines under cloches at Oxted ca1951

In 1951 Brock completed and submitted to his old university – London – a thesis entitled *Some Aspects of Viticulture in Southern England.* This thesis, which is over 100 pages long and crammed with very detailed scientific data about his experiments up to and including 1950, is unique and alone could serve as the *raison d'être* for the establishment and operation of the Research Station. In the back is a long list of

acknowledgements to various people who had helped him (Messrs Chase, Leyvraz, Hyams, Kessler, Duruz) the last one being to: *Mr E. G. Walker, the vinearon concerned with all the real work. His willingness to try anything and report on it carefully has been invaluable, apart from the very real hard work required to cope with the day to day work.* Sadly his thesis never gained him the Doctorate of Philosophy that he hoped it might, but he was awarded the 'Jones-Bateman Cup' (pictured left), awarded triennially for original research into fruit culture by the Royal Horticultural Society. This magnificent silver award was presented to him at the RHS Annual General Meeting on 22 February 1954.

Once it became known that England had its own living vine expert, Brock was called upon to write articles by a wide number of publishers. Apart from the *Pomona Britannica* (see below) Brock wrote the entry on *Vine-Growing Outdoors in England* in the *RHS Dictionary* in 1951, the entry on vines in the *Oxford Junior Encyclopaedia* in 1961, articles for the *RHS Journal*, *The Smallholder*, *Gardening Illustrated*, *The Grower*, *Country Life* and *The Field*. He also made several radio broadcasts.

Brock also liked to involve the wine trade in what he was doing and used to lecture on viticulture to those preparing for their Diploma and Master of Wine exams. In August 1960 he put on the Research Station's first official trade wine tasting and invited a number of tasters including 16 Masters of Wine. Guests included Harry Waugh, Sir Guy Fison, Michael Druitt, John Patrick, Denis Williams, John Vaughan-Hughes, Dr A. Pollard, Colin Fenton and a Mr Morgan-Grenville They were presented with 17 different wines – all served blind – and asked for their comments. Like the curate's egg, the general response seems to have been that they were good in parts. Some they appeared genuinely to like. Two samples of Riesling Sylvaner (Müller-Thurgau) and one of Seyval blanc came top, with a Précoce de Malingre and a Madeleine Angevine x Sylvaner III 28/51 in second place. Brock reported that the last wine had been a bit lacking in natural acidity and had been blended with one of the higher acid varieties (of which he had an ample supply). Denis Williams from Sichel & Co[7] even wrote asking whether he could buy a bottle of the Riesling Sylvaner to show to his boss, Walter Sichel, who eventually planted a small vineyard at his home

---

7   Sichels made Blue Nun, then the most popular white wine sold in the UK. When I started making wine in 1979, this was the style of wine I considered I should try and copy. How times change!

in Hertfordshire. (From this vineyard came a bottle of wine that I was offered when I went to see Sichels at their Mainz headquarters in 1975! Ricki Hess, then their Sales Director, took me under his wing and found me a job as a *praktikant* (apprentice) at a vineyard in the Rheingau which put me on the path to becoming a winegrower in the UK.) Harry Waugh wrote saying: *what you have been doing is quite remarkable and I am full of admiration for the results you have obtained. I suppose it is almost impossible for us to get another year like 1959* [a great European vintage year] *but it would appear from your experiments and experience that you are very much on the right lines*

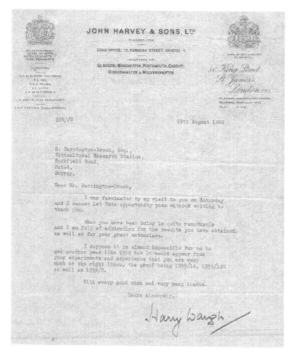

Letter from Harry Waugh following a visit to Oxted in August 1960

The worst of the bunch at the 1960 tasting were a Tissier-Ravat 578, a Baco No.1 (*which gave a very hard red wine with most excessive acidity* according to Brock) and a Brandt. This last variety, which H. M. Tod claimed to have introduced into the country in the early 1900s, featured on almost everybody's lists as one of *the* varieties for our climate. It was, however, summed up by Brock thus: *Brandt usually gives drinkable but uninteresting wine ... which we normally class as drinkable but poor. In 1959 it was barely drinkable.* These last three poor performers were soon taken off his 'recommended' list. Sparkling wines were also on offer at this Master of Wine tasting and three varieties – Riesling Sylvaner (Müller-Thurgau), Seyval blanc and Chasselas – showed promise. Brock told the assembled company that he had now demonstrated over a five year period that vines would crop at a rate of 500 gallons per acre (equivalent to around 3½ tonnes/acre or 55 hl/ha) which would be an acceptable commercial yield today. The guests all wrote effusive thank you letters, commenting on the excellence of the lunch that Mrs Brock had prepared, with slightly more guarded comments about the wines they had tasted. Brock did not mind this trade criticism, saying that it was the purpose of the Station to test varieties and it was just as important to eliminate poor performers, as it was to find good ones.

One of the major cultivation problems that Brock had to contend with was disease. *Oidium Tuckerii* or powdery mildew was well known as a major problem on both indoor and outdoor vines and was one of the factors that resulted in poor yields at the Castle Coch vineyards. He first noticed the disease on his vines in June 1947 and set about using the standard remedy, dusting sulphur. This appeared to work well, although it took considerable time to dust the cloched vines, which was most of them in the early years. Brock soon discovered that once signs of powdery mildew appear, it is almost too late to start dusting and the treatment must start well before the mildew shows itself on the vines. This is as true today as it was then and although growers in the UK now use wettable or liquid sulphur which can be sprayed on, the key element in control is timing. Powdery mildew continued to be a problem throughout the life of the Research Station and susceptibility to it was one of the major reasons why a vine might be written off as unsuitable for growing in our climate. It was also certainly one of the reasons why resistant hybrid varieties such as Seyval blanc, Seibel 13/053 and Léon Millot became popular with Brock and therefore with growers in general.

Downy mildew (*Plasmopara viticola*) was something not usually seen in Great Britain as vines grown indoors (which is where most vines were grown), in dry conditions, seldom suffer from it. However, outdoor vines are a different matter and the disease soon took up residence in the Oxted vineyards. At first, Brock was unsure whether it was downy mildew or not and had to call in an official, Joan Moore, from MAFF's Plant Pathology Department at Harpenden. She paid Brock a visit in November 1948 and confirmed that the outbreak was downy mildew, saying that it was the ninth in the country, the last one being from Yalding in Kent in 1947 (probably on George Ordish's vines). While she was there, Moore also had a look at some aphids found on the vines (Brock was very concerned about *Phylloxera*) but was relieved to find that they were just common aphids. Brock resorted to Bordeaux Mixture which, before the invention of modern fungicides, was the usual treatment for downy mildew. As ever, the scientist in Brock took over and he was forever inventing new combinations of copper sulphate and slaked lime – the major ingredients of Bordeaux Mixture – to get them to work more effectively. He consulted ICI's Jealott's Hill Research Station on the matter and they suggested using copper oxychloride which was then starting to replace Bordeaux Mixture on potatoes for the control of blight (a similar disease).

Botrytis (Grey Mould) on the other hand was another matter, and before the discovery of Benlate and the even newer fungicides, there was no real chemical control for it. Good hygiene, plenty of light and air and loose bunches are the greatest aid to avoiding the destructive rotting that occurs, but with the grapes under cloches, outdoors and in close proximity to the soil, Brock had his work cut out to keep a healthy crop. Time after time in his vineyard diaries and notebooks he reported tremendous losses from *Botrytis* and was often forced to pick early in order to save the crop. Today's winegrowers can have no idea what life must have been like before modern fungicides made the control of this disease relatively painless. Lack of a decent anti-*botrytis* chemical must surely rank as one of the major reasons why viticulture before the mid-1960s was such a risky and unrewarding venture.

Phylloxera was an ever present threat that Brock did his best to counter and it never surfaced at Oxted, despite the importation of thousands of rooted vines, both grafted and un-grafted, as well as bare wood cuttings. An outbreak would probably have finished the Research Station off as MAFF would have had no option but to demand the destruction of all non-grafted vines – which was most of them. *Phylloxera* was not unknown in Great Britain and there had been 17 distinct outbreaks in the British Isles (one was in Wicklow in 1867) since the original first sighting in a Hammersmith greenhouse in 1863. Brock established a selection of rootstock varieties (bought from Lepage et Cie, Angers in 1950) *so that grafting can commence if Phylloxera is found.*

The first sighting of *Phylloxera* in a modern vineyard was at Sir Guy Salisbury-Jones's at Hambledon in 1955 (three years after it was planted). Brock heard about this from an indiscrete MAFF official – the location of outbreaks was meant to be confidential – who had been called in to Hambledon to deal with the outbreak. It was then, as it is now, a notifiable pest that must be reported to the authorities. Brock also heard that *Phylloxera* had surfaced in vines imported by a commercial nursery and he wrote to the Horticultural Trades Association asking them to remind their members of the dangers. They responded that as long as the vines were accompanied by a phytosanitary certificate from the relevant authorities, MAFF officials had no option but to let the plants into the country. Brock replied by saying that as all vines on the Continent were on resistant grafted stock, the presence of *Phylloxera* eggs on rooted vines was very common and a phytosanitary certificate certainly did not mean that they were free of eggs. Brock was fairly incensed about Sir Guy Salisbury-Jones's attitude to the *Phylloxera* outbreak in his vineyard, saying that he was *adopting an 'I'm all right, Jack'* attitude to the problem as all the Hambledon vines were grafted onto resistant rootstock and therefore, in theory, not in danger. Mr Rhodes, the local MAFF plant health inspector, continued to inspect the Oxted vineyard from time to time to check that no *Phylloxera* had been imported.

Brock's other interests

It seems almost impossible to believe that Brock had any other interests during the heyday of the Research Station, so all-consuming does it seem to have been. However, nothing could be further from the truth. He was Managing Director of the aforementioned Townson and Mercer, a well-known firm of scientific instrument makers and suppliers founded in 1798, with offices and a factory in Croydon and factories in Ponders End and Slough. The firm made and sold scientific instruments and equipment, reagents and chemicals, and equipped laboratories and Brock worked for the company from 1938 until the end of 1960. In 1957 Brock became President of the Scientific Instrument Makers Association and was Master of the Worshipful Company of Scientific Instrument Makers in 1969–1970. After he left his old company, he took up a number of other pursuits and owned a colour printing works, a Renault dealership and an interest in a computer dealership at a time when computers were still in their infancy.

He became a director of Chase Organics Ltd and got involved with marketing a seaweed concentrate (SM3) that had been developed for them, as well as a new selective insecticide based on Polybutylene which used the seaweed concentrate as a base and stuck the insects to the plant. He also promoted 'Scaraweb', a rayon filament material that could be spread over fruit trees and bushes to keep off birds – bullfinches especially – which do much damage to the buds of apple and pear trees in the winter and which he had heard about from Switzerland where it was invented. He held demonstration trials at Oxted to which he invited officials from various MAFF Experimental Husbandry Stations and even at one stage tried to sell it to the Russian vine testing station with whom he had been in contact.

Brock with his HRG 'Scientific' which he built in 1948

Apart from work and the vineyard, Brock also had some serious hobbies, motor cars being one of them. In 1948 he had ordered a new HRG 'Aerodynamic' but fed up with the delay in delivery and finding out that a chassis could be bought off the shelf, he set to and designed and built his own version which he called the 'Scientific'. This rear-engined coupé with its 1.5 litre Javelin engine was capable of 100 mph and it was featured in Motor Magazine in a two part article in July 1955. For its time, its streamlined looks, rear engine and all-independent suspension were fairly revolutionary (at least for a British car). With its 'very quick' acceleration to 75 mph and a petrol consumption of 34/36 mpg, Brock was justifiably pleased with the results. He also enjoyed the ability to: *put it into a slide at every bend for the sheer pleasure of controlling it with two fingers* (hopefully on the race track rather than in the leafy lanes around Oxted). While he was completing the car, he was invited to take it to the Spa-Francorchamps racetrack in Belgium and race it in the 24-hour race. The car required some modifications if it was to be raced and these he got on with. On 7 July 1948 he noted in his garden diary: *all spare time spent preparing for motor race.* Brock and his team-mates – three HRGs were entered – drove the cars to Belgium, took part in the race and then drove them home. Brock was pleased to come third in class at an average speed of 59.35 mph and covering 1,425 miles. In 1949, he repeated the exercise and came second. He also raced at Goodwood, holding the up-to 2-litre class in 1948, took part in Swiss hill climbs, firstly in a Healey, with a body largely built by himself and then a works Jowett Javelin.

Brock also commented on races at Brooklands, Crystal Palace and Donington. During the early part of the war he was Head [air raid] Warden for the City of London, and was given the MBE for his work with unexploded bombs and made a Freeman of the City. At the age of 50 he tried the Cresta run and for a short time was brakeman in the British bobsleigh team, giving up after a nasty crash in which he broke several ribs. He was also interested in yachting and boating, and designed and built a steam launch called the *Silencia*.

In the last decade of his life he helped re-commission a Daimler Cannstatt (built in 1898) for the National Motor Museum at Beaulieu by hand-cutting some new drive gears on his lathe, rebuilt the rear axle of their 1909 Humber and helped restore several other classic cars. At his death he had almost completed the construction, from the ground up (this was *not* a kit) of a small steam car. The construction of this car was the idea of his wife's who told me that *poor Ray has been told he cannot drive any more* (he had an extremely fast Ford Sierra Cosworth and his doctor had decided he would probably kill himself if he continued to drive) and she was looking for a project that *would keep him busy*. Thus was the steam car born! My last memories of Ray are of him proudly showing me the single-cylinder steam engine that he and a friend, Tony Hillyard, had built (from raw materials naturally), clamped in the vice on his workbench and gently turning over on compressed air. The tiny car they had built, with two seats and every panel hand-beaten, waited at the end of the workshop to receive the engine.[8]

Brock's work on vines must be seen as really quite remarkable. That he should decide to establish a private research station to study a crop that did not have a natural home in our climate is quite a feat in itself; that he should do so with such effort, energy and diligence for little or no personal gain, apart from the satisfaction of seeing it done properly, is another matter. In retrospect, the site he chose could have been better – nearer to sea level and less exposed – and undoubtedly this would have resulted in riper grapes and better wine. He knew his site had limitations, but always countered this by saying that he felt comfortable in recommending a variety that had performed well at Oxted, knowing that it would therefore ripen on almost any site in the south of the country. The legacy of the Oxted Viticultural Research Station is to be seen in today's English and Welsh wine industry. While minute by the standards of other (more climatologically blessed) countries, it owes its existence in great part to his work. He lived to see an industry producing an average of two and a half million bottles of wine a year and an industry that was slowly gaining recognition. He died on 14 February 1999, aged 91. Ray Brock was a truly remarkable human being.

Edward Solomon Hyams 1910–1975

Edward Hyams, who first appears in the Oxted story at the harvest in 1949, shares with Brock the honour of being one of the fathers of the viticultural revival. Although his winegrowing and winemaking activities were never on the same scale as Brock's, through his writing and speaking he did much to publicise the subject and make the public aware that the revival was under way. Hyams was a prolific author, journalist, translator and broadcaster whose interest in vines and specifically in vines growing in Great Britain, was stimulated by reading a book which mentioned the historical evidence of British vineyards. (This book was one of a bundle sent to his ship – he was in the Navy during the Second World War – by the town that had adopted his ship's company as their own.) He had also read *The English Vineyard Vindicated* by John Rose, as well as the chapter on *Grapes Out of Doors* in Raymond Bush's book *Fruit Growing Outdoors*. Although born a Cockney, Hyams had been partially educated in France, spoke French fluently and claimed to have studied viticulture there, although to what extent was never made clear. In any event, he felt a natural affinity to the subject.

In 1938 Hyams and his wife had bought a small house – called Nut Tree Cottages – and 3-acres (1.21-hectares) of rough garden in Molash, a village between Faversham and Ashford in the eastern part of Kent. At the beginning of the war, as Hyams was away serving in the forces and his wife was in the Land Army and living on a farm

---

8   I am sure some readers will feel that this aspect of Brock's life is somehow outside the scope of a book on UK vineyards. However, I think most of us today would hesitate before hand-building a road-going car and it was with this degree of confidence that Brock carried out his viticultural experiments. I just feel it shows the man in his true light.

elsewhere, the house lay empty. At first, it was commandeered for evacuees, but later let to a local farmer who was a less-than-perfect tenant. By the end of the war, the cottage lay empty and almost derelict. It had been broken into and the contents stolen or vandalised.

In March 1946, Hyams was demobbed from the Royal Navy and he and his wife returned to Kent. Hyams, then 36, and his wife decided that: *the values by which they had lived before the war were morally, intellectually and spiritually unprofitable and they therefore decided to dispense with any more income than could be earned by work that was congenial, therefore liberating.* In this spirit of self-sufficiency, they started to clear the land and establish a vegetable and fruit garden which contained, among other things, their own small tobacco plantation! Before the war, Hyams and his wife had talked about planting some vines and as soon as this became a practical possibility, he set about contacting likely sources for suitable varieties.

From the outset, the intention was to plant both table grapes as well as varieties to turn into wine and Hyams estimated that he needed a litre per head per day to keep him and his wife happy. He made contact with some of the same institutions and nurseries with whom Brock was in touch and ended up with some of the same varieties. For the table he had Pirovano No.7 (Primus), Muscat de St Vallier, Landot's Oeillade de Conzieu and Muscadoule (all fairly obscure 1st Epoch varieties); for wine production he obtained Seyve-Villard 5/276 (Seyval blanc) directly from the Seyve-Villard nurseries in St Vallier on the Rhône as well as Baco No.1, Tissier-Ravat 578 (Téré Doré), Seibel 5279, Gamay Hâtif des Vosges and Riesling. These were planted in 1947 and 1948. Hyams made contact with Brock in 1948 and visited Oxted on 5 September of that year. After his visit he wrote to Brock asking for various varieties, including Riesling Sylvaner (Müller-Thurgau) which had been sent to Oxted in 1947 from Switzerland. Brock replied saying that: *there is not likely to be any big demand for this variety yet* and offered him plenty of cuttings as a present. These were sent the next year.

In 1950, Hyams received cuttings of three new varieties from Professor Dr B. Husfeld who ran the Geilweilerhof research institute at Siebeldingen bei Landau-Pfalz in Germany. These were Madeleine Angevine x Gutedal No.3 28/28, Madeleine Angevine x Sylvaner F2 31/16/52 and Madeleine Angevine x Sylvaner III 28/51. Two cuttings of each of these were passed on to Brock who put them into his collection. Although the first two of these proved less than satisfactory and were abandoned in 1958/9, the Madeleine Angevine x Sylvaner III 28/51 proved to be very effective and at one stage Brock rated it as one of his best. Brock shortened the name to Madeleine Sylvaner and it is still on the list of permitted varieties for the UK. Like Brock, Hyams was in contact with Georges Mariman who provided valuable advice and contact addresses. Hyams also corresponded with the grower in Sweden – Nils Endlandsson – who was in touch with Brock. They also swapped varieties and through Endlandsson, Hyams obtained information about growers in Denmark, Finland and Russia and he was able to make contact with them.

Hyams also went searching for old varieties already growing in Britain and through an appeal in one of his many articles, was told about a vine growing on a cottage wall at Wrotham in Kent. The cottage was located and cuttings taken to Oxted and propagated. As its leaves resembled those of Pinot Meunier, Hyams named it Wrotham Pinot.[9] Brock trialled it at Oxted and reported that it had: *a higher natural sugar content and ripened two weeks earlier* than supplies of Pinot Meunier obtained from overseas. Brock sold cuttings and it became quite popular in the early days of the revival.

Hyams kept in close contact with Brock ('too close' Brock told me) and offered his advice and suggestions whether asked for or not! He was also always coming up with new varieties to try and new treatments for vines to counter disease. In a an undated letter to Brock, Hyams said that he has been in touch with Vidal and Laffont (two well known French nurserymen) and had received a recipe for a better way of producing Bordeaux mixture to control downy mildew: *it involves steeping 125 grammes of copper tacks in one litre of concentrated nitric acid and one litre of water and keeping the resulting nitrate bouillie in quart beer bottles with a screw top.* This could then be diluted and sprayed onto the vines as required. In the letter, Hyams said that he intends to try this for two seasons and report the experiments in the *RHS Journal* and the *Gardener's Chronicle*.

Hyams and his wife left Kent in 1960 and moved to a house called Hill House near Ashburton in Devon, taking with him 1,500 unrooted cuttings which he proceeded to root in their kitchen garden. The next year he proceeded to plant another small vineyard, the history of which is recorded in *An Englishman's Garden* published in 1967. Despite Hyams' experience with vines, the Devon vineyard was not a success and after only a few years he reduced it in size and really only kept a few hardy hybrids for old time's sake and for decoration. He blamed the much wetter growing conditions of Devon (compared to East Kent) which led to too much lush growth, too much disease and poor fruit set.

Hyams greatest contribution to the advancement of viticulture in Great Britain was undoubtedly the massive amount of publicity he created through his writing and broadcasting. C. J. Greenwood of his publishers, The Bodley Head, suggested quite early on that he write a book on vineyards and in 1949 *The Grape Vine in England*, with a forward by the well known gardener and author Vita Sackville-West (of Sissinghurst Castle fame), was published. This book marked a milestone in the early years of the revival. It was, and remains to this day, a scholarly work on the subject and contains chapters on the history of the grapevine in England, the work of Brock at Oxted and the cultivation of the vine and winemaking. Given that viticulture was at a very undeveloped stage at the time, it shows that Hyams had a genuine interest and

---

9   See Appendix III for the full story of Wrotham Pinot.

regard for the subject. His recommendations to plant Riesling, Seyve Villard 5/276 and Seibel 5/279 for white wine and Gamay Hâtif des Vosges and Baco No.1 for red – while perhaps strange from today's perspective – then definitely 'showed promise'.

In 1948 Hyams had read Richard Church's book 'Kent' and noted what he (Church) had written about the possibility of a revival of viticulture in the county. In August 1949, Hyams wrote to Church to let him know what he was up to at Molash and informed him that a book on the subject was about to be published. Church then mentioned both Hyams' vineyard and his forthcoming book in his weekly article for *The Spectator* magazine on 2 September 1949. This alerted first the local and then the national press to Hyams' experiments. This flurry of press interest resulted in requests from general members of the public for information, advice and even cuttings, and Hyams realised that there was a wider audience to be reached on the revival of winegrowing. Church then suggested to *Country Life* that they commission Hyams to write an article, which he did, further fanning the flames of interest.

On 3 August 1950, Hyams gave a talk on the BBC's *Third Programme* called *Vineyards in England* which engendered yet another round of publicity. Hyams was very generous in recognising the part played by Brock in the whole story and ended his radio talk with a dedication, saying: *If it were the practice to dedicate radio talks, I should have dedicated this one to Brock, because any man who spends so much of his leisure time, his energy and money, not to speak of intelligence, on reintroducing a fruit plant, and that plant the source of wine, deserves all the honour one can give him.* The *Daily Mirror* of 17 August 1950 had an article entitled *A bottle of Maidstone '49* which praised the work of both Brock and Hyams. The article ended by saying: *perhaps ten years hence you'll be raising a glass of sparkling Canterbury in honour of the men who made an English wine industry possible.* In retrospect, these can be seen as quite prophetic words.

Hyams' interest in vines and wine stayed with him throughout his life. In 1952 he wrote *Grapes Under Cloches* which drew heavily ('rather too heavily' Brock told me!) on Brock's two published works: *Outdoor Grapes in Cool Climates* (1949) and *More Outdoor Grapes* (1950). Hyams dedicated this book to Brock, thanking him for his extraordinary generosity in making his research available and calling him *a notable vinearoon* – a term Hyams liked to use to mean *viticulteur* or *vigneron*. (Hyams had discovered this hitherto unknown word in a letter written by Lord Delaware in 1616 from New York to his Company in London when discussing the possibility of planting vines in Virginia). In 1953 Hyams edited *Vineyards in England*, a masterly work which consisted of 20 chapters, many written by different specialists (although Hyams himself wrote six of them and Brock two) covering every conceivable aspect of grape production in the British Isles. It included chapters on the history of viticulture, several on varieties including one on new French hybrids, soils and manures, climates, cloche and greenhouse cultivation, pests and diseases and winemaking. The book stands today as one of the most important for anyone contemplating growing vines in England or Wales and despite being published over half a century ago, much of it, apart from the choice of varieties, remains relevant.

Hyams was also, together with Allan Jackson of Wye College, the editor of Longman's *Pomona Britannica* and in 1956 he asked Brock to write the chapter on vines (for which Brock was offered 30 guineas). In 1959 Hyams wrote *Vin – the Wine Country of France* which was, at the time, when books on wine were not as plentiful as they are today, considered a major work on the subject. Perhaps not surprisingly (in a book on classic French wines) he makes no mention of his experiences of growing and making wine in England, although he does touch upon the then thorny question of hybrids. *La Viticulture Nouvelle* was being attacked from all sides and coming under pressure from the joint forces of the chemical industry, the vine-grafting fraternity and the established *appellations* who feared that these high-cropping varieties, which could be grown without fungicides, would threaten their markets.

Hyams' last book on a purely vine or wine related subject was *Dionysus – a Social History of the Wine Vine* published in 1965 which charted the history of the grape vine as a plant used by man from as early as 8,000 BC up to the present day. English and Welsh viticulture does feature in this book, but only really in passing. Indeed by then, Hyams appears to have become less convinced that viticulture was a viable venture in the UK and said that although there are a few vineyards in the country, they are not really economic. He wrote: *only by selling their wine at a price which has nothing to do with ordinary economic laws can they be made financially viable.*

Hyams was an extremely prolific writer and kept up a tremendous output of both fiction and non-fiction: books, articles in journals, magazines and newspapers all flowed from his pen. He wrote a weekly column in *The Illustrated London News*, in its day one of the most widely read magazines, especially among those interested in gardening and the countryside. In 1975, two years before he died, he wrote a well researched article in it about vineyards in Great Britain (which my father cut out and posted to me when I was training in Germany), in which he appears to have changed his mind somewhat about the financial viability of viticulture. At the end of this long article he wrote that: *the undertaking should be profitable if you can produce 2,000 bottles of wine per acre and very profitable at 3,000 bottles. There is no doubt that English vineyards in the right places can produce fine white wines, and that such wine should be the object of English viticulture.* By then of course the revival – for which he was in no small part responsible for instigating – was well under way.

George Ordish 1906–1992

George Ordish had two careers. He was by training an entomologist and economist who spent most of his life working for organisations such as the United Nations and the British and Commonwealth Office. He worked on horticultural problems in Europe, Latin America and Africa and took a keen interest in the great pests and diseases – those that caused the greatest damage both environmentally and economically. He was also a writer, not surprisingly one who specialised in writing about pests and diseases.

One of his first jobs was as an entomologist working in the Champagne region. On returning to his native Kent he was struck by the similarity in the climates and by the differences in the landscape. Where the *Champenoise* had vineyards and vines, Kent had none, but planted hops and apples instead. Why was this? He did some local research and discovered that England had a history of viticulture, but for a number of reasons, vines had ceased to be an economic crop. He therefore resolved to see whether he could get grapes to flourish and ripen and, in 1938, planted a few vines in his garden and on the walls of his cottage at Yalding on the Medway, near Maidstone.

The varieties he planted were those that were then considered to be the best bet for outdoor cultivation for wine production: the reds were Gamay Hatif des Vosges, Baco No.1 and Brandt; the whites, Madeleine Royale and Meslier Précoce. He also discovered a vine growing on the wall of an old house nearby and cuttings were taken. The first harvest from these vines – a small one – was in 1940. At the time, Ordish worked for an ICI subsidiary, Plant Protection Ltd, which had a factory nearby making, among other products, a rat poison that contained a substance extracted from the plant Italian Squill *(Hyacinthoides italica* – a member of the bluebell family). In the factory was an old wooden screw press which had previously been used in the squill extraction process, but now lay idle and unused. He therefore took it home, renovated it and put it into service for his first harvest.

Ordish was always a small scale winemaker and no wine was ever made for sale. However, he was by all accounts an accomplished winemaker and he soon saw that good wines could be made from outdoor grapes. His trial vineyard had proved that grapes would ripen in our climate and these trials prompted his first book on the subject, *Wine Growing in England*, published by Rupert Hart-Davis, which appeared in 1953. (It appeared as No.3 in their *The Countryman's Library* series – Nos 1 and 2 were *Keeping Pigs* and *Law and the Countryman* which says something about viticulture in the early 1950s.) This book, which came out in the same year as Hyams's second book on the subject, drew on many of the same sources. Ordish had been in contact with Brock and had visited Oxted on more than one occasion. How useful his book was to fledgling winegrowers is open to question. By this time, Brock had already dismissed varieties such as Brandt and Baco No.1 for wine production and had already started cropping Riesling Sylvaner (Müller-Thurgau) and Seyval blanc, which he had been growing since 1947. On the subject of diseases – which was after all one of Ordish's specialist subjects – he is very inaccurate. While he admits the possibility of getting both powdery and downy mildew, on *Botrytis* he states: *other fungus diseases such as Grey Mould (or Noble Fungus) can attack the grapes, but are very unlikely to occur in an open vineyard in England*! Although some of his varieties were resistant hybrids, it is barely possible to grow *viniferas* of any kind without encountering *Botrytis* problems and one has to question how much actual experience he had at that time.

One aspect of Ordish's *Wine Growing in England* that is of interest is the last chapter entitled *Commercial Production in Britain.* In it, he sets out the costs and returns from an acre of grapes. He estimates that the capital outlay on planting an acre of vines would be £255, the cost of winemaking equipment (suitable he says for a vineyard of five acres) another £215 and the annual running costs of one acre of vines £189.10.0. Based on a 'modest' crop of 2 tons per acre (35 hl/ha), he estimates the returns from selling 2,100 bottles at an average of 4 shillings a bottle would be £420 less excise duty at 1/9 per bottle. The net return would therefore be £46.15.0 which he says represent a return of 10 per cent which is not very much in view of the risks involved in starting a new industry (and especially as he had not included either the land or buildings or the cost of winemaking and selling). However, he does point out that the winery equipment will serve a much larger tonnage and that 2 tons per acre is really quite a low yield.

For all its inaccuracies, Ordish's book was yet another medium of publicity for the revival of winegrowing in Great Britain and helped spread the word. It certainly helped add to the number of people in the country who looked on outdoor grapegrowing as a possibility, rather than as an historical anomaly. Ordish went on to write two further books concerning viticulture, *The Great Wine Blight* (a study of the causes, effects and cure for *Phylloxera*) in 1972 (which was re-published, slightly amended, in 1987) and *Vineyards in England and Wales* in 1977. This last book, dedicated to the memory of Edward Hyams, was a much better researched and informative handbook on the subject than his first (he did at least admit that *Botrytis* was a serious problem) and was well received. By then, of course, the revival was well under way with 385 members of the English Vineyards Association who farmed over 500 acres of vines.

Ordish also wrote a number of books on a wide variety of agricultural and horticultural topics, as well as on Central and South America (he co-wrote *The Last of the Incas* with Edward Hyams in 1962) and after he retired, wrote and lectured on winegrowing in England and Wales. He died in 1992.

Between them, Ray Brock, Edward Hyams and George Ordish had questioned why it was that outdoor viticulture in the British Isles had all but died out and had shown how it might be revived. Although they had not discovered all the answers, they had, through a combination of practical demonstration, scientific research and publicity, generated sufficient enthusiasm for those with the inclination, to start planting vineyards again. The first modern vineyard, Hambledon in Hampshire, planted in March 1952, was the tangible evidence that a revival was under way.

CHAPTER 3

Commercial viticulture, 1952 onwards

The early vineyards 1952–1965

The planting of the Hambledon vineyard in the March of 1952[1] by Major-General Sir Arthur Guy Salisbury-Jones GCVO, CMG, CBE, MC DL (to give him his full name, title and decorations for the first and last time) marked a turning point in the history of winegrowing in Great Britain. This was the first vineyard to be planted specifically to produce wine for sale since Andrew Pettigrew planted the Marquess of Bute's at Castle Coch in 1875. Furthermore, the main varieties planted, Seyve-Villard 5-276 (Seyval blanc), Seibel 5279 (Aurore) and Seibel 10.868, all French-American hybrids, stood a good chance of resisting mildew and *Botrytis* and of ripening their fruit, problems which up until then had so troubled previous vineyard owners that all had eventually given up the battle. Why Salisbury-Jones chose these three varieties one can only speculate. He had visited Oxted and in Brock's first two *Reports*, Seyval blanc, which Brock and Hyams had been growing (albeit only since 1947/8), had been recommended as '*promising*'. Perhaps one of his contacts in Burgundy was a member of FENAVINO or subscribed to *La Viticulture Nouvelle*? Who knows? Whatever it was, Seyval blanc (if not perhaps the other two varieties) was an inspired choice and in retrospect, while it could be seen as possibly unadventurous, it did enable Salisbury-Jones to harvest crops of clean fruit with sufficient regularity to make wine every year.

Salisbury-Jones had ordered 3,620 vines, grafted onto 41B, 5BB and 161-49 rootstocks that he said: *were required because the chalky soil at Hambledon resembled that of Champagne* and those were the rootstocks used there.[2] The vines were trained in a very Burgundian way, with narrow 4-foot (1.22-metre) rows with the vines planted at approximately 3 feet (0.91 metres) apart and trelliswork of around 4-foot high. The area planted was almost exactly 1-acre (0.40-hectares). The vines grew

---

1   It is often stated that Hambledon vineyard was planted in 1951, but this is incorrect. It was not until the summer of 1951 that Sir Guy had the idea for the vineyard and he visited France in October of that year with his gardener, Mr. Blackman, to order the vines. He did plough the land in the winter of 1951, but the vines did not arrive until March 1952.
2   Rootstock 161-49, rated as low vigour, has rarely been used during the first 50 years of the revival, as it is seldom grafted by the German vine nurseries who supplied the majority of the vines planted in the first few decades. Now Champagne varieties are being planted, many on chalk-rich soils, this valuable rootstock, although slow and sometimes difficult to establish, is becoming more widely used. 5BB, is a much more vigourous rootstock than 161-49, but Seyval performs well on it as Seyval is a low-vigour variety.

well and produced their first crop in 1955. The wine – history does not record what it tasted like – was the first commercial vintage to be made in Great Britain since the 1911 Castle Coch. The fact that wine *was* now being produced, created much interest and Salisbury-Jones was besieged by the press and media anxious for a story. He was an imposing figure, with a colourful and honourable past, a name to conjure with and had the ability to hold an audience. This made him much in demand as a guest speaker. The name Hambledon soon became synonymous with English Wine and Brock's dream of re-establishing commercial wine production in Great Britain, some ten years after he started his trials at Oxted, became a reality.[3]

Vendange at Hambledon in the 1960s
Sir Guy Salisbury-Jones is on the left, with his wife, Hilda, by his side

The expansion of vineyards after the planting of Hambledon was painfully slow. Jack Ward, who had co-founded the Merrydown Wine Company at Horam in East Sussex, became interested in the subject. Being a cider and country winemaker, he looked at wine made from home-grown grapes as something which his company might get involved in. Ward made contact with Brock at Oxted and went to see what he was doing. In 1954 Ward planted six vines – really just to see how they would do at Horam – in the grounds of the Merrydown winery, known as Horam Manor, although the manor house had long before burnt down. The varieties chosen were Müller-Thurgau, Madeleine Royale and Gamay Hâtif des Vosges. No sooner had he

3   A longer version of the Hambledon story is to be found under their entry in Part 2 *Vineyards A-Z.*

done this than a property known as The Grange, a house across the road from the winery with several acres of garden, came up for sale and was bought by the company to provide accommodation for some of its employees. Ward's plans for establishing a vineyard were promptly brought forward and in 1955, taking charge of the gardens, he planted a 2-acre vineyard – the second commercial vineyard of the revival. Apart from Müller-Thurgau, it is not know what other varieties were planted, although it would be surprising if Seyval blanc was not also included. In later years, Ward, who had studied music at the *Frankfurt Conservatorium* before the war and spoke fluent German, visited Geisenheim and was instrumental in introducing varieties such as Reichensteiner, Huxelrebe and Schönburger to the UK. He was very much a driving force in the industry and was elected to be the first Chairman of the English Vineyards Association (EVA) when it was formed in 1967.[4]

The third vineyard to be planted in modern times was that of the Gore-Browne's at Beaulieu. In 1956 Lieutenant-Colonel Robert and Mrs Margaret Gore-Browne, who had recently returned to Great Britain from Africa, rented a house on the Beaulieu Estate (the Montagus were old family friends) called The Vineyards. On asking Lord Montagu why the house was so-called, they were told that the land behind the house had been the site of a vineyard planted by the Cistercian monks who had established Beaulieu Abbey in 1204. Despite initial reluctance from the Colonel, but no doubt encouraged by the success of the nearby vineyard at Hambledon (planted by a fellow soldier) the Gore-Brownes decided to re-establish the vineyard. In the spring of 1958 they planted four rows of Müller-Thurgau and Seyval blanc as well as a few Gamay noir Hâtif des Vosges, Précoce de Malingre and Madeleine Sylvaner III 28/51, all of which they bought from Brock at Oxted. Brock's account books show a sale to the Gore-Brownes on 24 December 1957 (perhaps a Christmas present?) of £112 worth of vines. The vineyard was gradually expanded with more of the same, plus some Wrotham Pinot. By 1960/61 they had planted almost 5.5-acres (2.23-hectares). Their first vintage, in 1961, was a rosé and was apparently well received. They also experimented with Baco No.1, Brandt, Pirovano 14 and Cascade – this last variety despite the fact that Mrs Gore-Browne had heard that it was prohibited by the Common Market *as it is said to have an injurious effect upon the liver*, a common scare story put out by the anti-hybrid growers in France. By 1967 however, they had decided to eliminate the experimental varieties – no doubt due to poor performance.

Winemaking in those early days was, from all accounts, a fairly hit and miss affair. Both Salisbury-Jones and Gore-Browne, as well as others in years to come, were helped by Anton Massel, a young German who had come across to work for the Seitz Filter company in the UK in 1956. In 1961 Massel opened his own laboratory at Water Lane in London which he moved to Ockley, a village to the south of Dorking in

---

4   The full story of Jack Ward, the Merrydown vineyards and the part played by the Merrydown Wine Company can be found in Appendix II.

Surrey, in 1969.[5] Before the first vintage at Hambledon (the 1955) Salisbury-Jones had built himself a small winery and equipped it cheaply with simple equipment and the first two vintages were made in what one might certainly call 'primitive conditions'. This showed in the results. When Massel appeared on the scene and offered his services, the first thing he did was persuade Salisbury-Jones to invest £6,000 in better equipment including a small Willmes air-bladder press – the first of many to enter the country. This press is believed to be still in use. It was first sold to Sir Reresby Sitwell Bt. at Renishaw Hall near Sheffield and subsequently to a grower in the south of the country. Massel also persuaded Salisbury-Jones that the vineyard needed to be at least three acres in size for it to be viable and to make use of the equipment that now sat in the winery. In fact Salisbury-Jones enlarged the vineyard to 4.5-acres (1.82-hectares). The Gore-Brownes likewise built themselves a winery and used Massel as their consultant. Being already involved with fermentation of cider and fruit wines Merrydown had their own winemaking equipment – albeit on a rather larger scale than they needed for their small vineyard – and did not need the services of a consultant.

What these very early wines were like is open to question – very few tasting notes survive and people's memories tend to be selective. Those who do remember them recall wines of high acidity, lean in structure and lacking fruit. The early growers battled to control disease, powdery mildew and *Botrytis* being the worst, and undoubtedly picked too early in order to get to the grapes before the birds or the rot. The wines were usually made in a fairly natural dry style, with little or no residual sugar and left to soften with age. Hambledon thought nothing of offering wines five or more years old and almost prided itself on their wines' long cellaring potential. The idea of bottling wines with a little residual sweetness to temper the acidity was something of an anathema to the early pioneers and this practice, now widespread, had to wait a few years.

The establishment of these three vineyards between 1952 and 1958, and the appearance of English wine on sale, was proof-positive that viticulture in the British Isles had been revived. While it would be an exaggeration to say that the industry then 'took off' there is no doubt that the number of both actual and potential vineyard owners suddenly expanded and small trial plots of vines appeared in all kinds of unlikely places. The real expansion of vineyards from which commercial quantities of wine for sale could be made started in the early to mid-1960s. People such as Trevor and Joy Bates at Nettlestead outside Maidstone, Norman Cowderoy at Rock Lodge, near Uckfield in West Sussex, Robin Don at Elmham Park in Norfolk, Nigel Godden at Pilton Manor in Somerset, Messrs. Gibbons and Poulter at Cranmore on the Isle of

---

5   This laboratory was sold by Massel in 1967 and eventually became Corkwise Ltd which still trades today and analyses most UK-grown wines. Massel also founded the International Wine and Spirits Competition (IWSC) which one of the largest and most respected of all international wine competitions. It is now owned by Harpers Wine and Spirit Weekly.

Wight, the Montagus at Beaulieu, Gillian Pearkes in Devon, Major Rook at Stragglethorpe Hall near Lincoln, Pam Smith at Flexerne, East Sussex and Philip Tyson-Woodcock at Brede, near Rye in East Sussex, all planted vineyards. Wales too became the home of several vineyards: Lewis Mathias at Lamphey Court, George Jones at Pembrey, plus several others belonging to or with advice from Margaret Gore-Browne (who was Welsh by birth).

This spread of vineyards geographically, coupled with a diversity of owners, sites, training and pruning systems and, above all, of vine varieties, meant that at last valuable experience was being gained across the whole country. Thus, potential winegrowers were better able to judge what varieties and what training systems were actually working, how vines should be managed and – last but by no means least – how grapes could be turned into palatable wine.

Vineyards become more commercial 1966–1975

Once wines from the early vineyards started to be produced in saleable quantities and could be bought, tasted and assessed by the wine trade and consumers alike, the publicity surrounding English and Welsh wine really started to gather momentum. It soon became clear that making wine in the UK, even with its marginal climate, was no longer entirely the joke it had long been considered and that grapes could perhaps be viewed as a commercial crop.

The real expansion of the vineyard area and the establishment of both sizeable vineyards and wineries started in earnest in the late 1960s and it was an era of rapid growth. One of the features of English and Welsh viticulture is the diversity of backgrounds of those who plant vineyards. In other countries where new vineyards are being planted, one would expect to see existing landowners – most usually those with land in the vicinity of established vineyards – planting up, together with a smaller number of entrants with no experience of growing at all, but with serious funds, usually made in a completely unrelated industry. In the UK, those planting vineyards came from a much wider cross-section of the community: a sprinkling of retired service people, a few farmers and landowners looking for alternative – hopefully more profitable – crops, some 'lifestyle' smallholders (generally under-funded) keen to be part of the Good Life brigade, as well as those with a few acres attached to their houses in the country who liked the idea of having their names on a wine label. Only one thing really seems to have united them: an almost complete lack of experience in growing vines (and in many cases of growing anything) or of making wine! Sadly this lack of experience often (although not always) showed in the quality of both the vineyards they planted and managed and of the wines they produced.

In the late 1960s a new crop of vineyards appeared: Ken Barlow at Adgestone, Isle of Wight, Richard and Joyce Barnes at Biddenden, Kent, Graham and Irene Barrett at Felsted in Essex, Walter Cardy at Pangbourne in Berkshire, the Crossland-Hinchcliffe's at Castlehouse in East Sussex, Jack Edgerly at Kelsale in Suffolk, Ian

Grant at Knowle Hill in Kent, Bill Greenwood at New Hall, Purleigh in Essex, Anton Massel at Ockley in Surrey, Gruff Reece at Gamlinglay, Bedfordshire, Bernard Theobald at Westbury, Berkshire and T. P. Baillie-Grohman at Hascombe, Surrey (whom some of us dubbed 'T. P. Barely-Growing', such was the state of his vineyard). These new ventures were in many cases quite substantial and their owners, several of whom were mildly (and in some cases quite wildly) eccentric, helped do two things: spread the word that establishing commercial vineyards was possible in the British Isles and reinforce the idea that to do so, in this climate, was something rather unusual and novel.

The next five years (the first half of the 1970s) saw yet another frenzy of planting: Sam Alper at Chilford Hall in Cambridgeshire, Bob Blayney at La Mare on Jersey, R. M. O. Capper at Stocks in Worcester, David Carr Taylor at Westfield near Hastings and William Ross at Barnsgate Manor, Crowborough, both in East Sussex, Peter Cook at Pulham St. Mary in Norfolk, J. R. M. Donald at Tytherley in Wiltshire, Colin and Sue Gillespie at Wootton in Somerset, Peter Hall at Breaky Bottom, Lewes, East Sussex, Kenneth McAlpine at Lamberhurst in Kent, Mary Macrae at Highwaymans near Bury St Edmunds, Basil Ambrose at Cavendish Manor and Ian and Eleanor Berwick at Bruisyard, all in Suffolk, Alan McKechnie at Three Choirs at Newent in Gloucestershire, Andrew and Ian Paget at Chilsdown in West Sussex, Chris Stuart at Aeshton Manor in Wiltshire and Bob Westphal at Penshurst in Kent. The above is by no means a comprehensive list of all those who planted vineyards – just the more substantial plantings – and scores of other growers were experimenting with smaller vineyards across the whole of the south of the UK. By the end of 1975, the total UK vine area was recorded by MAFF as being 196-hectares.[6]

The fabled summer of 1976 which, according to legend, was the hottest and driest on record (there were nine days over 30°C, which was a record at the time), gave further impetus to vinegrowing. In fact, although some vineyards did pick large crops in 1976 others were badly damaged by mid-April frosts and most vineyards suffered greatly from *Botrytis* as it started raining at the end of August, and September and October, the main ripening and harvesting months, were very wet. This however did

---

6   Until 1989, requests for information about the planted area of vines were only sent out to farmers and growers having a MAFF 'Holding Number' and who had recorded vines as part of their 'other crops' on their December returns (which each farmer is legally required to make). As these vine returns were voluntary, not all vineyard owners completed them. In addition, many vineyard owners, especially those with vines in back gardens, allotments and small paddocks, were not registered with MAFF and thus escaped scrutiny altogether. This means that the pre-1989 figures must be treated with suspicion. Post-1988, the data on vineyards and wine production has been collected by the Wine Standards Board (see Footnote 7) and because it covers all registered vineyards is much more reliable, although as vineyard owners do not have to register until they start producing a 'wine sector product' i.e. grapes, juice or wine, there is often quite a delay in registering and then collecting the data. A vineyard must be registered when it is 10 ares (1,000 square metres) or more in size. Vineyards under this size are not registered or recorded, although plenty exist in the UK.

not stop the general public believing that at last the Almighty had smiled on the country's winegrowers, further fuelling the interest in English and Welsh wines and with it the planting of more and more vineyards.

Vineyards established 1976–1993

The years between 1976 and 1993 saw a large number of vineyards planted, including some very sizeable ones. Growers such as Mark Lambert at Barkham Manor, Piltdown, East Sussex, Jon Leighton at Valley Vineyards (now Stanlake Park), Reading, Berkshire, Stuart and Sandy Moss at Nyetimber, Pulborough, West Sussex, the Quirk family at Chiddingstone, Edenbridge, Kent, the Sax family at Battle, East Sussex, Andrew Vining at Wellow, Romsey, Hampshire and Adrian White at Denbies, Dorking, Surrey all planted vineyards in excess of 8-hectares (20-acres) in size, the largest (Denbies) growing to 107-hectares (265-acres). In addition, existing vineyards such as those at Adgestone, Carr Taylor, Chilford, Highwaymans, Lamberhurst, New Hall and Three Choirs all increased in size as the market for their wines expanded. 1976 was also the year that I returned from Germany and in the spring of 1977 started planting vines at what was then called Spots Farm, which turned into Tenterden Vineyards and is now home to English Wines Group plc and more generally referred to as Chapel Down Wines.

The reasons for this spurt in planting were several-fold. A rumoured vine planting ban in 1990/91 persuaded many growers that if they were going to plant it had better be soon and between 1992 and 1993 an abnormally large number of vines were planted. Other reasons were the general buoyancy in the economy, coupled with a growth in wine-drinking in the UK, which seemed to make people with a spare bit of land think that owing a vineyard would be fun. English and Welsh wine continued to get plenty of publicity and this too, further fuelled the fires of vineyard planting. The official Wine Standards Board[7] (WSB) figures for 1993 showed that the national vineyard area had reached 1,065-hectares (2,631-acres), of which almost 28 per cent was not yet in production, and that there were 479 separate vineyards. This area total remained the highest until eclipsed by the 2008 figure of 1,106-hectares. The figure for vineyards still stands as a record.

To say that vineyard planting since the mid-1970s had followed a pattern of any recognisable sort would be brave, mainly because up until 1989 accurate data did not

---

7   The Wine Standards Board, was, until it was absorbed into the Food Standards Agency (FSA) in 2006 and became the Wine Standards Branch of the FSA, one of the more curious of quasi-governmental organisations. It was set up when the UK joined the European Union in 1973 to look after the legislation covering wine and was partially funded by the Vintner's Company. The Vintners felt that this was a good chance to put something back into the wine trade, from which they had become somewhat separated, and offered the WSB both office space and funding. The Vintners contributed 40 per cent of the funding which in 2005/6 amounted to £450,000 a year.

exist! MAFF's voluntary survey of 1975 revealed a total of 196-hectares (484-acres) of vines, but this was undoubtedly on the low side. By the time MAFF undertook their second survey in 1984, the figure had risen to 430-hectares (1,062-acres), but again, this was artificially low. The third survey in 1985/6 came up with 488-hectares (1,205-acres) and finally the fourth survey, in 1987/8, revealed a total of 546-hectares (1,349-acres) which triggered the need for a statutory (compulsory) survey so that a 'Vineyard Register' could be compiled.[8] In 1989 the first statutory vineyard census was undertaken and a much truer figure of 876-hectares (2,164-acres) was recorded. This showed that previous surveys had greatly underestimated the extent of vineyard plantings in the UK.

Decline in vineyard planting 1994–2004

The period between 1994 and 2004 saw a gradual decline in overall plantings, with the total area falling from the 1993 high of 1,065-hectares to a low of 761-hectares in 2004, a drop of almost 29 per cent. What is perhaps more telling is that the percentage of vineyards 'not in production' fell from 34.5 per cent of the total in 1991, to 18 per cent of the total in 2003. The area of vines 'in production' did not vary quite so spectacularly and reached its zenith in 1998 with 842-hectares and its nadir in 2004 with 747-hectares – a drop of a mere 11 per cent. Likewise, the number of vineyards fell by a massive 30 per cent from 479 in 1993 to 333 in 2003. What this shows is that the smaller vineyards disappeared more rapidly than the larger, and the larger ones that remained tended to get bigger.

The factors behind this large fall in the planted area and the number of vineyards is not hard to find and can be summed up thus: wrong varieties, wrong sites, poor winemaking, poor quality and lastly, and most importantly, marketing difficulties.

Most of the vineyards up to this period had been planted with German crosses plus Seyval blanc, varieties which (with one or two honourable exceptions) were getting beyond their sell-by date. The 1990 WSB vine varieties survey showed that Müller-

---

8 A 'Vineyard Register' is required in all Member States that have 500-hectares or more of vines. This details the location of every 'parcel' of vines together with the variety, clone and rootstock in the parcel. For over twenty years, I have been asking the WSB (and MAFF/DEFRA) if it could be made public, but was always met with the same response – NO. The reason given was that the data was collected under the Agricultural Census Act which guaranteed anonymity. In 2005, I decided to invoke the Freedom of Information Act and although initially my request was rejected, in May 2009 I asked again and after 6 months of stalling, the WSB decided that Regulation 436/2009 of August 2009 absolved them from the need to keep the Vineyard Register secret and sent me the full list of 417 vineyard names with declared hectarage, postal town and postcode – full addresses would take a little longer! Having cross-referenced the Vineyard Register with my own UK vineyards database, I discovered several things: the Vineyard Register is quite a bit out of date, and contains vineyards that have been dormant for a while and some that have even been grubbed up. However, I now have a list of 90 additional vineyard names to add to the 439 in this book, a total of 529!

Thurgau, Seyval blanc, Reichensteiner, Bacchus, Schönburger, Madeleine Angevine 7672, Huxelrebe, Ortega, Kerner and Würzer together accounted for 729-hectares (79 per cent) out of a total planted area of 929-hectares. At this time, Pinot noir and Chardonnay were fairly minor varieties and together only accounted for 51.9-hectares or 5.6 per cent of the total, most of which was planted on about three sites.

English and Welsh vineyards were finding it increasingly difficult to sell the wines they produced based upon these Germanic varieties, mainly because the public had been introduced to new styles of wines from places such as Australia, New Zealand, South Africa, Chile and the USA (principally California) and English and Welsh wines, with their Hock and Mosel bottle shapes and colours and their Teutonic varietal names required too much effort to get them to move off the shelves. Pricing too was always an issue and as costs rose, English and Welsh wines found themselves at even more of a disadvantage. Excise duties and VAT doubled between the late 1970s and 1991, while retail prices seemed (almost) to stand still. Taken together, these factors pushed many of the small vineyards, as well as quite a few of the larger ones, into oblivion.

It is a sobering thought that of the 352 vineyards in my 1989 book *The Vineyards of England*, less than half – 150 to be precise – were still around to be included in my 2001 book *The Wines of Britain and Ireland* and of those 150 only 84 remain to be included in this one. Among those that have disappeared are some 21 vineyards of 4-hectares (10-acres) or more – Barkham Manor, Bruisyard, Chiddingstone, Highwayman's, Pilton Manor, Pulham, Wellow and Westbury to name the biggest and best known. They went mainly because they were just unable to cope with the problem of selling their wines at anything approaching the right price – a price that gave both profit and return on capital. The British wine trade in general was fairly anti-English and Welsh wine and considered it, one has to say with some justification, as being mainly produced by amateurs who made indifferent wines and expected the trade to sell them at unrealistic prices. Even those vineyards who did produce reliable, good-quality (for the price) wines and had a realistic price structure that gave both wholesalers and retailers a proper margin, struggled.[9]

So if size wasn't a guarantee of success – was quality? When one looks at the roll-call of Gore-Browne Trophy winners – presumably some guide to excellence – between the Wine of the Year Competition's inception in 1974 and 1999 (the last year before the Champagne-variety based sparkling wines started winning it) it would seem apparently not. Of the 15 vineyards that won it in these 26 years, only five – Biddenden, Carr-Taylor, Wyken, Stanlake Park and Tenterden remain in anything like

---

9   For three years, 1988–1991, I was Winemaker and General Manager at Lamberhurst Vineyards, then the largest and most professional English wine producer. Under winemaker Karl-Heinz Johner their wines had won countless awards and medals and Lamberhurst was certainly the best known vineyard name in the UK. Even with all this behind it, the only way that their wines got onto supermarket and wine shop shelves was by attractive pricing.

rude health – another four linger on in a much changed format – Adgestone, Chiltern Valley, Felsted and Lamberhurst – and six have disappeared altogether – Barton Manor, Brede, Kelsale, Pilton Manor, Pulham St Mary and Wootton. It is a very sad fact, that very few vineyards survive from the early 1970s and even fewer survive under their original owners: Beaulieu, Biddenden, Bookers, Breaky Bottom, Carr Taylor, Chilford, New Hall and Syndale Valley come to mind – there may be a few others – but not many.

The surge of planting during the 1980s and early 1990s resulted in larger national yields and the average annual level of wine production for the eight years between 1989 and 1996 was 18,959 hl, a shade over 2.5 million bottles.[10] The 1992 UK harvest of 26,428 hl (3,523,733 bottles) was, and still remains, the largest ever recorded. This increase in the supply of UK-grown wine came at a time when demand appeared to be lessening and competition from overseas wines growing. The UK has one of the most sophisticated wine markets in the world and wines have to represent very good value for money if they are to succeed. The retail market is dominated by a small number of large chains of wine merchants and supermarket groups whose massive purchasing power allows them to squeeze keener and keener prices out of producers. Growers in marginal areas and whose production costs are relatively high and yields relatively low (such as the UK), are therefore at a very definite disadvantage. High levels of excise duty, levelled at a flat rate rather than on the value of the wine, also create further pressure in the UK market as certain 'price points' have to be met and wines have to be correctly priced in order for them to move off the shelf. In addition, the creation of the European Union Single Market meant that UK consumers could travel to the continent and import more or less unlimited quantities of wines at virtually nil rates of excise duty, which also put pressure on English vineyards and wineries, especially those situated in the counties bordering the channel where access to the ferries is easiest. At one time there were several vineyards in East Kent, near the Channel Ports: now there are very few. Taken together, these factors go some way towards explaining the miserable success rate of many vineyards planted in the late twentieth century.

Some vineyards were planted with the wrong varieties and on the wrong sites, and the problems of getting grapes to ripen under these circumstances were just too great. Others have fallen by the wayside through natural causes such as retirement, divorce and death. Quite a few vineyards, started by entrepreneurs in the boom years of the mid-1980s, were subsequently grubbed-up when their other interests came under pressure or failed. While many would like to believe it, not all vineyards that fail do so because the vineyard itself is in trouble. Other quite normal factors are often to blame. However, the desire to sink substantial sums of money into vineyards and wineries in

---

10   Contrast this with the average annual yield for the years 2000–8 which is 14,566 hl or just under 2 million bottles, a fair amount of which is sparkling wine and has gone into stock for future years.

the UK, where wine production has climatic and marketing problems that other countries do not share, has been quite remarkable. The profitability of growing grapes and making wine in the UK has always been open to debate and very many vineyards (mainly the smaller ones) have only survived because of a very high proportion of farm-gate sales at full retail prices, coupled with the ability of the owner to support the enterprise out of his or her own pocket in lean times. However, once a vineyard's production becomes too large to sell most of it over the farm-gate and the wine has to be sold through the normal wholesale and retail distribution channels that exist in the UK, the problems of marketing begin.

Before the first Hambledon vintage of 1955, no market for English and Welsh wines existed. To start with – probably up until the early 1970s – overall volumes were very small, English and Welsh wines were still a novelty and most growers could sell all they produced with little problem. However, as the number of vineyards expanded, so the amount of wine available for sale increased. A combination of relatively high prices, reflecting the difficulty of growing grapes in the UK and the scarcity of the product, and some wines of dubious quality, reflecting the inexperience of some growers and winemakers, made the British wine-trade i.e. wholesalers and retailers, somewhat wary of the product and they found it difficult to market. This led to some vineyards experiencing real problems with selling their wines at anything approaching a price that was required to fund their enterprises and they subsequently gave up the struggle. Many of these, it has to be said with the benefit of hindsight, completely misread their ability to market the volumes of wines they were able to produce. The UK wine market is a harsh place and English and Welsh wines have had to battle hard (and continue to battle hard) to maintain their place on the shelves against the endless stream of competing products.

One way out of the sales problem has been for vineyards to take the decision to sell some or all of their grapes to other, mainly larger concerns, whose marketing skills and abilities left them short of wines made from their own, home-grown grapes. Chapel Down was, and remains, the prime exponent of this method of securing grapes and they have around 75-hectares of vineyards under contract (plus around 38-hectares of their own). Although by far and away the largest buyer of grapes, Chapel Down is not the only winery to do so and several other wineries, large and small, buy grapes to supplement their own supplies. Come harvest time, there is a fair trade in grapes and lorry loads travel from east to west, and vice versa, seeking a home.

Vineyard plantings increase 2004–2009

The upturn in planting started in 2004, spurred on by two factors: the weather in 2003 and the Nyetimber effect. If anyone thought that global warming was not really happening in the UK, the summer of 2003 was a wake-up call. With ten days in the year when the temperature rose over 29°C, nine days over 30°C, five days over 33°C and two days over 35°C – the first year in the 360+ years of record keeping when this last temperature had been reached – it was evident that we were entering into uncharted territory. In Champagne, the situation was even worse. Apart from the worst frost for 80 years – the temperature fell to −11°C on 11 April – August saw the temperatures rise to 43°C, again a record, and grapes ripened far too quickly, losing the valuable acidity which is the hallmark of great sparkling wines. The general opinion was that little wine of note would be made in Champagne that year and if this was the shape of things to come, *vignerons* and the *Grande Marque* Champagne houses better find somewhere a bit cooler to plant their vines. Where? Well to go cooler, you need to go further north and where better than the home of their largest export market – England. The general feeling was that climate change had definitely arrived and the southern half of the UK was no bad place to establish a vineyard.

The other factor in the planting upturn was the Nyetimber effect. Planted between 1988 and 1991 by two reclusive Americans, Nyetimber kept itself to itself for years and just picked grapes and made wine, stacking up the vintages waiting for it to mature. Their first release was the *1992 Blanc de Blancs Première Cuvée* (a 100 per cent Chardonnay wine) which hit the ground running and won a Gold Medal and the English Wine Trophy in the 1997 IWSC Competition. Not content with this initial success, their next release, the *1993 Classic Cuvée* (a Chardonnay, Pinot noir and Pinot Meunier blend) went one better and won a Gold Medal, the English Wine Trophy *and* the Bottle Fermented Sparkling Wine Trophy in the 1998 IWSC. Suddenly, everyone woke up to the fact that good wine, even stunningly good wine, could be made from hitherto seemingly unworkable varieties – Chardonnay, Pinot noir and Pinot Meunier – and what was more, the wine could be sold at a premium price. Nyetimber went from strength to strength, winning the Gore-Browne Trophy in 2001, 2003, 2004, 2005 and 2006 and the IWSC International Sparkling Wine Trophy in 2006, 2008 and 2009. [11]

The second major producer making sparkling wines from the classic Champagne varieties was Sussex-based RidgeView who started planting in 1995. Their first release, the *1996 Cuveé Merret Bloomsbury*, was in fact a wine made from grapes sourced from other growers, Surrenden Vineyard near Ashford, Kent (who had been growing Champagne varieties since 1986), being the main one. This wine, released in 2000, won the Gore-Browne Trophy in that year, and added further impetus to the realisation that this was the way forward. They also won the Gore-Browne Trophy again, in 2002, with their *1998 Cuveé Merret Cavendish*, this time made from grapes from their own vineyards. They also won the IWSC International Sparkling Wine

---

11 Nyetimber was in fact far from the first to plant Champagne varieties and several growers had attempted to grow them previously, but with very mixed results. Hambledon planted some but they never ripened; the Paget brothers at Chilsdown, near Chichester also planted Chardonnay, but it too never ripened properly; and Piers Greenwood at New Hall, Essex first grew Chardonnay in the early 1980s and miraculously got it to ripen. This fruit was bought by Lamberhurst and was used in the Lamberhurst Brut launched in 1988-9.

Trophy in 2000 with the *1996 Cuveé Merret Bloomsbury*, in 2002 with the *1998 Cuveé Merret Bloomsbury* and in 2005 with the 2002 vintage of the same wine.

From 2005, the national area under vine, after eleven consecutive years of decline, showed a modest net increase in the first year of 32-hectares, thus starting a trend which continues today. The current spate of plantings has been overwhelmingly with Champagne varieties, mainly Chardonnay and Pinot noir, with a much smaller amount of Pinot Meunier. Official WSB figures show the planted area rising between 2004 and 2009 inclusive from 761-hectares to a total of 1,215-hectares, an increase of 454-hectares or almost 60 per cent. My guess is that new plantings are larger than that and I estimate that the figure for the total planted area today (including 2009 plantings) is nearer 1,350-1,400-hectares.

Several significant vineyards have been planted over the past five years: Nyetimber has expanded under its new ownership on various sites from its original 15.8-hectares to a whopping 142-hectares; Robert Fleming Wines in Essex 32-hectares; Chapel Down's new 'Kit's Coty' site at Aylesford near Maidstone 29-hectares (with possibly more to come in 2010), Gusbourne Estate 21-hectares, Squerryes Estate 11.5-hectares and Hush Heath 5-hectares, all in Kent; Court Gardens 4.8-hectares in East Sussex; Tinwood 18-hectares, Redfold 10-hectares, Tullens 7.5-hectares, Upperton 6.9-hectares, Wiston Estate 6.6-hectares, Stopham 5.6-hectares, all in West Sussex; Laverstoke Park 9-hectares, Exton Park 7.8-hectares, Jays Farm 4.4-hectares and Little West End Farm 4-hectares in Hampshire; Wodetone 11-hectares, Crawthorne 10-hectares and Furleigh Estate 5.5-hectares, all in Dorset; and Polgoon 4.7-hectares in Cornwall. By traditional UK standards, these are substantial vineyards. Apart from Nyetimber's and Chapel Down's new vineyards, both of which are owner-occupied, several of these larger vineyards are associated with either Chapel Down or RidgeView as suppliers under grape contracts or as co-producers. In this way, two of the three major brands, Chapel Down and RidgeView, are expanding by offloading some of the risk (and work) of growing grapes. This is in marked contrast to earlier times when growers tended to be very, even fiercely, independent and determined to do their own marketing and create their own brands which, as we have seen, quite often did not actually work.

Vineyards and wine production in the future

Although the history of planting vineyards in the UK would tend to suggest otherwise, ultimately it is the market for English and Welsh wines that will decide whether or not there should be a wine industry. There is no doubt that over the past 30 years, the market into which most of our wines are sold (there is very little English and Welsh wine exported) has become more competitive, with better and better wines being imported at cheaper and cheaper prices. The range and standard of wines available to the average consumer has never been better than it is today. English and Welsh wines, if they are to find a market among these imported wines, have to be available at the right price and of the right quality. In 1980, excise duty and VAT were less than half today's levels. Today[12], excise duty and VAT on still wine (at £1.46 a bottle and 17.5 per cent respectively) now, as can be seen from Table 3.1 absorb between 44 per cent and 29.5 per cent of still wines priced between £5 and £10 a bottle. If you then deduct a retailers normal margin of around 35 per cent GPM (this is margin – not mark-up) then the amount remaining for the producer looks alarmingly small, especially for the lower priced wines.[13]

Table 3.1   Still wines

Retail price	£5.00	£6.00	£7.00	£8.00	£9.00	£10.00
VAT	£0.74	£0.89	£1.04	£1.19	£1.34	£1.49
Excise Duty	£1.46	£1.46	£1.46	£1.46	£1.46	£1.46
Retailer's profit at 35% GPM	£1.49	£1.79	£2.09	£2.38	£2.68	£2.98
VAT, excise duty & retailer's profit	£3.69	£4.14	£4.59	£5.03	£5.48	£5.93
Balance left for producer	£1.31	£1.86	£2.41	£2.97	£3.52	£4.07
% taken by tax	44.1%	39.2%	35.8%	33.1%	31.1%	29.5%

Selling still wines at under £6 a bottle, based upon the above figures, looks increasingly like a challenge. Out of the £1.86 left for the producer must come all the production costs, including packaging and distribution, which must amount to over £1.50 a bottle, leaving perhaps a bare 36 pence to pay for the grapes. Taking 950 bottles per tonne as a standard, this would mean the value of the grapes would be around the £342 per tonne. With growing costs running at £1,750–£2,000 per acre (excluding picking), then a grower would need to be cropping at over 5 tonnes per acre just to stand still, let alone repay the cost of the vineyard or return on the land value. Of course many growers – especially but not only the smaller ones – manage to make ends meet and survive by selling a high proportion of their wines directly to the public at full retail prices. This is usually achieved by having an on-farm shop and attending county shows, farmer's markets and consumer fairs. Although this method of selling requires a level of commitment to the public that some find wearing, it does at least help the vineyard survive.

The alternative to poor returns through a combination of low yields and low prices is to produce added-value wines which achieve higher prices. The past 30 years has seen English and Welsh winegrowers making increasing amounts of wines such as

---

12 This section was written in 2008 and since then, Excise duty has risen for still wines to £1.61 and sparkling wine to £2.06 a bottle. VAT is currently 15%, although will revert back to 17.5% at 1 January 2010.

13   In case anyone thinks that you cannot buy good English wine under £6 a bottle, Waitrose, who claim to sell 28 per cent of all UK-grown wine sold via the UK off-trade, list (Oct 2009) three still English wines at £5.69. They also list eight between £6.16 and £7.59 and 10 between £8.02 and £10.44 and have ten sparkling wines from £14.24 to £24.69.

oak-aged white wines, red and rosé wines, sweet dessert wines and of course bottle-fermented sparkling wines, all of which sell at higher prices than the usual still wines. The costs of growing grapes for these 'speciality' wines is in most cases little different from standard wines, and apart from perhaps sparkling wines, where costs of production and excise duty rates are higher and oak-aged red and white wines where the cost of barrels has to be taken into account, the costs of production and packaging are more or less the same. The attractions therefore are obvious and undoubtedly these added-value wines will become the norm rather than the exception.

Oak-aged wines, once confined to the better wines from Burgundy and other traditional areas, are now commonplace in all price brackets and appear to have found favour with the average UK consumer. Winemakers in the UK have been making oak-aged wines since the mid-1980s, using not only oak barrels, the traditional, but costly method of imparting oak flavour to wine, but also by using oak staves and oak chips in the fermentation and storage tanks. There are now separate sections in the national and most regional competitions for 'oaked' wines.

In the general marketplace, red wines have been increasing their market share at the expense of whites – partly because of the increase in wine drinking at mealtimes and of the general maturity and sophistication of wine drinkers – but also because the perceived health benefits of modest wine drinking are greater for red than white wines. The amount of red wine produced in the UK is growing. In 1998 the five-year average was 8 per cent of total production; in 2007 the five-year average was 19 per cent, although this does include all shades of red, i.e. rosés as well. Although the quality of some red wines leaves a lot to be desired, a few winemakers do now consistently manage to produce very acceptable results. I used to think that blends using Dornfelder, Pinot noir, Regent and Rondo were probably the way forward, but the last few vintages (excluding 2007 and 2008) have shown us that the best wines are undoubtedly made from the right clones of Pinot noir. The Bernard Theobald Trophy for the Best Red in the EWOTYC was won every year between 2002 and 2008 by a Pinot noir (how Bernard would have loved to have seen that!): four times by Chapel Down and once each by Sharpham, Sandhurst and Titchfield Vineyards. Pinot noir has that all-important marketing edge which the Germanic varieties can never have and while some very good red blends can be made with Dornfelder, Regent and Rondo, my view is that plantings of these varieties will decline. If the weather continues to warm, then some of the Pinot noir clones currently being used for sparkling wine may well turn out to be suitable for red wine production, albeit at a lower level of yield. Having written the above in 2008, the 2009 Bernard Theobald Trophy promptly went to Mount Vineyards with a blend (Pinot noir, Rondo and Regent) called *Recession Red*. At least is was partly Pinot.

One category of wines which I do see increasing is that of rosés – both still and sparkling. Having won the President's Cup twice with rosé wines – in 1989 with the *1988 Tenterden Rosé*, a Pinot based still wine, and in 1994 with the *1992 Scott's Hall*

Bottle Fermented Sparkling Rosé – I have a soft spot for the category. In my view, many of those attempting to make red wines with varieties other than Pinot noir, should give up the struggle and make decent still and sparkling rosés. In the wider wine world, the category is booming, with retailers talking about 20 per cent growth across all types of rosé, so there is definitely a niche in the market for UK-grown rosé wines.

The production of sweet dessert wines – of which there used to be several – seems to have taken a downturn in recent years and very few of note have been produced recently. The first (in the mid-1990s) seemed to have been produced more by accident than design when rampant *Botrytis* infected varieties such as Huxelrebe, Ortega and Optima which led to classic *pourriture noble* as found in Sauternes or in German vineyards, rather than the damaging *pourriture gris* more commonly experienced in the UK. These early experiments, which on occasion produced wines of very high natural sugar levels and of superb quality, seem to have been just that – experiments – and very few vineyards make decent sweet wines on as regular basis. This is quite possibly a result of two factors which make the incidence of *Botrytis* less: warmer, drier summers and better chemical protection against the disease. Taken together, these mean cleaner crops and less chance of noble rot developing. A few growers make some acceptable semi-sweet wines – what the French might call *vin moelleux* – using varieties such as Ortega and Siegerrebe. Since Three Choirs won the 2008 Gore-Browne Trophy with their semi-sweet Siegerrebe, plantings of this early ripening variety have nudged upwards by almost 3-hectares.

However, it is the category of bottle-fermented sparkling wines that has come to dominate UK wine production. The attraction of selling sparkling wines, with their much higher prices, plus their other advantages, seems obvious. With still English and Welsh wines, age was always a problem, both retailers and consumers looking for the next vintage in the (probably rightly held belief) than the majority of our wines were best drunk within two years of harvest. In the initial years of a new vineyard, sales are always hard to come by and this meant that for still wine producers, stocks tended to build up alarmingly quickly and before you knew where you were, production would be outstripping sales and the vintages were piling up in store.

With sparkling wines, the production to sales route is much slower and the building up of stocks something that is a) necessary and b) contributes (within reason) to an improvement in the product. No one is going to worry (or even know if the product is non-vintage) how old the wine is when you offer it to them. With vintage sparkling wines, especially with UK-grown wines which tend to have high acidity which aids their keepability, it's a bit like the famous *Animal Farm* quotation turned on its head: two years good, four years better, six years even better still. Of course, the downside to having to age sparkling wines is that every vintage has to be grown, made, bottled and tucked away in expensive crates in expensive temperature controlled (or at least well-insulated) stores – all of which crank up the investment needed to create a business founded upon this sector of the wine market. With the 2009 IWSC Bottle Fermented Sparkling Wine Trophy going to the *1992 Nyetimber Blanc de Blancs* it will be interesting to see what other golden oldies come out of the cellar.

Table 3.2   Sparkling wines

Retail price	£15.00	£17.00	£19.00	£20.00	£22.00	£24.00
VAT [14]	£2.23	£2.53	£2.83	£2.98	£3.28	£3.57
Excise Duty	£1.87	£1.87	£1.87	£1.87	£1.87	£1.87
Retailer's profit at 35% GPM	£4.47	£5.06	£5.66	£5.96	£6.55	£7.15
VAT, excise duty & retailer's profit	£8.57	£9.47	£10.36	£10.81	£11.70	£12.59
Balance left for producer	£6.43	£7.53	£8.64	£9.19	£10.30	£11.41
% taken by tax	27.4%	25.9%	24.7%	24.2%	23.4%	22.7%

As can be seen from Table 3.2, if these prices are sustainable, and I believe that £15–£19 per bottle ought to be even with the larger volumes that will inevitably come onto the market, then the business model of sparkling wines, even with the greater production costs and much larger stock levels, is one that works. In the 2001 edition of this book, I wrote: *the production of bottle-fermented sparkling wines is likely to be one of the major growth areas in UK wineries over the next two decades*, perhaps not realising quite how quickly vineyards would be planted with Champagne varieties and wines produced. Sparkling wine production in the UK in fact goes right back to the first modern vineyards. In the 1978 English Wine of the Year Competition (EWOTYC), two sparkling wines, the *1976 Felstar Méthode Champenoise* and the *NV Pilton Manor De Marsac Brut Méthode Champenoise* both won medals. These early successes, however, didn't seem to help sales much and production seems to have faded out. The next appearance of a bottle-fermented sparkling wine in the EWOTYC (I am ignoring the carbonated *1983 Barton Manor Sparkling Rosé* that won a Gold Medal in the 1984 competition – delicious though it was) was in the 1987 EWOTYC when the first of Carr Taylor's sparkling wines won a medal.

In the mid-1980s both Carr Taylor and Lamberhurst vineyards started full-scale production of these wines and proved that both our 'native' vine varieties, as well as some early examples of Chardonnay, Pinot blanc and Auxerrois, could be used for producing good examples of this type of wine. For a few years Carr Taylor became the major producer – in fact almost the only producer – of bottle-fermented sparkling wines in the UK and appeared to achieve considerable sales success, although in the light of the financial problems they went through in the mid-1990s, perhaps prices

---

14 This section was written in 2008 and since then, Excise duty has risen for sparkling wine to £2.06 a bottle. VAT is currently 15%, although will revert back to 17.5% at 1 January 2010.

achieved were just not high enough.

The next on the UK sparkling wine scene was David Cowderoy who, working at his father's winery at Rock Lodge, produced the *1989 Rock Lodge Impresario* which won the IWSC English Wine Trophy in 1991.[15] When David joined forces with others to create Chapel Down Wines (in 1992) one of their first wines, the non-vintage *Epoch Brut*, made from a blend of Müller-Thurgau, Reichensteiner and Seyval blanc, was in fact a re-badged Rock Lodge wine. The fact that Chapel Down were not using the classic Champagne varieties (which, with the exception of New Hall Vineyards, were not being grown in enough quantity for them to buy), gave them something of a marketing advantage and enabled their prices to remain reasonable – under £10 – although at the time this was at least twice that of still wines. In the end though, once Chardonnay and Pinot based wines started to appear in 1997/1998, this marketing edge disappeared and their Müller-Thurgau, Reichensteiner and Seyval blanc based wines, although very good and well-priced, were always playing second fiddle to the Champagne lookalikes in quality (and quality perception) terms.

When first Nyetimber and later RidgeView started selling wines and achieving the sort of prices that many of us thought were unachievable, the way forward for UK-grown wines started to look a lot different. Again, what I wrote in 2001 bears repeating: *the quality of the wines* [those from Nyetimber and RidgeView] *to date has been very good, proving that it is possible to ripen these varieties sufficiently for this purpose. How easy it will be to obtain satisfactory crops of these varieties at the correct levels of sugar and acidity on all sites it is perhaps too early to tell, but undoubtedly, the success of these two individual vineyards will tempt other growers to attempt to emulate what they have achieved.* The question about ripening and crop levels appears (for the time being at least) to have been answered with most growers managing to harvest 7.5-10 tonnes per hectare (3–4 t/acre) from Chardonnay and Pinot noir (sparkling clones) and getting sugar and acid levels more than suitable for sparkling wines. Warm, but wet and overcast 2007 and outright chilly 2008 were a challenge for many growers, especially those who got hit by downy mildew, and, in some cases, yields were negligible. But after four brilliant vintages in a row – 2003, 2004, 2005 and 2006 – who's complaining? The fantastic 2009 harvest has certainly made most growers, but especially those in the south-east, where flowering conditions were perfect, forget the previous two years altogether.

The WSB's lists show that Pinot noir at 218-hectares and Chardonnay at 202-hectares occupy the top two slots and that together with Pinot Meunier, 49-hectares, take up 39 per cent of their figure for total planted area of 1,215-hectares. My educated guess is that these three Champagne varieties now (post-planting in 2009) occupy around 600-hectares of the UK's 1,400-hectares (43 per cent) and possibly more. However the impact of these three varieties upon UK wine production is

---

15   The next two years' IWSC English Wine Trophies were also won by sparkling wines: the 1989 Throwley Chardonnay in 1992 and 1987 Carr Taylor Vintage in 1993.

significantly greater than the bare figures suggest as most of the new plantings are large, professionally managed, correctly planted, trained and trellised and likely to yield at the higher end of the spectrum. Whereas the older Germanic-variety vineyards are often small, run by amateurs or part-timers and not always looked after very professionally, with often small, even very small, yields. At the moment, much of the sparkling wine produced from vineyards planted in the years between 2003 and 2006 is going into stock to mature *sur latte* and anything planted in 2007 or later is too young to crop. Therefore the impact of the new plantings upon the market will be slow and hopefully, as the wines become available for sale, the market itself will expand and any excess of supply over demand – which ordinarily would depress prices – will not do so.

The past 30 years have seen a marked change in wine styles and types sold in the UK. In the late 1960s and 1970s, when English wines started making an impact on consumers, the biggest selling wines in the UK were Liebfraumilches and other German and Germanic styles. While there is no doubt that price played a great part in their popularity, these wines did find favour with a large sector of the wine buying public who liked their easy, unpretentious style. In many respects the better English wines were similar – light and fruity, with a little residual sugar and not too heavy in alcohol – and they met with the approval of many consumers. In the 1980s, the tastes of UK wine drinkers started to change. Consumers seemed to want drier wines, perhaps because wine was appearing more and more at meal times, perhaps because palates were becoming more sophisticated. Wines from Australia started making a big impact on consumers and gradually the liking for German style wines reduced so that today's largest selling brands in the UK are the Australian Jacob's Creek and Hardy's ranges and Gallo's Californian wines.

English and Welsh wines have reflected these changes in the market, and today no growers (apart from Peter Hall at Breaky Bottom who uses a dark green *flute d'Alsace* for his still Seyval blanc) bottle in tall German-style Hock and Mosel bottles. Their preference today is to use the non-country specific Burgundy (in brown or green) and Bordeaux (in green or clear) bottles. Many growers also refrain from using the Germanic sounding varietal names such as Müller-Thurgau, Reichensteiner, Huxelrebe, etc. and will now give their wines more descriptive names (Stanlake Park, Downland Dry, etc.) believing (correctly in my view) that Germanic varietal names are both confusing and off-putting to the consumer. Those using varieties such as Bacchus, Ortega and Pinot noir, which appear to be more acceptable to consumers, continue to do so.

The future for sparkling wine production – which is the only category that in truth really matters – is an interesting one and I really wish my crystal ball worked properly. I have got a bit wary of making predictions about the English wine scene, so rapidly have things changed. Until the bulk of the wines produced from vineyards planted in the past five years come on the market and test the theory that they can be sold at sensible prices (by sensible I am talking about £15–£20), then I cannot see the planting boom stopping. I suppose another wet year like 2007 might make one or two people wonder if climate change means more (or should that be less?) than just endlessly hot sun-filled summers, but there will be lots of newcomers who won't worry about that I feel sure. If UK-grown sparkling wines can be successfully sold through the major multiples and retailers, which is where the bulk of sales in the UK have to take place, then those producing still wines will have an easier task than in previous decades. Every country that sells wine in the UK needs its own USP – New Zealand Sauvignon blanc, Australian Shiraz, Chilean Carménère – and there is no reason why Champagne look-a-likes cannot be ours.

The one thing that would really change the whole outlook for the future of sparkling wines is if (and I would really like to write 'when') the Champenoise get involved. The only Champagne house to investigate the prospect of planting with any degree of seriousness (at least the only one that I know about) was Duval-Leroy who instructed the Canterbury office of Strutt & Parker (well-known Estate Agents with strong farming links) to seek out suitable land for planting. Their brief was short, if slightly eccentric: the land must be within one hour of the Channel Tunnel, the soil must be chalky and there must have been no livestock on the land in recent years. This last request baffled most of those involved who were told that there might be residues in the soil which would interfere with the fermentation process! (I personally think that there was something lost in translation.) Although several sites were found, and lengthy negotiations entered into, nothing came of Duval-Leroy's quest and they retreated back to Epernay. I have recently heard that another Champagne house has been seriously looking for sites, but to date, no land appears to have been acquired. I showed Louis Roederer a few UK vineyards and possible sites, which fuelled a fair bit of speculation, but this was just a fact-finding visit. A grower from Champagne, Didier Pierson and his British-born wife, Imogen Whitaker, have planted 4-hectares of vines in the UK (see entry for Little West End Farm Vineyard) and to date, this remains the only Champagne-based involvement in UK viticulture. The Pierson-Whitakers live in Avize where they run their own small Champagne *maison* and Didier is a winemaker at the local co-operative. Their vineyard in Hampshire has been planted on land owned by a farmer, Sydney Chaplin, and if press reports are correct they have formed a joint venture. The first vines were planted in 2004, a few more in 2005 and the first harvest was in 2007. A small winery has been established on the farm. The site is very isolated (although it can be seen from a public road) and the top of the vineyard is on a very exposed hill at 203-metres above sea level. To my mind they would have done better by planting lower down on more sheltered land. I look forward to tasting their first wine.

The effect of climate change on UK viticulture

The final factor that has influenced viticulture in the UK – if not since 1951, then certainly in the past 10–15 years – is that of climate change. In 1989, when I wrote *The Vineyards of England* it didn't merit a mention. Why? Because it hadn't happened by then. Sure, there had been warm years. 1976, the year I returned from Germany, was certainly, at the time, the driest and hottest it had ever been since accurate records had been collected and, but that was a highly abnormal year and would not be repeated until 2003, almost 30 years later.

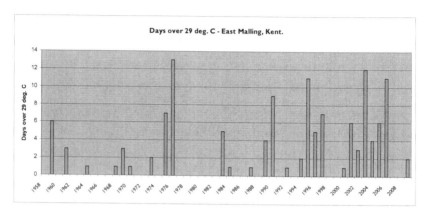

Days over 29°C, East Malling Research Station, Maidstone, Kent, 1959-2009

As you can see from the graph above, between 1959 and 1988, there were a total of forty-four days when the temperature rose to 29°C or higher, an average of just under 1.5 days per year. This period includes 1975 and 1976, both warm years, which together account for twenty of the forty-eight days in the total – take these out and the average falls to exactly 1 per year. You can also see that in-between 1977 and 1982 – the first six years of my winegrowing career in the UK – I never saw a single day when the temperature climbed over 29°C! Then things started to warm up and in 1989 and 1990 we had a total of thirteen days of 29°C or over. These two years were probably the first time that UK winegrowers realised that perhaps, just perhaps, the climate was looking up. The vintage in 1989 was very early. I started picking Schönburger on 19 September and pressed the last picking of Seyval blanc on 12 October. In 1990 a similar story, but a much heavier harvest: started on 4 October and finished on 23 October. (In contrast, in 1988, a much cooler year, I started picking Müller-Thurgau on 18 October and finished the Seyval blanc on 4 November.)

The next three years, 1991–1993, were cool and UK winegrowers saw only one day of 29°C or over: back to normal we thought, but then something very strange happened. In 1994, the weather improved and apart from 1998 and 1999, the temperature rose to 29°C or over in every year up to and including 2006 (which had the highest average annual temperature ever) until 2007 when things reverted back to normal with no days of 29°C or over and one of the wettest, coolest and most dismal summers ever, even though the average temperature for the year as a whole was, after 2006, the second highest since records began. 2008 followed much the same pattern, with no days of 29°C or over and a very low degree-day total (around 750), although sugar levels were exceptionally high, as were acid levels – an unusual combination. 2009 has (hopefully) got us back on track again, with a modest 2 days of 29°C or over, but with the highest sugar levels ever recorded in the history of modern UK winegrowing. But why – you may ask – do I consider 29°C to be of such significanc?

I have been convinced for many years that what made the UK such an unusual place (and sometimes a very unsatisfactory place) for growing grapes was the absence of really hot days in midsummer. We had quite a long, mild growing season with good light levels, long summer evenings, summer temperatures and degree days that didn't differ too much from some other winegrowing regions, yet several things were obvious: natural sugar levels were lower, acids were higher (and more malic), dry extracts lower and, very importantly for the economics of the business, yields were lower and more variable than any other winegrowing region. In addition, our spectrum of varieties was based around the ultra-cool-climate varieties: German crosses with the odd hybrid thrown in for good measure. None of the classic cool climate varieties got a look-in: Chardonnay, Chenin, Pinot noir, Riesling and Sauvignon blanc, none of them would ripen. Reims in Champagne, the UK's nearest winegrowing region travelling south, has very similar degree days to Kew in London, 869 to our 885, and the average temperature of the warmest month (July) is 17.8°C in Reims against that of 17.6°C in Kew. Yet it is plain to see that Reims could ripen 12–15 tonnes per hectare of Chardonnay and Pinot noir and make sublime sparkling wines, whereas UK growers struggled to ripen half to a third of that weight of varieties that often made second-rate wines. What then was the difference?

The idea that high summer temperatures are needed to grow a good crop of grapes which will ripen fully is not mine. In *Viticulture Volume 1 – Resources* (2nd edition 2005) edited by Peter Dry and Bryan Coombe, reference is made to work done by J. A. Prescott in 1969 and Smart and Dry in 1980, both of which take the Mean Temperature of the Warmest Month (MTWM) – January in Australia, July in Europe – as the single factor that governs the suitability of a site to grow certain varieties. And what governs the level of the temperature of the MTWM? – the number of days when the temperature rises into the high 20s or low 30s. You can take 28°, 29°, 30° or 31°C, the theory holds good at any of these temperatures.

The past 15–20 years have seen a gradual rise in the number of days when the temperatures rose above 29° and 30°, with a consequent rise in the average July temperatures which, for England as a whole, have risen from around 13.5–14.5°C in the 1970s and 1980s to 15–16.5°C – a rise of around 1.5–2.0°C in the past ten years. What this has meant to viticulturalists is that once marginal varieties – Pinot noir and Chardonnay being the most widely planted – have suddenly started to move into the mainstream. Natural sugars have increased, acids are still high in many years, but nowhere near as high as they were (for these varieties), the malic-tartaric balance is better and it would appear (although really reliable data is sadly lacking) that yields are steadier, less variable and starting to approach the averages where viticulture becomes economically viable. Whether 2007 and 2008's weather conditions were a wake-up call and we now face a spell of warm years, but years with warm winters and moist, overcast, warm summers without high July and August temperatures, who knows? Vintage 2007 in the UK was very late – some Chardonnay not picked until early November – and with very high acid levels. As if high acids were not bad enough, the malic acid content was much higher than normal, with lower tartaric acid levels, although this was common throughout northern Europe and we were not alone in having problems getting wines to complete their malo-lactic fermentations. 2009 has been a remarkable year and although the harvest is still under way as I write this (on 16 October) I think that I am safe to say that its going to be a truly vintage year. We are experiencing the best sugar levels *ever* seen (Chardonnay and Pinot noir with 11%-12% potential alcohol), near-perfect acid levels and some excellent yields. Even though the summer temperatures were not that high (only two days 29°C or over), we had a very good Spring and early Summer with high temperatures in June, a flowering period to die for which coincided with one of the driest Wimbledon tennis tournaments on record – no need of that new roof! July was wet and warm, August much the same, but September and October have been largely dry and warm.

The other change in the climate – apart from the higher mid-summer days – is the rise in night-time temperatures (if you don't believe me, go into your local bedding shop and ask them how many 13.5 Tog duvets they sell these days). This means that vines warm up more quickly, getting to the temperature where leaves can start photosynthesising more quickly, meaning that they can spend more time producing sugar. That is my theory anyway!

The Blue Fin bulding in London's Southwark, location of one of the UK's more obscure vineyards. See entry for Decanter Magazine.

CHAPTER 4

Vineyard associations

The English Vineyards Association

By the mid-1960s there were enough vineyards in the country for a growers' association to be formed and discussions were held with MAFF to determine how this could best be done. After much discussion it was eventually decided to form a company registered according to the Industrial and Provident Societies Act (IPSA) and under the auspices of the Agricultural Central Co-operative Association Ltd. In October 1965 a meeting was held at Lord Montagu's house at Beaulieu to elect a Steering Committee and to choose a name for the new association. It was agreed that it would be called The British Viticultural Association. This name, however, was rejected by the Board of Trade (why, history does not tell, but perhaps the absence of vineyards in Scotland had something to do with it) but an alternative, The English Vineyards Association (EVA), was accepted. Wales was not included in the name as a Welsh Vine Growers Association had already been formed in September 1965. A Steering Committee was elected and held its first meeting over a year later (the naming problems had taken up the intervening 12 months) on 15 November 1966. The first Annual General Meeting was subsequently held on 18 January 1967 at which the following were elected: President, Sir Guy Salisbury-Jones; Vice President, Lady Montagu of Beaulieu; Chairman, Jack Ward; Vice Chairman, P. Tyson-Woodcock; Secretary, Irene Barrett; and Director, Robin Don. In addition to the elected officers, there were eight full members and 12 associates.

The growth of interest in winegrowing in the country over the next few years was quite remarkable. By the end of 1968, although the number of full members – those owning at least half an acre of vines – had only risen to 15, the number of associate members had shot up to over 100. This was the start of the era of much larger, more commercially orientated vineyards and over the next five years, a number of major vineyards were planted. These, together with a large number of smaller vineyards, really caused the public, especially the wine-buying and vineyard-visiting public, to take an interest in the country's vineyards and their wines. By the end of 1972, the EVA had 330 members and associates, farming 200 acres of vines, with an additional 100 acres ready to be planted in the spring of 1973.

In the early years, the EVA was run very much on a shoestring and the amount it could do to help winegrowers was necessarily limited. Members' events included annual tastings, visits to overseas shows, and symposia on winegrowing. It also published an annual newsletter which continued until 1978 when the *Grape Press*, a bi-monthly publication, replaced it. The EVA also recognised that it had a duty to members of the public who were interested in buying English and Welsh wines, and therefore did what it could to promote them as well as answering the many enquiries it received on the subject. The Association also felt it had a duty if not actually physically to help growers improve their wines, then to do what it could to recognise those wines that were good. In 1978, after six years of negotiations with the authorities, the EVA received permission to introduce a Certification Trade Mark – known as the EVA Seal of Quality – which gave wines, after they had been analysed and been before a tasting panel – and approved on both counts – a recognised seal of approval that could be affixed to bottles. (This scheme ran until 1995 when the official EU approved Quality Wine Scheme, the UK's *appellation* system, was introduced.) In 1974, the EVA established the English Wine of the Year competition and Margaret Gore-Browne donated a magnificent silver bowl in memory of her husband Robert (who had died in 1972) which was to be presented to the best wine in the competition. Since then, as the number and styles of wines entered has increased, several other trophies have been donated and today the Gore-Browne Trophy has been joined by the Jack Ward Memorial Salver and the President's, the Wine Guild of the United Kingdom, the Vintner's, the Dudley Quirk Memorial, the McAlpine Winemaker of the Year, the Montagu, the Tom Day, the Berwick, the Waitrose Rosé and the Maggie McNie Trophies. The competition has, by showing growers and winemakers what their peers have been making, greatly helped to improve wine quality.

Another function of the EVA was the need to represent the interests of growers and winemakers and as soon as it was founded, it held regular meetings with the various authorities who had a hand in regulating and controlling the industry: the Home Office, MAFF and its successor, the Department for Environment, Food, and Rural Affairs (DEFRA), HM Customs and Excise (now HM Revenue and Customs – HMRC) and the Wine Standards Board (now the Wine Standards Branch of the Food Standards Agency) being the main ones.

By 1978, for legal reasons, substantial changes to the status of the EVA were needed and in February 1979 it was incorporated as a company limited by guarantee, rather than one registered under the IPSA. The finances of the Association were always balanced fairly finely, and during the early 1970s subscription income rarely covered expenses. In 1976, in addition to an annual subscription, a levy on each acre of vines in production (vines under four years old were exempt) was introduced and this greatly helped matters. In 1980, the management of the association also required changes as Irene Barrett of Felsted Vineyards, who had been unpaid Secretary since its inception, retired. Her place was taken by Kenneth McAlpine, owner of Lamberhurst Vineyards, which at that time was by far the largest wine producer in the UK. McAlpine also became Treasurer. In April 1981, Sir Guy Salisbury-Jones decided to retire from his position as President of the EVA and his place was taken by Lord Montagu of Beaulieu. Jack Ward also stepped down from his position as

Chairman of the Board of the EVA, a post he had held since the founding of the Association in 1967 and his place was taken by Colin Gillespie of Wootton Vineyards. With these changes in place it felt very much like the 'old guard' stepping down in favour of a new, more commercially minded, management team taking over.

As more and more vineyards were planted and production levies started to produce solid income, the finances of the EVA improved, and at the AGM in April 1985 the membership felt that the Association was sufficiently strong to consider appointing its first full-time employee. In October 1985, Commander Geoffrey Bond RN (rtd) was appointed to the post of Chief Executive and for the next ten years he ran the EVA from an office in his house in Eltham in south London, dealing with a multitude of enquiries from all and sundry, handling press enquiries, talking to groups and associations and generally being 'Mr English Wine' whenever required. The EVA also appointed Anthony Steen, MP for South Hams in Devon, as its official (paid) parliamentary adviser, and for six years Steen made sure that the industry's concerns were heard in Westminster.

During the 1980s, the EVA prospered, with new vineyards being planted all over the south of the country, some good harvests and a buoyant membership list. A combination of subscription income and production levies allowed the association's reserves to build to a considerable size.

As a result of this optimism in the industry the regional associations, which had been formed to cater for the local needs of vineyard owners, also became strong and started, to a certain extent, to take over some of the functions of the EVA, considered to be the central body and therefore more concerned with national issues.[1] Some members of the regional associations saw no need to belong to the EVA as they felt that they were getting all the benefits locally and therefore why should they belong to both associations? From about 1990, the membership of the EVA began to fall and with it, its income, while its work continued to grow. More was spent on publicity, the duties of its staff did not contract and negotiations with the authorities grew as changes to the EU Wine Regime threatened to harm growers. By 1992/3 it had become clear that the situation could not continue indefinitely and changes to the way the EVA was both constituted and funded had to be made.

The United Kingdom Vineyards Association

The next 18 months were taken up with the long and, at times difficult, process of changing the entire structure of the EVA. After considerable discussion and debate with both its own members and those of the six regional associations, a situation was

1   There are today six regional vineyard associations: East Anglian Winegrowers' Association, South East Vineyards Association (which started out life as the Weald and Downland Vineyards Association), the Wessex Vineyards Association, the South West Vineyards Association and the Thames and Chilterns Vineyards Association. There is also an English Wine Producers (EWP) Larger Growers and Producers Group.

reached where it was generally agreed that the EVA would be disbanded and a new company, the United Kingdom Vineyards Association (UKVA), would be formed in its place and take over both its assets and its duties. This company would be owned, managed and financed by the six existing regional associations, its members would be those who were members of those regional associations and no others and its board of directors would be nominated by the regional associations, plus one representative from the English Wine Producers who represented the Larger Growers and Producers Group. The UKVA would have no independent means of raising revenue from its members and all funding would come from the affiliated regional associations.

On paper this looked a workable solution and a further twelve months were taken up with the practicalities of drawing up and approving the new company's Memorandum and Articles of Association. By the midsummer of 1996, everything was in place for a handover of control and assets from the EVA to the UKVA. In the event, only five out of the six eligible regional associations decided to become affiliated. The Thames and Chilterns Vineyards Association (T&CVA), which had been party to the negotiations and deliberations right up until the last moment, decided (somewhat churlishly in my view) that they did not wish to be affiliated. They had reservations about some of the decisions taken by the EVA Board (even though they had a non-voting representative on it) and decided that this was not the best way forward for the association. They therefore felt that they could not support the Board's decisions and decided to remain independent. It was a pity that unanimity could not have been maintained to the end, but the remainder felt, in the event, that five out of six was actually not too bad a result.[2] The first meeting of the UKVA was held on 15 July 1996.

The functions of the UKVA remained much the same as those of the EVA. Organising meetings for members, the AGM and the Symposium, publishing the *Grape Press*, running the annual Wine of the Year Competition and the House of Lords prizegiving, operating the Quality and Regional Wine Schemes (see below), liaising with members of the public, winetrade and media who wanted information about English and Welsh wine, arranging tastings of one sort or another, organising council meetings, meetings with DEFRA, HMRC, WSB, plus the hundred and one other things that a national association gets asked to do. The fact that the regional associations were now both responsible for the running and financing of the association meant that some of the work previously carried out by the central organisation could now be left to the regions. In 1998, the UKVA formed a UK Winegrowers Committee under the auspices of the Wine and Spirit Association of Great Britain (now the Wine and Spirit Trade Association), thus giving it a more powerful voice when looking after the interests of its members.

---

2 One of my stated aims when I took over the Chairmanship of the UKVA in 1999 was to get the T&CVA back in the fold and in 2000 they were persuaded to affiliate.

MAFF, DEFRA and the EVA-UKVA

In the early days of the viticultural revival, MAFF took an active interest in the subject and for 20 years there was an official National Vines Adviser who could be called upon to advise growers through MAFF's own consultancy arm, the Agricultural Development and Advisory Service (ADAS). The first person to occupy this position was Tony Heath, a soft-fruit adviser based at the Efford Experimental Husbandry Station (EHS) at Lymington near Southampton. Although principally a strawberry specialist, he took a great personal interest in vines and was responsible for writing two MAFF publications on the subject: *Outdoor Grape Production* in 1978 and *Grapes for Wine* in 1980. Both of these books were very well written and apart from some mis-information about what varieties we were actually allowed to plant (the books stated, incorrectly, that any variety not on the Recommended or Authorised lists may be regarded as being under test in the UK and used for commercial wine production) contained much useful information for growers. After Heath retired, his position was taken in turn by Joanna Wood, Sheila Baxter and Jerry Garner, all of whom gave advice to growers on matters viticultural. Efford EHS had its own vineyard, planted in 1975, which undertook variety and trellising trials, as well as trials on vine nutrition, fungicides and weed control. It published several useful reports, hosted open days and while it lasted, provided some useful information to the UK's small but growing band of winegrowers. In 1986 MAFF decided that running the vineyard was an expense it could do without and it was grubbed-up. One serious flaw in MAFF's approach to helping those growing grapes in the UK – given that these were solely wine varieties which growers were being advised upon – was that it was adamant that its job finished at harvest time and winemaking matters were totally outside its remit. Many felt that it would have been more helpful if MAFF's advice could have covered all aspects of wine production. In recent years, with the privatisation of ADAS, the position of National Vines Adviser has lain dormant, and advice, certainly free advice, on viticulture is no longer available.

Relations with MAFF, as the authority governing the production of wine both before we joined the European Union (EU) and, since 1973, after we joined, have always been important for UK grape growers and winemakers. To begin with, the EVA was invited by MAFF to meetings on an irregular basis to discuss matters that affected the industry, such as vine varieties, winery practices, labelling legislation, pesticide registrations and a wide range of other topics. This committee, which became known as the English and Welsh Wine Liaison Committee, was purely advisory and its deliberations and decisions carried no official weight. Once the number of area of vines in the UK was known to exceed 500-hectares (which happened in 1987) relations between the industry and MAFF was put on a more formal basis, with meetings held on a regular basis. In addition, a Vine Varieties Classification Committee (VVCC) was formed, whose task was to oversee changes to the lists of vine varieties permitted to be grown in the UK (more on the workings of the VVCC can be found in Chapter 7).

Today, the UKVA is lean, but fit and in co-operation with the committees of the six affiliated regional associations, looks after the interests of both its members and promoting, as far as its finances allow, English and Welsh wines. It secured a grant of £30,000 from MAFF/DEFRA to create an English Wine Quality Marque, which although short-lived, was a genuine attempt to create a distinguishing mark which could be used by growers to publicise the quality of their products. It persuaded Food From Britain to support the annual English Wine Producer's St George's Day tasting which has become the showcase where winewriters and the wine trade can taste a comprehensive selection of the best of UK-grown wines.

The UKVA's most recent contribution to the well-being of UK winegrowers was to assist DEFRA in their negotiations with the EU over the reform of the Wine Regime. By supplying valuable data about the growth of vineyards and wine production in the UK and by showing that the UK was by no means 'the far-away country of whom we know little', DEFRA was able to support the other Zone A countries (the northerly EU wine-producing Member States) who wished to retain the right to enrich (aka chaptalise) their wines with sucrose, to keep the enrichment level at 3 per cent, plus an additional 0.5 per cent in 'difficult' years (2.5 per cent had been proposed) and last, but by no means least, to secure for ever the right of the small producing Member States (the UK, Belgium, Holland, Denmark and Ireland) to plant vines in the future without the threat of a planting ban.

Chairmen of the EVA

Jack Ward OBE	1967–1981
Colin Gillespie	1981–1987
Anthony Goddard	1987–1990
Ian Berwick OBE	1990–1993
Robin Don	1993–1995

Chairmen of the UKVA

Ian Berwick OBE	1995–1999
Stephen Skelton	1999–2003
Roger Marchbank	2003–2007
Bob Lindo	2007–

Secretaries of the EVA and UKVA

Irene Barrett	1967-1980
Kenneth McAlpine DL, MBE	1980-1996
Ian Berwick OBE	1996-2004
Robert Beardsmore	2004-2007
Sian Liwcki	2007-

CHAPTER 5

Quality and Regional Wine Schemes

The reaching of the 500-hectare limit in 1988 caused the WSB to start the process of drawing up a Vineyard Register – a national list of all vineyards containing exact plot (parcel) locations and sizes, together with the number of vines and the variety, clone and rootstock types. The following year MAFF conducted a statutory survey of all vineyards over one-tenth of a hectare (100 ares) then known to exist. Given that it was not – and is still not – obligatory to register the ownership of a vineyard unless it is producing a 'wine sector product' (grapes, grape juice or wine), this survey was bound to be a little bit hit and miss. However, comprehensive or not, the survey showed a remarkable increase in the area under vines. From 546-hectares with 382-hectares in production in 1988, the total jumped in one year by over 60 per cent to 876-hectares with 652-hectares in production. More interesting were the yield figures. From a declared production of 4,110 hl – equivalent to 548,000 75 cl bottles – in 1988, the 1989 figure had shot to 21,447 hl or 2,859,600 75 cl bottles – a 520 per cent increase! Although this was partly due to better weather in 1989 and therefore a larger yield, it was obvious that the pre-1989 surveys were only picking up the smaller, less productive vineyards and those with larger yields had, for whatever reason, declined to send in returns.

The reason for concern over the high yield figure, both within the industry and with UK officialdom, was the existence of an EU-wide vine-planting ban which applied in all Member States whose annual production was in excess of 25,000 hl of wine. (This limit had originally been set at 5,000 hl and a planting ban had been mooted in 1979 to take effect in 1980–1981, but the EVA had successfully petitioned MAFF at the time and the limit was raised to 25,000 hl.) In 1993, when a 26,428 hl yield was announced for the 1992 harvest, MAFF successfully appealed to the Commission to take a five-year average yield figure (2003–2007 this was 16,135 hl.) rather than one single year. This was accepted and remained the situation until in 2007, as part of the general EU wine regime reforms, it was announced that a planting ban in those Member States that did not already have one, would never take place.)

The only official way around the planting ban was either to buy planting rights from a grower who was permanently giving up growing vines (the usual way for growers in the remainder of the EU to expand their vineyard holdings) or to apply to the authorities for permission to plant vines. In this latter case, growers who wished to plant new vineyards could only do so for: *the production of certain* [still] *Quality Wines which could be shown to be in demand by the market.* The discovery that the

UK had what was probably nearer a 1,000-hectares of vines than 500-hectares and that in good years was capable of producing well over 25 hl/ha, meant that we were in serious danger of breaching the 25,000 hl barrier which would, according to the strict interpretation of the regulations, precipitate a planting ban in the UK. Given that we had no Quality Wine Scheme (QWS), a crop in excess of his figure would have ended all new vine planting in the UK.

In early 1990, as soon as the results of the 1989 vineyard survey were known, MAFF decided that the answer to this potential problem was to set up a Quality Wine Scheme Committee (QWSC) whose task it would be to draw up a full 'Quality Wine Produced in a Specified Region' (QWpsr) scheme to give still (i.e. not sparkling) English and Welsh wines full *appellation contrôlée* status. The membership of the committee was largely based on that of the VVCC and it was set to work as soon as it could. Over the next 18 months the committee met on an almost monthly basis in an attempt to hammer out a scheme that would satisfy the demands of a diverse number of interested parties. The scheme had to conform to existing EU regulations and ultimately be approved by the Commission; it had to be practical with regard to the conditions governing wine production in England and Wales and to be one that growers found both acceptable and affordable; above all it had to be a scheme that, as far as was possible, guaranteed to the wine trade, the wine press and to the wine buying public in general, that a wine that had passed through the scheme was of genuine 'quality' status – whatever that word meant!

To satisfy the EU regulations was in one sense the easiest, and in another the hardest of the committee's problems. The regulations had been drawn up with a fairly broad brush so that they could cope with the myriad of different production conditions across the climatic and cultural spread of Europe. They had also been drawn up with one eye on the preservation of each region's 'traditional practices'. The fact that the UK had played no part in drawing up the original regulations and in any event was a relative newcomer to winegrowing and winemaking, meant that our tally of 'traditional practices' was fairly small. The one big impediment to getting a scheme that satisfied both the regulations and the majority of growers was the thorny problem of hybrids (vines with some non-*vitis vinifera* genetic material in them). These were denied the right – in whatever proportions – to be made into Quality Wine by a clause in the EU regulations.

For many growers in the UK the exclusion of hybrids was a difficult pill to swallow. As well as Seyval blanc, which at the time was the third most widely planted variety in terms of area and the most widely planted in terms of the number of vineyards having the variety, there were a number of older hybrid varieties (Cascade, Léon Millot, Maréchal Foch and Triomphe) together with some newer ones (Orion, Phoenix, Regent and Rondo[1]) which growers found useful. Hybrids covered over 15

---

1   These last four varieties have since been declared as 'true' viniferas and can now be made into Quality Wine. See Chapter 7 for more details.

per cent of the total UK vine area and produced approximately 25 per cent of the UK's wine – a higher percentage than their area because of two factors: their higher than average yield and the fact they were often blended with wines from *vinifera* varieties. Their exclusion from Quality Wine production was a hangover from history. Apart from the fact that they existed in many UK growers' vineyards and, in most cases, were useful, disease resistant varieties, the grapes from them made perfectly good wine.

A majority on the committee thought that the UK should have a scheme that would promote, protect and guarantee English and Welsh wines solely on a objective, scientifically backed basis and to introduce a scheme that discriminated against one class of vines solely on the basis of their 'race' was flawed and would, if not bring the scheme into disrepute, at least lower its attraction to growers wishing to enter their wines into it. Wines containing even the slightest trace of wine made from hybrids would be excluded, so for many wineries, most of their wines would be ineligible. The EVA representatives on the committee urged that the scheme should be drawn up so that it recognised our national circumstances.

The arguments over whether hybrids could or could not, should or should not, be included in the QWS went on for many meetings. Representations were made to the Commission and their ruling was that they could not, and furthermore the basic regulations could only be altered by a qualified majority of the Council of Ministers. MAFF pointed out quite forcefully to the EVA committee members that this was a highly unlikely occurrence. MAFF, knowing that a 25,000 hl yield could be just around the corner and knowing that a Brussels imposed vine planting ban would not reflect well upon them and would not help relations with the general farming community ('MAFF introduces vine planting ban' was not the headline anyone wanted to see), decided that a scheme should go ahead without the inclusion of hybrids. Once the basic framework of the scheme had been drawn up, a number of options and alternatives were still open and a 'consultation exercise' was carried out among interested parties: growers, wine producers, EVA members and associates, academic institutions, consumer and promotional organisations, central and local government departments, press and winewriters, and the wine trade. In March 1991, a consultation document was sent to out to 942 addresses (including those of 420 registered growers) and 183 were returned. MAFF considered this a very good response. Analysis of the survey showed that an overwhelming majority (90.44 per cent) of respondents felt that hybrids ought to be allowed in the scheme and that without them included, the scheme would have less validity. Only 7 per cent of respondents wanted a scheme that excluded hybrids. Despite this overwhelming response in favour of hybrids, MAFF insisted that the scheme go ahead without them.[2]

---

2   In the margins of committee meetings the pro-hybrid members were left in no doubt that matters viticultural were already taking up far too much Ministry time and money (all those meeting rooms, First Class railway fares, biscuits and – occasionally – sandwiches) and that

In many other respects, the QWS was fairly straightforward to design. Apart from the issue of varieties, there was less contention over such subjects as minimum natural alcohols, the geographical areas covered, whether wines could be made in one area from grapes grown in another, whether irrigation should be allowed (it was not) and what the yield restrictions should be. As to what should actually constitute a 'Quality Wine', the committee relied heavily on the existing EVA Seal of Quality regulations. With only a few amendments and adjustments to the analytical requirements, it was able to lift the Seal regulations in their entirety and place them into the QWS. Wines would be subject to a fairly stringent analysis which looked at not only the simple physical aspects such as the alcohol, acid, sulphur dioxide, iron and copper contents, but also the wine's sterility status (bacteria and yeasts) and its stability with regard to both proteins and tartrates. It had been found with the operation of the Seal that the sterility and stability requirements had been valuable in weeding out those winemakers whose winemaking and bottling practices were not really up to standard and while they might have been able to produce wines of fine quality on the day of the tasting, they did not keep once in the hands of the wine merchant or final customer. The wines would be tasted by a panel of between five and seven members, at least two of whom would be Masters of Wine,[3] and would follow the twenty point tasting scheme that had proved simple and workable for the Seal. The minimum natural alcoholic strength of wines eligible for Quality Wine status i.e. their potential alcohol level at harvest and before enrichment (chaptalisation) was set at 6.5 per cent (1.5% more than the level for Table Wine). A derogation existed that allowed Member States to reduce this to 6 per cent and this was applied for but was not granted until December 1991, too late for it to apply to wines from the 1991 vintage.

By the early summer of 1991, a basic scheme had been drawn up and was almost ready to be submitted to the Commission for its comments. The issue of hybrids remained unsettled, with a majority on the committee unwilling to see a scheme introduced which discriminated against these varieties. This majority suggested that the scheme be held in abeyance until such time as a planting ban was threatened. MAFF however, thought otherwise. Fearing the arrival of a crop higher than 25,000 hl, they were determined to press ahead with its introduction for the 1991 harvest. In an attempt to placate the pro-hybrid lobby, the then Junior Agriculture Minister, David Curry, went to Brussels and on 30 May 1991 returned waving a piece of paper (in what some of us thought was a rather Neville Chamberlainesque 'Peace for our Time' sort of way) which promised that: *the Commission will study the possibility of*

---

vines were such a small crop that MAFF would gain little in the way of kudos by fighting to gain concessions. We (the pro-hybrid brigade) prolonged the debate for as long as we could on the grounds that if we could never win, at least the battle would be remembered and you never knew what might happen in the future!

3   This last requirement was changed as it proved difficult to get MWs to turn out (unpaid) for what were often only tastings of five to ten wines. Today, there is no requirement for any MWs to be present, although there is usually at least one on the tasting panel.

including inter-specific [hybrid] *varieties in the list of varieties deemed suitable for the production of Quality Wine produced in a specified region.*[4]

Neville Chamberlain on his return from meeting Hitler in Munich

The last hurdle to be overcome before the scheme could be submitted to the Commission was that of the geographical delineation and naming of the 'specified regions' of production. Various suggestions as to how the UK might be split up into separate Quality Wine production regions had already been made. An obvious solution was to create regions based upon the existing regional vineyards associations' areas – East Anglia, South East, Wessex, South West, etc. – but this was quickly found to be unacceptable once the rules on the naming of Quality Wine regions had been fully digested. Under the rules contained in Council Regulations 823/87 (as amended by Reg. 2043/89) grapes grown in one region could only be made into a Quality Wine in the same region or in an administrative region (taken to mean a county) that was in immediate proximity (taken to mean having a common border) to the one where the grapes were grown. This meant that grapes from Essex, for example, could not be made into Quality Wine in East Sussex had these two counties been in non-adjacent Quality Wine regions. The only derogation to these rules was if the practice was both traditional and had taken place continuously since before 1973 and which met other specified conditions. Since the first two restrictions could not be met by any winery in the UK, no one bothered to enquire what the other specified conditions were! As a trade in grapes between vineyards and wineries across the UK

---

4   In the same way that the people of Britain in 1939 knew that they were being fobbed off by both Chamberlain and Hitler with their promises of peace, the pro-hybrid lobby took the view that we would believe this 'study' when we saw it. Annual requests for it to be undertaken were partially satisfied with a financial provision for it making an appearance in the EU's budget. There was then more delay as the Commission couldn't find anyone impartial enough to undertake it. Eventually, over 12 years after the promise was first made, a wholly unsatisfactory paper exercise took place, in which the UK wine industry took no part. Having said that the method of its undertaking was unsatisfactory, the result was even less so. The study concluded that, under certain circumstances – surprise, surprise – hybrids could be made into perfectly satisfactory wine. This result of course did nothing to sway the Commission and non-viniferas are still prohibited from being made into Quality Wine.

existed, it was felt that the 'multiple region' approach was too inflexible for most UK growers and winemakers and that a 'two region' approach (where one region was entirely contiguous with another) would be best. Another problem which a multiple region system would have exacerbated was that juice used for sweetening Quality Wines (*süss-reserve*) had to originate from the same region in which the grapes were grown and two large regions would make for more flexibility than several small ones. The option favoured by the industry members of the committee was to split the UK into two adjacent regions – England and Wales – which would have resulted in two descriptors: English Quality Wine psr and Welsh Quality Wine psr. Given these two regions, Welsh grapes could be taken to wineries in English counties bordering Wales (and of course vice versa), which was an important consideration given the location of the Three Choirs winery in Gloucestershire which made wines under contract for several smaller Welsh growers. Everyone agreed that this was a practical, pragmatic solution and was incorporated into the draft regulations.

The question of what to call Table Wines also had to be addressed, given that the WSB – responsible for policing labelling in the UK – felt that English Quality Wine psr and English Table Wine (and the Welsh equivalents) would not have been acceptable to the Commission. One solution, which had the approval of the industry members of the QWC, was to call them all United Kingdom Table Wines. This solution was accepted by the committee and a final draft of the 'Pilot Quality Wine Scheme' (as it was initially known) was sent out to all growers in August 1991 so that wines from the 1991 vintage would be able to be considered for Quality Wine status. The WSB stated that they felt that the scheme was being hurriedly introduced and that they were really not ready to handle the additional work as the Vineyard Register was not fully completed.

Feedback from the industry soon showed that it was less than keen on renaming their Table Wines by the proposed descriptor United Kingdom Table Wines, especially those with wines which, because they were made wholly or partly from hybrids, were not eligible for inclusion in the QWS. Once the WSB also pointed out that certain information on labels, such as the name of the vine variety and the vintage, could only appear on wines where the Geographical Indication (GI) covered an area smaller than the Member State, this solution was effectively dead. The industry members of the committee urged MAFF to reconsider the idea to have both English Quality Wine and English Table Wine or some other variant which incorporated the words England or English (and their Welsh/Wales equivalents), but it was felt that the Commission would not accept this, despite there being examples in, for instance, French wine labelling (*Vin de Pays du Jardin de la France*). After considerable discussion and several additional committee meetings, and with the 1991 harvest already completed, a typical bureaucratic solution was arrived at. Two regions would be created, one called Northern Counties (Durham, Humberside, South Yorkshire and West Yorkshire) which contained almost no vineyards and one called

Southern Counties (i.e. the rest of the UK) which contained almost all existing vineyards. In addition, vines for Quality Wine production had to be situated below 220 metres above sea level, a height chosen with some care, as it was known that no vineyards were planted above this height, yet it further defined the geographical limits of the region.

However bizarre it seemed, this solution did allow grapes and juice to be shipped around the wine producing counties, got round the problem of re-naming Table Wines and satisfied MAFF and the Commission. Despite general industry opposition, letters to the Minister and a leader in *Decanter Magazine*, in January 1992 this solution was steamrollered through the committee. With the 1991 wines already made and eligible for Quality Wine status, a decision had to be made quickly and the committee was advised that this was the best stop-gap solution. Industry members of the committee felt that MAFF should have been more forceful in interpreting the regulations to suit the UK's geographical and climatic circumstances, especially as MAFF was prepared to base regions on nothing other than what was, in reality, administrative convenience. The regulations stated that a Quality Wine region had to: *describe a wine-growing area ... which produces wines with particular quality characteristics*, but this did not seem to bother anyone from MAFF or the Commission too much. With the best will in the world, wines from the Southern Counties (i.e. the whole of the UK's vineyard area) could hardly be said to show any particular quality characteristics that would distinguish them from those of the Northern Counties especially as no wines from this area existed!

At the same January meeting, the use of two alternative wine descriptors was accepted and it was agreed that wines could be labelled Quality Wine or Designated Origin. Originally it had been hoped, at least by most industry committee members, that a single descriptor – that of Designated Origin (similar to that used in *all* other EU Member States apart from Germany) would have been acceptable to MAFF. The thinking behind this was that growers whose wines were ineligible to be entered for the scheme – mainly because they were made in whole or in part from non-*vinifera* grapes – would be at a disadvantage by the appearance of the word Quality on some wines, but not on theirs, even though they might be of equal – or even better – quality. However, MAFF officials announced that the Minister could not ban the term Quality Wine produced in a specified region and risked prosecution if he did so. Again, the fact that most wine-producing Member States *had* interpreted the regulations to suit their own purposes and had effectively banned the use of this alternative term counted for nothing – another example of UK officials playing by the rules to the disadvantage of its own citizens!

The completed scheme was quickly agreed by the Commission, the necessary Statutory Instruments were drawn up and issued, and the Pilot Quality Wine Scheme was incorporated into UK legislation. The English Vineyards Association had been appointed to be the Recognised Industry Body (RIB) which was responsible for handling applications to the scheme and sending wines to be analysed and tasted. The first tasting was held on 18 May 1992 at which ten wines, which had already been analysed and had cleared the analytical requirements, were tasted. All passed and after the producer's winemaking records were inspected, were given Quality Wine status.

Over the years since the original 'Pilot' scheme was incorporated into UK legislation, several changes have been made. Some sort of sense prevailed in the naming of the regions and after considerable argument in committee about what other Member States were allowed to do (i.e. get away with) MAFF accepted that the terms English Vineyards and Welsh Vineyards could be used as the names of the 'Specified Regions'. These regions covered all English and Welsh counties that contained vineyards, so long as those vineyards were no more than 220 metres above sea level. These terms were felt to be sufficiently different from English Table Wine and Welsh Table Wine not to incur the displeasure of the Commission. In 1996, when a Regional Wine Scheme (equivalent to the French *Vin de Pays* category) was introduced to give some sort of status to wines made from non-*vinifera* varieties, the terms English Counties and Welsh Counties were adopted, covering exactly the same geographical areas as the Quality Wine regions, but being sufficiently different as vines growing over 220 metres above sea level were accepted (despite the fact that no vines were being grown – or indeed would be likely to ripen grapes – at this altitude), but below 250 metres above sea level.

Thus, in the naming of the three categories of wine allowed to be produced in the UK –Table Wine, Regional Wine and Quality Wine – the three descriptors and the regions they covered are, while in fact the same, on paper sufficiently different to satisfy the *amour-propre* of both ministers and officials, as well as offering lip service to the regulations in order to keep Brussels happy! What a strange world we inhabit.

It has now been almost twenty years since the Quality Wine regulations were 'imposed' upon UK winegrowers and despite initial misgivings from some that it would lead to alarm and panic in the shires, the net affect has been – surprise, surprise – a gradual improvement in the quality of the wines being produced in the UK. At the time of its introduction, I was one of the most vociferous against its introduction because of the hybrid problem. While I have not changed my mind that the exclusion of the old hybrids (principally Seyval blanc which still occupies over 7.5 per cent of the UK planted area and because of blending accounts for more than this percentage in wine) is divisive and has *nothing* to do with wine quality, I knew that the imposition on growers of a set of rules and regulations which related directly to the quality of the wines they were producing would, in the long-run, be a good thing.

In 2004 DEFRA (as MAFF had then become) were informed by the EU that the terms English Table Wine and Welsh Table Wine were illegal as a Table Wine may not bear a GI smaller than the area covered by the Member State, unless that Table Wine has some redeeming features and has been adjudged to be a Regional Wine. This in itself was no surprise to me at all and was something that had already been pointed out in committee several times. In all probability, EU officials thought that England was an alternative name for Great Britain, an understandable mistake since most foreigners refer to anyone from across the Channel as 'English'. The upshot of this was that the categories of wine able to be produced were, once again, changed: basic Table Wine, untested and untasted, was to be called 'UK Table Wine', with the categories Regional and Quality Wine remaining much as before, although Regional Wine now has to be grown at below 250 metres above sea level (Quality Wine remaining at below 220 metres and UK Table Wine can be grown at any height above (or I suppose even below) sea level.

The good thing about these changes was that a UK Table Wine would be unable to bear a vintage or the name of any vine variety used in its production. Thus most growers, used to having both a vintage and a vine variety on their labels, would be more likely to put their wines up for Regional or Quality Wine status and therefore their wines would be tested and tasted before being offered to the public. While at the time I kept my own council about this benefit (not wishing to make myself any more unpopular with some growers than I already was), the result of this change is exactly as I surmised. Very few wines, and certainly very few wines of interest, were labelled as UK Table Wines and the overall quality of the still wines produced in the UK has gradually risen over the years. An additional benefit of these changes was that UK Table Wines could be made from vine varieties listed under Category 4, the experimental varieties (see Chapter 7 for an explanation of Categories 1-4).

Other changes to the rules for the production of Quality and Regional Wine were small and mainly aimed at making the schemes more user-friendly. Wines entered for Regional Wine status could be accompanied by an analysis certificate drawn up by the producer, rather than requiring (an expensive) one from a laboratory and tastings for Regional Wine status could now take place as part of a properly organised tasting competition. Thus wines entered for the UKVA's national competition or one of the Regional Association's competitions, if they achieved the correct score and were accompanied by the correct paperwork, gained Regional Wine status automatically. Regional Wines were also permitted to bear the name of a county (or unitary authority) and there were 18 English GIs and 11 Welsh GIs – thus bottles can be labelled Cornish Regional Wine or Pembrokeshire Regional Wine.

The one big hole in the whole apparatus of Quality and Regional Wine status is the exclusion of sparkling wines. Under current EU legislation, there are three basic types of sparkling wine: Aerated Sparkling Wine, a wine produced by the addition of carbon dioxide (which must be stated on the label); Sparkling Wine, a sparkling wine produced by tank fermentation (Charmat method), transfer method or bottle fermentation, but which has not spent a minimum time on the lees; and Quality Sparkling Wine, a wine which has spent a minimum of nine months on lees.[5] (This is a

---

5   There are also semi-sparkling wines and aerated semi-sparkling wines, but no UK winegrower currently produces these.

very brief summary of the categories and there are a myriad of additional requirements which define each of these three types of wine.) This means that most producers of sparkling wine in the UK, virtually all of whom produce wine by bottle-fermentation and who leave it on the lees to mature, are able to call their wines 'Traditional Method Quality Sparkling Wine', thus immediately gaining (in the eyes of all but anyone extremely familiar with both winemaking and wine labelling regulations) instant recognition for their wines, irrespective of its intrinsic quality. The added (and of course being an EU regulation, wholly illogical) bonus is that the word 'Quality' in 'Quality Sparkling Wine' refers to the method of production, *not* the base materials from which it has been made. Therefore, the much-maligned hybrid varieties (Seyval blanc, being fairly neutral in character and well-suited to yeast/lees ageing is the main one) instantly achieve *faux*-Quality status. This last aspect I don't actually mind – being an old dyed-in-the-wool Seyval grower at heart – but what I do object to is winemakers putting on the market sub-standard sparkling wines bearing a label with the words 'Quality Wine' on them. This cannot be to the benefit of all those producers making good quality sparkling wines and the sooner the UK develops regulations to cover 'Quality Sparkling Wines Produced in a Specified Region' (QSWpsr) the better. These need not be onerous, the analytical requirements have already been drawn up and agreed by the major sparkling wine producers, and the tastings required to judge these wines are already being held for still wines. If this requirement was in place it would start the process of weeding out – as the QWS and RWS have with still wine producers – those whose wines are damaging the profile of UK-grown sparkling wines.

At the March 2008 *Decanter Magazine* grand tasting of 68 English and Welsh sparkling wines, the top 13 wines were all made from the Champagne varieties and in the top 29 wines, only four were made from non-Champagne varieties. Of the bottom nine wines, all but one were made from non-Champagne varieties and overall wines made from Champagne varieties scored an average of 14.17 points, against an average for non-Champagne varieties of 12.94. This is not to say that those growing Champagne varieties are necessarily better winemakers (although this is demonstrably the case), but that there are unfortunately a lot of wine producers jumping on the sparkling bandwagon and producing wines of questionable quality from indifferent and probably unsuitable varieties. It is to be hoped that the many new entrants to the UK sparkling winegrowing scene will see the sense of this proposal and start agitating for the introduction of a QSWpsr scheme.

Changes in wine regulations - 2009

After much discussion between the major wine producing countries – and in which the UK played little part – major changes to the terminology used on labels and some slightly less major changes to wine production processes have been agreed by Brussels.

On the labelling front, the terms Quality Wine PSR, Regional Wine and Table Wine will cease, to be replaced respectively by Protected Designation of Origin (PDO) wine, Protected Geographical Indication (PGI) wine and 'wines with no PDO or PGI'. Until 31 December 2011, the current QWS and RWS schemes may continue as they are currently formulated, but by this date, new rules must have been submitted to, and agreed by, Brussels. Wines produced before, and labelled by, 31 December 2010 may be sold with their old labels until used up.

The most important change – which I consider to be detrimental as it undoes all the benefits we saw from the introduction of the category UK Table Wine – is that wines, still and sparkling, without a GI (geographical indication) i.e. those wines which have not been through the QWS, RWS, or any subsequently agreed schemes, will be allowed to be labelled as English Wine, Wine of England, Product of England or Produced in England (and the Welsh equivalents). These wines will also be allowed to show the vintage and grape variety or varieties – something that UK Table Wines were not allowed to do – if they go through a 'Certification Process' prior to sale. What this 'process' will comprise has yet to be agreed, although we do know that the 'winery records must show details of production for wine intended for this category'. Once they have passed this process they will be known as 'Varietal Wines'.

Pure Seyval blanc from Peter Hall's Breaky Bottom Vineyard in East Sussex

CHAPTER 6

Viticulture and vinification

This book is not intended to be a practical handbook for grape growers or winemakers, but some mention of both growing systems and winemaking techniques used in the UK is necessary if the wines are to be fully understood and appreciated. For anyone looking for more information on either subject there are a large number of excellent books on both topics available from around the world (and even closer to home). I think it also helpful to look at where we seem to have gone wrong in the past, so that we can learn from our mistakes.

Training and experience

There is no doubt that many of those who planted vineyards in the past were rank amateurs when it came to growing vines (or for that matter, growing anything). They seem to think that vines were an undemanding crop, farmed by generations of growers overseas who seemed to muddle by without much bother, and therefore it couldn't be that difficult – could it? Many also took the view that vinegrowing was an occupation they could fit into their spare time, weekends and summer evenings, forgetting that sometimes a week is a long time in a vine's life, especially if rain disrupts the spraying or weed control programme. This fairly casual approach to the process resulted in some very poorly established vineyards, with inadequate site preparation, inadequate trellising and some unusual pruning techniques. It also resulted in high levels of disease which meant poor crops in both terms of quantity and quality. A lack of quantity only impinges on one's own finances; a lack of quality impinges on the whole of the English and Welsh wine fraternity. Most vineyards were also fairly small, too small to make employing anyone (with or without experience in growing vines) possible and this too gave rise to problems.

Very few of the early growers also had anything approaching a formal training in vinegrowing. Several were farmers. This helped, but they were usually large-scale arable farmers and not growers used to looking after fruit crops. Ken Barlow, who owned Adgestone Vineyard on the Isle of Wight, had spent some time in Germany learning what he could about viticulture, as well as having spent over 20 years in agricultural research. This experience showed and he won the Gore-Browne Trophy twice in the mid-1970s. (I was also lucky enough to spend almost two years working in a vineyard and winery and attending lectures at Geisenheim in Germany before I planted a vineyard and started making wine, a fact that seemed to go against me when I won the Gore-Browne Trophy with my second vintage. 'You've been trained!' a friend said. 'That's cheating'!)

A few growers were large enough to employ specialists, the most notable being Kenneth McAlpine at Lamberhurst Vineyards. The scale of that enterprise meant that right from the start, before the first vines were planted, everything from site selection to winemaking was in the hands of trained professionals brought over from Germany. It helped that his farm manager, Bob Reeves (whose wife was from Germany) spoke the language. When Lamberhurst started winning all the prizes, the reasons were not hard to find: a professional approach from the outset resulted in quality fruit which, using the right equipment and a talented winemaker, could be turned into good, even very good, wine. Although good wines had been made 'BL' (Before Lamberhurst) – Ken Barlow at Adgestone, Peter Cook at Pulham, Colin Gillespie at Wootton, and Nigel Godden at Pilton were all early Gore-Browne Trophy winners – everything changed once Karl-Heinz Johner arrived at Lamberhurst as winemaker and established himself as the man of the moment in English Wine. Since then, the realisation that viticulture requires both investment and expertise if good wines are to be the end result, has become lodged in the viticultural psyche of UK winegrowers. Of course there will always be a few who think that the 'dog and stick' approach to farming will work with vines, but these are today very much in the minority.

Since those early days, the level of professionalism at all levels in the UK wine production chain has greatly improved. Plumpton College, which started in a very low-key way in 1988, has over the years expanded its range of courses and its *alumni* (and even *alumnae*) are to be found not only in UK vineyards, but also in vineyards and wineries around the world. Their new £1 million training facility, opened by Jancis Robinson in June 2007, is a testament to the change in attitudes and approach to growing vines and making wine in the UK. Others in the business are graduates of viticulture and winemaking colleges in France, the USA, Australia and New Zealand. Some UK vineyards are now being run by the very experienced sons of their founders (Piers Greenwood at New Hall and Julian Barnes at Biddenden come to mind) and I feel sure it will not be long before a third generation also become involved.

The advent of sparkling wine as a serious commercial product has also helped change attitudes. The level of investment required and the length of time from planting to first sales are both substantially higher than for still wines and this tends to exclude all but the serious and those without access to capital. The average size of these new enterprises is considerable. There are around 100 vineyards over 2-hectares that have been planted since 2003 (most of which have been planted with Champagne varieties) and together these 100 (out of a total of around 435 in this guide) represent about 65 per cent of the total UK planted area. Many of these are far too large to be owner-operated and must rely on good trained staff to make them function which must augur well for the future of the UK's viticulture and winemaking and, eventually, its wines.

Site selection

Historically, poor site selection has probably been one of the major reasons why many English and Welsh vineyards have failed to last the course. The desire to own a vineyard and to have one's name on a label has led growers in the past to plant vineyards on sites of dubious quality – sites chosen on the 'because it was there' principle, rather than for the site's intrinsic quality for wine production. The usual errors were sites that were too exposed, at too high an altitude and too windswept and where no consideration was given to providing shelter; sites which were in frost pockets; and sites where the soil conditions required drainage and none was done. Add to this inaccessible sites which tended to get neglected on the 'out of sight, out of mind' principle and you have a fair recipe for disaster. Several vineyards come to mind as I write those words.

Highwayman's Vineyard near Bury St Edmunds in Suffolk (a vineyard of almost 10-hectares planted in 1974) was, according to the farm manager I spoke to (a man I am fairly sure was called Bonaparte), planted on the worst land on the farm as he'd heard that 'vines liked poor soil' and the land in question 'wouldn't grow sugar beet'. The fact that the site seemed to catch all the easterly winds going and consequently rarely produced worthwhile crops seemed to have escaped his notice. Take another – Barnsgate Manor near Crowborough in East Sussex. This grand enterprise, the subject of an ADAS Farm Walk (those were the days – 90 per cent Drainage Grants available to all!) consisted of about 20-hectares of vines planted in a steep bowl which, at 50 metres above sea level, would have been perfect. Unfortunately it lay between 125 and 150-metres above sea level with wonderful views towards the Channel and far too exposed to be successful. Add to this the proximity of unfenced woodland teeming with rabbits and deer, and the idiosyncratic way in which the enthusiastic owner, a Mr William Ross, had planted the vines using a cabbage planter, and the recipe was not a good one. Unsurprisingly, the picking machine, which Ross confidently spoke of buying, never materialised and as far as I am aware, no bottle of wine was ever produced under his ownership. These two were, unfortunately, not rare and many other examples could have been chosen.

You can still ask vineyard owners the question 'Why did you plant here?' and the answer is still often (depressingly) the same: 'Because it was there!' Many growers plant land that they already own, convinced for some reason that it will be good enough and ignoring what could be learnt from past grower's mistakes. Of course, site selection is not down to just picking the most suitable piece of land in the neighbourhood and planting it. It has to be for sale, it has to be accessible, in many instances it has to come with a house to live in and some buildings to make wine in. Compromises often have to be made and one of the surprising things about English and Welsh wines – given the degree of care that went into site selection – is that some of them are as good as they are!

Overseas, where vines have been growing in some regions for centuries, site selection is less of a problem. The Old World wine regions are mapped in the minutest detail and *appellation* boundaries are based on the suitability of certain sites to produce wines true to the *appellation's* ideals. In any event, in climates warmer than the UK's, the pressure to find sites where vines can fruit and grapes can ripen is less as there are many more of them. It always has to be remembered that we are growing vines in the coolest winegrowing region in the world bar none and we must grasp whatever natural advantages there are by correct site selection. Lighter, sandy soils, with good natural drainage are to be favoured and soils that overlie even leaner sand and gravel deposits are best of all. MAFF used to publish an excellent booklet called *Soils and Manures for Fruit* (Bulletin 107) which listed all the suitable fruit soils in the UK, together with their attributes. Prospective vine growers should ignore the advice given on page 14 (of the 1975 edition) which states that vines are: *less susceptible to drought or adverse drainage conditions than most fruit crops* but take the advice which says that: *shallow or coarse sandy soils are acceptable*. The advice on page 2 that: *aspect is not of great importance except for vines which need a southerly slope* and that: *land above 400'* [122 metres] *is not suitable* should also be noted. Suffice it to say that one can drag a horse to water but making it drink is another matter!

Despite the availability of advice from both books and consultants, many vineyards in the UK, both past and present, have been planted on sites unlikely to allow vines to prosper and this, sadly, has been reflected in the quality of the wine produced. The importance of choosing south-facing slopes, rather than flat sites (the second choice if south-facing sites are not available) or sites facing in other directions, especially north, is set out by George Ordish in great detail in his book *Vineyards in England and Wales* (1977). Any prospective vineyard owner searching for a site to grow vines on in the UK should read it. In an appendix, Ordish quotes a thesis written by Nick Poulter of Cranmore Vineyards which accurately states that: *although the amount of sunshine reaching a 30° south facing slope compared to a level site will only be 8% more in midsummer (which is towards the beginning of the growing season), by October, when the grapes are struggling to amass sugars, it will be 70% more*. To owners of level sites, let alone those with east, west or heaven forbid, north facing sites, this is frightening information.

However, the tide in site selection appears to be turning with the many of the newer, post-2003 vineyards, planted on sites where considerable thought has gone into site selection. This is partly because of the size of the enterprises – it is, perversely, easier to buy 100-hectares containing the 20-hectares you would like to plant with vines, than just the 20-hectares you need – partly that many of the new *vignerons* are better capitalised and therefore more able to pick and choose land, and partly because as many of these vineyards are planted with Champagne varieties, growers have gone out looking for chalk-rich soils that resemble the *Vallée de la Marne* and the *Côte de Blancs* in order to give their wines a suitable home and heritage. 'Planted on soil similar to that found in the best Champagne vineyards' looks so much better on a back label than 'Planted on some of the toughest Wealden Clay it was possible to find'! (My only concern in the hunt to find chalk-rich soil in the UK is that much of this land is at 100 metres or more over sea-level and much of it very exposed to prevailing winds. Chalk is not the only component in the Champagne mix.) In truth though, better site selection is part of the realisation, after over 55 years of commercial viticulture, that if you don't have a good site, you cannot grow good grapes and of you don't have good grapes, you cannot make good wine.

Rootstocks

The selection of the correct rootstock is something of a black art and wherever one goes throughout the winegrowing world, growers debate the matter endlessly. Most, but not all, rootstocks stem from crossings made in northern European nurseries. In France, Germany and Hungary the great vinebreeders of the late nineteenth century developed many crosses using wild American *Vitis* species as crossing partners to produce *Phylloxera* tolerant rootstocks. Over the intervening 145 years since the aphid struck in Europe, the colleges and universities that specialise in vinebreeding have clonally selected and improved those original varieties, increasing their *Phylloxera* tolerance, improving their resistance to drought, to calcium rich soils and to nematodes (which spread viruses). There are hundreds of rootstocks available worldwide, with scores in regular use. On the UK's list of permitted rootstocks there are 46 separate rootstock varieties, although probably no more than ten are in use.

Which ones should be used in UK vineyards? This is a very debatable matter. Traditionally, since most of our vines were Germanic in origin, they came from German nurserymen and were only available on what would be, to a German grower, a standard rootstock. Whether these were the most appropriate for our varieties and soils is another matter altogether. Many of the UK's problems in growing and ripening grapes in sufficient quantity and quality stem from the fact that our vines suffer from excess vigour and shaded canopies and as many of the rootstocks in use in the UK – 5BB, SO4, 125AA and 5C – are classed as 'medium vigorous' to 'very vigorous', they may not be helping this situation. Rootstocks with less vigour such as *Riparia Gloire de Montpelier* (RGM), 420A, 41B, 101-14, 161-49 and 3309C, all of French origin, might just help in this battle. Luckily, since the increase in planting of the Champagne varieties, many more of the vines we plant (although by no means all, as some UK vine dealers still source from Germany) have come from French *pépiniéristes* (nurserymen) for whom these rootstocks are standard fare. Add on to this the chalk factor (rootstocks suitable for planting on land with a high active calcium carbonate content tend to be less vigorous than others) and the rootstock spectrum used in the UK starts to look more respectable. My only worry is about the continuing use by many of SO4 as a suitable rootstock in all situations. Although it is classed as a 'medium' vigour rootstock, on some soils (although not chalky soils) it still seems to make vines fairly pushy. Time will tell. The new chalk-tolerant rootstock Fercal appears to be quite growy in its youth (it is classed as 'medium' for vigour) and I just hope that once it gets it roots down into the sub-soil, some of its energy will dissipate.

The number of UK vineyards now planted on their own roots must be fairly small and there cannot be many remaining, even though the results from own-rooted vines can be encouraging. Vines on their own roots are usually less vigorous than their counterparts on rootstocks and in many situations appear to break bud earlier, leading to a longer growing season. If a complete *cordon sanitaire* could be guaranteed around one's vineyard, these benefits (and those of cheaper home-produced rooted cuttings) might be worth taking. However, with *Phylloxera* an ever-present threat – another outbreak occurred in 2008 in the UK – no grower with aspirations to be around to see his or her vines into their old age would consider planting on anything else but good resistant rootstocks.

Trellising, training and pruning systems

Even after more than 55 years since the first modern vineyard was planted in the UK, few in the business would claim that the question of how best to trellis, train and prune vines for our varieties and climate had been completely answered. However, over the last ten to fifteen years, some methods of trellising, training and pruning have fallen out of favour and growers appear to be reaching some sort of consensus that straightforward Vertically Shoot Positioned (VSP) Guyot trained vines are best.

In the early days of the revival there was great debate between those predisposed towards the wide-planted extensive spur-pruned GDC system and those who favoured a more European approach with more intensively planted, Guyot (cane) pruned vines. Did GDC offer all the benefits its proponents suggested were there for the taking? Was it as cheap to establish as they said? Was the manpower required to manage a hectare of GDC trained vines really that low? Were crops really that large? The intensively planted Guyot growers claimed much earlier cropping (in year two to three, rather than year six to seven for GDC), better disease control and better wine quality. These benefits had to pay for the extra costs of establishing and growing cane-pruned vines planted relatively close together.

Since those early days, the debate over GDC versus Guyot seems to have quietened down, largely because many of the large GDC vineyards have disappeared! The original GDC vineyard, Bernard Theobald's at Westbury, soon disappeared following his death sometime in the early 1990s and many planted under the aegis of David Carr Taylor, another great GDC proponent, followed suit. Many of these were large vineyards beaten eventually by the sheer volume of work involved in managing vineyards in our climate or beaten by dealing with (i.e. selling) the large volume of grapes and therefore of wine, which was often produced. I have never felt that the quality of fruit coming from GDC trained vines was as good as that coming from VSP Guyot vines, mainly I suspect because many GDC vineyards did not get the attention to detail in such matters as shoot positioning and leaf removal that are so much easier with upright-trained vines.

However, there is no doubt that in some years, GDC does work well in the UK. Whether this is because the vines are big and therefore individually stressed so that they fruit rather than grow excess canopy (known as the 'big vine' theory) is debatable. GDC trained vines in the UK seem just as vigorous as their Guyot-pruned counterparts. It may be, however, that the basal buds – which in a spur pruned system are the only buds there are – are more fruitful because, being close to a large body of permanent wood, they are better supplied with reserves. These reserves (carbohydrates) also help the buds withstand spring frosts and in addition, bring about a slightly earlier bud-burst leading to a marginally longer growing season. Disease control is still a problem in GDC vines, partly because there tends to be a lot of crossing-over of canes leading to much of the fruit getting covered up, but also because many growers do not possess sprayers of sufficient power capable of putting spray onto the target. When these two problems are addressed – by canopy management and by using more powerful air-blast sprayers – results do seem to improve.

I like to think that when I started growing vines, I adopted a more technical approach to the problem of trellising and training, having had the good fortune to spend a considerable time studying the subject while at Geisenheim. I came back from Germany in 1976/7, having worked in the densely planted vineyards in the Rheingau, convinced that a 2-metre row width, with vines planted at 1.2 to 1.4-metres in the row, was right for UK conditions and essentially have not changed my mind over the 30 years since then. The new science of 'Canopy Management', the term invented by Dr Richard Smart and Mike Robinson and the basis for their seminal work *Sunlight into Wine – A Handbook for Winegrape Canopy Management* (published in 1991), became essential bedtime reading for modern viticulturalists worldwide, myself included. Whether all of its advice was suited to UK conditions is open to debate. Our average yields are so much lower than those in many other countries (especially compared to New Zealand and Australia where much of the research work that led to *Sunlight* was done) that some of the 'Golden Rules' advocated by Smart and Robinson in the book and by Richard during several Canopy Management Workshops that he has held in UK vineyards, do not really apply. However, the basic philosophy that underperforming vines with low yields can be helped by both leaving more fruiting wood per metre run of vine and by opening up the canopy to allow in as much light, heat and air as possible, still holds good, albeit to a lesser degree. Despite the extra growing costs involved, the yields from Guyot trained vines are higher, more consistent and of better quality. The additional capital costs of establishing a closely spaced, intensively planted vineyard are a reality, but taken over the 25+ year life of a vineyard, these do not add significantly to annual overheads. (GDC growers will also admit that a cheaply established vineyard, where the quality and quantity of posts and end-anchors have been skimped, is a false economy.) Growing costs in closely planted Guyot vineyards can be lowered with the mechanisation of some vineyard operations – summer pruning in particular – and a more relaxed view of how often, and how severely, vines should be tucked in.

In the 2001 edition of this book I wrote:

> *It is interesting to note that one fairly recent vineyard – Nyetimber – which is specialising in sparkling wine and which has been established using advice from Epernay, has planted narrow 1.60-metre wide rows with single Guyot trained vines at 1.00-metre apart – a planting density of 6,250 vines/hectare (2,530 vines/acre). This is very near the original planting scheme that Hambledon adopted when they planted in 1951 and was followed by many others at the time. Most decided that it was an unmanageable system for UK conditions – the costs of summer pruning and training were too high – and very few vineyards survived with vines trained in this way. However, with the high quality of product coming out of Nyetimber, it cannot be long before their planting scheme is copied on the basis of 'if they can do it, so can we'. Of course quality is not the only criteria to take into account and a prudent grower would wish to be satisfied that this system can produce the correct yields (and yield means income per hectare, not just tonnes of grapes) as well as the correct quality.*

Since the above was written, much has happened. A lot of vineyards have been planted and many, while perhaps not adopting quite such tight spacing as Nyetimber's original plantings (even Nyetimber themselves plant at 2.20-metres now), have planted with a row width of between 2.00 and 2.40 metres, with VSP trained, Guyot pruned vines. Most of the bigger, new Champagne-variety vineyards have been planted like this, although Didier Pierson at Little West End Farm has stuck to the 1.20 x 1.00-metres planting that he uses in Champagne, but has had to import an *enjambeur* (straddle tractor) to cope with the narrow rows.

Of the many other growing systems available, very few have found much favour in UK vineyards. There are a handful of Scott Henry growers in the UK, but, like the many ex-Scott Henry growers I met on a recent visit to Adelaide and Melbourne's winegrowing regions, there are even more that have tried and given up on the system. Why? Too much work and not enough benefit over VSP Guyot trained vines. There are the odd one or two growers who use the Lyre system, but it shows no distinct advantage over either GDC or Guyot and establishment costs are higher. Following a three week visit to New Zealand in 1998, a trip sponsored by the Canterbury Farmers Club (Canterbury, Kent, UK) in order for me to study the rootstocks and viticultural systems used there, I came back convinced that vines trained onto a single high wire (which could be called a high Sylvoz system, but which I dubbed the Blondin system after Charles 'The Great' Blondin, the first man to cross the Niagara Falls on a tightrope) could achieve as much yield and as good a quality as other systems, yet both establishment and growing costs are lower. This system does have several advantages over both GDC and Guyot and with experience can be made to perform well. It seems to incorporate some of the advantages of GDC (lower capital costs, more fruitful buds, better frost resistance and lower growing costs) with the better yields and more effective disease control associated with Guyot-trained vineyards. Weed control is also easier (or less demanding which comes to much the same thing) and the ability to vary the bud-count by leaving longer or shorter spurs could be an advantage. I trialled this system on 4 rows of Seyval blanc in my old Scott's Hall vineyard and Chapel Down adopted a version of this system when they planted their Pinot noir vineyard at Tenterden and the vines have produced a Bernard Theobald Trophy winning red wine. I note however, on their new Kit's Coty, Aylesford site, where they have planted 29-hectares of Champagne varieties, they have reverted to a 2.00 x 1.20-metre VSP Guyot system, exactly the one I used when first planting vines at Tenterden in 1977.

Whether training and trellising in UK vineyards will change in the future is open to debate. Growers tend to get used to the systems they initially adopt, partly one suspects because change is either impossible or prohibitively expensive and also because no one likes to admit that they were wrong! Given that they are stuck with their chosen system, they tend to adapt and modify it to suit their individual circumstances and equipment and put up with its imperfections. Whether this attitude can be sustained is one that ultimately comes down to economics – few can support really low yields for ever. I suspect however, given that the most successful and high-profile vineyards – Nyetimber, RidgeView, Chapel Down plus many of the new ones – are all planted on more or less the same VSP Guyot system, this will remain the *de facto* system of growing vines in the UK.

Viticultural equipment

The viticultural equipment used in UK vineyards has not changed that much since the early days and in any event, there is nothing that different about UK vineyards that means they require specialist equipment not seen overseas. Tractors have got more powerful and four-wheel drive tractors, with cabs, are now quite common. Sprayers are more efficient with low and ultra-low volume nozzles widespread (although not always that effective for controlling diseases such as powdery mildew) with quite a few vineyards now using re-circulation sprayers. These capture any excess spray that passes right through the row, which is then filtered and returned to the spray tank. This reduces the volume (and therefore the cost) of the chemicals used by up to 50 per cent. Many vineyards now mechanise their summer pruning with tractor mounted trimmers and a few have modern air-operated leaf strippers. Most vineyards control weeds below the vines with chemicals, although a few, especially those farming organically, do use automatic under-vine hoes or cultivators. Most vineyards have grass alleyways which are kept mown. In truth, the old problem facing many growers is one of size: most are simply not large enough to be able to justify any very sophisticated equipment. Most grapes are still hand-harvested and the picking machine at Denbies remains the only one in use in the UK. The increase in the area of Champagne varieties, where hand-harvesting and whole bunch pressing is part of the process, means that picking machines are unlikely to be very common in the future.

Winemaking and wine styles

Again, as with viticulture, there is little in the production of wine in England and Wales that differs from winemaking in other parts of the world. While we do have natural sugar levels that some winemakers might find discouragingly low and acid levels that would have winemakers from warmer climes rushing for their text books, in essence the task of turning UK grown grapes into wine is much the same as it is in wineries worldwide.

When the first few vineyards of the revival started cropping, the level of winemaking knowledge was, by all accounts, fairly basic. Jack Ward at Merrydown had some technical expertise to draw on, but his staff had little experience of making wine from grapes at this time – cider and fruit wines were their specialities. Dr Alfred Pollard and Fred Beech, who ran the Cider Department at Long Ashton Research Station, near Bristol, helped Ray Brock with his winemaking. However, from what Pollard wrote in the winemaking section of the 1953 book *Vineyards in England*, he too had had little experience of working with grapes. Sir Guy Salisbury-Jones had help from a Monsieur Chardon (a friend of Allan Sichel's from Bordeaux) for the first Hambledon vintage (in 1955) and the results were decscribed as 'encouraging'! What this meant in terms of wine quality one can only hazard a guess at. About the only person who professed to know anything about the job was Anton Massel. He quite quickly became involved with the fledgling wine industry and supplied both advice and equipment to Salisbury-Jones, the Gore-Brownes at Beaulieu, Major Rook at Stragglethorpe Hall, as well as a number of others. Nigel Godden at Pilton Manor took a different tack: he employed a cousin of the famous opera singer Mario Lanza to help in the vineyard and winery. Since Pilton Manor won the Gore-Browne Trophy two years running (1975 and 1976) they must have been doing something right.

From all accounts, the early English and Welsh wines were, at their best, 'interesting', at their worst, fairly thin and austere. Vineyards tended to suffer from bird damage which forced growers to pick early and rely upon chemicals to remove excess acidity rather than allowing the grapes to ripen naturally. Without today's modern anti-*Botrytis* and mildew sprays, the grapes suffered badly from disease which again led growers to pick early. The equipment found in many wineries was also fairly primitive and in some cases, very unsuitable for the production of the fresh, fruity wines which today we are able to produce with regularity. There were almost no stainless steel tanks in the early wineries and up until the mid-1970s, most wineries were equipped with second-hand fibreglass tanks, many of which had already seen 20 years' service in the cellars and railway arches of the wine companies that used to bottle wines in the UK. Many wineries had small vertical screw presses, more suited to red wine production than white, although Massel did persuade Salisbury-Jones to import a Willmes airbag press in 1965 which greatly improved both the efficiency of the operation and the quality of their wines. In 1969, Ward started the Merrydown Co-operative Scheme which gave smaller growers the chance to have their wine made by professionals and greatly helped raise the general standard of UK produced wines. Ward employed Kit Lindlar,[1] who had worked on the Mosel and spoke German, to work in the winery from 1976 until the last vintage under this scheme in 1979.

Until Lamberhurst started producing wine in 1974, very few English and Welsh wines had been produced (intentionally) with noticeable residual sugar. Up until then, wines tended to be fairly dry and crisp, relying on time in the bottle to soften the acidity, rather than any added sweetness. The arrival of two German trained winemakers (Ernst Abel and Karl-Heinz Schmitt) to make the first Lamberhurst wines marked the start of a new era. Their first wines were naturally – for they were Geisenheim trained – sweetened slightly with sterile grape juice (*süss-reserve* as it is usually known by UK winemakers) and bottled through sterile filters. The results were something of a revelation. The sweetness balanced the acidity and the fruity grape juice gave the wines an added dimension which pleased, if not some purists, then at least the public who were becoming increasingly interested in English and Welsh wines. With hindsight, it is easy to say that the wholesale addition of grape juice – much of it imported from Germany – was perhaps overdone and in some cases used as a mask to cover excess acidity and unripe phenolic flavours. However, at the time, when the wines were being appreciated by ordinary customers, many winemakers saw the technique as a very valuable one.

As the size and importance of Lamberhurst, both as an individual wine producer and as a contract winemaker for many different vineyards in the UK, grew, so did the influence of their style of wine. Karl-Heinz Johner, another Geisenheim graduate, who took over winemaking in September 1976 and was there for 12 vintages until 1988, continued to make many wines in what one might call a German style – then extremely popular. It has to be remembered that at this time, brands such as Blue Nun, Golden Oktober and Black Tower, as well as a large number of generic Hocks, Mosels and Liebfraumilches dominated the entry-level and mid-markets in wine. More and

---

1 Christopher (or more usually Kit) Lindlar was one of the most experienced winemakers working in the UK in the late 1970s to mid-1990s. After Merrydown, he ran a contract winemaking business based at Biddenden Vineyards, built his own winery, High Weald Winery, near Maidstone, Kent where he co-made the first three vintages of Nyetimber (1992–1994) as well as a large number of other wines. After that closed, he became winemaker at Denbies for two years before retiring from winemaking to take up Holy Orders. I guess that his experience of praying for good weather and good winemaking conditions gave him something of an advantage at theological college!

more wine was being sold through the rapidly growing national supermarket chains and their wine-buying customers – many of them female – found this style suited their palates. Many of the newer, larger UK vineyards opened shops to sell wines directly to the public and it was very evident that when buyers had the chance to taste them first, wines with residual sugar found greater favour. Lamberhurst was also the first of the 'super wineries' built at a UK vineyard. With the financial clout of its proprietor, Kenneth McAlpine, behind it, the winery was lavishly equipped with the latest equipment and became a place of pilgrimage for vineyard owners and winemakers.

The years since Lamberhurst was the major player in the English and Welsh wine industry have seen many changes. Other large vineyards and wineries have been established, with just as impressive facilities and capable of producing wines of equal technical quality. Growers have, through a combination of better vineyard management, better chemical sprays to control *Botrytis* and mildews and an appreciation that quality really does start (and often end) in the vineyard, been delivering higher quality grapes to their winery doors. Winemakers such as John Worontschak, then based at Valley Vineyards (now called Stanlake Park), but who also worked as a consultant to many other wineries and David Cowderoy, at Chapel Down Wines until 1999, both of whom graduated from Australian winemaking universities, brought with them new ideas and new techniques which have resulted in softer, more approachable wines – much more in the New World style. The fact is that while some would like to believe that English and Welsh wines are somehow immune from market forces, the truth is that they are not. The domination of the lower and middle market by the big German and German-style brands has ended and been replaced by softer New World styles. Old fashioned English and Welsh wines, packaged as they almost always were, in brown Hock or green Mosel bottles, with their funny-sounding varietal names have largely – thank goodness – disappeared.

While many of the smaller wineries still retain simple equipment and use techniques suited to their scale, there are now a number of wineries of considerable size and complexity: wineries such as those at Biddenden, Bookers, Camel Valley, Chapel Down, Davenport, Denbies, Nyetimber, RidgeView, Three Choirs, Stanlake Park and Wickham would not look out of place in any winemaking region. They are mostly well equipped with stainless steel tanks (often refrigerated), airbag presses, modern filtration equipment and good bottling lines, including a few with screw-capping facilities. Those vineyards specialising in sparkling wines have presses with Champagne programmes, gyro-pallets and modern disgorging and corking machinery. Both RidgeView and Nyetimber have a Coquard PAI Champagne presses, considered by many to be the Rolls Royce of sparkling wine presses.

In the winery too, practices have changed. Winemakers have come to appreciate the benefits of gentler handling techniques, whole-bunch pressing, cold maceration of fruity varieties to extract more flavour, cold settling to produce clearer juice at the point of fermentation and the use of certain yeast strains to enhance flavours or add complexity. Until 1986, the use of oak barrels for the maturation of white wines was unheard of in UK wineries, whereas today, while not perhaps to be found in every winery, they are quite widely distributed. As winemakers have gained experience with barrels, learning which of the different oaks suit their wines and how long to leave them on the yeast lees, so the quality of these wines has risen. A number of wineries also now produce 'oaked' wines, a term used to denote that the oaking is carried out with oak chips or oak staves, and that the wines have generally only fleetingly seen a barrel or often not seen a barrel at all. The use of oak chips and staves, made from the same wood and treated (toasted) in the same way as the wood used for making barrels, is nothing new and while it may not be openly admitted as such on labels, it is a common practice in wineries throughout the world. Both chips and staves can be introduced into tanks of juice or wine at any stage and the amount used and the length of time they are left in contact will determine the degree of 'oakiness' imparted. While these techniques do not give the same effect as using barrels, they can be very effective and impart an oaked character at a lesser cost. The use of the malolactic fermentation (the conversion of the harsher malic acid to the softer lactic acid by bacteria) to soften both white and red wines and add complexity during lees ageing, is also a practice that some UK winemakers have now taken to – until the late 1980s it was a unheard of. In most cases, pHs were too low and acid levels too high for a spontaneous secondary fermentation (as it is often known) to take place. Now, by picking later when acids are lower and pHs higher and by using malolactic cultures to induce the secondary fermentation, this is a technique seen very much more often.

Table 6.1

Year	Total Yield in Hl.	% White	% Red
1990	14,442	93.37%	6.63%
1991	15,429	93.75%	6.25%
1992	26,428	93.44%	6.56%
1993	17,504	90.52%	9.48%
1994	17,693	91.63%	8.37%
1995	12,651	92.75%	7.25%
1996	26,080	91.87%	8.13%
1997	6,460	91.56%	8.44%
1998	11,202	90.70%	9.30%
1999	13,272	90.80%	9.20%
2000	14,215	89.69%	10.31%
2001	15,817	90.05%	9.95%
2002	9,385	85.62%	14.38%
2003	14,503	80.43%	19.57%
2004	19,071	84.63%	15.37%
2005	12,806	81.42%	18.58%
2006	25,267	79.88%	20.12%
2007	9,948	77.92%	22.08%
2008	10,087	77.65%	22.35%

Red wines, which once only accounted for a very small percentage of the total wine produced, are increasing in quantity and improving year on year. As can be seen from Table 6.1 red wines (which also includes rosé wines) have grown from around 6–7 per cent of total production (1990 was the first year in which accurate data was collected) to just over 22 per cent in 2008. While much of this increase is down to winemakers responding to the rise in demand for rosé wines (both still and sparkling) by UK wine drinkers, some of this increase is believed to be for what one might call technical reasons: wines have to be declared by their producers as whites, reds or rosés by 15 December of the year of harvest, the date by which annual production returns have to be made to the WSB. In fact some of these wines may well be white wines made from the red Champagne varieties Pinot noir and Pinot Meunier and which ultimately will end up as white sparkling wine.

The newer vine varieties, Regent, Rondo and Dornfelder, have definitely helped to produce much deeper coloured and fuller bodied red wines over the past decade, and the increasing use of oak for ageing is a significant factor in their improvement in quality. However, since 2002, it is wines made from Pinot noir that have been the most successful, with the Bernard Theobald Trophy for the Best Red Wine going to this variety every year for seven consecutive years – four times to Chapel Down and once each to Sandhurst, Sharpham and Titchfield. With Pinot noir now officially the most planted vine variety and with the increase in average summer temperatures, it would seem likely that even more reds from this variety will be produced. (There is more on red vine varieties in Chapter 7.)

A few growers have produced successful sweet wines and while this is an even smaller category than red wines, it certainly one where value can be added. Early ripening varieties such as Ortega, Optima and Siegerrebe, together with *Botrytis*-prone varieties such as Bacchus and Huxelrebe, which can all produce high sugars if allowed to ripen fully, have been used to make some excellent sweet late-harvest style wines. Using Optima and Ortega, Denbies made, for several years running, an amazingly powerful dessert wine called 'Noble Harvest' which, in 1992, had a potential alcohol at picking of 22 per cent. Jim Dowling at Pilton Manor won the Gore-Browne Trophy in 1994 with his '1992 Westholme Late Harvest', made from Huxelrebe which had succumbed to *Botrytis*. Northbrook Springs made a Gold Medal winning wine called 'Noble Dessert' in 1994 from *Botrytis*-infected Bacchus, Huxelrebe and Schönburger. Today, these wines are but a memory, brought about I suspect by better vineyard management and better anti-*Botrytis* sprays which prevent noble rot appearing. However, Tony Skuriat at Eglantine Vineyard in Nottinghamshire, consistently (and completely legally) produces a *faux* icewine by freezing Madeleine x Angevine 7672 grapes which quite often wins medals in the UKVA Competition, as well as overseas and Three Choirs usually make a semi-sweet dessert wine using the early ripening Siegerrebe which can be good. In general though, this is not a burgeoning category for UK wines.

The production of sparkling wines, as has already been discussed in an earlier chapter, will, I believe, come to dominate UK wine production in the not too distant future. Almost all UK sparkling wine is bottle-fermented and almost all carried out according to the strict *méthode Champenoise* as laid down by the CIVC (Comité Interprofessionnel du Vin de Champagne). A few producers in the past have used carbonation to produce sparkling wines: Barton Manor won a Gold Medal with their Sparkling Rosé in 1984 and Chris Hartley at Meon Valley Vineyard produced many carbonated sparkling wines under contract. Today, however, the story that sells best is that our wines 'are as good as Champagne' and to back that up, serious producers are concentrating on using the three standard grape varieties (Chardonnay, Pinot noir and Pinot Meunier) and using the the officially approved CIVC equipment and techniques. The four top UK producers – Camel Valley, Chapel Down, Nyetimber and RidgeView – have all upgraded their equipment in recent years and as they sail clear of the pack, others trying to catch them up will undoubtedly be forced to follow suit. Growers and winemakers making sparkling wines from non-Champagne varieties and adopting techniques not CIVC approved will, I feel sure, never reach the quality heights that have been shown to be possible.[2] Perhaps more importantly, those not using the classic varieties and processes will be viewed by the wine trade and consumers – at least by those that care about such things – as country cousins and not really trying hard enough.

Winemaking rules and regulations

The regulations governing the production of wine from home-grown grapes have altered little since the UK joined the Common Market in 1973. The minimum natural (i.e. potential) alcohol level which grapes have to reach before they can be harvested and made into wine remains at the generously low level of 5 per cent for Table Wines and 6 per cent for Regional and Quality Wines. For enriched (i.e. chaptalised) Table and Regional Wines, there is a maximum *total* alcohol level (total alcohol is the sum of the actual plus the potential alcohol) of 11.5 per cent for white and 12 per cent for red and rosé wines and a maximum of 15 per cent *total* alcohol for un-enriched Table and Regional Wines of whatever colour. Wines with more than 15 per cent *total* alcohol cannot be Table or Regional Wines and have to qualify for Quality Wine status before they can be sold in the EU. It is important therefore to exclude non-vinifera grapes from these wines as only 100 per cent pure *vinifera* wines qualify for Quality Wine status. For all categories of wine, enrichment levels used to be + 3.5 per cent in normal years, with an additional + 1 per cent allowed in years when climatic conditions are 'exceptionally unfavourable', but in 2009 these were lowered to + 3 per cent and an additional + 0.5 per cent in poor years. This extra 0.5 per cent allowance may be restricted to certain parts of the country or certain grape varieties. Some growers have experimented with 'cryo-extraction' or 'freeze concentration' where grape juice is concentrated by cooling to freezing point and removing the resultant ice. This technique is allowed up to a point where the volume is not reduced by more than 20 per cent and where the natural alcohol level is increased by no more than 2 per cent.

Table and Regional Wines must have at least 8.5 per cent *actual* alcohol when bottled, whereas Quality Wines must have a minimum actual alcohol of 9 per cent,

---

2   Having said that, both Camel Valley and Chapel Down make perfectly respectable – even very good, award-winning – wines using other suitable varieties such as Seyval blanc, Pinot blanc, Auxerrois, even M-T and Reichensteiner. In time, however, I feel sure these will be replaced with the more 'noble' varieties.

although unenriched white wines may, subject to EU approval, be bottled with 8.5 per cent alcohol. Acid levels of finished Table Wines must be at least 3.5 g/l (total acidity expressed as tartaric acid) and of Regional and Quality Wines, 4 g/l. De-acidification of juice and wines still in fermentation[3] is allowed without limit, but finished wines may only be de-acidified by a maximum of 1 g/l. The acidification of still wines is not allowed, whereas wine for the production of sparkling wine (the *cuvée*) may be acidified by up to 1.5 g/l. These are only the very basic rules governing the production of wine in the UK and the full regulations can be downloaded from the 'Food and Drink' section of the DEFRA website.

The restrictions on total alcohol levels of enriched Table and Regional Wines to 11.5 per cent for whites and 12 per cent for reds and rosé wines can lead to problems. A medium-dry wine with say 9 g/l of residual sugar, which equates to a potential alcohol of just over 0.5 per cent may only have an actual alcohol of, at the very maximum, 11 per cent in order to keep under the 11.5 per cent total figure. In reality winemakers have to aim slightly lower than the 11.5 per cent total alcohol figure as there are always inaccuracies in the initial measurement of sugar levels and sugar to alcohol conversion rates are never that predictable. This means that many wines are bottled with between 10 per cent and 10.5 per cent actual alcohol which, by today's standards, is quite low. Wines from around the world are much more likely to be bottled with 12.5 per cent to 13.5 per cent actual alcohol and this relative lack of alcohol in our wines is noticeable to wine drinkers more used to modern wines from overseas. One solution to this problem is to make more Quality Wines where there are no upper limits on total alcohol levels. However, this does not help those wines made in whole or in part from hybrids which may not, under present EU legislation, be Quality Wines! This means that producers of red wines, which are the wines that really might benefit from having actual alcohols in the 12.5–13.5 per cent range, have to make sure that they don't use any Triomphe or Léon Millot in their blends as both of these varieties are hybrids. Luckily, the 2002 ruling by DEFRA (following, I have to say, five years of lobbying by myself) that four modern interspecific-crosses – Orion, Phoenix, Regent and Rondo – would henceforth be considered to be *viniferas* has helped red wine producers as Rondo and Regent are both successful red varieties and quite widely used.

The question of the use of *süss-reserve* which seemed to exercise minds greatly in the 1980s, no longer seems to do so quite so much. Many winemakers now rely on naturally stopped fermentations, using strains of yeast that are easier to stop, as well as racking-off and cooling, easier now that many wineries have tanks with cooling coils or jackets. *Süss* – as it tends to be called when it is used – is either imported (almost entirely from Germany with Müller-Thurgau and Bacchus being the most popular varieties) or is home-grown, where Müller-Thurgau and Reichensteiner (and

---

3   'Still in fermentation' is defined as before the wine is racked off its gross lees.

occasionally Bacchus) are the preferred varieties. This change has come about partly because it is a requirement for Quality Wines that material used for sweetening originates in the same region of production as the wine being sweetened. Stopping fermentations of course gets round the problem of finding suitable English or Welsh *süss-reserve*. In any event, residual sugar levels in English and Welsh wines have come down over the past 15 years, mainly because of the change in tastes of the wine buying public, many of whom now prefer wines with relatively low levels of residual sugar. Geoff Taylor, whose 'Corkwise' analytical laboratory has been the principal analyst to English and Welsh winegrowers since 1988, says that most English and Welsh wines now fall into the official 'dry' and 'medium dry' categories where, with sufficient acidity, wines can have up to 9 g/l (dry) and 18 g/l (med-dry) of residual sugar. Very few English and Welsh wines are now bottled with more than 25 g/l of residual sugar which was far from the case in the 1980's. Taylor also says that in the 20+ years that he has been analysing English and Welsh wines he has noticed that acidity levels have come down, due to riper grapes, better de-acidification and the use of malolactic fermentation. He also says that alcohol levels have risen (as they have worldwide) which he feels is due to growers leaving their grapes to ripen more fully, coupled with the use of yeasts with better sugar-to-alcohol conversion rates and the wider use of refrigeration in UK wineries. This leads to gentler fermentations and less loss of alcohol. He also says that without a doubt, the overall quality of English and Welsh wines has risen over the past 15 years very substantially and many of the poorer producers now appear (thankfully) to have given up the struggle. This is surely good news for the industry. One slight caveat to the above is that in the 2009 regulation changes already referred to, sweetening of wines now falls outside the levels for total alcohols at fermentation and winemakers may increase the total alcohol of their wines through sweetening by 4% or less.

One thing is certain: winegrowing and winemaking will continue to change and develop to the benefit of UK-grown wines. In the past 50+ years, huge advances have been made in every aspect of wine production and there is nothing to suppose that similar changes will not happen over the next 50 years. In sparkling wine production we have only just started to understand how to grow and make good wines and as the large number of new vineyards planted with Champagne varieties start cropping and their grapes are made into wines, much experience will be gained for producers to learn from.

CHAPTER 7

Vine varieties

The success of a winegrowing region depends, to a very large extent, on the marriage of those elements that go to make up what the French call *terroir*: climate, sites, soils and vine varieties. While the first three elements remain largely fixed and unchangeable, the fourth, that of vine varieties, is not. Better varieties can be chosen and better clones of varieties selected to create wines more in tune with the market. The rise of varietal wines, a phenomenon of the past 30–40 years, bears witness to the importance of the vine variety in determining both the style and quality of wine from any given region. The UK, while different in many ways from any other wine producing area in the world, still has to produce wines that find favour with the consumer and is not insulated against varietal changes and fashions.

Pre-revival vineyards

Which varieties were used in British vineyards before the modern revival is open to conjecture. Of Roman viticulture, so little evidence exists, that discussion about what varieties they grew in the British Isles is meaningless (and the idea that the original Wrotham Pinot vine was left behind by the Romans has already been discussed and declared fanciful at best). In the mainland northern regions that the Romans conquered the variety Elbling – now found on the Moselle in Luxembourg – is held to be a 'Roman' variety, but this is as much folklore as fact.

The monks who established vineyards following the Norman invasion of 1066 and kept them going throughout the next five centuries no doubt brought vines with them from their home monasteries and also from the nearest continental winegrowing regions – the Rhine and Mosel, the Loire, Champagne and the Paris basin (which before the railways allowed wine to be brought from much greater distances was a large centre of wine production). Belgium had a history of vineyards attached to monasteries going back to 854 AD and, with a very similar climate to ours, would have been a good place to find suitable varieties. Our medieval Bordeaux connection must also have enabled vineyard owners to gather varieties from this region.

The quest to find new and better varieties for growing in vineyards, and perhaps more importantly, in the glass roofed and walled 'vineries' which started to be built all over the country from the 1600s onwards (once it was discovered how to make glass large enough and thin enough to be used for this purpose) was one which yielded hundreds of varieties from all over the world. Table grape production became an important feature in Britain and no grand house or mansion was without its vinery to produce grapes for almost every day of the year. Britain's gardeners became adept at the cross-pollination of vines and it is quite remarkable how many of the world's leading table-grape vine varieties originated in this country (Foster's White Seedling for instance, raised in 1835 by Mr Foster, gardener to Lord Downe) or were brought to this country and improved through clonal selection. Varieties for outdoor ripening – whether for the table or for wine – were, however, less available.

In 1666, John Rose wrote in his book *The English Vineyard Vindicated* that the best varieties were: *the small Black Grape, by some call'd the Cluster Grape, the white Muscadine, the Parsley Grape, the Muscadella, the Frontiniaq, both white and red, together with a new white grape which I found in his Majesty's garden in St James* – which he did not name. In 1670 Will Hughes wrote in *The Compleat Vineyard* that the best varieties to grow outside were: *the lesser and greater white Muscadine, the red Muscadine, the Frantinick, the Parsley-grape (more for show and rarity than profit) and the Rhenish-wine vine.* At least these two commentators seem to show some degree of uniformity in their choice of varieties (unless Hughes just copied the varieties Rose had suggested!)

In the 1727 book *The Vineyard*, the un-named author, a 'Gentleman' we know only by the initials S. J., states that: *the Vines I would advise as most proper for this climate, and as being the hardiest, are the small black Muscadine, which are the same planted by the Champaigners and the Burgundians, in their vineyards.* No other varieties, at least for outdoor cultivation, appear to have met with his favour. Philip Miller, in his *Gardener's Dictionary*, the first edition of which was published in 1731, lists over 20 varieties and says: *I shall not trouble the reader with an enumeration of all the sorts of grapes which are at present known in England as this would swell this work much beyond its intended bulk, and be of little use, since many of them are not worth the trouble of cultivating.* The only one that he recommends for wine production is: *the Auverna* [sic] *or true Burgundy grape, sometimes called Black Morillon* (Robinson 1986 gives Morillon as a synonym for both Chardonnay and Pinot noir). Sir Edward Barry, writing in 1775, quotes his friend, the Hon. Charles Hamilton, who had planted the Painshill vineyard between 1740 and 1743. Barry says that Hamilton planted: *two sorts of Burgundy grapes, the Auvernat, which is the most delicate, but the tenderest, and the Miller grape, commonly called the black cluster, which is more hardy.* We can probably assume that the Auvernat was a forerunner of Pinot noir and the Miller grape was what we today call Pinot Meunier. In a letter written by Hamilton's vineyard worker, David Geneste (and already quoted in the chapter on the history of UK viticulture) other varieties were also planted at Painshill. They were: *the Pied rouge, Muscat blanc, Muscat rouge, Guillan blanc, and Sauviot* plus a few other un-named *hatif* (early) varieties. Guillan (possibly Malbec) and Sauviot appear to have been varieties then common in Bordeaux, Geneste's home region, but would have been unlikely to ripen well in the British climate.

William Speechly, writing in the 1790 edition of his *Treatise on the Culture of the Vine*, lists 50 separately identified and described varieties suitable for growing indoors for the table and adds that he has: *above 100 sorts growing at Welbeck*, the Duke of Portland's estate, where he was head gardener. In the chapter *On Vineyards*, Speechly states: *that there would be the greatest possibility of success with those kinds of grapes which have been known to thrive in the most Northern latitudes. I should therefore recommend the kinds of Vines cultivated in Germany and particularly the sort producing the grapes of which the Rhenish wine is made, in preference to any kind cultivated in France.* (It has to be said that when one looks at the selection of varieties upon which the modern revival was founded, Speechly was here giving some good advice, although sadly unheeded for another 160 years.)

As has already been related, the last vineyard enterprise of the pre-revival era, Castle Coch, was planted with Gamay noir and Millie Blanche, although the latter was soon abandoned. H. M. Tod, who grew over 40 different varieties, recommended seven as being 'absolutely safe, year by year'. They were: *the Miller, the Miller's Burgundy*, [the difference between these two is not explained], *the Common or Royal Muscadine, Black Cluster, Esperione, Cambridge Botanic Garden and Brandt*. None of these today – with the exception of Miller's Burgundy if we assume that this variety was Pinot Meunier – are worth considering.

Between the end of the Bute vineyards and 1946, when Brock started his experiments at Oxted, no serious attempt appears to have been made to find better varieties for the production of wine. Indeed, why should anyone have wanted to? Cheap wine was available from the colonies – Australia and South Africa especially – and no one seemed interested in planting vineyards in the UK. What little viticultural activity there was, was confined to growing grapes for the table or for home winemaking using varieties that today would be considered most unsuitable for either purpose.

Vine varieties of the revival

As has already been discussed in Chapter 2, the revival of commercial viticulture in the early 1950s was based upon the discovery by Brock and Hyams that Müller-Thurgau and Seyval blanc were varieties that would both fruit and ripen in our climate. The early vineyards, Hambledon, Horam Manor and Beaulieu, together with those that followed in the 1960s, were planted overwhelmingly with these two varieties. In 1970, when the first of the annual Vintage Reports appeared in the EVA's *Grape Press* No.5 (based on the 1969 harvest), Müller-Thurgau, Seyval blanc, Madeleine x Angevine 7672, Seibel 13/053 (later to be called Cascade), Scheurebe and Siegerrebe were the only varieties giving crops worth reporting. By then, Jack Ward (Horam Manor) had made several forays to Germany to find better varieties and returned with Bacchus, Faberrebe, Huxelrebe, Ortega and Reichensteiner which started to make appearances in some of the newer vineyards.

Faced with a blank field and a desire to plant a vineyard, a grower in this country in the early stages of the viticultural revival was faced with a dilemma – the dilemma of what varieties to plant. The track record of the two major varieties – Müller-Thurgau and Seyval blanc – was patchy to say the least. Both growing and winemaking skills were in short supply and most of the pioneer growers adopted a rather amateur approach to the problems. After all, in other winemaking regions, growing grapes and making wine didn't appear to be too difficult and if your average French *paysan* could do it seemingly with little specialist education, why shouldn't a Brit? The results of this attitude led to poorly managed vineyards, often with high levels of disease. In those days, the main chemical control of *Botrytis* was with a product called Benlate (whose active ingredient was called Benoymyl) which became renowned for its ineffectiveness and for the way in which the disease was able to mutate and produce Benlate-resistant strains. Canopies were also very vigorous and consequently dense (as they so often are with very young vines) leading to shaded, unripe grapes. Attacks from wasps and birds – problems upon which the early editions of the *Grape Press* seem to dwell quite a bit – exacerbated the problem of harvesting grapes fit for winemaking. In the cellars, lack of experience showed in the resulting wines. While some good wines were made and early vineyards such as Adgestone, Pilton Manor and Wootton soon got a reputation for the quality of their wines, many wines were too acidic, too dry and lacking both fruit and body – the inevitable result of picking grapes at low levels of natural sugar and not fully appreciating how to correctly de-acidify or use low levels of *süss-reserve* to balance excess acidity.

Growers looking to plant vineyards therefore tended to do two things: plant Müller-Thurgau and Seyval blanc as their core varieties, but also to plant a selection of different ones, hoping that they might find one or more that would do better than the two standard varieties. This inevitably led to a large number of cultivars being planted as growers sought the holy grail of British vineyard owners – the perfect variety for our conditions. To a certain extent, those that did have some knowledge about the subject and who also sold vines to growers – Ray Brock, Jack Ward at Merrydown and Anton Massel at Ockley – all had a vested interest in seeing as many new varieties planted in commercial quantities as possible. Otherwise how was anyone going to learn what varieties really did work? Brock offered both rooted and bare-wood cuttings of a large number of varieties (for both table-grape and wine-grape production) and to start with cornered the market. With hindsight, many of the varieties Brock offered were fairly obscure and today would not be remotely considered as suitable. His 1970/1 list (and by this time he had been growing vines for almost 25 years) included – for wine production – Gamay Hâtif des Vosges and Marshal Joffre, varieties which it is doubtful anyone has ever made a good bottle of wine from in an English or Welsh vineyard. However, he was also offering Müller-Thurgau, Seyval blanc, Madeleine x Angevine 7672, Léon Millot, Seibel 13/053, Siegerrebe and Madeleine x Sylvaner III 28/51, not all of which today we might consider when planting a vineyard, but which, in their time, contributed greatly to the revival. Both Ward and Massel imported grafted vines from overseas and looked upon Brock as a bit of a renegade who sold ungrafted vines without really informing growers of the dangers of *Phylloxera*, as well as a rather wide (and wild) selection of different cultivars. They, on the other hand, only imported grafted vines. They also only imported those varieties that the Germans (and to a certain extent the French) wanted us to have. There is no doubt that had it not been for German insistence that Müller-Thurgau was the only variety likely to ripen in our climate (which Germans think is 'foggy'[1] for 12 months of the year) we might have discovered some of their better cultivars a bit sooner. As it was, Müller-Thurgau, which was sweeping through their own vineyards at the time, was seen as the saviour of their war-torn industry (instead of which it turned out to be the destroyer) and they felt that it would also be ideal for the UK.

A look through the EVA's Vintage Reports of the early years (from the 1969 harvest onwards) show that over 20 different varieties were being grown. This resulted in yet more problems for growers as they struggled with unknown and in many cases, unsuitable varieties, leading to yet more trouble in their wineries. How it could have been otherwise is, of course, a question that has no answer. MAFF at the time had neither the experience, inclination – or probably the power – to impose restrictions on what growers could or could not plant. However, with hindsight, had MAFF had the powers to dictate that vineyards could only be planted with Bacchus, Reichensteiner, Seyval blanc and Schönburger, how many vineyards would have saved themselves the heartache of struggling to grow decent crops of Müller-Thurgau, Huxelrebe and Kerner and a whole host of other unsuitable varieties? As it was, the free-for-all approach has left us with a very wide spectrum of varieties, not all ideal for our climate, but just good enough for growers to keep them in their vineyards, rather than going to the expense of replacing them or grubbing them up altogether. Writing this from the safety of 2008, one is able to use 20/20 hindsight to say that had MAFF dictated that only sparkling wine be made and that only the Champagne varieties be used, many, many millions of pounds of hard-earned grower's funds would have been saved and a much more viable wine industry established decades earlier.

The UK is often compared – viticulturally – to New Zealand which was once dominated by Müller-Thurgau and other varieties less suitable for today's market. In

---

1   When I lived in Germany in the mid-1970s, the Germans constantly referred to the UK as *zehr neblische* (very foggy). I got rather fed up with this so went to the official weather station in Geisenheim (where I was studying) and asked them for the data on the number of foggy days there. (Officially, a foggy day is a day when the visibility falls to below 1,000 metres.) When this turned out to be a few days less than some similar data I obtained from the UK, I was able to counter the locals' aspersions on the British climate with some accurate figures. The fact that Geisenheim is right on the banks of the Rhine and often suffers from river-mists I conveniently avoided mentioning!

1985–1986, a new Labour government in New Zealand – hoping perhaps to find a few votes in the rural community – instigated a vine-pull programme which paid growers to grub out old vineyards, yet unlike most grubbing-up schemes, allowed them to replant. The result of this generosity was that in one season, over 25 per cent of all vines in the country were taken out and over the next few years, vineyards were replanted with varieties such as Sauvignon blanc, Chardonnay and Pinot noir which today form the basis for one of the most remarkable winegrowing regions in the world. If only our government had this type of foresight!

Before the UK joined the Common Market in 1973, MAFF was asked by the Commission to produce a list of acceptable vine varieties. MAFF consulted the EVA and a meeting was held at the National Farmers Union's *Agriculture House* in 1971 to discuss the varieties to be included. The EVA wanted Müller-Thurgau and Seyval blanc as the only Recommended varieties, with a whole host of others in the lesser category, Authorised.[2] However, when MAFF produced the lists for presentation to the EU, they contained a few surprises. As well as Müller-Thurgau, both Auxerrois and Wrotham Pinot had been added to the Recommended list and Seyval blanc left off. Auxerrois was barely grown in the UK and had not been even mentioned by the EVA; Wrotham Pinot was the name given to the vine found by Edward Hyams growing on a cottage wall in Wrotham, Kent, had no official status and was again, not widely planted; and Seyval blanc, then the most planted variety, had been downgraded to Authorised. Apparently, despite 'strenuous argument' by MAFF in Brussels, the Commission was not prepared to accept Seyval blanc on the Recommended list as it was a hybrid variety. The EVA was told that they would have to be happy with its Authorised classification although MAFF did agree that its status would be reviewed *at a later date* (the first of several 'fobbings off' that MAFF doled out to the EVA). In fact, it was not until July 1990 that Seyval blanc was elevated to the Recommended list, but of course not able to be made into Quality Wine owing to it being a hybrid.

When the EU Commission were presented with the list, they had several observations. They were concerned about the naming of the varieties Madeleine Angevine and Madeleine Sylvaner as they felt (quite rightly as it happened) that there would be confusion. These were the names that Brock gave to the varieties he had been sent as Sämling 7672 and Madeleine Angevine x Sylvaner III 28/51, but which he felt were unwieldy. The shortened names were more user-friendly to the growers who bought vines from him. Reichensteiner, which Jack Ward felt sure was going to be a good variety for our climate, was not permitted to be classified as its track record was too recent. (Reichensteiner and Schönburger were eventually added as Temporarily Authorised in 1986). The omission of Reichensteiner however, did not really pose a problem as it was agreed with MAFF that any other varieties being

---

2   At that time, Recommended varieties were those that could be made into Quality Wine (as long as they were 100 per cent *vinifera*). Authorised varieties could only be made into Table Wine. These distinctions do not now apply.

grown in the UK would be considered as being 'on trial' and could continue to be used for wine production. The list as accepted by the EU in 1973 looked like this:

Recommended
Müller-Thurgau
Wrotham Pinot (Pinot Meunier)
Auxerrois

Authorised

Bacchus	Madeleine Royale
Chardonnay	Mariensteiner
Ehrenfelser	Ortega
Faber (Faberrebe)	Perle
Huxelrebe	Pinot noir
Kerner	Ruländer (Pinot gris)
Kanzler	Seyval blanc
Madeleine Angevine	Siegerrebe
Madeleine Sylvaner	

Although the EVA was not very happy with the list, for practical purposes its contents made no difference to UK vinegrowers. After the UK joined the Common Market on 1 January 1973, the only varieties permitted to be planted (in theory) were those on the Recommended and Authorised lists. In practice, MAFF took little notice of this regulation and until the 500-hectare limit was reached, neither MAFF nor the WSB appeared to be concerned about what was being planted. As has already been pointed out, MAFF (no doubt unwittingly) helped exacerbate the situation of 'illegal' planting by issuing two publications, *Outdoor Grape Production* in 1978 and *Grapes for Wine* in 1980, both of which stated that: *any variety not in the 'Recommended' or 'Authorised' list may* [be planted and] *be used for commercial wine production.*

In November 1971, Wye College, the University of London's agricultural department near Ashford in Kent, which specialised in research into hops, had suggested that it might undertake some research into grapevines by planting a trial vineyard. The EVA launched an appeal and the sum of £10,000 was raised towards the costs, with donations coming from members and interested organisations. Vines were donated by various German, Swiss and Austrian universities, together with some from Weingut Louis Guntrum in Nierstein. In total, 850 vines of 17 different varieties were obtained (not all of them on the permitted lists) and planted in 1973, with more to follow in 1974, 1975, 1980 and 1981. The vineyard eventually covered 1.3 acres (0.526 ha). The vines were trained on three different trellising systems: Double Guyot, Lenz Moser and GDC. Bob Farrar, then in charge of the management of the College's hop gardens, took great personal interest in the vineyard, and was really responsible for seeing that it was maintained at minimal expense to the EVA, making sure that it was sprayed with fungicides left over from spraying the hop gardens. The yield and performance statistics gathered gave valuable information about the different varieties being grown there. The grapes harvested were either sold to Merrydown or sent to Long Ashton Research Station in Bristol to be made into wine. Eventually, the vineyard site was required by Wye College for a new hop garden and in 1984 the vines were grubbed-up. Although it only lasted just over a decade, the Wye College vineyard introduced Regner, Würzer, Bacchus, Faberrebe and Zweigeltrebe to UK vineyards.

In 1976 the categories of vines were extended to include the following:

Temporarily Authorised Varieties growing in the United Kingdom on 31 December 1976 and not included in any of the other lists of permitted vines. In theory, these varieties could be grown and made into wine for a further 25 years, but no new vines of these varieties could be planted after this date.

Experimental Varieties that were subject to officially approved trials or were being grown for the production of cuttings or of scion wood for export to non-EC countries.

Provisionally Authorised Varieties whose suitability has been determined by approved trials and which were subject to a further five to seven-year wait until they are eligible to be added to the Authorised list.

Unauthorised Varieties that did not fall into any of the permitted categories. Wine from them could not be sold in an EC country, but it could be exported to a non-EC country, distilled, converted into vinegar or consumed by the winegrower and his family.

In order to comply with EU regulations, which required the relevant authority to monitor the area of vines being grown in a Member State, MAFF carried out four voluntary surveys, in 1975, 1984, 1986 and 1988 and, in addition, it made estimates of the area of vines in 1979, 1980 and 1982. The first statutory survey was held in 1989.

Table 7.1   Ha of vineyards in the UK, 1975–1988 (MAFF voluntary surveys) & 1989 (statutory survey).

Year	1975	1979	1980	1982	1984	1986	1988	1989
Ha not in production	46				105	132	164	224
Ha in production	150				325	356	382	652
Total ha	196	250	350	400	430	488	546	876

The voluntary nature of the four surveys, in which growers were requested to supply details of varieties grown and yields, meant that the data collected must be viewed with some suspicion. A comparison between the 1988 and 1989 surveys, the first voluntary, the second statutory, shows that there was a very considerable rise in vineyard area. Hectares not in production rose by 37 per cent to 224-hectares, hectares in production rose by 71 per cent to 652-hectares and the overall area by 60 per cent to 876 hectares – rises far too large to be accounted for by plantings in the spring of 1989. However, inaccurate as they were, the 1975–1988 surveys probably gave a fair indication of the rise in the level of interest in viticulture over the period.

The three later voluntary surveys (1984, 1986 and 1988) also looked at individual vine variety areas (Table 7.2) and again, although not that reliable, probably give a general indication of the changes in the varietal makeup of the UK's vineyards. Varieties such as Bacchus, Huxelrebe, Reichensteiner and Schönburger rising in terms of percentage of the area with Madeleine x Angevine 7672, Müller-Thurgau and Seyval blanc falling. Müller-Thurgau showed the greatest fall, from 34.6 per cent of the total area, down to 26.7 per cent.

Table 7.2   Distribution of vine varieties in the UK: 1984, 1986 and 1988 (MAFF)

Variety	Ha planted 1984	Ha planted 1986	Ha planted 1988
Auxerrois			5
Bacchus	10	14	34
Cascade (Seibel 13/053)			2
Chardonnay			7
Dunkelfelder			2
Ehrenfelser			3
Faberrebe			6
Gamay			2
Gewürztraminer			1
Gutenborner			4
Huxelrebe	23	26	30
Kerner			17
Kernling		11	12
Léon Millot			1
Madeleine x Angevine 7672	26	26	24
Madeleine Sylvaner III 28/57			1
Müller-Thurgau	149	155	146
Optima			3
Ortega			16
Pinot gris (Ruländer)			6
Pinot Meunier			5

Pinot noir	11	13	20
Regner			6
Reichensteiner	47	55	62
Riesling			2
Sauvignon blanc			1
Scheurebe			6
Schönburger	16	27	34
Seyval blanc	46	45	53
Siegerrebe			6
Triomphe			2
Würzer			7
Zweigeltrebe			3
Miscellaneous	102	116	17
Total	**430**	**488**	**546**

Yields of major vine varieties

The 1984, 1986 and 1988 voluntary surveys also looked at yields of individual varieties. As with the area data (or perhaps even more so) the accuracy of these figures must be questioned, although they probably reflect the comparative cropping levels of the major varieties such as Müller-Thurgau, Bacchus, Reichensteiner, Schönburger and Seyval blanc,

Table 7.3 Yields of major varieties in hl/ha (MAFF voluntary surveys 1984–1988)

Variety	*1984*	*1986*	*1988*	*Averages 1984–1988*
Bacchus	48	13	3	21
Huxelrebe	31	19	5	18
Kerner	/	16	5	10
Madeleine x Angevine 7672	26	10	11	16
Müller-Thurgau	39	13	7	20
Pinot noir	23	12	5	13
Reichensteiner	36	15	10	20
Schönburger	43	19	13	25
Seyval blanc	40	23	13	25
Miscellaneous varieties	54	31	21	35
All varieties average	42	18	11	24
Total UK yield	**13,510 hl**	**6,531 hl**	**4,110 hl**	**8,050 hl**

As can be seen from Table 7.3, yields were never very high and in poor years, 1987 being a case in point, they were downright disastrous. Taking 17.5 hl/ha to equate to 1 tonne per acre and reckoning that 3 tonnes per acre are needed to cover one's costs, it can be seen that during the 1980s very few growers were making much money out of English Wine.

Since the 1987 survey there have been other surveys which have charted the progress of varietal change in UK vineyards. These have been statutory surveys, rather like the annual MAFF June Census, where farmers and growers can be prosecuted for not supplying data. However, since the establishment of the 'Vineyard Register', data on both the area of vines being grown and the varieties has been (one assumes) accurate. The only proviso that one must add to the question of accuracy is that with growers under 10-ares (1,000 square metres) not required to register at all and with growers over 10-ares not required to register until they produce a 'wine sector product' (grapes, juice or wine) – which often means that they are not discovered until they take their grapes to a winery for their first vintage and the winemaker includes them on the 15 December annual 'Harvest Declaration' – it could be up to three or four years after planting before they are included in the WSB's figures. Add on to this the fact that the Vineyard Register is kept up to date on the basis of visits once every three years to known vineyards and there is no system of annual reporting of grubbings-up and plantings by registered vineyards, then the term 'accurate' need to be taken with a pinch of salt.

I have long campaigned to make both the planting and grubbing-up of vineyards something that must be registered with the WSB – they have the power now to prosecute growers who refuse to register once they are known about, so this would be no more draconian than the powers they already have – and to make the Vineyard Register, as it is in other EU countries, a public document. It worries me that in a time of rapid expansion of the vineyard area in the UK, such as we have seen since 2004, those thinking of planting have no real idea of exactly what is being planted (i.e. varieties and clones) or how much. I suspect that if some growers or potential growers really appreciated just how many hectares of vines have been planted in the past five years, they might have second thoughts about planting.

As can be seen from Table 7.4, once growers were required by law to admit to exactly which varieties they were growing and how many hectares of each, a long list was produced. The 1990 survey revealed a total of 56 varieties grown in excess of 0.1 hectare on at least two different sites (for reasons of confidentiality, a variety which was unique to one site could not be identified). By any winegrowing country's standards, let alone for one as minor as the UK, it is a very large number of different cultivars.

Table 7.4   UK Vine varieties 1990–2007 (WSB Vineyard Register)

Variety	1990	% of area	2007	% of area
Albalonga	0.1	0.01%		
Auxerrois	9.1	0.98%		
AZ 15477	0.2	0.02%		
Bacchus	76.0	8.18%	104.4	10.53%
Blauberger	0.6	0.06%		
Cascade	1.2	0.13%		
Chardonnay	19.9	2.14%	119.6	12.06%
Chasselas (Gutedal)	2.5	0.27%		
Comtessa	0.2	0.02%		
Domina	0.2	0.02%		
Dornfelder	5.4	0.58%	16.2	1.63%
Dunkelfelder	3.5	0.38%	2.8	0.28%
Ehrenfelser	2.4	0.26%		
Elbling (Red & White)	3.8	0.41%		
Faberrebe	10.3	1.11%	4.9	0.50%
Findling	3.3	0.36%		
Gamay	1.4	0.15%		
Gewürztraminer	0.8	0.09%		
Gutenborner	3.7	0.40%	2.2	0.22%
Heroldrebe	0.2	0.02%		
Huxelrebe	43.9	4.73%	25.0	2.52%
Kanzler	0.2	0.02%		
Kerner	21.4	2.30%	8.0	0.80%
Kernling	4.2	0.45%	5.8	0.58%
Léon Millot	2.0	0.22%	2.9	0.29%
Madeleine Sylvaner III 28/51	3.7	0.40%		
Madeleine x Angevine 7672	54.6	5.88%	48.6	4.90%
Maréchal Foch	0.3	0.03%		

Variety	1990	% of area	2007	% of area
Marienfeldt	0.4	0.04%		
Merlot	0.2	0.02%		
Müller-Thurgau	184.5	19.87%	71.2	7.18%
Optima	4.6	0.50%	2.0	0.20%
Orion	0.7	0.08%	9.7	0.98%
Ortega	29.5	3.18%	27.2	2.74%
Perle (from Alzey)	0.4	0.04%		
Phoenix	0.4	0.04%	16.3	1.65%
Pinot blanc			13.0	1.31%
Pinot gris (Ruländer)	2.6	0.28%	5.5	0.56%
Pinot Meunier	5.5	0.59%	27.4	2.77%
Pinot noir	32.0	3.45%	121.4	12.24%
Pinot noir Précoce			8.2	0.83%
Portugieser	0.8	0.09%		
Regent			14.8	1.50%
Regner	9.7	1.04%	5.2	0.52%
Reichensteiner	113.9	12.27%	93.6	9.43%
Riesling	5.5	0.59%		
Rondo (Gm 6494/5)	2.0	0.22%	38.7	3.90%
Sauvignon blanc	0.5	0.05%		
Scheurebe	2.3	0.25%		
Schönburger	75.3	8.11%	47.0	4.74%
Senator	0.9	0.10%		
Seyval blanc	122.7	13.21%	91.2	9.19%
Siegerrebe	9.3	1.00%	10.0	1.00%
Triomphe	7.5	0.81%	15.1	1.52%
Würzer	14.3	1.54%	5.7	0.57%
Zweigeltrebe	3.9	0.42%	1.8	0.19%
Miscellaneous/Unauthorised	24.1	2.60%	26.4	2.66%
Totals	**928.6**	**100.00%**	**991.8**	**100.00%**

A comparison between the 1990 MAFF survey (the first statutory survey which included vine varieties) and the Vineyard Register figures for 2007 (collected during 2006) shows how the varietal spectrum has changed in 17 years. The big losers are the old standbys that once occupied the top slots: Müller-Thurgau (−61%), Huxelrebe (−43%), Schönburger (−38%), Seyval blanc (−26%), Reichensteiner (−18%), Madeleine Angevine 7672 (−11%) and Ortega (−8%). Nineteen very minor varieties (those with less than 2 hectares in 1999) have gone altogether, together with another nineteen varieties (of those planted in excess of 2 hectares in 1999) which are listed below:

Auxerrois	Gutenborner	Regner
Chasselas	Kerner	Riesling
Dunkelfelder	Kernling	Scheurebe
Erhenfelser	Léon Millot	Würzer
Elbling	Optima	Zweigeltrebe
Faberrebe	Madeleine Sylvaner III 28/51	
Findling	Pinot gris	

Table 7.5   Top 20 varieties by hectares planted in 2007 (WSB Vineyard Register)

2007 rank	Variety	1990	2007	% +/−
1	Pinot noir	32.0	121.4	279.5%
2	Chardonnay	19.9	119.6	501.2%
3	Bacchus	76.0	104.4	37.4%
4	Reichensteiner	113.9	93.6	−17.9%
5	Seyval blanc	122.7	91.2	−25.7%
6	Müller-Thurgau	184.5	71.2	−61.4%
7	Madeleine x Angevine 7672	54.6	48.6	−10.9%
8	Schönburger	75.3	47.0	−37.6%
9	Rondo	2.0	38.7	1,836.0%
10	Pinot Meunier	5.5	27.4	398.7%
11	Ortega	29.5	27.2	−7.9%
12	Huxelrebe	43.9	25.0	−43.1%
13	Phoenix	0.4	16.3	3,982.5%
14	Dornfelder	5.4	16.2	199.1%
15	Triomphe	7.5	15.1	101.3%
16	Regent		14.8	
17	Pinot blanc		13.0	
18	Siegerrebe	9.3	10.0	7.1%
19	Orion	0.7	9.7	1,288.6%
20	Pinot noir Précoce		8.2	

Since both Müller-Thurgau and Seyval blanc were the first varieties to be planted in the UK, it is not surprising that they feature more prominently in older vineyards and in the smaller, more 'amateur' vineyards, both of which are more likely to be grubbed-up on the grounds of age, either of the vines or of the owner. While many of the varieties on the 'completely disappeared' list were never likely to make old bones in the UK, it is ironic that some of them, with the increase in temperatures that global warming has given the UK, are being replanted. In 2008 I hear of growers planting Auxerrois, Faberrebe, Gutenborner, Pinot gris, Regner, Riesling and Sauvignon blanc – all varieties that were planted in the 1980s and grubbed-up in the 1990s and 2000s!

Bottle-fermented sparkling wines 1990-2007

The varieties that have risen most in area of course are the Champagne varieties[3] – Pinot noir almost quadrupled, Chardonnay up six times and Pinot Meunier up five times – an impressive rise by any measure, but actually *well below* what I estimate the totals of these varieties to be. The total area for these three varieties is officially 268.4-hectares, but I would be very surprised if the actual planted area was under 375-hectares and it could possibly be even more.[4]

As I have already pointed out at the end of Chapter 3, the reasons for the surge in the planting of these varieties are not hard to find: apparent ease of marketing, high prices and global warming. What I said in the 2001 edition of this book perhaps bears repeating:

> *There is no doubt that bottle-fermented sparkling wines (of all types and from all countries) are gaining in popularity with British consumers and many consider that the UK now has an ideal climate in which to produce them. Much of the sparkling wine has, up to now, been produced from 'standard' varieties – Müller-Thurgau, Reichensteiner and Seyval blanc – and whilst this does not always find favour with wine-writers and purists, who consider that the UK ought to concentrate on making wine from the 'classic' varieties, the results to date have in general been promising, although of course there is always room for improvement. However, the rise in the planted areas of the classic sparkling wine varieties – Chardonnay, Pinot Meunier and Pinot noir – although small in terms of their share of the total planted area (+9.8%), represents a significant shift towards this type of wine. Whether in the long term these are the correct varieties to grow is open to debate for they must be considered as marginal for many sites, average yields are bound to be lower*

---

3   Undoubtedly a fair percentage of the Pinot noir planted is actually for the production of red and rosé wine, but since there is no distinction made by the WSB or even usually by the growers themselves, I have, for the purposes of this chapter, referred to all of the Pinot noir planted in the UK as a 'Champagne' variety.

4   This section was written in 2007. See later for 2009 update.

and therefore the cost of grapes higher. Take the higher cost of grapes, add on the additional costs of making, storing and financing bottle-fermented sparkling wines, and the result is a product that needs a premium in the marketplace in order for it to survive. The market in non-Champagne sparkling wines – Cava, Sekt, Cremant and a myriad of wines from other countries and regions – is a tough one and if UK produced sparkling wines are going to survive, they will have to fight hard. Having additional burdens in the shape of low yields and expensive grapes may, in the long term, prove too much. To date, the quality of wines being produced by the specialist 'classic' variety producers – most notably Nyetimber Vineyard and RidgeView Estate – has been good, if not excellent, and one can only hope that they can find (or carve out) a niche for their premium products. They deserve to succeed, not only on a personal level, but also for the good of the whole UK wine industry.

Since writing those words in 2001, much seems to have changed. The market for UK-grown sparkling wines appears to be holding up, prices keep rising, £20+ a bottle is being achieved for the better wines and the weather continues to surprise us (and after 2007 is has to be said, not always pleasantly). The real challenge will come when the *tsunami* of sparkling wine, that the large plantings of Champagne varieties must one day unleash onto the market, has to be sold. Perhaps by then, the current banking crisis will have blown itself out, the Labour party will have been replaced and Boris will have made London a great place to live – and drink English and Welsh sparkling wine – in! Who can tell? May be it will all get drunk during the 2012 Olympics?

Red vine varieties 1990-2007

As can be seen in Table 7.6, in 1990, red wine varieties totalled 70.1-hectares (excluding those too minor to be separately recorded), which was just over 7.5 per cent of the total UK area. By 1999 the area had risen to 104.1-hectares, 11.9 per cent of the total, and by 2007, the total, including Pinot noir and Pinot Meunier, had reached 249.3-hectares or just over 25 per cent of the total, a surprising amount.

If you exclude the Champagne varietals, the total area of purely red wine varieties has more than trebled since 1990 from 32.6-hectares to 100.5-hectares. The winners since 1990 have been newcomer Regent which has come from nowhere and is now the fourth most widely planted red wine variety; Rondo up almost twenty times to take top slot; Dornfelder has trebled; and Pinot noir Précoce (or Blauer Frühburgunder if you prefer its German synonym) came from nowhere and now totals 8.2-hectares.[5]

---

5   The rise of Pinot noir Précoce (or Blauer Frühburgunder) from nowhere is the result of a bit of varietal tidying up on the part of the WSB. Growers who planted it, believing it to be an early clone of Pinot noir, were told that in fact it is a separate self-standing variety (and has been since the early 1800s), and although a close relation of Pinot noir, must be labelled as Pinot noir Précoce or Blauer Frühburgunder.

Dunkelfelder, Léon Millot and Triomphe more or less remained static and Zweigeltrebe (thankfully) retreated. The minor varieties Blauburger, Cascade, Domina, Red Elbling, Gamay noir, Maréchal Foch, Marienfeldt, Portugieser, Senator and Heroldrebe disappeared altogether (or have become too thinly planted to be separately recorded.)

Table 7.6   Hectares of red vine varieties in the UK (WSB Vineyard Register)

Variety	1990	1999	2007
Dornfelder	5.4	11.2	16.2
Dunkelfelder	3.5	2.5	2.8
Léon Millot	2.0	3.6	2.9
Pinot Meunier	5.5	8.0	27.4
Pinot noir	32.0	44.0	121.4
Pinot noir Précoce			8.2
Regent		2.2	14.8
Rondo	2.0	9.5	38.7
Triomphe	7.5	15.0	15.1
Zweigeltrebe	3.9	2.6	1.8
Miscellaneous Reds	8.3	5.5	0.0
Total Red Varieties	**70.1**	**104.1**	**249.3**

What of the future for reds? Well I see no stopping Pinot noir taking over as the major red wine variety in the UK and if the summers continue to improve, then so should the wines. The inbuilt marketing advantage of the name on the label, plus the instantly recognisable style, help sales enormously.

The promise held out by Rondo in its early days has, I am afraid to say, not been realised. I am sad about this, if only because the variety was a direct link back to my old Professor at Geisenheim, the much loved and missed Helmut Becker who, in 1983, gave 50 vines each to Ken Barlow at Adgestone, Karl-Heinz Johner at Lamberhurst and me, to see how they would do. That it is now planted on almost 39-hectares – almost 100-acres in old money – surprises me, but one must assume the WSB's vine-hounds are correct. The variety does have a lot of things in its favour: early ripening, good yields, great colour and low(ish) acids. The only problem was that however much work you did on the wine, however much oak you threw at it, the taste was just not quite right. If you didn't know what you were drinking, good examples could be passed off as Syrah or perhaps Tempranillo from somewhere coolish, but in general wines from Rondo always have a slight *fremdtone*. In blends with other varieties – Regent and Dornfelder – the variety can be OK, but probably best turned into a deep pink rosé with a touch of residual sugar and a light *pétillance.*

Dornfelder, the second most widely planted purely red wine variety, has its moments. Colours are good, acids manageable and in good years, it crops well. Against Pinot noir though, there is no contest. Regent, one of the new interspecific-crosses for which I fought so hard to gain *Vinifera* status, I fear might turn out to be another Rondo, although I have tasted some decent blends based upon it. It's not as disease-resistant as we hoped, but then none of the new hybrids are (at least not when compared to Seyval blanc.) Of the others, I am surprised that Léon Millot and Triomphe have held on – I feel sure they will disappear as the owners of the vineyards they are in retire – and I am not surprised by the reduction in area and/or disappearance of the others.

On the list of permitted varieties, there are another four red wine varieties: Cabernet Sauvignon and Merlot, which are only on the list to get Mark Sharman at Beenleigh Manor out of trouble with the labelling of his (usually very good) plastic tunnel-grown red wine; Elbling, a variety once grown by Denbies but now no longer; and Acolon, a 1971 Limberger x Dornfelder variety from Weinsberg. It doesn't appear on the WSB's current lists, so one must assume that it is either only grown on one site or only in very small amounts (or possibly both). In any event, I doubt that it will take over from the varieties we already have, even though several German growers I know think it better than Dornfelder.[6]

Red vine varieties - 2009 update

As Pinot noir and Pinot Meunier become more and more planted for sparkling wine production, it becomes increasingly difficult to separate what is grown for sparkling wine and what is grown for rosé and red wines. Apart from the additional 118-hectares of Pinot noir and Meunier that were planted between 2007 and 2009, an additional 28-hectares of other reds were also planted. Pinot noir Précoce up 9-hectares, Acolon, Regent and Rondo up 4-hectares each, Dornfelder up 2-hectares and Gamay and Merlot up just over 1-hectare each. Some other minor reds also showed small increases of less than 1-hectare each.

Current situation (written in 2007)

In the 2001 edition I wrote:

> *Over the next few years, it would be surprising if the overall planted area did not fall slightly as growers take stock of the condition of their vineyards and the market for their grapes and wines. Once the trelliswork holding up the vines requires substantial repairs or even complete replacement (which depending on the quality of the wooden stakes used will be between the 10th*

---

6   Acolon has now appeared on the WSB's 2009 list with 4.59-hectares.

and 20th years) growers, who are perhaps experiencing low returns through a combination of poorly yielding varieties (Müller-Thurgau in particular) and low grape prices, or are having problems selling wine into what is a very competitive market, will take the decision to grub up their vines. Those growers who have been able to attend to the upkeep of their vineyards, who have managed to create a market for their wines and who have perhaps developed a niche for their 'speciality' wines – oak-aged, red, dessert and sparkling wines – will continue to expand and plant more vines as they see fit.

While not claiming to be a fortune-teller, what I surmised above was more or less right. The planted area fell for the next five years and quite large areas of the old varieties disappeared. What I did perhaps underestimate was a) the changing weather patterns, in particular the very warm summer in 2003 which I blame for much of the increased interest in plantings and b) the strength of the Nyetimber effect (and maybe I am being unkind if I don't rename this the Nyetimber/RidgeView effect) which post-2003 provided some of the impetus for the mass plantings of Champagne varieties that has taken place since then.

With the planting boom showing no sign of stopping, it would be a brave person who can predict the future. As I have said already in another chapter in this book, there are two things which will bring this to an end, or at least slow it down: the weather and the market for UK-grown sparkling wines. Another summer like those of 2007 and 2008, and some of us might start to wonder whether global warming is all its cracked up to be – this one really is in the lap of the gods. As for the market in sparkling wine, the event I am looking forward to is the advent of wine from Nyetimber's new vineyards. With most of these having been planted in 2004–2006, it will be a couple of years yet before they reach their full potential, but when they do, they will have significantly more wine to place on the market than currently. Where, and at what price it will sell, remains to be seen. RidgeView will also have significantly more wine to sell at some stage, but their major plantings are a year or two behind Nyetimber's.

Vine varieties for the future

In 2001 I wrote quite enthusiastically about varieties that we might be planting in the future and said that: *to pretend that no change will take place in UK's vine varieties in the future would be to ignore the experience of the past.* I wrote encouragingly about the new interspecific-crosses being turned out by German colleges and vine-breeding institutions and even some that the Eger Vine Breeding Station in Hungary had produced. I waxed lyrical (at the bequest of Julian Jeffs, Iberian expert and then my editor at publishers Faber and Faber) about Albarino, Loureira Blanco and even Ondarribi Zuri (or Hondarribi Zuri if you must) which is one of the constituent varieties in a favourite wine of mine: Txakoli. I surmised that were Orion, Phoenix,

Regent and Rondo to be granted *Vinifera* status, they would be more widely planted, which turned out to be the case, up from a total of 20.1 to 79.5-hectares. I did muse on the fact that there were some 80 clones of Chardonnay and 65 clones of Pinot noir to choose from (since having researched this subject, I now know that there are at least ten times this number) and that growers ought to be taking a bit more notice of what they planted (they did) and finished by pondering on the possibility of 'transgenic vines' making an appearance. That last likelihood still seems a long way off.

What in fact I now think will happen is that unless something drastic occurs to seriously dent the sparkling bandwagon, vineyards will be one of two types: serious Champagne-variety growers and sparkling wine producers, who as they gain experience with their sites, their soils and their clones, will become ever more proficient at turning out a great product; and the smaller mixed-variety vineyards, producing a wide range of wines, red, white and rosé, still and sparkling, selling much of their output from the gate or into local markets – local supermarkets included. I see Pinot noir and Chardonnay as gaining ground and eventually (by 2015?) taking up 75 per cent of the UK's planted area. In white varieties, I think that Bacchus, Reichensteiner and even good old Seyval blanc will hold their own, being turned into good wines and finding friends; and Müller-Thurgau, Madeleine x Angevine 7672, Schönburger, Ortega, Huxelrebe and Siegerrebe will all continue to slide, eventually becoming quite minor varieties. Red varieties I have covered above and the future can be summed up in two words: Pinot noir.

Vine varieties update 2009

Since 2007, the following varieties have increased by a total of 286.97-hectares:

Pinot noir	96.53 ha	Solaris	4.74 ha
Chardonnay	82.06 ha	Acolon	4.59 ha
Pinot Meunier	21.27 ha	Regent	4.47 ha
Bacchus	14.35 ha	Rondo	4.18 ha
Pinot noir Précoce	9.12 ha	Phoenix	3.91 ha
Auxerrois	9.05 ha	Siegerrebe	2.83 ha
Pinot blanc	8.09 ha	Dornfelder	2.07 ha
Pinot gris	5.07 ha	Misc. varieties	14.64 ha

Since 2007, the following varieties have decreased by a total of 63.69-hectares:

Müller-Thurgau	9.65 ha	Seyval blanc	2.31 ha
Reichensteiner	9.13 ha	Madeleine Ang.	1.84 ha
Huxelrebe	7.15 ha	Kerner	1.42 ha
Schönburger	4.82 ha	Misc. varieties	27.40 ha

Table 7.7   *Variety situation August 2009, Wine Standards Branch*

	Variety	2009		Variety	2009
1	Pinot noir	217.97	21	Pinot gris (Ruländer)	10.59
2	Chardonnay	201.69	22	Auxerrois	9.05
3	Bacchus	118.75	23	Kerner	6.56
4	Seyval blanc	88.86	24	Kernling	5.02
5	Reichensteiner	84.43	25	Solaris	4.74
6	Müller-Thurgau	61.53	26	Acolon	4.59
7	Pinot Meunier	48.70	27	Würzer	4.55
8	Madeleine x Angevine 7672	46.80	28	Regner	4.37
9	Rondo	43.00	29	Faberrebe	3.62
10	Schönburger	42.17	30	Dunkelfelder	3.32
11	Ortega	27.77	31	Léon Millot	2.74
12	Pinot blanc	21.04	32	Gutenborner	2.13
13	Phoenix	20.24	33	Optima	1.99
14	Regent	19.30	34	Scheurebe	1.91
15	Dornfelder	18.22	35	Zweigeltrebe	1.34
16	Huxelrebe	17.85	36	Madeleine Sylvaner	1.32
17	Pinot noir Précoce	17.31	37	Gamay	1.23
18	Triomphe	14.77	38	Merlot	1.13
19	Siegerrebe	12.79	39	Miscellaneous varieties	6.84
20	Orion	10.80		Total ha	1215.15

The increases over the years 2007-9 are fairly predictable to anyone who has been paying attention. The rise of the Champagne varieties and quasi-Champagne varieties – Auxerrois and Pinot blanc – continues in a seemingly unstoppable way, with Bacchus also increasing on the back of the wine's popularity. Pinot gris also puts in a surprising increase. The planting of additional vineyards in the more extreme regions of the UK (well I think they're extreme) and the rise in the number of organic vineyards has resulted in more plantings of the newer interspecific varieties: Solaris, Regent, Rondo, Phoenix, and the new *vinifera* variety Acolon. The increase in Siegerrebe is no doubt on the back of Three Choirs' success in the EWOTYC. The decreases – 64-hectares – again, show nothing surprising, although the total decrease is fairly small, only 6 per cent of the 2007 total. The old Germanic varieties are the main casualties, with Seyval blanc also showing a small decline.

Of course, these are only the official figures and, as ever, they lag (perhaps this time even further) behind reality. Having got hold of the Vineyard Register, I now know that this is not only out-of-date, but also inaccurate and has failed to keep up with vineyards that have been grubbed and also of both increased plantings on existing vineyards and also completely new ones. Still, I appreciate that the keeping of the Vineyard Register is not the only thing the WSB has to do.

My database has an additional 265-hectares of vines to add on to the Vineyard Register's total of 1,044-hectares, making 1,309-hectares and whilst this is nearer the 1,215-hectares given in the WSB's varietal information (why these two don't tally is beyond me) it is still around one hundred hectares short. Add on to this the vineyards that neither I nor the WSB know about – and there surely must be a few – and the total planted UK vine area, as of the end of 2009, is probably nearer 1,350 to 1,400-hectares

The Vine Varieties Classification Committee

When the 1986 voluntary MAFF survey showed that the area under vines in the UK had risen to 488 hectares, two things became self-evident: the voluntary nature of the survey meant that the area was almost certainly under-reported and therefore probably over 500 hectares and in addition, there was a far wider range of varieties being grown than those allowed under the regulations. These fears were confirmed two years later when the next survey revealed that the area under vines had risen to 546 hectares. Action had to be taken.

Under the Community regulations then in force, each Member State with 500 hectares of vines or more not only had to have an official Vineyard Register but it also had to have a committee whose task was to monitor and manage the lists of vine varieties being grown and make proposals to the Commission for changes. Therefore, at the next English and Welsh Wine Liaison Committee meeting, it was agreed that a Vine Varieties Classification Committee (VVCC) would be established whose task it would be to look at the existing lists of varieties permitted to be grown in the UK and suggest changes. This committee was made up of industry representatives from around the country, together with representatives from the National Farmer's Union (NFU), ADAS, the WSB and the Welsh Office Agricultural Department (WOAD). I was on the committee as the south-east representative.

At its first meeting, held on 3 July 1989, the VVCC came up with a proposal to reorganise the lists of varieties and in July 1990 the Recommended list for the UK was officially changed so that it consisted of the six most widely grown and successful varieties, which were, in alphabetical order: Huxelrebe, Madeleine x Angevine 7672, Müller-Thurgau, Reichensteiner, Schönburger and Seyval blanc. Auxerrois and Wrotham Pinot were dropped to Authorised. Likewise, the list of Authorised varieties was substantially altered to reflect the then current plantings. It also proposed that four varieties, Kanzler, Madeleine Royale, Mariensteiner and Perle, which were being grown in minute quantities and for which there was no grower support, be downgraded to Temporarily Authorised. This allowed them a further 25 years of use, but no new vines of these varieties could be planted. The revised list contained the following varieties:

Recommended   (* Denotes interspecific-cross or hybrid vine)
Huxelrebe
Reichensteiner
Madeleine x Angevine 7672
Müller-Thurgau
Schönburger
Seyval blanc *

Authorised
Auxerrois
Bacchus
Chardonnay
Ehrenfelser
Faberrebe
Kerner
Madeleine x Sylvaner III 28/51
Ortega

The 1987 survey had also shown that 13 'illegal' varieties were being grown in enough volume for them to be noticed by the Commission and therefore had to be legalised. The varieties were:

Dunkelfelder	2 ha	Sauvignon blanc	1 ha
Gamay noir	2 ha	Scheurebe	6 ha
Gewürztraminer	1 ha	Seibel 13/053 (Cascade)	4 ha
Gutenborner	4 ha	Triomphe	2 ha
Optima	3 ha	Würzer	7 ha
Léon Millot	1 ha	Zweigeltrebe	3 ha
Regner	6 ha		

Apart from Gamay noir, Gewürztraminer and Sauvignon blanc, which most growers accepted were very marginal for UK conditions, the VVCC proposed that over the course of the next three years, the ten remaining varieties be proposed for the Provisionally Authorised category. This happened and they were incorporated into the permitted lists.

The work of the VVCC was ongoing, with Bacchus being upgraded from Authorised to Recommended and others from Provisionally Authorised to Authorised. Newer varieties, which had been on unofficial trial in UK vineyards, were proposed for introduction into the lists as Provisionally Authorised and data sheets showing full details about the variety in question were prepared and submitted to the Commission. The main reason for reorganising these lists was not, rather surprisingly, to give growers guidance about which varieties were suitable for growing in the UK, but to legalise those varieties growers had already chosen to grow so that the variety names could appear on wine labels.

Following changes in EU legislation, the concept of Recommended and Authorised varieties disappeared and the permitted varieties were grouped into four categories. Category 1 were 'Varieties suitable for a wide section of appropriate sites'; Category 2 were 'Varieties that are more site demanding or suitable for specific uses'; Category 3 were 'Varieties than can no longer be recommended for general use'; and Category 4 were 'Experimental varieties'. Categories 1–3 could be used to make wine for sale, subject to the four old hybrids, Cascade (Seibel 13/053), Léon Millot, Seyval blanc and Triomphe, being excluded from Quality Wine production and Category 4 could only (in theory) be used for wine production with specific permission. These category lists were intended to give growers information they might find helpful when it came to deciding which varieties to plant – something which the previous lists had never tried to do. As is the way of these things, no sooner had the Category 1–4 lists been adopted, than further changes to EU wine legislation were made and it was felt that as far as UK law was concerned, *no* distinction should be made between the varieties and with the exception of 11 very minor varieties,[1] all the others were lumped into one general list.[2]

Table 7.8   Permitted vine varieties for UK wine production in 2008

Acolon	Merlot
Auxerrois	Müller-Thurgau (Rivaner)
Bacchus	Optima
Cabernet Sauvignon	Orion
Cascade (Seibel 13/053) *	Ortega
Chardonnay	Perle of Alzey (Perle)
Chasselas (Gutedal)	Phoenix
Dornfelder	Pinot blanc
Dunkelfelder	Pinot Meunier (Wrotham Pinot)
Ehrenfelser	Pinot noir
Elbling (red)	Pinot noir Précoce
Elbling (white)	Regent
Faberrebe	Regner
Findling	Reichensteiner
Gutenborner	Riesling
Huxelrebe	Rondo (Gm 6494/5)

---

1   Albalonga, Az 15477, Blauburger, Blauer Portugieser, Cabernet Franc, Gamay noir, Garanoir, Gewürztraminer, Jubilaumsrebe, Maréchal Foch and Nobling.

2   Page 28 of the current 'WSB Guide to EU Wine Regulations' still refers to vine varieties being in 'Categories 1–4' but I am assured by the WSB that this is a technical oversight.

Kerner	Ruländer (Pinot gris)
Kernling	Scheurebe
Kanzler	Schönburger
Léon Millot *	Seyval blanc *
Madeleine x Angevine 7672	Siegerrebe
Madeleine Royale	Triomphe *
Madeleine Sylvaner III 28/51	Würzer
Mariensteiner	Zweigeltrebe

* Denotes interspecific-cross or hybrid vine
Permitted synonyms are in brackets.

In 2008, any variety on Table 7.7 could be used for the production of UK Table Wine and Regional Wine, and with the exception of the four interspecific-crosses – Cascade, Seyval blanc, Léon Millot and Triomphe – they may all be used for Quality Wine. Any variety may be used for any category of sparkling wine.

Vine variety situation in 2009

In October 2008, the UK government issued a new SI (Statutory Instrument) which abolished the requirement for a National Vine List and, with the exception of six old American varieties, Noah, Othello, Isabella, Jacquez, Clinton and Herbemont (originally banned in France in 1934), any variety could be used for making wine. The rule about Quality Wines (or PDO wines as they will become known) only being made from *vinifera* varieties (plus the new interspecific crosses granted *vinifera* status) still remains in force. This varietal freedom will hold good all the while the UK is below a 50,000-hectolitre annual production level, the average to be calculated over five consecutive vintages. This level was raised from 25,000-hectolitre and should keep us clear of any problems for a very long while.

Availability of accurate yield and performance data

Despite the advent of the Quality and Regional Wine Schemes, despite the WSB's collection of Production Returns from every grower, every year and despite the interest that DEFRA takes in UK winegrowing, the one thing that is sadly lacking is a reliable yield recording system for individual varieties, as can be found in every other winegrowing country with pretensions to professionalism. True the WSB collects an overall yield figure which is released around six months after the harvest, but since this includes both immature and mature vineyards, as well as vineyards that have more-or-less been abandoned (some growers make production returns even with virtually no crop, just so that they can keep their vineyards 'alive' in the event of a planting ban), its worth is negligible.

Until 1993, the EVA collected valuable yield figures which were submitted when growers entered their wines for the 'EVA Seal of Quality'. While these figures only related to those growers and those actual wines entered, it did give a valuable guide to the yields being achieved in better managed vineyards. Despite the inbuilt inaccuracies of the system, the most problematic being that of returning yield data from immature or very badly performing vineyards, the results do show a consistency in line with the expectations of vineyard owners. The following figures were collected over the ten-year period 1983–1992.

Table 7.9   Yield data collected for the EVA Seal of Quality 1983–1992

Variety	Hl per ha	Tonnes per acre
Müller-Thurgau	36.6	2.1
Reichensteiner	40.6	2.3
Seyval blanc	51.8	3.0
Bacchus	31.3	1.8
Schönburger	32.7	1.9
Madeleine x Angevine 7672	35.9	2.1
Huxelrebe	32.8	1.9

As can be seen from Table 7.9, most varieties averaged around the 35 hl/ha (2 tonne/acre) mark, apart from Reichensteiner, a touch ahead at 40.6 hl/ha and Seyval blanc which can claim another 50 per cent, bringing it up to nearer 52 hl/ha or 3 tonnes/acre. In reality, given a mature vineyard and good management (especially pest and disease control) capable growers would expect to better these figures – on all varieties – by a further 30–50 per cent. Indeed, the economics of growing grapes and making wine in the UK would suggest that for most standard wines i.e. not sparkling, red, oak-aged, late-harvest or other speciality wines, 52 hl/ha or 3 tonnes/acre would be considered the bare minimum for the long term viability of the enterprise.

Since the demise of the 'Seal', no accurate yield data that reflects what is happening across a range of vineyards has been collected and collated. That it was not a requirement of the QWS and RWS for actual harvest data – yields, natural alcohol and acidity levels – to be submitted with applications and, after collating, made available to the industry, was a great pity. That it is also not a requirement for this type of data to be submitted by every grower along with the mandatory 15 December Production Declaration is also a loss to the industry. Without accurate figures of at least yields (but hopefully other data as well) it becomes very difficult to assess which varieties and clones are performing well. No doubt the already stretched WSB would have other views about the collection and collation of even more data.

The actual yield from a vineyard will depend on many factors and it is almost impossible to be dogmatic about the causes of high or low crops. Yields in vineyards, especially under UK growing conditions, can vary widely and inconsistency of harvests is one of the problems that have to be faced. The annual yield figures that are collected by the Wine Standards Board demonstrate this dramatically.

Table 7.10   Vineyard area and yield data, 1989–2008 (WSB Vineyard Register) [3]

Year	Total ha	Ha. In production	Ha. Not in prod.	% of total not in prod	Total Yield in Hl.	Yield per ha.	No. of Vineyards	No. of Wineries
1989	876	652	224	25.57%	21,447	32.89	442	147
1990	929	629	300	32.29%	14,442	22.96	445	147
1991	992	650	342	34.48%	15,429	23.74	454	150
1992	1054	701	353	33.49%	26,428	37.70	457	157
1993	1065	767	298	27.98%	17,504	22.82	479	148
1994	1035	733	302	29.18%	17,693	24.14	435	123
1995	984	745	239	24.29%	12,651	16.98	413	115
1996	965	775	190	19.69%	26,080	33.65	408	123
1997	949	791	158	16.65%	6,460	8.17	386	114
1998	901	842	59	6.55%	11,202	13.30	382	108
1999	872	835	37	4.29%	13,272	15.90	373	106
2000	857	822	35	4.08%	14,215	17.29	363	106
2001	836	801	35	4.15%	15,817	19.75	350	105
2002	812	789	23	2.83%	9,385	11.89	333	114
2003	773	756	18	2.26%	14,503	19.20	333	109
2004	761	722	39	5.12%	19,071	26.41	339	106
2005	793	722	71	8.95%	12,806	17.74	353	90
2006	923	747	176	19.07%	25,267	33.82	362	102
2007	992	697	295	29.74%	9,948	14.27	383	98
2008	1,106	785	321	29.04%	10,087	12.85	416	116

An inspection of Table 7.10 shows just how variable yields can be in the UK. The long-term average across twenty years is a lamentable 19.53 hl/ha, a barely over one tonne per acre. No vineyard in the UK can make economic sense at those yields. The lowest yielding year (8.17 hl/ha or under half a tonne per acre) in 1997, was one where a sharp, late frost (down to −6° on 6 and 7 May) caused many vineyards to harvest very little, even though yields in unaffected vineyards were actually quite good. The next lowest year, 2002, was down to a damp summer when mildew caused many growers to lose their crops (much the same as happened in the low yielding years, 1998, 2007 and 2008).

The four years in which average crops exceeded 30 hl/ha – 1989 (32.89 hl/ha), 1992 (37.70 hl/ha), 1996 (33.65 hl/ha) and 2006 (33.82 hl/ha) were all years which were preceded by years when early summer growing conditions had been good for

---

3 Given all the additional vineyards that have been planted since 2003, I suspect that the 2007 figure for 'Hectares in production' of 697 ha is something of a statistical 'blip' and even the WSB cannot explain it. I cannot believe that the cropping area has fallen by 50 ha in one year and it wouldn't surprise me to see the 2008 figure for cropping vineyards nearer – or even over – 800 ha.

fruit bud initiation and show how close to the margin of success UK growers are. The average over these four years of 34.52 hl/ha actually compares quite favourably with the long-term average yields of Spain and Portugal, both 30 hl/ha, not so favourably when compared to Italy, 68 hl/ha, France, 66 hl/ha, New Zealand, 56 hl/ha and the USA, 50 hl/ha, and look downright sick compared to those of Germany, 117 hl/ha, South Africa, 85 hl/ha and Australia, 83 hl/ha. 2009 looks like being another big year – possibly with the increase in productive hectares – the biggest ever and I would not be surprised to see the total near to 30,000-hl.

Table Wines and Quality Wines

As can be seen in Table 7.11, the amount of Quality Wine produced in the UK has varied between 12 per cent in 2002 and almost 66 per cent in 2004. For the past few years it has been around 40 per cent. Apart from Germany, where usually only 1–2 per cent of their wines are Table Wines, the UK's figures don't look too bad when compared to other EU wine producing countries and if you take Regional Wines into account (which are in practice Quality Wines for hybrids and for smaller growers who do not want the expense of a QWS application), the figures look even more encouraging. It's a pity that the WSB doesn't collect and distribute the RW figures.

Table 7.11   Volumes of UK Table and Quality Wines 1997–2008 (WSB-DEFRA)

Year	Table Wines		Quality Wines		All Wines		Total Yield in Hl.	% of Quality Wine
	White	Red	White	Red	White	Red		
1997	3,523	444	2,392	101	5,915	545	6,460	38.6%
1998	6,712	772	3,448	270	10,160	1,042	11,202	33.2%
1999	10,003	1,025	2,048	195	12,051	1,221	13,272	16.9%
2000	10,799	1,409	1,950	57	12,749	1,466	14,215	14.1%
2001	12,180	1,414	2,063	160	14,243	1,574	15,817	14.1%
2002	7,035	1,219	999	131	8,035	1,350	9,385	12.0%
2003	6,315	1,437	5,350	1,401	11,665	2,838	14,503	46.5%
2004	5,559	958	10,581	1,973	16,140	2,931	19,071	65.8%
2005	6,269	1,324	4,158	1,055	10,427	2,379	12,806	40.7%
2006	12,437	2,928	7,747	2,155	20,184	5,083	25,267	39.2%
2007	4,754	824	2,997	1,373	7,751	2,197	9,948	43.9%
2008	4,499	1,145	3,334	1,109	7,833	2,254	10,087	44.0%

Natural sugar and acidity levels

Most growers in the UK record natural sugar levels using the German system of degrees Oechsle (°OE), mainly because winemakers in the early days were very often guided and helped by both German trained winemakers and by German textbooks. In addition, most of the varieties grown in the early decades had their origins in that country. In addition, the WSB issues conversion tables for winemakers to convert °OE into a figure of potential alcohol in order to calculate amounts of sugar required for enrichment. While this may be confusing to growers and winemakers used to using Brix, Baumé, Ballung, Klosterneuberg or any other system, it is the one which all UK vineyards and winemakers accept. Acidity levels are always recorded in grams per litre of total acidity expressed as tartaric acid which – apart from France and French influenced winemaking regions – is the universal way of recording acid levels.

Having said above that yield figures can be difficult to obtain and when obtained, open to interpretation, the same has to be said about natural sugar and acid levels. Again, as with the yield figures, the industry would have benefited greatly had these figures been requested as part of the annual return required to be completed by all growers. In the 2001 edition of this book I attempted to give what I considered to be average figures for both natural sugar and acidity levels for each of the major varieties, but in this edition, with one or two exceptions, I have not. Why? – in general because accurate data across a spread of varieties and sites is unobtainable. While I know figures from vineyards I work with and from winemakers I trust, these are relatively small in number compared to the 380+ vineyards harvesting grapes in the UK.

Many, many factors will influence both sugar and acid levels. The most significant influences on these – apart from the general warmth and length of any particular growing season – will be the general 'quality' of the vineyard in all aspects, as well as the level of yield obtained. Some sites consistently produce grapes with significantly higher natural sugar levels than the average and this can be put down to a variety of factors: the height above sea-level, the angle of the vineyard to the sun, the amount of shelter, the date bud-burst occurs, the quality of the management, the trellising and pruning systems employed, plus several more.

Yields, especially in more marginal areas and vineyards, can also have a very marked effect upon both sugar and acid levels. This of course is not a particular UK phenomenon and is something that all growing regions encounter. However, under our very cool growing conditions there would appear to be a definite cut-off level of yield for any given site, variety and year. Over and above this point, natural sugar levels will be lower and acid levels higher by far more than can be explained by say, a 20 per cent increase in yield. It would appear that the limited amount of heat and light that we have in our vineyards can only be spread so far.

As I have said above, several times and will probably continue to do so, until there are officially collected and therefore verifiably accurate yield figures for all the varieties and clones we are growing and on all sites (or at least on all the major ones), growers are flying blind and have no way of comparing their own efforts with those of the wider winegrowing world. One day, hopefully not too far away, my wish will become reality – maybe.

CHAPTER 8

Vine variety descriptions A–Z

This chapter contains detailed descriptions of the following thirty-three varieties, each of which is grown in the UK on 2-hectares or more for the production of wine:

Acolon	Phoenix
Auxerrois	Pinot blanc
Bacchus	Pinot gris (Ruländer)
Chardonnay	Pinot Meunier
Dornfelder	Pinot noir
Dunkelfelder	Pinot noir Précoce
Faberrebe	Regent
Gutenborner	Regner
Huxelrebe	Reichensteiner
Kerner	Rondo
Kernling	Schönburger
Léon Millot	Seyval blanc
Madeleine x Angevine 7672	Siegerrebe
Müller-Thurgau	Solaris
Optima	Triomphe
Orion	Würzer
Ortega	

The following seventeen varieties, although they are on the WSB's 2009 list of varieties currently being grown in the UK, have not been described in detail as they occupy less than 2-hectares and must, for the moment at least, be considered very 'minor' varieties for UK wine production. However, this is not to say that they may not be valuable varieties (grown in plastic tunnels for instance like Cabernet Sauvignon and Merlot) or may not one day, with better summer temperatures, become part of the UK vine variety scene – Gewürztraminer, Riesling and Sauvignon blanc for example.

Blauburger	Marechal Foch
Cabernet Sauvignon	Merlot
Cascade (Seibel 13/053)	Perle of Alzey
Chasselas	Riesling
Ehrenfesler	Sauvignon blanc

Findling

Scheurebe

Gamay

Senator

Gewürztraminer

Zweigeltrebe

Madeleine Sylvaner III 28/51

Notes on vine variety names

Madeleine x Angevine 7672 (MA)

I have used the name Madeleine x Angevine 7672 and the abbreviation MA throughout this book and on the following pages, even though this name is not strictly correct. Please refer to the entry on this variety for the reasons why.

Sylvaner

I have kept to the old spelling of Sylvaner when referring to both 'Madeleine x Sylvaner III 28/51' and 'Riesling Sylvaner' (Müller-Thurgau or Rivaner) in preference to the modern German spelling 'Silvaner', except where this variety was one of the parents of another variety. The Swiss (and others) continue to use the spelling Sylvaner.

Pinots

The Pinots (blanc, gris, Meunier and noir) I have referred to by their French names in preference to their German names, even though many growers will have imported their vines from Germany.

Müller-Thurgau

When referring to Müller-Thurgau in the individual variety descriptions I have used M-T.

German vine-breeding establishments

References are made in the following variety descriptions of the following vine-breeding establishments, all of them in Germany:

Alzey, Rheinpfalz

Geilweilerhof, Rheinpfalz

Geisenheim, Rheingau

Weinsberg, Würtemburg

Würzburg, Franken

Acolon

Type: *Vinifera*
Colour: Red
Area in the UK: 4.6 hectares, 0.38 per cent of the planted area in 2009
Origin: Limberger x Dornfelder

Acolon is newish German *vinifera* cross bred in 1971 at Weinsberg and its parents – Limberger (known also as Blaufränkisch in Austria) and Dornfelder – are both staples of German red wine production. Dornfelder itself is Helfensteiner (Blauer Frühburgunder x Black Hamburg) and Heroldrebe (Portugieser x Limburger), so its antecedents are impeccable. In Germany, plantings have risen from its release in 2000 to a total of 428-hectares by 2005, but have then risen more slowly to 478-hectares in 2008. In Germany it is planted as a deep coloured variety that adds colour to Dornfelder wines of which there are plenty – there are 8,100-hectares of Dornfelder in Germany – with higher sugars and a slightly lower yield.

In the UK, it has been planted for only a short time, New Hall Vineyards being the first to plant, and even now it is only found in around twelve vineyards, including several in the more northerly regions. As to whether it is a good variety for the UK – who can tell? To date there have been very few single-variety wines made from Acolon. My guess is that it will not take-over from the more mainstream reds and as (if?) the climate continues to improve, Pinot noir, with its heritage, class and consumer acceptability, will continue to be the red variety of choice.

Auxerrois

Synonym: Pinot Auxerrois
Type: *Vinifera*
Colour: White
Area in the UK: 9.05 hectares, 0.75 per cent of the planted area in 2009
Origin: Original variety

Auxerrois, said to be related to Chardonnay, is widely grown in Alsace where it is usually blended into *Edelzwicker* (although it can also be labelled as Chardonnay or Pinot blanc) or used for sparkling wine. It can also be found in Burgundy and Luxembourg in the Old World and Canada, New Zealand and the USA in the New. Geisenheim has produced some more productive clones and in 2006, 167 hectares were being grown in Germany. It was included on the original list of Recommended varieties for the UK submitted to the EU in 1973, even though it was not widely grown and had not been suggested by the EVA.

Auxerrois is a variety of moderate vigour, fairly resistant to *Botrytis* and ripens its wood well. It is quite a late variety, ripening in the UK after M-T but before Seyval blanc. As a neutral Pinot blanc/Chardonnay style variety which would be useful for barrel ageing or for sparkling wine base, it should be more widely planted in the UK – perhaps on the more challenging sites – as it has lower acid levels than other similar varieties. It is a steady yielding variety and it is a pity that it appears to have fallen out of favour in the UK, but I guess that if you can ripen Chardonnay, why would you want to grow Auxerrois? There were 9-hectares in 1990, none recorded in 2007, but it has made a reappearance on the 2009 list! Perhaps it's the same 9-hectares?

Bacchus

Type: *Vinifera*
Colour: White
Area in UK: 118.75 hectares, 9.77 per cent of the planted area in 2009
Origin: (Silvaner x Riesling) x Müller-Thurgau

Bacchus is a crossing made by Peter Morio and Prof. Husfeld at Geilweilerhof, was first registered in 1972 and was known in the Rheinpfalz as the 'Early Scheurebe'. It is the second most popular white *neuzüchtung* (new-crossing) in Germany (after Kerner) and in 2008 there were 2,015-hectares planted. It first appeared in the UK in the Wye College vineyard in 1973 and was upgraded to Recommended in 1998. Bacchus as a variety for the UK is here to stay (unless it warms up another notch or two so that we can start growing *echt* Sauvignon blanc) and the area under cultivation has risen from 76 hectares in 1990 to 118.75-hectares in 2009 and it is the third most widely planted variety.

Bacchus is probably the best white variety being grown in the UK today – at least for the production of still wines – and wines from it regularly win many of the major prizes. In growth habit it is similar to M-T, although perhaps not quite as vigorous, but just as prone to *Botrytis*. It appears to ripen readily in most years with 8–10 per cent natural alcohol achievable. Acids tend to be high and care needs to be taken that they are not too high in the bottle, especially with wine made from grapes harvested at lower sugar levels.

In the bottle Bacchus falls into two camps: what one might term the *Sauvignon de Touraine* or pretend *Sancerre* camp, where the wine is light, fruity, with a modest spiciness, but of no great weight; and the full-on Marlborough Sauvignon style with luscious spicy, even catty, fruit with enough body and weight to carry the flavour. These tend to be the riper (higher natural sugar) examples and are best when they are bottled with perhaps a few grams of residual sweetness (as are many Marlborough wines). Chapel Down's *Bacchus Reserve* is often a fine example of this latter (and to me, more preferable), style. I like Bacchus as a variety, both to grow and to consume. The one *really* good thing about Bacchus is the name – none of your funny Teutonic names complete with umlauts and *–burger* or *–rebe* at the end – just a name everyone recognises and thinks has something to do with wine. Who was that Bacchus guy, some sort of God?

Chardonnay

Type: *Vinifera*
Colour: White
Area in the UK: 201.69 hectares, 16.6 per cent of the planted area in 2009
Origin: Original variety

With its origins lost in the mists of viticultural time, Chardonnay is now found in virtually every grapegrowing region in the world, from the hottest parts of Australia, South Africa and California to the coolest of all growing regions, the UK. With it being the dominant (often the only) variety in white wines from Burgundy, Chablis and Champagne, it is not surprising that early vineyard owners in Britain were seduced into thinking that it would do well here. Brock had it in his collection at Oxted, but could never get it to ripen properly. Salisbury-Jones planted it at Hambledon in the late 1950s and had the same problems: excessively high acid levels and low natural sugars. Ian and Andrew Paget at Chilsdown planted Chardonnay and I seem to recall one year (1981?) when the acidity (in grams per litre) was higher than the degrees Oechsle! Ouch. Extreme unripeness was a common finding among those early growers who persevered with it, although most decided to give up and removed the offending variety. Only in really hot years would it produce anything like ripe grapes and tolerable wine.

In the late 1980s, some growers – New Hall, Surrenden and Nyetimber – started to plant Chardonnay for the production of bottle-fermented sparkling wines using better clones, ones perhaps more suited to our climate. In the 2001 edition of this book I wrote: *through a combination of good site selection and traditional training systems (aided by a degree of global warming) they have started to produce some interesting results. While acids are still high at harvest (15 g/l is not uncommon) the combination of a full malolactic-fermentation and the traditional secondary bottle fermentation, renders them manageable.* Well, the 'interesting results' turned out to be more than interesting and since then some extremely good wines, almost all sparkling, and very occasionally (especially in warm years such as 2003 and 2005) some respectable still wines, have been produced. High acids are still a problem and to my palate Nyetimber's 100 per cent Chardonnay *Première Cuvée Blanc de Blancs* is often a touch too acidic. RidgeView, planted since 1995, appears to get their Chardonnay a touch riper and their 100 per cent Chardonnay *Grosvenor 2001* scored my highest score (19+) in the *Decanter Magazine* March 2008 mega-tasting of English and Welsh sparkling wines, whereas for Nyetimber's *2001 Première Cuvée Blanc de Blancs* I only gave it 15 points. I suspect that the problem is partially clonal – growers will need to be sure that they are planting the right clones on the right rootstocks to get as low acids as they can – and partially site related. Nyetimber appears better at growing the Pinots than Chardonnay, whereas RidgeView has a less exposed, and therefore warmer, site.

As a variety for the UK, Chardonnay appears to be more and more at home. Viticulturally it is no more demanding to grow than most varieties. It buds up quite early and in frost prone sites this could be a problem. It is susceptible to powdery and downy mildew and *Botrytis* and even vines in their planting year need spraying. Until it can be demonstrated otherwise, simple Guyot single or two-cane pruning appears to work well. While we might like to have them, we do not get the very high yields common in Champagne (15–20 tonnes/ha is not uncommon), so I don't think Cordon pruning is required. It benefits from an open canopy and some leaf removal 3–4 weeks prior to picking. It ripens late and is usually not harvested until the third week of October. (Late, of course, is subjective and having rarely enjoyed sharing Guy Fawkes night with my children in the late 1970s and 1980s as I was always pressing Seyval blanc, today's Chardonnay growers shouldn't complain.) Sugar levels are usually in the 8–10 per cent region – ideal for sparkling wine. Acid levels, as already said, can be a problem; 12 g/l is typical with a fair crop and 15 g/l not unheard of in some years. In 2008, a cool, late year when acids were generally very high – and malic acid proportions were higher than typically seen – some Chardonnay was harvested at 15-16 g/l which must be seen as a negative. Growers with higher altitude, more exposed sites have been warned. In 2009, the tables were turned and many vineyards in the southern half of the UK harvested Chardonnay with between 11% and 12% potential alcohol (81-88°OE) and acids in the 10-11 g/l range. These are truly amazing results and 5 years ago, I would never have throught these sugar levels possible.

I have had good experiences with clones 76, 95, 96, 124 and 277, but many others are being tried (the CIVC lists 11 clones). The area under cultivation in the UK has risen from 19.9 hectares in 1990 to 201.69-hectares in 2009, making it the second most widely planted variety (after Pinot noir), although my private estimate is that the total is nearer 250-hectares.

The combination of a classic name, its Champagne heritage and some excellent wines from the leading sparkling wine producers, have made Chardonnay a must-have for any UK vineyard with pretensions to seriousness. I am not convinced that it suits all the sites it has been planted on in the last five years, and some growers may yet struggle to ripen it and/or find that their wines need years (5+) in the bottle to come round – not a recipe that I think will guarantee financial success.

Dornfelder

Type: *Vinifera*
Colour: Red
Area in the UK: 18.22 hectares, 1.50 per cent of the planted area in 2009
Origin: Helfensteiner x Heroldrebe

Dornfelder is one of the new(ish) wave of German crossings, bred at Weinsberg in the heart of Germany's red wine producing region, Würtemburg. Here, the traditional varieties – Trollinger (Black Hamburg) and Limberger – suffer from a lack of colour and substance and Dornfelder was bred to produce more of both. The crossing was made in 1955 by August Herold and released to growers in 1980. Dornfelder's parents are two other Weinsberg varieties: Helfensteiner (which is Blauer Frühburgunder x Black Hamburg) and Heroldrebe (which is Portugieser x Limburger).

Now the most widely grown, and still expanding (up by almost 50 per cent in five years) 'new variety' in Germany, its 8,101-hectares (2008) occupy 22 per cent of their red vine area and just under 8 per cent of their total vine area. It is capable of producing some fine wines, albeit in a spicy Rhône style, rather than a classic Bordeaux style, although some German examples can be fairly light and insubstantial.

Dornfelder first appeared in the UK in the late 1980s and is able to produce some interesting red wines, especially in combination with other varieties. Although plantings have expanded over the last twenty years (5.4 hectares in 1990 and 18.22-hectares in 2009) it is probably due for a slow lingering death as varieties such as Regent do better and of course Pinot noir becomes the market leader. My advice: no need to rip it out, but think twice before planting any more.

Dunkelfelder

Type: *Vinifera*
Colour: Red
Area in the UK: 3.22 hectares, 0.27 per cent of the planted area in 2009
Origin: Crossing of unknown parents

Dunkelfelder is a crossing made by G. A. Froelich in Edenkoben in the Rheinpfalz in the early 1900s and its exact parentage is unknown. It was discovered in the Geisenheim vine collection in the 1930s and clonally selected in the 1970s. It was officially classified for wine production in Germany in 1980 where there are now 352 hectares (2009), although few varietal wines are made from it and it is primarily used as *deckwein* (colouring wine).

Dunkelfelder first appeared in the UK in mid-1980s (I believe I was the first grower to plant it) and in 1990 there were 3.5 hectares. Today it is down to 3.22-hectares which probably sums up its attractiveness to UK growers: small and falling. Viticulturally it is undemanding with fairly low vigour, but does not usually run to large crops. It needs regular spraying and *Botrytis* can be a problem. It ripens very early and is susceptible to bird and wasp attack. It is the best *teinturier* variety grown in the UK and can produce massive colour. On its own, the wine is fairly neutral with low acidity and is best blended with other red varieties. As part of a red blend it is fine, but it is never likely to be anything else. One that red wine growers should have a few rows of to liven up their reds or rosé growers should have to add extra colour.

Faberrebe

Type: *Vinifera*
Colour: White
Area in the UK: 3.62 hectares, 0.3 per cent of the planted area in 2009
Origin: Pinot blanc x Müller-Thurgau

Faberrebe (often incorrectly called Faber) is a crossing made by Georg Scheu at Alzey in 1929. It is valued in Germany for its high sugars and crisp fruity acidity and is used for blending with M-T, although the area under cultivation has fallen quite quickly: 1998 1,657-hectares, 2008 587-hectares.

In the UK it is declining in area (10.3-hectares in 1990, 3.62-hectares 2009) and has probably had its day. Bacchus makes better wines, is easier to grow, far easier to ripen and has a more user-friendly name. My advice: leave it there if you have it, but don't plant any more.

Gutenborner

Type: *Vinifera*
Colour: White
Area in the UK: 2.13 hectares, 0.18 per cent of the planted area in 2009
Origin: Müller-Thurgau x Chasselas Napoleon

Gutenborner is a Geisenheim cross from the 1930s and now not found in Germany except in very small amounts. It was first introduced into the UK in the mid-1970s – David Carr Taylor planted it in 1973 and I planted it, on the advice of Professors Becker and Kiefer, at Tenterden (now Chapel Down) in 1977. With less vigour overall than M-T, smaller leaves and more resistance to disease, this variety is a much easier variety to grow. Wine quality is good, with a pronounced fruity Muscat flavour. Although in 1999 I wrote: *another one for the history books and not likely to be around much in the next century* I hear that Chapel Down are considering planting some more! Of all the varieties that I originally planted at Tenterden – M-T, Gutenborner, Reichensteiner and Seyval blanc – Gutenborner is the sole survivor and certainly it makes great wine. I won a Gold Medal with the 1982 vintage and it was always the wine I would take indoors after a tasting. Perhaps it will make a comeback?

Huxelrebe

Type: *Vinifera*
Colour: White
Area in the UK: 17.85 hectares, 1.47 per cent of the planted area in 2009
Origin: Chasselas x Courtillier Musqué

Huxelrebe is another Georg Scheu crossing (Alzey 1927) and named after Fritz Huxel, a grower from near Worms who first recognised its potential. In Germany (635 hectares in 2008), it is capable of producing very large yields of grapes (or as the Germans say 'trägt wie ein Esel' – 'carries like a donkey'), with high natural sugars.

Huxel – as it is usually called – was first introduced to the UK via the Wye College vineyard in 1972 and on account of its higher yielding ability was quite widely planted. In 1990 there were 43.9-hectares although today (2009), the area planted has fallen and is down to 17.85-hectares.

Huxel can be extremely vigorous, with great fat canes and very large leaves and is probably best grown on a spur system (GDC) where vigour can, to a certain extent, be tamed. Bunches are very large and contain an unusually high number of seedless grapes which ripen readily and achieve very high natural sugars, although loved by wasps. It undoubtedly benefits from thinning and pre-harvest leaf removal as it suffers badly from *Botrytis*.

The wine can be very fruity with a pronounced Sauvignon blanc character, although acid levels can be high and to obtain the best wines, the grapes must be allowed to ripen fully. Unripe examples can be rather too herbaceous and catty and can be detected even when disguised in a blend. It has been used for a few late-harvest sweet wines, but only when *Botrytis* has got the better of it. In 2001 I wrote: *a variety that is probably worth persevering with on account of its good quality wine and higher than average yields. With a new generation of anti-Botrytis fungicides now available, will Huxelrebe become more viable to grow?* Well, nine years on, I can answer the question: no. It is still a pushy monster in the vineyard, overcropping when it feels like it and suffering from wasps and rot in equal measure. Its falling area sums up its attractiveness to UK growers and I cannot see it lasting that much longer and I doubt anyone is planting it now.[1]

---

1   The best UK-grown Huxel I ever tasted was the late Bill Ash's 1982 Staple St James Huxelrebe, one of the very few English wines I have ever bought a case of. The interesting story about this wine is that Bill sold half the grapes to Lamberhurst (he was always strapped for cash) and they made a wine with it, sweetened with some high-strength Auslese Gewürztraminer *süss-reserve* that Karl-Heinz Johner had prised out of the local co-op winery where he lived in Baden. This wine won the 1983 Gore-Browne Trophy, largely on account of the great *süss* used, but fell apart after a while and the Staple wine, with as I recall 12 per cent natural alcohol, aged into a really great wine. The *süss* trick was one I remembered and when I was winemaker at Lamberhurst I used the same Gewürztraminer *süss* in the 1988 Schönburger which won the Gore-Browne in 1990! They say all's fair in love, war and winemaking.

Kerner

Type: *Vinifera*
Colour: White
Area in the UK: 6.56 hectares, 0.54 per cent of the planted area in 2009
Origin: Trollinger x Riesling

Kerner is a crossing made in 1929 by August Herold at Weinsberg. It is popular in Germany where, over Riesling, it has several advantages: it ripens more easily, has a lower acidity and better frost resistance, yet still retains the wine quality of the noblest of its parents, Riesling. It is Germany's sixth most planted white variety (3,712-hectares in 2008, although falling) and, after Dornfelder, the second most popular of the 'new crosses'. It is also popular with growers in the Alto Adige and the wines from there can often be good.

Kerner first appeared in the UK in the Wye College vineyard in the mid-1970s and was widely promoted as a quality variety, although just why I am still not sure. It was always extremely vigorous with great big, dark green, leaves and lots of side-shoots. Acids were always high and the wines, which seldom did well in tastings, were always fairly hard and uncompromising. With time, some of them came round, but who wants to wait for a Kerner to come round? The area has dropped from 21.4-hectares in 1990 to under 7-hectares today – a fair measure of its popularity. Another one for the history books and if I had any I would pull it up.

Kernling

Type: *Vinifera*
Colour: White
Area in the UK: 5.02 hectares, 0.41 per cent of the planted area in 2009
Origin: Mutation from Kerner

Kernling is a mutation from Kerner selected by Ludwig Hochdörfer from the Pfalz, Germany and first registered in 1974. It is said to be similar to Kerner, but without the excessive side-shoots that make Kerner difficult to grow. It was introduced into the UK in the late 1980s as an alternative to Kerner and promoted quite strongly in the West of the UK by certain viticultural consultants in that region. However, despite being planted on quite a large area in 1990 (21.4 hectares) very few wines of note have ever been produced and its high acidity and unsympathetic wine did not find favour with wine drinkers. Today it is down to 5.02-hectares and, I predict, destined for the dustbin.

Léon Millot

Type: Hybrid
Colour: Red
Area in the UK: 2.74 hectares, 0.23 per cent of the planted area in 2009
Origin: *Riparia-Rupestris* x Goldriesling

Léon Millot is an old French-American hybrid bred by Eugene Kuhlmann (1858–1932) in the late 1890s and popular at one time in France. It can still be found in many vineyards in the United States.

Introduced into the UK by Brock at Oxted in the early 1950s, it was one of the first red varieties to be grown commercially. It is, like many red hybrids, very vigorous and canopies can be extremely dense, although it is very resistant to disease and can be grown with minimal spraying. The bunches are small, as are the grapes on them, and yields are never that high. Colour is good – the skin, flesh and juice are all red – and the variety is useful for adding colour to a blend of different red varieties or for a rosé with other white varieties. Its flavour, while not 'foxy', does have a certain non-*vinifera* element which must be counted against it. For the UK, it has probably now been superseded by better red varieties and one would not think of it as a first-choice red variety. Some report that there is a lot of clonal variation and it might be that the good clones will survive and it is difficult to obtain stock except as rooted cuttings. Although the area is slightly up from 2-hectares in 1990 to 2.74-hectares in 2009, I suspect it's another one for the history books.

Madeleine x Angevine 7672

Type: *Vinifera*
Colour: White
Area in the UK: 46.80 hectares, 3.85 per cent of the planted area in 2009
Origin: Freely pollinated seedling of Madeleine Angevine

The variety we loosely call 'Madeleine Angevine' is more properly called Madeleine x Angevine 7672 for reasons which I will explain. In 1957 Brock at Oxted was sent cuttings of several varieties by Dr Zimmerman from Alzey and one of them was labelled 'Sämling [seedling] 7672'. Just when this crossing was made is not known, although the timing would suggest that it was while Georg Scheu – responsible for varieties such as Huxelrebe, Faberrebe, Kanzler, Regner, Scheurebe, Septimer, Siegerrebe and Würzer – was the Alzey Institute's Director.

By 1960 Brock was able to report that it was: *giving large crops which ripen with Riesling Sylvaner* [M-T]. *Considered to be a promising variety.* Not having been given the crossing details of Sämling 7672, Brock wrote to Zimmerman and asked for them. He was informed that it was a 'freely pollinated seedling of Madeleine Angevine'. When Brock started to sell cuttings of the variety (as he did with all promising varieties) he gave it the name Madeleine x Angevine 7672 and it was under this name that it was known for many years. As it became quite popular, the name on wine labels became shortened to simply 'Madeleine Angevine'. This was an unfortunate name as another variety already existed under this name.

The true Madeleine Angevine (also sometimes called Madeleine d'Angevine), is a female only table-grape variety, a crossing of Précoce de Malingre and Madeleine Royale[2] made by Pierre Vibert at the Moreau-Robert nurseries in Angers in 1857 (some reports say 1859). It is one of the earliest table-grape varieties for open cultivation in France. Having only female flowers and being very early, it has been used by plant breeders in a number of crosses over the years. Morio and Husfeld used it for Forta and Noblessa and it is one grandparent of Reichensteiner. Scheu himself used it to produce Siegerrebe and interestingly, this variety, which at one time was credited with being a Madeleine Angevine x Gewürztraminer crossing, was unmasked by Heinz Scheu – Georg's son – as also being a freely pollinated Madeleine Angevine seedling. It is conceivable that the variety we now grow in the UK as Madeleine x Angevine 7672 comes from the same crossing programme that produced Siegerrebe. In 1992, I asked Professor Dr Alleweldt, then head of the Geilweilerhof State Institute for Grapevine Breeding, to see if he could discover more about our Mad Angie (as it is often known). He located Georg Scheu's old breeding books in the Alzey archives and found that 'Sämling 7672' was – as Brock was originally told – an 'open pollinated progeny of Madeleine Angevine'.

Madeleine x Angevine 7672 found favour with many of the early UK growers and it became fairly widespread. At one time it was the third most popular variety (after M-T and Seyval blanc) and Gillian Pearkes, in the West Country, thought highly of it. Unfortunately, owing to the confusion over the name and the fact that this variety was not available from any other source other than Brock's original stock or vineyards planted with vines obtained from Brock, some growers were sold vines of the true table grape variety Madeleine Angevine, which was barely suitable for the UK, except in the very best years. Unless it was being grown in proximity to other early varieties for pollination, it seldom set a good crop and in some years, ripened at the end of August. The wines from this table grape variety were flabby and never really acceptable, except for blending. The confusion over this variety – foreseen in a rare moment of sanity (as far as rules and regulations governing UK viticulture is concerned) by the EU Commission in 1973 when MAFF submitted vine varieties for classification – has meant that it gained something of a chequered reputation.

Today, the area planted is 46.8-hectares and under 4 per cent of the UK's planted area – down from 54.6-hectares in 1990, but not drastically so. Its supporters like it: it ripens early, gives good crops and the wines have a light Muscat tone. It has a low

---

2   Madeleine Royale, a table-grape vine variety developed from a Chasselas seedling, has now been 'outed' by the gene-jockeys as the father of Müller-Thurgau, with Riesling being the mother.

acidity (usually a blessing) and is easy to grow. In 1988 I took wood from genuine Madeleine x Angevine 7672 vines growing in Robin Don's Elmham Park vineyard in Norfolk, which Robin had planted with cuttings supplied by Brock. Buds from this wood were then sent to France and grafted onto resistant rootstock. The resultant grafted vines were sold to various growers around the country. Sharpham Vineyard in Devon is probably the best known and the wines they make from these vines, 'Sharpham Barrel Fermented' and 'Sharpham Estate Selection', sell well and regularly win prizes.

For the long term I doubt whether Mad Angie will survive the Pinot-Chardonnay storm-troopers lining up against her. I suspect that as the growers get older and give up, sell up or go to that vineyard in the sky, the area will dwindle. Pity, as it can make good wine.

Müller-Thurgau

Synonym: Rivaner, Riesling Sylvaner
Type: *Vinifera*
Colour: White
Area in the UK: 61.53 hectares, 5.06 per cent of the planted area in 2009
Origin: Riesling x Madeleine Royale

Professor Dr H. Müller, a Swiss from Thurgau near Zurich, produced this crossing while working at Geisenheim in 1882. Returning to Switzerland in 1891 to become Director of the Wädenswil Research Institute, Prof. Müller asked for 150 of his best crossings to be sent to him at Wädenswil, including No.58, which was eventually to become M-T. Owing to some confusion with the labelling at the time the crossings were delivered, the true parentage of No.58 was never discovered and it eventually became known as 'Riesling Sylvaner' on account of its wine style, said to resemble a blend of Riesling and Sylvaner. Professor Becker, head of Geisenheim in the 1970s and 1980s, attempted to recreate the variety by making multiple Riesling and Sylvaner crossings, but failed. He was, however, of the opinion that it more resembled a Riesling x Riesling crossing than any other.

In 1996 an Austrian, Dr Regner from the viticulture school in Klosterneuburg, proved that the crossing was between Riesling and a member of the Chasselas family, a table-grape vine variety (that he thought) was called *Admirable de Courtiller*. It was then discovered that the reference vine of this variety in Klosterneuburg's collection was in fact another variety altogether – it turned out to be Madeleine Royale (a Chasselas seedling variety). In 2001, two researchers in Germany, Erika Dettweiler and Andreas Jung, were able to unravel the DNA in M-T and prove that it was a crossing between Riesling and Madeleine Royale. After 119 years M-T's parents were finally found.

In 1912, wet-sugaring (the use of sugar in solution to chaptalise wines) was forbidden in Switzerland and M-T started to replace Elbling, up until then a widely grown variety but high in acid. M-T then began to find favour in Germany and in the early 1920s, was taken up by Georg Scheu, then at Alzey in the Rheinland-Pfalz. He subjected it to clonal selection and helped improve its yield. Following the Second World War, when many vineyards were suffering from *Phylloxera* as well as the ravages of the war, M-T was widely planted and its large yields, early ripening and soft wines, lower in acidity than either Riesling or Sylvaner, were much appreciated.

It is today Germany's second most widely planted vine variety (13,721 hectares in 2008, 13.4 per cent of the total vine area) after Riesling and just ahead of Pinot noir and is to be found in all their winegrowing regions, especially Franken, Saale-Unstrut and Sachsen in the east of the country. In Luxembourg – where it is called Rivaner – it is still a popular variety (31 per cent of total area in 2002). Until 1987, it was New Zealand's most widely planted variety and accounted for 42 per cent of their vineyard area although plantings have now almost disappeared and only 116 hectares remain (producing 1,573 tonnes of grapes in 2006). It is popular in high-altitude vineyards in Italy's German-speaking Alto Adige (*Sud Tyrol*) region, where it can make very fine wines. It is also to be found in many Eastern European countries, such as Slovakia and the Czech Republic. EU regulations forbid the use of the name Riesling Sylvaner, although this name can still be found in non-EU countries such as Switzerland.

Its introduction into the UK stems from Ray Barrington Brock's visit to Switzerland in 1946 when he met Mr Leyvraz at the Swiss Federal Vine Testing Station at Caudoz-sur-Pully. In 1947 vines of various varieties were sent by Leyvraz to Brock, including 'Riesling Sylvaner'. Brock gave cuttings to Edward Hyams in 1949 and they both trialled it for a number of years. Brock first harvested grapes from M-T on 14 October 1950. In Hyams' 1953 book *The Grapevine in England* Brock wrote in his chapter on vine varieties that: *Riesling Sylvaner is known to give an outstandingly fine wine in cool climates.*

Jack Ward was recommended it when he looked for vines for the Horam Manor vineyard which he planted in 1954. Ward was a very influential figure in the early days of the revival (the EVA's first Chairman) and undoubtedly did much to persuade growers to plant M-T. Ward's company – the Merrydown Wine Company – sold vines and gave advice and ran a winemaking co-operative between 1969 and 1979 to which many of the early growers belonged. MT was top of my list when I selected varieties for planting in 1976–1977 and it was almost unthinkable to plant a vineyard in the UK then without it. Most German wine and viticulture experts considered England to be a country of mists and not-very-mellow fruitfulness and thought that a high-cropping, early ripening, low acid variety (which is what M-T is in Germany) was just what we needed.

M-T is a vigorous variety, especially in its early years, and it will grow thick canes and large leaves leading to excess shading. This often results in poor cropping, especially in years with low light and heat levels in the previous season. It suffers from *Botrytis*, *Oidium* and downy mildew and requires regular spraying and can benefit from leaf removal to expose fruit. In heavy-yielding years, stem-rot can be a problem. The wood often ripens poorly and does not over-winter well, often showing active *Botrytis* in mild winters. It is probably a variety best avoided by organic growers. Since the advent of better anti-*Botrytis* chemicals such as Scala, Teldor and Switch, disease control has become easier (if more costly) and clean crops of M-T are the norm, rather than the exception they were in the 1970s and 1980s.

M-T grapes can have good fruity flavours with light Muscat hints and at their best, the wines made from them can be very good. However, when less than fully ripe, they tend towards the herbaceous and catty. The acidity is usually average to low and with some balancing residual sugar, the wine can be very attractive and fresh when young and will keep well, although probably best drunk within two to three years after bottling.

In 1990 the area being grown in the UK was 184.5-hectares, making it by far the largest variety (Seyval blanc was second with 122.7-hectares) so it has fallen by almost exactly two-thirds to 61.53-hectares in 2009. I fully expect by the time the next area data is published that it will have fallen by another 10 to 15-hectares and will have effectively disappeared from UK vineyards within ten years. With hindsight, it was a variety that the UK could probably have done without, although one must not forget that the most popular wine at the time it was mainly being planted was the light, fruity *Liebfraumilch* style that M-T is so suitable for. Its extreme vigour, especially in the early years, coupled with its on–off cropping pattern and disease problems make it a difficult variety for UK conditions.

Optima

Type: *Vinifera*
Colour: White
Area in the UK: 1.99 hectares, 0.16 per cent of the planted area in 2009
Origin: (Silvaner x Riesling) x Müller-Thurgau

The crossing for Optima was made by Peter Morio and Prof. Dr B. Husfeld at Geilweilerhof and first registered in 1970. Germany had 184 hectares in 2001, but it has fallen since then and no longer appears in their national wine statistics as a separate variety.

In the UK, Optima can ripen very early, certainly by mid-September and is capable of reaching high natural sugars and therefore suitable for 'late-harvest' style dessert wines. Birds and wasps are always going to be a problem with this type of sweet, early variety and may preclude it being grown widely. It is not very resistant to disease (about the same as M-T) and needs a full spray programme to keep it clean. It will get *Botrytis* easily, which might be an advantage if sweet wines are required. Although it has its fans, (perhaps that ought to be *had* its fans) Optima is unlikely to become very widespread in the UK and the area has more than halved since 1990, down from 4.6-hectares to 1.99-hectares. If an early variety is needed, then Ortega and Siegerrebe are probably better bets.

Orion

Type: *Vinifera* (complex hybrid) [3]
Colour: White
Area in the UK: 10.8 hectares, 0.89 per cent of the planted area in 2009
Origin: Optima x Seyve Villard 12-375

Orion is one of the many crossings made by Prof. Dr Alleweldt at Geilweilerhof and was first registered in 1984. It is a crossing of another Geilweilerhof crossing, Optima, which is [(Silvaner x Riesling) x M-T], and Seyve Villard 12-375 which is known as Villard blanc. Orion is one of the new generation of hybrid varieties (or complex interspecific-crosses to give them a more scientific title) which have been bred for both wine quality and disease resistance. It is not as resistant to fungal attack as some of the older hybrids (Seyval blanc for instance) and usually requires spraying against *Oidium*, but is good against *Botrytis* and ripens its wood well. It also shows better resistance to winter frost damage than M-T (not often a problem in the UK) and its basal buds are said to be very fruitful. Orion was introduced to the UK in the late 1990s and by 1999 there was 8.4-hectares being grown. This area has grown only slowly since then to stand at 10.8-hectares (2009), which makes me think that it is probably not going to be the answer to all our dreams. 100 per cent Orion wines seldom surface, so it is difficult to judge its true worth, but the wine is said to be fruity and aromatic. As they say in the *Good Food Guide* – more reports needed.

Ortega

Type: *Vinifera*
Colour: White
Area in the UK: 27.77 hectares, 2.29 per cent of the planted area in 2009
Origin: Müller-Thurgau x Siegerrebe

Ortega is a crossing made by Dr H. Breider at Würzburg between M-T and

---

3   Orion is one of the four complex interspecific-crosses grown in the UK (Phoenix, Regent and Rondo being the others) that were judged to be as good as *Vinifera* varieties by the German Bundessortenamt (the regulatory body that grants plant breeder's rights and classifys new cultivars) as their non-*Vinifera* traits had been so bred out of them that they resembled *Viniferas* in every respect – apart from their superior natural disease resistance. This judgement was accepted by the EU and German winegrowers could then make Quality Wines from them. After five years of lobbying by the UKVA and of MAFF/DEFRA dragging its heels, they finally agreed that what the Germans had done was legal and these four varieties could then be made into English and Welsh Quality Wine.

Siegerrebe. Siegerrebe is a freely pollinated Madeleine Angevine seedling with Gewürztraminer the most likely culprit as father. Ortega was first registered in 1971 and is named (somewhat curiously) after the Spanish philosopher José Ortega y Gasset, (but good for pub quizzes when 'what's the name of a famous Spanish philosopher' comes up.) In Germany there are 634-hectares (2008) and it is said to be popular on the Mosel. However, it is a declining variety (down from 951 hectares in 2001), so not universally popular. It ripens early, achieves high natural alcohol levels and low acidity levels and with its rich spicy tones, makes a good blending partner for higher acid varieties such as Riesling.

In the UK, Ortega was introduced by Jack Ward who planted it at Horam Manor in 1971 and it has steadily grown in popularity. It ripens early – just after Siegerrebe and Optima – has high sugars, low acids and plenty of flavour. An early bud burst makes it susceptible to spring frost damage and it is sensitive to poor flowering conditions and will suffer from *coulure* in poor years. It can be quite vigorous and canopy management needs to be good to get the best fruit. It will also get *Botrytis* towards the end of ripening which will turn to 'noble rot' if sugar levels are high enough. Given good canopy management and attention to timely spraying, this variety can provide high quality grapes, useful for both normal still wines and dessert wines.

When fully ripe, wines are rich and zesty with good balance, although warm years may result in wines with rather low acidity and care needs to be taken to pick at the correct time. Biddenden Vineyards have won five Gold medals with Ortega wines and won the Gore-Browne Trophy with one in 1987. Surprisingly it takes to new oak well and Chapel Down's barrel-aged Ortega can be very good – Viognier-based *Condrieu* comes to mind. Growers of Ortega seem to like the variety and the small decline in area from 29.5-hectares in 1990 to 27.77-hectares in 2007, must be seen as a positive vote in its favour. It's a variety that I suspect will not be planted much these days, even though the new-generation fungicides make it easier to grow and keep clean.

Phoenix

Type: *Vinifera* (complex hybrid)
Colour: White
Area in the UK: 20.24 hectares, 1.67 per cent of the planted area in 2008
Origin: Bacchus x Seyve Villard 12-375

Phoenix (and not Phönix) is another of the many complex hybrid crossings made by Prof. Dr Alleweldt at Geilweilerhof and was first registered in 1984. Although not as resistant to fungal attack as some of the older hybrids, it ripens its wood very well. It first appeared in the UK in the late 1990s – there were only 1.9-hectares planted in 1999 – and it has slowly risen to cover 20.24-hectares, which, all things considered, is relatively respectable. Although only planted on a few sites in the UK, the wine quality can be good (Three Choirs' is usually the best), with higher sugars and lower acids than M-T and is Bacchus-like, although not as powerful. It is one of the four complex hybrids that can be made into Quality Wine in the UK.

Whether Phoenix really has a place in UK vineyards when Bacchus is now easier to grow given the warmer summers and better fungicides I doubt and I don't expect it to increase in area much in the future.

Pinot blanc

Synonym: Weißer Burgunder
Type: *Vinifera*
Colour: White
Area in the UK: 21.04 hectares, 1.73 per cent of the planted area in 2009
Origin: Original variety

Pinot blanc is one of the most widely distributed of varieties across Europe and is one of the vast family of Pinots. It is often confused (one suspects mostly on purpose) with Chardonnay – the style of wine they produce can be similar – and in general terms it is less demanding than Chardonnay, will ripen more easily and has a higher yield. In Germany in 2008 there are 3,731 hectares, making it the sixth most widely planted white variety and it is to be found in France, Alsace especially, and in many Italian regions in great quantity.

In the UK it is a fairly new introduction (since 1990) and is mainly used for the production of sparkling base-wine and very few 100 per cent varietal wines exist. Chapel Down's version (usually made from grapes grown at New Hall, although they now have their own vines cropping at Tenterden) is one of their best wines and more growers should emulate them. Like Chardonnay, it requires a good site and careful management to ripen it fully and get the acids down. It will find a good home in sparkling wines (Chapel Down use it) and it deserves to be planted a bit more. In 2008 I said 'I cannot really see it expanding much more, given the onward march of Chardonnay' but since it has risen by 8-hectares in two years, someone is planting it and maybe, that as an alternative to Chardonnay for more marginal sites, it will come into its own in the UK?

Pinot gris

Synonym: Ruländer
Type: *Vinifera*
Colour: White
Area in the UK: 10.59 hectares, 0.87 per cent of the planted area in 2009
Origin: Original variety

Pinot gris is another variety from the large Pinot family and it appears to have almost as many clones as there are winegrowing regions that use it. In Alsace, its most respected home (where until recently it was known as Tokay d'Alsace), it is capable of producing exceptionally fine late-harvest dessert wines; in Germany – where it is known as Ruländer – there were 4,481-hectares in 2006 making it the fifth most widely planted white vine variety and it makes an easy-drinking soft wine; in Italy (as Pinot grigio) it makes a very neutral, quite crisp wine, ideal with food. It seems to be able to change its style to suit the region.

In the UK, where it has been grown since the late 1970s, it is an unexceptional variety and although it has a lower acidity than Pinot blanc, really has few other attributes and ahs not produced many wines of interest. In 2008 I said that 'the area planted is fairly static, 6.0-hectares in 1987 and 5.52-hectares in 2006. Not a variety to stir too many hearts, although wines can be acceptable.' In two years though (2007-9), an additional 5-hectares has been planted almost doubling its area in the UK, so someone likes it. Watch this space.

Pinot Meunier

Synonym: Meunier, Schwarzriesling, Müllerrebe – and in the UK only – Wrotham Pinot
Type: *Vinifera*
Colour: Red
Area in the UK: 48.70 hectares, 4.01 per cent of the planted area in 2009
Origin: Original variety

Pinot Meunier is the most widely grown variety in Champagne (40 per cent of their vineyards) and while it is seldom spoken about in the same breath as its nobler companions – Chardonnay and Pinot noir – it is used in some of the finest *cuvées* (Krug for example). It is said to be a hairy-leaved mutation from Pinot noir, although I have seen it surmised that in fact it's the other way round – Meunier came first and all the other Pinots stemmed from it.

In the UK, Meunier has had a somewhat chequered career. In the early 1950s, Edward Hyams discovered a vine growing on a cottage wall at Wrotham which he named Wrotham Pinot which he gave to Brock at Oxted. Brock reported that it had: *a higher natural sugar content and ripened two weeks earlier* than supplies of Meunier obtained from overseas. Brock sold cuttings and it became quite popular with some of the early vineyards.[4] It is doubtful now whether any cuttings from Hyams or Oxted still survive in British vineyards and all plantings of Meunier stem from France or Germany (where it is known as Schwarzriesling or Müllerrebe). However, the name Wrotham Pinot is still a permitted synonym for Meunier in the UK.

Although it has been grown for over 50 years in UK vineyards, Meunier has never really shone as a variety capable of making interesting wines on its own and most of it has been blended with other varieties. However, the rise in the planting of Champagne varieties has meant a resurgence of interest in the variety and my experiences to date, despite my former misgivings about its suitability for our climate, has been

---

4   See Appendix IV for the full Wrotham Pinot story.

favourable. The quality of the Nyetimber *2003 Blanc de Noirs Pinot Meunier* which won a Gold Medal in both the 2006 and 2008 EWOTYC and for me (and for Tom Stevenson) was the best wine in the *Decanter Magazine* March 2008 mega-tasting of UK sparkling wines, has opened my eyes to its possibilities. In 1999 there were only 5.5-hectares being grown in the UK, most of it fairly old and unloved I suspect, but since 2004, plantings have shot up and today (despite the official figure being 48.70-hectares) I suspect that it is nearer 75-hectares. I like clones 817, 865, 900 and 916; there are many others – the CIVC lists 11. In 2001 I wrote:

it needs a good site and year to get it to ripen properly for still wine production and most of the upsurge in planting in recent years is for making sparkling wine base. In this rôle it may be more successful, especially if blended with other, lower acid varieties. It is not suitable for the production of red wines in the UK. The amount of colour in the skins, except in very exceptional years, is not high, it ripens late and there are other better varieties.

I am still of the opinion that it is unsuitable for reds, but as a component of sparkling wines – and even as a 100 per cent varietal from good vintages – it must be worth considering. I still feel that it needs a good, sheltered site and is best not overcropped, but viticulturally it is no more problematic than Pinot noir and in ripe years has better colour. In 2009 it performed exceptionally well and of all the Champagne varieties, had some of the highest sugar levels.

Pinot noir

Synonym: Blauer Spätburgunder
Type: *Vinifera*
Colour: Red
Area in the UK: 217.97 hectares, 17.94 per cent of the planted area in 2009
Origin: Original variety

Pinot noir is one of the most ancient of varieties and probably has more clones and variants than any other variety. It sometimes seems as if every grower and every site spawns its own sub-variety or clone. While its home is often thought of as Burgundy, where undoubtedly many of the finest examples can be found, it seems to thrive in both very warm and very cool climates and good examples can be found in Chile, California, Australia, Spain, South Africa and New Zealand. Norway's only vineyard – yes, Norway – is planted with Pinot noir and the wine can (so one is told) be very good. It is also of course one of the classic sparkling wine grapes, found not only in Champagne, but wherever good sparkling wines are made.

In the UK it was one of the earliest varieties to be grown. Brock trialled it at Oxted, but was not pleased with it and by 1961, when he issued *Report No.3 Progress with vines and wines,* he stated that Pinot noir: *appears to be very much later* [than on the continent] *in this climate ... and has been discontinued.* His lack of success was probably due to the fact that, at the vineyard's elevation of 125–137 metres above sea level, the site was just too cool. In addition, Brock was not, at least not in the early years, looking to make sparkling wines, although he did make some later on. Jack Ward was likewise somewhat dismissive of the variety and also thought it too late.

Despite the reservations of these pioneers, it seems to have been planted quite widely, if not in any great quantity. Many of the early growers seemed to limit their investigation of continental vineyards to a quick visit to Champagne and returned enthused with the idea that Pinot noir, and for that matter Chardonnay, were naturals for our climate. The truth of the matter is that in those early days they were not and good wines were *very* few in number. Whatever Bernard Theobald claimed in the 1970s and 1980s, Pinot noir was *not* the best variety to be growing then. What I wrote in 2001 (I hope) bears repeating:

> *The rise in interest of bottle-fermented sparkling wines and the results to date, from those vineyards that have gone into the job seriously, is impressive. There have also been a number of very creditable red wines made from the variety in recent years – only it has to be said in the warmer years – but it is an exciting trend.*

> *There are a number of factors which might make Pinot noir a more acceptable variety for the UK. There is no doubt that vine breeders have done much to change Pinot over the last 50 years. Clones are available now that ripen earlier, are more consistent, produce better quality wines and are more disease resistant. The upsurge in interest in making bottle-fermented sparkling wines seems set to continue and Pinot noir must be considered as a major variety in this respect. Today's fungicides, especially for the control of Botrytis are markedly better than they were only a decade ago and this undoubtedly allows growers to leave their grapes to hang for longer and to ripen more fully.*

> *Whether or not global warming is affecting the UK now – or will do in years to come – is open to debate. However, most winegrowers sense that weather patterns are changing and we are now experiencing earlier bud-bursts (although this is coupled with a higher incidence of spring frost damage) and therefore longer growing seasons. This does mean that the more marginal varieties – of which group the Pinots and Chardonnay are members – may fare better in the next decade than the last. One other factor to be considered is that of marketing. There is no doubt that the public will buy wines bearing names that they recognise and Pinot noir is one that has its devotees.*

The upsurge in plantings over the past 19 years, up from 32-hectares in 1990 to

217.97-hectares in 2009 (and that's only the official WSB figure; the actual figure is probably nearer 275-hectares) is due to two factors: the Nyetimber effect and the weather. The first factor showed that good, even great, sparkling wine could be made using the classic varieties (although the first Nyetimber wine was a *Blanc de Blanc*) and since then, all of the major players in the sparkling wine business have shown that this was no fluke. The second factor has meant that the acids are manageable and – if you want some colour – colours are acceptable. It has also meant that it crops adequately – another not-to-be-forgotten aspect of the variety. It is now the most widely planted vine variety in the UK and likely to stay that way, possibly for ever.

On the red wine front, I am still hesitant about Pinot noir as many of the examples I see are less than impressive and although Pinot noir wines have won The Bernard Theobald Trophy for the Best Red in the EWOTYC every year between 2002 and 2008 (four times by Chapel Down and once each by Sharpham, Sandhurst and Titchfield), these wines were the exceptions, rather than the rule. The best UK reds made from Pinot noir are generally light in colour (although no lighter than many top class Burgundies) and have simple red-fruit bouquets perhaps with a touch of oak, adequate tannins and a fresh, fruity crispness about them that says 'attractive' rather than 'serious'. They are never very substantial wines and must be put in context with wines from other cooler growing regions: the Loire (Sancerre especially), Burgundy and even Alsace. Against warmer climes they stand no chance. Many UK-grown Pinot noirs are, however, thin, acidic and charmless and would be much better presented as light, fruity rosés with a touch of sweetness and a very light *petillance*.

Viticulturally Pinot noir presents no great problems to the seasoned grower. It buds up quite early, making it unsuitable for frost-prone sites, but it will shoot from secondary buds. It gets all the usual ailments and requires good management to keep it *Botrytis* free if the fruit is needed for whole-bunch pressing or for fermenting on the skins as a red wine. With a good spray regime and some leaf removal prior to harvest, clean fruit is achievable. On the cropping front, I have been very impressed by the level of the yields and while another summer like 2007 might set the averages back, 70 hl/ha (4 tonnes per acre) would appear to be achievable, ideal if sparkling wines are being made. For reds, the quality of the site and the year will play a major rôle in fruit quality, but it is probably wiser to aim for nearer half this figure if good red wines are to be made.

Clonally, Pinot noir (as well as the other Pinots and Chardonnay) is very diverse and I have no doubt that we have only scratched the surface of this aspect of growing. To date, growers have looked at the CIVC lists, made some assumptions about the weather and hoped for the best.

For sparkling wine, I am not as concerned about the question of clones. There is so much that happens in sparkling wine production between picking and drinking that can substantially alter the nature, flavour, style and quality of the wine (blending, lees contact and dosage being the main ones) that the clone is of secondary importance. It would be nice to plant those clones with the lowest acidity and highest yield and in time these will hopefully make themselves known. Until that happens I like 114, 115, 292, 374, 375, 386, 459, 521, 528 and 583. Given that the CIVC list 18, ENTAV-INRA 43 and FPS[5] a whopping 74, this is quite a short list.

Pinot noir Précoce

Synonym: Blauer Frühburgunder
Type: *Vinifera*
Colour: Red
Area in the UK: 17.31 hectares, 8.19 per cent of the planted area in 2009
Origin: Original variety

When growers starting planting Pinot noir in earnest in the UK, the search went out for the earliest ripening clones in the belief that it was a late ripening variety (it's not, but that's another matter) and they were offered what many thought was an early German clone of Pinot noir by some UK vine suppliers. This was what the Germans call Blauer Frühburgunder. Vines were imported and planted and the wine was sometimes called by its correct name, (Blauer) Frühburgunder, but was more usually called Spätburgunder or Pinot Noir, occasionally Early Pinot noir.

All was fine and dandy until some eagle-eyed WSB inspector noticed Blauer Frühburgunder on a label and realised that this variety was not on the list of permitted vine varieties for the UK and therefore any wine made from it could only be sold as UK Table Wine. After some discussion within the industry, it was agreed that the synonym Pinot noir Précoce (PNP) would be a permitted name (as it is already called this in other EU Member States and it is so much nicer than Blauer Frühburgunder) and growers with this variety were asked to confess their misdeeds and re-register their vineyard parcels containing this 'clone'. This is why it has suddenly appeared from nowhere on the variety lists.

In fact Frühburgunder is a relatively old variety, known in the 1800s in Germany's most northerly winegrowing region, the Ahr, named after a tributary of the Rhine, which joins the main river just south of Bonn. By the 1900s the variety had migrated to the town of Ingelheim am Rhein, '*Die Rotweinstadt*' and it became that town's dominant variety for which they became very well known.[6] Geisenheim has done some work on it, cleaned it up (the old clones had Leaf Roll and cropped very poorly) and today there are five clones listed that are worth growing (in Germany).

---

5   FPS (or FPMS) stands for Foundation Plant Materials Services and is the UC Davis centre for the collection, evaluation and distribution of grape vine material.
6   Ingelheim, situated on the southern side of the Rhine, about halfway between Mainz and Bingen, is where Charlemagne built a palace (in about 800). According to legend, he noticed that the snows melted first on the south-facing slopes opposite and could see that the area had a unique microclimate. His son, Ludwig the Pious, started growing grapes there and the slopes eventually became the site for what is today Schloss Johannisberg.

Whether PNP is a suitable variety for the UK is another matter. It ripens up to two weeks earlier than Pinot noir and is said to achieve better sugars and better colour. It is just as *Botrytis* prone and offers no other advantages. Its drawback is the name; Pinot noir Précoce sounds a bit odd and Blauer Frühburgunder dreadful. It may well turn out to be a great blending partner for Pinot noir and kept below 15 per cent of the blend, would not upset the WSB's labelling inspectors. In the 2008 edition of this guide I wrote: *I don't anticipate a huge surge in plantings, although I suspect that more will emerge over the next few years as the WSB ask growers to look back and see what they actually planted. Luckily, ampelographers are fairly thin on the ground in the UK.* In fact the area has more than doubled in two years from 8-hectares to 17-hectares, mainly I suspect by growers with more marginal sites (probably those northern counties again), hoping that it will ripen more easily than straight Pinot noir. The only problem with this strategy is that I am not sure the wine is that good.

Regent

Type: *Vinifera* (complex hybrid)
Colour: Red
Area in the UK: 19.30 hectares, 1.59 per cent of the planted area in 2009
Origin: Diana x Chambourcin

Regent (pronounced in Germany not as in Regent Street, but as Rehgent with hard G) is another of Alleweldt's Geilweilerhof crossings (see Orion and Phoenix). Its parents are Diana, a Silvaner x Müller-Thurgau crossing and Chambourcin, a Joannès Seyve crossing of unknown parentage. In Germany it was released in 1995 and it has become quite widely grown and at 2,161 hectares (2008) is their sixth most widely grown red vine variety. It has very good colour, is more disease resistant than *Viniferas* and the wine quality is good to very good (always a help).

In the UK, Regent has only been around since the late 1980s and in 1990 there were 9.7 hectares. Today (2009) the area stands at 19.30-hectares, up by 4.47-hectares since 2007. If deep red wines are required and if labelling is not an issue, then I think it the best of the lot, better than Dornfelder or Rondo. It takes oak well, has great colour, soft tannins and acids are manageable. It requires a good site, good management and some leaf removal prior to harvest, but no more so than other red varieties It is certainly less disease prone than Dornfelder and Rondo, so on that score alone, could be a better bet. However, as I have said about the other red varieties, Pinot noir will take a lot of beating.

Regner

Type: *Vinifera*
Colour: White
Area in the UK: 4.37 hectares, 0.36 per cent of the planted area in 2009
Origin: Luglienca bianca x Gamay Früh

Regner is an Alzey crossing from Georg Scheu, made in 1929 and first released in 1978, and is another of Scheu's crossings that used a commercial table grape (Luglienca Bianca, known as Gelbe Seidentraube in Germany) as one parent and a standard wine grape (Early Gamay) as the other. It is not widely planted in Germany and in 2001 they grew only 124 hectares. It is not now separately listed in Germany, so one must assume that the area has fallen below 100 hectares.

Regner first appeared in the UK in the Wye College vineyard and quickly proved capable of good yields and had grapes that ripened mid-early (before M-T) with high sugars and low acid levels – in short – an ideal variety for our climate. I have long felt that it had a place in the UK and when I was winemaker at Lamberhurst, we used to buy it from a local vineyard and make good wine from it. Jon Leighton at Valley Vineyards (now Stanlake Park) used to grow it and was always pleased with the results and Wroxeter Vineyard in Shropshire have it and like it very much. With the UK area having fallen slightly (8-hectares in 1999, 4.37-hectares in 2007) I assume that it is on its way out, but I recently heard that Plumpton College, no less, were thinking of planting some Regner, so perhaps it's due for a modest revival?

Reichensteiner

Type: *Vinifera*
Colour: White
Area in the UK: 84.43 hectares, 6.95 per cent of the planted area in 2009
Origin: Müller-Thurgau x (Madeleine Angevine x Calabreser-Froelich)

Reichensteiner is a Geisenheim cross produced by Prof. H. Birk in 1939 by crossing Müller-Thurgau with a cross between two other varieties: Madeleine Angevine, the female French table grape used by Scheu (among others) for a number of his vines, and Calabreser-Froelich, an early white Italian table grape. Together, these have combined to produce an early ripening variety, capable of producing large crops of relatively neutral grapes, high in natural sugars and low(ish) in acidity.

In Germany, Reichensteiner was seen as a substitute to the practice of 'wet-sugaring' (where up to 20 per cent by volume of water could be added to the must during the enrichment process in order to lower the acidity) – a practice that only came to an end in the late 1970s. In 2008 there were 106-hectares of it in Germany. In warm climates, it is capable of producing massive crops – up to 200 hl/ha (12 tonnes/acre) is not uncommon – and it is used as a blending partner for varieties with more acidity. Apart from a small, but highly productive area in New Zealand (where in 1998, 74 hectares cropped at an average of 23 tonnes/ha) its only other real home is the UK.

Reichensteiner was introduced into the UK by Jack Ward when he extended the Brickyard vineyard in Horam in 1971. Early results showed that it was a consistent cropper, with good yields and high sugars. Although it can be vigorous in its youth, it settles down after a few years and is less vigorous than M-T at the same age. It has a good open habit and a leaf-wall that is less crowded and better ventilated than M-T, both of which help disease control.

As a varietal wine, it does not have the character of fruitier varieties, but has lower acid levels, more body and extract and higher natural sugars. It is probably best used in a blend. It has been used for sparkling wine (Chapel Down use it in their NV Brut), as well as for the production of *süss-reserve*. Although it has slightly fallen in area (from 113.9-hectares in 1990 to 84.43-hectares in 2009) this cannot be seen as a wholesale flight out of the variety and I suspect that those with it, will hang on to it for a while yet, although there will be very few new plantings.

Rondo

Synonym: Gm 6494/5
Type: *Vinifera* (complex hybrid)
Colour: Red
Area in the UK: 43.00 hectares, 3.54 per cent of the planted area in 2009
Origin: Zarya Severa x St Laurent

If ever there was a variety with a complicated, not to say convoluted, history attached to it, then Rondo has to have one of the twistiest. Having thought that I had got it sorted out in the 2008 edition, I have new information which has meant some changes for this edition.

The original *Vitis amurensis* vines from which Rondo is derived were wild vines and came from Manchuria, in the north of China, where the River Amur marks the border between China and Russia. Here, on account of the early onset and severity of the winters, wild vines need be able to withstand deep winter temperatures and therefore colour up and ripen early. In 1910, a Russian breeder, Ivan Vladimirovich Michurin (1855-1935) – pictured on the left – selected an open-pollinated seedling of Précoce de Malingre – probably pollinated by a *Vitis amurensis* in Michurin's vine collection – which he called Seyanets Malengra. Michurin was a famous plant breeder whose work was recognised by Lenin and whose private research station at Tambov, about 435-km south-east of Moscow, became the Michurin Central Genetic Laboratory in 1934. Seyanets Malengra is a female vine and used in Russia and Ukraine as a table grape variety. In 1936, two Russian plant breeders, Yakov Potapenko and E. Zakharova, working at the the All-Russia Research Institute of Viticulture and Winemaking (later called the Potapenko All-Russia Research Institute of Viticulture and Winemaking), situated at Novocherkassk in Rostov Province, crossed Seyanets Malengra with another *Amurensis* vine to produce a variety called Zarya Severa. This crossing then found its way to Lednice in Moravia, Czechoslavakia where Prof. Dr. Vilem Kraus crossed it, in 1964, with St Laurent, an old Austrian wine variety. This crossing then travelled to Geisenheim where Prof. Helmut Becker improved it and gave it a breeding number Gm 6494/5. With me so far? It was then trialled at Geisenheim and proved capable of producing good crops of early ripening, deeply coloured grapes. In 1983 Prof. Becker gave me 50 vines to plant at Tenterden, as well as 50 to both Ken Barlow at Adgestone and Karl-Heinz Johner at Lamberhurst, to see what the results would be. From the first harvests it showed itself well adapted to UK conditions and plantings have been increasing since then. The UK had 2-hectares in 1990 and 43-hectares in 2009.

Initially, Rondo had all the makings of a good variety for the UK: early to ripen, with a good crop of deep red grapes and wine quality that was certainly better than anything else in the mid-1980s – Léon Millot, Triomphe d'Alsace (as it was then called) and Maréchal Foch being the alternatives. It was very, very vigorous, with great big leaves (almost like the leaves of Kiwi fruit) and canes that could stretch for several metres if allowed to run. Consequently, canopies tended to be a bit crowded and shaded and although a hybrid, it was still fairly susceptible to *Botrytis*. The wine colour was excellent, deeper than anything then seen and the quality was passable. It took oak well – American oak seemed to suit it – and for a while I had high hopes for it. We got it a name – Rondo – and eventually persuaded DEFRA to classify it as a *Vinifera* (as the Germans had done five years earlier). The future looked rosy; the future looked Rondo.

Chapel Down made two versions: a straightforward wine and a Reserve, both from grapes from Anthony Pilcher's Chapel Farm vineyard on the Isle of Wight. The Reserve, with enough oak and some time, could be very good, although the flavour was always very slightly unusual. I always likened it to a Syrah-Tempranillo blend – the American oak helped – and I tried to persuade myself for years that it had a future. However, reluctantly, and in the face of the onslaught from Pinot noir and Regent, I don't think the wine quality is high enough for it to succeed in the long term. As I say in Chapter 7, this is a pity as apart from anything else, I value the direct link back to Helmut Becker and those first 50 vines, but sentimentality never helped make good wine and plantings of Rondo, I fear, will slowly, probably very slowly, wither away, although there have been just over 4-hectares planted in the last two years.

Schönburger

Type: *Vinifera*
Colour: White
Area in the UK: 42.17 hectares, 3.47 per cent of the planted area in 2009
Origin: Pinot noir x IP1

Schönburger is a crossing made at Geisenheim by Prof. Dr H. Birk in 1939 and first registered for use in 1979. Like many of the crosses from this era, it combined an early ripening table grape variety (in this case a crossing from an Italian, I. Pirovano and called IP1 which is Chasselas rosa x Muscat Hamburg) with a classic winemaking variety (Pinot noir) in the hope that a unique German table grape could be produced. Schönburger is very little planted in Germany (in 2001 there were only 35 hectares) and countries such as Canada, New Zealand and the UK have more – some can even be found in South Africa!

It has been grown in the UK since the late 1970s and on account of its quality grapes, low acidity and regular crops, it became quite widely planted. In 1990 there were 75.3-hectares, making it then the fifth most planted variety. It is an undemanding variety, more disease resistant than M-T and not so on–off in its cropping habits. Yields are never large, but what is picked is almost always of excellent quality, with high sugars and low acids. As they ripen, the grapes change colour from a light lime-green to, at first, light pink and then, when fully ripe, to an almost tawny brown colour. This gives a very good visual indication to the pickers as to which bunches are ripe and allows for some selective picking. This can only aid wine quality. The wines are almost always light and very fruity, with some good Muscat tones (some resemble a less powerful version of Gewürztraminer) that are best balanced with a slight amount of residual sugar. Wines age well and have been known to keep for up to seven years. Schönburger is one of the few varieties we grow that can be eaten with pleasure and although the berries are small, they are packed with flavour.

Despite all these attributes, the area being grown has fallen by almost 44 per cent to 42.17-hectares (2009) and I suspect that this decline will continue. Why? The name is tricky – an *umlaut* and -burger on the end never helped any grape variety become popular – and in style its just a bit to – well it has to be said – a bit too weak and washy (I was going to say 'girly' but I realise that might upset some readers). I say this even though a well-made Schönburger, with a touch of residual sweetness, nicely chilled and served as an apéritif is as good an English Wine experience as you could want – not serious, light, and slightly frivolous. Why has this counted against it? Who knows, fashion is a fickle thing and while I like Gewürztraminer, Muscat and other aromatic, flowery varieties, I know that I am in the minority. Another variety that, I fear, will dwindle in years to come.

Seyval blanc

Synonym: Seyve Villard 5/276
Type: *Hybrid*
Colour: White
Area in the UK: 88.86 hectares, 7.31 per cent of the planted area in 2009
Origin: Seibel 5656 x Seibel 4986

Seyval blanc, a crossing made by Bertille Seyve (the younger) at the nursery of his father-in-law, Victor Villard, in St Vallier on the Rhône in 1921, was originally known as Seyve-Villard 5/276. In some references, the crossing is given as Seibel 4996 x Seibel 4986, but Pierre Galet (probably the most famous ampelographer in the world) assured me in a letter that Bertille Seyve's son stated in the *Viticulture Nouvelle* of 1961 (p. 182) that the crossing was Seibel 5656 x Seibel 4986. S. 4986 is known as *Rayon d'Or*. At one stage there were over 1,300-hectares in France (1968) but plantings have declined since then. It can be found in many different parts of North America, most notably in New York State and Ontario.

It was first grown in the UK by Edward Hyams who, in 1947, obtained vines directly from the Seyve-Villard nurseries (as they had become known by then) and planted them in his small vineyard at Molash near Canterbury, Kent. Brock also imported the variety from the Swiss Federal Vine Testing Station at Caudoz-sur-Pully a year later in 1948. These two pioneers tested it and soon found that it was a very suitable variety for our climate and together with M-T, it became the standard variety for almost all the early vineyards. When Sir Guy Salisbury-Jones planted his vineyard at Hambledon in 1952 he chose Seyval blanc on the advice of a helpful Burgundian grower to whom he sat next at a *Confrérie des Chevaliers du Tastevin* dinner.

Seyval blanc has many attributes. It sets good crops even in cool years, is not vigorous and has a good open habit with small leaves and only a few side-shoots. It is unusual in that the flowers appear and are very prominent before many of the leaves really develop. It is almost totally resistant to disease, although *Botrytis* will occur in riper years, and it yields well – in some years very well. Although the grapes are never very high in natural sugar (I remember plenty of years in the 1970s and 1980s when only 5–6 per cent natural alcohol was reached), wine quality can be good *if* the winery knows what it is doing. On the downside, apart from the low natural sugars, the wine can be very neutral, high in acidity and if not pressed with care, can get a rather grassy herbaceous tone. However, it takes to oak-ageing well, is a good foil for lees-ageing and *battonage* and is great for sparkling wine. What's not to like about it one might ask?

Seyval blanc suffers from a bad press and, rather like Meunier in Champagne – it's a useful variety, but don't let's frighten the horses by talking about it too much. Most winewriters and many wine merchants, faced with the word 'hybrid', seem to recoil into their shells a bit, strike an arrogant pose, and declare without a *shred* of evidence, let alone experience in winegrowing or winemaking, that 'of course you cannot make good wine from a *hybrid*'. The truth is of course that you can and people do. Wines made from Seyval win their share of medals and awards: I won the Gore-Browne Trophy with Seyval twice (in 1981 and 1991) and Colin Gillespie at Wootton won it in 1986 with a Seyval blanc. It can still be found in some good sparkling wines (Breaky Bottom, Camel Valley, Denbies, Monnow Valley and Stanlake Park for instance) as well as a lot of good still wine. Many growers like it and although the area is down from a high of 122.7-hectares in 1990 to 88.86-hectares in 2009, it is still the fourth most widely planted variety, having overtaken Reichensteiner. We fought hard for it when the Quality Wine Scheme was put together as I knew the exclusion of hybrids from the scheme would mean the start of their decline. To deny wines made in whole or in part from a grape variety solely on the grounds of its parentage were does seem somewhat perverse, but that's the EU for you.

When I imported my first Seyval, I obtained stock from one of Professor Becker's friends, Ernest Pfrimmer who had a nursery at Hurtigheim near Strasbourg, and the results were always good. When I started importing a lot of Seyval vines from France, I spent a considerable time searching for a good source-block of vines and together with François Morisson (from the Morisson-Couderc Nursery) found an ideal one in Blois on the Loire. From this vineyard he took wood and grafted many thousands of vines for me. Having seen a fair few Seyval vineyards, both in the UK and overseas, I am convinced that there is quite a bit of clonal variation and some of the UK's vineyards are planted with some inferior clones. This might account for some of the grassy, herbaceous notes that are sometimes seen, although that could just be harsh pressing. Recently I have seen some Seyval that is plainly another variety altogether – possibly another Seyve-Villard hybrid – and plainly unsuited for UK conditions.

Having said all that, I know when I am beaten and I accept that Seyval's glory days are numbered and tomorrow's *vignerons* are unlikely to plant it much. A pity, but there we are. The sight of a heavy crop of Seyval gently turning golden in late October was always a welcome one and it is such an *easy* variety to grow and turn into wine! Too easy – perhaps that's the problem?

Siegerrebe

Type: *Vinifera*
Colour: White
Area in the UK: 12.79 hectares, 1.05 per cent of the planted area in 2009
Origin: Freely pollinated seedling of Madeleine Angevine

Siegerrebe is another Georg Scheu crossing from Alzey, made in 1929 and released to growers in 1958. The variety was originally said to be Madeleine Angevine x Gewürztraminer, but it was later revealed by Scheu's son, Heinz, to be a freely pollinated seedling of Madeleine Angevine (which is the same as the UK's Madeleine x Angevine 7672). In Germany (103-hectares in 2008) it is capable of reaching very high natural sugar levels and consequently used for making sweet dessert wines. The grapes have a strong Muscat character and when ripe, can be very concentrated and almost overpowering. Consequently it is more often used for blending with other, less distinctive varieties.

It has been in the UK since 1957 when Brock was sent cuttings from Alzey. By 1960 he was able to report: *exceptionally early and the grapes have a strong bouquet* and he highly recommended it as suitable for both the table and winemaking. Despite its attributes of early ripening, low acidity and strongly flavoured grapes, it has really failed to be planted in anything like serious amounts and although one or two vineyards do make interesting varietal wines from it, it mainly gets lost in blends. Maybe because it does ripen very early and falls so far outside what most growers consider their normal harvest time, it is rather disruptive? Wasps are a particular problem and good wasp nest control needs to be practised if real damage is to be avoided. Birds likewise, tend to be a nuisance. The area planted has risen slightly: 9.30-hectares in 1990 and 12.79-hectares in 2009. Three Choirs consistently make an interesting semi-sweet wine with the variety (its usually one of their better wines) and their 2006 Estate Reserve Siegerrebe won the Gore-Browne Trophy in 2008 and their 2007 Three Choirs Siegerrebe won a Gold medal in 2009. Siegerrebe can add a nice piquancy to an otherwise dull blend and is probably worth considering as a minor variety. As the slight rise in the area would suggest, there is some interest in the variety and it will probably hold its own and possibly expand slightly.

Solaris

Type: *Vinifera* (complex hybrid)
Colour: White
Area in the UK: 4.74 hectares, 0.39 per cent of the planted area in 2009
Origin: Merzling x Gm 6493

Solaris is a new Freiburg interspecific-cross, once known as Fr 240-75, bred by Dr. Norbert Becker in 1975 and released in 2001. In 2007 there were 54-hectares planted in Germany, mainly in the south and it is also found in Switzerland. Its parents are Merzling and Gm 6493. Merzling is a crossing between our old friend Seyval blanc and a (Riesling x Pinot gris) crossing. Gm 6493 is a Geisenheim *Vitis Amurensis* influenced crossing and is Zarya Severa x Muscat Ottonel, Zarya Severa being one of the parents of Rondo! Complicated or what? The *Taschenbuch der Rebsorten* says that it is very vigorous, with very large leaves, and that it ripens early with very high sugars, usually over 100°OE (13.8% potential alcohol) and often nearer 130°OE (18.4% potential alcohol). Its also states that the acidity is less than Ruländer (Pinot gris) – which would mean that its acidity is towards to bottom of the acid spectrum i.e. 5-6 g/l as tartaric acid. Being a hybrid, it has a good resistence against the major diseases, especially *Botrytis* to which high-sugared varieties are usually prone and its loose bunches help in this respect. It sounds very similar in many ways to Reichensteiner, but with better disease resistence.

In the UK it is planted on 4.74-hectares and has found favour in vineyards in the more northerly counties. To date, little single-variety wine has been made from Solaris and the jury is still out over its long-term potential. However, as vineyards spread ever further north in the UK – a vineyard in Scotland is surely only just be round the corner – perhaps Solaris will fill a small, but useful, niche. Early reports suggest a vigourous variety, with loose bunches and good disease resistence. One to watch.

Triomphe

Type: *Hybrid*
Colour: Red
Area in the UK: 14.77 hectares, 1.22 per cent of the planted area in 2009
Origin: Unknown parentage

Triomphe is an old French–American hybrid bred by Eugene Kuhlmann in Alsace in the late 1900s. Its breeding number is Kuhlmann 319.3 and was originally known as *Triomphe d'Alsace* and for many years was labelled as such. When, in 1992, the UK tried to register it under that title, the EU Commission objected (because it contained the name of an *appellation contrôlée* region – Alsace) and the name was shortened to Triomphe. Its exact parentage appears to be unknown, but is probably from the same *riparia-rupestris* x Goldriesling selections that produced two other Kuhlmann crosses, Léon Millot and Maréchal Foch. (Goldriesling is Riesling x Courtillier Musqué).

Triomphe was first introduced into the UK by Brock at Oxted, quite widely planted by the early growers and together with Cascade, Léon Millot and Maréchal Foch became one of the most widely planted red varieties. It is a vigorous variety and needs a bit of canopy management to keep it under control. However, disease resistance is fairly good and it has the small berries and dark red skin, red flesh and red juice of the other Kuhlmann hybrids. However, its wine quality is not that good, certainly below that of Dornfelder and Regent, with a slightly non-vinous tone about it. It is probably best blended with other varieties.

Despite the fact that it is an old hybrid and despite the fact there is said to be a lot of clonal variation, the planted area expanded from 7.5-hectares in 1990 to 14.77-hectares in 2009, although this is very slightly down on the 2007 figure of 15.10-hectares. It is the fourth most widely planted purely red variety – after Rondo, Regent and Dornfelder – and I am surprised that it has held up as well as it has. I really do not think it has much of a future in the UK.

Würzer

Type: *Vinifera*
Colour: White
Area in the UK: 4.55 hectares, 0.37 per cent of the planted area in 2009
Origin: Gewürztraminer x Müller-Thurgau

Würzer is a crossing made by Georg Scheu at Alzey in 1932 and released to growers in 1978. It is another of Scheu's spicy crosses (Scheurebe, Faberrebe and Huxelrebe being the other ones used in the UK) and in a similar mould. There were 97-hectares in Germany in 2001.

For the UK it is really rather too late for most sites, has high, often unripe acids and does not show any real advantages over several other varieties (Bacchus for instance) and the decline in the area from 14.3-hectares in 1999 to 4.55-hectares in 2009 is probably a good indication of its usefulness. Not one for the future.

The collection of sarsen stones, known as Kits Coty House, which dates from 4,300 BC adjoins Chapel Down's new Kits Coty vineyard.

PART II

Vineyards A–Z

This section lists the details of 439 vineyards: 415 in England, 18 in Wales, 2 in Scotland, 3 in Ireland & 1 in the Channel Isles which cover 1,270-ha (3,138-acres).

English County	Ha. of vines	English County	Ha. of vines
West Sussex	211.84	Lincolnshire	7.17
Kent	154.49	Warwickshire	6.46
Hampshire	122.78	Hertfordshire	6.29
Surrey	119.89	North Somerset	6.25
Essex	114.35	Nottinghamshire	5.55
East Sussex	92.68	North Yorkshire	4.55
Devon	49.40	Rutland	4.62
Dorset	46.69	West Yorkshire	4.14
Gloucestershire	35.25	Leicestershire	3.81
Suffolk	34.21	Northamptonshire	3.46
Cornwall	25.49	Isles of Scilly	2.42
Oxfordshire	19.60	Derbyshire	1.70
Herefordshire	17.68	Bedfordshire	1.62
Somerset	17.64	Cheshire	1.20
Wiltshire	16.87	London	0.72
Isle of Wight	15.54	South Yorkshire	0.57
Buckinghamshire	13.01	South Gloucestershire	0.50
Staffordshire	12.62	West Midlands	0.25
Berkshire	12.24	Avon	0.20
Shropshire	12.01	Lancashire	0.20
Norfolk	9.96	County Durham	0.10
Cambridgeshire	8.93	Manchester	0.02
Worcestershire	7.75	**Total for England**	**1232.75**

Welsh County	Ha. of vines	Welsh County	Ha. of vines
Monmouthshire	10.28	Pembrokeshire	1.00
Vale of Glamorgan	6.25	Cardiff	0.30
Powys	4.00	Wrexham	0.25
Gwynedd	2.83	**Other Areas**	
Anglesey	2.62	**Channel Islands**	**5.00**
Ceredigion	2.43	**Ireland**	**1.22**
Carmarthenshire	1.00	**Scotland**	**0.01**

Vineyards by county and by size

The vineyards in this section are listed by county and within their county, alphabetically. Several wine producers – Abbey Vineyards, Chapel Down, Davenport, Nyetimber, Pebblebed, Plumpton College, RidgeView Estate, Sedlescombe Organic and possibly several others – have more than one vineyard site under their ownership and rent or lease vineyards. These vineyards are, wherever possible, shown as separate entries. Many of the above vineyards also have growers under contract or have some other arrangement to supply them with grapes. Wherever possible, individual vineyards have been listed irrespective of ownership or ultimate destination of their grapes. The total area of vines under the control of the vineyards listed above will be found under the entries for the the individual producers.

Trying to decide what constitutes an English or Welsh 'county' is today no easy task given the division of England and Wales into Metropolitan Counties, Non-Metropolitan Counties (not having a County Council), Unitary Authorities and Administrative Areas. I have generally taken the county name given to me by growers, even though technically they may lie in a differently named local authority. Some vineyards also lie right on the border between two counties and although the Post Office has them in one county, they prefer to be listed in another.

England   416 vineyards

Avon	*1 vineyard*		
Avonwood	0.2000 ha		
Bedfordshire	*1 vineyard*		
Warden Abbey	1.6194 ha		
Berkshire	*4 vineyards*		
Binfield	2.0240 ha	Stanlake Park	10.0000 ha
North Court Farm	0.0719 ha	Theale	0.1400 ha
Buckinghamshire	*8 vineyards*		
Claydon	0.1000 ha	Magpie Lane	4.3000 ha
Daws Hill	1.7862 ha	Manor Fields	0.8907 ha
Dropmore	0.6600 ha	Shardeloes	4.0000 ha
Hale Valley	0.6200 ha	Tyringham Hall	0.6510 ha
Cambridgeshire	*4 vineyards*		
Chilford Hall	7.4000 ha	Elysian Fields	1.0000 ha
Coton Orchard	0.2000 ha	Gog Magog	0.3300 ha

Cheshire   *1 vineyard*
Carden Park   1.2000 ha

Cornwall   *11 vineyards*

Bosue	1.5000 ha	Polgoon	3.6000 ha
Camel Valley	7.0000 ha	Pollaughan	2.8000 ha
Cobland Mill	1.6200 ha	Polmassick	1.0000 ha
Cornish Garden	0.5000 ha	Struddicks Farm	2.3000 ha
Lambourne	2.0000 ha	Trevibban Mill	3.0000 ha
Penberth Valley	0.1700 ha		

County Durham   *1 vineyard*
Whitworth Hall   0.1000 ha

Derbyshire   *2 vineyards*
Renishaw Hall   0.2024 ha   Sealwood Cottage 1.5000 ha

Devon   *33 vineyards*

Alder Farm	1.0000 ha	Otter Farm	1.5000 ha
Ashwell	0.0365 ha	Pebblebed Clyst	3.2376 ha
Beenleigh Manor	0.1300 ha	Pebblebed Ebford	4.2376 ha
Blackdown Hills	1.5000 ha	Pebblebed West	2.4282 ha
Borough Hill Farm	2.6460 ha	Redyeates Wedge	2.4000 ha
Brick House	0.6552 ha	Rock Moors	0.2141 ha
Clawford	0.2000 ha	Sandridge Barton	1.6194 ha
Eastcott	1.4900 ha	Sharpham	3.4000 ha
Ebford Eden	0.2000 ha	Silverland	0.8200 ha
Higher Bumsley	0.8300 ha	Southwood	0.4340 ha
Huxbear	4.0000 ha	Summermoor	1.4170 ha
Kenton	2.7500 ha	Torview	1.6700 ha
Knightshayes	0.0720 ha	Watchcombe	1.0000 ha
Lily Farm	0.3830 ha	Wier Quay	0.1000 ha
Manstree	1.8219 ha	Willhayne	0.1550 ha
Oakford	1.0500 ha	Yearlstone	3.0000 ha
Old Walls	3.0000 ha		

Dorset   *16 vineyards*

Castlewood	1.0100 ha	Doles Ash Farm	0.7500 ha
Charlton Barrow	0.3000 ha	English Oak	8.0600 ha
Crawthorne	10.0000 ha	Furleigh Estate	5.5000 ha
Cross Tree Farm	3.2000 ha	Higher Sandford	0.2500 ha

Dorset – continued

Melbury Vale	0.8000 ha	Sherborne Castle	2.8000 ha
Parhams	0.4000 ha	Stalbridge Weston	0.2000 ha
Portesham	1.0000 ha	Timberline	0.5000 ha
Purbeck	1.0000 ha	Wodetone	10.9200 ha

East Sussex   *33 vineyards*

Albourne	0.2900 ha	Herons Ghyll	3.6500 ha
Barnsgate Manor	1.4171 ha	Hidden Spring	1.4000 ha
Battle Wine Estate	8.5020 ha	Hobdens	1.6000 ha
Bewl Water	2.6135 ha	Methersham	1.2000 ha
Black Dog Hill	4.9203 ha	Mount Harry	2.6000 ha
Bluebell Estates	3.7900 ha	New House	4.0000 ha
Bodiam	1.8219 ha	Pippins	2.1200 ha
Breaky Bottom	2.2000 ha	Plumpton College	0.4600 ha
Burwash Weald	1.2550 ha	RidgeView Estate	6.4800 ha
Carr Taylor	6.0700 ha	Rosemary Farm	3.3818 ha
Charles Palmer	2.0000 ha	Sculdown	0.4900 ha
Chingley Manor	0.8093 ha	Sedlescombe Org.	7.3500 ha
Court Garden	5.0000 ha	Sheffield Park	1.2145 ha
Davenport	1.6700 ha	Spilsted	2.2267 ha
Ditchling	1.8200 ha	Springfields	3.0000 ha
Forstal Farm	3.4431 ha	Ticehurst	1.0567 ha
Henners	2.8340 ha		

Essex   *15 vineyards*

Bardfield	1.0000 ha	Ollivers Farm	0.0170 ha
Carters	2.6100 ha	Potash	0.1000 ha
Clayhill	4.0000 ha	Robert Fleming	31.5789 ha
Coggeshall	0.4000 ha	Russetts	0.1380 ha
Felsted	4.0000 ha	Saffron Grange	2.0000 ha
Gravel Lane	1.0000 ha	St. Mary Magdelen	0.2000 ha
Mersea Island	3.5000 ha	Sandyford	0.8097 ha
New Hall	63.0000 ha		

Gloucestershire   *10 vineyards*

Compton Green	2.1000 ha	St Anne's	0.3600 ha
Cowley Estate	0.0200 ha	Strawberry Hill	1.8000 ha
Kents Green	0.2000 ha	Three Choirs	30.0000 ha
Kilcott Valley	0 2000 ha	Winner Hill	0.2700 ha
Little Foxes	0.0011 ha	Newtown	0.3000 ha

Hampshire	*16 vineyards*		
Beaulieu	1.8000 ha	Jenkyn Place	2.9000 ha
Beeches Hill	0.0100 ha	Laverstoke Park	9.0000 ha
Birchenwood	2.0000 ha	Leckford Estate	4.6977 ha
Bishops Waltham	2.0000 ha	Little West End	4.0000 ha
Chalk Vale	25.1000 ha	Marlings	0.8600 ha
Coach House	0.4000 ha	Northbrook Spr.	5.1000 ha
Cottonworth	4.8000 ha	Priors Dean	0.8000 ha
Court Lane	0.6000 ha	Setley Ridge	2.4800 ha
Danebury	3.0000 ha	Somborne Valley	7.3752 ha
Deans Farm	0.5000 ha	Sour Grapes	0.4049 ha
Dunley	0.2000 ha	Titchfield	1.1000 ha
East Meon	0.4000 ha	Webbs Land	3.2100 ha
Exton Park Estate	7.8056 ha	Westward House	0.1000 ha
Hambledon	4.0300 ha	Wickham	6.2000 ha
Hattingley Valley	7.3000 ha	Winchester	0.0100 ha
Jays Farm	4.2000 ha	Wooldings	6.0729 ha

Herefordshire	*16 vineyards*		
Backbury House	0.3000 ha	Lulham Court	1.2146 ha
Beeches	0.2020 ha	Old Grove House	0.0210 ha
Broadfield Court	5.4656 ha	Pengethley Manor	0.2000 ha
Castle Brook	2.4300 ha	Sparchall	1.0089 ha
Coddington	0.6000 ha	Sunnybank	0.3400 ha
Croft Castle	0.1822 ha	Tarrington Court	0.2500 ha
Four Foxes	3.2500 ha	Townsend Farm	0.5140 ha
Frome Valley	1.5000 ha	Treago	0.2000 ha

Hertfordshire	*7 vineyards*		
Broxbournebury	1.6000 ha	Mimram Valley	0.4800 ha
Frithsden	1.2320 ha	Moat House	0.4000 ha
Hazel End	1.2199 ha	Wareside Wines	0.3330 ha
Herts Oak Farm	1.0300 ha		

Isle of Wight	*4 vineyards*		
Adgestone	2.9100 ha	Rosemary	6.4778 ha
Ashey	2.4500 ha	Rossiters	3.7000 ha

Isles of Scilly	*2 vineyards*		
St Martin's	0.6000 ha	St. Mary's	1.8200 ha

Kent   *38 vineyards*
Barnsole   1.2000 ha
Biddenden   8.0000 ha
Bourne Farm   4.0000 ha
Broadway Green   0.6073 ha
Budds Farm   2.0000 ha
Chalksole Estate   2.1342 ha
East Sutton Vine   4.0000 ha
Elham Valley   0.7200 ha
Friday St. Farm   4.6500 ha
Groombridge Place 1.0120 ha
Gusbourne   20.6478 ha
Harbourne   1.2000 ha
Harden   2.2500 ha
Horsmonden   6.4780 ha
Hush Heath Estate 5.0481 ha
Kempes Hall   0.1000 ha
Kit's Coty   29.4000 ha
Lamberhurst   8.1000 ha
Leeds Castle   1.3500 ha

Little Knoxbridge 0.5330 ha
Marden Organic   3.5000 ha
Mayshaves   0.0991 ha
Meopham Valley   2.0000 ha
Mount   3.6800 ha
Mystole Members   2.0500 ha
National Fruit Coll. 0.2400 ha
Port Lympne   0.0250 ha
Sandhurst   6.0000 ha
Squerryes Court   11.5471 ha
Stanford Bridge   0.1000 ha
Surrenden   1.0000 ha
Syndale Valley   4.0520 ha
Tenterden   8.3300 ha
Terlingham   1.5000 ha
Throwley   1.3800 ha
Westwell Wines   4.8400 ha
Wootton Park   0.8100 ha
Wrangling Lane   0.0675 ha

Lancashire   *1 vineyard*
Mount Pleasant   0.2000 ha

Leicestershire   *6 vineyards*
Chevelswarde   0.5300 ha
High Cross   0.0150 ha
Keyham   2.2500 ha

Kingfisher's Pool 0.2400 ha
Manor Farm   0.1300 ha
Walton Brook   0.6500 ha

Lincolnshire   *5 vineyards*
Good Earth   0.0144 ha
Lincoln   0.0900 ha
Mill Lane   0.4500 ha

Somerby   6.0000 ha
Three Sisters   0.6189 ha

London   *7 vineyards*
Alara Wholefoods 0.0350 ha
Clocktower   0.0237 ha
Decanter Magazine 0.0001 ha
Forty Hall   0.4000 ha

Mill Hill Village 0.0600 ha
Olding Manor   0.0100 ha
St. Andrew's   0.1940 ha

Manchester   *1 vineyard*
Plot 19   0.0222 ha

Norfolk	*8 vineyards*		
Chapel Field	0.8100 ha	South Pickenham	2.0300 ha
Congham	0.3035 ha	Sustead Lane	1.6200 ha
Crown Vines	0.2500 ha	Tas Valley	1.2146 ha
Railway	2.8430 ha	Thelnetham Lodge	0.9000 ha

North Somerset	*1 vineyard*
Aldwick Court	6.2500 ha

North Yorkshire	*6 vineyards*		
Acomb Grange	0.0336 ha	Ryedale	2.5000 ha
Bolton Castle	0.2000 ha	Womack's	0.0200 ha
Helmsley Walled	0.0001 ha	Yorkshire Heart	1.8000 ha

Northamptonshire	*8 vineyards*		
Fleurfields	1.5000 ha	Ravensthorpe	0.0250 ha
Harlestone	0.0759 ha	Vernon Lodge	0.0900 ha
Kemps	0.2000 ha	Welland Valley	0.8000 ha
New Lodge	0.2300 ha	Windmill	0.2600 ha

Nottinghamshire	*3 vineyards*		
East Bridgeford	3.0000 ha	River Walk	1.2500 ha
Eglantine	1.3000 ha		

Oxfordshire	*15 vineyards*		
Bothy	2.0243 ha	Hendred	2.2031 ha
Bridewell Organic	0.9300 ha	Linch Hill	1.0000 ha
Brightwell	4.5000 ha	Meadowgrove	0.1125 ha
Childrey Manor	1.0000 ha	Pheasants Ridge	0.6478 ha
Chiltern Valley	1.0000 ha	Springfield	0.1349 ha
Fawley	0.2620 ha	Wyfold	1.1880 ha
Floreys	2.5000 ha	Rossi Regatta	2.0000 ha
Grange Farm	0.1020 ha		

Rutland	*3 vineyards*		
Old Oak	1.5000 ha	Tixover	1.5000 ha
South Shore	1.6194 ha		

Shropshire	*8 vineyards*		
Clee Hills	0.2000 ha	Habberley	0.2000 ha
Commonwood	0.8065 ha	Hargrove	1.2500 ha

Shropshire - continued

Ludlow	4.0000 ha	Tern Valley	1.6700 ha
Morville St Greg.	1.2000 ha	Wroxeter Roman	2.6850 ha

Somerset	*16 vineyards*		
Aller Hill	1.0500 ha	Mumfords	1.6194 ha
Avalon	0.9100 ha	Oatley	1.0000 ha
Carpenters	0.1012 ha	Quantock Hills	0.0600 ha
Coxley	1.6194 ha	Secret Valley	2.0000 ha
Dunkery	1.4200 ha	Staplecombe	0.7300 ha
Dunleavy	1.2146 ha	Wayford	1.7000 ha
Head of the Vale	0.1500 ha	Wootton	0.1000 ha
Lopen	1.6817 ha	Wraxall	2.2800 ha

South Gloucestershire	*2 vineyards*		
St Augustine's	0.3035 ha	Thornbury Castle	0.2000 ha

South Yorkshire	*1 vineyard*
Summerhouse	0.5720 ha

Staffordshire	*2 vineyards*		
Buzzard Valley	2.8000 ha	Halfpenny Green	9.8200 ha

Suffolk	*16 vineyards*		
Brook Farm	3.7390 ha	Oak Hill	0.4000 ha
Giffords Hall	4.0000 ha	Old Rectory	1.6200 ha
Heveningham Hall	1.0121 ha	Shawsgate	5.5000 ha
Ickworth	0.8000 ha	Shotley	7.5000 ha
Kemp's	0.6310 ha	Staverton	0.5300 ha
Knettishall	1.2000 ha	Valley Farm	3.2000 ha
Melbury	0.2500 ha	Willow Grange	0.4000 ha
Melton Lodge	0.6700 ha	Wyken	2.7600 ha

Surrey	*17 vineyards*		
Albury	2.0510 ha	Greyfriars	0.6072 ha
Alexandra Road	0.0100 ha	High Clandon	0.5000 ha
Burnt House	4.0000 ha	Iron Railway	0.8100 ha
Denbies	107.2874 ha	Painshill Park	0.7300 ha
Fernhurst	0.8097 ha	Primrose Hill	0.1820 ha
Godstone	1.0000 ha	Shere	0.8097 ha
Goose Green	0.0285 ha	Thorncroft	0.4000 ha

Surrey - continued

Virginia Water	0.0240 ha	Wisley RHS	0.2400 ha
Warren Farm	0.4000 ha		

Warwickshire   *4 vineyards*

Bearley	0.5384 ha	Hunt Hall Farm	4.0000 ha
Heart of England	1.2145 ha	Welcombe Hills	0.7100 ha

West Midlands   *1 vineyard*

Spring Cottage	0.2500 ha

West Sussex   *27 vineyards*

Bookers	16.8000 ha	Roman Villa	21.2000 ha
Brinsbury College	1.2000 ha	Rother Valley	1.6280 ha
Chanctonbury	1.4710 ha	Southlands Valley	1.0000 ha
Ebernoe	1.0000 ha	Standen	1.0000 ha
Halnacker	2.6565 ha	Stopham	6.0000 ha
Highdown	2.5000 ha	Storrington Priory	1.0396 ha
Netherland	37.3000 ha	Tinwood	18.1764 ha
Nutbourne Lane	6.4000 ha	Tullens	7.5000 ha
Nutbourne	7.2874 ha	Upperton	5.7700 ha
Nyetimber	24.0500 ha	Upperton Nyet'r	8.0000 ha
Nyetimber private	8.3000 ha	Warnham Vale	1.0000 ha
Redfold Farm	8.0850 ha	Wiston Estate	6.5460 ha
River	11.3000 ha	Wychwood House	0.0120 ha
Rock Lodge	4.6700 ha		

West Yorkshire   *2 vineyards*

Holmfirth	1.9300 ha	Leventhorpe	2.2100 ha

Wiltshire   *12 vineyards*

a'Beckett's	1.8700 ha	New Mill	0.8000 ha
Avonleigh Organic	2.2000 ha	Pear Tree at Purton	0.7000 ha
Bow-in-the-Cloud	1.2400 ha	Quoins Organic	1.0000 ha
Fonthill Glebe	3.5000 ha	Southcott	0.6000 ha
Leigh Park Hotel	0.5000 ha	Tytherley	0.6600 ha
Littlebredy	0.2000 ha	Wylye Valley	3.6000 ha

Worcestershire   *5 vineyards*

Astley	2.0000 ha	Rose Bank	0.7200 ha
Church Farm	3.2927 ha	Tiltridge	0.7400 ha
Nash	1.0000 ha		

Wales   18 vineyards

Anglesey	*1 vineyard*		
Llanbadrig	1.0000 ha	Ty Croes	1.6194 ha
Cardiff	*1 vineyard*		
Gelynis	0.3000 ha		
Carmarthenshire	*1 vineyard*		
Jabajak	1.0000 ha		
Ceredigion	*1 vineyard*		
Llaethliw	2.4291 ha		
Gwynedd	*1 vineyard*		
Pant Du	2.8340 ha		
Monmouthshire	*16 vineyards*		
Ancre Hill	3.4244 ha	Sugarloaf	2.0000 ha
Monnow Valley	1.6100 ha	Wernddu	0.5000 ha
Parva Farm	0.9940 ha	White Castle	1.7500 ha
Pembrokeshire	*1 vineyard*		
Cwm Deri	1.0000 ha		
Powys	*1 vineyard*		
Penarth	4.0000 ha		
Vale of Glamorgan			
Bryn Ceilog	1.8000 ha	Llanerch	2.8000 ha
Glyndŵr	1.6488 ha		
Wrexham			
Worthenbury	0.2500 ha		

Scotland   2 vineyards

Isle of Lewis	
Poly Croft	0.0050 ha
Perthshire	
Ardeonaig	0.0069 ha

Ireland   3 vineyards

Cork	*2 vineyards*		
Longueville House	0.1575 ha	Thomas Walk	0.9800

Dublin
Lusca   0.0750 ha

Channel Islands   1 vineyard

Jersey
La Mare   5.0000 ha

Organic and biodynamic vineyards

The following vineyards are farmed according to organic or biodynamic principles, although not all are registered with an appropriate certification authority.

Albury (in conversion)   Marden Organic
Avalon   Olivers Farm
Avonleigh Organic   Pebblebed
Bodiam   Penarth
Bridewell Organic Gardens   Quoins Organic
Chevelswarde   Ryedale (partly)
Davenport   Sedlescombe Organic
Forty Hall   Spilsted
Horsmonden   Springfields (Biodynamic)
Laverstoke Park (Biodynamic)   Thomas Walk
Llaethliw   Trevibban Mill (in conversion)
Lopen
Wernddu

Vineyards of 4-hectares or more

The 72 vineyards of 4-hectares or more listed below total 875-hectares, which is 69 per cent of the total area in this guide, but only 17 per cent of the number of vineyards. Whilst Denbies still has the largest single vineyard, Nyetimber is top of the list with 141.65-hectares spread over eight sites. Some wineries – Chapel Down, RidgeView, Camel Valley are the main ones, but there are others – source their grapes from a combination of: vineyards they own and farm, vineyards which are under contract, and vineyards they buy grapes from on an annual basis. Vineyards marked with an asterisk* are made up of two or more different vineyards and details can be found under their main entry. Abbey Vineyards Group own nine vineyards: East Bridgeford, Floreys, Keyham, Magpie Lane, Old Oak, River Walk, South Shore, Sustead Lane and Tas Valley.

Nyetimber*	141.6500 ha	Tullens	7.5000 ha
Denbies	107.2874 ha	Chilford Hall	7.4000 ha
New Hall	63.0000 ha	Somborne Valley	7.3752 ha
Chapel Down*	37.7300 ha	Hattingley Valley	7.3000 ha
Robert Fleming	31.5789 ha	Nutbourne	7.2874 ha
Three Choirs	30.0000 ha	Camel Valley	7.0000 ha
Gusbourne	20.5200 ha	Wiston Estate	6.5460 ha
Abbey Vineyards*	18.3531 ha	RidgeView Estate	6.4800 ha
Tinwood	18.1764 ha	Rosemary	6.4778 ha
Bookers	16.8000 ha	Aldwick Court	6.2500 ha
Wickham*	13.7000 ha	Carr Taylor	6.0700 ha
Squerryes Court	11.5471 ha	Somerby	6.0000 ha
Sedlescombe*	11.3986 ha	Stopham	6.0000 ha
Wodetone	10.9200 ha	Upperton	5.7700 ha
Wooldings	10.4000 ha	Furleigh Estate	5.5000 ha
Crawthorne	10.0000 ha	Shawsgate	5.5000 ha
Sandhurst*	10.0000 ha	Broadfield Court	5.4656 ha
Stanlake Park	10.0000 ha	Northbrook Sp.	5.1000 ha
Halfpenny Green	9.8200 ha	Hush Heath Estate	5.0481 ha
Laverstoke Park	9.0000 ha	Court Gardens	5.0000 ha
Battle Wine Estate	8.5020 ha	La Mare	5.0000 ha
Pebblebed*	9.9034 ha	Black Dog	4.9203 ha
Lamberhurst	8.1000 ha	Westwell Wines	4.8400 ha
Redfold Farm	8.0850 ha	Cottonworth	4.8000 ha
Davenport*	8.1478 ha	Leckford Estate	4.6977 ha
English Oak	8.0600 ha	Rock Lodge	4.6700 ha
Biddenden	8.0000 ha	Friday Street	4.6500 ha
Exton Park Estate	7.8056 ha	Brightwell	4.5000 ha

Magpie Lane	4.3000 ha	Giffords Hall	4.0000 ha
Jays Farm	4.2000 ha	Hunt Hall Farm	4.0000 ha
Syndale Valley	4.0520 ha	Huxbear	4.0000 ha
Hambledon	4.0300 ha	Little West End	4.0000 ha
Burnt House	4.0000 ha	Ludlow	4.0000 ha
Clayhill	4.0000 ha	New House Farm	4.0000 ha
East Sutton	4.0000 ha	Penarth	4.0000 ha
Felsted	4.0000 ha	Shardeloes	4.0000 ha

Notes to vineyard entries

Vineyards are listed in alphabetical order apart from La Mare which is listed under L. English Wines Group plc is referred to as Chapel Down throughout and grape varieties are listed in order of area, largest first. The grape varieties listed below are referred to as indicated:

MA = Madeleine x Angevine 7672
MT = Müller-Thurgau
Madeleine Sylvaner = Madeleine x Sylvaner III 28/51
Pinot noir Précoce = Blauer Früburgunder

The following abbreviations for wine competitions have been used:
Decanter WWA – *Decanter Magazine* World Wine Awards
EWOTYC – UKVA annual 'English Wine of the Year' Competition
IWC – International Wine Challenge
IWSC – International Wine and Spirit Competition
SEVA – South East Vineyards Association competition

Maps – there are no maps

With over half the vineyards in this guide having websites, most of which have maps and directions, Google Maps and other similar resources and the ever-increasing access to sat-nav and other direction finding devices, finding one's way around the country has never been easier. I therefore decided that maps were a luxury this guide could do without. If you need a vineyard map, the EWP has an excellent one.

a'Beckett's Vineyard

High Street, Littleton Panell, Devizes, Wiltshire SN10 4EN
Telephone: 01380 816669
E-mail: info@abecketts.co.uk
Website: www.abecketts.co.uk
Contact: Paul Langham
Vineyards: 1.87 hectares
Grape varieties: Pinot noir, Dunkelfelder, Seyval blanc, Reichensteiner, Auxerrois
Open to the public: Thursday, Friday, Saturday and Bank Holidays, 10.30 am to 5.30 pm; at other times by appointment. See website for details. Wine tours are run for groups and wine tour gift vouchers can be bought for 2 and 4 people. The vineyard and orchard are available for use by schools, Scouts, Guides & other youth groups. Please ask for details.

Situated halfway between Avebury and Stonehenge on the edge of Salisbury Plain, a'Beckett's Vineyard sits on Upper Greensand soil with chalk lying between 0.60 and 3 metres below the site giving the vineyard warm, well-drained soils. All the vines are Guyot trained. The site also has Wiltshire's last commercial apple orchard with some 600 trees now renovated and back in production. They make cider and apple juice on-site with longer term plans to have a winery as well. The vineyards will be expanding with further plantings of Pinot Noir & Chardonnay and the long-term intention is to increase the vineyards to around 10 hectares.

a'Beckett's wines have done well in competitions, their 2006 Pinot Noir Précoce and their 2005 Estate Reserve winning Silver Medals at the 2008 EWOTYC, 2007 Estate Rosé winning Bronze at the 2008 EWOTYC and their 2006 Estate Rosé winning Silver and their 2005 Estate Red Bronze in the 2007 EWOTYC.

Acomb Grange Vineyard

Grange Lane, York, North Yorkshire YO23 3QZ
Telephone: 0871 288 4763
E-mail: carolbrown@acombgrange.co.uk
Website: www.acombgrange.co.uk
Contact: Carol Ann Brown
Vineyards: 0.0366 hectares (estimate)
Grape varieties: Not known
Open to the public. See website for details.

Adgestone Vineyard

Upper Road, Adgestone, Sandown, Isle of Wight PO36 0ES
Telephone: 01983 402503
E-mail: enquiries@english-wine.co.uk
Website: www.english-wine.co.uk
Contact: Alan Stockman
Vineyards: 2.91 hectares
Grape varieties: Reichensteiner, Seyval blanc, Rondo, Bacchus, MT, Phoenix, Gewürztraminer
Open to the public. See website for details.

Alara Wholefoods Vineyard

110-112 Casmley Street, London, NW1 0PF
Telephone: 020 7387 6077
Fax: 020 7388 6077
E-mail: info@alara.co.uk
Website: www.alara.co.uk
Contact: Alex Smith, Ed Inett
Vineyards: 0.035 hectares
Grape varieties: Rondo
Not open to the public.

Albourne Vineyard

Yew Tree Farm House, Church Lane, Ditchling, East Sussex, BN6 9BX
Telephone: 01273 835382
Mobile: 07801 665159
Contact. Gywnn Price
Vineyards: 0.29 hectares
Not open to the public.

Albury Vineyard

c/o Weston Lodge, Albury, Guildford, GU5 9AE
Vineyard location: Behind Silent Pool car park, GU5 9BW
Telephone: 01483 202017
Mobile: 07768 863650
E-mail: nick@wenmans.co.uk
Website: http://alburyvineyard.blogspot.com
Contact: Nick Wenman
Vineyards: 2.051 hectares
Grape varieties: Chardonnay, Pinot noir, Pinot Meunier, Seyval blanc
Not open to the public.

Albury Vineyard is a new vineyard planted on land leased from the Duke of Northumberland by Nick Wenman. This new venture has been several years in gestation – I first met Nick about 5 years ago and did my best to disuade him – and is his response to having turned 50 and having sold his successful software business. As if owning a vineyard was not enough, Nick has burdened himself with the decision that it ought to be ORGANIC. However, with characteristic thoroughness and with the help of an experienced consultant (yours truly) he has forged ahead and planted the first *tranche* of what will be a total of around 6 hectares. Organic status has been applied for though Organic Farmers and Growers (www.organicfarmers.org.uk) and the vineyard should be fully certified for its first crop in 2011. Weed control in the first year has been achieved (as I write we are still ahead of the weeds) by using a mulch of compost (organic from Laverstoke Park) and woodchips (also certified organic) and spread in the rows. Powdery and Downy Mildews have been kept at bay with biodynamic preparations. The aim is to avoid using sulphur and copper and rely on building up the plant's own defence mechanisms.

Although the main product will be a bottle-fermented sparkling wine, 0.2-hectares of Seyval blanc have been planted which will form the basis of a still rosé which will be a joint venture between Nick and myself. Further land has been

optioned should Nick feel the desire to expand the vineyard. An additional 2.83-hectares will be planted in 2010, including a trial plot of Pinot gris.

Compost and woodchip mulch used for weed control

Alder Farm Vineyard

Lewdown, Oakhampton, Devon, EX20 4PJ
Telephone: 01566 783480
Mobile: 07813 752805
E-mail: hodgetts@henerysgarden.wanadoo.co.uk
Contact: Sarah amd Michael Hodgetts
Vineyards: 1 hectares
Grape varieties: MA
Not open to the public.

Aldwick Court Farm Vineyard

Aldwick Court Farm, Redhill, Bristol, North Somerset, BS40 5RF
Telephone: 01934 862305
Fax: 01937 863308
Mobile: 07799 847537
E-mail: mark@acfhospitality.co.uk
Website: www.acfhospitality.co.uk
Contact: Mark Fanning, Chris Watts
Vineyards: 6.25 hectares
Grape varieties: Bacchus, Pinot noir, Seyval blanc, Solaris
Not open to the public

Alexandra Road Allotments Vineyard

Copse End Road, Epsom, Surrey, KT17 4EQ
Telephone: 01372 729601
Mobile: 07766 544687
E-mail: david@epsomelectrical.co.uk
Website: www.epsomandewellhistoryexplorer.org.uk/Allotments.html
Contact: David Cremer
Vineyards: 0.01 hectares
Grape varieties: Pinot noir, Dornfelder, Seyval blanc, MA, Kerner, Faberrebe, MT, Schönburger
Not open to the public.

Alexandra Road Allotments

Aller Hill Vineyard

Higher Plot Farm, Aller Road, Langport, Somerset TA10 0QL
Telephone: 01458 259 075
E-mail: guy@bibelotwine.co.uk
Website: www.higherplot.co.uk
Contact: Guy Smith
Vineyards: 1.05 hectares
Grape varieties: Pinot noir, Chardonnay, Pinot Meunier
Not open to the public.

Ancre Hill Vineyard

Ancre Hill Estates, Monmouth, Monmouthshire NP25 5HS, Wales
Telephone: 01600 714152 Fax 01600 713784
Mobile: 07885 984918
E-mail: info@ancrehillestates.co.uk
Website: www.ancrehillestates.co.uk
Contact: Richard and Joy Morris
Vineyards: 3.4224 hectares
Grape varieties: Pinot noir, Chardonnay, Seyval blanc, Triomphe
Open to the public. See website for details.

Ancre Hill Vineyard trained
to GDC

Ardeonaig House Hotel Vineyard

South Road Lock Tay, Ardeonaig, Perthshire, Scotland, FK21 8SU
Telephone: 01567 820400
Contact: Peter Gottgens 07958 792799
E-mail: info@ardeonaighotel.co.uk
Website: www.ardeonaighotel.co.uk
Vineyards: 0.0069 hectares
Grape varieties: Seyval blanc, Orion, Bacchus, Phoenix

Calling the 48 vines at Ardeonaig House Hotel a 'vineyard' stretches the description
somewhat, but if global warming is set to continue, this might be the first of many in
Scotland. See website for more details.

Ashey Vineyard

Ashey Road, Ryde, Isle of Wight, PO33 4BB
Telephone: 01983 611357
Fax: 01983 563328
Contact: Bob Pakes
Vineyards: 2.45 hectares
Grape varieties: Not known
Not open to the public.

Ashwell Vineyard

East Street, Bovey Tracey, Devon TQ13 9EJ
Telephone: 01626 830031
E-mail: bill.riddell@ukgateway.net
Contact: Bill Riddell, Diane Riddell
Vineyards: 0.0365 hectares
Grape varieties: Regent, MA, Seyval blanc
Not open to the public.

Astley Vineyards

Astley, Stourport-on-Severn, Worcestershire DY13 0RU
Telephone and fax: 01299 822907
Website: www.astley-vineyards.co.uk
Contact: Jonty Daniels, Janet Baldwin
Vineyards: 2 hectares
Grape varieties: Kerner, MA, Siegerrebe, Bacchus, Sauvignon blanc
Open to visitors Monday and Thursday to Saturday, 10 am to 5 pm. Sunday, 12 noon to 5 pm. Closed Tuesday and Wednesday. At other times by appointment.

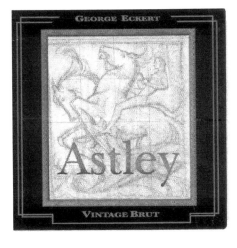

Astley Vineyards is situated in an area that possibly has historical connections with viticulture, as the steep, south-facing slope adjacent to the Norman church in Astley is known as The Vineyard and could have been connected to the Benedictine Monastery that existed locally until the reign of Henry V. In 1971 local solicitor Michael Bache and his wife Betty planted some experimental vines at a time when a vineyard in this relatively northern part of the UK was a true rarity. They trialled the vines for eight years before planting a 2-hectare commercial block in 1979. In 1993 the current owners, Jonty Daniels and Janet Baldwin, bought the vineyard.

The site, which is within 750 metres of the western bank of the River Severn and 5 kilometres south of Stourport-on-Severn, is north-facing and situated at 55 metres above sea level. The soil is sandy loam derived from old red sandstone. Prior to vines being planted, the land was unimproved permanent pasture and before the war was a cherry orchard. The natural fertility of the site is low and with a density of vines of around 1,730 per hectare and no additional fertiliser, yields are inherently low.

Currently, Astley only produces white wines, although there are plans to test Pinot noir for both sparkling wines and rosé. There are currently an impressive nine wines on their wine list including dry, off-dry, medium-dry and sweet, as well as a sparkling wine made from Kerner. All wines are made at Three Choirs and have been since the first vintage. Since 1996, all Astley wines have achieved Quality Wine status, a record that I doubt anyone else in the English Wine world can match, and their record at winning awards and medals is an enviable one. The longevity of their wines is shown by the fact that a *1984 Kerner* won the 'Best off-dry wine' at the 2000 Mercian Vineyards Association's competition. In 2009 their *2008 Late Harvest* dessert wine won 'Wine of the Year' and a Gold medal (the only one awarded) in the SWVA's competition.

Avalon Vineyard

The Drove, East Pennard, Shepton Mallet, Somerset BA4 6UA
Telephone: 01749 860393
E-mail: pennardorganicwines@mail.com
Website: www.pennardorganicwines.co.uk
Contact: Hugh Tripp
Vineyards: 0.91 hectares
Grape varieties: Seyval blanc, Orion
Open to the public. See website for details.

Avonleigh Organic Vineyard and Orchard

c/o 14 Otago Terrace, St Saviours Road, Bath, Avon BA1 6SX
Location of vineyard: BA15 2RD
Telephone: 01225 867119 and 01225 312762
Contact: Di Francis 07503 999906   E-mail: vineyard@avonleighorganics.co.uk
Contact: Ingrid Smith 07775 129205   E-mail: wine@avonleighorganics.co.uk
Website: www.avonleighorganics.co.uk
Vineyards: 2.44 hectares
Grape varieties: Orion, Pinot noir, Rondo, Dornfelder, Chardonnay, Seyval blanc
Open to the public. See website for details.

The vineyard and orchard are located on a south-facing slope just outside the beautiful historic Saxon town of Bradford-on-Avon. The soil is predominantly clay on limestone which provides a high level of nutrients to the vines and trees but also allows good drainage. The vineyard and orchard were planted in 2005/6 on agricultural land that had been setaside for a number of years. Conversion to organic status was started immediately which meant that the land had to be cultivated and prepared without the use of any chemicals. The vineyard and orchard are registered with the Soil Association and received full organic status in 2006.

The grape varieties were selected to produce the sorts of wines this vineyard wants to specialise in – sparkling, rose and white – but also with some regard to the disease resistance of the vines. The first crop of grapes was harvested in 2008 producing 730 bottles of rosé and 400 bottles of sparkling wine. The rosé received a Bronze award in the 2009 EWOTYC and the sparkling will be available to purchase early in 2010.

They have also planted a commercial orchard predominantly for eating apples but the intention is to juice a percentage of the fruit as well as in the future making a cider.

Avonwood Vineyard

Seawalls Road, Sneyd Park, Bristol, Avon, BS9 1PH
E-mail: vineyard@avongorge.co.uk
Contact: Peter Walters
Contact: Ingrid Bates 07779 085420 E-mail: ingridbates@mac.com
Vineyards: 0.2 hectares
Grape varieties: MA, Schönburger, Pinot noir
Not open to the public.

Backbury House Vineyard

Checkley, Hereford, Herefordshire HR1 4NA
Telephone: 01432 850255
Mobile: 07528 474114
Contact: John Lee
Vineyards: 0.3 hectares
Grape varieties: Phoenix, Seyval blanc
Open by appointment.

Bardfield Vineyard

Great Lodge, Great Bardfield, Braintree, Essex CM7 4QD
Telephone: 01371 810776
Fax: 01371 811398
E-mail: alanjordan@thegreatlodgeexperience.com
Website: www.thegreatlodgeexperience.com
Contact: Alan Jordan
Vineyards: 1 hectare
Grape varieties: Bacchus, Reichensteiner
Open to the public. See website for details.

Barnsgate Manor Vineyard

Herons Ghyll, Uckfield, East Sussex TN22 4DB
Telephone: 01825 713366
Fax: 01825 713543
E-mail: info@barnsgate.co.uk
Website: www.barnsgate.co.uk
Contact: Keith Johnson
Vineyards: 1.417 hectares
Grape varieties: Rondo, Reichensteiner
Open to the public. See website for details.

Barnsole Vineyard

Fleming Road, Staple, Canterbury, Kent CT3 1LG
Telephone: 01304 812530
Mobile: 07770 482883
E-mail: vineyard@barnsole.co.uk
Website: www.barnsole.co.uk
Contact: Dr John Danilewicz
Vineyards: 1.2 hectares
Grape varieties: Reichensteiner, Huxelrebe, Regent, Rondo, Pinot noir Précoce
Open to the public. See website for details.

Barnsole Vineyard was planted by the Danilewicz brothers in 1993 after some 16 years of research into both varieties and growing systems. The vines are planted on a south-facing site between 17 and 20 metres above sea level in the middle of the Kentish fruit and vegetable growing area known as 'The Garden of England'. The soil is heavy loam on clay and the vines are planted on a 2 x 1.8 metre double Guyot system. Every effort is made to achieve high fruit quality by developing a large leaf area and by careful canopy management to compensate for the cooler UK climate. At one time there were several vineyards in the immediate area – Ash Coombe, Staple St James, St Nicholas and Three Corners – but one by one they have gone and Barnsole is the sole survivor. The winery at Barnsole is well equipped and insulated with a crusher and de-stalker, Willmes WP500 pneumatic press, stainless steel tanks with a total capacity of 13,000 litres and GAI eight-head rotary filler. There are also two separate insulated wine stores. White grapes are crushed and given 12 to 24 hours skin contact with pectinase treatment to obtain as much varietal character as possible. Red grapes undergo long fermentation on the skins to produce dark wines with a firm tannic character.

Barnsole Vineyard, Staple, Canterbury

Generally four wines are produced under the 'Canterbury Choice' label: two dry white wines, 'Dry Reserve' (Reichensteiner) and 'Kent Classic' (Huxelrebe); a medium dry white wine, 'Pilgrim's Harvest' (a blend of the above two grape varieties); and a red wine, 'Red Reserve' (blend of the three red grape varieties but mainly Rondo). All wines produced over the past 11 years have achieved official Quality Wine status except for the red wines which were classified as Regional Wines until Regent and Rondo became approved for Quality Wine production. The 2003 'Red Reserve' and 2002 'Kent Classic' both obtained Silver medals in the South East Wine of the Year Competition, the latter also being awarded the Charles Laughton Trophy for the second best wine in the competition. The 2003 and 2007 'Red Reserve' and 1998 'Pilgrim's Harvest' also achieved Silver medals in the EWOTYC. Twelve Bronze medals have also been obtained in this competition.

Battle Wine Estate

Leeford Vineyards, Whatlington, Battle, East Sussex TN33 0ND
Telephone: 01424 870449
E-mail: pam@battlewineestate.co.uk
Website: www.battlewineestate.com
Contact: Pam Butcher
Vineyards: 8.5020 hectares
Grape varieties: Reichensteiner, Pinot noir, Schönburger, Blauer Zweigeltrebe, Kerner, Huxelrebe
Not open to the public.

Bearley Vineyard

The Beeches, Snitterfield Road, Bearley, Stratford-upon-Avon, Warwickshire CV37 0SR
Telephone: 01789 731676
E-mail: bearleyvineyard@aol.com
Contact: Richard Le Page, Jo Le Page
Vineyards: 0.5384 hectares
Grape varieties: Pinot noir Précoce, Seyval blanc, Regent, Rondo
Not open to the public.

Beaulieu Vineyard

John Montagu Building, Beaulieu, Brockenhurst, Hampshire SO42 72N
Telephone: 01590 614621
Fax: 01590 612624
E-mail: estate@beaulieu.co.uk
Website: www.beaulieu.co.uk
Contact: Rachel Pearson
Vineyards: 1.8 hectares
Grape varieties: Bacchus, MT, Reichensteiner, Huxelrebe
Vineyard open by appointment.
Beaulieu Vineyard is now leased by Roger Marchbank (Coach House Vineyard, David Balls (Marlings Vineyard) and Jeremy Broyd (keen to learn).

Beaulieu Abbey and its vineyard occupy a special place in the history of viticulture in the UK. Legend has it that following a dream in which King John (1199–1216) was beaten by a group of monks because of his oppression of them, he gave them a tract of land on his royal hunting grounds on the south coast known as *Bellus Locus Regis*, meaning 'the beautiful place of the King'. The monks, who came from France, rechristened it in their own language as Beuli. It was King John's only religious foundation. The Cistercians, an enclosed order, are required to provide their own food, drink and clothing and, being from a winegrowing country, it was only natural that they should plant a vineyard. How good the wine was though, is debatable. The only clue we have is that during a visit by the king, on being offered the local wine, he tasted it and then called his steward and said 'send ships forthwith to fetch some good

French wine for the Abbot'! During the turmoil of Henry VIII's dispute with Rome, the monastery was dissolved and the monks and their vineyard disappeared. It re-appeared in the mid-eighteenth century and there are records showing that brandy was produced, but this appears to have been a short-lived revival.

Lord Montagu inspecting the crop from Beaulieu Vineyard in about 1965

As has already been recounted, the modern vineyard at Beaulieu was planted by Lieutenant-Colonel Robert and Mrs Margaret Gore-Browne in the spring of 1958 when they planted four rows of Müller-Thurgau and Seyval Blanc as well as a few Gamay Noir Hâtif des Vosges, Précoce de Malingre and Madeleine Sylvaner. These they bought from Brock and his account books show a sale to the Gore-Brownes on 24 December 1957 of £112 worth of vines – a nice Christmas present! The vineyard was gradually expanded with more of the same, plus some Wrotham Pinot. By 1960/1 they had almost 5½ acres (2.23-hectares). Their first vintage, in 1961, was a rosé and was apparently well received. They also experimented with Baco No.1, Brandt, Pirovano 14, and Cascade (this despite the fact that Mrs Gore-Browne had heard that: *it was prohibited by the Common Market as it is said to have an injurious effect upon the liver* – a scare story put out by the anti-hybrid growers in France) but by 1967 had decided to eliminate the experimental varieties – no doubt due to poor performance.

Margaret Gore-Browne was a great supporter of British viticulture, and in particular Welsh viticulture (she came from strong Welsh stock) and in September 1965 she helped Lewis Mathias and George (or was it Gwilym?) Jones, together with the Development Corporation for Wales, form a Welsh Vine Growers Association. This Association does not seem to have prospered, and at some stage obviously died out. In 1967, she wrote a small book called *Let's plant a vineyard; 6000 vines, 600 or 60 or 6* published by Mills and Boon (which in itself sounds unlikely given this publisher's current reputation) in which she mentions some vineyards in Wales, one in Glamorganshire which was destroyed by a herd of Welsh mountain goats and another two in Carmarthen and Pembroke where: *healthy vines had mysteriously died due to vibration and drying out of the grafts on the long journey.* In the EVA newsletter of 1970, she is shown as the owner of '1,000 plus vines at Lamphey in Pembrokeshire' and '1,100 vines at Trimsaran in Carmarthenshire'. Whether any of these vineyards survived to produce wine is not known. The Gore-Brownes' success with their 'Beaulieu Abbey' wine continued throughout the 1960s with reports of 7,000 bottles in 1966, 1,800 bottles in 1967 and 8,000 bottles in 1968. The wine was made in a small, but well-equipped winery, built in the vineyard at Beaulieu, which is still there and used today as a wine store. The Gore-Brownes continued to run the vineyard until January 1974 when it was given to Margaret's godson, Lord Montagu's eldest son, Ralph. It was then taken over by Beaulieu Enterprises Ltd, and is adjacent to the National Motor Museum tourist attraction. Visitors wishing to see the vineyard need to make an appointment.

The Gore-Brownes were involved with the fledgling English Vineyards Association and Margaret donated a magnificent silver bowl, the Gore-Browne Trophy, in memory of her husband, who died in 1973. This trophy has been awarded annually to the top wine in the national competition since 1974. Margaret Gore-Browne died in 1976.

The Montagu family have been supporters of English Wine for many years, and at one time maintained another small vineyard at Blackfield, Southampton, called The King's Rew Vineyard. Belinda, Lady Montagu (Lord Montagu's first wife) was Vice-President of the English Vineyards Association from its founding in 1967 until 1977 and the first English Wine Festival (catalogue above) was staged at Beaulieu on 14–15 September 1974. Lord Montagu became President of the EVA in 1981 on the retirement of Sir Guy Salisbury-Jones.

The current vineyard, which is on the same site as that planted by the Gore-Brownes, consists of 1.8 hectares of vines. The oldest vines were planted in 1980 and various sections have been replanted over the years, the latest being in 2000. The vines are all planted on a 3.6 x 1.8-metre GDC system. Over the years, the wines have been made in a number of wineries: Merrydown, Lamberhurst and Lymington. Today a sparkling wine – Beaulieu Bubbly – is made at Stanlake Park and still wines, dry or medium-dry, are made at Setley Ridge. In 2009 the vineyard was leased for five years by three local growers, Roger Marchbank (Coach House), David Balls (Marlings) and Jeremy Broyd. The Seyval blanc have been grubbed and in future, the wines will be made at Marlings and Setley Ridge.

Beeches Hill Vineyard

3 Margaret's Cottages, Beeches Hill, Bishop's Waltham, Hampshire, SO32 1FE
Telephone: 01489 892356
E-mail: Richardharris388@btinternet.com
Contact: Richard Harris, Nancy Harris
Vineyards: 0.1 hectares
Grape varieties: Schönburger, Seyval blanc
Not open to the public.

Beeches Vineyard

Beeches, Upton Bishop, Herefordshire HR9 7UD
Telephone: 01306 886124
Mobile: 07770 908391
E-mail: info@beechesvineyard.com
Website: www.beechesvineyard.com
Contact: Karin Wilkins
Vineyards: 0.202 hectares
Grape varieties: MA, Regent, Rondo, Triomphe, Seyval blanc
Not open to the public, but please email for details of wines for sale.

Beenleigh Manor Vineyard

Owls Roost, Beenleigh, Harbertonford, Totnes, Devon TQ9 7EF
Telephone. 01803 732305
Fax: 01803 732979
E-mail: mark@sharpham.com
Contact: Mark Sharman
Vineyards: 0.13 hectares
Grape varieties: In polytunnels – Cabernet Sauvignon, Merlot
Open by appointment. Wines are available from Sharpham Vineyard.

Bewl Water Vineyard

Little Butts Lane, Cousley Wood, Wadhurst, East Sussex TN5 6EX
Telephone: 01892 782045
Mobile: 07768 510131
E-mail: d.corney@hotmail.co.uk
Contact: David Corney
Vineyards: 2.6135 hectares
Grape varieties: Bacchus, Pinot noir
Not open to the public.

Biddenden Vineyards

Gribble Bridge Lane, Biddenden, Ashford, Kent TN27 8DF
Telephone: 01580 291726
Fax: 01580 291933
E-mail: info@biddendenvineyards.co.uk
Website: www.biddendenvineyards.com
Contact: Julian Barnes
Sales: 07595 081634
Vineyards: 8 hectares
Grape varieties: Ortega, Huxelrebe, Bacchus, Schönburger, Reichensteiner, Pinot noir, Gamay, Dornfelder
Open to the public. Free guided tour for individuals on the third Saturday of each month, April to October. Booking essential. See website for further details.

Biddenden Vineyards is the oldest commercial vineyard in Kent, vines having first been planted there in 1969. Richard and Joyce Barnes, parents of the current owner, came from their native Lancashire in 1958 to what was then a compact fruit farm. In 1969 they planted a small area of vines (0.135 hectares) as an experiment and had their first vintage in 1972. Today the area under vines has expanded to 8 hectares. The

site is between 52 and 65 metres above sea level, south and south-east facing in a small sheltered valley. Most of the vines are GDC trained, originally chosen in order to help with frost protection. Over the years, Biddenden wines have been a very established part of the English wine scene, winning numerous awards and medals, including, in 1987, the Gore-Browne Trophy for their 1986 Ortega. Their latest award was for the 2008 Ortega medium-dry which won a Gold medal, plus the Jack Ward Memorial Salver (best wine from the previous vintage) and the Berwick Trophy (best unchaptalised wine) in the 2009 EWOTYC. Their 2008 Ortega Dry also won a Gold medal.

As well as producing English wine, Biddenden Vineyards, also produces (and I suspect sometimes relies upon) over 500,000 litres of high-quality, farm pressed apple juice every year and over 350,000 litres of Kentish cider. The award-winning cider produced has an alcohol level of 8.4 per cent and is made from a blend of culinary and dessert apples grown on a local farm. The apple juice, non-carbonated and free from additives, is also made from culinary and dessert apples and is of an exceptionally high quality. The business is very much a family run one, with the second generation of Barnes now running the show, with the third generation helping out when needed. It was good to see them celebrate their 40th anniversary this year.

Geneva Double Curtain trained vines at Biddenden Vineyards, Kent

Binfield Vineyard

Forest Road, Wokingham, Berkshire RG40 5SE
Telephone: 01344 411322
Fax: 01344 488622
E-mail: sales@championwine.co.uk
Website: www.championwine.co.uk
Contact: John Hickey
Vineyards: 2.0243 hectares
Grape varieties: Scheurebe, Pinot noir, Chardonnay
Open to the public. See website for details.

Birchenwood Vineyard

Brook, Lyndhurst, Hampshire SO43 7JA
Telephone: 02380 812595
Mobile: 07831 315838

Fax: 02380 812595
E-mail: feabriggs@aol.com
Contact: Joan Briggs
Vineyards: 2 hectares
Grape varieties: Pinot noir, Dornfelder, Triomphe, Bacchus, Reichensteiner
Open by appointment.

Bishop's Waltham Vineyard

Tangier Lane, Bishop's Waltham, Southampton, Hampshire SO32 1BU
Telephone: 01489 896803
E-mail: johnyoules@hotmail.com
Contact: John Youles
Vineyards: 2 hectares
Grape varieties: Schönburger, Triomphe, Pinot noir, Rondo
Open by appointment.

Bishop's Waltham Vineyard was established on a bare site by the John Youles in 1982. Subsequently, planning permission for a house was applied for and was granted, and in 1986, having built a house and an adjacent winery, the first crop was harvested. The vineyards originally covered 4.14-hectares, but they have now been reduced to 2-hectares. The wine is made on site.

Black Dog Hill Vineyard

Clayes, Underhill Lane, Westmeston, West Sussex BN6 8XG
Telephone: 01273 844338
Mobile: 07710 572974
E-mail: anjanolan@aol.com
Contact: Anja Nolan
Vineyards: 4.9203 hectares
Grape varieties: Chardonnay, Pinot noir, Pinot Meunier, Rondo, Dunkelfelder
Not open to the public.

Blackdown Hills Vineyard

Oaklands Farm, Monkton, Honiton, Devon, EX14 9QH
Telephone: 01404 47442
Fax: 01404 45539
E-mail: r.boote@btinternet.com
E-mail: marcelle.boote@btinternet.com
Website: www.blackdownhills-vineyard.co.uk
Contact: Roger & Marcelle Boote
Vineyards: 1.5 hectares
Grape varieties: Pinot noir Précoce, Reichensteiner, Dunkelfelder, Auxerrois, Rondo, Bacchus, Triomphe, Chardonnay
Open to the public. See website for details.

Bluebell Vineyard Estates

Glenmore Farm, Sliders Lane, Furners Green, East Sussex TN22 3RU
Telephone: 01825 790395
Mobile: 07785 333417
Fax: 01825 790395
E-mail: bluebellvineyardestates@gmail.com
E-mail: andrewjhope@gmail.com
Contact: Andrew Hope
Vineyards: 3.79 hectares
Grape varieties: Pinot noir, Chardonnay, Pinot Meunier
Not open to the public.

Bodiam Vineyard

Court Lodge Farm, Bodiam, East Sussex TN32 5UJ
Vineyards: 1.8219 hectares
Grape varieties: Auxerrois, Bacchus, Blauburger, Faberrebe, Kerner, Optima, Ortega, Pinot noir, Regner, Reichensteiner, Seyval blanc
Not open to the public.
Vineyard rented by Sedlescombe Organic Vineyard.

Bolton Castle Vineyard

Bolton Castle, Leyburn, North Yorkshire DL8 4ET
Telephone: 01969 623981
Fax: 01969 623332
E-mail: info@boltoncastle.co.uk
E-mail: tom@boltoncastle.co.uk
Website: www.boltoncastle.co.uk
Contact: Tom Orde-Powlett
Vineyards: 0.2 hectares
Grape varieties: Rondo
Open to the public. See website for details.

Bookers Vineyard

Bolney Wine Estate, Foxhole Lane, Bolney, West Sussex RH17 5NB
Telephone: 01444 881575   Fax: 01444 881399
E-mail: sam@bookersvineyard.co.uk
E-mail: info@bookersvineyard.co.uk
Website: www.bookersvineyard.co.uk
Contact: Samantha Linter
Tours and tastings: Susan Monro and Jules Churchill 01444 881894
Vineyards: 16.8 hectares
Grape varieties: Rondo, Pinot noir, Pinot gris, Dornfelder, Chardonnay, Dunkelfelder, MT, Schönburger, Würzer, Merlot
Open to the public. See website for details of tours and tastings.

Bolney Wine Estate was started by Janet and Rodney Pratt in 1972 when 1.2 hectares of vines were planted and is today run by their daughter, Sam Linter. The site is around 150 metres above sea level, faces south and south-west and the soil is a mixture of mostly sandstone and a little clay. The vineyard has slowly been expanded since those early days and now extends to 16.8 hectares, the latest 3.5 hectares of vines having been planted in 2009. In 2005 a brand new winery was completed with help of a DEFRA grant which takes them some way towards their intended goal of making top-quality white and red still wines and traditional method sparkling wines. The sparkling wines are aged for a period of at least 2 to 3 years. Bookers produce a wide range of wines, red, white and rosé, and over the years a number of awards and medals have been gained.

Wide-trained vines at Bookers Vineyard

Borough Hill Farm Vineyard

Wiggaton, Ottery St. Mary, Devon, EX11 1PZ
Telephone: 01404 811006
Mobile: 07966 490517
E-mail: graham@boroughhill.eclipse.co.uk
Contact: Graham & Kathy Archer
Vineyards: 2.646 hectares
Grape varieties: Nine varieties – too many to remember!
Not open to the public.

Bosue Vineyard

St Ewe, St Austell, Cornwall PL26 6EU
Telephone: 01726 843159
Mobile: 07721 689378
E-mail: p.sibley@cornwallwines.co.uk
Website: www.cornwallwines.co.uk
Contact: Paul Sibley
Vineyards: 1.5 hectares
Grape varieties: Orion, Phoenix, Rondo, Regent, Johanniter
Open to the public. See website for details.

Bosue Vineyard was first established in 1996 with some experimental varieties, with further plantings in 1999, 2004, 2005 and 2009. The vineyard is in a sheltered south-facing valley, on a good loam soil and considerable effort is expended in the management of the canopy in the summer months to control vigour. Spraying is kept to a minimum on these disease-resistant varieties, with the emphasis on feeding the vines through foliar feeds and *botrytis* control. The wines are made in a winery on site, and the policy is to retain the delicate fruit flavours by fermentation control and cooling. Both white and red still wines are produced, which gain Regional status, and they also produce a sparkling wine, usually made from Orion.

This is a family run operation and visitors are always welcome, though it is always advisable to ring first to ensure that someone is there and to obtain directions as there are no signs to Bosue! Wines can be tasted and bought at the winery and are available in local wine merchants, farm shops, restaurants and hotels.

Bothy Vineyard

Frilford Heath, Abingdon, Oxfordshire OX13 6QW
Telephone: 01865 390067
E-mail: office@bothyvineyard.co.uk
Website: www.bothyvineyard.co.uk
Contact: Sian and Richard Liwicki
Vineyards: 2.0243 hectares
Grape varieties: Albalonga, Findling, Huxelrebe, Optima, Ortega, Perle, Rondo, Dunkelfelder, Dornfelder, Acolon, Bacchus, Solaris, Regent
Open to the public. See website for details.

Bothy Vineyard was established thirty-one years ago by the late Roger Fisher and his wife, Dorothea, and continues a tradition of wine making in the Vale of the White Horse, Oxfordshire, dating back at least to medieval times. The excellent microclimate, deep sandy soils, long-ripening season, careful cultivation and mature, low-yielding vines help produce wines of consistent depth and quality.

The Liwicki's philosophy is to produce the highest quality wines from grapes cultivated in as an environmentally friendly way as possible. The former has been borne out by the fact that Bothy wines have won the award for the best white wine in

the Thames region over several years. In 2008, Bothy's Paradox won a national trophy – the Berwick Trophy for the best unchaptalised wine – which was produced from Ortega and Findling grapes.

In 1978 six grape varieties were planted at the vineyard on 1.2145-hectares of land. These are vinified and blended to produce a variety of dry and off-dry white wines in the on-site winery. Today 2.0243-hectares are under cultivation. The current owners, Sian and Richard Liwicki, have introduced new grape varieties which will enable a wider range of styles to be produced. However, the dry and off-dry whites will remain the backbone of this boutique vineyard.

The grapes are picked as late as possible in the Autumn to ensure maximum ripeness and flavour, and the wines are often not chaptalised. Careful cooling during fermentation and minimum intervention means that the aromatic notes of the rosé and white wines are captured, while the blending of various red varieties and the assiduous use of oak means that the vineyard's first red (the 2008) will be an event to savour.

Bourne Farm Vineyard

c/o Sandhurst Vineyards, Hoads Farm, Crouch Lane, Sandhurst, Cranbrook, Kent TN18 5PA
Location of vineyard: Bourne Farm, Bourne Lane, Sandhurst, Kent, TN18 5NT
Telephone: 01580 850296
E-mail: ca.nicholas@btinternet.com
Website: www.sandhurstvineyards.co.uk
Contact: Anne Nicholas, Chris Nicholas
Vineyards: 4 hectares
Grape varieties: Chardonnay, Pinot noir, Pinot Meunier
Not open to the public. Vineyard under contract to Hush Heath Estate.

Bow-in-the-Cloud Vineyard

Noah's Ark, Garsdon, Malmesbury, Wiltshire SN16 9NS
Telephone: 01666 823040
E-mail: wine@bowinthecloud.co.uk
Website: www.bowinthecloud.co.uk
Contact: Keith Willingale
Vineyards: 1.24 hectares
Grape varieties: Bacchus, Seyval blanc, Schönburger
Open by appointment only.

Bow-in-the-Cloud Vineyard is planted on very well-drained soil, well sheltered by woodland and is an ideal location for vines. In 1992 Keith and Esther Willingale planted three varieties of vines, initially trained on double Guyot, but later converted to GDC. Their grapes are taken to Three Choirs and halfpenny Green wineries for processing and to date their wines have done well, all qualifying for Quality or Regional Wine status and several have already won awards. Two of their wines were chosen by Malmesbury Town Council for the reception and lunch during the visit of HM the Queen in December 2001, their sparkling was selected for the inauguration of the High Sheriff of Gloucestershire at Gloucester Cathedral in April 2007, and their pink sparkling is currently used as a welcome gift to honeymooners at the nearby and über-posh (2 Michelin Stars plus host of other awards) Whatley Manor Hotel. A rent-a-vine scheme has recently been started.

Bow-in-the-Cloud Vineyard is in a unique geographical location, being in the hamlet of Noah's Ark. As Noah (the one with the ark) planted the first vineyard, Keith claims to have the second at Noah's Ark, and the presentation of the wine develops this theme with the bubbly and blend being named 'Cloud Nine', and the single varietals being named 'Arkadian'.

Keith Willingale amongst his
vines at Bow-in-the-Cloud

Breaky Bottom Vineyard

Rodmell, Lewes, East Sussex BN7 3EX
Telephone: 01273 476427
E-mail: breakybottom@btinternet.com
Website: www.breakybottom.co.uk
Contact: Peter Hall
Vineyards: 2.2 hectares
Grape varieties: Seyval blanc, Chardonnay, Pinot noir
Open by appointment. See website for details.

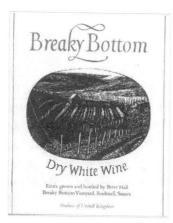

In many ways Breaky Bottom is the archetypal English vineyard: the name is slightly quirky, the site is very picturesque, it is situated down the end of a long, rough, very English track[1], and it appears small in a compact, cosy sort of way. Oh – and I almost forgot – it manages (usually) to produce wines of interest and quality. However, as ever, there is more behind the image than meets the eye. I first met its owner, Peter Hall (no, not the theatrical one) in early 1977, a few weeks before I planted my first vines at Tenterden. Having spent the previous two years training in Germany, I guess he thought I knew something about viticulture and he asked for my advice about his vines which had just been sprayed (by his then father-in-law) with hormone weedkiller. We have been friends ever since.

Hall, a graduate of Newcastle University and sometime pig farmer, started the vineyards at Breaky Bottom in a fit of enthusiasm in 1974, planting three main varieties: Müller-Thurgau, Reichensteiner and Seyval blanc. His first vintage in 1976 was ruined by another winery into whose hands he had delivered his grapes (I think that it is now long enough ago to state that it was Lamberhurst Vineyards) and since then he has always made his own wines. The winery is housed in a lovely old Sussex flint barn (built in 1827) that sits square in the middle of his vines, waiting for the harvest. Today, there are stainless steel tanks, a 1.5 tonne Vaslin press, a seven-head filler and all the other paraphernalia required in a small winery. In recent years, improvements have been made to the storage facilities and there is now a temperature-controlled wine store to hold maturing stocks of sparkling wine (plus home-made *cassis* – a constituent of his very successful *Kir Royale*)..

---

[1] After over 30 years of visiting Breaky Bottom and hitting the undersides of each and every one of my cars, I am pleased to say that in July 2009 the track was greatly improved. It's not quite the *autostrada del sol* but its getting close!

The history of calamities that have struck Breaky Bottom over the years seem to have induced a Job-like patience in Peter and he doggedly refuses to give in: the spray drift already mentioned ruined one harvest; damage from supposedly beneficial chemical sprays ruined another; an underground fungus attacked the roots of some young vines which destroyed them; infestations of grape-eating badgers and pheasants took their share of the crop; extensive flooding and soil deposits from further up the valley brought damage and destruction on an unimaginable scale (at one stage Peter and family had to move into a mobile home for two years); and small, conical snails managed to eat their way through hundreds of young vines. However, all of these have been endured, insurance claims have been made and won, grapes have been harvested and wines made.

Peter's approach to winemaking has changed little over the 30 years that he has been making wine. In essence, it is to let the grapes speak for themselves, a practice possibly inherited from his French mother. In the first two decades, when only still wines were made, the vineyard would be netted against birds and the grapes allowed to ripen at their own pace. The grapes were then harvested by a loyal band of friends, carefully pressed, allowed to ferment with the minimum of physical disturbance and left on the lees to gain some extra character. After that they were bottled in as calm a way as possible. Both de-acidification and the use of *süss-reserve* were avoided. Occasionally wines were oaked with chips, which added another layer of complexity. This style of winemaking brought individual results and the wines, austere in their youth, gradually developed as they matured and often turned from ugly ducklings into quite nice swans. His best (still) wines had an austere, Loire-like quality, with plenty of body and character, rather like their maker. Many Breaky Bottom wines aged exceptionally well and could be even better after ten years in bottle - they were often compared to the wines from *Savennières*. Those made from Seyval blanc had a *goût de terroir* not found in other wines from this variety and we often joked that it was due to the volumes of Old Holborn that were consumed in their making. In 1994, the first bottle-fermented sparkling wine was made and since then, sparkling wines have become a larger and larger part of the output until today, still wines are no longer made. Over the years he has built up a loyal clientele and rarely has a problem selling what he produces.

Breaky Bottom wines have notched up quite an impressive list of medals and awards and although Peter is not one to set great store by winning competitions, they are some sort of recognition that his wines do have commercial appeal. His 1989 Seyval blanc won the 1990 South East Wine of the Year Competition, the 1990 Seyval blanc won Gold at the 1993 IWSC and the 1992 Seyval blanc Oaked Fumé won Silver in the 1996 IWC and Silver in 1996 and Gold in 1997 in the EWOTYC. The 1995 Seyval blanc won a Silver and the 1996 won a Bronze in the EWOTYC, together with the UKVA's Best Presentation Trophy. In the 2003 EWOTYC the first medal was awarded to a Breaky Bottom sparkling wine, a Silver for the *1999 Cuvée*

Remy Alexandre (named after his late brother) and his sparkling wines are regularly ordered by the Government Hospitality for serving at official functions. In recent years, some of the older vines have been grubbed-up and replaced with Chardonnay and Pinot noir. These are just starting to yield and will hopefully add a little something extra to the wines in the years to come. In the 2008 EWOTYC Peter won two Silver and one Bronze medals and in the 2009 SEVA competition, his *2005 Cuvée Brian Jordan* (named after a late friend) won the Charles Laughton Trophy (runner-up award) and a Gold medal.

Yields at Breaky Bottom have been very variable and occasionally non-existent and those that know Peter wonder at his stamina. However, he has managed over the years, with much hard work and help from friends and family, to keep going and one has to admire his tenacity. In 1994, he and his wife Christina managed to buy the farm (he was previously a tenant) and thus make the future a little bit more certain. Although he has had to give up smoking and his intake of hard spirits seems to have lessened somewhat, I don't think he is ready to give up yet and whenever I am down there, there is always talk of what should be done in the future. There are very few UK vineyards of over 30 years old still run by their original owners, and it is a great testament to Peter's (and Chris's) stamina that Breaky Bottom is one of them. I hope to be able to share a glass or two with them for many years to come.

Breaky Bottom Vineyard keeping its head below the parapet

Brick House Vineyard

Brick House Farm, Mamhead, Exeter, Devon EX6 8HP
Telephone: 07802 246270
E-mail: gary.bullard@btopenworld.com
Contact: Gary Bullard
Vineyards: 0.6552 hectares
Grape varieties: Pinot noir, Faberrebe, Regent, Sauvignon blanc, Cabernet Sauvignon, Merlot
Not open to the public.

Bridewell Organic Gardens

The Walled Garden, Wilcote, Oxfordshire OX7 3EB
Telephone: 01993 864530 and 01993 868313
E-mail: info@bridewellorganicgardens.co.uk
Website: www.bridewellorganicgardens.co.uk
Contact: Alex Taylor
Vineyards: 0.93 hectares
Grape varieties: Orion, Phoenix and Regent
Open by appointment only. See website for details.

Bridewell Organic Gardens is an innovative and award-winning charity operating in West Oxfordshire, providing land-based therapeutic support to adults who are suffering from a range of mental health illnesses. Their objective is to improve the emotional well-being of clients and to help them rebuild lives.

Since their formation in 1994, Bridewell has operated from a walled garden, provided by a local estate. In 1999 they acquired a further 2-hectare site adjacent to the garden that is now one of the few organic, and probably the only therapeutic, vineyards in the country. The vineyard is registered with Organic Farmers and Growers Ltd, one of the leading organic certification bodies in the UK.

The vineyard was first planted in 2001 with Orion and Phoenix grapes varieties and the first vintage was in 2004. As there is no winery on site, the grapes are sent to Davenport Vineyards in East Sussex who are one of the few UK wineries processing organic grapes. Both still and sparkling wines are produced.

Brightwell Vineyard

Rush Court, Shillingford Road, Wallingford, Oxfordshire OX10 8LJ
Telephone: 01491 832354 and 01491 833605
Mobile: 07771 516376
Fax: 01491 832354
E-mail: wines@brightwines.co.uk
Website: www.brightwines.co.uk
Contact: Bob and Carol Nielsen
Vineyards: 4.5 hectares
Grape varieties: Bacchus, Dornfelder, Chardonnay, Reichensteiner, Pinot noir, Huxelrebe, Dunkelfelder
Wine store open on Fridays, Saturdays and Sundays, 12 noon to 6 pm. At other times by appointment. See website for details.

Brightwell Vineyard is planted on the flinty chalk greensand and gravel of the Thames Valley and is ideal for vines. The site, on the south side of the Thames, sits in the upper Thames Valley bowl sheltered by surrounding hills and is consequently one of the driest areas of the UK. The vineyard was planted between 1987 and 1990 with six varieties, all grown on the GDC trellising system. The current owners, Bob and Carol Nielsen, bought the vineyard in 1999, renovated it and have changed some of the vine varieties, expanding the area planted with Chardonnay and, in 2006, planting Pinot noir. They have also built and equipped a winery which was first used for the 2008 harvest.

Brightwell now produces three different white wines, a rosé, a red and a traditional method sparkling Chardonnay. Their wines have been successful in winning awards at home and abroad: Silver medal, Nîmes 2006; Gold and Silver medals, Angers 2007; Runner-up, Tesco Drinks Awards 2008; Bronze medal Decanter WWA, London 2007, Commended IWC 2008. Brightwell wines are now sold abroad.

Brightwell Vineyard, Oxfordshire – GDC trained vines

Brinsbury College Vineyard

c/o East Clayton Farm Trust, Penlands Vale, Steyning, West Sussex BN44 3PL
Location of vineyard: RH20 1DL
Telephone: 01903 814998
E-mail: hobo@farmersweekly.net
Contact: Robin Hobson
Vineyards: 1.2 hectares
Grape varieties: Bacchus, Rondo
Not open to the public.

Keeping the birds at bay at
Brinsbury College!

Broadfield Court Vineyard

Bowley Lane, Bodenham, Herefordshire HR1 3LG
Telephone: 01568 797483   Fax: 01568 797859
E-mail: enquiries@broadfieldcourt.co.uk
Website: www.broadfieldcourt.co.uk
Vineyards: 5.4656 hectares
Grape varieties: Huxelrebe, MA, MT, Reichensteiner, Seyval blanc
Open to the public: See website for opening details.

Broadway Green Farm Vineyard

The Broadway, Petham, Canterbury, Kent CT4 5RX
Telephone: 01227 700058
Mobile: 07801 551553
E-mail: richard@cammegh.com
Contact: Annette Cammegh
Vineyards: 0.6073 hectares
Grape varieties: Pinot noir, Chardonnay
Not open to the public.

Brook Farm Vineyard

Brook Farm, Cock Lane, Brent Eleigh, Sudbury, Suffolk CO10 9PB
Telephone: 01787 248590
Mobile: 07870 340033
E-mail: info@lavenhamheritageproducts.co.uk
E-mail: chrisanddenise@homecall.co.uk
Website: www.lavenhamheritageproducts.co.uk
Contact: Nick Thomson or Denise Thomas
Vineyards: 3.739 hectares
Grape varieties: Bacchus and Pinot noir Précoce
Open by appointment.

The initial 0.5-hectare of Brook Farm Vineyard was planted by Nick Thomson in 2002 as part of a new farming venture as he gradually retired from a city career. Further plantings in 2005 and 2008 increased the numbers of vines to around 10,000 and each time a 50:50 split of Bacchus and Pinot Noir was maintained as these varieties have proved they enjoy the gentle south-facing slope and grow well in the chalky boulder clay.

The first two plantings are supported by wooden trellising but its questionable longevity persuaded Nick to use steelwork throughout the new section. The vines crop on a VSP Double Guyot training system and each year they have produced excellent quality, clean grapes. Although these have been sold to other wine producers so far, future plans are to make wines that will complement the farm's other products which include Red Poll beef, Suffolk lamb, Ixworth chicken, Appleyard duck and free range eggs. The older vines share their field with a small orchard of eight heritage varieties of apple tree that are pruned to a traditional, open-centred shape with the apples being sold as top-fruit and high quality juice. The vineyard fits well into the mixed farm, enabling labour and machinery to be shared with the other enterprises in the business and the long term nature of their planting adds further ecological benefits to the rich flora and fauna of the farm.

Broxbournebury Vineyard

c/o 35 Park Avenue, Palmers Green, London, N13 5PG
Location of vineyard: Cock Lane, Hoddesdon, Hertfordshire, EN11 8LS
Telephone: 020 8886 2168
Mobile: 07503 461113
E-mail: wdmartin.knight@blueyonder.co.uk
Contact: Martin Knight
Vineyards: 1.6 hectares
Grape varieties: Seyval blanc, Reichensteiner, Pinot noir, Huxelrebe, Faberrebe, MT
Open to the public by appointment.

Bryn Ceilog Vineyard

c/o Fairfield, 14 Clinton Road, Penarth, Vale of Glamorgan CF64 3JB, Wales
Location of vineyard: Beggan Farm, Leckwith, Vale of Glamorgan CF11 8AS
Telephone: 029 20711017
E-mail: ian.d.symonds@btinternet.com
Contact: Ian Symonds
Vineyards: 1.8 hectares
Grape varieties: Orion, Phoenix, Reichensteiner, Bacchus, Findling, Kernling, Rondo, Dornfelder, Regent
Not open to the public.

Budds Farm Vineyard

Budds Lane, Wittersham, Tenterden, Kent TN30 7EL
Telephone: 01797 270245
Fax: 01797 270 113
Mobile: 07785 997816
E-mail: charlie@charlieparsons.co.uk

Budds Farm Vineyard, Kent with Wittersham church in the distance

Burnt House Wines

Lansdowne, Hound House Road, Shere, Surrey, GU5 9JJ
Mobile: 07980 306575
E-mail: ken@kinsey-quick.com
Contact: Ken Kinsey-Quick
Vineyards: 4 hectares
Grape varieties: Chardonnay, Pinot noir, Cabernet Sauvignon, Merlot, Sauvignon blanc
Not open to the public.

Burwash Weald Vineyard

Burnt House Farm, Burwash Weald, Etchingham, East Sussex TN19 7LA
Telephone: 01424 441979
Mobile: 07836 655570
Contact: Peter Etherton
Vineyards: 1.255 hectares
Grape varieties: Bacchus, Pinot Meunier, Huxelrebe
Open by appointment.

Buzzard Valley Vineyard [2]

37 Shirrall Drive, Drayton Bassett, Tamworth, Staffordshire B78 3EQ
Telephone: 0121 3081951
Fax: 0121 323 2805
E-mail: buzzardvalley@btconnect.com
Website: www.buzzardvalley.co.uk
Contact: André Jones
Vineyards: 2.8 hectares
Grape varieties: Rondo, Regent, MA, Pinot noir, Reichensteiner, Seyval blanc, Phoenix
Open to the public. See website for details.

Ivan and Pat Jones came to the site in 1962 as dairy farmers and over the years, along with their family, have committed themselves to arable farming, market gardening and also, during the 1980s, the growing of flowers for drying and dyeing. This business grew very big and now occupies the same site but caters for trade only. As dried flowers were gradually replaced by silk flowers in the 1990s, much of the land was freed up, allowing them to plant Christmas trees which are still sold today. Along with Christmas trees, more woodland was planted and eventually, in 2001, they decided to plant a vineyard.

Buzzard Valley Vineyard is set in the Staffordshire countryside overlooking beautiful woodlands and lakes on a south-facing slope. The soil is very clay-like and

2 Eagle-eyed readers (or perhaps that ought to be buzzard-eyed readers) will have noticed that although the vineyard name, website etc is 'Buzzard', singular (which I am assured is correct), the wine labels honour more than one buzzard.

gives a good character to the wine while holding sufficient water to keep the vines happy even in the driest of years. The 8,000 vines consist of the following varieties: Pinot noir, Rondo and Regent for red wines; MA, Reichensteiner and Seyval blanc for white and sparkling wines.

In 2006 Leon and André Jones started to build the modern winery and tea rooms which were opened in late 2007. Also during this time the nine lakes were completed, landscaped and stocked, with the fishing pegs being scheduled for early 2008. Future projects include a touring park and holiday lodges if all goes to plan. See website for details of opening hours, vineyards tours and talks, and functions suite.

Camel Valley Vineyard

Nanstallon, Bodmin, Cornwall PL30 5LG
Telephone and Fax: 01208 77959
E-mail: bob@camelvalley.com
Website: www.camelvalley.com
Contact: Bob Lindo
Vineyards: 7 hectares
Grape varieties: Seyval blanc, Pinot noir, Bacchus, Reichensteiner, Dornfelder
Open to the public. See website for details.

Camel Valley is the largest vineyard in Cornwall and in just under 20 years has established itself as among the best in the UK. Their toll of trophies, awards and medals, for both their wines and their tourism and business achievements is impressive, but only the just rewards of hard work, innovation and attention to detail.

The vineyards, situated on sunny slopes above the River Camel, are halfway between Cornwall's Atlantic and Channel coasts. In 1989, Bob and Annie Lindo planted Seyval blanc, Reichensteiner and Triomphe vines and won a Bronze medal in the EWOTYC with their first Seyval blanc vintage. Bob soon established himself as a more than proficient winemaker, winning the President's, Jack Ward, Waitrose and Dudley Quirk Trophies. In 2005 the IWC awarded a Gold medal for the *2001 Camel Valley Cornwall Brut*. Bob also won several Gold medals for tourism and in 2006 was awarded the Cornwall Tourist Board Gold Medal for outstanding services to tourism, won by Rick Stein the year before. The vineyard was also awarded a Gold Medal in the South West Business Challenge for 'creating wealth in the rural community'.

The vineyard has grown from the original 2 to 7 hectares with new plantings of Pinot noir, Dornfelder and Bacchus but the removal of the Triomphe. The winery, the first in the UK to be built with grant-aid from EU funds, soon grew to a 200,000-litre capacity with the arrival into the business of the next generation, son Sam Lindo in 2002. Sam, a maths graduate from the University of Bath, installed a cooling system for fermentations and in 2005 Camel Valley became the first UK winery to use Stelvin screwcaps for the still wines. Sam had previously done a spell at Kim Crawford's winery in New Zealand.

Camel Valley has concentrated on winning top awards and features regularly in everything from the IWC, Decanter WWA and the IWSC to the Japanese Wine Challenge. In the 2007 EWOTYC, Sam Lindo was the 2007 McAlpine Winemaker of the Year and won three Gold medals with his sparkling wines, together with the Gore-Browne and Vintner's trophies, another IWC Silver and topped the Decanter WWA with his Bacchus still wine. In the 2008 EWOTYC Camel Valley wines won three Gold Medals, this time two for sparkling wines and the third for a 2006 Bacchus, together with the President's, Dudley Quirk and Vintner's Trophies. However, coming second, only to Bollinger, in the World Sparkling Wine Championships in Verona was probably the most remarkable achievement for 2008. In 2009, Camel Valley scored a double first: simultaneous Gold Medals in both IWC and Decanter WWA for the *2005 Camel Valley White Pinot Sparkling*. They were awarded the IWC Trophy, an IWC Silver and three bronze medals. A further two Decanter WWA silvers and four bronzes, added the Dudley Quirk and the Waitrose Rosé Trophies, plus two Golds, four Silvers and four bronzes in the 2009 EWOTYC capped an outstanding year for Camel Valley. In addition to being featured on television by 'Oz and James' and 'Rick Stein, their wines have received praise in the past from several noted wine writers: Jancis Robinson said on the BBC's *Today* programme that she was 'very impressed' with the 1995 Red and Tom Stevenson so liked their Camel Valley Brut that after a tasting 'he and his wife – unusually – drank the whole bottle'. In 2009, Jane Macquitty became a convert describing their 2006 fizz: 'perfect now' and listing Camel Valley in her 'top 100 wines of the World under £25'.

Sam Lindo – McAlpine Winemaker of the Year 2007

The Camel Valley wine range is over 50 per cent bottle-fermented and includes a Seyval blanc blend, Pinot noir *blanc de blanc* and Pinot noir rosé. Bob and Sam very much try to be distinctive with a fruit forward style and are definitely not trying to make a Champagne substitute. The winery supplies 150 trade outlets including Rick Stein's restaurant empire and Waitrose and welcomes over 20,000 visitors a year to the winery. It has recently developed a sparkling wine for Fortnum and Mason.

Camel Valley is without doubt one of the leading wine producers in the UK and whilst in one sense quite old fashioned (in that they are not like the new sparkling-wine-only producers who appear to be ruling the English wine roost) with their devotion to visitors, tourists and local trade, as well as selling to the wider trade, they are the ideal template for what can be achieved with a vineyard in the UK. They make a wide and attractive range of wines – something for everyone you might say – and don't mind taking the money wherever it is. Opening to the public does not suit everyone and it can be hard work and sometimes wearing. But the rewards, the ability to create a viable business from a relatively few acres, are there. Bob, Annie and Sam are to be congratulated.

Carden Park Hotel Vineyard

Carden, Chester, Cheshire CH3 9DQ
Telephone: 01829 731000
Contact: Peter Pattenden 07920 597318
E-mail: peter.pattenden@devere-hotels.co.uk
Website: www.devere.co.uk/deluxe/Carden-Park
Vineyards: 1.2 hectares
Grape varieties: Seyval blanc, Pinot noir
Open to the public. See website for details

Carden Park Vineyard was originally planted in 1988 by serial entrepreneur John Broome (ex-Alton Towers and very ex-Battersea Power Station) who had bought the 550-hectare Carden Park Estate (his home was in a nearby village) and was busy turning it into one of the finest leisure and sporting estates in this part of Cheshire. I was engaged as his vineyard consultant and such was the lateness of the season, that the Seyval blanc vines had to be flown in from a nursery in Canada which was the only supplier that I could find at that time. This part of the world is known as the Cheshire Gap because it is sandwiched between the Welsh mountains to the east and the Penines to the west and is, given its northerly location, surprisingly mild. Warm winds come off the Irish sea down the Dee estuary and farmers are able to grow good crops of early vegetables. Seyval was chosen because of its hardiness – the climate tends towards the damp – and Madeleine x Angevine 7672 because of its earliness. The vines established well and there were three very good vintages – 1990, 1991 and 1992 (the last a huge 36,000 bottle's worth) which I made into wine at Lamberhurst and then Tenterden – before John Broome's business empire crumbled under the enormity of developing the wreck that was Battersea Power Station. He the entered into an IVA (Individual Voluntary Arrangement) with his creditors, owing somewhere in the region of £26m.

The hotel, golf courses and other leisure facilities that Broome had developed changed hands and are now part of the DeVere empire (owned by Altenative Hotels Group whose Chairman and significant shareholder is Hush Heath Vineyard owner Richard Balfour-Lynn). Estates Manager, Peter Pattenden and his team, have been given the task of resurrecting what remained of the 3.3-hectare vineyard. The cropping area is now down to 1.2-hectares and consists of both Seyval blanc and some newly planted Pinot noir.

Carpenters Vineyard

Carpenters, High Street, Norton-Sub-Hamdon, Somerset TA14 6SN
Telephone: 01935 881255
E-mail: mikecumbo@hotmail.com
Contact: Mike Cumberlege
Vineyards: 0.1012 hectares
Grape varieties: Siegerrebe, MA, Seyval blanc, Bacchus
Not open to the public.

Carr Taylor Vineyards

Wheel Lane, Westfield, Hastings, East Sussex TN35 4SG
Telephone: 01424 752501   Fax: 01424 751716
E-mail: sales@carr-taylor.co.uk
Website: www.carr-taylor.co.uk
Contact: David Carr Taylor Sales: Linda Carr Taylor
Winemaker: Alex Carr Taylor alex@carr-taylor.co.uk
Vineyards: 6.07 hectares
Grape varieties: Bacchus, Gutenborner, Kerner, MT, Ortega, Pinot noir, Reichensteiner, Schönburger
Open to the public all year round, every day 10 am to 5 pm. Closed from Christmas Day to New Year.
See website for more details.

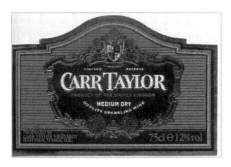

Carr Taylor Vineyards is one of the oldest vineyards in the UK, having been planted in 1973. It was also one of the first vineyards in the UK to use the GDC system of trellising and training (although not *the* first – Bernard Theobald at Westbury claimed that distinction). However, David Carr Taylor was one of the system's greatest protagonists and his enthusiasm for it persuaded many to follow his example.

The site at Westfield is less than 6 miles from the coast at Hastings and is well sheltered by the gentle rolling countryside as well as windbreaks positioned strategically throughout the vineyard. The initial plantings in 1973 consisted of Müller-Thurgau and Reichensteiner, and these gave their first crops in 1976. There was, at that time, no winery at Carr Taylor Vineyards and the grapes were processed at Lamberhurst Vineyards. Crops continued to be modest up until 1982, when a good crop of 56,000 bottles coincided with the installation of a winery. Vintage 1983 followed and was a huge year with Reichensteiner cropping at 15 tonnes per acre and a total harvest of some 186,000 bottles! This rapid increase in wine stocks enabled the Carr Taylors to really get to grips with their marketing, and since those days, their wines have seldom been out of the news.

Carr Taylor Vineyards is probably best known today for its bottle-fermented sparkling wines. Their first year of production was in 1983 when the ample crop gave them sufficient wine to start putting stocks away. Although not the first to make this type of wine – both Pilton Manor and Felsted produced very modest amounts in the early days of English wine production and Lamberhurst a bit later on – Carr Taylor was certainly the first to make serious commercial quantities of it, a fact that tends to get forgotten in these days of the mega-vineyards planted with Champagne varieties.

In the mid-1990s, the recession forced the Carr Taylors to look for additional backers and the vineyard went through uncertain times with a short-lived merger with both Chapel Down Wines and Lamberhurst Vineyards. Since then a new limited company, Carr Taylor Wines, has taken over the business, with David and Linda's son Alexander (winner of the 2005 Wine and Spirit Education Trust 'Vintner's Cup' – awarded to the top WSET Diploma student) in the winery.

Over the years since production started, Carr Taylor wines have been successful in many national and international competitions winning awards, medals and commendations in abundance. Their sparkling wines in particular have done well and in 1998, their NV Quality Sparkling was joint winner of the Country Landowners English and Welsh wine competition. In 1998 David Carr Taylor was awarded a Gold medal at the *Challenge International du Vin* in Bordeaux for his sparkling wines. In

1999 Alexander was awarded a gold medal and in 2008 a bronze medal in the same competition.

Carters Vineyard

Green Lane, Boxted, Colchester, Essex CO4 5TS
Telephone: 01206 271136
Fax: 01206 273625
E-mail: enquiries@cartersvineyards.co.uk
Website: www.cartersvineyards.co.uk
Contact: Ben Bunting
Vineyards: 2.61 hectares
Grape varieties: Bacchus, Chardonnay, Dornfelder, Dunkelfelder, Orion, Phoenix, Pinot noir, Reichensteiner
Open to the public. See website for details.

Castle Brook Vineyard

Cobrey Farms, Coughton, Ross-on-Wye, Herefordshire HR9 5SG
Telephone: 01989 562770
Fax: 01989 562622
Mobile: 07971 541775
E-mail: john@cobrey.co.uk
Website: www.wyevalleywine.co.uk
Contact: John Chinn
Vineyards: 2.43 hectares
Grape varieties: Chardonnay, Pinot noir, Pinot Meunier
Not open to the public.

Located on the south facing slopes of a old River Wye meander valley and possibly the site of a Roman vineyard, vines were first planted by the Chinn Family in 2004. Traditional champagne varieties are grown with the aim of producing top quality sparkling wines. The first release will be from the 2006 vintage and the wine is being produced by RidgeView.

Castlewood Vineyard

Castlewood Farm, Musbury, Axminster, Dorset, EX13 8SS
Telephone: 01297 552068
Mobile: 07812 554861
E-mail: robcorbett@hotmail.com
Contact: Rob Corbett
Vineyards: 1.01 hectares
Grape varieties: Pinot noir, Chardonnay, Riseling, Pinot Meunier, MA, Reichensteiner, Rondo
Open to the public by appointment. Also have self-catering accommodation.

Chalk Vale Vineyard

c/o Nyetimber Vineyard, Gay Street, West Chiltington, West Sussex RH20 2HH
Location of vineyard: Chalk Vale, Kings Somborne, Hampshire, SO20 6RE
See entry for Nyetimber Vineyard for contact details
Vineyards: 25.1 hectares
Grape varieties: Pinot noir, Chardonnay, Pinot Meunier
Not open to the public.

Nyetimber's Chalk Vale vineyard – planted May 2009

Chalksole Estate Vineyard

Chalksole Green Lane, Alkham, Folkestone, Kent CT15 7EE
Telephone: 01304 828881
Mobile: 07917 411588
E-mail: claire@chalksolevineyard.co.uk
Contact: Claire Joblin
Vineyards: 2.1342 hectares
Grape varieties: Chardonnay, Pinot noir, Pinot Meunier
Open by appointment.

Chanctonbury Vineyard

North Lane, Ashington, Pulborough, West Sussex, RH20 3DF
Telephone: 01903 892721
Mobile: 07930 641665
Contact: Hendryk Szterbin, Joanna Szterbin
Vineyards: 1.417 hectares
Grape varieties: Being replanted with red varieties
Not open to the public.

Chapel Down Wines

Tenterden Vineyard, Small Hythe, Tenterden, Kent TN30 7NG
Telephone: Office 01580 763033
Telephone: Shop and tours 01580 766111
Fax: 01580 765333
E-mail: sales@englishwinesgroup.com
E-mail: retail@englishwinesgroup.com
Website: www.chapeldownwines.co.uk
Contact: Frazer Thompson
Winemaker: Owen Elias
Vineyard Manager: Craig Daly
Visitor Services: Rebecca Hirst
Vineyards: See Kit's Coty Vineyard and Tenterden Vineyard
Open to the public. Guided tours May to October – booking is advised – and there is a very good wine and food shop, plus great catering facilities. See website for full details.

The first vines were planted at Tenterden Vineyard in 1977 when I returned to the UK having spent the previous two years in Germany with my wife and family. There, I had been working in a vineyard and winery (Schloss Schönborn in the Rheingau), studying at Geisenheim and formulating my plans for planting vines in England. The farm at Tenterden, at that time called Spots Farm, had been purchased by my then father-in-law in 1976 for us to establish a vineyard. The farm was chosen for its closeness to sea level, good light soil, its well-sheltered sites and the presence of buildings suited for conversion into a winery, wine store and farm shop. There was also a pair of cottages for us to live in. An initial 2.33-hectares of vines were planted with varieties selected in consultation with my mentor, Professor Helmut Becker from Geisenheim. The varieties were Müller-Thurgau, Reichensteiner, Gutenborner and Seyval blanc. All were planted on a 2.0 x 1.1 to 1.3-metre Pendlebogen system.

For the first vintage in 1979 a winery was installed in the old oast house on the farm and equipped with mainly second-hand equipment, the press being a 25-year-old Willmes pneumatic which I found in Germany. The next harvest, although not large, proved to be something of a milestone. The 1980 Spots Farm Seyval blanc, of which only 1,250 bottles were made, was, much to my astonishment, awarded the Gore-Browne Trophy for the English Wine of the Year. One of the features of this wine was its high level of natural carbon dioxide, achieved by stopping the fermentation before it was completely finished and sterile filtering it to retain some residual sugar. This early success gave the vineyard plenty of publicity (including a three-page colour spread in *The Sunday Times Magazine* with an interview conducted by a very young, pre-MW Jancis Robinson) which enabled wine sales to get off to a good start.

Over the next few years more vineyards were planted, a shop, tasting bar and functions room built in the barn where the hop-picking machine once stood and the farm opened to visitors. In 1980 my then wife, Linda, planned and planted a large herb garden as an additional visitor attraction. After the large 1983 harvest (50 tonnes of grapes from 3 hectares) it became obvious that the winery needed upgrading and expanding and a Chemo Harvest Trailer and Willmes UP1800 press with central filling were purchased. In 1986 we took a decision, which surprised many in the industry at the time, to sell the farm as a going concern to two businessmen, Bill Garner and Derek Todd, who had already dipped their toes in the viticultural water by buying Felsted Vineyard the year before. The reason for selling was simple: the bank manager wanted the deeds to our house if he was to extend the overdraft and we felt that was a step too far. At Easter 1986 the new owners took over, retaining me as winemaker and consultant. Garner and Todd immediately embarked on an impressive spending spree, making substantial investments in both the winemaking and visitor facilities, as well as expanding the vineyard acreage. The winery was equipped with Möschle stainless-steel tanks, all housed in the existing temperature-controlled cold store (built to store apples), a new Seitz Tauch-Stella bottle steriliser and a Tirax eight-head filler and a dozen new French *barriques* were bought. A large insulated bottling hall and wine store was erected, the shop was enlarged and the catering facilities improved.

The wines produced at Tenterden between 1980 and 1989 had their fair share of success in competitions: the Gore-Browne Trophy was won twice, in 1981 with the 1980 Seyval blanc and in 1991 with the oak-aged 1989 Seyval blanc Special Reserve; UKVA gold medals were gained in 1983 with the 1982 Müller-Thurgau Dry, 1982 Spots Farm Medium-Dry and 1982 Gutenborner; the President's Trophy went to the 1988 Tenterden Rosé in 1989; and the Wine Guild of the UK Trophy was awarded to the 1989 Seyval blanc Special Reserve. Tenterden wines were served at Downing Street and Lancaster House for a G8 summit and by the Queen at the Commonwealth Prime Minister's Conference in India.

Towards the end of 1989, Garner and Todd decided that the English wine business was not for them and the business and farm was put on the market. Just before the 1990 harvest it was bought by Malcolm Kay who already owned Ashburnhams Vineyard near Battle (now no longer) and needed processing facilities. Kay owned the vineyard until 1995, during which time more investment was made in the visitor facilities, in packaging, presentation and in marketing. Unfortunately, Kay's other business interests (property, hotels and restaurants) suffered badly in the recession and by mid-1992 he was effectively bankrupt. In early 1993 Kay entered into an Individual Voluntary Arrangement (IVA) with his creditors and the farm became the property of Dunbar Bank who had been his main lenders. For the next two years the vineyards suffered badly as money for sprays and general maintenance was short and only a little wine was made. The bank took almost no interest in what was going on and apart from the occasional telephone call, we were left alone. The visitor facilities remained open, generating enough income to pay the staff and I continued to make wine for contract customers and to bottle the stock of Tenterden wines from the 1990 and 1991 harvests. In September 1995, after over six months of negotiations with Kay and the bank, Chapel Down Wines Ltd purchased the business and property and proceeded to move their entire operation from Burgess Hill to Tenterden.

Chapel Down Wines traces its origins back to Chapel Farm Vineyard on the Isle of Wight, owned then, as now, by ex-Lloyds underwriter Anthony Pilcher[3]. This vineyard had been planted

and managed by Ken Barlow of nearby Adgestone vineyard and for a number of years the grapes had been incorporated into his wines. However, owing to a drop in Adgestone's sales, this arrangement had ended and Pilcher was contemplating what to do with his grapes. Jan Trzebski, owner of neighbouring Morton Manor vineyard (now also grubbed), suggested that a close friend of his, David Cowderoy, with whom he had been at Wye Agricultural College, might be interested in taking the grapes. David, son of Norman Cowderoy who had been growing grapes at Rock Lodge Vineyard since 1965, had recently returned from Australia where he had been studying winemaking at Roseworthy College.

Cowderoy's idea was to create what today we might call a 'virtual vineyard' by contracting out the grapegrowing to others and concentrating on the two aspects of the wine business that required the most expertise: winemaking and marketing. By sourcing grapes from a number of different vineyards spread about the UK and by making wines on a much larger scale than would normally (in the UK at least) be the case, economies of scale in production would be achieved which would enable the wines to be marketed at a competitive price. A company was formed in 1992 with Pilcher as Chairman, Nicky Branch, an accountant, as Managing Director, Carl Koenen, whose family had been in the UK wine trade since 1925 as Sales Director and Cowderoy as Winemaker. The winery would concentrate on making a new style of English wine and would also specialise in making sparkling wines, a product they felt was very suited to our climate. They would also offer contract winemaking services for making both still and sparkling wines.

To start with, the winery at Rock Lodge vineyards was used as a base and grapes from both Chapel Farm and other vineyards were purchased and made into wine. The company soon outgrew these premises and in 1993 a building on a factory estate in Burgess Hill was rented and speedily transformed into a winery. For the next two vintages this was home to the fledgling enterprise. As volumes grew and as stocks of maturing wines, especially sparkling, became larger, it was obvious that another move would have to be made. A chance conversation between Carl Koenen amd myself in February 1995 about the search for new premises led eventually to the company buying Tenterden Vineyards from the bank – the 25-hectare farm, vineyards, winery,

---

[3] Chapel Farm vineyard is due to be grubbed in 2009.

business and stock – for £500,000. Nicky Branch, in his characteristically flamboyant style and with his flair for financial engineering, managed to persuade Dunbar Bank to give the company a five-year loan covering 100 per cent of the purchase price at a 0 per cent interest rate for the first 12 months, rising (as I recall) by 1 per cent a year for the next five years. In September 1995, with the harvest already under way, the complete winery was shipped from Burgess Hill to Tenterden and re-assembled as best it could be, in between loads of grapes arriving to be pressed. I became a director of the company and made the wines coming from the vineyards at Tenterden itself and negotiated a deal whereby I could use the facilities to make and bottle wine for my contract winemaking customers.

The next five years were something of a roller-coaster in several different ways. Significant investments were made in both premises and facilities. The tank capacity was increased to over a million bottles, all stainless steel and mostly temperature controlled, as well as three inclined-plane drainage tanks for cold-soaking to extract maximum flavours from varieties such as Bacchus and Schönburger. New equipment was bought and put into service: an RDV filter, a bank of gyro-pallets for riddling sparkling wine, a semi-automatic disgorging and dosage line and new labelling and packaging equipment. New buildings for the winery, the public and for the increasing numbers of staff were erected or converted and acres of concrete were poured. Although they tended to get a bit forgotten in this winemaking and marketing led company, the vineyards were not totally neglected. Some of the older vineyards – those approaching 20 years old – were re-trellised and 1.77 hectares of new vineyards were planted with Dornfelder, Rondo and four clones of Pinot noir: 115, 667, 777 and the *teinturier* clone *Tête du Nègre* (their 2004 Pinot Noir which in 2006 won a EWOTYC Gold medal and the Theobald 'Best Red' trophy came from this vineyard).

In order to increase the volume of wine made, grapes were sourced from a very wide selection of vineyards around the UK. Chapel Farm on the Isle of Wight continued to be a major supplier, but others were brought into the fold. Piers Greenwood at New Hall Vineyards in Essex became (and remains) a significant supplier and for a time, Denbies sold around 50 per cent of its total crop to Chapel Down. In addition, a large number of smaller growers were signed up to grape-supply contracts and 1999 saw grapes from 26 different vineyards arrive at the winery. Amounts purchased varied according to the vintage and stock requirements, but it was usually in the 300–400 tonnes range, although it did rise to 600 tonnes in big vintages. In addition to winemaking on their own account, Chapel Down also made still and sparkling wines for a large number of growers.

From the outset, Chapel Down decided to break the mould of English winemaking and refused to make the easy drinking *ersatz-Liebfraumilch* that the other big vineyards (Lamberhurst, Denbies and Three Choirs were then the major players) seemed to think was what mass-market English wines ought to be. Chapel Down's wines tended to be slightly drier than most English wines, more akin to modern New

World styles, with acids under control. Oak was used in all its forms – barrels, staves and chips – with considerable success and large-scale malolactic fermentation and lees-ageing and lees-stirring (of still wines) was practised. Wines made from Bacchus became something of a trademark – the 1997 Bacchus won the Jack Ward Memorial Salver in the 1998 EWOTYC – and its red wines were most definitely a leap forward. The best reds were made either from super-ripe Rondo, usually sourced from Chapel Farm, or a blend of Rondo and Dornfelder. Their Epoch Reserve and Epoch I were among the very best UK reds at the time and Cowderoy's use of micro-oxygenation and his understanding of oaking certainly helped.

The first Chapel Down wine to feature in the EWOTYC medals list was the 1994 Epoch Reserve which won the Bernard Theobald Trophy for 'Best Red' and, in the 1995 IWSC, the 1993 Epoch I won the English Wine Trophy, the first (and only) red wine ever to have won this particular accolade. Chapel Down's performance in the 1999 UKVA competition was even better: the Gore-Browne Trophy, Jack Ward Memorial Salver and Dudley Quirk Memorial Trophy – all for their 1998 Bacchus, the Wine Guild of the UK Trophy for their 1997 Schönburger and the McNie Trophy for their non-vintage Downland Oak. In the 2000 EWOTYC, they again won the McNie Trophy as well as the Dudley Quirk Memorial Trophy with the Downland Oak. In late 1999, Cowderoy, who had always spent some of the spring months winemaking in the southern hemisphere, decided to leave Chapel Down to work for International Wine Services as manager of their team of flying winemakers. Owen Elias, his long-time assistant, took over as winemaker, assisted by two young winemakers, Andy Hollis and Hugh Girling. Despite Cowderoy's sometimes eratic working methods and general disregard for putting things back where they belonged or ever tidying up, his winemaking could not be faulted.

On the commercial front, life was not such a bed of roses. Although there were some significant sales coups – supplying British Airways with 20,000 litres at a time with a medium-dry white (Chapel Down Horizon) in quarter bottles for three years running was probably the best – getting quantities of English Wine onto supermarket and retailers shelves was never going to be easy, at least not at a price that made any commercial sense. Some retailers helped more than others – Waitrose featured one of the Chapel Down wines as 'Wine of the Month' (miraculously without demanding too much up-front marketing money) and managed to shift 29,000 bottles in just four weeks – but successes like this were memorable for their scarcity. On the whole, it was a tough slog for Koenen and his sales team (which waxed and waned according to the prevailing financial circumstances) and financially, life got tougher and tougher. Existing shareholders were asked for more funds, bank loans were re-negotiated and a feverish search went out for new investors, business angels, indeed anyone who might be interested in helping out.

In July 2000, after much negotiation, a 'merger' was announced between Chapel Down Wines, Lamberhurst Vineyards and Carr Taylor Vineyards (the last two being owned by Adrian Drewe and Simon Hume-Kendall from Stenoak Fencing who had previously purchased the Lamberhurst site and business) who joined together to form English Wines plc. In reality, this was a last-ditch attempt by Branch to rescue Chapel Down Wines from oblivion and in March 2001 he and Pilcher left the company, considerably the wiser and sadly, considerably the poorer. I decided to give up contract winemaking and, after 22 vintages in the same winery, vintage 2000 became my last.

Since the formation of English Wines plc, which became English Wines Group plc in January 2002, there have been several changes in the company. Frazer Thompson, previously in marketing at brewer Heineken, was brought in as CEO and appointed to the board in March 2002. In 2004 two new investors appeared: Nigel Wray, often described as a 'serial investor' and best known for his investments in Saracens Rugby Club, Domino Pizzas and the Prestbury property company, who ended up owning around 35 per cent of the company; and Richard Balfour-Lynn, Chief Executive of Marylebone, Warwick, Balfour, the company behind Malmaison Hotels, Hôtel-du-Vin, Liberty Stores and a number of other companies, who now owns around 11.5 per cent of the company. Balfour-Lynn also has his own vineyard at nearby Hush Heath Manor and produces the award-winning Balfour Brut Rosé (made at Chapel Down). The other major shareholder is the Chairman, ex-CEO of Thomson Travel, Paul Brett, with almost 23 per cent. In October 2004, the Chapel Down board was restructured. Drewe and Hume-Kendall resigned and sold their shareholdings and the board pared down to just five: non-executive Chairman, Paul Brett, CEO Frazer Thompson, Finance Director Richard Woodhouse, plus non-executives Wray and Balfour-Lynn[4].

Since 2004 Chapel Down has made slow but steady progress with a gradual reshaping of the company, more investments in the buildings and facilities and a gradual switch of emphasis towards more sparkling wine. The tank chiller refrigeration unit caught fire in August 2004 which caused a barn housing a large number of tanks to burn down. This meant that some of the winemaking shifted for a while to a temporary building which has now been replaced by a permanent one and a new labelling line installed in September 2008. Plans for a complete new winery seem to be on hold. Elias continues as winemaker and having won the EWOTYC McAlpine Winemaker of the Year Trophy in 2002, 2003, 2005 and 2006 has shown beyond doubt that he has a talent for the job. In 2007 alone, his wines gained a Gold, two Silvers, nine Bronzes and three Highly Commendeds, plus the Wine Guild and Tom Day trophies. In 2008, although no Golds, a tally of twelve Silvers and seven Bronzes is still a good total and in 2009, one Gold, eight Silvers, three Bronzes, one Highly Commended and the Wine Guild Trophy[5] for their *2006 Cinque Port Classic* still beats all other UK wine producers. They also do well in other areas: they were the

---

4   Richard Balfour-Lynn resigned as a director on 30 June 2009. He remains a shareholder.
5   The Wine Guild Trophy is awarded to the best, large production wine (10,000 litres or more) from a vintage other than the previous vintage.

2008 Taste of Kent winners and also won the 2009 Kent Small and Medium Sized Enterprise of the Year award.

Shop, tasting room and visitor facilities at Chapel Down, Tenterden

Chapel Down is the only UK winemaker to be quoted on the stock exchange (on the PLUS-Markets exchange) and is, at the moment, by far the largest UK wine producer by volume. Sales to 31 December 2008 were £2,337,041 (6% down on the previous year owing to the short 2007 vintage) with a pre-tax profit of £105,995, the second year in a row that the company has been profitable. In July 2009, the company rasised £1.1m (before expenses) to provide "additional working capital to purchase the increased supply of grapes, the acquisition of winery equipment to process them, the improvement of the car park, access road and other facilities at Chapel Down Winery and investments in developing exports and marketing materials." In the process, a PLUS-Markets listed company, Worship Street Investments, became a shareholder with just under 2% of the company.

In July 2008, a brand new, very classy restaurant was opened in what had been the café and functions area above the shop. 'Richard Philips at Chapel Down' is run by Michelin starred chef Richard Philips (his other restuarants are 'Thackeray's' in Tunbridge Wells and 'Hengist' in Aylesford, near Maidstone) and it is gaining great reviews and getting praise all over the place. Having eaten there three times, I can also say it is very good. The visitor facilities at Chapel Down – shop, tearooms, restaurant and friendly staff – are among the best in the country and certainly offer the newcomer a great introduction to English wine.

In late 2007, a 47-hectare block of land on the North Downs just south of the Pilgrim's Way near Bluebell Hill, Maidstone (see entry under 'Kit's Coty Vineyard') was purchased. This site, which had taken them some years to find, has very good, freely draining chalk soil and mostly slopes to the south, should provide some good fruit. In May 2008 it was planted with 122,500 vines – Chardonnay and Pinot noir (why no Pinot Meunier?) – at 2-metre row width by 1.2 metres in the row which equates to 29.4 hectares. The development of the vines has been quite slow – the hard winter of 2008/9 didn't help – and it will be 2011 before very much fruit is harvested here. This major investment of over £1.25 million opens another chapter in the Chapel Down story as up until now they have mainly relied on other growers to supply them with grapes. By 2010, Thompson has stated that they will be drawing grapes from around 200 hectares of vineyards with 20–30 per cent owned and up to 45 per cent managed by Chapel Down. At the moment they have seven vineyards (either in whole or in part) signed up on long-term contracts – Budds Farm, New Hall, Forstal Farm, Rosemary Farm, Sandhurst, Squerryes, and Tullens – and also buy grapes on an annual basis from several others. They are expecting to process 500-plus tonnes in 2009 for their own wines, as well as making wines for other vineyards under contract.

The history of Chapel Down reflects in many ways the history of the revival of UK viticulture. From enthusiastic, if under-capitalised beginnings via a series of owners, each of them pumping in funds to keep the place afloat (sometimes succeeding, sometimes not quite), to today's substantial business (at least by UK winegrowing standards) with a workforce of around 25 and wines available in over 200 outlets. I take some pride in having planted the first vines at Tenterden and while I can take no credit for its progress since 2000, I am pleased that it is where it is today and has not joined the ranks of those that are no longer. The future of course is unpredictable, but with a bit of luck, the continuation of global warming and the rise in popularity of, and demand for, English sparkling wine, I really hope that Chapel Down will be even bigger and even more profitable by the time I next update this guide.

Chapel Field Vineyard

Pilgrim's Barn, Chapel Road, Spooner Row, Wymondham, Norfolk, NR19 9LN
Telephone: 01953 602749
Contact: Mike McAully
Mobile: 07590 188488
E-mail: michael@designcompany.net
Contact: Chris Hatto
Mobile: 07882 792434
E-mail: helena.hatto@tiscali.co.uk
Website: www.chapelfieldvineyard.co.uk
Vineyards: 0.81 hectares
Grape varieties: Auxerrois, Pinot noir, Rondo, Bacchus
Not open to the public.

Charles Palmer Vineyard

c/o Wickham Manor, Wickham Rock Lane, Winchelsea, East Sussex TN36 4AG
Location of vineyard: Opposite lay-by off A269 just outside Winchelsea towards Hastings
Telephone: 01797 226216
Mobile: 07808 086480
E-mail: info@wickhammanor.co.uk
Website: www.charlespalmer-vineyards.co.uk
Website: www.wickhammanor.co.uk
Contact: Mason Palmer
Vineyards: 2 hectares
Grape varieties: Chardonnay, Pinot noir
Open to the public. See website for details.

Charlton Barrow Vineyard

Charlton Marshall, Blandford Forum, Dorset, DT11 9DD
Mobile: 07528 644396
E-mail: craigdoug1@hotmail.co.uk
Contact: Craig Clapcott, Richard Bonham Christie
Vineyards: 0.3 hectares
Grape varieties: Bacchus, Orion, Phoenix, Seyval blanc, MT, Sylvaner
Not open to the public.

Chevelswarde Vineyard

Chevel House, The Belt, South Kilworth, Lutterworth, Leicestershire LE17 6DX
Telephone: 01858 575309
E-mail: john@chevelswardeorganics.co.uk
Website: www.chevelswardeorganics.co.uk
Contact: John Daltry
Vineyards: 0.53 hectares
Grape varieties: Regent, Rondo, Solaris, Phoenix
Open to the public. See website for details.

Childrey Manor Vineyard

Childrey Manor, Wantage, Oxfordshire OX12 9PQ
Telephone: 01235 751244
Contact: T. Marks
Vineyards: 1 hectare
Grape varieties: Bacchus, Reichensteiner
Not open to the public.

Chilford Hall Vineyard

Linton, Cambridge, Cambridgeshire CB21 4LE
Telephone: 01223 895600
Fax: 01223 895605
E-mail: mark@chilfordhall.co.uk
Website: www.chilfordhall.co.uk
Contact: Mark Barnes
Vineyards: 7.2 hectares
Grape varieties: MT, Schönburger, Reichensteiner, Ortega, Pinot noir, Rondo, Regent, Siegerrebe, Dornfelder
Open to the public. See website for details.

Chiltern Valley Vineyard

Old Luxters, Hambleden, Henley-on-Thames, Oxfordshire RG9 6JW
Telephone: 01491 638330
Mobile: 07788 723835
Fax: 01491 638645
E-mail: donald@chilternvalley.co.uk
Website: www.chilternvalley.co.uk
Contact: Donald Ealand
Vineyards: 1 hectare
Grape varieties: Bacchus, MA, Reichensteiner
Open to the public. See website for details.

Chiltern Valley vineyard is perhaps best remembered as being one of only three UK wine producers ever to have been prosecuted by the Wine Standards Board (WSB). The problem arose with the 1992 vintage of their *botrytis* affected dessert wine, Old Luxters Noble Bacchus. The vineyard had achieved considerable success with this wine, winning a Gold medal and the President's Trophy for the 1989 vinage and a silver medal and the Jack Ward Trophy for the 1990 vintage. Many of us who tasted these wines were impressed by their quality, and especially interested by the subtle 'peachy' character that gave it a certain distinction. The 1992 vintage was again, good, but slightly sweeter and, more importantly, the peachy character was ever – perhaps even more so – present.

The previous vintages of this wine had been under 15% total alcohol (actual alcohol plus potential alcohol) and therefore could be sold as Table Wines. The 1992 vintage however, was over 15% total alcohol and therefore could only be sold as a Quality Wine. This meant that it had to go through the Quality Wine Scheme (QWS), then only in its second year of operation. The wine was duly entered, analysed by Geoff Taylor at Corkwise and presented to the tasting panel. At the time, I was running the QWS tastings and I assembled a tasting panel which included two Masters of Wine, Sir Guy Fison and Christopher Tatham. Both Taylor and I were very suspicious of this wine and we both felt that the impressive peachy character had taken a definite step upwards in concentration and character. At the tasting, both MWs, but especially Tatham, were astonished by the wine and Tatham immediately said that it had to have been flavoured with something to achieve that level of fruit character. When asked for his score for the wine, Tatham said that he couldn't give it one as he felt it wasn't made 100% from grapes. I told him to write this on his score sheet and the wine therefore could not be passed as a Quality Wine. The problem was handed over to the WSB.

The next stage in the saga was for the WSB to establish whether there was anything in the wine of a non-grape origin. No laboratory in the UK could be found to analyse the wine and, at a cost said to be around £700 per sample, two wines – the 1991 and 1992 vintages – were sent to Germany to be analysed. They were found to contain peach flavouring.

In August 1995 the case came to court, and we all assembled in High Wycombe Magistrate's Court. David Ealand and his winemaker, Peter Arguile, were both charged with adding peach essence to two wines and of failing to keep proper winemaking records After the usual presentation of evidence and cross-questioning, Arguile, who had argued in the dock that he had added the peach essence as an experiment and never expected the wine to be sold, was found guilty of adding the essence and of failing to keep adequate winemaking records i.e. he did not record that he had added the essence. He was fined £6,000 and ordered to pay £6,000 costs. Ealand was cleared of the charge of adding the essence but found guilty of the record keeping charge and fined £2,500 and ordered to pay £2,000 costs. On appeal, the charge against Arguile for adding the essence was turned around on the grounds that the wine had never been labelled and sold as English Wine.

Surprisingly, the court case, although reported in the Times, the Daily Telegraph and other organs of quality, created very little interest and whereas other wine scandals – the Austrian 'anti-freeze' and the Italian 'methanol' scandals come to mind – had a long-lasting effect upon the reputation of their country's wines, the effect upon the reputation of UK-grown wines was absolutely zero. The upshot of the case was that Ealand delved into the labelling regulations and continued to sell the offending wine, at £9.95 per half-bottle, as a 'flavoured grape-based drink' and went on to higher things with his winery and brewery, winning the Royal Warrant for supplying beer to Her Majesty, and establishing what appears to be a very successful business high in the Chiltern Hills. After the prosecution, some other wines produced at Chiltern Valley came under scrutiny and many of us thought that a wine from the now-defunct Cane End Vineyard near Reading also displayed a remarkable fruit character. Arguile left the winery and went on to found a drinks production consultancy called Liquid Solutions.

As might be expected, Chiltern Valley Vineyard withdrew from membership of the UKVA and concentrated rather more on its brewing and functions business. The vineyard today is very neglected and most of the wines they make – I assume – must come from bought-in grapes. Ealand continues to run it, aided by his son Donald, although the complete business has been on the market (for £3.5m) for some while. A buyer, Christina Domecq – not of the Sherry firm, but co-founder and Chief Executive of SpinVox – apparently signed a contract and paid a 10% deposit but problems at her company (it is alleged that the software she helped develop to convert voice messages to text messages doesn't work properly) caused her to pull out of the deal before completion, leaving behind her £350,000!

Chingley Oast Vineyard

Chingley Manor Oast, Flimwell, Wadhurst, East Sussex TN5 7QA
Telephone: 01580 879528   Mobile: 07711 077366
Fax: 01580 879736
E-mail: gfbowden@gmail.com
Contact: Graham Bowden
Vineyards: 0.8093 hectares
Grape varieties: Reichensteiner, Würzer
Not open to the public.

Church Farm Vineyard

Church Lane, Shrawley, Worcestershire, WR6 6TS
Telephone: 01905 620283
Mobile: 07515 538357
E-mail: curradinebarns@btconnect.com
Contact: John Ballard
Website: www.curradinebarns.co.uk
Vineyards: 3.2927 hectares
Grape varieties: Seyval blanc, Pinot noir, Pinot noir Précoce
Curradine Barns is a wedding venue. See website fro details.

Clawford Vineyard

Clawton, Holsworthy, Devon, EX22 6PN
Telephone: 01409 254177
Mobile: 07554 124700
E-mail: john.ray@clawford.co.uk
Website: www.clawford.co.uk
Contact: John Ray
Vineyards: 0.2 hectares
Grape varieties: Not known
Not open to the public.

Claydon Vineyard

c/o 3 Sandhill Farm, Middle Claydon, Buckinghamshire, MK18 2LD
Location of vineyard: The Allotments, Botolph Claydon, Buckinghamshire
Telephone: 01296 730730
E-mail: richesjohn@hotmail.com
Contact: John Riches
Vineyards: 0.1 hectares
Grape varieties: Rondo, Seyval blanc
Not open to the public.

Clayhill Vineyard

c/o 3 Tyle Cottages, Lower Burnham Road, Latchingdon, Chelmsford, Essex, CM3 6HE
Location of vineyard: Lower Burnham Road, Latchingdon, Chelmsford, Essex, CM3 6HF
Telephone: 0800 211 8515
Fax: 01621 743753
Mobile: 07771 995460
E-mail: info@clayhillvineyard.co.uk
E-mail: dale@clayhillvineyard.co.uk
E-mail: vicky@clayhillvineyard.co.uk
Website: www.clayhillvineyard.co.uk
Contact: Dale Symons, Vicky Symons
Vineyards: 4 hectares
Grape varieties: Chardonnay, Pinot noir
Open to the public at certain times. see website for details.

Clees Hill Vineyard

Clee St. Margaret, Craven Arms, Shropshire, SY7 9DT
Telephone: 01584 823441
E-mail: cleeshillvineyard@hotmail.com
Contact: Robin Talbot
Vineyards: 0.2 hectares
Grape varieties: MA, Seyval blanc, Reichensteiner, Rondo, Regent, Léon Millot
Not open to the public.

Clocktower Vineyard

Twickenham Road, Redlees Park, Isleworth, London, TW7 6DW
Vineyards: 0.0237 hectares (estimate)
Grape varieties: Riesling, Pinot noir, Dunkelfelder
Not open to the public (although you can see it from the road).
http://www.hazelmurray.com/vineyardvision/vineyard-story.php.

Clocktower Vineyard was planted in 1996 by Dominic Di Chiera and Hazel Murray (then one of Sky TV's weather presenters and also a garden designer) and consists of

100 vines planted in a public park on what was once an allotment. The first vintage was in 1999 (only 23 bottles!) which was made by Will Davenport. Although the vineyard appears to be looked after, it is not known by whom or what happens to the grapes. If anyone knows – please make contact!

Clocktower Vineyard, Isleworth, London

Coach House Vineyard

Salisbury Road, West Wellow, Romsey, Hampshire SO51 6BW
Telephone: 01794 323345
E-mail: roger.marchbank@btinternet.com
Contact: Roger Marchbank
Vineyards: 0.4 hectares
Grape varieties: Bacchus, Reichensteiner
Open by appointment.

Coach House Vineyard was started in 1989 by Roger and Margaret Marchbank and is just inside the New Forest National Park. The vines are planted in the very sandy soil, typical of the area, at around 80 metres above sea level. The Bacchus and Reichensteiner vines, the first to be planted, have been joined by enough Pinot noir and Triomphe to enable the production of rosé wines in addition to the standard dry white. The grapes are crushed and wines produced by Roger in the winery at Setley Ridge Vineyard in nearby Brockenhurst.

Cobland Mill Estate

Eglarooze, Torpoint, Cornwall PL11 3DY
Telephone: 01503 230656
Mobile: 07739 212171
E-mail: malcolm.cross@gmail.com
Website: www.coblandmill.co.uk
Contact: Malcolm Cross
Vineyards: 1.62 hectares
Grape varieties: Phoenix, Orion, Reichensteiner, Regent, Merlot, Syrah
Open to the public. See website for details.

Cobland Mill Estate, which extends to about 4.45-hectares, is located in a hidden valley only a few hundred metres from the coastal path on the Rame Peninsula in South East Cornwall. The Old Mill was built in approximately 1830 but had lain abandoned as part of the Port Eliot Estate until 2001. Since then it has been converted into a house adjacent to the vineyard. At the centre of the estate is a large lake converted from an old reservoir originally constructed in 1922 to bring fresh water to the citizens of Torpoint. The 1.62-hectares of vines are on a south-facing slope immediately above the lake which is stocked with coarse fish and features abundant wildlife. The rest of the estate is woodland which is gradually being restored.

The vines were planted in three phases. Initially in 1998, 750 vines were planted in the 'old' vineyard consisting of equal proportions of Phoenix, Orion and Reichensteiner and in 2003, 250 Seyval Blanc were added. The remaining half of the total area was planted in 2007 with 300 Regent vines for red wine production, plus an additional planting of 500 Phoenix. A further planting of Merlot and Syrah (Shiraz) was made in 2007. These vines will be protected with polytunnels for red wine production after 2009. Currently the estate produces the 'Cobland Mill White' which is a dry fresh wine with delicate fruit aromas. It is hoped to produce the first red wines in 2010. For harvest 2009 a new winery will open which will incorporate the restored water wheel from the old mill. This will only handle red wines to start with, with whites still being made at Yearlstone.

Coddington Vineyard

Ledbury, Herefordshire HR8 1JJ
Telephone: 01531 640668
E-mail: denis@coddingtonvineyard.com
Website: www.coddingtonvineyard.com
Contact: Denis Savage
Vineyards: 0.6 hectares
Grape varieties: Bacchus, Ortega, Pinot gris
Open to the public. See website for details.

Coggeshall Vineyard

c/o Danes Vale, Wethersfield, Essex, CM7 4AH
Location of vineyard: West Street, Coggeshall, Essex CO6 1NS
Telephone: 01371 851509
Mobile: 07941 224938
E-mail: janemohan@yahoo.co.uk
Website: www.coggeshallvineyard.co.uk
Contact: Jane Mohan
Vineyards: 0.4 hectares
Grape varieties: Faberrebe
Not open to the public. Wine centre to be be built in 2010-2011.

Commonwood Vineyard

Weavers Loft, Commonwood, Nonely, Wem, Shropshire SY4 5SJ
Telephone: 01939 236193
E-mail: alangoddard@madasafish.com
Contact: Alan Goddard
Vineyards: 0.8065 hectares
Grape varieties: Phoenix, Rondo, Regent, Dornfelder
Open by appointment.

Compton Green Vineyard

c/o Maxstoke, Aston Ingham, Ross-on-Wye, Herefordshire HR9 7LS
Location of vineyard: Between Newent and Redmarley, Gloucestershire
Telephone: 01989 720465
E-mail: alan@oastlers.fsnet.co.uk
Contact: Alan Oastler
Vineyards: 2.1 hectares
Grape varieties: MA, Phoenix, Triomphe, Seyval blanc, Schönburger
Not open to the public.

Compton Green Vineyard is owned by Alan Oastler who was influenced by the late
Gillian Pearkes, a renowned pioneer and prime-mover in the revival of viticulture in
the UK. The vineyard is situated in a rolling landscape, 60 and 75 metres above sea

Gloucestershire Regional Wine
Triomphe
11.5% vol   75cl ℮

Produced for Compton Green Vineyard Redmarley
Gloucestershire by 1473UK

level and facing south to south-east towards the Severn Valley in the lea of May Hill. The area around is very suitable for winegrowing and its high-grade, well-drained soil, is renowned for horticulture. Several successful vineyards are situated in the region, including Three Choirs, one of the UK's largest, and the winery where Compton Green's wines are made.

All earlier plantings are at a 2.75-metre row width, double Guyot trained, but the latest plantings – of the variety Phoenix – are GDC trained at a 3.35-metre row width. The reliable Madeleine Angevine – highly regarded in this area – is the major variety in the vineyard and produces characteristic wines, both dry and medium, crafted by the skilled Three Choirs winemakers. Triomphe only started to produce after about eight years but has excelled in 2003, 2005 and 2006. Seyval blanc, as elsewhere, has produced some fine sparkling wines in the past few years.

Congham Vineyard

Heath House, Hillington, King's Lynn, Norfolk, PE31 6BZ
Telephone: 01485 600153
E-mail: john.lilley@rocketmail.com
ContactJohn Lilley, Helen Lilley
Vineyards: 0.3035 hectares
Grape varieties: Rondo, Acolon, Orion, Phoenix
Not open to the public.

Cornish Garden Nurseries

Barras Moor Farm, Perran-ar-worthal, Truro, Cornwall TR3 7PE
Telephone: 01872 864380
E-mail: peter@afa-ltd.co.uk
Contact: Peter Hall
Vineyards: 0.5 hectares
Grape varieties: Not known.

Cotton Orchard Vineyard

Coton Orchard, Madingley Road, Coton, Cambridge, Cambridgeshire, CB23 7PJ
Telephone: 07808 161945
E-mail: info@cotonorchard.com

Contact: Albert Gazeley
Vineyards: 0.2 hectares
Grape varieties: Not known
Not open to the public.

Cottonworth Vineyard

Fullerton Farms, Cottonworth, Andover, Hampshire SP11 7JX
Telephone: 01264 860221
Mobile: 07825 664936
E-mail: jr@jrliddell.co.uk
E-mail: hughliddell@yahoo.co.uk
Contact: James Liddell, Hugh Liddell
Vineyards: 4.8 hectares
Grape varieties: Chardonnay, Pinot noir, Seyval blanc, Rondo, Regent, Riesling
Open by appointment.

Court Garden Vineyard

Orchard Lane, Ditchling, East Sussex BN6 8TH
Telephone: 01273 844479
Fax: 0871 2364601
E-mail: howard@corney.co.uk
Website: www.courtgardensfarm.co.uk
Contact: Howard Corney
Vineyards: 5 hectares
Grape varieties: Pinot noir, Chardonnay, Pinot Meunier, Pinot gris, Ortega, Dornfelder, Rondo
Open to the public by appointment.

Court Garden Vineyard was planted in 2005 on a south-facing slope in the middle of an ancient farm. Their 2007 sparkling wine will be available from the farm shop from December 2009.

Court Lane Vineyard

Ropley, Alresford, Hampshire SO24 0DE
Telephone: 01962 773391
Contact - Owner: Stephen Flook stephenflook@onetel.com
Contact - Vineyard Manager: Jeremy Broyd jeremybroyd@btinternet.com 07748 059831
Vineyards: 0.6 hectares
Grape varieties: MT, Reichensteiner, Seyval blanc, Huxelrebe
Not open to the public.

Cowley Estate Vineyard

c/o 14 Bowly Crescent, Siddington, Cirencester, Gloucestershire
Location of vineyard: GL7 5UH
Telephone: 01285 640974
Mobile: 07907 649098
E-mail: robertcowley@cowley-estate.com
Website: www.cowley-estate.com
Contact: Robert Cowley
Vineyards: 0.02 hectares
Grape varieties: Siegerrebe, Seyval blanc, Phoenix, MA, Chardonnay, Pinot noir Précoce
Not open to the public. See website for further information.

Coxley Vineyard

Coxley, Somerset BA5 1RQ
Telephone: 01749 670285
E-mail: max@orofino.freeserve.co.uk
Website: www.coxleyvineyard.com
Contact: Max Orofino, Vince Ferro
Vineyards: 1.6194 hectares
Grape varieties: Not known
Open to the public. See website for details.

Crawthorne Vineyard

Dewlish, Dorchester, Dorset, DT2 7NG
Telephone: 01258 817446
E-mail: justin@langhamfarm.co.uk
Contact: Jutsin Langham
Vineyards: 10 hectares
Grape varieties: Chardonnay, Pinot noir, Pinot Meunier
Not open to the public.

Croft Castle Vineyard

Yarpole, Leominster, Hereford, Herefordshire HR6 9PW
Telephone: 020 7435 9814 and 01568 780246
E-mail: notcomp@googlemail.com
Contact: Caroline Compton
Vineyards: 0.18 hectares
Grape varieties: Phoenix
Vineyard is within walled garden of Croft Castle (a National Trust property) and can be visited during their usual opening hours.
Website : www.nationaltrust.org.uk for details of opening dates and times.

Cross Tree Farm Vineyard

c/o The Court House, Litton Cheney, Dorchester, Dorset, DT2 9AW
Location of vineyard: Cross Tree Farm, Litton Cheney, Dorchester, Dorset
Telephone: 01308 482367
Concact: Arabella Spurrier 07818 052090
Contact: Steven Spurrier 07894 230470 & 020 7385 3855
E-mail: bellaspurrier@hotmail.com
E-mail: steven@stevenspurrier.com
Vineyards: 3.2 hectares
Grape varieties: Chardonnay, Pinot noir, Pinot Meunier
Not open to the public.

I am not quite sure to say who has planted this vineyard – whether its Steven Spurrier on his wife's farm or Bella Spurrier at the request (insistence?) of her husband, Steven. In any event, after quite a few false starts, the Spurriers-both have, between them, established 3.2 hectares of Champagne varieties on a chalky bankside at around 100-metres above sea level on Bella's farm in the little Dorset village of Litton Cheney, which is between Bridport and Weymouth and just under 3 miles from the coast. I say false starts, as Steven and I started talking in August 2006 about the cost of planting vines and then I was involved with two attempts to get French wine companies interested in the idea of planting a vineyard here. Firstly with Champagne house Duval-Leroy, who talked, visited and then (as they had done at Squerryes Court in Kent) offered such onerous terms that Steven declined to take up their offer, and then with the huge Burgundy-based wine company of Boisset. Again, after meetings and discussions, Boisset could not make sense of the economics (basing their sales projections on a £12 a bottle shelf price) and walked away.

After going down these two *cul-de-sacs* Steven bit the bullet and declared that he would do it on his own. Steven, of course, is one of the best-known characters on the British wine scene, having been the man responsible for what has come to be known as the 'Judgement of Paris' when he pitched top Californian wines against top French wines, the former fairly comprhehensively trouncing the latter, much to the annoyance of the French judges who took part. Since those heady days, Steven has made a name for himself as a man-about the tasting rooms of the world, as a journalist, a wine educator and as an a consultant editor to Decanter. He also has the distinction of having been at the LSE with a certain Mr. Michael Jagger!

Time will tell whether this site can produce good sparkling wine. They have chosen the best piece of land on the farm (that is to say the most sheltered) and if global warming continues as predicted, they ought to succeed. It is planned that the grapes will be taken to Ian Edwards at nearby Furleigh Estates for winemaking.

Crown Vines

Crown Farm House, 25 Mill Road, Burston, Norfolk IP22 5TW
Telephone: 01379 741081
Fax: 01379 740221
E-mail: crown.vines@virgin.net
Contact: Juliette Atkinson
Vineyards: 0.25 hectares
Grape varieties: Seyval blanc, MA, Pinot noir, Rondo, Regent
Not open to the public.

Cwm Deri Vineyard

Martletwy, Narberth, Pembrokeshire SA67 8AP, Wales
Telephone: 01834 891274
Fax: 01834 891464
E-mail: mike@cwm-deri.co.uk
Website: www.cwm-deri.co.uk
Contact: Mike Caine
Vineyards: 1 hectares
Grape varieties: MA, Seyval blanc, Triomphe
Open to the public. There is a vineyard and nature walk; restaurant and coffee shop; pet's corner; Caravan Club CL; and a holiday cottage. See website for full details.

Danebury Vineyard

Nether Wallop, Stockbridge, Hampshire SO20 6JX
Telephone: 01264 781851
Fax: 01264 782212
E-mail: liz@danebury.com
Website: www.danebury.com
Contact: Liz Vincent
Vineyards: 3 hectares
Grape varieties: Auxerrois, Schonburger, MA, Pinot gris
Open by appointment.

Davenport Vineyard

Limney Farm, Castle Hill, Rotherfield, East Sussex TN6 3RR
Telephone: 01892 852380
E-mail: will@davenportvineyards.co.uk
Website: www.davenportvineyards.co.uk
Contact: Will Davenport
Vineyards: 1.67 hectares
Grape varieties: Pinot noir, Auxerrois
Open to the public. See website for details.

Will Davenport, who also runs Horsmonden Vineyards (see separate entry) is one of the more serious and talented winegrowers in the UK today. After training at Australia's Roseworthy College, assisting in cellars in Alsace, California and Australia, helping at the International Wine Challenge and two years in the wine trade in London, he planted vineyards on his parent's farm at nearby Horsmonden in 1991 and at Limney Farm, a 15-hectare traditional cattle farm (managed under DEFRA's Countryside Stewardship Scheme) which helps promote wildflower meadows, traditional hedges etc) in 1993. All the vineyards are farmed organically, certified by the Soil Association, using minimum inputs of fungicides and no herbicides, insecticides or any artificial fertilisers. At Limney Farm there are 1.67-hectares of vines, planted in 1993, on a west-facing, heavy loam site on a 2.7 x 1.5-metre Double Guyot system.

The winery, set up in the farm's old dairy buildings, contains some of the best facilities and equipment in the UK. It has a Willmes WCP 1500 press (the only one in the UK), a Rotary Drum Vacuum filter, GAI monoblock filler, temperature-controlled sparkling wine storage building, fully automatic CDA labeller and full bottle-fermented sparkling wine facilities. All fermentations and storage of wine are in stainless steel. Will's approach to winemaking is to combine nature with technology, letting wines ferment and clarify slowly — sometimes this can take until the summer following the harvest — using as little sulphur dioxide as possible and allowing the natural fruit flavours to shine through. All wines are made to organic and vegetarian/vegan standards, finings are kept to a minimum (usually only Bentonite and sometimes no fining at all) and still wines are fermented using natural yeasts. Most wines are bottled without any filtration. De-acidification is completely avoided. Will also makes wine for several vineyards that do not have wineries and has achieved success with many of their wines as well.

The production from the original 1991 planting at the Horsmonden vineyard goes into the Horsmonden Dry white wine. A bottle-fermented sparkling wine, made from the Pinot noir and Auxerrois planted at Limney Farm specifically for the purpose, is sold as the Limney Estate sparkling wine. A red wine, the Diamond Fields Pinot Noir, is made (in tiny volumes) from younger vines grown at Horsmonden and matured in old oak barriques. All three wines carry the Limney branding and logo on the label. Will has also formed a partnership in 2004 with Duchy Originals Ltd to make an organic sparkling wine for them which today sells for £19.99.

Several of Davenport's wines have done well in both regional and national competitions, with every vintage of the Horsmonden dry wine gaining an award at the UKVA wine of the year competition since 1995. Highlights include twice getting into the top three in the Country Landowners Association's (CLA) competition, three times being shortlisted for the Waitrose Small Producer of the Year competition, 1st prize in the Rosé category at the 1999 English Wine Festival at Plumpton College for the 1998 Rosé, winning the Gold Medal in the 2007 Soil Association Organic Food Awards with the 2005 Horsmonden dry white, winning a Gold Medal in the 2009 EWOTYC with the 2005 Limney Estate sparkling wine (which only won a Bronze in the 2008 competition), plus many Bronze medals and commended wines in the International Wine Challenge, the SEVA and UKVA competitions. All of the still wines achieve Quality Wine status.

Will Davenport has established himself as one of the brighter stars in the English and Welsh wine firmament. His choice to use only organic methods are driven by his belief that this is the way to make the purest wine, maximising the wine's individual character and fully reflecting of the terroir of each site. He has tackled the planning and establishment of both the vineyard and winery in a thoroughly professional manner and deserves his success. If you can find it - it must be one of the most tucked away vineyards in the country - it is well worth a visit (but please make an appointment first).

Daws Hill Vineyard

Town End Road, Radnage, High Wycombe, Buckinghamshire HP14 4DY
Telephone: 01494 483358   Mobile: 07748 829453
E-mail: nigel@jefferson.co.uk
Website: www.dawshillvineyard.co.uk
Contact: Nigel Morgan
Vineyards: 1.7862 hectares
Grape varieties: Pinot noir, Chardonnay, Auxerrois, Pinot Meunier, Merlot, Cabernet Sauvignon
Open by appointment.

The Daws Hill Vineyard was initially planted in 2004 on a south-facing slope in an Area of Outstanding Natural Beauty and extended in 2008. The soil is loam over chalk and was tested in France prior to planting and pronounced to have a 'similar profile to Champagne'. The site is known locally to be a very warm one. The vines are planted at 2.5 x 1.3 metres and are single and double (arched) Guyot trained. Over 80 per cent of the planting is with Champagne varieties, plus the easier to ripen Auxerrois and a few Merlot and Cabernet Sauvignon 'just for fun'.

A winery at Daws Hill is being established in old loose boxes and all winemaking will be done on site. Bottle-fermented sparkling wines will have a minimum of 18 months *sur lattes*. Bottle fermented sparkling cider from locally sourced apples is also made using the same *méthode* as for the wine. The first vintages of sparkling wine were in 2007 and the 2,000 bottles of English sparkling wine and 500 bottles of sparkling cider will be available at the end of 2009. Production should rise to 8,000–10,000 bottles per year.

Deans Farm Vineyard

Weston, Petersfield, Hampshire, GU32 3NP
Telephone: 01730 269111
E-mail: dihughes66@o2.co.uk
Contact: David Hughes
Vineyards: 0.5 hectares
Grape varieties: Pinot noir
Not open to the public.

Decanter Magazine Vineyard

Blue Fin Building, 110 Southwark Street, London, SE1 0SU
Telephone: 020 3148 5000
E-mail: editor@decanter.com
Website: www.decanter.com
Vineyards: 0.001 hectares
Grape varieties: Furmint, Cabernet Sauvignon, Palomino, Pinot noir, Sangiovese, Syrah
Not open to the public.

To call a collection of six vines a 'vineyard' is stretching things somewhat, but I felt that Decanter's unique collection of vines worth a mention. Planted in 2007 in a flowerbed on the 10th floor terrace of IPC Media's Blue Fin Building and right outside Decanter's palatial tasting room, the vines were all donated by notable châteaux and wine estate owners:

Furmint from Royal Tokaji Wine Company, Hungary
Cabernet Sauvignon from Château Lynch Bages, Bordeaux
Palomino from Domecq, Jerez
Pinot noir from Louis Roederer, Champagne
Sangiovese from Antinori, Florence
Syrah from Marcel Guigal, Ampuis

The terrace is north-facing – marvellous views of the Tate Modern's chimney with St. Paul's Cathedral behind – and rather windswept. Despite these natural disadvantages, the vines produced their first bunches of grapes in 2009. What Decanter's plans are for the winemaking I have no idea, although perhaps the girls from "Nuts" magazine from the floor below could crush them with their bare feet? I am their honorary viticulturalist and keep my eye on them (the vines that is) whenever I am there for tastings. They suffered a little bit from what looked like mildew, but might actually have been scorch from the spotlights that light them up all night.

Denbies Wine Estate

London Road, Dorking, Surrey RH5 6AA
Telephone: 01306 876616   Fax: 01306 888930
E-mail: jsimpson@denbiesvineyard.co.uk
Website: www.denbies.co.uk
Contact: Jeanette Simpson
General Manager: Christopher White
Operations Director: John Worontschak
Winemaker: Marcus Sharp
Vineyard Manager: Sue Osgood
Vineyards: 107.2874 hectares
Grape varieties: MT, Reichensteiner, Pinot noir, Ortega, Bacchus, Chardonnay, Dornfelder, Seyval blanc, Schönburger, Pinot gris, Pinot Meunier, Rondo, Regent
Wine and gift shop: January to March: Monday to Friday, 10 am to 5 pm; Saturday 10 am to 5.30 pm; Sunday, 11.30 am to 5.30 pm. April to December: Monday to Saturday, 10 am to 5.30 pm; Sunday, 11.30 am to 5.30 pm. Closed Christmas Day, Boxing Day and New Year's Day.
Vineyard visits: The visitor facilities are extensive and there is a range of different tours. In addition, there are several different opportunities for corporate functions, meetings, weddings, etc. See website for full details.

Denbies Wine Estate was planted between 1986 and 1990 when English wine based upon German crosses and German know-how was approaching its peak. It was an impressive operation from the start and in my 2001 book I wrote: *It is difficult to know quite where to start in describing Denbies Wine Estate, such is the scale and scope of the undertaking.* Although today other vineyards have been planted of an (almost) equal size and other vineyards have achieved more success in terms of wine quality and awards and medals, Denbies still stands out from the crowd. The scale is still grand – over 100 hectares of vines in one block is big by any country's standards – and the winery building, sitting as it does surrounded by vineyards and so very visible from the main road, still makes a great statement of individuality.

When Adrian White (head of Biwater, the very successful water supply and treatment company based in Dorking) who is the prime mover behind this remarkable venture, let it be known that he was preparing to plant over 100 hectares of vineyards, most in the industry – and probably many outside it – questioned his sanity.[6] The UK, with, at that time, around 750 hectares of vines (figures are approximate as at the time no official records were kept) was not really ready for one vineyard that would increase the area under vine, and the production of wine, by almost 15 per cent. However, undeterred by any criticism, over the four years between 1986 and 1989 the bulk of the vineyards were planted using a laser-guided planting machine imported from Germany, the first to be used in the UK.

Denbies Estate was once the property of the Cubitt family (the nineteenth-century builders and property developers) and there used to be a very large mansion on the estate, overlooking the town of Dorking. This mansion was demolished after a war-time fire and initially there were plans to excavate the old basements, cover the roof over with soil and grass so that the whole building would blend in with the countryside and put a winery in there. However, the Mole Valley District Council did not view this as the correct place for a winery and were frightened that it might become 'another Lamberhurst' as the Planning Committee put it. The access to that part of the estate was poor and they were concerned about the large number of vehicles that would visit the winery.

The land planted with vines stretches from the top of the hills overlooking the town of Dorking, right down to the A24 which defines the southern limit of the site. Cutting across the lower end of the vineyards is the London to Dorking railway line, at this point raised up on an embankment some 5 metres above the surrounding land. Apart

---

6   I recall meeting Adrian White for the first time when he came over to see Kenneth McAlpine at Lamberhurst Vineyards (where I was then winemaker and General Manager). We all had lunch together in our Oast House restaurant and I well remember saying that if Denbies ever hoped to sell all the wine they would be producing, it could only be via a public outlet (such as we then had at Lamberhurst) and that Adrian would find himself running a tourist enterprise with 'over 100 people on the payroll'. At the time I thought I was exaggerating (although Lamberhurst then employed almost 40 people), but only slightly. With Denbies payroll now at 155 people, I was in fact out by quite a big margin!

from making access to the site impossible for anything over 3.66 metres (12 feet), the embankment traps any downward rolling frost which might otherwise escape. Parts of the site are ideal south-facing slopes, some undulating sections which are warm in the summer, but frost-pockets in the spring and much of the lower section, that surrounding the winery and running down to the main road, is relatively flat.

Advice from the Trier Viticulture Institute on the Mosel was sought before planting and a selection of varieties chosen, some of which at the time were seen as rather wild cards. Since the first issue of this book (1989), Auxerrois, Ehrenfelser, Elbling (both red and white), Gewürztraminer, Huxelrebe, Kerner, Pinot blanc, Riesling and Siegerrebe have gone and Chardonnay, Dornfelder, Pinot Meunier and Rondo have all made an appearance. Slowly but surely, the vineyards are being replanted with the older varieties being removed, although MT and Seyval blanc are being retained. More Pinot noir, Chardonnay and Pinot Meunier are going in (they now have 20.1 hectares of these three varieties) partly in order to increase the production of sparkling wines, but also for both red and rosé wines. Riesling, one of the original varieties, was eventually taken out ('only ripens once in five years', I was told), even though when wine was produced, it could be very good. Now, however, it is being replanted on a more favourable part of the site and in the hope that climate change continues to improve growing conditions for this high-acid variety.

The vines are planted at either 2.9 x 1.2-metres or 2.5 x 1.2-metres and are trained to both double and single Guyot training. It is said that the fairly wide row spacings were chosen to cope with the Braud SB60 grape harvesting machine, something I do not really understand as models are available to cope with narrower rows. To my mind the wide spacings do not really make best use of the available land and crops are lower (on a per hectare basis) than in more closely planted vineyards. The harvester is the only one in use in UK vineyards at the present time.

A vineyard of this size and complexity can never be planted – especially in a country as marginal as the UK – without problems and with hindsight one can always see the pitfalls. The vineyards have suffered from frost and efforts to overcome these have not been without difficulties. Anti-frost 'windmills' – large two-bladed propellers which stir up the colder air that sinks to the valley floor with the warmer air that remains above it (an inversion frost) – were imported from California (where they are widely used in both vineyards and citrus orchards) at a cost reputed to be near £250,000 and installed across the lower vineyard areas in preparation for the next frost. Unfortunately, the powers of the local authority's enforcement officer had not been reckoned with (planning permission should have been obtained) and after a few nights of noise and alarm when the giant blades stirred up the air and the nearby residents in about equal amounts, a halt was called to their use. Efforts were made to make them quieter. The world famous Hoffmann Propellor Company from Germany designed and built a new propeller at a cost of £150,000, but it failed to move enough air to shift the frost and eventually the windmills were dismantled and sold.[7] The next (and current) idea is to use oil-powered burners that sit silently among the vines in the dangerous mid-April to mid-May period, waiting for the temperature to drop, whereupon all hands set to and light them in ever-increasing numbers as the temperature sinks. These can be effective if the number of burners and the depth of the frost are matched, although a really deep frost might defeat them. Their big drawback is that they need to be placed out among the vines each year, filled with oil and lit, one by one, usually at very unsociable hours. Inversion frosts usually strike after midnight and keep going until nine in the morning. To date, they are using several hundred of these and more are on order. They do give off a rather eerie glow and when they are all alight at the dead of night, there is a touch of Dante's Inferno about the place!

Denbies Wine Estate - winery and visitor centre

For the first harvest, in 1989, a winery was installed in the old cattle buildings and for three years it remained there while the new winery was in both the planning and building stages. Mole Valley Council again had views about the desirability of the whole enterprise and while they could do nothing about someone wanting to plant vineyards, they could – and did – put objections in the way of building the winery. In the end, planning permission was gained and a magnificent flint and brick building, complete with central tower and viewing gallery, atrium-cum-conservatory style servery, superb visitor centre and, of course, well-appointed winemaking areas and

---

7   On a visit to New Zealand in 1998, I was talking to Richard Riddiford, MD of Palliser
    Estates in Martinborough, and he pointed out of his office window at a frost windmill and
    said 'you'll never guess where that came from'. I couldn't – it was Denbies!

underground storage cellars, was constructed. Today it is the very busy nerve centre of the operation. The shop and restaurant seem always to be filled with both local visitors and tourists, there are good conference and wedding facilities and it is widely used for this purpose. Denbies have won many tourist awards, including the South East Visitor Attraction of the Year in 2002. When the Queen came to Surrey on one of her perambulations around the shires, she visited Denbies, planted a tree and was presented with some of their wines.

The winery must be the finest in the UK in terms of facilities and equipment (at least until Nyetimber's new winery see the light of day). Glass, tiles and stainless steel dominate and the place has the look of the Napa Valley, rather than the outskirts of leafy Dorking. It is magnificently equipped with over 500,000 litres of temperature controlled stainless steel tanks (mainly made in South Africa), two 8-tonne Sharfenburger Europresses, RDV and DE filters, a GAI fully automatic filler and Bertani labeller, a Clemens sparkling wine disgorging line and a whole host of other winemaking paraphernalia. Running through the winery are the hidden tracks of the 'people mover' that ferries visitors across its floors and down into its cellars.

The winemaking at Denbies has, over the years since the first harvest, been something of a roller-coaster with winemakers coming and going at rather too frequent intervals. The first winemaker was Hans Schleifer (still active in UK winegrowing) who arrived from Germany just at a time when most UK winemakers were attempting to shed the *ersatz-Liebfraumilch* image that English and Welsh wine had achieved for itself. Although some good wines were made – most noticeably some sweet wines and those made from the Bacchus grape – many did not really live up to the quality that the trade had been expecting. The General Manager at this time was a South African, living in the UK, Michael Trull, whose marketing skills were brought to bear on selling the first few vintages. Special crested bottles were created and the presentation was (and remains) very good, but without the quality in the bottle, sales were slow and Denbies' reputation suffered. Schleifer then left.

The second winemaker was an Australian called Keith Bown. He supervised the 1995 vintage before returning home in 1996 just before the harvest. The third was Kit Lindlar (a well-known English winemaker who had been busy making the first few vintages of Nyetimber, but had recently closed his own winery and was fortuitously available to take over at short notice), who was retained almost minutes before the first grapes of the 1996 season were harvested. He acted on a consultancy basis for two seasons until the fourth winemaker arrived, a young New Zealand-trained Englishman, Nick Patrick, who remained there for four vintages. For the 1999 vintage John Worontschak, the well-known flying winemaker, Australian-born, but UK-based, was brought in to oversee production. Worontschak's style was – as one would imagine – more New World than old, with an accent upon appealing, fresh fruity whites. His list of achievements in the field of English Wine (to say nothing of his overseas ventures) is impressive. His winemaking skills have won him the Gore-

Browne Trophy five times, the President's Trophy three times, the Bernard Theobald (best red) four times, the Vintner's Trophy once and the Jack Ward Salver twice, to say nothing of the other awards and medals that wines either made by him or from wineries where he is a consultant have won. He remained at Denbies in this capacity for two vintages.

The fifth (and current) winemaker was Marcus Sharp, who took over when Nick Patrick left in 2003. Marcus had already worked at Denbies in the vineyard for two

years and the winery for another two before he took over as winemaker and, as he is still there, it makes him by my reckoning their longest-serving winemaker. In 2008, however, John Worontschak re-emerged from the woodwork and has been employed on a consultancy basis as Operations Director.

With all the changes in the winemaking department, it is hardly surprising that the style of wines produced at Denbies in the past changed with some regularity and never seemed to settle down into a recognisable pattern. There seemed to be a lot of quite ordinary, although sometimes great value, wines and just a few very good ones. At one stage, Denbies most successful wines were their dessert wines, made from a selection of varieties depending on the vintage and sugar content of the grapes. Their 1992 'Noble Harvest', a wine with a natural alcohol level of almost 22 per cent, an actual alcohol of 16.5 per cent and made from Optima and Ortega, would have been a remarkable wine wherever it was made. To have made it in England was nothing short of a miracle.

Today however, after almost twenty years of winemaking, things have greatly settled down, many of the early varieties have been replaced and their range of wines is probably one of the most consistent available from any of the major wineries, although with the accent on still rather than sparkling wines. Their two 'Estate Range' wines, Surrey Gold and Flint Valley, are usually excellent quality for the price (that is when compared to the price of many English wines of the same quality). The 'Cellarmaster's Choice' range consists of about seven or eight wines, some of which can be very good. Their 2003 'Hillside Chardonnay' gained an EWOTYC Gold medal (and was one of my favourite wines of the year) as well as the McNie Trophy for best oak-aged wine. The 'Coopers Brook', – a Chardonnay blend – and their Bacchus varietal can also be good. The best red that Worontschak made when he was first there – the 1999 'Redlands' – won a Silver medal, the Jack Ward and the Bernard Theobald (Best Red) trophies in the 2000 EWOTYC and the 'Rose Hill' rosé often wins medals and certainly pleases the palate.

Denbies' most successful wine in recent competitions has been their 'Greenfields' bottle-fermented sparkling wine. The 1999 vintage won several medals (Gold at the 2005 EWOTYC and Wine of the Year at the SEVA competition, but it is with the 2003 that they have hit the jackpot. This won Gold at the 2006 IWSC and 2007 IWC, as well as gaining them the IWC English Wine Producer Trophy. It also won the Charles Laughton Trophy (for runner-up) at the 2006 SEVA competition. In the 2008 EWOTYC their 2007 Rose Hill Rosé won a Gold Medal and the Jack Ward and Waitrose Rosé Trophies. Other wines gained a very respectable seven Silver and two Bronze Medals.

It would appear that in warm years (such as 2003 and no doubt 2009) when the Champagne varieties – in particular the Chardonnay – can be persuaded to ripen, Denbies scores well. The wines are still mainly sold from the premises and only 20 per cent finds its way to the outside world, although into some quite prestigious outlets: Fortnums, Harrods, the Dorchester, Claridges, Houses of Parliament, P&O Cruises and Waitrose are a few.

In my 2001 edition, with Worontschak newly appointed, I wrote: *It is to be hoped that with Worontschak's guiding hand – and he is without doubt one of the most experienced and arguably the most successful winemaker in the UK today – the wines produced at Denbies will settle down.* His 1999 harvest report ended with a statement which at the time I said 'sums up for the whole industry and not just for Denbies, the state of UK wines today'. John wrote: *With the far greater understanding we now have of how to handle the viticulture and winemaking in this climate, a greater desire by the general public to buy local produce and the past and future investments of this industry, I am sure that finally wine of interest, quality and volume can be profitably produced in this country.*

In 2001 I concluded this report on Denbies by saying: *there are perhaps a few winemakers who will chuckle at Worontschak's inclusion of the word 'finally' in his report – but in essence he is correct. We have all been learning how to grow grapes and make wines and it has taken time. What is also certain is that Denbies, as the biggest vineyard in the UK and one of its most visited and noticed, must produce wines of real quality and interest if English and Welsh wines are to be taken seriously.*

Well, it's been ten years since I wrote that and in that time, John Worontschak has left Denbies and rejoined them. General Manager Michael Trull was replaced by Mike Allen who in turn was replaced (in 2002) by Christopher White, Adrian's eldest son. With 155 employees (only 20 of whom are employed in the vineyards and winery) Denbies is by any measure a substantial enterprise and it is nice to see someone now in charge who really wants it to succeed. While Denbies is not quite 'an ace café with a nice vineyard attached' (to paraphrase what Saatchi and Saatchi once said about the Victoria and Albert Museum), it has sometimes felt in the past that the vineyards were an adjunct to what was essentially a tourist business. Worontschak's appointment to oversee the complete winegrowing and winemaking side of the enterprise shows a determination to improve Denbies wines as much as is possible. There will be, in the next ten years, a lot of competition for the title 'The UK's Best Vineyard' and I have no doubt that Denbies will be up there fighting it out at the top with the others.

Ditchling Vineyard

Beacon Road, Ditchling, East Sussex BN6 8XB
See entry for Plumpton College for contact details
Vineyards: 1.82 hectares
Grape varieties: MT, Ortega, Reichensteiner, Pinot noir, Dornfelder, Triomphe, Kerner, Regner, Optima
Not open to the public. Vineyard rented by Plumpton College

Doles Ash Farm Vineyard

Doles Ash Farm, Piddletrenthide, Dorset, DT2 7RE
Telephone: 01300 348248
Mobile: 07831 544544
E-mail: tom@mallows.plus.com
Contact: Tom Mallows, Tania Mallows
Vineyards: 0.75 hectares
Grape varieties: MA, Bacchus, Scyval blanc, Triomphe
Not open to the public.

Dropmore Vineyard

Brook End Farmhouse, Dropmore Road, Littleworth Common, Buckinghamshire, SL1 8NF
Telephone & Fax: 01628 664376
Mobile: 07767 662622
E-mail: johnjpetersen@aol.com
Website: www.dropmorewines.co.uk

Contact: John Petersen, Fiona McEwan
Vineyards: 0.66 hectares
Grape varieties: Bacchus, Ortega, Chardonnay, Pinot noir, Pinot Meunier
Not open to the public.

Dunkery Vineyard - Exmoor

Wootton Courtenay, Minehead, Somerset TA24 8RD
Telephone: 01643 841505
E-mail: derek@winegrowers.info
Website: www.exmoor-excellence.com
Contact: Derek Pritchard
Vineyards: 1.42 hectares
Grape varieties: Reichensteiner, Dornfelder, Regent, MA, Kernling, Merzling, Rondo, Pinot noir, Chardonnay, Orion, Dunkelfelder, Phoenix
Open by appointment.

Dunkery Vineyard

Dunleavy Vineyards

c/o 18 Wolseley Road, Bishopston, Bristol, Somerset, BS7 8EN
Location of vineyard: Nates Lane, Wrington, Bristol, Somerset, BS40 5RS
Telephone: 0117 9245 415
Contact: Stephen Dunleavy E-mail: stephendunleavy@mac.com
Contact: Ingrid Bates 07779 085420 E-mail: ingridbates@mac.com
Website: www.dunleavyvineyards.com
Vineyards: 1.2146 hectares
Grape varieties: Pinot noir Précoce, Seyval blanc
Not open to the public.

Dunley Vineyard

Dunley House, Dunley, Whitchurch, Hampshire, RG28 7PU
Telephone: 01256 892876

Mobile: 07850 491320
E-mail: capnersq@btinternet.com
Contact: Gareth Capner
Vineyards: 0.2 hectares
Grape varieties: Auxerrois, Phoenix, Regent, Pinot noir Précoce, Dunkelfelder
Not open to the public.

East Bridgeford Vineyard

c/o Abbey Vineyards Group, Irnham Grange, Irnham, Corby Glen, Grantham, Lincolnshire, NG33 4NE
Location of vineyard: Hill Lane, East Bridgeford, Nottinghamshire, NG13 8LP
Telephone: 01476 550191
Fax: 01476 550080
E-mail: info@abbeyvineyards.co.uk
Contact: Phil Kerry 07815 308838
Contact: Jonathan Kerry 07805 315763
Vineyards: 3.00 hectares
Grape varieties: Pinot noir, Riesling, Bacchus, Triomphe
Not open to the public.

East Meon Vineyard

The Court House, East Meon, Hampshire GU32 1NJ
Telephone: 01730 823274
E-mail: gandcbartlett@tiscali.co.uk
Contact: George Bartlett
Vineyards: 0.4 hectares
Grape varieties: Pinot noir, Chardonnay
Not open to the public.

East Sutton Vine Garden

Brissenden, East Sutton Road, Headcorn, Maidstone, Kent, ME17 3DU
Telephone: 01622 844811
Mobile: 07973 213699
E-mail: dvrac@hotmail.co.uk
Contact: Dave Rackham
Vineyards: 4 hectares
Grape varieties: Pinot noir, Bacchus, Reichensteiner
Not open to the public.

Eastcott Vineyard

Lower Eastcott, Northlew, Okehampton, Devon EX20 3PT
Telephone: 01837 811012
Mobile: 07770 656522
E-mail: wallerr@hotmail.com
E-mail: wallerh@hotmail.com
Website: www.eastcottvineyard.co.uk

Contact: Richard Waller, Hilary Waller
Vineyards: 1.49 hectares
Grape varieties: Chardonnay, Rondo, Pinot noir Précoce, Pinot Meunier, Dunkelfelder, Solaris
Open to the public. See website for details.

Richard & Hilary Waller moved to Devon in 2007 to establish a vineyard. This will be completed in 2010 with the addition of some Phoenix. They have converted an agricultural barn into an on-site winery and are now licensed to sell direct to the public. Their aim is to focus on the production of sparkling wines, with a still white and rosé in most years and perhaps even a red in a good year. Their first wine – Two Moors Rosé – achieved a Highly Commended in the 2009 EWOTYC.

Ebernoe Vineyard

Petworth, West Sussex GU28 9LH
Telephone: 01428 707269
Fax: 01428 707629
E-mail: sales@simmonds-saws.co.uk
Contact: Peter Simmonds
Vineyards: 1 hectare
Grape varieties: Seyval blanc, MT
Not open to the public.

Ebford Eden Community Vineyard

c/o The Wine Cellar, 46a Fore Street, Topsham, Devon EX3 0HY
Location of vineyard: Ebford Lane, Ebford, Exeter, Devon
See entry for Pebblebed Wines for contact details
Vineyards: 0.2 hectares
Grape varieties: Seyval blanc, MA
Open to the public by appointment.

Eglantine Vineyard

Ash Lane, Costock, Loughborough, Nottinghamshire LE12 6UX
(NB Despite the Leics. postcode, the vineyard is in Notts.)
Telephone: 01509 852386
E-mail: tony@skuriat.freeserve.co.uk
Contact: Tony Skuriat
Vineyards: 1.3 hectares
Grape varieties: MA, Pinot noir, Chardonnay, Seyval blanc, Regent, Rondo
Open daily between 10 am and 6 pm, but please telephone in advance to confirm. Guided tours for

groups need to be booked in advance and last about two hours. Please telephone for details and charges.

The 1.3 hectares of vines at Eglantine were originally planted between 1979 and 1984. The site is 75 to 83 metres above sea level, slightly sloping south by south-east and the soil is glacial drift over calcareous clay over discontinuous hydraulic limestone. Some replanting was carried out in 1999 and then again in 2007–2008. The vines are planted at 2.25 x 1.5-metres to a VSP trellis and are spur-pruned. Apart from the main varieties listed above, there is also a vine trials collection of over 200 varieties, which has played a significant role in deciding which varieties to grow in the main vineyard.

All wines are made at the vineyard in the purpose-built winery which has recently been re-equipped with modern processing machinery, including a *Vaslin-Bucher*

membrane press, a sparkling wine line and a screwcapping machine for still wines. This was necessary in order to cope with the increasing amount of contract winemaking being undertaken. The wines have won many awards. Their premium product, the dessert wine North Star, has consistently won Gold and Silver awards in international competitions (IWSC, Decanter WWA, and *Vignerons Independents)* and in March 2008 this wine was awarded Gold at the International Paris Competition (*Vinalies Internationales*) and was the only UK wine to receive a medal and only the third Gold for an English wine in this prestigious competition in the past ten years. The 2004 North Star won an EWOTYC Gold Medal in 2008.

Tony Skuriat (pictured above) has played an active part in the progress of the English wine industry having founded the Mercian Vineyards' Association on 30 October 1994 and serving as its first Chairman. As the MVA representative he was involved in the formation of the UK Vineyards Association and served as the association's first Treasurer. In 2009 he was the MVA's 'Personality of the Year'.

Elham Valley Vineyard

Breach, Barham, Canterbury, Kent CT4 6LN
Telephone: Office 01227 832022 Tea Room 01227 831266
E-mail: familyinvest@tiscali.co.uk
Website: www.kentattractions.co.uk/ElhamValleyVineyard.htm
Contact: Mike Cheoff   mike@familyinvestmenthomes.com Mobile: 07843 153440
Vineyards: 0.72 hectares
Grape varieties: MT, Seyval blanc, Reichensteiner
Open to the public.

Elysian Fields Vineyard

Bedwell Hey Farm, Ely Road, Little Thetford, Ely, Cambridgeshire CB6 3HJ
Telephone: 01353 662722
Mobile: 07860 663510
Fax: 01353 663774
E-mail: rg.parish@farmline.com
Contact: John Parish
Vineyards: 1 hectare
Grape varieties: Bacchus, Acolon
Open by appointment.

English Oak Vineyard

Flowers Drove, Lytchett Matravers, Poole, Dorset BH16 6BX
Telephone: 01258 858205
Fax: 01258 858205
Mobile: 07799 713566
E-mail: am.pharoah@btopenworld.com
Website: www.englishoakvineyard.co.uk
Contact: Andrew Pharoah
Vineyards: 8.06 hectares
Grape varieties: Chardonnay, Pinot noir, Pinot Meunier
Open to the public. See website for details.

English Wine Centre

Alfriston Roundabout, Alfriston, East Sussex BN26 5QS
Telephone: 01323 870174
Fax: 01323 870164
E-mail: bottles@englishwine.co.uk
Website: www.englishwine.co.uk
Contact: Colin Munday, Christine Munday
Vineyard: No vineyard on this site, but a wine shop selling very large selection of English wines. See website for details of opening times and wine selection.

Exton Park Estate Vineyard

Exton, Southampton, Hampshire SO32 3NW
Mobile: 07792 122690
Contact: Fred Langdale
Vineyards: 7.8056 hectares
Grape varieties: Pinot noir, Chardonnay, Bacchus
Open by appointment.

Fawley Vineyard

The Old Forge, Fawley Green, Henley-on-Thames, Buckinghamshire, RG9 6JA
Telephone: 01491 413071
Telephone: 01491 577998
Fax: 01491 577477
E-mail: wsargent@skillbondplc.co.uk
Contact: Wendy Sargent
Vineyards: 0.262 hectares
Grape varieties: Bacchus
Open by appointment.

Felsted Vineyard

Crix Green, Felsted, Essex CM6 3JT
Telephone: 01245 361504
E-mail: felstedvineyard@supanet.com
Contact: Marcello Davanzo
Vineyards: 4 hectares
Grape varieties: Chardonnay, MA, Madeleine Sylvaner, MT, Pinot Meunier, Pinot noir, Seyval blanc
Open by appointment.

Fernhurst Vineyard

c/o Gospel Green Cottage, Haslemere, Surrey GU27 3BH
Location of vineyard: GU27 3NW
Telephone: 01428 654120
Mobile: 07981 259810
E-mail: gospelgreen@hotmail.co.uk
Contact: James Lane
Vineyards: 0.8097 hectares
Grape varieties: Chardonnay, Pinot noir
Open by appointment.

Fleurfields Vineyard

Hill Farm House, Brixworth, Northamptonshire NN6 9DQ
Telephone: 01604 880197
E-mail: info@fleurfields.co.uk
Website: www.fleurfields.co.uk
Contact: Bill Hulme
Vineyards: 1.5 hectares
Grape varieties: Seyvel blanc, Solaris, Triomphe
Open to the public. See website for details.

Floreys Vineyard

c/o Abbey Vineyards Group, Irnham Grange, Irnham, Corby Glen, Grantham, Lincolnshire, NG33 4NE
Location of vineyard: Chipping Norton Road, Little Tew, Oxfordshire OX7
Telephone: 01476 550191
Fax: 01476 550080
E-mail: info@abbeyvineyards.co.uk
Contact: Phil Kerry 07815 308838
Contact: Jonathan Kerry 07805 315763
Vineyards: 2.5 hectares
Grape varieties: Regent, Chardonnay, Solaris, Acolon
Open by appointment.

Fonthill Glebe Vineyard

The Winery, Teffont Evias, Salisbury, Wiltshire SP3 5RG
Telephone: 01722 716770
Mobile: 07703 353518
E-mail: sales@fonthillglebewines.co.uk
Website: www.fonthillglebewines.co.uk
Contact: John Edginton
Vineyards: 3.5 hectares
Grape varieties: Seyval blanc, Pinot blanc, Reichensteiner, MT, Triomphe, Pinot noir
Open to the public. See website for details.

Forstal Farm Vineyard

Old House Farm Lane, Peasmarsh, East Sussex TN31 6YD
Telephone: 020 7303 6321
Mobile: 07770 311311
E-mail: egkock@btopenworld.com
Contact: Egmont Kock
Vineyards: 3.4413 hectares
Grape varieties: Chardonnay, Pinot noir, Pinot Meunier
Not open to the public.

Forty Hall Vineyard

Forty Hall Farm, Forty Hill, Enfield, London, EN2 9HA
Telephone: 020 8800 1358
E-mail: enquiries@fortyhallvineyard.org.uk
Website: www.fortyhallvineyard.org.uk
Contact: Sarah Vaughan-Roberts
Vineyards: 0.4 hectares
Grape varieties: Bacchus

Forty Hall Vineyard is a community vineyard in the London Borough of Enfield. The vineyard is located at Forty Hall Organic Farm which is leased to, and managed by,

Capel Manor Horticultural College from the local authority. The vineyard is being supported by Capel Manor College during its early development phase, but a steering group is in the process of exploring the most suitable legal structure for the enterprise in the long term, with support from Cooperatives UK. The aim is establish the vineyard as a self-sustaining, not-for-profit, social enterprise delivering educational, social and mental health benefits to local people. The vineyard forms part of a wider college initiative to develop the farm as a hub of community organic food production, distribution and skills education. Any profits generated from the sale of wine from the vineyard will be ring-fenced for local food growing and educational projects on the farm. The grapes will be taken to Davenport Vineyards for winemaking.

The College Governors have donated the long term use of up to 6-hectares of land for the vineyard and have funded the establishment of the first 0.4-hectares of vines which were hand planted by over 100 volunteers in 2009. Organic Certification will be sought from the Soil Association in two years time.

Four Foxes Vineyard

Longworth Lane, Bartestree, Hereford, Herefordshire, HR1 4BX
Telephone: 01432 850065
Contact: Peter Crilly
Vineyards: 3.25 hectares
Grape varieties: Not known
Not open to the public.

Friday Street Vineyard

Friday Street Farm, East Sutton, Maidstone, Kent ME17 3DD
Telephone: 01622 842162
Mobile: 07761 262894
E-mail: skinner@fsfarm.f9.co.uk
Website: www.fridaystreetfarm.com
Contact: Jack Skinner
Vineyards: 4.65 hectares
Grape varieties: Chardonnay, Pinot noir, Meunier
Open by appointment.

Frithsden Vineyard

Frithsden, Hemel Hemsptead, Hertfordshire HP1 3DD
Telephone: 01442 878723
E-mail: info@frithsdenvineyard.co.uk
Website: www.frithsdenvineyard.co.uk
Contact: Simon and Natalie Tooley
Vineyards: 1.232 hectares
Grape varieties: Solaris, Phoenix, Rondo, Seyval blanc
Open to visitors. See website for details.

Frithsden Vineyard was originally planted in 1971 but when owner Peter Latchford retired from winemaking, the vines were grubbed-up, the winery dismantled and the equipment sold. The present owners noticed the vineyard was marked on an OS map and decided to take a look at it, but when they got there found nothing! Further enquiries were made and in 2006 they were able to buy the site and within a month had planted over 5,000 vines. Further plantings of Solaris were made in 2008. The site, which is south-facing and about 125 metres above sea level, is silty loam over chalk. All vines are planted at 2 x 1.1 metres and the white varieties are trained on an arched double Guyot system and the Rondo on a high-wire single cordon. The winery has been re-equipped and the first harvest from the new vineyard was picked in 2007. The intention is to make three wines: Solaris, Phoenix and a Rondo rosé and a bottle-fermented sparkling wine from Seyval blanc.. A new shop and tasting room were opened in 2009 and it also sells clothing and gifts (hope the planners know about this!). It is good to see this old vineyard revived and in view of one of the grape varieties planted, I cannot resist adding 'rise Phoenix-like from the ashes'.

Frome Valley Vineyard

Paunton Court, Bishops Frome, Herefordshire WR6 5BJ
Telephone: 01885 490768
Mobile: 07886 700976
E-mail: jeanie@fromewine.co.uk
Website: www.fromewine.co.uk
Contact: Jeanie Falconer
Vineyards: 1.5 hectares
Grape varieties: Huxelrebe, MA, Schönburger, Bacchus, Reichensteiner, Seyval blanc, Pinot noir, Pinot noir Précoce, Rondo, Chardonnay, Siegerrebe
Open: April to October, Wednesday to Sunday, 11 am to 5 pm and at other times by arrangement. Groups are very welcome to tour the vineyards by arrangement. Admission free for individuals and groups under ten people.

Frome Valley Vineyard was established nearly 20 years ago and is set among Herefordshire's hop-yards and cider orchards. In addition to the main 1.50-hectare vineyard, they have a small model vineyard which demonstrates different trellising systems for different climates, geography or geology. Their wines have won a

consistent stream of awards at both national and regional level from their earliest days and since the Falconers inherited the vineyard in 2005, they have kept up this tradition, winning a Silver with their 2006 Rosé and Bronze with their 2006 Huxelrebe in the EWOTYC. They sell their wines at the cellar door, at the major regional food and drink shows and some farmers' markets including the Teme Valley Market at The Talbot at Knightwick, one of the longest-running markets in the country. Their wines can also be found in a variety of restuarants, bars and delicatessens in the region.

Jeanie Falconer in her vineyard at Frome Valley

Furleigh Estate

Salway Ash, Bridport, Dorset DT6 5JF
Telephone: 01308 488991
Mobile: 07740 286385
E-mail: iemail@btinternet.com and rhmail@btinternet.com
Contact: Ian Edwards
Vineyards: 5.5 hectares
Grape varieties: Chardonnay, Pinot noir, Bacchus, Rondo
Open by appointment.

Gelynis Vineyard

Gelynis Fruit Farm, Morganstown, Cardiff CF15 8LB, Wales
Telephone: 02920 844440
E-mail: gelynisfarm@btconnect.com
Website: www.gelynisfarm.co.uk
Contact: Edward Watt
Vineyards: 0.3 hectares
Grape varieties: Seyval blanc
Open to the public. See website for details.

Giffords Hall Vineyard

Hartest, Bury St Edmunds, Suffolk IP29 4EX
Telephone: 01284 830559
E-mail: linda@giffordshall.co.uk
E-mail: linda.howard1@btinternet.com
Website: www.giffordshall.co.uk

Contact: Linda Howard
Vineyards: 4 hectares
Grape varieties: MA, Bacchus, Reichensteiner, Rondo
Open to the public. See website for details.

Glyndŵr Vineyard

Llanblethian, Cowbridge, Vale of Glamorgan CF71 7JF, Wales
Telephone: 01446 774564
E-mail: glyndwrvineyard@hotmail.com
Website: www.glyndwrvineyard.co.uk
Contact: Richard Norris
Vineyards: 1.6488 hectares
Grape varieties: Seyval blanc, Reichensteiner, MA, Triomphe, Rondo, Regent, Siegerrebe
Open to the public by appointment.

Glyndŵr Vineyard, the oldest in Wales, has been managed by the Norris family of Llanblethian since it was established in 1982 and has been expanded over the years to its present size. The vines are all double Guyot trained. Apart from the vineyards and cellars beneath the farmhouse which can be visited, there are extensive gardens, orchards, woods and areas with ponds open to the public.

The wines, which are produced at Three Choirs, include three whites, a rosé, a red and a vintage sparkling wine. The three whites consist of a medium, medium-dry and dry, the latter being made from Siegerrebe and Madeleine Angevine. The rosé is made from Seyval blanc and Triomphe and the red, which is aged in American oak, is made from Rondo, Regent and Triomphe and is something of a rarity in Wales. The sparkling wine is bottle-fermented and made from Seyval blanc. The wines are sold extensively throughout Wales and can be found in a wide variety of outlets in the region. A new tour centre is planned to coincide with the launch of their new rosé sparkling wine.

Godstone Vineyard

c/o Flower Farm, Flower Lane, Godstone, Surrey RH9 8DE
Location of vineyard: Quarry Road, Off Godstone Hill, Godstone, Surrey RH9 8DQ
Telephone: 01883 742367
E-mail: mail@godstonevineyards.com
Website: www.godstonevineyards.com
Contact: June Deeley
Vineyards: 1 hectare
Grape varieties: Seyval blanc
Open to the public. See website for details.

Gog Magog Vineyard

Great Shelford, Cambridge, Cambridgeshire CB22 5AN
Telephone: 01223 844075
Fax: 07092 111369
E-mail: vines@gogmagogvineyard.co.uk
Website: www.gogmagogvineyard.co.uk
Contact: Colin Ross
Vineyards: 0.33 hectares
Grape varieties: Chardonnay
Not open to the public.

Gog Magog vineyard was planted in March 1995 and the vines are Single Guyot pruned on a low vertical trellis.The site is an ideal, south-facing slope on a chalk hill (the Gog Magog Hills) just south of Cambridge. The first harvest was in 1997 and for the first five years a still Chardonnay was produced but in 2002 they started making a bottle-fermented sparkling wine.

Good Earth Vineyard

c/o 9 Lea View, Ryhall, Stamford, Lincolnshire PE9 4HZ
Location of vineyard: Stamford, Lincolnshire PE9 2QH
Telephone: 01780 762859
E-mail: phil@philreeve.com
Website: http://an-english-vineyard.blogspot.com
Contact: Phil Reeve
Vineyards: 0.0144 hectares
Grape varieties: Pinot noir
Not open to the public.

Goose Green Vineyard

c/o 292 Stafford Road, Wallington, Surrey SM6 8PN
Location of vineyard: Beddington, Croydon CR0 4TB
Telephone: 020 8688 1797

Telephone: 01737 642557
Mobile: 07952 753911
E-mail: dave_spinks@hotmail.com
Contact: Dave Randall, Dave Spinks
Vineyards: 0.0285 hectares
Grape varieties: Phoenix, Orion, Pinot noir
Not open to the public.

Goose Green was conceived in 2003 ('we started with just a couple of vines') with the majority of the 130 vines being planted in 2005. The vineyard is two-thirds Phoenix, with the balance spread equally Orion and Pinot noir. Although the Phoenix were originally Scott Henry trellised, they have now been converted to join the other vines on double Guyot. Two wines are made: Autumn Gold from the Phoenix and a bottle-fermented sparkling wine from the Pinot noir and Orion. There are plans to plant additional vines for red wine production. Despite rumours to the contrary, this vineyard is not in the Falkland Islands.

Grange Farm Vineyard

Swerford, Chipping Norton, Oxfordshire OX7 4AX
Telephone: 01608 737313
E-mail: grangefarm3@onetel.net
Contact: Jonathan and Jane Abbott
Vineyards: 0.102 hectares
Grape varieties: Pinot gris, MA, Pinot blanc, Rondo, Auxerrois, Huxelrebe
Open by appointment only. Winery also produces organic apple and pear juices.

Grange Farm Vineyard

Gravel Lane Vineyard

c/o 1-7 Garman Lane, Tottenham, London, N17 0UR
Location of vineyard: Gravel Lane, Chigwell, Essex, IG7 6DQ
Telephone: 020 8885 5888
Mobile: 07952 964260
E-mail: mainlineplantltd@btconnect.com
Contact: Graham Bayliss
Vineyards: 1 hectare
Grape varieties: Pinot noir, Pinot noir Précoce, Bacchus, Schönburger, Acolon
Not open to the public.

Greyfriars Vineyard

Greyfriars Farm, The Hogs Back, Puttenham, Guildford, Surrey GU13 1AG
Telephone: 01483 813712
Website: www.greyfriarsvineyard.com
Contact: Bill Croxon 07970 525377
Contact: Philip Underwood 07771 633599
Vineyards: 0.6072 hectares
Grape varieties: Chardonnay, Pinot noir
Open to the public: See website for opening details.

Groombridge Place Vineyard

Groombridge, Tunbridge Wells, Kent TN3 9QG
Telephone: 01892 861444
Mobile: 07831 123 987
E-mail: office@groombridge.co.uk
Website: www.groombridge.co.uk
Contact: Jill Todd
Vineyards: 1.012 hectares
Grape varieties: Schönburger, Seyval blanc
Open to the public. See website for details.

Gusbourne Estate Vineyard

Kenardington Road, Appledore, Ashford, Kent TN26 2BE
Telephone: 01233 758666
Fax: 01233 758666
E-mail: gusbourne.estate@gmail.com
Owner: Andrew Weeber 07808 714735
Vineyard manager: Jon Pollard 07919 131233
Vineyards: 20.52 hectares
Grape varieties: Chardonnay, Pinot noir, Pinot Meunier
Vineyard open to visitors by appointment with Jon Pollard.

At over 20-hectares, Gusbourne Estate is one of the largest vineyards in the UK and I feel sure it is set to be one of the finest. The vineyards are planted on the south-facing slopes of the ancient coastal escarpment facing towards the Romney Marsh just outside Appledore in Kent. The land falls away towards the Royal Military Canal (the 30 km canal which runs from Folkestone to Rye and which was built during the Napoleonic War to stop an invasion by French troops) and stretches towards the Channel coast which is approximately 10 km away.

The soil in this part of Kent is an interesting mixture of Weald Clay, Tunbridge Wells Sand and a very light sandy loam, a similar soil to that at Chapel Down Wines at nearby Tenterden which I know well and think is a very good soil for vines. Gusbourne's site has high sunshine hours and below-average rainfall for the area which ensure good conditions for the ripening of the three traditional Champagne varieties that have been planted. The *encepagement* is 51 per cent Chardonnay, 34 per cent Pinot noir and 15 per cent Pinot Meunier and the vineyards were planted over four successive years: 2004–2007. There is an additional 120-hectares suitable for vines. The first harvest in 2006 was processed at RidgeView and went on sale in 2009. Plans are under way to establish a state-of-the-art winery (computer simulation below) which will include full visitor facilities, and planning permission has been applied for. At the time of writing the 2009 harvest was under way and vineyard manager Pollard was expecting 120 tonnes (and maybe a touch more) with half going to RidgeView and half to other buyers.

Gusbourne Estate is one of the most impressive and exciting new vineyards that I have seen in the UK (and it takes quite a lot to get me excited) and is a testament to its owner, Andrew Weeber, a man who leaves no stone unturned in his quest for the

answer – whatever the question. His research into the how, why and wherefore of growing grapes in the UK appears to have no bounds and the fruits of his research are plain to see. He is also lucky to have a very dedicated and obviously capable vineyard manager in Plumpton-trained Jon Pollard. This is, as they say, one to watch.

Habberley Vineyard

Habberley, Shrewsbury, Shropshire SY5 0TR
Telephone: 01743 790144
E-mail: silverslugs@aol.com
Contact: John Crook, Susan Crook
Vineyards: 0.2 hectares
Grape varieties: Phoenix, Rondo, Solaris
Not open to the public.

Hale Valley Vineyard

Boddington East, Hale Lane, Wendover, Buckinghamshire HP22 6NQ
Telephone: 01296 623730
Fax: 01296 623730
E-mail: chap@halevalley.freeserve.co.uk
Contact: Antony Chapman
Vineyards: 0.62 hectares
Grape varieties: Bacchus, Findling, Kernling
Open by appointment.

Halfpenny Green Vineyard

Tom Lane, Bobbington, Staffordshire DY7 5EP
Telephone: 01384 221122
E-mail: sales@halfpenny-green-vineyards.co.uk
Website: www.halfpennygreenvineyards.co.uk
Contact: Clive Vickers
Vineyards: 9.82 hectares
Grape varieties: Huxelrebe, Reichensteiner, MA, Rondo, Triomphe, Seyval blanc, Schönburger, Dornfelder, Regent, Pinot noir, Faberrebe, Chardonnay
Open to the public. See website for details.

Halnaker Vineyard

Thicket Lane, Halnaker, Chichester, West Sussex, PO18 0QS
Telephone: 01903 730140
Contact: Nicola Ogilvie
E-mail: ogilvie@bluewin.ch
Mobile: +41 7620 54903
Vineyards: 2.6565 hectares
Grape varieties: Chardonnay, Pinot noir, Pinot Meunier
Not open to the public.

Hambledon Vineyard

Mill Down, Hambledon, Hampshire PO7 4RY
Telephone: 012392 632066
Mobile: 07887 823909
E-mail: ian.kellett@brookespartnership.com
Contact: Ian Kellett
Vineyards: 4.03 hectares
Grape varieties: Chardonnay, Pinot noir, Pinot Meunier
Open by appointment.

Major General Sir Guy Salisbury-Jones, and his wife, Hilda (pictured left), planted the first commercial vineyard of the modern revival at Hambledon in the spring of 1952. It has often been recounted that Salisbury-Jones acquired his love of wine during the Great War, when, finding himself sharing a trench with some French soldiers, he was invited to share their wine ration. His love of both France and its wines started then and stayed with him throughout his life. He was the first Englishman to train at the famous French Military Academy at *Saint-Cyr* and was taught military history and tank warfare there by one Charles de Gaulle! He was Military Attaché at the British Embassy in Paris between 1946 and 1949 (and also His, and then, Her Majesty's Marshal of the Diplomatic Corps between 1950 and 1961). As an acknowledged Francophile, it was perhaps only natural that Salisbury-Jones' dreams included owning his own vineyard.

After his time at the British Embassy in Paris, Salisbury-Jones retired to Mill Down in Hambledon and, looking at the south-facing field where once his daughter's pony had grazed, the thought came to him, and encouraged by his son Raymond, that perhaps it would be a good place to plant a vineyard. The idea that vines could flourish in the United Kingdom had at that time been receiving a fair bit of publicity, generated by two people: Ray Brock and Edward Hyams. Salisbury-Jones admitted that it was the writings of these two – especially Hyams' *The Grape Vine in England* – that really inspired him to carry on and plant his vineyard.

As would be expected of a man with a military bent, a visit to France to reconnoitre the ground ahead was called for and in the autumn of 1951, Salisbury-Jones and his loyal gardener Mr Blackman, taking with them a sack of their chalky Hampshire soil, crossed the Channel. Blackman had not been there since his time in the Army in the 1914–1918 war, but had: *still remembered a few of those essential French words which enabled the British soldiers of the war to get along with their allies – 'Napoo',[8] 'Madamezel' and 'Promenade' were among them.* They drove and stopped in Paris for lunch and fortified by *a bottle of 'convenable' claret* continued on to Burgundy. After visiting *acre upon acre of vineyards along the Côte d'Or and numbers of wineries and cellars, plying our kind French hosts with questions* they ended their visit by attending a dinner on 16 November given by the *Confrérie des Chevaliers du Tastevin* at the former Cistercian Monastery of Clos-Vougeot to celebrate the 400th anniversary of its foundation. The dinner, which was preceded by *pretty girls in picturesque dress* [who] *offered us us the pure juice of grapes which had just been picked and had barely started to ferment,* was obviously a great success and as a result Salisbury-Jones returned to England having ordered 3,620 vines while, as he put it, *under the influence of Burgundian hospitality.*

The main varieties he selected for his new venture were French-American hybrids: 1,440 Seyval blanc (Seyve-Villard 5-276), 1,440 Aurore (Seibel 5279) and 300 Seibel 10-868, grafted in equal numbers onto three different rootstocks: 41B, 5BB and 161-49. He also ordered 60 Aligote and 20 Chardonnay to see how they would fare. As an experiement, he also ordered some red varieties, again, all French-American hybrids: 120 Seibel 545560, 120 Seibel 10587,[9] and 120 Baco Noir (Baco No.1). As to why Salisbury-Jones chose his three main white varieties one can only speculate. He had visited Oxted and in Brock's first two *Reports,* Seyval blanc, which Brock and Hyams had been growing (albeit only since 1947/8), had been recommended as *'promising'.* Perhaps at the Clos-Vougeot dinner he sat next to a member of FENAVINO or someone who subscribed to *La Viticulture Nouvelle?* Who knows? Whatever it was, Seyval blanc (if not perhaps the other two varieties) was an inspired choice and in retrospect, while it could be seen as possibly unadventurous, it was resistant to mildew and *Botrytis* and did enable Salisbury-Jones to harvest crops of clean fruit with sufficient regularity to make wine every year – something that had eluded most vineyard owners of former times. Why he chose those rootstocks is more obvious. They were required, Salisbury-Jones said: *because the chalky soil at Hambledon resembled that of Champagne and those were the rootstocks used there.*[10]

During the winter of 1951 the land for the vineyard was deeply ploughed and left until the spring. In March 1952, the vines arrived *beautifully packed in wooden boxes and enclosed in sawdust* and were planted. They were planted in rows, 4-feet apart and approximately 3-feet in the row   the spacings were not exact – and in total,

---

8   Napoo (in French 'il n'y a plus') means 'there's no more' which in soldier's slang meant 'finished' or 'dead'.

9   Seibel 545560 and Seibel 10587 were, according to Bill Carcary, the variety names written on the original Hambledon planting plan, although I can find no reference to varieties having these numbers in any literature or database. Seibel 5455 exists – known as Plantet – and one of the most widely planted of all hybrids in France, but of Seibel 10587 I have no clues.

10   Not sure that 5BB is a Champagne rootstock – its certainly not approved by the CIVC today.

seventy rows were planted which filled almost exactly one acre (0.4-hectares). They were trellised in a very Burgundian manner with posts only about 4 feet (1.22 metres) out of the ground.

The vines grew well, pests (rabbits especially) and diseases were kept at bay and in 1955 the vineyard produced its first crop. Salisbury-Jones had been in contact with Bordeaux-based Allan Sichel (well-known *negociant*, proprietor of Ch. D'Angludet and part-proprietor of Ch. Palmer) who had arranged for a Monsieur Chardon to come and help with the winemaking. Unfortunately, the 1955 *vendange* in Bordeaux was a late one and by the time Chardon arrived, the birds had eaten most of the Hambledon grapes. Salisbury-Jones wrote that: *Every day the lovely green bunches grew less. Here and there, tucked away under the foliage, a few bunches still defied the invaders. Elsewhere, only the naked hideous stalks remained. It reminded me of moments in the First World War, when some lovely wood, under the ceaseless pounding of the guns, would slowly be transformed into a gaunt array of skeletons that had once been trees.*

Despite the avian onslaught, a few grapes hung on and within two hours of Chardon arriving, the remaining grapes were picked, pressed and the juice run into barrels, to which was added some sugar. Chardon had brought with him a saccharometer, titration equipment to measure the acidity and some yeast. Within two days, with an ear pressed to the bung-hole, signs of life were heard and the first commercial vintage of wine produced in Great Britain since the 1911 Castle Coch vintage was under way. The fact that wine *was* now being produced aroused much publicity and Salisbury-Jones was besieged by the press and media anxious for a story. He was an imposing figure, with a colourful and honourable past, a name to conjure with and the presence to hold an audience, which meant that he was much in demand. Hambledon soon became synonymous with English Wine and Brock's dream, ten years after he started his trials vineyard at Oxted, had become a reality.

What that first Hambledon vintage tasted like, history does not record and it did not go on sale. The next two vintages, 1956 and 1957 were much better and with improved disease control and the use of netting to keep the birds out, more serious quantities of grapes were harvested from their bare acre. The 1957 vintage was decribed as 'excellent' and Salisbury-Jones said *that the wine should be even more agreeable and a little more 'serious'* than the previous two vintages. Anton Massel had persuaded Salisbury-Jones to invest in a proper winery and more suitable equipment (at an overall cost of £6,000) was purchased and Massel took over the vinification. Writing at the end of 1957, Salisbury-Jones wrote: *I wish that I could find words to describe the scene at our home on that October day, in 1957, on the occasion of our third vendange. The weather was as perfect as on that day seven years before when I had first dreamed of the vineyard. The dream had now come true. There below me in the vineyard with their baskets were the pickers – my daughter and her young friends. A benevolent sun shone down upon their gaily coloured head-scarves and skirts and the sound of their laughter and young voices filled the air, just as I hoped.*

The heartening beam of Bacchus banished all our cares.

In 1960 it was decided to concentrate on white wine production (presumably the three red varieties had not been a success) and expand the vineyard. An additional 2,000 Seyval blanc – which had been the best performing of the varieties initially chosen – were planted on rootstock 41B at 4 x 3-feet (1.22 x 0.91-metres). The rootstock chosen, 41B, was at the time the most chalk-resistent variety available, so perhaps 161-49 and SO4 had not been resistant enough. The new vines were used to expand the area planted and to gap up where there had been failures. This brought the vineyard up to 1.5-acres (0.6-hectares) which was an area that Salisbury-Jones had been told by the French *would be enough to support a family.* In UK conditions this proved patently untrue and further plantings were planned.

By 1966, production at Hambledon had risen to *380 gallons or 2,380 bottles* and it was decided to plant more vines. In 1967, another 8,000 Seyval blanc, again on 41B, were planted. It was said at the time that the total planted area was *nearly 4½ acres,* although in fact the number of vines at that time – almost 13,500 – planted at 4 x 3-feet is around 3.7-acres (1.5-hectares). In 1970, it was decided to introduce some Chardonnay, and 2,000 on 161-49 and 41B were ordered. Unfortunately, the nursery the vines had been ordered from could not fulfil the whole order and two different nurseries were used. After two years, it was noticed that in fact whilst the original nursery had sent the correct vines – 1,000 Chardonnay on 41B – the second nursery had, in error, supplied 1,000 Pinot Meunier on SO4! In the end, this turned out to be an advantage as the Meunier performed better than the Chardonnay. In 1973, there was, according to Bill Carcary (see below), *a bit of filling-in*, and 1,000 Pinot Meunier and 500 Pinot noir were planted. The *bit of filling-in* was needed because there were quite large areas of the original plantings that had never thrived, most probably those on 161-49 which struggled in the very chalky soil. It was also decided that the vineyard had got too big to be sprayed by hand with a back-pack and, from an agent in Champagne, a Jacquet *tracteur-enjambeur*[11] complete with 475 cc Citroen engine was purchased with which to keep the vines sprayed.

The next addition to the Hambledon blend was in 1982, when 6,000 more vines were planted: 2,000 Auxerrois on SO4, 2,000 Pinot Meunier on SO4 and 41B and 2,000 Seyval blanc, again on SO4 and 41B. The fact that more Chardonnay were not planted was an admission that they were, at that time, an impossible variety to ripen for still wine production. The site at Hambledon is almost 100 metres above sea level and fairly open and exposed. As an experiment, eleven rows were planted at 8 x 4-feet (2.44 x 1.22-metres) on a high trellis (a variation of GDC) to see whether this would make life easier.

In the vineyard, Salisbury-Jones had the help of Bill Carcary who started work there after he left the Army in 1966 and continued to manage the vineyards and make

---

11 This *tracteur-enjambeur* (straddle tractor) was the only one in the UK until Frenchman Didier Pierson planted vines at Little West End Farm 3½ miles away to the north in 2004.

the wines until the late 1980s. (Carcary still lives in the cottage by the entrance to the vineyard, and keeps a watchful eye on the vines.) 1973 was one of their most successful and over 14,000 bottles were made. In the mid-1970s the Champagne house of Pol-Roger took an interest in the vineyards and one of their viticulturalists, Serge Martin, made several visits to give practical help and advice. By 1975, the vineyard was said to cover *a total of 5 acres and the average annual production had reached 10,000 bottles* and in a good year *production has exceeded 15,000 bottles.* In 1976 Hambledon had its best year ever, with yields of over 4-tonnes an acre (68-hl/ha) and a blend of Chardonnay and Meunier was produced – known as *Hambledon Gold Seal* – which went on to win a Gold medal at the Bristol Wine Fair in 1978.

The Hambledon name under Salisbury-Jones's ownership was widely known and their wine sold from many different outlets, could be found on Cunard and P&O cruise ships and they were one of the first vineyards to export their wine to the United States. I seem to recall that Neiman Marcus bought some for a British Week in their Dallas store. According to an undated booklet (probably written in 1968 or 1969) called *A Short History of Hambledon Wine*, a banquet was given by the Belgian *Académie du Vin* at the Restaurant Savoy in Brussels in honour of Hambledon's wines on 15 March 1966. Under the *Presidency of the Under-Secretary for the Development of External Commerce* (I am not sure whether this was a British or Belgian official) 36 bottles of (vintage not stated) Hambledon wine were consumed to accompany *Le Saumon d'Ecosse* which was served with a *Sauce Mousseline*. One wonders what the Belgians made of this wine, but since they were then treated to *Ch. Beychevelle 1961* and *Les Charmes Chambertin 1959* (both wines from fabled vintages), they probably didn't worry too much. They also consumed Sherry with the soup, a lesser Claret and Port with the Stilton, so I am sure it was an enjoyable occasion.

Sir Guy Salisbury-Jones – properly attired in jacket and tie – supervising the grape harvest

In 1976 Hambledon won the Farmer's Weekly Trophy (with which vintage is not recorded) and in 1978 they achieved their only success in the EWOYTC when they won a Bronze medal with their 1976 blend. Whether this singular award was because they rarely entered the competition, or because their wines were not made in an 'award-winning' style, is not known. However, their high-acid varieties would have performed better than usual in the exceptionally hot and dry 1976 conditions, resulting in a better than usual wine. Hambledon wines tended to be very dry and fairly austere – in the best traditions of French winemaking – and benefited from (perhaps *needed* would be more correct) bottle age. In my first guide, *The Vineyards of England,* written in 1989, the current vintage was the 1984, on sale at £3 a bottle. In 1979, Massel experimented with the production of a bottle-fermented sparkling wine with favourable results. However, Sir Guy considered that the production costs were too high and the length of time the wine needed to mature was too long to make the product commercially viable. *Hambledon 1982* also won a Gold medal and the English Wine Trophy in the 1984 IWSC.

Salisbury-Jones was founder President of the English Vineyards Association and remained at its head until 1981, when he relinquished this position and was appointed Honorary Life Patron. His time spent in the Diplomatic Corps was put to good use during his Presidency, and he worked diligently at securing such things as the grower's duty-free allowance, as well as pleading often against the absurdity of a lower rate of duty on 'British Made-Wines' which was then the case. Salisbury-Jones died on 8 February 1985 at the age of 88. In many ways Salisbury-Jones was the typical English winegrower of his time and many retired servicemen followed his example and planted vines. He was a magnificent spokesman for the industry (if one could have called it that in the early days) and certainly awoke the public to the existence of English wine.

Salisbury-Jones was also a published author and wrote a biography of Marshal de Lattre de Tassigny who had been in charge of *Saint-Cyr* when he was a student there and was a much-decorated professional soldier in the French Army. While Her Majesty's Marshall of the Diplomatic Corps, he was also asked to perform some unusual duties. After the independence of Morocco in 1963, he was called in to help organise their ceremonial occasions and in 1970 helped them design a royal coat of arms and their heraldic devices.

After Salisbury-Jones's death in 1985, the house and vineyards were sold to John Patterson, founder of the (pre-computer) dating service *Dateline.* In 1987, in a departure from the narrow-rowed, dense plantings that had been used up until then (almost 9,000 vines per hectare), another 3.04-hectares were planted on a 3.5 x 2.0-metre GDC system. At that stage the vineyards reached their maximum size of 6.22-hectares. Patterson also invested in the production facilities and a new winery, bottling hall and underground temperature controlled bottle store were built. In 1993, following his divorce, Patterson sold the house and estate and under the new owner, a

Canadian called Jim Larock – whose view was that *English Wine will never make money* – the vineyards went into something of a decline. Most of the vineyards were grubbed up leaving only 1-hectare of Seyval blanc and Pinot Meunier and the grapes were not always harvested. In 1999 it was sold to the current owner who eventually decided to replant the vineyards and resurrect Hambledon as a wine producing estate. In 2004, all the old vines having been removed, new vineyards were planted with

 Chardonnay, Pinot noir and Meunier and the area under vine is now just over 4-hectares. With a small harvest in 2007, wine production got under way and the grapes were sent to RidgeView for processing. In time, the winery and cellars will be refurbished so that the whole production process can take place on site.[12]

Hambledon Vineyard 2009

Harbourne Vineyard

c/o Wittersham, Tenterden, Kent TN30 7NP
Location of vineyard: High Halden, Tenterden, Kent TN26 3HD
Telephone: 01797 270420
E-mail: laurence@harbournevineyard.co.uk
Website: www.harbournevineyard.co.uk
Contact: Laurence Williams
Vineyards: 1.2 hectares
Grape varieties: Ortega, MT, Seyval, Bacchus, Pinot Meunier, Blauer Portugieser, Schönburger
Open to the public. See website for details.

Harden Vineyard

Grove Road, Penshurst, Kent TN11 8DX
Telephone: 01892 871443
E-mail: gerard.morris@talk21.com
Contact: Gerard Morris
Vineyards: 2.25 hectares
Grape varieties: Reichensteiner, Schönburger, Regent, Pinot noir Précoce
Not open to the public.

---

12   My thanks go to Bill Carcary for his help in putting the Hambledon story together.

Hargrove Estate

Wall-under-Heywood, Church Stretton, Shropshire SY6 7DP
Telephone: 01694 771722
E-mail: gbwainwright@aol.com
Contact: Gerard Wainwright
Vineyards: 1.25 hectares
Grape varieties: Siegerrebe, Bacchus, Phoenix, Regent
Not open to the public.

Harlestone Allotment Vineyard

10 Lower Harlestone, Northampton, Northamptonshire NN7 4EW
Telephone: 01604 616679
E-mail: spleasance@standrew.co.uk
Contact: Steve Pleasance
Vineyards: 0.0759 hectares
Grape varieties: Regent, Pinot noir, Pinot blanc, Orion, Solaris, Seyval blanc
Not open to the public.

Hattingley Valley Vineyard

c/o Kings Farm, Lower Wield, Alresford, Hampshire SO24 9RX
Location of vineyard: Medstead, Alton, Hampshire GU34 5NQ
Telephone: 01256 389188
Mobile: 07827 850487
E-mail: office@kingsfarm.co.uk
Contact: Simon Checketts, Simon Robinson
Vineyards: 7.3 hectares
Grape varieties: Chardonnay, Pinot noir, Pinot Meunier, Pinot Gris, Chenin blanc
Not open to the public.

Hazel End Vineyard

Hazel End Farm, Bishop's Stortford, Hertfordshire CM23 1HG
Telephone: 01279 812377
Fax: 08707 052463
Mobile: 07768 264766
E-mail: corylus@corylet.com
Website: www.corylet.com
Contact: Charles Humphreys
Vineyards: 1.2199 hectares
Grape varieties: Bacchus, Huxelrebe, MT, Reichensteiner
Not open to the public.

Charles Humphreys planted his first vines in 1978 but it was only in 1990 that the present site (the third!) was planted, producing the first commercial vintage in 1996. Still wines were produced initially under the Hazel End label and, since 2001,

sparkling wine under the Three Squirrels label has been successfully added. In 2009, an additional 1,500 Bacchus were planted on the original site first planted 30 years ago. The wines are made at Chapel Down in Kent and are sold from the farm. The Lemon Tree restaurant in nearby Bishop's Stortford offers Three Squirrels by the glass.

Head of the Vale Vineyard

Mitchells Farm, Stoke Trister, Wincanton, Somerset BA9 9PH
Telephone: 01963 33316
E-mail: david.jordan@mitchellsfarm.co.uk
Contact: David Jordan
Vineyards: 0.15 hectares
Grape varieties: Rondo, Regent
Not open to the public.

Heart of England Vineyard

Welford Hill Farm, Welford-on-Avon, Stratford-upon-Avon, Warwickshire, CV37 8AE
Telephone: 01789 750565   Mobile: 07775 805806
E-mail: sales@heart-of-england.info
Contact: Meryl Stanley, Nick Richards
Vineyards: 1.2145 hectares
Grape varieties: Phoenix, Seyval blanc, Rondo, Triomphe
Not open to the public.

Helmsley Walled Garden Vineyard

Cleveland Way, Helmsley, North Yorkshire YO62 5AH
Telephone: 01439 771427
E-mail: info@helmsleywalledgarden.org.uk
Website: www.helmsleywalledgarden.org.uk
Contact: Neil Booth
Vineyards: 0.0001 hectares
Grape varieties: Rondo, Regent, Phoenix, Orion, Siegerrebe, plus vines on garden walls
Open to the public. See website for details.

Hendred Vineyard

Allins Lane, East Hendred, Wantage, Oxfordshire OX12 8HR
Telephone: 01235 820081
Mobile: 07771 921210
E-mail: hendredvineyard@btinternet.com

Website: www.hendredvineyard.co.uk
Contact: Steve and Viviane Callaghan
Vineyards: 2.2031 hectares
Grape varieties: Seyval blanc, MA, Pinot noir
Open to the public. See website for details.

Henners Vineyard

c/o The Granary, Ladham Road, Goudhurst, Kent TN17 1LS
Location of vineyard: Church Road, Herstmonceaux, East Sussex BN27 1QJ
Telephone: 01580 211134   Mobile: 07971 464202
E-mail: larrywarr@hennersvineyard.co.uk
Website: www.hennersvineyard.co.uk
Contact: Larry Warr
Vineyards: 2.8340 hectares
Grape varieties: Chardonnay, Pinot noir, Pinot Meunier
Open by appointment.

Herons Ghyll Estate

Newnham Park, Chillies Lane, Crowborough, East Sussex TN6 3TB
Telephone: 07956 388272
E-mail: marshslatter@blueyonder.co.uk
Website: www.heronsghyllestate.co.uk
Contact: Marsh Slatter
Vineyards: 3.65 hectares
Grape varieties: Huxelrebe, Reichensteiner

Herts Oak Farm Vineyard

c/o 165 High Road, Broxbournebury, Hertfordshire EN10 7BT
Location of vineyard: Beaumont Road, Wormley West End, Broxbourne, Hertfordshire, EN10 7QJ
Contact: Carmelo Galione 01992 448537
Contact: Ben Roberts 07867 971166
E-mail: ben.roberts@ntlworld.com
Vineyards: 1.03 hectares
Grape varieties: Bacchus, Reichensteiner, Dunkelfelder, Regent, Rondo, Acolon, Nero

Heveningham Hall

Heveningham Hall, Heveningham, Halesworth, Suffolk IP19 0PN
Telephone: 07773 816344
E-mail: grahambroadhurst@btinternet.com
Contact: Graham Broadhurst
Vineyards: 1.0121 hectares
Grape varieties: 14 varieties on trial
Not open to the public.

Hidden Spring Vineyard

Vines Cross Road, Horam, Heathfield, East Sussex, TN21 0HF
Telephone & Fax: 01435 812640
E-mail: hiddenspring@btconnect.com
Website: www.hiddenspring.co.uk
Contact: David Whittingham, Tamzin Whittingham
Vineyards: 1.4 hectares
Grape varieties: Reichensteiner, Faberrebe, Pinot noir, Dunkelfelder
Open to the public on Saturdays or by appointment. See website for details.

High Clandon Vineyard

Clandon Downs, High Clandon, Surrey, GU4 7RP
Telephone: 01483 225660
Mobile: 07711 266918
E-mail: Sibylla.tindale@tecres.net
Contact: Sibylla and Bruce Tindale
Vineyards: 0.5 hectares
Grape varieties: Chardonnay, Pinot noir, Pinot Meunier
Not open to the public.

High Cross Vineyard

c/o Tanglewood, 1 Main Road, Claybrooke Magna, Leicester, Leicestershire, LE17 5AJ
Location of vineyard: High Cross Road Allotments, Claybrooke Magna, LE17 5
Telephone: 01455 209116
Mobile: 07946 722934
E-mail: robvaldeacon@aol.com
Contact: Robin Deacon
Vineyards: 0.015 hectares
Grape varieties: Solaris, Regent
Not open to the public.

Highdown Vineyard

Littlehampton Road, Ferring, West Sussex BN12 6PG
Telephone: 01903 500663
Mobile: 07719 858282
E-mail: wine@highdown-vineyard.co.uk or karinhay@hotmail.co.uk
Website: www.highdown-vineyard.co.uk
Contact: Karin Hay, Ross Hay
Vineyards: 2.5 hectares
Grape varieties: Pinot noir, Rondo, Dornfelder, Reichensteiner, Bacchus, Schönburger, Chardonnay
Open to the public. See website for details.

Higher Bumsley Vineyard

Higher Bumsley Farm, Parracombe, Devon EX31 4PT
Telephone: 01598 763325
E-mail: brakebrook@btinternet.com
Contact: Pamela Smith, Peter Smith
Vineyards: 0.83 hectares
Grape varieties: MA
Open by appointment.

Higher Sandford Vineyard

Higher Sandford House, Sandford Orcas, Sherborne, Dorset, DT9 4RP
Telephone: 01963 220275
Mobile: 07831 458468
E-mail: candreskell@btinternet.com
Contact: Christopher and Rosanne Eskell
Vineyards: 0.25 hectares
Grape varieties: Reichensteiner, Bacchus
Not open to the public.

Hobdens Vineyards

Hobdens, Mayfield, Rotherfield, East Sussex TN20 6HH
Telephone: No telephone numbers available – please e-mail
E-mail: hello@hobdensvineyards.com or foxes@seva.uk.com
Website: www.hobdensvineyards.com
Contact: Gerard and Jonica Fox
Vineyards: 1.6 hectares
Grape varieties: Pinot noir, Chardonnay, Pinot gris, Pinot Meunier, Pinot blanc
Not open to the public. Only sparkling wines are produced.

Hobdens Vineyards

Holmfirth Vineyard

Woodhouse Farm, Woodhouse Lane, Holmbridge, Holmfirth, West Yorkshire, HD9 2QR
Telephone: 0113 815 5588
Mobile: 07910 400152
E-mail: bec@holmfirthvineyard.com
E-mail: contactus@holmfirthvineyard.com
Website: www.holmfirthvineyard.com
Contact: Rebecca and Ian Sheveling
Vineyards: 1.932 hectares
Grape varieties: Solaris, Ortega, Acolon, Regent, Rondo
Open by appointment.

Horsmonden Vineyard

c/o Davenport Vineyards, Limney Farm, Castle Hill, East Sussex TN6 3RR
Location of vineyard: Hazel Street Farm, Horsmonden, Kent, TN12 8EF
See entry for Davenport Vineyards for contact details
Vineyards: 6.4778 hectares
Grape varieties: Ortega, Bacchus, Huxelrebe, Faberrebe, Siegerrebe, Pinot noir, Chardonnay, Pinot Meunier
Open by appointment.

Horsmonden Vineyard was Will Davenport's first venture as a viticulturalist and was planted in 1991 on his parent's fruit farm on a south-facing site between 80 and 90 metres above sea level. The soil is a typical Wealden clay with a sandy-loam topsoil. The site is well sheltered with windbreaks and areas of woodland and has never suffered from spring frost damage. This is the heart of the 'Garden of England', the fruit-growing region famed for its hops, cherries, apples and pears, plus soft fruit. Whilst hops and fruit may have declined over the last 50 years, there is still plenty of intensive fruit farmed here, including vines. The vines have been productive since 1993 and the grapes are taken to the winery at Limney Farm (Davenport Vineyards). Further vines were planted in 2000 (Pinot noir) and in 2007 (Chardonnay, Ortega, Bacchus, Siegerrebe and Pinot Meunier). The vines are all now Double Guyot trained.

Hunt Hall Farm Vineyard

Hunt Hall Lane, Welford-on-Avon, Stratford-on-Avon, Warwickshire, CV37 8HE
Telephone: 01789 750349
Mobile: 07742 540150
E-mail: ni.richards@btinternet.com
Contact: Nick Richards
Vineyards: 4 hectares
Grape varieties: Too many to list (and remember)!
Not open to the public.

Hush Heath Estate Vineyard

Hush Heath Farm, Cranbrook, Kent TN17 2NG
Telephone: 020 7479 2900
Fax: 020 7479 9109
Website: www.hushheath.com
Contact: Richard Balfour-Lynn 07703 393111 E-mail: rbl@mwb.co.uk
Contact: Karen Hargreaves 07768 594669 E-mail: hushheath@mwb.co.uk
Contact: Sheila O'Hare 020 7479 2914
Vineyards: 5.0108 hectares
Grape varieties: Chardonnay, Pinot noir, Pinot Meunier
Open by appointment.

Hush Heath Estate sits in the middle of the plain to the south of Maidstone, known as the Weald of Kent, famed for its fine apples, soft fruit and hops, and, since the mid-1960s, its vineyards. In 2002 an initial 1.53 hectares of Pinot noir and Chardonnay were planted by owner Richard Balfour-Lynn who had a year or two earlier managed to buy the farmland that surrounded his beautiful half-timbered Tudor manor house. Since then, further plantings have taken place: 0.15 hectares of Pinot Meunier in 2004 and 0.3 hectares (2007) and 3.1 hectares (2008) of the three Champagne varieties. The overall *encépagement* is 45 per cent Pinot noir, 45 percent Chardonnay and 10 per cent Pinot Meunier.

I was brought in as consultant at an early stage and helped select the site for the initial planting of vines – an old Bramley apple orchard – and advised on all aspects of the vineyard. After some initial discussions and tastings, Balfour-Lynn decided that his goal was to produce one product – a top-quality, bottle-fermented sparkling rosé. The vines were hand-planted, trellised in their first year and made very good growth, so good in fact that in 2003 we managed to harvest just over 2 tonnes of grapes. Balfour-Lynn had by that time become a part-owner of Chapel Down and the grapes were taken there for processing. Since that first harvest, the site has proved itself capable of producing both good quality and good yields of fruit: 12-tonnes in 2004, 21-tonnes in 2005, 32-tonnes in 2006, 9-tonnes in 2007, 14-tonnes in 2008 and 20.5-tonnes in 2009 – an average yield (not including 2003) of 4.20-tonnes per acre or 10.37 tonnes per hectare. The average yield over the same period (2004-9) for the individual varieties has been: Chardonnay 10.62 t/ha; Pinot Noir 11.21 t/ha; and Pinot Meunier 8.18 t/ha. Sugar and acid levels have also been good, especially considering the age of the vines and the relatively high yields. Sugars have been between 8.3% and 11.1% and acids (as tartaric) between 8.5 g/l and 15.5 g/l, ideal for sparkling wine.The first small vintage, the 2003, was not released, but served as a test-bed for the commercial vintages that followed. The *2004 Balfour Brut Rosé*, released in October 2006 after a bare 18 months *sur latte,* turned out to be of excellent quality, winning a Silver medal in the EWOTYC and gaining critical acclaim from many different sources. The wine was well received by the trade and sold out by mid-2008. In the 2008 IWC it was awarded the only Gold Medal awarded to an English Wine and picked up the prestigeous English Wine Trophy. The 2005 vintage, released in May 2008, tasted even better than the previous vintage did at the same stage and in its first competition outing won the prestigious SEVA 'Wine of the Year' Trophy together with a Gold Medal. It also won a Gold medal and the English Wine Trophy in the 2009 Decanter World Wine Awards. At the time of writing, the 2006 has just been launched and is selling in both Waitrose and Marks and Spencers, packaged in a very smart box, at £34.99 a bottle.

That the Balfour Brut Rosé has had such early success is very satisfying to all concerned. Balfour-Lynn is certainly the most enthusiastic (and occasionally demanding) of all the clients I have ever worked for and when he puts his energy behind something, things tend to happen. Although his day job – running several different companies with interests in: hotels (Malmaison Hotels, Hôtel du Vin, De Vere), sports clubs (Green's Health and Fitness), conference facilities (De Vere Venues), serviced offices (MWB Business Exchange), retail (Liberty of Regent Street), drinks (G and J Greenall), catering (Searcy), and property (Marylebone, Warwick, Balfour) – means that he leads a busy life, I always get the feeling that Balfour Brut Rosé is one of his real passions. Planning permission has been obtained to build a winery at Hush Heath to produce around 100,000 bottles a year. In 2009 Sandhurst Vineyards planted 4-hectares of Champagne varieties which are under contract to Hush Heath.

Hush Heath Estate, Kent

Huxbear Vineyard

Chudleigh, Newton Abbot, Devon, TQ13 0EH
Mobile: 07846 407713
E-mail: ben.hulland@gmail.com
Website: www.huxbear.com
Contact: Ben Hulland
Vineyards: 4 hectares
Grape varieties: Chardonnay, Pinot noir, Pinot Meunier, Bacchus, Siegerrebe, Schönburger
Not open to the public.

Ickworth Vineyard

c/o Fortlands Sicklesmere Road, Bury St Edmunds Suffolk IP33 2BN
Location of vineyard: Ickworth House, Horringer, Bury St Edmunds, IP29 5QE
Note: Ickworth House is a National Trust property
Telephone: 01284 723399 Fax: 01284 748021
Mobile: 07980 208442
E-mail: macready@ickworthvineyard.co.uk
Website: www.ickworthvineyard.co.uk
Contact: Jillian Macready
Vineyards: 0.8 hectares
Grape varieties: Rondo, Auxerrois, Bacchus, Pinot noir
Open to the public. See website for details.

The National Trust took over Ickworth House from the Marquises of Bristol (the Hervey family) in 1956 but in 1995 - the Trust's centenary year - the walled garden was turned over to the cultivation of grapevines. Jillian and Charles Macready (along with family and friends) planted 1 hectares of vines, which had grown within the walls in Victorian times. This time the emphasis was on the production of fine English wine. It is the only commercial vineyard on National Trust land and the south facing slope and the walls provided a sheltered and idyllic setting for it.

Bacchus and Auxerrois were planted on the east side and in 1996 the west side was planted with a fairly new red variety known (rather unpromisingly) at the time as GM 6494/5 and now known as Rondo, a rather apt for a vine grown on a property famous for it's Rotunda and which has an impressive Italiante garden. Seventy Pinot Noir vines were also planted against the south-facing wall, as these would need a little more global warming to be really happy in the main vineyard. Pinot Noir was chosen to give complexity to the sparkling wine.

Four wines are produced. The rosé, the white and the sparkling were made, up until 2008, by Chapel Down Winery in Kent and the red is made by Carter's Vineyard in Essex. The Lady Geraldine's Blush is made from Rondo grapes and is treated as a white wine, without being left on the skins like many rosés. It has damsons, cranberries and raspberries on the palette with a long redcurrant finish. This wine was launched in the summer of 2007 in response to a 30% increase in rosé drinking – nice to see a tiny boutique vineyard taking account of marketing trends! Suffolk Pink is Ickworth's bottle-fermented sparkling pink wine which won a silver medal in the 2006 EWOTYC. It is worth noting that the only sparkling wine to receive a higher accolade in that year was Nyetimber's. Pinot Noir can impart colour to wine, but the pink in this wine comes from about 15 ml of Rondo wine added at dosage time. Those interested in old Suffolk houses will know that the wine shares its name with the colour of some of the traditional houses in the area.

The Earl Bishop's Reserve is red and made 100% from Rondo grapes. It is deep in colour, has a rich, plummy aroma and satisfyingly smooth lingering flavour not unlike a Montepulciano of Italy. This too has won a decent amount of medals in it's time, the best of which was East Anglian Wine of the Year 2000 when the wasps took all but 20% of the grapes leaving the rest with a very high concentration of sugar. This was exploited by Mary Mudd, our winemaker at Carters, who was able to make a wonderfully rich and complex red that year.

The Walled Garden Bacchus 2005 was winner of the President's Trophy for the Best Small Production wine in the 2007 EWOTYC. Needless to say it was much in demand and soon ran out since there was so little of it produced.

If you are visiting Ickworth Park you can wander around the vineyard on your own, but please close all gates after you as deer are partial to tender vine and rose shoots! Group tours and wine-tastings can be arranged at any time, by appointment. If you want to taste the wines before you buy, Open Days are on the second Sunday of the month, June to October. Visitors can do a self guided tour following interpretation boards; take in the wonderful view of the vineyard from across the lake and end up at the gazebo in the vineyard for a wine tasting and short talk by Jillian and Charles Macready. Children have activities to do and are offered grape juice to drink.

There is a cost for the vineyard Open Days, even if you are a National Trust member: £3.50 for adults and 50p for children. (Please note that if you are not an NT member, there is a charge to enter the park payable at the kiosk on entry. See the NT website for details).

Iron Railway Vineyard

c/o 11 Vincent Road, Coulsdon, Surrey CR5 3DH
Location of vineyard: RH1 3BA
Telephone: 01737 551829
Contact: John Dicken
Vineyards: 0.81 hectares
Grape varieties: MA, Phoenix, Orion, Solaris
Open by appointment.

Jabajak Vineyard

Blanc-Y-Llain, Llanboidy Road, Whitland, Carmarthenshire SA34 0ED, Wales
Telephone: 01994 448786
E-mail: info@jabajak.co.uk
Website: www.jabajak.co.uk
Contact: Amanda and Julian Stuart-Robson
Vineyards: 1 hectare
Grape varieties: Reichensteiner, Phoenix, Huxelrebe, Seyval blanc, Pinot noir Précoce
Open to the public. See website for details.

Jays Farm Vineyard

Embley Lane, East Wellow, Hampshire SO51 6DN
Telephone: 01794 511314   Mobile: 07773 848994
E-mail: sales@embleywine.co.uk
Website: www.embleywine.co.uk
Contact: Jamie King
Vineyards: 4.2 hectares
Grape varieties: Seyval blanc
Open by appointment. See website for details.

Jenkyn Place Vineyard

Hole Lane, Bentley, Alton, Hampshire, GU10 5LU
Telephone: 020 7736 3102
Telephone: 01420 22561
Mobile: 07973 318061
Fax: 020 7731 7614
E-mail: simon.bladon@westella.org
Contact: Simon Bladon
Vineyards: 2.9 hectares
Grape varieties: Chardonnay, Pinot noir, Pinot Meunier
Open by appointment.

There are two separate vineyards at Jenkyn Place, both planted on former hop-gardens and both on Greensand over marlstone and chalk. The westernmost, called Dogkennel Vineyard (1.6 hectares), was planted in 2004, 2005 and 2009 and is 15 per cent Pinot Meunier, 25 per cent Pinot noir and 60 per cent Chardonnay, all Double Guyot trained. The second vineyard, known as Inwoods (1.3 hectares), was planted in 2007 and is very much within the village of Bentley with houses on all four sides. This vineyard is 50 per cent Chardonnay, 50 per cent Pinot noir and is also Double Guyot trained. Both vineyards are adjacent to the gardens of Jenkyn Place which were very well known and open to the public before the current owner purchased the property. A further 2 ha is planned for 2010.

The first harvest was in 2006 and both that and the 2007 harvest were sent to RidgeView for processing. The first wine – a bottled-fermented sparkling wine – was released in June 2009 and won a bronze medal at the 2009 EWOTYC. From 2008, the grapes have been sent to a new winery at Wiston Estate (see separate entry) which is masterminded by Dermot Sugrue, the former Nytimber winemaker, who will be making a Jenkyn Place Brut, and also a Sparkling Rosé.

Kempes Hall Vineyard

Kempes Corner, Wye, Ashford, Kent TN25 4ER
Telephone: 01233 812217
Contact: Tony Denne
E-mail: tony@tonydenne.fsnet.co.uk
Vineyards: 0.1 hectares
Grape varieties: Chardonnay, Schönburger, Seyval blanc
Not open to the public.

This vineyard was originally owned by Charles Laughton (no, not the actor) who planted it in 1976 and who was for many years Treasurer of the SEVA. The trophy awarded to the runner-up in the SEVA competition is named after him.

Kemps Vineyard

Church Street, Hargrave, Northamptonshire, NN9 6BW
Telephone: 01933 623497
E-mail: marie@kempsvineyard.eclipse.co.uk
Contact: Joe Rawlings, Marie Rawlings
Vineyards: 0.2 hectares
Grape varieties: Dunkelfelder, Dornfelder, Triomphe, Merlot, Pinot noir, Chambourcin, Reichensteriner, Phoenix
Not open to the public.

Kemp's Vineyard

The Winery, Dales Meadow, Bury St Edmunds, Suffolk IP29 4EY
Telephone: 01359 271497
Mobile: 07785 163252
E-mail: johnkemp296@btinternet.com
Contact: John Kemp
Vineyards: 0.75 hectares
Grape varieties: MA, Bacchus, Rondo
Not open to the public.

Kenton Vineyard

Helwell Barton, Kenton, Exeter, Devon EX6 8NW
Telephone: 01626 891091
Fax: 01626 891091
E-mail: info@kentonvineyard.co.uk
Website: www.kentonvineyard.co.uk
Contact: Matthew Bernstein
Vineyards: 2.75 hectares
Grape varieties: Pinot noir Précoce, Ortega, Bacchus, Seyval blanc, Solaris, Rondo, Auxerrois, Dornfelder.
Open to the public. See website for details.

Kenton Vineyard was established in 2003 and 2004 by Matthew Bernstein, previously a solicitor who studied viticulture and winemaking at Plumpton College. The site, chosen after an 18 month search, is ideal for grape-growing being on south-facing slopes with free-draining sandy soil. It is located in an area historically renowned for horticulture and arable farming, partly because of the weather protection afforded by the Haldon Hills. The vines are planted at 2.2 x 1.4-metres, on a Scott Henry trellis.

An existing farm building was converted to create a winery, fitted out with all-new stainless steel tanks and equipment, in time for the 2006 harvest. The wines produced include a red, a rosé, a single varietal Ortega, a single varietal Bacchus, and a sparkling wine. An adjoining shop was opened to the public in May 2007. The 2006 wines proved very successful and sold out within a few weeks. As a result the vineyard was expanded in 2008, which doubled the Ortega and Pinot Noir Précoce plantings, as well as introducing Seyval blanc and Solaris. A Kreyer cooling system is being fitted to the winery for the 2009 harvest, which will allow complete control of fermentation temperatures.

Kents Green Vineyard

Kents Green House, Kents Green, Taynton, Gloucestershire GL19 3AJ
Telephone: 01452 790171
Mobile: 07771 732319
E-mail: charliepeak@yahoo.com
Website: www.kentsgreenwine.co.uk
Contact: Charlie Peak
Vineyards: 0.18 hectares
Grape varieties: MT
Not open to the public.

Keyham Vineyard

c/o Abbey Vineyards Group, Irnham Grange, Irnham, Corby Glen, Grantham, Lincolnshire, NG33 4NE
Location of vineyard: Hungarton Lane, Keyham, Leicestershire, LE7 9JU
Telephone: 01476 550191
Fax: 01476 550080
E-mail: info@abbeyvineyards.co.uk
Contact: Phil Kerry 07815 308838
Contact: Jonathan Kerry 07805 315763
Vineyards: 2.25 hectares
Grape varieties: Seyval blanc, Rondo, Solaris, Ortega, Acolon
Not open to the public.

Knightshayes Vineyard

c/o Knighshayes Court, Bolham, Tiverton, Devon, EX16 7RQ
Location of vineyard: EX16 7RD
Telephone - Gardens Department: 01884 253264
Fax: 01844 243050
Mobile: 07969 239599
E-mail: kightshayes@nationaltrust.ork.uk
Website: www.nationaltrust.org.uk
Contact: Lorraine Colebrook
Vineyards: 0.072 hectares
Grape varieties: Regent, Orion
Open to the public as part of a National Trust property.

Kilcott Valley Vineyard

Bank Cottage, Lower Kilcott, Wotton-under-Edge, Gloucestershire GL12 7RL
Telephone: 01454 238007
Mobile: 07951 331351
E-mail: info@kilcottvalley.com
E-mail: davidandjojones@yahoo.co.uk
Website: www.kilcottvalley.com
Contact: David Jones

Vineyards: 0.2 hectares
Grape varieties: Seyval blanc
Not open to the public.

Kingfishers' Pool Vineyard

43 Westfield Lane, Rothley, Leicestershire LE7 7LH
Telephone: 0116 207 8701
E-mail: lizrobson@kp43.fsnet.co.uk
E-mail: eerobson@dmu.ac.uk
Contact: Liz Robson
Vineyards: 0.24 hectares
Grape varieties: Siegerrebe, Orion, Solaris
Not open to the public.

This amateur vineyard is situated behind a house which is located within the former grounds of a Knights of St. John monastery, the Rothley Temple. This is where William Wilberforce drafted the Act of Parliament to abolish the slave trade, and is now a hotel. Further along Westfield Lane lie the ruins of a Roman villa and a steam railway station.

The 550 vines were chosen to suit the sandy soil with a low pH, and are planted on a GDC system. Further vines may be planted when Liz and Matthew have some spare time from their university careers. The first harvest is anticipated to be in 2010, and the grapes will be sent to a commercial vineyard to be made into wine. It is unlikely that wine will be available to the public until a few years have passed.

Kit's Coty Vineyard

Location of vineyard: Pilgrims Way, Eccles, Aylesford, Maidstone, Kent ME20 7EF
See entry for Chapel Down Wines for contact details
Vineyards: 29.4 hectares
Grape varieties: Chardonnay, Pinot noir
Not open to the public. This 47-hectare site was bought in early 2008 and 29.4 hectares have been planted. More vines will be planted in the future.

Knettishall Vineyard

Hall Farm, Heath Road, Knettishall, Diss, Suffolk IP22 2TQ
Telephone: 07968 106549
E-mail: jbucher@netcom.co.uk
Contact: James Bucher
Vineyards: 1.2 hectares
Grape varieties: Bacchus, Pinot noir, Auxerrois
Open by appointment.

La Mare Vineyards and Distillery

St Mary, Jersey JE3 3BA, Channel Isles
Telephone: 01534 481178
Fax: 01534 48521
E-mail: info@lamarevineyards.com
E-mail: tim@lamarevineyards.com
Website: www.lamarewineestate.com
Contact: Tim Crowley
Vineyards: 5 hectares
Grape varieties: Seyval blanc, Reichensteiner, Pinot noir, Regent, Rondo
Open to the public. See website for details.

Lamberhurst Vineyard

The Down, Lamberhurst, Kent TN3 8ER
Telephone: 01892 890412
Fax: 01892 891242
E-mail: info@lamberhurstvineyard.net
Website: www.lamberhurstvineyard.net
Contact: Ruth Smart
Vineyards: 8.1 hectares
Grape varieties: Bacchus, Rondo, Pinot noir, Pinot blanc, Regent, Ortega, Reichensteiner
Open to the public. See website for details.

In its heyday, Lamberhurst Vineyard was by far the best-known vineyard in the UK and its wines were considered the model to which other growers aspired. It was at its peak the largest producer, had the most modern winery and the most charismatic winemaker (Karl-Heinz Johner). Today, it is, as they say, but a shadow of its former self, brought down by a combination of changing tastes and changing owners, although now undergoing something of a revival.

The Lamberhurst story started in 1971 when Kenneth McAlpine, a member of the Sir Robert McAlpine construction family, who lived (and still lives) at Lamberhurst Priory and had substantial farming interests in the village, thought that some land he had just purchased overlooking the village would be suitable for vines. Although the land was north-facing, it was well sheltered from the prevailing south-westerly winds, quite steeply sloping and had often produced early crops of raspberries, strawberries and other fruit. Vines would fit in well with some of the other crops being grown on his farms which included both hops and fruit. Bob Reeves, his farm manager, who was fluent in German from his time in the army and had a German-born wife, visited Germany and went to Geisenheim to see the head of viticulture, Professor Kiefer, who suggested varieties and trellising systems that could be used in the UK. In 1972 an initial 3.64 hectares were planted with Müller-Thurgau, Seyval Blanc and Madeleine x Angevine 7672, all on a 2.6 by 1.3-metre Pendlebogen training system. In 1974 Professor Kiefer came over from Geisenheim to see how the first plantings were coming along, and encouraged by his advice, another 1.6 hectares were planted the following year.

In the spring of 1974, as the first grapes were appearing on the vines, an apple farm, called Ridge Farm, facing onto Lamberhurst Down was purchased and a relatively simple winery installed in what had been the old apple grading room and cold stores. Reeves had always looked more to Germany than to France for help and encouragement and for the first vintage in 1974, two young Germans, Ernst Abel, who worked at Geisenheim and Karl-Heinz Schmitt, a Geisenheim graduate, came over for the vintage. Abel returned soon after the harvest, leaving Schmitt to carry on. Only 700 bottles of 1974 wine were produced, with quite a few grapes having been lost before harvest to birds and *Botrytis*. The following year, 1975, was generally a good year for English vineyards and some 7,000 bottles were made from their own vineyards and in addition they began taking in grapes from other vineyards and making wines under contract. In 1976, Schmitt decided to return home, and another young winemaker was sought. In September, just before the harvest, Karl-Heinz Johner, also a graduate from Geisenheim, came over with his wife and two young children, and took over as winemaker.

The 1976 harvest was large and showed that the existing winery was far from adequate, and for the next harvest a brand new winery, certainly the largest in the UK, and equipped to a better standard than many overseas, was built. With its underground fermentation and storage cellars capable of holding 300,000 litres, its insulated bottle store with a capacity of 500,000 bottles, its Willmes pneumatic presses, Westphalia centrifuge and fully automatic bottling line, it was for many the proof they needed that English Wine had arrived. Of course it helped to have access to the McAlpine millions and the funding of the new winery was rumoured to have come from McAlpine's share in the proceeds of the sale of the Dorchester Hotel which the family had owned since the 1930s.

In 1977 another 5.24 hectares of vines were planted, bringing the total up to 10 hectares, and in 1979 another 4 hectares making them by far the largest vineyard in the country. It was not all plain sailing, however. The initial area of Madeleine Angevine proved very unsatisfactory, with many plants dying and the remainder refusing to crop and they were grubbed-up in 1975. They were replaced with Ortega which a neighbour promptly sprayed with 2-4-5-T weedkiller, killing over half of them! During 1975, areas of newly planted vines appeared to be dying for no apparent reason and Professor Stellwag-Kittler (head of viticulture at Geisenheim) was brought over to see if he could see what the problem was. A flight for him in McAlpine's helicopter over both Lamberhurst's and some nearby vineyards failed to pinpoint the cause. However, one of the women working in the vineyards noticed a small grub emerging from a dead vine and it transpired that the Dock Sawfly had taken to laying its eggs in the stems of the young vines, and the hatching larvae were the problem. This was put right by getting rid of the docks in the vineyards and covering the grafts of newly planted vines with grafting wax.

After the large 1976 yield, harvests during the period 1977 to 1981 were generally poor, and it was at this time that the spare capacity in the new winery was put to good use by the production of a 'British Wine'. The first batch was made from a quantity of table grapes destined for Covent Garden that had become over-ripe in transit and the resulting wine was known as Olympus, named after the variety of grape used. As production grew, it was decided to use fresh grape juice from Germany, and the name was changed to Festival. At this time, British Made-Wines (as they were officially called) carried a lower rate of duty than either imported or home produced wines, and this enabled Festival to be sold at the very competitive price of £1.49 a bottle. With the advent of the large crops in 1982 and 1983 however, the decision was taken to drop the production of Festival, much to the relief of many growers of English Wines who felt that too much confusion was being caused over the distinction between British and English wine. It also showed English wines, then selling in the £2.99–£4.99 price range, in a poor light, many consumers not realising the intrinsic difference between the products.

However, this relief was short-lived as, in 1984, with another large crop of grapes harvested from vineyards all over the country and over 1 million bottles in stock in both tank and bottle, McAlpine took the decision to cut the retail price of his basic English Wine, the blended 'Lamberhurst White', to an unheard-of price of £1.99 (a full £1 below the price that anyone else was then selling English Wine for), together with attractive wholesale prices. Sales of this wine naturally took off and suddenly there was an English Wine which could be found on the shelves of wine merchants all over the country, spreading the word that the product was good, available and, at that price, no longer the elitist product it had seemed to be to many wine drinkers and, perhaps more importantly, wine merchants as well.

The harvests between 1982 and 1986 were relatively good for the south-east, and during this period Lamberhurst was able to consolidate its position as the leading vineyard in the country. The vineyards were extended to over 20 hectares and the output of wine increased. A grape purchase scheme was started which contracted growers in other parts of the country to supply grapes on a regular basis and a range of services from winemaking to vineyard management as well as a wide variety of supplies for both vineyards and wineries were offered for sale. In 1988, Johner, who since 1982 had been commuting weekly between Lamberhurst and his home and vineyards in Baden, decided to leave. He had recently started selling wines from his German vineyards in England and as this was taking more and more of his available time, he decided that he could no longer devote enough time to the Lamberhurst operations. After a little problem over some midnight blending and an exchange of views with management, he thought it best to leave.

Johner's 12 years as winemaker at Lamberhurst were ones of remarkable change in the English Wine industry. While he was winemaker, the winery won many awards and medals for both its own wines and the many it made under contract. Their 1982 Huxelrebe (made with grapes purchased from Bill Ash's Staple Vineyards) and their 1984 Schönburger both won the Gore-Browne Trophy. They also won four Gold and seven Silver medals (which were then far more difficult to win than today) and their wines were regularly awarded the EVA's Seal of Quality. During this time, Johner also started experimenting with oak-aged wines, bottle-fermented sparkling wines and red wines – all types of wine that were then far from commonplace. With the supportive backing of McAlpine he was able to use techniques and equipment unavailable to most UK wineries at the time and did much to pave the way for today's wine styles. Lamberhurst's seemingly unbeatable position in terms of both wine quality and the market certainly goaded the rest of us in the industry to sharpen up our collective acts. Johner also started production of their successful range of fruit liqueurs which helped support the marketing of their wines.

Lamberhurst's wines from this era were often criticised for being too 'Germanic' and for their over-reliance on imported *süss-reserve* which was used quite liberally in most of the more popular and widely distributed wines. With hindsight, it easy to say this, but the market for high-volume wines was then very different to today's and almost all the top-selling brands were Liebfraumilch or of a similar style: Blue Nun,

Golden Oktober and Black Tower were then the leading wines in the light-wine sector. Whatever the supposed failings of Lamberhurst's wines, the professionalism with which they were produced, packaged and marketed – at least when compared to how most of the growers at that time presented their wines – did much to put English Wines in front of both the public and the wine trade.

In July 1988 I received a telephone call from Diana Hibling, McAlpine's personal assistant, who said that 'Mr Kenneth' (as he was usually known) would like to speak to me. In a few minutes he explained that he had sacked Johner and asked if I would like to take over as 'Winemaker and General Manager'. After considerable deliberation and a promise from McAlpine that I would be free for three months at the start of 1989 to write the first edition of this guide to vineyards in the UK, I agreed. It was not an easy decision to make because only two years before I had sold my vineyard and winery at Tenterden with the intention of spending my time writing in the summer and contract winemaking in the winter. However, running Lamberhurst, then the largest producer of English Wines, was a challenge I felt I could not let pass (plus there was the salary and the Golf GTI which helped).

For the three years that I was at Lamberhurst, things more or less continued where Johner had left off. More vineyards were planted including 0.75 hectares of the new red *Vitis amurensis* hybrid Rondo which had been on trial from Geisenheim and 5 hectares of Seyval blanc which had proved over its years the most productive variety on the farm. During my time there I relied very heavily in the winery on Stephen Donnelly, who had been Assistant Winemaker since 1987, and I like to think that we made some interesting wines. We were all certainly very pleased, in 1990, to win both the Gore-Browne[13] and the Wine Guild Trophy with the 1988 Schönburger. It was also during this time that Lamberhurst launched the first brandy made from English Wine – an event which seemed to interest the media far beyond its commercial importance. Substantial improvements to both the visitor and office facilities were also carried out while I was there. In 1991 McAlpine decided that as he was now approaching retirement age he would like to retire from active management of the business and started to look for a purchaser for the whole enterprise. In the light of what were obviously going to be substantial changes to the place, I decided that I would continue where I left off – making wine under contract and writing. It had been an enjoyable and enlightening time and for someone who had been largely self-employed for their whole working life, something of an eye-opener.

---

[13] Winning the Gore-Browne Trophy gave rise to one of my more unusual moments at Lamberhurst. Having accepted the trophy at the House of Lords annual prizegiving, it was retained as it needed engaving. Consequently, when the local press turned up at the vineyard to take a photograph, there was no trophy. McAlpine said "not to worry, I have a cupboard full of silverware at home" and duly returned home, to reappear a short while later with a magnificent silver cup which his Connaught F1 motor racing team acquired by winning the 1955 Syracuse Grand Prix (for the avoidance of doubt, that's Syracuse in Sicily) driven by Tony Brooks in his first race.

Perhaps not surprisingly, finding a buyer for an undertaking of this size and of this very specialised nature was bound to take time and it wasn't until late 1994 that buyers emerged and then not for all of the property. The area of vineyards had already been reduced during the three years that the business was up for sale and only the 10.6 hectares of vines at Ridge Farm (which surround the winery) were purchased by the new owners, Paul Cooper and Derek McMillen. This dynamic duo, one (Cooper) from the PR/advertising world, the other a local builder/property developer, proposed to use the facilities and the well-known name of Lamberhurst Vineyards to import and sell a range of foreign wines, in addition to continuing the English Wine business. As soon as they signed the contract to buy the place, winemaker Donnelly handed in his notice, so I was asked to come back to assist on a consultancy basis and subsequently hired Simon Day to take over as winemaker. The highlight of the Cooper/McMillen tenure of Lamberhurst was their involvement with Manchester United with whom Cooper negotiated a deal to sell wine bearing the team's colours and logo. A launch party was held, complete with several players (not being much of a football fan, I do not remember which ones) plus their wine-loving manager, Alex Ferguson and star-fan Gary Rhodes. The only time I ever recall seeing a bottle of the Manchester United wine on sale was in a wine shop in Hermanus in South Africa. Unfortunately, trading conditions did not favour the business and in March 1998 their company was put into administration and although it continued to trade, the property was, at the end of 1999, once again sold.

The new owners were Stenoak Fencing, a major fencing contractor from nearby Uckfield who wanted to establish their offices and depot there, but also wanted to revitalise the vineyard and continue the production of English Wine. The company was run at the time by Adrian Drewe and Simon Hume-Kendall, two entrepreneurs who already had an involvement with vineyards as they had earlier baled out Carr Taylor Vineyards. Chapel Down, who at this stage were starting to flag under financial pressures, thought that an alliance with Messrs. Drewe and Hume-Kendall might offer them some salvation and entered into negotiations to effect a merger or tie-up of some sort. In July 2000, English Wines plc was formed which consolidated the combined vineyard interests of Lamberhurst, Chapel Down and Carr Taylor Vineyards. Together, these three enterprises had around 100 hectares of vines under their ownership or contractual control and a million bottles worth of winemaking capacity. The idea was that all winemaking would be moved to Chapel Down's Tenterden site, allowing Stenoak to redevelop the old winery, although the temperature-controlled underground cellars would still be used for sparkling wine maturation. On the face of it the merger stood a chance of succeeding, although external observers, knowing some of the personalities involved, thought that it might, at times, be a rocky ride. In the event, the old problem surfaced: sales, or lack of them. However many vineyards you control and however modern and efficient your winemaking facilities, at some stage the product has to be sold to generate income and without enough sales, problems are bound to occur. Eventually, Chapel Down became the dominant partner in the combined business and in October 2004, with new blood and new money injected into the company, Drewe and Hume-Kendall sold their shares in English Wines plc and resigned their directorships. Since then, Lamberhurst Vineyards has become the sole property of Hume-Kendall, who also has a number of other leisure-based businesses in the area. The old winery, both the ground floor premises as well as the old cellars, have been converted into offices, the shop, restaurant and entertaining facilities are (yet again) undergoing improvements, new vineyards are being planted and there is generally an air of optimism about the place. Long may it continue.

Those of you who have read this far (and you probably deserve at least a good-conduct medal for doing so) may wonder why I have written so much about Lamberhurst. It is easy to forget the past and difficult for those not intimately involved to understand or appreciate the significance of this one vineyard in the development of our industry. Before Lamberhurst was a force on the English Wine scene, winegrowing used to be thought of as one for retired servicemen, the gentleman farmer, and the enthusiastic amateur. English Wines pre-Lamberhurst were made to appeal to an elitist consumer and not for the generality of high street wine buyers. The Lamberhurst operation however, was something else. It was big and professional, it made wines to appeal to ordinary wine drinkers, and what was more, ordinary wine drinkers seemed to want to buy them. More than any other vineyard in modern times it helped establish English Wine as a commercial product. Its success during those halcyon days was due almost entirely to the support, financial and personal, given to it by Kenneth McAlpine. His MBE, awarded in the 1997 New Year's Honours list for 'Services to English Wine' was justifiably given.

Lambourne Vineyard

Ruanhighlanes, Truro, Cornwall TR2 5NL
Telephone: 01872 501212
Mobile: 07890 902039
E-mail: wine@lambournevineyard.co.uk
E-mail: info@lambournevineyard.co.uk
Website: www.lambournevineyard.co.uk
Contact: Graham Sherratt
Vineyards: 2 hectares
Grape varieties: Rondo, Regent, Orion, Phoenix, Pinot noir Précoce
Open to the public. See website for details.

Lambourne Vineyard, planted between 1996 and 2007, is situated in the heart of the beautiful Roseland Peninsula between the Channel coast and the creeks of the River Fal Valley in Cornwall. The vineyard is south-west facing and is between 43 and 50 metres above sea level and the land previously grew cereals. The shelter of the site

was improved with the planting of windbreaks of Red Alder, Willow and Escallonia which help with the microclimate. The vines are planted at 2.0 x 1.4 metres on both double and single Guyot training systems.

A winery was first established in one of the disused farm buildings but in 2004 a new winery was built, fully equipped with stainless steel tanks and equipment. Wines now produced include red, white and rosé, some of which are barrel-aged. In 2008 a bottle-fermented sparkling wine is to be released.

Laverstoke Park Vineyard

Overton, Hampshire RG25 3DR
Telephone: 01256 772659
Mobile: 07595 651825
E-mail: darryl@laverstokepark.co.uk
E-mail: office@laverstokepark.co.uk
Website: www.laverstokepark.co.uk
Contact: Darryl Kemp, Katie Swinton-Clark
Vineyards: 9 hectares
Grape varieties: Chardonnay, Pinot noir, Pinot Meunier
Open to the public. See website for details.

Laverstoke Park is owned by South African-born Jody Scheckter who was F1 World Champion, driving for Ferrari, in 1979. He moved to the US and invented a computer-based firearms training system (FATS) which was eventually used by a large number of police forces and armed services around the world. In 1996 he sold the company (very successfully) and decided to move back to the UK where he bought the 1,000-hectare estate which is now home to him and his family. He also owns 53-hectares of glasshouses in Lymington, Hamsphire. The Laverstoke Estate is known as the "University of Organics" and is 100% biodynamic (Demeter certified) and equipped with its own state-of-the-art laboratory for both soil and tissue analysis. Apart from the 9-ha of vineyards, it supports a 400-head herd of grass-fed Hereford and Aberdeen Angus beef cattle, who live on pasture comprising 31 different types of grasses, clovers and herbs. The estate also supports water buffalo (great mozzarella), wild boar, sheep, poultry, a hop garden and a few other delights. It also has a 2 ha slab of concrete (that's about three football pitches-worth) which houses a composting plant. Here, up to 40,000 tonnnes a year of green waste from local authorities and processing plants is mixed with wood chips, animal manures and biodynamic prepartions to produce top-quality organic/biodynamic compost for use on their own land (up to 25-

tonnes/ha per year) and for sale to other organic/biodynamic growers.

The vineyard was established in 2006 when 1-hectare of Champagne varieties were planted and expanded in 2007 with another 8-hectares. The *encépagement* is 49% Chardonnay, 49% Pinot noir and 2% Pinot Meunier, with several different clones and all planted on rootstock 41B. The vines are planted at 2.0 x 1.0-metres, Single Guyot trained and (somewhat bizarely) all fitted with irrigation drippers (although I am told it has never been used). The rows are planted with a green-manure comprising 21 different herbs, legumes, wild-flowers and grasses and biodynamic mulch has been liberally applied around the vines to aid weed control. The vineyard is managed by New Zealander Darryl Kemp (ex-Nyetimber and ex-Exton Park). The vines are regularly sprayed with various compost teas and other preparations to keep diseases at bay and no sulphur or copper are used. The aim is to build up the vines' own defence mechanisms to mildews and *Botrytis*. When viewed in early August 2009, after one of the wettest Julys on record, the vines did look remarkably free of mildew, so something is working!

The consultant used by Scheckter to plan and plant the vineyard was California-based Frenchman, Dr. Michel Salgues who established and was the first winemaker at Roederer Estate in California's cool(ish) Anderson Valley. Salgues advised that the vines be planted at the top of one of Laverstoke's rolling chalky hills at between 125-metres and 150-metres above sea-level, fully exposed to the prevailing south-westerly winds. This altitude and exposure, coupled with the additional pressures associated with growing vines without the protection of chemicals, has meant that the vines have been slow to establish and so far, no crops have been harvested. In selecting the top of a hill, Salgues was only doing what they do in Champagne where the tops of the hills are preferred as disease is far less of a problem with good air drainage, but where the vine density is 10,000 per hectare. Only time will tell if he got it right! Dr. Tony Jordan (who – amongst many other vinous achievements – started and for 21 years ran Domain Chandon for Moët et Chandon in the Yarra Valley and now oversees this winery, plus Cape Mentelle and Cloudy Bay) has now been brought on board for the next phase, the building of a winery to handle the "65 to 80 tonnes" of grapes which Laverstoke expect to harvest.

To get organic, let-alone biodynamic, vines to establish, grow and fruit in the UK is never going to be easy and even if the weed control can be successfully (and economically) handled, the pressures from disease on both the vines and the grapes will be considerable. Laverstoke, with their enthusiastic approach to natural farming, which lacks nothing when it comes to know-how and machinery, stand a better chance than most of making this system work. They will hopefully become a blueprint for other like-minded vinegrowers.

Leckford Estate Vineyard

c/o The Estate Office, Leckford, Stockbridge, Hampshire, SO20 6JF
Location of Vineyard: Winchester Street, Leckford, Stockbridge, Hampshire, SO20 6JG
Telephone: 01264 810634
Fax: 01264 810441
Website: www.waitrose.com/ourcompany/leckfordestate.aspx
Contact: Iain Dalton 07764 674192   iaindalton@leckfordestate.co.uk
Contact: Justin Coleman 07872 157396   justincoleman@leckfordestate.co.uk
Vineyards: 4.6977 hectares
Grape varieties: Pinot noir, Chardonnay, Pinot Meunier
Leckford Estate is open to the public at certain times. See website for details.

Leckford Estate Vineyard must rate as one of the more unusual in this guide in that it is part of the John Lewis Partnership, owners of major UK retailer, Waitrose. The Leckford Estate, a 1,600-ha mixed farm in the heart of the Test Valley, was once the estate of John Spedan Lewis, son of the founder of the John Lewis empire, who gave the company to its employees. The estate is known as 'The Waitrose Farm' and most of its produce – milk, wheat, apples and pears, apple juice, cider, mushrooms, free-range chickens and free-range eggs – ends up on their shelves.

The idea for an 'own-label' vineyard came about after some of the Waitrose wine-buying team – principally Justin Howard-Sneyd MW and Dee Blackstock MW – suggested that since they sold a considerable quantity of English and Welsh wines (according to retail research company Nielsens they sell 27% of all UK-grown wine sold on the high street) and since they owned a large chunk of chalk downland which has suddenly become so fashionable for vineyards in the UK, why not plant one? After considerable discussions with myself and others, agreement from various committees that control the investment pursestrings, the go-ahead was given and a steeply sloping south-facing site just outside the village of Leckford was chosen.

The vineyard was planted in May 2009 and is 54% Chardonnay (4 clones), 33% Pinot noir (4 clones) and 13% Pinot Meunier (2 clones). As the land has a pH of between 7.9 and 8.4 all vines are on either 41B or Fercal rootstock. The vines are planted at 2.0 x 1.2-metres and will be Double-Guyot trained and the site has been both rabbit and deer fenced. So far the vines have established well and ought to produce their first small crop in 2011. The aim is to produce a bottle-fermented sparkling wine for sale through the John Lewis and Waitrose outlets. No decision has yet been made about winemaking.

Although plenty of UK retailers have wines made to their specification and several employ winemakers to oversee winery operations, I don't think that there are any that actually own their own vineyards or wineries. Being employee-owned and not always having to think about the bottom-line, enables the John Lewis Partnership to take a different view on life to their competitiors and it will be interesting to see how this enterprise progresses.

Leeds Castle Vineyard

Penfold Hill, Leeds, Maidstone, Kent ME17 1PL
Telephone: 01622 765400
E-mail: enquiries@leeds-castle.co.uk
Website: www.leeds-castle.com
Contact: Trevor Fermor
Vineyards: 1.35 hectares
Grape varieties: MT, Seyval blanc, Reichensteiner, Schönburger
Open to the public. See website for details.

Leigh Park Hotel Vineyard

Leigh Road West, Bradford-on-Avon, Wiltshire BA15 2RA
Telephone: 01225 864885
Fax: 01225 862315
E-mail: info@leighparkhotel.eclipse.co.uk
Website: www.latonahotels.co.uk/best-western-leigh-park.html
Contact: Pamela Duckett
Vineyards: 0.5 hectares
Grape varieties: Reichensteiner
Open by appointment.

Leventhorpe Vineyard

Bullerthorpe Lane, Woodlesford, Leeds, West Yorkshire LS26 8AF
Telephone: 0113 2889088
Fax: 0113 2667892
E-mail: janet@leventhorpevineyard.freeserve.co.uk
Contact: George Bowden, Janet Bowden
Vineyards: 2.21 hectares
Grape varieties: MA, Seyval blanc, Triomphe, Regent, Rondo, Pinot noir
Open to the public. See website for details.

Leventhorpe Vineyard is siutated within the boundaries of the City of Leeds and is Yorkshire's longest established commercial vineyard. The Cistercians of Kirkstall Abbey, Leeds, and the Benedictines at St. Mary's Abbey, York, had been making wine in Yorkshire up until the end of the 1500s, so viticulture to this region is not new. George and Janet Bowden re-introduced commercial winegrowing to Yorkshire by establishing their vineyard in 1986. At latitude 53° 49', Leventhorpe is probably the most northerly commercially producing vineyard in the United Kingdom[14]. It is planted on a sheltered south-facing slope, which leads down to the River Aire, and helps protect the vines against spring frosts, and the well-drained hungry soil is free-draining and warms quickly. The site is between 18 and 26 metres above sea level, and the soil is sandy loam overlying sand and broken sandstone. The vines are planted on a 2 x 1.5-metre double Guyot system or a 4 x 1.5-metre Lenz Moser system.

Leventhorpe has its own well-equipped winery and its wines are given a long fermentation to preserve nose and delicacy. They regularly achieve medals at competitions and many achieve Yorkshire Regional Wine status. The vineyard is recommended in Rick Stein's Guide and Leventhorpe Madeleine Angevine was included as one of the Wines of the Week in the *Daily Telegraph* in July 2006. It was also recommended by Jancis Robinson in the *Financial Times* in May 2007.

In July 2007, HRH The Duke of Kent made an official visit to Leventhorpe Vineyard in connection with George Bowden's nomination for the Queen's Award for Enterprise due to his pioneering work in the reintroduction of commercial winegrowing in Yorkshire. This has encouraged others to follow, and more vineyards are now being planted or planned in Yorkshire. The Duke spent some time in both the vineyard and winery and was 'astonished by the quality of the wine'. Leventhorpe is one of the few UK vineyards to have received a royal visitor. Oz Clarke and James May visited the vineyard for their 2009 BBC series 'Oz & James Drink to Britain' and included it in his 'Pick of the Best' six British vineyards for the May 2009 issue of the BBC Countryfile Magazine.

George Bowden and The Duke of Kent discuss the finer points of grapegrowing at Leventhorpe

---

14 The competition for the 'most northerly vineyard' is divided between those vineyards that produce wine commercially and vineyards that exist, but produce wine seldom, if ever. Leventhorpe probably wins the prize for the former category as it does produce wine with regularity. The most northerly in this guide is at Whitworth Hall (54° 42' 25.28").

Lily Farm Vineyard

c/o 7 Moormead, Budleigh Salterton, Devon EX9 6QA
Location of vineyard: EX9 7AH
Telephone: 01395 443877
Mobile: 07929 488245
E-mail: alanandfayepratt@googlemail.com
Website: www.lilyfarmvineyard.com
Contact: Alan Pratt
Vineyards: 0.383 hectares
Grape varieties: Rondo, Pinot noir Précoce, Seyval blanc, Bacchus.
Open to the public. See website for details.

Linch Hill Vineyard

Linch Hill Farm, Stanton Harcourt, Oxfordshire OX29 5BB
Telephone: 07775 583737
E-mail: Rob@aml.co.uk
E-mail: dr@lhvineyard.wanadoo.co.uk
Contact: Rob Santilli
Vineyards: 1 hectare
Grape varieties: Seyval blanc, Phoenix
Open by appointment.

Lincoln Vineyard

Bishop's Palace, Minster Yard, Lincoln, Lincolnshire LN1 1DH
Telephone: 01522 873542
Telephone: 01522 527468
E-mail: kate.fenn@lincoln.gov.uk
Website: www.english-heritage.org.uk/server/show/nav.11756
Contact: Kate Fenn
Vineyards: 0.09 hectares
Grape varieties: Madeleine Sylvaner, MT, Ortega, Blauer Portugieser
Open to the public. See website for details.

Little Foxes Vineyard

111 Gloucester Road, Stonehouse, Gloucestershire GL10 2HB
Telephone: 01453 828930
E-mail: n.h.munro@btinternet.com
Contact: Neil Munro
Vineyards: 0.0011 hectares
Grape varieties: Auxerrois
Not open to the public.

Little Knoxbridge Vineyard

Cranbrook Road, Staplehurst, Kent TN12 0EU
Telephone: 01580 893643
Mobile: 07934 454840
E-mail: loftys1@hotmail.co.uk
Contact: Paul Loftus
Vineyards: 0.533 hectares
Grape varieties: Auxerrois
Open by appointment.

The vineyard was originally planted in 1983 and bought by Paul Loftus in 1996 who now runs it as a partnership with three friends. Only Auxerrois is grown, high double Guyot trained at 2 x 1.3-metres, and the site is 60-metres above sea level, flat with a silty clay soil. Both still and sparkling wines are made, mainly for home consumption.

Little West End Farm Vineyard

c/o 14 Route d'Oger, 51190 Avize, France
Location of vineyard: Little West End Farm, Chidden, Hambledon, Hampshire PO7 4TE
Telephone: 0033 326 577704
E-mail: champagnepiersonwhitaker@club-internet.fr
Contact: Imogen Whitaker, Didier Pierson
Vineyards: 4 hectares
Grape varieties: Chardonnay, Pinot noir, Pinot Meunier
Not open to the public.

Little West End Farm Vineyard is the work of Frenchman Didier Pierson and his British-born wife, Imogen Whitaker. In 2004 and 2005 they established 4-hectares of vines, planted at 1.2 x 1.0-metres, on a very low *Champenoise* trellis, on a farm high up in the Meon Valley. They live in Avize, in Champagne, where they run their own small *maison* and Didier is a winemaker at the local co-operative and to date, this remains the only Champagne-based involvement in UK viticulture. Their vineyard in Hampshire has been planted on land owned by a farmer, Sydney Chaplin, and if press reports are correct they have formed a joint venture. The first vines were planted in 2004, a few more in 2005 and the first harvest was in 2007. A small winery has been established on the farm. The site is very isolated (although it can be seen from a public road) and the top of the vineyard is on a very exposed hill at 203-metres above sea level. To my mind they would have done better by planting lower down on more sheltered land, but perhaps the very low trellis and high planting density will give them some advantages. Certainly if Chardonnay and the Pinots can be persuaded to ripen at this altitude, it opens up a lot of chalkland to vineyards. I very much look forward to tasting their first wine.

Littlebredy Vineyard

The Walled Garden, Littlebredy, Dorchester, Wilsthire, DT2 9HL
Telephone: 01305 898055
Website: wgw.org.uk/littlebredy.com/index2.html
Contact: secretary@wgw.org.uk
Vineyards: 0.2 hectares - estimate
Grape varieties: Not known
Not open to the public.

Llaethliw Vineyard

Neuaddlwyd, Aberaeron, Ceredigion, SA48 7RF, Ceredigion, Wales
Telephone: 01545 571879
E-mail: sheepevans@aol.com
Contact: Richard Evans, Siw Evans
Vineyards: 2.4291 hectares
Grape varieties: Solaris, Rondo, Regent, Orion
Not open to the public. Vineyard is organic.

Llanbadrig Vineyard

Gwinllan Padrig, Cae Owain, Cemaes Bay, Anglesey LL67 0LN, Wales
Telephone House: 01407 710416   Winery: 01407 710999
E-mail: thomas.barlow@btinternet.com
Website: www.llanbadrigvineyard.com
Contact: Tom Barlow
Vineyards: 1 hectare
Grape varieties: Open air - Triomphe, MA, Phoenix, Regent, Seyval blanc. In polytunnels - Cabernet Sauvignon, Merlot
Open to the public. See website for details.

Llanerch Vineyard

Hensol, Pendoylan, Vale of Glamorgan CF72 8GG, Wales
Telephone: 01443 225877
E-mail: enquiries@llanerch-vineyard.co.uk
Website: www.llanerch-vineyard.co.uk

Contact: Carole Growcott, Scott Williams
Vineyards: 2.8 hectares
Grape varieties: Bacchus, Huxelrebe, Kernling, Reichensteiner, Seyval blanc, Triomphe
Open to the public. See website for details.

Longueville House Vineyard

Longueville House Hotel, Mallow, County Cork, Ireland
Telephone: 00353 22 47156
E-mail: info@longuevillehouse.ie
Website: www.longuevillehouse.ie
Contact: Michael O'Callaghan
Vineyards: 0.1575 hectares
Grape varieties: Reichensteiner
The vineyards is part of the hotel grounds. See website for opening dates and times.

Michael O'Callaghan's vineyard is planted at the country-house hotel he owns and which his son, William, now runs. He first planted vines there in the '70s and once grew Müller-Thurgau as well as Reichensteiner. The vines that remain today are in a sheltered garden to the side of the hotel in a partially walled garden. There are 6 long rows of what looks like Reichensteiner, plus a long south-facing wall also planted with vines. Geisenheim's Professor Helmut Becker paid at least one visit to Longueville House and encouraged O'Callaghan in his efforts, offering him some of the new German crosses which he hoped would better withstand the cold, damp flowering weather which is the bane of Irish *vignerons*. When I visited in August 2009, there were plenty of shoots and leaves, but only a scattering of grapes. The vines on the wall were faring a little better and had a fair scattering of grapes, showing how close Ireland is to being able to successfully grow vines.

The winery is in a converted coach house across the stable yard from the hotel and also, so I am told, houses a small pot still for the (entirely legal and above-board) production of spirit for apple brandy and other spirit-based drinks. At one time, Dr. Billy Christopher (the Mallow GP) who owned 2-ha of vines nearby (Blackwater Valley Vineyard) and O'Callaghan made the wine together, but since Dr. Billy grubbed his vines, O'Callaghan has made it on his own. For some years it seems that the small crop (sometimes very small) from the Longueville vines has been supplemented by grapes from the Thomas Walk Vineyard in Kinsale, some 60 km away, and the only Irish wine currently on the Longueville House wine list is a *2006 Amurensis Walk.* The label has the words "Rogha Gacha Dighe" above the picture of the hotel, which translates (so I am told) as "The Choice of the Gods". It also bears the legend "Made and Bottled by Vin du Longueville" which probably makes a couple of châteaux owners in Bordeaux a bit upset! I was told by the hotel receptionist that there had been no grapes at either vineyard in 2007 or 2008.

If you want to see a video clip of someone tasting the 2006 Amurensis Walk go to www.sourgrapes.ie and search for 'amurensis' or go to: http://tinyurl.com/nagnn8. I am told that the wine is available from a shop in Dublin – *The Corkscrew* – for €11.95. More details about the *2006 Amurensis Walk* can be found under the entry for the Thomas Walk Vineyard.[15]

Lopen Vineyard

Meadowhaze House, The Bartons, Yeabridge, Somerset TA13 5LW
Telephone: 01460 249119
Mobile: 07977 471962
E-mail: lopenvineyard@mac.com
Contact: Paull Robathan (yes, two 'l's)
Vineyards: 1.6817 hectares
Grape varieties: Pinot noir, Pinot Meunier, Pinot gris
Open by appointment.

Lopen Vineyard in South Somerset is a fairly new vineyard, planted in 2003 and 2004 and is dedicated to natural methods. No pesticides, herbicides and non-organic fertilisers are used. The vines are all Pinots, mainly Pinot noir (3,000 vines) with

smaller plantings of Pinot Meunier and Pinot gris (500 vines each). The Pinot noir is made up of a number of different clones to increase the diversity of picking and blending opportunities. Their first vintage was 2006 and a delicate rosé made at the Bagborough Winery that

---

15   See Appendix IV for a brief history of vineyards in Ireland.

was awarded Regional Wine Status and sold out in no time to local restaurants, shops and stately homes. Choosing not to use most of the normal (chemical) methods for controlling mildew is always going to be tough in a climate like the UK's, as 2007 proved when they lost their entire crop due to disease. However, they intend to forge ahead with confidence and are sure that the great start they made in 2006 will continue. They are looking forward to working with the other new and re-invigorated Somerset vineyards and hope to put the area firmly on the map for sparkling, red, white, rosé and dessert wines.

Ludlow Vineyard

Wainbridge House, Clee St Margaret, Craven Arms, Shropshire SY7 9DT
Telephone: 01584 823356
E-mail: mike.hardingham@btinternet.com
Website: www.ludlowvineyard.co.uk
Contact: Mike Hardingham
Vineyards: 4 hectares
Grape varieties: Kernling, MA, Madeleine Sylvaner, Seyval blanc, Triomphe
Not open to the public.

Ludlow Vineyard was planted between 1995 and 2003 on a south-facing slope high up in the hills above Ludlow at between 180 and 240-meters above sea level. Owner Mike Hardingham experimented with both Guyot training and GDC and eventually decided that GDC at 3.0 x 2.0-metres worked better (I cannot think why!). Mike says that qualities are "reasonable" and he has won both bronze and silver medals in the EWOTYC, but yields are "poor" and he will be "pleasantly surprised if we ever get an average yield of more than 1 tonne per acre (17 hl/ha)".

Ludlow Vineyard

Lulham Court Vineyard

Madley, Hereford, Herefordshire HR2 9JQ
Telephone: 01981 251107
E-mail: phil@lulhamcourtvineyard.co.uk
E-mail: lulhamcourt@freenetname.co.uk
Website: www.lulhamcourt.co.uk
Contact: Phil Pennington
Vineyards: 1.2146 hectares
Grape varieties: MT, Reichensteiner, Seyval blanc, Regent
Open to the public. See website for details.

Lusca Vineyard

Quickpenny Road, Lusk, County Dublin, Republic of Ireland
Telephone and Fax: +353 1843 1650
Mobile: +353 87284 3879
E-mail: pureapple@eircom.net
Contact: David LLewellyn
Vineyards: 0.075 hectares
Grape varieties under cover: Cabernet Sauvignon, Merlot, Sauvignon blanc, Chardonnay, Schönburger, Gewürztraminer
Grape varieties open air: Rondo, Regent, MA, Phoenix
Open to the public by appointment.

David Llewellyn's interest in vines stems from his time as a horticulture student at Warrenstown College, County Meath when he spent a summer working on a mixed fruit and vines farm in Germany. After Warrenstown he took a degree in horticulture at UC Dublin and started, although never finished, a master's thesis on suitable micro-

climates for viticulture in Ireland. Llewellyn was in my 2001 guide *The Wines of Britain and Ireland* with a small vineyard planted in 2000 at Swords just north of the city of Dublin, but this vineyard has been grubbed up. His current vineyard, Lusca, is 15-km north of Dublin, about 4-km from the coast and some 40-metres above sea level. The vineyard is planted with a selection of varieties and the first crop was in 2005. He has vines both under polythene protection and without. The polythene is kept on for the summer months and then removed after harvest and none of the vines receive any sprays. This region is reputed to be the dryest and sunniest in Ireland which may explain how Llewellyn has been able to get his vines to both produce and ripen grapes, although the polythene undoubtedly helps.

Llewellyn makes several wines, depending on the season: a cuvée of Chardonnay and other white grapes; a Sauvignon blanc; a red made from Cabernet Sauvignon and Merlot; and occasionally a red from Rondo. Total annual production is only about 350-litres and the wines sell for €40 for 75 cl and €25 for a half-bottle. The wines are sold direct and can be mailed anywhere or are available from Fallon & Byrne and Wines on the Green in Dublin. John Wilson, an Irish Times reporter, tasted both wines in November 2008 and found them: *not in line for Gold medals* but said that they *made for interesting drinking and, served blind, would fox any wine buff who thinks he or she knows it all.* Not a bad write up, and much better than for the *2006 Amurensis Walk* which is about the only other Irish wine being made.

Llewellyn also sells apples, apple juice and balsamic vinegar at the local farmer's markets. This is a brave venture in such a viticulturally harsh climate, but who knows how the weather will behave in the future?[16]

Magpie Lane Vineyard

c/o Abbey Vineyards Group, Irnham Grange, Irnham, Corby Glen, Grantham, Lincolnshire, NG33 4NE
Location of vineyard: Magpie Lane, Coleshill, Amersham, Buckinghamshire, HP7 0LU
Telephone: 01476 550191
Fax: 01476 550080
E-mail: info@abbeyvineyards.co.uk
Contact: Phil Kerry 07815 308838
Contact: Jonathan Kerry 07805 315763
Vineyards: 4.3 hectares
Grape varieties: Pinot noir, Pinot Meunier, Chardonnay, Ortega
Not open to the public.

Manor Farm Vineyard

Main Street, Botcheston, Leicester, Leicestershire LE9 9FF
Telephone: 01455 822657
Mobile: 07889 862370
E-mail: bernvines@aol.com
Contact: Phil Johnson, Kaye Johnson
Vineyards: 0.13 hectares
Grape varieties: Rondo, Regent
Not open to the public.

---

16 See Appendix IV for a brief history of vineyards in Ireland.

Manor Fields Vineyard

Northcroft, Weedon, Aylesbury, Buckinghamshire HP22 4NR
Telephone: 01296 641178
Mobile: 07989 863932
E-mail: vigneron@manorfieldsvineyard.co.uk
Website: www.manorfieldsvineyard.co.uk
Contact: Nigel Smith
Vineyards: 0.8907 hectares
Grape varieties: MA, Bacchus, Chardonnay, Pinot noir, Pinot Meunier, Pinot gris
Open to the public. See website for details.

Manstree Vineyard

New Barn Farm, Shillingford St George, Exeter, Devon EX2 9QR
Telephone: 01392 832218
Fax: 01392 833712
E-mail: boyces@manstree.freeserve.co.uk
Website: www.boyces-manstree.co.uk
Contact: Tim Boyce
Vineyards: 1.8219 hectares
Grape varieties: MA, Seyval Blanc, Phoenix, Siegerrebe, Rondo
Open to the public. See website for details.

Manstree Vineyard is situated 1½ miles south-west of the Exeter city boundary and has been producing light, fresh and fruity white wines for the past 26 years. The Boyce family have been there for 15 years and although Tim and Simon Boyce both have College Diplomas in Commercial Horticulture, they had no previous viticultural experience so initially it was a very steep learning curve.

The vineyard is in an area referred to as 'Devon's frying pan' on account of the unusually low rainfall due to the double rain-shadow effect from Dartmoor and the Haldon Hills. The vineyard was established by former owner Gerry Symons over a ten year period between 1979 and 1989 and the site was selected because of the well-drained soil, good shelter, and good air drainage reducing the risk of spring frost.

Manstree has never had its own winery but has successfully used local contract winemakers. Currently two are used: Juliet White of Yearlstone Vineyard who makes the Siegerrebe and dry 'Old-Vine' Madeleine and Seyval Blanc wines; and Sam Lindo at Camel Valley who makes the extremely popular Mayval (Madeleine Angevine and Seyval) blend dry.

Successive Manstree wines have won many awards over the years in regional, national and international competitions. Recently they won a Silver for their 2007 Old-Vine Madeleine and 3 bronze awards for the 2006 and '07 Mayval and the 2007 Phoenix medium dry in the 2008 SWVA annual competition. They also gained a bronze for the 2008 Old-Vine Seyval in the 2009 EWOTYC.

Marden Organic Vineyard

Plain Road, Marden, Tonbridge, Kent TN12 9LS
Telephone: 07956 163519
E-mail: nmh@herberthall.co.uk
Website: www.herberthall.com
Contact: Nicholas Hall
Vineyards: 3.5 hectares
Grape varieties: Chardonnay, Pinot noir, Pinot Meunier
Not open to the public.

Marlings Vineyard

Mead End Road, Sway, Hampshire SO41 6EE
Telephone: 01590 681606
Mobile: 07904 526375
E-mail: david@marlingsvineyard.co.uk
Website: www.marlingsvineyard.co.uk
Contact: David Balls
Vineyards: 0.86 hectares
Grape varieties: Dornfelder; Léon Millot, Triomphe, Seyval blanc, Reichensteiner, Schönburger; Findling; Bacchus, Chardonnay; Pinot noir
Open by appointment.

Marlings Vineyard was planted between 1989 and 1995. It is a south-east sloping site 25 metres above sea level, with a clay-gravel soil. The vines are planted at 2 x 1.5 metres and Double Guyot trained. A new planting of Bacchus in 2009 replaced some underperforming varieties. Their 2005 & 2008 Three Cows Dry White have won Bronze medals in the EWOTYC, along with the 2006 Three Cows Red, and 2007 and 2008 Three Cows Rosé which achieved Highly Commended.

Mayshaves Vineyard

Mayshaves Farm, Woodchurch, Ashford, Kent TN26 3PT
Telephone: 01233 820 286
E-mail: roy.adams1@virgin.net
Contact: Roy Adams
Vineyards: 0.0991 hectares
Grape varieties: MT, Reichensteiner, Seyval blanc. Not open to the public.

Meadowgrove Vineyard

Letcombe Road, Wantage, Oxfordshire, OX12 9NA
Telephone: 01235 767913
E-mail: andy@meadowgrove.com
Website: www.meadowgrove.com
Contact: Andy McLeod
Vineyards: 0.1125 hectares
Grape varieties: Phoenix, MA, Reichensteiner
Not open to the public.

Melbury Vineyard

School Lane, Borley, Sudbury, Suffolk, CO10 7AE
Telephone: 01787 376800
E-mail: davey59er@googlemail.com
E-mail: dave@melbury.org
Contact: David House
Vineyards: 0.25 hectares
Grape varieties: Triomphe
Not open to the public.

Melbury Vale Vineyard

c/o 9a Lambourn Road, Speen, Newbury, Berkshire RG20 8AA
Location of vineyard: Barfoot Farm, Redmans Lane, Melbury SP7 0DB
Contact: Clare Kelly, Joseph Pestell
Telephone: Clare Kelly 07730 955593
Telephone: Joseph Pestell 07752 865232
E-mail: enquiries@melburyvaleco.co.uk
Website: www.melburyvaleco.co.uk
Vineyards: 0.8 hectares
Grape varieties: Pinot noir, Solaris, Rondo, Seyval blanc
Open by appointment.

Melton Lodge Vineyard

Melton, Woodbridge, Suffolk IP12 1LU
Telephone: 0879 999 4404
E-mail: leggettjjr@aol.com
Contact: Jeremy Leggett
Vineyards: 0.67 hectares
Grape varieties: Bacchus, Pinot noir, Reichensteiner, Siegerrebe
Not open to the public.

Meopham Valley Vineyard

Norway House, Wrotham Road, Meopham, Kent DA13 0AU
Telephone: 01474 812727
Telephone: 020 7353 3563
Fax: 020 7353 3564
E-mail: david@davidgreyco.com
Website: www.meophamvalleyvineyard.co.uk
Contact: David Grey, Pauline Grey
Vineyards: 2 hectares
Grape varieties: Chardonnay, Pinot noir, Pinot gris, Reichensteiner, MA, Triomphe
Open to the public. See website for details.

David Grey and his wife Pauline set this vineyard up in 1991 with the help and encouragement of the late Gillian Pearkes and attended a course at her vineyard in Devon (Yearlstone). The south-east-facing site is between 107 and 137-metres above sea level and the soil is loam with a limestone subsoil. The vines are planted at 1.83 x 1.23-metres and double Guyot trained. Only sulphur and a seaweed mixture are used to guard against disease and no other fungicides, pesticides or herbicides are used in the vineyard. The vineyard is fertilised by mulching the vine prunings and using the services of a flock of sheep from the adjacent farm between harvest and the start of pruning. The first harvest was in 1994 and they now sell a range of wines including a white, rosé and a sparkling.

Mersea Island Vineyard

Rewsalls Lane, East Mersea, Colchester, Essex CO5 8SX
Telephone: 01206 385900
Fax: 01206 383600
E-mail: info@merseawine.com
Website: www.merseawine.com
Contact: Roger Barber
Vineyards: 3.5 hectares
Grape varieties: MT, Ortega, Reichensteiner, Chardonnay, Pinot Meunier
Open to the public. See website for details.

Methersham Vineyard

Hobbs Lane, Beckley, Rye, East Sussex, TN31 6TX
Telephone: 01797 260491
Fax: 01797 260491
Mobile: 07963 346887

Contact: Neil Holcombe   neil@fieldgreen.eclipse.co.uk
Contact: Wendy Holcombe   wendy@fieldgreen.eclipse.co.uk
Vineyards: 1.2 hectares
Grape varieties: Schönburger, Würzer, Reichensteiner, Rondo
Not open to the public.

Mill Hill Village Vineyard

c/o 68 Millway, Mill Hill, London NW7 3QY
Location of vineyard: NW7
Telephone: 020 8959 2214
E-mail: andy.creighton@btinternet.com
Contact: Andy Creighton
Vineyards: 0.06 hectares
Grape varieties: Pinot noir, Chardonnay, Huxelrebe, Kerner, Ortega, Reichensteiner, Schönburger,
Seyval blanc, Siegerrebe (25 vines of each variety except PN which is 50 vines)
Not open to the public.

This small experimental non-commercial vineyard was planted between 1986 and 1993 and is situated on a local authority allotment, facing gently to the south-east and is between 125 and 135-metres above sea level. The soil is a fairly rich loam over London clay. The different varieties are vinified separately and enough grapes are normally harvested from each to produce at least twenty-five litres of wine and the wines are made and stored in an insulated and partially air-conditioned converted garage. With no commercial pressures to sell, the white wines are usually kept for a minimum of two years in glass containers before bottling and the wines have won a number of 'Best Non-commercial Wine' awards in the T&CVA competitions.

2003 harvest under way with Schönburger to the left and Pinot noir to the right. The very hot weather had induced a lot of leaf-drop into the Xironets!

Mill Lane Vineyard

Brantedge Farm, Webourn Road, Brant Broughton, Lincolnshire LN5 0SP
Telephone: 01522 788784
Mobile: 07885 460489
E-mail: booth.william@btinternet.com
Contact: William Booth
Vineyards: 0.45 hectares
Grape varieties: Regent, Rondo, Bacchus, Pinot noir Précoce, Phoenix
Not open to the public.

Mimram Valley Vineyard

The Garden House, Tewin Water, Welwyn, Hertfordshire AL6 0AB
Telephone: 01438 714395
E-mail: keith.cox@talk21.com
Contact: Keith Cox
Vineyards: 0.48 hectares
Grape varieties: Bacchus, Huxelrebe, MA, Reichensteiner
Not open to the public.

Moat House Vineyard

New Hall Green, Wareside, Hertfordshire, SG12 7SD
Telephone: 01920 468733
E-mail: david.briscoe2@btopenworld.com
Contact: David Briscoe
Vineyards: 0.4 hectares
Grape varieties: Pinot noir Précoce, Bacchus
Not open to the public.

Monnow Valley Vineyard

Great Osbaston Farm, Monmouth, Monmouthshire NP25 5DL, Wales
Telephone: 01600 716209
E-mail: wine@monnowvalley.com
Contact: Peter Baker
Vineyards: 1.61 hectares
Grape varieties: Huxelrebe, MA, Seyval blanc
Open by appointment.

Morville St Gregory Vineyard

Valentine Cottage, Aston Munslow, Craven Arms, Shropshire SY7 9EW
Telephone: 01584 841021
E-mail: jillrallings@valentinecottage.co.uk
Contact: Richard Rallings

Vineyards: 1.2 hectares
Grape varieties: Orion, Phoenix, Seyval Blanc, Pinot noir, MA
Open to visitors by appointment.

Mount Harry Vines

Mount Harry House, Ditchling Road, Offham, Lewes, East Sussex BN7 3QW
Telephone: 01273 474456
Mobile: 07787 153081
E-mail: mountharry@btopenworld.com
Contact: Alice Renton
Vineyards: 2.6 hectares
Grape varieties: Chardonnay, Pinot noir, Pinot Meunier
Not open to the public.

Mount Pleasant Vineyard

Mount Pleasant, Mount Pleasant Lane, Bolton-le-Sands, Carnforth, Lancashire LA5 8AD
Telephone: 01524 732038
E-mail: graham.michael09@yahoo.co.uk
Contact: Michael Graham
Vineyards: 0.2 hectares
Grape varieties: MA, Rondo
Not open to the public.

Mount Vineyard

The Mount, Church Street, Shoreham, Sevenoaks, Kent TN14 7SD
Telephone: 01959 524008   Fax: 01959 525809
E-mail: jon.moulton@btconnect.com
E-mail: sara.everett@btconnect.com
Website: www.themountvineyard.co.uk
Contact: Jon Moulton
Vineyards: 3.68 hectares
Grape varieties: Pinot noir, Rondo, Regent, Bacchus, Siegerrebe, Seyval blanc, Phoenix
Not open to the public.

The Mount Vineyard was established in 2004 when 8,500 vines were planted. The site, which is in the middle of the charming Kent village of Shoreham, is on a gentle, south-facing slope which runs down to the River Darenth and the soil is a mixture of flints and chalk. The owner, Jon Moulton, is a well-known figure in the City and until recently ran Alchemy Partners and could often be heard on the radio talking about financial matters. The vineyard was expanded in 2006 when an additional 4,500 vines were planted. Surprisingly for a vineyard planted in this century, NO Chardonnay or Champagne clones of Pinot noir were planted and the varieties hark back to the old days, although I guess Phoenix and Rondo one might consider quite 'modern'. The grapes are taken to Wickham Vineyard for vinification and success has come early to this vineyard. Their 2007 Recession Red, complete with label bearing a (rather unkind) drawing of our great and glorious leader, Gordon Brown, won a Bronze at the

2009 SEVA awards and Gold and the Bernard Theobald 'Best Red' Trophy at the 2009 EWOTYC. At £13.50 a bottle, its on the high side, but who can argue as it's in short supply and is getting lots of publicity.

Jon Moulton picking grapes

Mumfords Vineyard

Shockerwick Lane, Bannerdown, Bath, Somerset BA1 7LQ
Telephone: 01225 858367 and 01225 852385
E-mail: enquiries@mumfordsvineyard.co.uk
Website: www.mumfordsvineyard.co.uk
Contact: Tony Cox
Vineyards: 1.6194 hectares
Grape varieties: MA, Kerner, Reichensteiner, Seyval blanc, Triomphe
Open to the public. See website for details.

Mystole Members Vineyard

The Orangery, Mystole, Canterbury, Kent CT4 7DB
Telephone: 01227 738348
E-mail: rex@mystole.fsnet.co.uk
Contact: Rex Stickland
Vineyards: 2.05 hectares
Grape varieties: Bacchus, Dornfelder, Regent, Kerner, Seyval blanc, Pinot noir, Chardonnay
Open by appointment.

The Nash Vineyard

The Nash, Kempsey, Worcester, Worcestershire, WR5 3PB
Telephone and Fax: 01905 821397
E-mail: info@the-nash.com
Contact: Mr W. T. Davies, Mrs B. Bennett
Vineyards: 1 hectare
Grape varieties: Reichensteiner, Regent, Rondo, Seyval blanc, Bacchus, Phoenix
Not open to the public.

National Fruit Collection - Brogdale

Brogdale Farm, Brogdale Rd, Faversham, Kent, ME13 8XZ
Telephone: 01795 536250
Website: www.brogdalecollections.co.uk
Contact for visitors: Sally Roger sallyroger@brogdalecollections.co.uk
Contact for technical inquiries: Dr. Matthew Ordidge   contact@nationalfruitcollection.org.uk
Vineyards: 0.24 hectares
Grape varieties: 40+ varieties in collection
  Open to the public. See website for details.

Brogdale Farm, just outside Faversham in north Kent, has been the home of the National Fruit Collection since 1952, and consists of almost 4,000 different varieties of apple, pear, plum, cherry, bush fruit, vine and nut cultivars. The collection is owned by our old friends DEFRA and is part of an international programme to protect plant genetic resources for the future. The collection is looked after by the University of Reading and FAST – Farm Advisory Services Team – who are based at Brogdale. 'Brogdale Collections' manage the 65 ha site and open it to visitors. Brogdale is also famous (possibly only in climatalogical circles) for recording the highest ever temperature in the UK when on 10 August 2003 it reached 38.3°C (101.3°F) – so probably a perfect place for vines!

The current collection dates from 1987 when I sold them five vines of each of 40 varieties. Since then, Brogdale has gone through several incarnations and a while ago had to be saved for the nation by 'friends', one of whom was Prince Charles. The vine collection became, at one stage, very neglected, but has since been revived. It also has (had?) a small collection of vines against a south facing office wall, from one of which – Madeleine Angevine Oberlin – I took some cuttings in around 1977, hoping that it would prove to be the same variety as UK growers were calling Madeleine Angevine. It wasn't!

Netherland Vineyard

c/o Nyetimber Vineyard, Gay Street, West Chiltington, West Sussex RH20 2HH
Location of vineyard: Tillington, Petworth, West Sussex GU28 0PQ
See Nyetimber Vineyards entry for contact details
Vineyards: 36.4372 hectares
Grape varieties: Pinot noir, Chardonnay, Pinot Meunier
Not open to the public.

New Hall Vineyards

Chelmsford Road, Purleigh, Chelmsford, Essex CM3 6PN
Telephone: 01621 828343
E-mail: piers@newhallwines.co.uk
Website: www.newhallwines.co.uk

Contact: Piers Greenwood
Vineyards: 68.5 hectares
Grape varieties: Bacchus, Pinot noir, Pinot blanc, MT, Huxelrebe, Schönburger, Acolon, Reichensteiner, Chardonnay, Ortega, Zweiegltrebe, Pinot gris, Rondo, Perle
Open to the public. See website for details.

New Hall Vineyards is one of the oldest and largest vineyards in the country and in an area climatically ideal for growing vines. rleigh is four miles from the River Blackwater estuary, has an annual rainfall of only 430-mm and frost is seldom a problem. Bill Greenwood, Pier's father, first planted vines on his 249-hectare arable farm in 1969. Despite initial drainage problems with the heavy clay soil, crops are now usually very good and consistent. The first harvest at New Hall was a modest 2½ tons in 1973 and in those days, with no winery on the farm, the grapes were shipped to Merrydown to be vinified. Today, New Hall has its own winery, fully equipped with two Vaslin 1200 litre presses, a 12 head Seitz Velox filler and all the other usual equipment. The winery has a capacity of 150,000 litres, about half in stainless steel, the balance in glass fibre.

New Hall is not the village of Purleigh's first vineyard as records show that there was one at nearby Purleigh Hall in the twelfth century. In 1169 the 'vintager', as the winegrower was called, received 19s 10d for repairs to the vineyard for two years. In 1187 the cost of making and transferring the wine to London was 11/- and in 1207, two 'tuns' or barrels were taken to Bury St. Edmunds in readiness for the arrival of King John. The vineyard crops up in the records throughout the next two hundred years, with a final mention being in 1402, when 8 men were employed at 1½d per day to dig the vineyard and cart manure from the rectory. The carting was a separate item and cost 4/- for two four-horse carts for two days!

Today, Purleigh's vineyards are under a more modern management regime. The wide spaced Guyot system suits the equipment on the farm and makes for a more open growth of vines than one sees in other vineyards. In 1988 approx. 20-hectares of vines were established, planted under contract by Lamberhurst Vineyards using a Wagner planting machine specially brought over from Germany. This new area was planted at the unusual row width of 3.96-metres but with a very good reason. The vineyards had been interplanted with lucerne which was destined for a local grass drying plant and the forage harvester needed to cut the crop required this distance to get down the rows. The trellising system is also of interest. The wide rows enable a proportion of the growth to grow without being tucked In, which is unusual for Guyot systems and makes for both savings in labour and a well ventilated leaf canopy. Crops at New Hall must be amongst the best in the country and are usually high in natural sugars. Quite a large proportion of the New Hall crop is sold under contract to other wineries and some of the major UK producers source their grapes here. Today the vineyards extend to 68.5-hectares – one of the largest in the UK – and they also manage the 31.6-hectares of vines that belong to Robert Fleming Wines at nearby Mundon.

New House Farm Vineyard

c/o Carr Taylor Wines Ltd, Wheel Lane, Westfield, Hastings, East Sussex TN35 4SG
Location of vineyard: Lane adjacent to Castle Inn, Bodiam, Robertsbridge, East Sussex, TN32 5UB
Telephone: 01424 752501
Fax: 01424 751716
E-mail: alex@carr-taylor.co.uk
Website: www.carr-taylor.co.uk
Contact: Alex Carr Taylor
Vineyards: 4 hectares
Grape varieties: Chardonnay, Pinot noir, Bacchus
Not open to the public.

New Lodge Vineyard

Earls Barton, Northampton, Northamptonshire NN6 0HF
Telephone: 01604 811311
E-mail: joyce@vineyard2000.fsnet.co.uk
E-mail: mail@newlodgevineyard.co.uk
Website: www.newlodgevineyard.co.uk
Contact: Joyce Boulos-Hanna
Vineyards: 0.23 hectares
Grape varieties: Phoenix, Bacchus, Seyval blanc
Open to the public. See website for details.

New Lodge is a small vineyard of only 400 vines, and was planted in 2000. The vineyard is just outside the village of Earls Barton (famous for the Barkers shoe factory) and overlooks the Nene Valley, where readers who paid attention in the historical section of this book, will know that there was in all probability one of the *very* rare Roman vineyards.

The first harvest was in 2004 and the wines are being made by Tony Skuriat at Eglantine Vineyard. Their 2006 wine, named 'Earls Baron' [sic], was awarded Regional Wine status.

New Mill Vineyard

Totteridge Farm, Littleworth, Milton Lilbourne, Pewsey, Wiltshire SN9 5LF
Telephone: 01672 562402
E-mail: totteridgepat@aol.com
Contact: David and Patricia Wells
Vineyards: 0.8 hectares
Grape varieties: Pinot noir Précoce, Seyval blanc, Phoenix
Open by appointment.

Newtown Nurseries Vineyard

Strawberry Hill, Newent, Gloucestershire, GL18 1LH
Telephone: 01531 821847
Contact: Michael Sinclair
Vineyards: 0.3 hectares
Grape varieties: Phoenix, Schönburger, Seyval blanc
Not open to the public.

North Court Farm Vineyard

c/o 100b High Street, Hampton, Middlesex, TW12 2ST
Location of vineyard: North Court Farm, Wick Hill, Finchampstead, Berkshire, RG40 3SN
Telephone: 020 8979 6556
Fax: 020 8979 2091
Mobile: 07811 166791
E-mail: marc@mesvconsultancy.com
Contact: Marc Verstringhe
Vineyards: 0.0719 hectares
Grape varieties: MA, Reichensteiner, Siegerrebe, Pinot noir
Not open to the public.

Northbrook Springs

Beeches Hill, Bishops Waltham, Southampton, Hampshire SO32 1FB
Telephone: 01489 892659
Fax: 01962 777668
E-mail: vineyard@northbrooksprings.fsnet.co.uk
E-mail: jtuttiett@newbyassociates.co.uk
Contact: James Tuttiett
Vineyards: 5.1 hectares
Grape varieties: Kornor, Bacchus, Reichensteiner, Schönburger, Huxelrebe
Open by appointment.

Nutbourne Lane Vineyard

c/o Nyetimber Vineyard, Gay Street, West Chiltington, West Sussex RH20 2HH
Location of vineyard: Nutbourne, Pulborough, West Sussex RH20 2HS
See entry for Nyetimber Vineyard for contact details

Vineyards: 6.4778 hectares
Grape varieties: Pinot noir, Chardonnay, Pinot Meunier
Not open to the public.

Nutbourne Vineyards

Gay Street, Pulborough, West Sussex RH20 2HH
Telephone: 01798 815196
E-mail: sales@nutbournevineyards.com
Website: www.nutbournevineyards.com
Contact: Bridget Gladwin
Vineyards: 7.2874 hectares
Grape varieties: Pinot noir, Reichensteiner, Bacchus, Schönburger, Huxelrebe, MT, Rondo
Open to the public. See website for details.

Nyetimber Vineyard

Gay Street, West Chiltington, West Sussex RH20 2HH
Telephone: 01798 813989
Fax: 01798 815511
E-mail: info@nyetimber.com
Website: www.nyetimber.com
Contact: Ros McCall E-mail: ros@nyetimber.com
Winemaker: Cherie Spriggs E-mail: cherie@nyetimber.com
Vineyard Manager: Paul Woodrow-Hill Email: paul@nyetimber.com
Vineyards:
24.05 hectares at above address, RH20 2HH
25.1 hectares, Chalk Vale, King's Somborne, Stockbridge, Hampshire, SO20 6RE
37.3 hectares, Netherland, Tillington, Petworth, GU28 0PQ
6.4 hectares, Nutbourne Lane, Nutbourne, Pulborough, RH20 2HS
11.3 hectares, River, Petworth, West Sussex, GU28 0PQ
21.2 hectares, Roman Villa, Bignor, Pulborough, RH20 1PQ
8.3 hectares, Undisclosed location
8.0 hectares, Upperton, New Road, Upperton, Petworth, GU28 9BG
Total vineyard area: 141.65hectares
Grape varieties: Pinot noir, Chardonnay, Pinot Meunier
Not open to the public.

Over the 50 years since the revival in UK viticulture started and the first modern commercial vineyard was planted at Hambledon, there have been many brave adventurers who, bitten by 'milady vine' (as Sir Guy Salisbury-Jones used to put it), have taken the plunge and planted vineyards. Many of these have chosen the most unlikely sites, planted the wildest of varieties and forged ahead with seemingly little regard for the amount of work ahead. When it was heard (in 1988) that there were some 'crazy Americans' (Stuart and Sandy Moss) planting acres of Chardonnay high up (60-metres) in the hills near Pulborough, many in the industry (including myself I will admit) said 'not another one' and waited for the inevitable outcome. The vines were planted at 1.6 x 1.0-metre (6,250 vines/ha – a high density for the UK), single Guyot trained and with a fairly low leaf-wall. With their 100 per cent herbicide regime one could be duped into thinking one was in Champagne.

This time, however, it was different. Tales were told of the dedication which the two from Chicago were putting into the venture, of the French consultant (Jean-Manuel Jacquinot) drafted in to help and of the serious equipment bought to make the wine and temporarily installed at Kit Lindlar's High Weald Winery while their's was being designed and built. Even more fascinating was the fact that even after a winery had been built at Nyetimber and several harvests had taken place, no wines were forthcoming. What was going on? The answer was that the Mosses were slowly, painstakingly getting it right. They were determined to come to the market with a product that was as good as they had ever hoped it would be and with packaging that lived up to the product.

The first wine released was the *1992 Nyetimber Première Cuvée Blanc de Blancs* (100 per cent Chardonnay) which was entered into the 1997 IWSC and promptly nabbed a Gold medal and the English Wine Trophy. The second release, the *1993 Nyetimber Classic Cuvée* (a Chardonnay, Pinot noir, Pinot Meunier blend) went one better: a Gold medal, the English Wine Trophy *and* the Bottle Fermented Sparkling Wine Trophy for the best (non-Champagne) sparkling wine in the 1998 IWSC. The third wine was the *1993 Nyetimber Première Cuvée* which was again awarded a Gold medal, the English Wine Trophy and – just to ring the changes – the IWSC 'Most Impressive Wine Presentation Trophy' in the 1999 IWSC. These awards, not given lightly, attest to both the quality in the bottle and the excellence of the packaging. There could be no doubt that whatever the cost, whatever the hard work and single-mindedness that had gone into getting this whole project off the ground, the overall quality of the product was *not* in doubt and that English Wine had turned some sort of corner. I never thought that they would do it and was genuinely amazed at the results. However, a combination of patient and well-heeled patrons with the good luck (possibly foresight) to choose a good site, together with two talented winemakers, Lindlar and Jacquinot, resulted in something that was, for its time, quite revolutionary.

In 1995 the winery at Nyetimber was built and equipped. It was housed in a purpose-built steel-framed building (since expanded), was clean and functional and contained the latest French Champagne making equipment: a 8,000-litre whole berry Magnum press, stainless steel fermentation tanks, cold stabilisation unit, a double-cage Gyro-pallet for riddling and semi-automatic disgorging and dosage line. Bottling is still done under contract by a team from Epernay, as it is at several other sparkling wine vineyards. With the winery complete, Sandy Moss, with the continuing help of Jacquinot, took over officially as winemaker. The Mosses remained in ownership until

2001 when they decided to sell. Stuart was approaching retirement age and without a member of the family interested in continuing their work, buyers were sought and Andy Hill and his wife Nichola became proprietors. Andy Hill, a songwriter, is best known as co-writer and producer of the 1981 European Song Contest winner 'Making your mind up' for Buck's Fizz (an apt name given that some of the proceeds went into buying a sparkling wine producer) and for later masterminding their musical careers. He has also written for artists such as Celine Dion, Cher, Cliff Richard and Leo Sayer, plus a number of other well-known artists (see Wikipedia for a full biography).

With the change of ownership came a change of winemaker. Sandy stayed on to help for a while, but in March 2002, Peter Morgan, an ex-Plumpton student who had been winemaking in Gaillac and had worked at both RidgeView and Davenport, took over. Morgan stayed for two vintages, 2002 and 2003, before returning to Plumpton College as winemaker. He was replaced by Irishman Dermot Sugrue who had been recruited as assistant winemaker the previous year and went on to oversee what were arguably Nyetimber's most successful years, 2004 and 2006, in terms of production, sales, awards and global recognition. Sugrue quickly forged close relationships with Andy Hill, consultant Jacquinot, Jill Stephens (who ran the sales office) and the vineyard team, many of whom had been there since the vineyard was planted 15 years previously. Sugrue inherited the 2002 and 2003 vintages which were still in tank, having only been fermented and racked, and produced six different wines, releasing one after only 18 months on lees, rather than Nyetimber's traditional 5 years of ageing. One of these wines, the 100 per cent Pinot Meunier *2003 Blanc de Noirs*, won a Gold Medal at the 2006 EWOTYC (and then promptly disappeared from view, re-surfacing 18 months later on sale at Harvey Nichols at £35 a bottle). Both I and Tom Stevenson rated this wine as probably Nyetimber's greatest to date.

The next three years were really all Nyetimber's in terms of English Sparkling Wine as Sugrue disgorged as many of the 1995 and 1996 wines as possible so that they could be released at their peak of quality. This resulted in an unprecedented tripling of sales between 2003 and 2005. These two vintages were then followed by the 1997, 1999 and 1998 wines (released in that order) to great critical acclaim. The *1998 Classic Cuvée* won a Gold medal and the Bottle Fermented Sparkling Wine Trophy in the 2006 IWSC – at that time, the second time that Nyetimber had won this prestigious trophy. Suddenly Nyetimber's sales rate started to meet the level of its annual production, gaining huge volumes of publicity in the process.

The 2004 harvest was, at 136 tonnes, the biggest handled at that time. For the 2005 vintage Sugrue introduced barrel fermentation for selected base wines, producing a new style of *Blanc de Blancs* that has yet to be released. It appeared that Hill was initially as committed as the Mosses to Nyetimber and under his tenure more Pinot noir vines were planted (in 2005) and a much-needed semi-automatic labeling machine was placed on order. However, in August 2005, it was announced that the Hills were splitting up (although in true rock-and-roll style they remained 'good friends') and the place was once again on the market.

Prior to Nyetimber being offered for sale as a going concern, a full financial report (69 pages long) was produced which detailed every facet of the production process, of the stocks of wine (£1.28 million worth) and of the costs of everything. It made interesting reading. It showed that production was 'inefficient', that stock control was 'poor' and that the assumed cost of a bottle of wine of £5 a bottle was incorrect and was actually £8.84 and that there was 'no cohesive sales or marketing plan'. It also showed that 'the staff decided what needed doing and when' and that 'leadership was required'. The company's major problem was 'the amount of cash tied up in stock'. On the plus side, sales had risen: 16,581 bottles in the year ending 31 March 2003, 25,859 bottles in the year ending 31 March 2004 and a massive 45,356 bottles in the year ending 31 March 2005. The price to the trade per bottle had also risen and stood at £11.28 a bottle (duty-paid, ex-VAT). It also showed that 15 customers accounted for 70 per cent of sales, top customers being Waitrose, Majestic, Raymond Reynolds and Berry Bros. The report concluded that the aim should be to sell 50,000–55,000 bottles a year, to raise the trade price to £13.75 (inc. duty and ex-VAT), to trim £50,000 from the annual production costs and to instigate a 'long-term business plan'. In short, there was a good business there, capable of making a profit, but it was under-managed and under-capitalised. Yields at Nyetimber have been quite variable over the years and generally on the low side which cannot have helped the financial situation. Yields for the years 1997–2005 have been as follows: 1997 2.4 hl/ha; 1998 12.1 hl/ha; 1999 20 hl/ha; 2000 11 hl/ha; 2001 25.3 hl/ha; 2002 7.5 hl/ha; 2003 18.1 hl/ha; 2004 53 hl/ha; 2005 26 hl/ha. (These yields are of actual bottles produced and since only the *première cuvée* is used and the *taille* – the pressings – sold to another vineyard this needs to be taken into account.)

When the sale was announced, various parties appeared who were interested in buying Nyetimber and even Champagne houses were talked of as possible buyers although none actually seems to have been interested. English Wines Group (Chapel Down) certainly was interested but could not make sense of the £7.5 million price tag. They estimated the house was worth £3 million, the 16 hectares of vineyards then planted perhaps another £0.5 million, the winery, winery equipment and stock another £2 million and then there was the goodwill – maybe another £0.5 million, maybe £1 million – either way it was well off the asking price. The eventual buyer, Eric Heerema, then enters the picture.

Heerema, who was variously reported as being an 'ex-lawyer, ex-venture capitalist and businessman' had been living in the UK with his family for over a decade and had made his home here. He had already dipped his toes into English Wine and had planted an 8.3-hectare vineyard at his country home nearby. In 2004 he had decided that he wanted to create *a commercially viable project of quite considerable scale* and do for English sparkling wines *what McAlpine did for still wines in the 1980s at Lamberhurst.* To this end, in April 2005, he had meetings with Hill to see whether he would sell Nyetimber, but negotiations foundered as their ideas of value were fairly far apart. In August 2005, the Hills having announced their separation and with lawyers involved, Hill's need to sell became more acute and he got back in touch with Heerema. After several months of negotiations, not helped by the divorce proceedings, a price was agreed and on 3 March 2006, for £7.4 million, Heerema became the proud owner of Nyetimber.

Prior to the purchase, Heerema had already been looking for land in the area to expand the vineyards and between February and April 2006 was able to buy several suitable blocks. Within weeks of taking over he was able to expand the vineyards and in 2006, 2007 and 2008 an additional 81.4-hectares of vines – over 300,000 vines – were planted: 51.7-hectares at nearby Upperton, Tillington and Nutbourne Lane; 21.2-hectares at Bignor alongside the Roman Villa; and 8.5-hectares at Nyetimber itself. These plantings brought the total under vine, including the 8.3-hectares at Heerema's house, to 105.25-hectares.

Not wishing to be left out of the hunt for chalkland to plant – very few of Nyetimber's vineyards up to this point were on calcarious soil – Heerema was also able to find a gently sloping, chalky, south-facing 30-ha site near Stockbridge, Hampshire, situated at between 65 and 50-metres above sea level. This site, which ticks almost all the viticultural boxes, was bought for a reputed £40,000 per hectare from the Plymouth Brethren, apparently large (and very lucky) landowners in the area. A total of 25.1-hectares were planted here, as well as an additional 11.3-hectares at River, just to the west of Petworth. As of the end of the 2009 planting season, the total under vines stands at 141.65-hectares (350 acres). All the new vineyards have been planted at a spacing of 2.2 x 1.2-metres (3,788 vines per hectare). Heerema would like to acquire additional land and his aim is to bring the total under vine to 200-hectares as soon as possible.

Almost as soon as Heerema took over, a hot-shot general manager, Chris Varley, was appointed and new staff taken on to look after the greatly expanded vineyards. Things, however, didn't go quite as smoothly as presumably Heerema hoped as before the 2006 vintage both Sugrue and Jill Stephens left, followed quite soon after by Varley. Harvest 2006 was something of a trial for all concerned. A freshly graduated Plumpton student, Belinda Kemp, took over as winemaker for six months, assisted by consultant Jacquinot – only there as usual for a few days to get the vintage under way – and with *Botrytis* taking the crop as it ripened (it is estimated that 40% of the crop was lost), picking was brought forward by two weeks. Despite these setbacks, around 68,000 botttles were produced. A search for a new winemaker produced Canadian Cherie Spriggs, who studied in Canada (Ontario and British Columbia) and Adelaide and whose husband, Brad Greatrix, also helps run the winery. Cherie and Brad's winemaking CVs includes time spent at wineries in Australia, Canada, France, New Zealand and the USA (Oregon) and they come to the UK with considerable international experience. Spriggs' first harvest was the difficult 2007, followed by the even more challenging 2008 – two vintages which would test any winemaker's patience. A new sales manager, Stephen Clark (who spent 22 years with Laurent-Perrier in the UK) was appointed in April 2008 to replace Nina Walters (who left after only a short while in the position), but Clark also left after a very short spell and was gone by Christmas. After a considerable search, his place was taken, in May 2009, by Francis Brackley, who left Lay and Wheeler after they were bought by Majestic. Charlie Mount, who has been brand manager for Krug, has also been taken on as London account manager to support what will, in the fullness of time, become a 1,000,000-plus bottle brand.

The legend of Nyetimber was founded on wine quality. Granted the story of two mysterious, almost reclusive Americans, followed by a moderately flamboyant rock-and-roll couple and now a former venture capitalist, makes for good copy, but when all is said and done, it's the wines that have made – and must continue to make – Nyetimber's reputation. Twenty-seven Nyetimber wines were entered into the EWOTYC between 2001 and 2009 (before 2001 the Mosses declined to enter this competition and in 2007 no wines were entered) and have won an outstanding array of awards and trophies: the Gore-Browne Trophy five times, the Vintner's Trophy and the Wine Guild Trophy four times each, the Dudley Quirk three times and the Tom Day once. In 2001 Sandy Moss was the inaugural McAlpine Winemaker of the Year (and would have won it in 2002 had the rules not been changed!). On the medals front the same twenty-seven wines won an unprecedented seventeen Gold medals, six Silvers, three Bronzes and one Highly Commended. Nyetimber also won the IWSC UK Wine Producer of the Year Trophy in 1999, 2001, 2003, 2004, 2006, 2008 and 2009, and as has already been mentioned, the IWSC International Sparkling Wine Trophy in 1998 and 2006. Their most recent triumph has been with their first ever release, the *1992 Nyetimber Première Cuvée Blanc de Blancs* – which won a Gold medal and the English Wine Trophy in 1997 – was awarded another Gold medal in the 2009 IWSC, plus the Bottle Fermented Sparkling Wine Trophy. That a wine – an English Wine – can, after over 15 years *sur latte* and only recently disgorged, win a trophy of such prestige, is a real testament to the longevity of Nyetimber's 100% Chardonnay-based wines. To these you can add a host of other awards and medals from around Europe and their wines have been served at countless Royal and other public occasions. If you asked a reasonably (wine) informed man on the Clapham omnibus to name an English sparkling wine, the hot money would be on Nyetimber coming up more times than any other name.

Having said that wine quality was their *raison d'être* it has not always been plain sailing as perhaps the Bronze medals and the Highly Commended above indicate. I have tasted their wines at every UKVA competition between 2001 and 2009 (except 2007 – see above) and on countless other occasions and there has sometimes been bottle variability. A few years ago, especially in the period around the sale of the business, it seemed to get worse with wines from the 2000 vintage being especially prone, although a batch of poor corks may have accounted for some of these problems. Happily it now seems to be a thing of the past and the 2000 vintage is sold out. The 2001s I tasted at the 2008 EWP St George's Day tasting were very 'fresh' (unkindly one might say acidic) and comparatively youthful tasting compared to the Nyetimber toasty, oaky old-vintage style. To my palate at least, these wines appeared somewhat light on residual sugar with their high acidity rather prominent. However, these were recently disgorged samples and I thought that some additional time on the cork would result in a bit more harmony.

In July 2009, I tasted the whole range of Nyetimber's wines, and am pleased to say that the *2001 Blanc de Blancs*, whilst still crisp, is starting to show signs of the usual *brioche* on the nose, and the *2001 Classic Cuvée* is a really classy wine. I am not surprised that it won a Gold medal in the 2008 IWSC. Their 2003 offerings, which are just starting to come on to the market, are softer (as one would excpect from the vintage) and should do very well in competitions, especially the *2003 Classic Cuvée* which, after over four years *sur lie* and nine months on cork, had excellent length and great balance. This wine didn't go through a malolactic fermentation and is all the better for it. I also tasted the *1998 Blanc de Blancs,* which recently won a Gold at the *Chardonnay du Monde*, and finished in the top ten of over 1,200 Chardonnay-based still and sparkling wines from all over the world. This just shows that UK-grown wines will age beautifully and can go on getting better and better. It is planned to launch a 2007 Rosé at the end of 2010 and, in the fullness of time, a non-vintage blend. The retail prices of Nyetimber are still at the top end of the range for UK-grown sparkling wines – around £24-25 for the *Classic Cuvée* and £28-30 for the *Blanc de Blancs*[17] – which is right where Moët, Taittinger, Lanson and the other major Champagne brands want to sell. Nyetimber's quality can certainly justify these prices, but they are at the top-end of where most casual consumers for UK-grown wines want to find them.

On the winery front, Cherie Spriggs and her team have settled in (French consultant Jacquinot was dispensed with in May 2009 and is no longer involved) and they are well into planning what will be the next big development at Nyetimber – the construction of a new 1,000,000-plus bottle winery. Owing to planning problems, it is not possible (and perhaps given the access, not really practical) to expand the winery at Nyetimber itself, and an agreement has been entered into with Brinsbury College to establish the new winery on land opposite their main campus which is about five minutes away. It is planned that the winery will be operational for 2012. To cope with the grapes now coming from the new plantings, an 8-tonne Coquard press was installed at Nyetimber for the 2008 harvest, but this will be moved temporarily to a facilty at Tillington, near to their large new plantings, and after pressing, the juice will be tankered to Nyetimber for fermentation. In 2008, 160 tonnes were harvested and it

---

17 October 2009: Waitrose Wine Direct has 2003 Classic Cuvée at £24 and 2001 Blanc de Blancs at £27 which shows a slight softening of prices.

is anticipated that the 2009 harvest, from 105-hectares, will be nearer to 1,000 tonnes. With Hereema's aim to get to 200-hectares, the total crush could rise to 2,000 tonnes in a good year which will result in 1.5 m bottles.

Heerema and his team have certainly, in under four years, taken Nyetimber to a completely new level – one unseen in UK winegrowing circles, even in the heyday of Lamberhurst's domination of the still wine market in the late 1980s and early 1990s. The scale of the Nyetimber enterprise, in both the obvious investment in vineyards, buildings and winemaking equipment, but also in the commitment and dedication on the part of Heerema and his staff is huge. Their desire to produce wines of world-beating quality is obvious and it will be fascinating to see the "Heerema" vintages when they first appear. Despite changes in ownership, changes in personnel and the vagaries of the UK climate, the pre-2006 vintages have had an amazing amount of success in both national and international competitions, yet I feel certain that these will be eclipsed in the future.

The next few years promises to be the most interesting one in the history of the post-war revival of UK-grown wines. The massive plantings of the Champagne varieties (well, massive in the context of UK wine production) will, global warming willing, produce wines which will come to market and they will need a brand to lead them to the promised land of milk and honey (aka profitability) and it falls to Nyetimber to play the Moses part. Their reputation, their current market position and their sheer volume means that they will certainly be in the spotlight. I look forward to the next few years with interest.

Oak Hill Vineyard

Willow House, Fressingfield, Eye, Suffolk IP21 5PE
Telephone: 01379 586868
E-mail: mail@oak-hill.co.uk
Website: www.oak-hill.co.uk
Contact: Carol Spenser
Vineyards: 0.4 hectares
Grape varieties: Bacchus
Vineyard not open to the public. Wine sales by appointment. See website for details.

Oakford Vineyard

The Old Rectory, Holme Place, Oakford, Tiverton, Devon EX16 9EW
Telephone: 01398 351486
E-mail: prot@oakford57.fsnet.co.uk
Contact: Peter Rostron
Vineyards: 1.05 hectares
Grape varieties: Kernling, Orion, Rondo, Siegerrebe
Open by appointment.

Oatley Vineyard

Cannington, Bridgwater, Somerset TA5 2NL
Telephone: 01278 671340
E-mail: wine@oatleyvineyard.co.uk
Website: www.oatleyvineyard.co.uk
Contact: Iain and Jane Awty
Vineyards: 1 hectare
Grape varieties: Kernling, MA
Open by appointment. See website for details.

The vineyard was planted in 1986 and 1987 on a gentle, south-east facing slope, 37 metres above sea level, between the Quantock Hills and the Bristol Channel on red sandy loam. The 0.6 hectares of Kernling are Guyot pruned on the upper slopes of the site and on a high single wire on the lower slopes. The 0.4 hectares of Madeleine Angevine are spur-pruned on a low single wire. The alleyways are close-mown permanent pasture and the vineyard is managed to maximise biodiversity and minimise environmental impact.

Oatley is a well-established small commercial vineyard and the owners concentrate on achieving interest and character in their wines. They aim to reflect the innate characteristics of the grapes and the terroir by producing high-quality, fully ripened grapes that need minimum intervention during vinification and produce dry white wines of character and distinction. There can be significant differences in the wines from year to year, depending on what the weather brings, including an occasional medium Kernling where high natural sugars in the grapes have caused fermentation to stop a little early. Oatley wines are never sweetened artificially and are suitable for vegans.

Two distinct 'series' of wines are made: rose-red Kernling grapes produce 'Leonora's' white wines with body, length and fruit to complement fine food; and golden Madeleine Angevine grapes produce 'Jane's' wines which typically have more flowery flavours, lower acidity and perhaps a shorter finish and make a good *apéritif* and excellent summer afternoon drinking. Oatley wines have won many awards in both UK and international competitions, including 15 awards in 13 years of entries to the IWC. The vineyard has a following of regular customers who await the release of each new vintage with anticipation. Interested visitors get a warm welcome but it is best to phone first. Wines are available by the case from the informative website, by telephone or after a vineyard tasting. Case deliveries are free to Somerset, Devon, Avon, Gloucestershire, Wiltshire, Dorset and Hampshire.

Old Grove House Vineyard

Llangrove, Ross-on-Wye, Herefordshire HR9 6HA
Telephone: 01989 770754
Fax: 01989 770754
Mobile: 07774 291546
E-mail: emdservices@msn.com
Contact: Robin Drewett, Sally Ashworth
Vineyards: 0.0210 hectares
Grape varieties: Triomphe, Rondo, Phoenix
Not open to the public.

Old Oak Vineyard

c/o Abbey Vineyards Group, Irnham Grange, Irnham, Corby Glen, Grantham, Lincolnshire, NG33 4NE
Location of vineyard: Uppingham Road, Preston, Uppingham, Rutland, LE15
Telephone: 01476 550191
Fax: 01476 550080
E-mail: info@abbeyvineyards.co,uk
Contact: Phil Kerry 07815 308838
Contact: Jonathan Kerry 07805 315763
Vineyards: 1.5 hectares
Grape varieties: Pinot noir, Chardonnay, Reichensteiner, Regent
Not open to the public.

Old Rectory Vineyard

The Street, Bredfield, Woodbridge, Suffolk, IP13 6AX
Telephone: 01394 386339, 01394 385223
E-mail: rjbdarcy@aol.com
Contact: Robin D'Arcy
Vineyards: 1.62 hectares
Grape varieties: Seyval blanc, Rondo
Not open to the public.

Old Walls Vineyard

Old Walls Road, Bishopsteignton, Teignmouth, Devon TQ14 9PQ
Telephone: 01626 770877
Mobile: 07929 870908
E-mail: ken@oldwallsvineyard.co.uk
Website: www.oldwallsvineyard.co.uk
Contact: Ken Dawe
Vineyards: 3 hectares
Grape varieties: Bacchus, Reichensteiner, Auxerrois, Rondo, Regent, Dunkelfelder, Pinot noir Précoce
Open to the public. See website for details.

Vines at Old Walls were first planted in 2002 and occupy a series of fairly steep south-facing slopes just outside the picturesque village of Bishopsteignton. The name 'Old Walls' is derived from the fact that the ruins of the Bishop of Exeter's Summer Palace, which dates from 1275, can still be seen in the vicinity.

Old Walls winery, wine shop and tea rooms

The vineyard and winery is run by the Dawe family, Ken and Lesley and their son, Paul, with winemaking overseen by Hans Schleifer. The winery is well equipped with modern tanks and machinery and produces around 30,000 bottles a year. Wines come in all colours – white, red and rosé – both still and sparkling, and many wines have achieved Quality Wine status. Visitors are very well catered for with a shop, tearooms and the usual facilities and for someone wishing to see the ins and outs of running a small vineyard, this is an ideal place to start.

Olding Manor Vineyard

c/o 42 Pitfold Road, Lee, London SE12 9HX
Location of vineyard: SE12 0TF
Telephone: 020 7652 3151
Mobile: 07970 155303
E-mail: paul@oldingmanor.co.uk

E-mail: paul.olding@bbc.co.uk
Website: www.oldingmanor.co.uk
Contact: Paul Olding
Vineyards: 0.01 hectares
Grape varieties: Phoenix, Orion, Regent
Not open to the public.

Ollivers Farm Vineyard

Toppesfield, Halstead, Essex CO9 4LS
Telephone: 01787 237642
Fax: 01787 237602
E-mail: blackiejames@hotmail.com
E-mail: james@trickerblackie.co.uk
Contact: James Blackie
Vineyards: 0.017 hectares
Grape varieties: MA
Not open to the public.

OLLIVERS FARM

MADELEINE ANGEVINE

English wine grown, made and bottled by James Blackie
at Ollivers Farm, Toppesfield, Essex.

75 cl ℮

Ollivers Farm Vineyard (which if nothing else has gained an extra 'l' to its name since the last publication – apparently this is how it was spelt on a 1738 map of the farm) is in a village containing one of the few vineyard sites in Essex recorded in the Domesday Book. It is on the north side of an east–west running valley with about 2 miles of south-facing slope which runs down to the Toppesfield Brook. It is between 70 and 73 metres above sea level and the soil is chalky boulder clay. The vines, all Madeleine x Angevine 7672, were planted between 1980 and 1990 and are on their own roots, planted at 1.2 x 1.2 metres and double Guyot trained. The vines are grown organically and, increasingly, biodynamic principles are being followed. The wine – which is not sold – is 'unashamedly English' says James Blackie, 'and does not attempt to imitate the product of any other country or region, i.e. it is low in alcohol with hints of elderflower and gooseberry on the nose, fruity with a touch of Muscat and a long finish'. Sounds delicious to me!

Otter Farm Vineyard

Weston, Honiton, Devon EX14 3PA
Telephone: 01404 548927
Mobile: 07870 771535

E-mail: mark@otterfarm.co.uk
Website: www.otterfarm.co.uk
Contact: Mark Diacono
Vineyards: 1.5 hectares
Grape varieties: Seyval blanc, Pinot noir, Sauvignon blanc, Gewürztraminer
Not open to the public.

Painshill Park Vineyard

Portsmouth Road, Cobham, Surrey KT11 1JE
Telephone: 01932 868113
E-mail: info@painshill.co.uk
E-mail: markebdon@painshill.co.uk
Website: www.painshill.co.uk
Contact: Mark Ebdon
Vineyards: 0.73 hectares
Grape varieties: Chardonnay, Pinot noir, Seyval blanc
Open to the public. See website for details.

Painshill Park is one of Europe's finest eighteenth-century landscape gardens and was created by the Hon. Charles Hamilton between 1738 and 1773. He transformed barren heathland into ornamental pleasure grounds and parkland of dramatic beauty and contrasting scenery, dominated by a 6-hectare lake fed from the river by an immense waterwheel. The lake is overlooked by a steeply facing slope upon which he planted a vineyard. The vineyard outlasted Hamilton by only a few years and the last known vintage was in 1779.[18]

I first saw the site in the early 1980s when I had accompanied Anthony Goddard (at that time owner of Barton Manor vineyard on the Isle of Wight), who had been invited to visit the site to advise on the possible replanting of the vineyard. Owing to the demands of the many other restoration projects in the park, the idea to replant the vineyard was left for several years. The replanting of the Painshill vineyard was part of the overall re-creation of Hamilton's masterpiece and, as such, had to be as true to the original as possible. The only real record of how the vineyard looked were two contemporary paintings which show closely planted vines, trained up thin single poles, a type of training and pruning still seen on the Mosel and in vineyards in other steeply sloping

---

18 A fuller history of this vineyard can be found in Chapter 1.

regions. The modern vineyard, in order to accommodate a tractor and mower, was more widely spaced with rows at 7-feet (2.13-metres) wide, although the vines were trained up individual poles at 4-feet (1.2 metres) apart, but with pruning and training wires as in a normal vertically shoot positioned system.

The original varieties were said by Hamilton to be: *two sorts of Burgundy grapes, the Auvernat, which is the most delicate, but the tenderest, and the Miller grape, commonly called the black cluster, which is more hardy* and that the wine *had a finer flavour than the best Champaign* [sic] *I ever tasted.* The decision therefore was taken to plant varieties suited for the production of bottle-fermented sparkling wine. As a gesture to history, Chardonnay and Pinot noir were planted, but supplemented with Seyval blanc – a reliable variety with a good track record for producing sparkling wines in this climate.

The first task to be undertaken before the vineyard could be replanted was the clearing of the site which was covered with immense Scot's Pines which had established themselves over the intervening two centuries. At that time I was

winemaker at Lamberhurst Vineyards, then owned by Kenneth McAlpine, a member of the Sir Robert McAlpine construction company family, who volunteered in the winter of 1989 to provide some heavy earth-moving equipment and operators. (McAlpine, who at one time financed, and drove for, the 'Connaught' motor racing team – one of their cars is shown above – knew the site as he had once been part of a consortium, which included Bernie Eccleston, who were considering buying it to build an F1 racing circuit). The site was duly cleared of trees and undergrowth, graded to a uniform slope and then sown with grass seed to stabilise the site. After two years the site was ready for replanting and in 1992 I personally undertook the replanting of the vines, some 230 years after the original vineyard had been planted. To my knowledge, it is the only vineyard today that occupies exactly the same site as an original pre-revival one.

The vines were slow to establish – badgers, deer and rabbits have all had to be contended with – and over 1,000 vines had to be replanted. The first very small harvest of Pinot noir was taken in 1996 and was blended with some bought-in Dunkelfelder to make a rosé. In 1997 and 1998 spring frosts affected the site and very few grapes were harvested. Yields in 1998 and 1999 were better, with the Seyval blanc producing most of the crop. Vineyard manager Mark Ebdon says that his major problem is getting the acids of the Chardonnay down to a manageable level and keeping the birds – especially parakeets – off. Netting was tried once, but the costs proved prohibitive. The grapes are taken to Stanlake Park and a rosé is generally made as a first choice wine, with a sparkling wine made (I wonder how close to Hamilton's *best Champaign* it is?) as and when quantities allow. Wines are exclusively sold in the on-site shop to the many visitors that visit the park. Current wines include a 2006 Rosé at £6.95 and the 2005 Painshill Brut (Pinot noir and Seyval blanc) at £10.50.

Pant Du Vineyard

Y Wern, Pant Du, Hen Lon, Penygroes, Gwynedd LL54 6PY, Wales
Telephone: 01286 880806
Mobile: 07831 578516
E-mail: richaiola@aol.com
Website: www.pantdu.co.uk
Contact: Richard Wyn Huws
Vineyards: 2.834 hectares
Grape varieties: Bacchus, Seyval blanc, Pinot noir Précoce, Rondo, Regent, Siegerrebe, Pinot noir
Open by appointment.

Parhams Vineyard

Melbury Abbas, Shaftesbury, Dorset SP7 0DE
Telephone: 01747 853122
Fax: 01747 853122
E-mail: royphillips.parhams@tiscali.co.uk
Contact: Roy Phillips
Vineyards: 0.4 hectares
Grape varieties: Reichensteiner, Bacchus
Open by appointment.

Parva Farm Vineyard

Tintern, Chepstow, Monmouthshire NP16 6SQ, Wales
Telephone: 01291 689636
Mobile: 07899 980826
E-mail: parvafarm@hotmail.com
Website: www.paravafarm.com
Contact: Judith Dudley
Vineyards: 0.994 hectares
Grape varieties: Bacchus, Regent, Seyval blanc, Pinot noir, MT, plus 12 other varieties in small amounts
Open daily, except Wednesdays, 11.30 am to 6 pm. Best to ring first.

Parva Farm Vineyard was planted in 1979 on a steep south-facing slope overlooking Tintern and its historic abbey. The region has historical links to both the Romans and medieval monks, so it is quite possible that vines are not new to the area. In 1996 the 23-hectare hill farm was bought by Colin and Judith Dudley who found the vineyard in a sad state of neglect, overgrown with brambles and with many of the posts rotten.

Undeterred, they set to and restored as much as they could. Although most of the vines date back to the early days, 750 Regent vines were planted in 2002–2005 to supplement the Pinot noir so that a red wine could be made. The Dudley's first harvest, all 65-kilos of it, was in 1997. Since then, yields have improved and in 2001 they picked 5.5-tonnes and in 2006, 11.5-tonnes. The grapes are taken to Three Choirs

for processing. Their 2006 Bacchus won a silver medal in the 2008 EWOTYC and was awarded a commended in the 2009 Decanter World Wine Awards. They also won bronzes with their 2006 Dathliad Sparkling Rosé in the 2008 EWOTYC and for the 2007 Bwthyn Rhosyn Rosé in the 2009 EWOTYC.

Pear Tree at Purton Vineyard

Church End, Swindon, Wiltshire SN5 4ED
Telephone: 01793 772100
Fax: 01793 772369
E-mail: francis@peartreepurton.co.uk
Website: www.peartreepurton.co.uk
Contact: Francis Young
Vineyards: 0.7 hectares
Grape varieties: Seyval blanc, Bacchus, Pinot noir
Open to the public. See website for details.

Pebblebed Clyst St George Vineyard

Location of vineyard: Bushayes Farm, Clyst St George, Exeter, Devon
For contact details see entry for Pebblebed Wines
Vineyards: 3.2376 hectares
Grape varieties: Seyval blanc, Rondo
Open to the public by appointment..

Pebblebed Ebford Vineyard

Location of vineyard: Ebford Lane, Ebford, Exeter, Devon
For contact details see entry for Pebblebed Wines
Vineyards: 4.2376 hectares
Grape varieties: Pinot noir Précoce, Seyval blanc, Rondo, MA
Open to the public by appointment.

Pebblebed West Hill Vineyard

Location of vineyard: Off Toad Pit Lane, West Hill, Ottery St Mary, Exeter, Devon
For contact details see entry for Pebblebed Wines
Vineyards: 2.4282 hectares
Grape varieties: Pinot noir Précoce, Seyval blanc, Rondo
Open to the public by appointment.

Pebblebed Wines

Shop: The Wine Cellar, 46a Fore Street, Topsham, Devon EX3 0HY
Telephone: 01392 875908
Mobile: 07814 788348
E-mail: geoff@pebblebedwines.co.uk
Website: www.pebblebedwines.co.uk
Contact: Geoff Bowen
Vineyards: See separate entries. 10.1034 hectares in total.
Grape varieties: Seyval blanc, Rondo, Pinot noir Précoce, MA, Cabernet Sauvignon, Merlot
Open to the public by appointment. See website for details of visiting arrangements, events and wine sales.

The vineyards which provide the grapes for Pebblebed Wines come from four different vineyards: Clyst St George, West Hill, near Ottery St Mary, and two in the village of Ebford. They are all to the south-east of Exeter. The first vines were planted in 2000, further expanded with commercial plantings in 2002 and again in 2005 and 2006. All vineyards are organic and working practices are based on strong environmental principles. It is hoped that biodynamic status can be achieved in the future. Pebblebed Wines involves the local community as much as possible with part of the Ebford vineyard set aside for local families to manage and more than 200 local people assisted with the harvest in 2007.

Pebblebed Wines currently produces a dry white, rosé, red and sparkling rosé and their wines regularly win awards in both national and regional competitions. Their 2006 Sparkling Rosé was awarded a Silver Medal in the 2008 EWOTYC. All wines are currently made by Juliet White at Exe Valley Wines (aka Yearlstone Vineyard) and the wines have been environmentally assessed for Carbon Labelling purposes. Their continental-style tasting cellar near the quay in Topsham is very busy with tastings of both their own and other Devon wines and is open most evenings serving tapas-style food. Their adopt-a-vine package is proving very popular and there are plans to build a carbon-neutral winery in 2010.

Penarth Vineyard

Pool Road, Newtown, Powys, SY16 3AN, Wales
Telephone and Fax: 01686 610383
E-mail: tanya@penarthvineyard.co.uk
E-mail: penarthvineyard@aol.com
Website: www.penarthvineyard.co.uk
Contact: Grace Dowley
Vineyards: 4 hectares
Grape varieties: Chardonnay, Pinot noir, Pinot Meunier, Cabernet Franc, Merlot, Sauvignon blanc plus others
Open to the public by appointment.

Penarth Vineyard is located in Newtown, in the Montgomeryshire region of Powys. Newtown is best known for its famous sons, Robert Owen and Pryce Jones, for its fine flannel, and as the home of the world's first mail-order business. Penarth House (below) which is shown on the wine labels, was built in 1485 as an original aisled hall and began its life as a residence in the eighteenth century. It is listed as a Grade 2* building and the main feature of the house is its stunning façade. Internally it retains many of its original features.

The vineyard sits on an old riverbed with views up to the surrounding hills in all directions providing shelter and creating a unique microclimate. Planting began in

1999 and in 2002 the first crop was harvested. Grapes are taken to Three Choirs for processing and both white and rosé sparkling and still wines are produced. In the 2009 Decanter WWA, the NV Penarth Estate Pink Sparkling gained a Commended award.

Penberth Valley Vincyard

Penberth Valley, St Buryan, Penzance, Cornwall TR19 6HH
Telephone: 01736 810714
E-mail: robinjuliabryant@hotmail.com
Contact: Robin Bryant
Vineyards: 0.17 hectares
Grape varieties: Triomphe, Léon Millot, Rondo
Not open to the public.

Pengethley Manor Hotel Vineyard

Pengethley Park, Ross-on-Wye, Herefordshire HR9 6LL
Telephone: 01989 730211
Fax: 01989 730238
E-mail: reservations@pengethleymanor.co.uk
Website: www.pengethleymanor.co.uk
Contact: Mr P. Whisker
Vineyards: 0.2 hectares
Grape varieties: Reichensteiner, Seyval blanc, Phoenix
Open to the public. See website for details.

Pheasants Ridge Vineyard

Hambleden, Henley-on-Thames, Oxfordshire RG9 6SN
Telephone: 01491 576087
E-mail: michael@pheasantsridge.co.uk
Website: http://www.gilbeygroup.com/pheasants-ridge
Contact: Michael Gilbey
Vineyards: 0.6478 hectares
Grape varieties: Bacchus, Faberrebe
Open by appointment.

Pheasants Ridge Vineyard is owned by Michael and Lin Gilbey and is planted below the Gilbeys' house in a truly beautiful valley near the village of Hambleden. The soil is light with some chalky elements and well-suited for vines (and the local red kites make it even more-so) and all the vines are planted on a traditional (well, traditional at the time they were planted in the late 1980s) GDC system at 3.65 x 2.44-metres. Two varieties are grown, Bacchus and Faberrebe. The vineyard is looked after by the Gilbeys and a loyal team of local (unpaid!) volunteers and all profits from the vineyard go to the village church and associated charities. Since 2004, the profits have been £17,500 of which £11,500 has been given away to date (March 2009). The balance represents the investment in future vintages. Apart from a few local sales,

most of the wine is sold through one of the Gilbeys' two restuarants: one in Eton and the other in Old Amersham. The grapes are taken to Stanlake Park for vinification. Two wines are produced: a bottle-fermented sparkling wine from the Faberrebe and a still white from the Bacchus. In 2009 almost 5.5-tonnes were harvested at record sugar levels.

Pippins Vineyard

Tickerage Lane, Blackboys, Uckfield, East Sussex, TN22 5LT
Telephone: 01825 890525
E-mail: the4budds@btinternet.com
Contact: Anthony Budd
Vineyards: 2.12 hectares
Grape varieties: Not known
Not open to the public.

Plot 19 Vineyard

c/o 23 Clifton Road, Urmston, Manchester M41 5RU
Location of vineyard: Brook Road, Flixton, Manchester, M41
Telephone: 0161 749 9348
Mobile: 07717 784045
E-mail: michael@michaeltait.wanadoo.co.uk
Contact: Michael Tait
Vineyards: 0.0222 hectares
Grape varieties: Phoenix, Triomphe, Rondo, Siegerrebe, Léon Millot, Seyval blanc
Not open to the public.

Plumpton College Vineyard

Ditchling Road, Lewes, East Sussex BN7 3AE
Telephone: 01273 890454   Fax: 01273 890071
E-mail: enquiries@plumpton.ac.uk
Website: www.plumpton.ac.uk
General contact: Chris Foss (chris.foss@plumpton.ac.uk)
Vineyard: Kevin Sutherland (kevin.sutherland@plumpton.ac.uk)
Winemaker: Peter Morgan (peter.morgan@plumpton.ac.uk)
Wine Sales: Paul Harley (harleyp@plumpton.ac.uk)
Vineyards: 0.46 hectares. Rock Lodge (4.67 ha) and Ditchling (1.82 ha) are leased by the college.
Grape varieties: Bacchus, Regner, Schönburger, Seyval blanc plus collection of 26 varieties and 22 rootstocks
Not open to individuals, but group tours by appointment.

Plumpton College was founded in 1926 and is at the centre of a 647-hectare farm which is used to teach many different land-based courses. The vineyards were established in 1988 when the college started offering courses in viticulture and winemaking. At first these were done in conjunction with a college in Brighton and offered a City and Guilds qualification. Since then, the wine studies courses have expanded and there are now three full-time undergraduate degrees (in partnership with the University of Brighton) in Wine Production (FdSc), Wine Business (FdA) and a Bsc (Hons) in Viticulture and Oenology. They also offer WSET Foundation, Intermediate, Advanced and Diploma courses. A new £1.5 million Wine Studies Centre was opened in June 2007 by Jancis Robinson MW which includes science labs, tiered lecture seating, a state-or-the-art tasting room with individual booths and a fully equipped commercial winery. The 'Vintners Room', with its vaulted ash ceiling and panoramic views of the downs is the focus for wine events, both educational and social (and can be hired).

Plumpton has 0.46-hectares of its own vineyards, planted with a number of different varieties, plus a collection of cultivars and rootstock varieties. They also lease two other local vineyards: Rock Lodge (4.67-hectares) and Ditchling (1.82-hectares). Both the Plumpton and Ditchling vineyards are planted on the chalk soil of the South Downs; Rock Lodge is on sandstone. Plumpton produces a range of wines, using fruit from both its own and the leased vineyards. These include two sparkling wines, two whites, a rosé and two reds. Plumpton's wines continue to improve in quality and it is pleasing to see them winning prizes. Recent successes include Bronze at the 2009 Decanter WWA for the NV Cloudy Ridge Dry White and a Silvers for both the 2008 Cloudy Ridge Rosé and the NV The Dean Blush sparkling at the 2009 SEVA competition. In the March 2008 *Decanter Magazine* mega-tasting of English Sparkling Wines I was surprised (and pleased) to see their sparkling wine 'The Dean' achieve the second highest marks.

Pollaughan Vineyard

c/o Deviock Wine Company, Looe Hill, St. Martin, Looe, Cornwall, PL13 1PA
Location of vineyard: Pollaughan, Portscatho, Truro, Cornwall, TR2 5EH
Telephone: 01752 812178
Contact: Adrian Derx 07815 196199
E-mail: adrian_derx@hotmail.com
Contact: Alex Davidson   07882 097339
E-mail: larajo36@hotmail.com
Vineyards: 2.8 hectares
Grape varieties: Pinot noir Précoce, Seyval blanc, Bacchus, Riesling, Rondo, Dornfelder, Dunkelfelder, Chardonnay, Pinot noir
Not open to the public.

Polgoon Vineyard

Rosehill, Penzance, Cornwall TR20 8TE
Telephone: 01736 351680
Mobile: 07770 815704

E-mail: john@polgoon.co.uk   E-mail: kim@polgoon.co.uk
Website: www.polgoon.co.uk
Contact: John and Kim Coulson
Vineyards: 3.6 hectares
Grape varieties: Rondo, Pinot noir Précoce, Seyval blanc, Bacchus, Ortega
Open to the public. See website for details.

Polgoon Vineyard

Polmassick Vineyard

St Ewe, St Austell, Cornwall PL26 6HA
Telephone: 01726 842239
E-mail: polmassick@btconnect.com
Contact: Barbara Musgrave
Vineyards: 1 hectare
Grape varieties: MT, Kernling, Seyvla blanc, Pinot noir, Ortega, Orion
Open by appointment.

Poly Croft Vineyard

Riverviw House, South dell, Isle of Lewis, HS2 0SO, Scotland
Telephone: 01851 810396
E-mail: thepolycroft@aol.com
Website: www.the-poly-croft.co.uk
Contact: Donald Hope
Vineyards: 0.0050 hectares
Grape varieties: Black Hamburg
Open by appointment.

The Poly Croft Vineyard – at 20 vines all grown indoors – barely rates the title
'vineyard' but who knows, in 50 years time Scotland might be the new Bordeaux?
Situated on the northern tip of the Isle of Lewis and at 58°28' it certainly rates as the
UK's most northerly grapegrowing enterprise. The Black Hamburgh table grapes can
be bought in Stornaway Crofters and Farmers Market.

Port Lympne Vineyard

Port Lympne Wild Animal Park, Lympne, Hythe, Kent, CT21 4PD
Telephone: 01303 264647
Mobile: 07816 541568
E-mail: jeremy@howletts.net
Website: www.totallywild.net
Contact: Jeremy Edmond
Vineyards: 0.25 hectares
Grape varieties: Unknown
Port Lympne is open to the public, but access to the vines is only by appointment.

The vines at Port Lympne, a spectacular mansion built in 1912 for Sir Philip Sassoon (a prominent MP, politician and civil servant between the wars and cousin of the 1st World War poet Siegfried Sassoon) were originally planted as part of the garden and occupy some south facing terraces about halfway down the garden and opposite a "figery" – if that is what a fig plantation is called. None of the original vines remain and it is unclear what varieties the existing ones are. They have been somewhat neglected recently.

Portesham Vineyard

East Portesham, Brookside, Waddon, Weymouth, Dorset DT3 4ER
Telephone: 01305 871444
Website: www.porteshamvineyard.co.uk
Contact: Peter Biddlecombe
Vineyards: 1 hectare
Grape varieties: Not known
Open to the public. See website for details.

Potash Vineyard

Abberton Road, Layer de la Haye, Colchester, Essex CO2 0JX
Telephone: 01206 734734
E-mail: p.w.rowe@talk21.com
Contact: Peter Rowe
Vineyards: 0.1 hectares
Grape varieties: Bacchus, Reichensteiner, Dornfelder, Pinot noir
Not open to the public.

Primrose Hill Vineyard

Bunch Lane, Haslemere, Surrey GU27 1AJ
Telephone: 01428 643360
E-mail: robjmacqueen@talktalk.net
Contact: Robert Macqueen

Vineyards: 0.182 hectares
Grape varieties: Orion, Phoenix, Regent, Rondo, Seyval blanc
Not open to the public.

Priors Dean Vineyard

c/o 5 St Mary's Road, Liss, Hampshire GU33 7AH
Location of vineyard: Buttons Lane, Selborne, Alton, Hants, GU34 3SD
Telephone: 01730 894147
E-mail: pamelaelkins@ukonline.co.uk
Website: www.priorsdeanvineyard.co.uk
Contact: Pamela Morley
Vineyards: 0.8 hectares
Grape varieties: Bacchus, MA, Seyval blanc
Open by appointment.

Priors Dean Vineyard, planted in 1988, is set on a steep, south-facing slope, high up (120 to 150-metres) in the Hampshire countryside. The soil is light loam over chalk (similar to that found in Champagne) and provides excellent drainage. Unusually, the vines are not planted in blocks, but the three varieties are planted in sequence across the vineyard and the vines are high-trained, keeping them out of the way of the frost and badgers. The aim is to produce high-quality grapes rather than large yields and the vines are pruned with that in mind. The three varieties of grapes go to be made into a single blended wine at Stanlake Park. To date, the results from this small vineyard have been impressive with several good awards and commendations. Their 2006 Classic Dry White was awarded a Highly Commended in the 2009 EWOTYC and a Silver in the WVA competition.

Purbeck Vineyard

Valley Road, Harmans Cross, Wareham, Dorset BH20 5HU
Telephone: 01929 481525
E-mail: theresa@vineyard.uk.com
Website: www.purbeckvineyard.co.uk
Website: www.vineyard.uk.com
Contact: Robert and Theresa Steel
Vineyards: 1 hectare
Grape varieties: Pinot Noir, Phoenix, Seyval blanc, Regent, Rondo, Chardonnay
Open to the public. See website for details.

Quantock Hills Vineyard

Greenway Barton, Rhode, Bridgwater, Somerset TA5 2AD
Telephone: 01278 663775
E-mail: ghubregtse@doctors.org.uk
Contact: Dr Geer Hubregtse
Vineyards: 0.06 hectares
Grape varieties: Phoenix
Not open to the public.

Quoins Organic Vineyard

Little Ashley, Bradford-on-Avon, Wiltshire BA15 2PW
Telephone: 01225 862334
Mobile: 07835 265082
E-mail: alan@quoins.demon.co.uk
Website: www.quoinsvineyard.co.uk
Contact: Alan Chubb
Vineyards: 1 hectare
Grape varieties: MA, Orion, Rondo
Open to the public. See website for details.

Quoins Organic Vineyard is one of the oldest vineyards in the UK producing organic wines and both the vineyard and the winery are certified by the Soil Association. The

vineyard is planted on Cotswold limestone near the old town of Bradford-on-Avon where the Domesday Book records the presence of a vineyard.

Two medium-dry white wines from Orion and Madeleine Angevine 7672 are produced, as is a red wine from Rondo. Guided tours of the vineyard are organised throughout the summer.

Railway Vineyard

c/o Pilgrim's Barn, Chapel Road, Spooner Row, Wymondham, Norfolk, NR19 9LN
Location of vineyard: Junction of A11 and Wymondham Road, Spooner Row, Wymondham, NR19
Telephone: 01953 602749
Contact: Mike McAully
Mobile: 07590 188488
E-mail: michael@designcompany.net
Contact: Chris Hatto

Mobile: 07882 792434
E-mail: helena.hatto@tiscali.co.uk
Website: www.chapelfieldvineyard.co.uk
Vineyards: 2.834 hectares
Grape varieties: Bacchus, Pinot noir Précoce, MA, Rondo
Not open to the public.

Ravensthorpe Vineyard

The Hollows, Ravensthorpe, Northamptonshire NN6 8EN
Telephone: 01604 770463
E-mail: ellison@hollows2.fsnet.co.uk
Contact: Nick Ellison
Vineyards: 0.3 hectares
Grape varieties: Bacchus, Ortega, Phoenix, Regent
Not open to the public.

Ravensthorpe Vineyards is a non-commercial vineyard of 110 vines, first planted in 2000 on allotments. The main wine is a Bacchus/Ortega blend and there is a small winery on site equipped with a basket press, stainless tanks and a plate filter. Regent was planted in 2009 after experimenting with red production using grapes from

elsewhere. After a run of increasing vintages, culminating in the bumper crop of 2006, the lesson on wine quality v quantity was truly learned and the policy now is to limit annual yield to approximately one bottle per vine. All wine is for consumption by family and friends and the owners (both industrial food technologists) have "absolutely no intention of going commercial!"

Redfold Farm Vineyard

Nutbourne Lane, Nutbourne, Pulborough, West Sussex RH20 2HS
Telephone: 01798 817202
Telephone: 07711 138805
Mobile: 07776 180033
E-mail: charles.outhwaite@btinternet.com
Contact: Charles Outhwaite
Vineyards: 8.085 hectares
Grape varieties: Chardonnay, Pinot noir, Pinot Meunier
Not open to the public.

Redyeates Wedge Vineyard

Chapel Hill, Cheriton Fitzpaine, Devon EX17 4HG
Telephone: 01823 256741
Mobile: 07866 630575
E-mail: emmaken@bennevitis.com
Website: www.bennevitis.com
Contact: Ken Bennett
Vineyards: 2.40 hectares
Grape varieties: Regent, Rondo, Orion, Phoenix, Seyval blanc
Not open to the public.

Renishaw Hall Vineyard

Renishaw, Sheffield, Derbyshire S21 3WB
Telephone: 01246 432310
Fax: 01246 430760
E-mail: info2@renishaw-hall.co.uk
Website: www.renishaw-hall.co.uk
Contact: David Kesteven, Head Gardener
Vineyards: 0.2024 hectares
Grape varieties: Phoenix, Seyval blanc, MA
Open to the public. See website for details.

Renishaw's vineyard was planted in 1972 by Sir Reresby Sitwell Bt. in the "Top Paddock" where his great-grandfather, Sir Sitwell Sitwell, had his racehorses exercised. The site is 38-metres above sea level and the vines are close planted at 1.50 x 1.37-metres. Until 1986 was certified as the most northerly in the world at 53 degrees 18 minutes North. Received wisdom at the time of planting was that grapes

would only succeed south of a line from the Wash in the east to South Wales in the west. However, due to global warming (or perhaps man's adventurous spirit and unscientific optimism), there are vineyards planted near Leeds, in the Lake District and even one in Norway. Two consecutive hot summers are needed for the best crops, the first to ripen the fruit bearing wood and to initiate flower bud formation, the second to ripen the grapes themselves. This, however, is a course of perfection and grapes suitable for wine making are usually harvested at Renishaw even in typical English summers. Of the many varieties planted in the 1970s only Seyval blanc remains which ripens in mid to late October. Seyval blends well and is often used as the base for sparkling wines. In 1997 a programme of replanting was started, using

Seyval blanc, MA and Phoenix. The planting was completed in 2002 and the first full crop from the new vines went on sale in 2006.

In 2001, the Renishaw Hall Wine achieved Regional Wine Status; in 2003 there was a record harvest of 2,000 bottles with the grapes picked between October 3 and 7; and in 2006 the 2004 Renishaw Hall won a Bronze Medal at the MVA wine competition. Sir Reresby Sitwell, who had been involved with the wine trade as a Director of Ellis Son and Vidler in Hastings, died on March 31 2009 and Renishaw Hall and its 5,000 acre estate, was inherited by his daughter, Alexandra.

RidgeView Wine Estate

Fragbarrow Lane, Ditchling Common, East Sussex BN6 8TP
Telephone: 0845 345 7292
Telephone: 01444 241441
Fax: 01444 230757
E-mail: info@ridgeview.co.uk
Website: www.ridgeview.co.uk
Contact: Mardi Roberts
Vineyards: 6.48 hectares
Grape varieties: Chardonnay, Pinot noir, Pinot Meunier
Wine sales and vineyard visits: See website for details.

RidgeView estate was created in 1995 by Christine and Michael Roberts, both previously in the computer industry, who wished to establish a vineyard for the production of high-quality bottle-fermented sparkling wine. With advice from both French consultants and Kit Lindlar (a well known winemaker and viticultural consultant who has already been mentioned in relation to both Merrydown and Nyetimber), 13 different clones of the classic Champagne varieties were planted, each variety on two different rootstocks. Drainage on the site is not naturally good and land drains have been installed at 5-metre intervals. The south-facing site is between 40 and 50-metres above sea level and the site lies on a Paludina limestone ridge on sandstone with clay loam over clay alluvial drift. The vines are planted at 2.2 x 1.2-metres and are single Guyot pruned. The site is only 7 miles from the sea and the high hills to the south create a rain shadow which gives RidgeView a dry microclimate and helps keep fungal diseases at bay.

For their first vintage in 1996 a modern winery was built, housed in a purpose-built building with an underground maturing cellar which will hold 250,000 bottles. The winery was equipped with the latest sparkling wine-making equipment so that the complete *méthode Champenoise* could be followed from harvest to sale. It had two Willmes presses, 44 temperature-controlled stainless-steel tanks which can be heated or cooled, a dedicated cold stabilisation unit, a bottling line and a complete sparkling wine disgorging, corking and muzzling line. Giro-pallets are used for riddling. Their 1998 harvest amounted to 24,000 bottles, in line with expectations.

Since those early days, plenty has happened at RidgeView. The team has been strengthened by the addition of son and daughter-in-law, Simon and Mardi and daughter Tamara. The winery has been expanded and developed (with the aid of a DEFRA grant). A new 4 tonne Coquard press has been installed and a new bottling and disgorging line installed. Planning permission for a winery extension has been obtained which will take the storage capacity to 750,000 bottles. Various partnerships and grape-supply arrangements have been entered into so that today the area of vines that supplies grapes totalled 31 hectares in 2007, which will rise to 45 hectares in 2008 and 60 hectares by 2010. Their stated aim is to reach a production level of 350,000 bottles by 2012. In 2007, 25 per cent of the company was sold to the Tukker family for £600,000. The Tukkers, who are one of the largest growers of lettuces and salad crops in the UK, have planted 18 hectares of vines at Tinwood Vineyard at Halnaker just outside Chichester, West Sussex. The Tukker's investment in RidgeView appears to be a win–win event – it gives the Roberts family an injection of cash with which to improve facilities and continue the build up of sparkling wine stocks, plus it gives the Tukkers a home for their grapes, as well as an involvement in one of the best sparkling wine producers in the UK.

RidgeView's first shipment of wine was in June 1999 to *The Sunday Times* Wine Club and their South Ridge sparkling wines (a white and a rosé) are still among the Club's most popular wines. Since that first release, they have produced a range of wines, all named after London squares or areas – Belgravia, Bloomsbury, Cavendish, Fitzrovia, Grosvenor, Knightsbridge and Pimlico – and their tally of awards has been impressive. They won the Gore-Browne Trophy in 2000 and 2002, together with a clutch of Gold, Silver and Bronze medals in the EWOTYC. They have also been IWSC UK Wine Producer of the Year in 2000, 2002 and 2005. In the 2008 EWOTYC they won Gold Medals for both the 2005 Bloomsbury and Cavendish. In 2009 RidgeView had its best year ever in the EWOTYC, winning three Gold medals, one Silver and one Bronze, together with the Gore-Browne and Vintner's Trophies for the *2006 Blanc de Noir Knightsbridge* and Mike Roberts won the McAlpine Winemaker of the Year Trophy. In 2009 their Bloomsbury 2006 won the SEVA Wine of the Year Trophy, with the 2006 Cavendish and 2006 Knightsbridge winning Gold medals.

RidgeView have also won a number of overseas awards – the latest being for the 2004 Fitzrovia which won the Best International Rosé in the 'Le Mondial de Rosé' competition. In 2007 Mike Roberts awarded Egon Ronay's 'Grand Prix of Gastronomy' for *the person, venture or product that has done most for UK gastronomy in the last twelve months.* On the wine quality front, there is no doubt that

Mike and Simon Roberts have the edge for consistency and reliability over all other UK sparkling wine producers. While their wines may not have won as many Gore-Browne Trophies or Gold medals as the long-aged Nyetimber wines – the reason being that RidgeView's wines generally have less bottle age (because they sell out too fast) and are therefore less impressive on the tasting bench – the fact that more or less the same team has been making the wines for 12 vintages stands them in good stead.

Another factor which sets RidgeView apart from other producers at the top end is their prudent pricing policy. Their Cavendish and Bloomsbury wines are still under £20 (£19 from Waitrose Wine Direct) and their Fitzrovia – which I rate as one of their best – is £21.95 (£21 from Waitrose Wine Direct). With Chapel Down's NV Brut (not made from Champagne varieties) now at £17 and Nyetimber's wines at £24/25 and £27/28, RidgeView's pricing is to be commended and in the long term, when the larger volumes of English sparkling wine start appearing on the market, I am sure that it will pay dividends. RidgeView were the first wine producer to whom I gave four stars in the UK section of Hugh Johnson's *Pocket Wine Book* [19] (for which I supply the copy) as they come closest to the concept of a proper *Grande Marque* Champagne house. I was very pleased to be able to serve their *2005 Cavendish* and *2006 Bloomsbury* at my son's wedding in September 2008 and to introduce it to some of my daughter-in-law's American and Italian friends and relations.

The Roberts family with their awards – the Gore-Browne Trophy to the fore – at the House of Lords in July 2009

19 Hugh Johnson's editor unfortunately refuses to allow the four-star rating to appear, as this is "reserved for wineries that are grand, prestigious, expensive". For the next edition, I will try and get both RidgeView and Nyetimber upgraded to this rating – watch this space!

Ridgeview's success has only come through a single-minded approach to all aspects of the business – grapegrowing, winemaking and marketing – and it shows. One wishes that other producers would take a leaf out of their book. As I said at the end of the 2001 edition of this book, I wish them *bonne chance* and every success in the future. I meant it and they deserve it.

River Walk Vineyard

c/o Abbey Vineyards Group, Irnham Grange, Irnham, Corby Glen, Grantham, Lincolnshire, NG33 4NE
Location of vineyard: Granby Lane, Bingham, Nottingham, Nottinghamshire, NG13 9
Telephone: 01476 550191
Fax: 01476 550080
E-mail: info@abbeyvineyards.co.uk
Contact: Phil Kerry 07815 308838
Contact: Jonathan Kerry 07805 315763
Vineyards: 1.25 hectares
Grape varieties: Ortega, Solaris, Pinot noir
Not open to the public.

Robert Fleming Wines

c/o Roundbush Farm, Mundon, Maldon, Essex CM9 6NP
Location of vineyard: CM3 6RW
Telephone and Fax: 01621 828837
Mobile: 07850 734057
E-mail: roundbushfarms@btinternet.com
Contact: Duncan McNeil
Vineyards: 31.5789 hectares
Grape varieties: Bacchus, Pinot blanc, Pinot noir, Chardonnay
Not open to the public.

Rock Lodge Vineyard

Location of vineyard: Scaynes Hill, Haywards Heath, West Sussex RH17 7NG
See Plumpton College entry for contact details
Vineyards: 4.67 hectares
Grape varieties: Seyval blanc, Acolon, Chardonnay, Dornfelder, Bacchus, Pinot Meunier, Rondo, Pinot noir, Reichensteiner, Schönburger, MT, Triomphe, Riesling
Not open to the public. Leased by Plumpton College.

Rock Moors Vineyard

Woodland Head, Yeoford, Crediton, Devon EX17 5HE
Telephone: 01647 24743 and 01647 24744
E-mail: gleneverton@msn.com
Contact: Glen Everton

Vineyards: 0.2141 hectares
Grape varieties: MA, Léon Millot, Triomphe
Not open to the public.

Roman Villa Vineyard

Location of vineyard: Bignor, Pulborough, West Sussex RH20 1PQ
See Nyetimber entry for contact details
Vineyards: 28.745 hectares
Grape varieties: Pinot noir, Chardonnay, Pinot Meunier
Not open to the public.

Rose Bank Vineyard

247 Droitwich Road, Fernhill Heath, Worcester, Worcestershire WR3 7UH
Telephone: 01905 451439
E-mail: winesales@rosebankvineyard.co.uk
Contact: Richard Tomkinson
Vineyards: 0.72 hectares
Grape varieties: Phoenix, MA, Reichensteiner, Regent
Open Saturdays, 9 am – 5 pm or by appointment. Groups welcome.

Rosemary Farm Vineyard

Rosemary Lane, Flimwell, Wadhurst, East Sussex TN5 7PT
Telephone: Peter Reeves 07710 111800
Telephone: Michael Reeves 07773 361542
E-mail: peter@arenapursuits.com
E-mail: michael.reeves@farmline.com
Website: www.arenapursuits.com
Vineyards: 3.3818 hectares
Grape varieties: Chardonnay, Pinot noir, Pinot Meunier
Not open to the public.

Rosemary Vineyard

Smallbrook Lane, Ryde, Isle of Wight PO33 4BE
Telephone: 01983 811084
Fax: 01983 812899
E-mail: info@rosemaryvineyard.co.uk
Website: www.rosemaryvineyard.co.uk
Contact: Conrad Gauntlet, David Hunt
Vineyards: 6.4778 hectares
Grape varieties: Schönburger, Orion, MA, Bacchus, Triomphe, Rondo
Open to the public. See website for details.

Rosemary Vineyard was planted in 1986 in a small valley with a mostly south facing aspect at around 18 metres above sea level. The vineyard is ideally placed to benefit from the mild island climate and the valley situation helps retain summer warmth and offers shelter from the south-westerly winds. The gentle slopes allow excellent frost drainage in the spring to protect the vines, whilst the soil, a clay-silt loam overlying greensand, is not only free-draining but also retains sufficient moisture for healthy growth.

The winery can be visited during opening hours and display boards, packed with information, will enable visitors to get a detailed understanding of the complete winemaking process. The winery is in operation on selected days throughout the year and visitors are welcome on these operational days by appointment. There is a wine and gift shop selling a wide range of wines and liqueurs, together with other island produce and a café for snacks and light meals.

Rossi Regatta Vineyard

Benham Orchard, Benhams Lane, Fawley, Oxfordshire, RG9 6JG
Telephone: 01491 410018/412637
Vineyards: 2.0 hectares
Grape varieties: Not known
Not open to the public.

Rossiters Vineyard

Main Road, Wellow, Isle of Wight PO41 0TE
Telephone: 01983 761616
Fax: 01983 760263
E-mail: rossitersiow@fsmail.net
Website: www.rossitersvineyard.com
Contact: Rod Thompson
Vineyards: 3.7 hectares
Grape varieties: Orion, Bacchus, Dornfelder, Rondo
Open to the public. See website for details.

Rother Valley Vineyard

Rother Farm, Elsted, Midhurst, West Sussex GU29 0JS
Telephone: 01730 816888   Mobile: 07979 505950
E-mail: lizajanemeredith@aol.com
E-mail: LizaNieddu@aol.com
Website: www.rothervalleyvineyard.co.uk
Contact: Liza Meredith, Giovanni Nieddu
Vineyards: 1.628 hectares
Grape varieties: Dunkelfelder, Pinot gris, Phoenix, Gewürztraminer, Pinot Meunier, Seyval blanc, Chardonnay
Not open to the public.

Russetts Vineyard

Bumpstead Road, Hempstead, Saffron Walden, Essex, CB10 2PW
Telephone: 01799 599775
Contact: Fiona Walsh, Damian Walsh
Mobile: 07957 821075
E-mail: dpwa@btinternet.com
Vineyards: 0.138 hectares
Grape varieties: Phoenix, Bacchus, Auxerrois, Pinot noir, MA
Not open to the public.

Ryedale Vineyards

Farfield Farm, Westow, York, North Yorkshire YO60 7LS
Telephone: 01653 658507
Mobile: 07763 109458
E-mail: stuart@thevinehouse.fsnet.co.uk
E-mail: elizabeth@thevinehouse.fsnet.co.uk
Website: www.ryedalevineyards.co.uk
Contact: Stuart Smith
Vineyards: 2.5 hectares
Grape varieties: Solaris, Rondo, Ortega, Regent, Phoenix, Seyval blanc, Siegerrebe, Bacchus, Pinot noir, Chardonnay
Open to the public. See website for details.

Saffron Grange Vineyard

Rowley Hill Farm, Little Waldon, Saffron Waldon, Essex, CB10 1UZ
Telephone: 01799 516678, 01799 516597
Fax: 01799 516657
Website: www.saffrongrange.com
Contact: Paul Edwards 07805 643414 paul.edwards@pacific.net.sg
Contact: Rossalyn Edwards edwaross@hotmail.com
Vineyards: 2 hectares
Grape varieties: Pinot noir, Chardonnay, Seyval blanc, Pinot Meunier
Not open to the public.

Saffron Grange's newest vines
planted in 2009

St Andrew's Vineyard

c/o 24 Bolton Road, London NW10 4BG
Location of vineyard: Dors Close Allotments adjacent to NW9 8DE
Telephone: 020 8961 3029
E-mail: tonycastle2@tiscali.co.uk
E-mail: r.castle@tiscali.co.uk
Contact: Tony Castle, Roger Castle
Vineyards: 0.194 hectares
Grape varieties: Rondo, Dornfelder, Pinot noir, Schönburger, MA
Not open to the public.

St Anne's Vineyard

Wain House, Oxenhall, Newent, Gloucestershire GL18 1RW
Telephone: 01989 720313
E-mail: david@stannesvineyard.fsnet.co.uk
Contact: David Jenkins, Paula Jenkins
Vineyards: 0.36 hectares
Grape varieties: Madeleine Angevine, Seyval blanc, Triomphe, Phoenix
Open to the public. Call for details.

St Augustine's Vineyard

Passage Road, Aust, South Gloucestershire BS35 4BG
Telephone: 01454 632236
Mobile: 07970 802019
Contact: Adam Hall
E-mail: theoldparsonage@mac.com
Vineyards: 0.75 hectares
Grape varieties: Reichensteiner, MA, Kernling
Open by appointment.

St Martin's Isles of Scilly Vineyard

4 Signal Row, St Martin's, Isles of Scilly TR25 0QL
Telephone: 01720 423418
E-mail: grahamw.thomas@tiscali.co.uk
Website: www.stmartinsvineyard.co.uk
Contact: Graham Thomas
Vineyards: 0.6 hectares
Grape varieties: Orion, Seyval blanc, Reichensteiner, Findling, Siegerrebe, MA, Rondo, Regent, Triomphe
Open to the public. See website for details.

St. Mary Magdalen Vineyard

143 High Street, Billericay, Essex, CM11 2TR
Telephone: 01277 651315
E-mail: amerigo@soldani.co.uk
Contact: Amerigo Soldani
Vineyards: 0.2 hectares
Grape varieties: MT, Huxelrebe, Seyval blanc, Pinot noir, Gagarin Blue, Pinot gris, Chardonnay
Not open to the public.

St. Mary's Vineyard

c/o Star Castle Hotel, St. Mary's, Isles of Scilly, TR21 0TA
Location of vineyards: Holy Vale, Maypole, Silver Carn, Helvear
Telephone: 01720 422317
Mobile: 07775 568242
E-mail: info@star-castle.co.uk
Website: www.star-castle.co.uk
Contact: Robert Francis, Theresa Francis
Vineyards: 1.82 hectares
Grape varieties: Pinot noir, Chardonnay, Pinot gris
Oen to the public by appointment.

Sandhurst Vineyards and Hop Farm

Hoads Farm, Crouch Lane, Sandhurst, Cranbrook, Kent TN18 5PA
Telephone: 01580 850296
E-mail: ca.nicholas@btinternet.com
Website: www.sandhurstvineyards.co.uk
Contact: Anne Nicholas, Chris Nicholas
Vineyards: 6 hectares at TN18 5PA and 4 ha at Bourne Farm, Sandhurst, TN18 5NT
Grape varieties: Reichensteiner, Schönburger, Bacchus, Rondo, Pinot noir, Regent
Open to the public. Bed and breakfast rooms available. See website for details.

The vineyards at Sandhurst were established in 1988 (when I helped plant the first plot of Seyval blanc) on this 142-hectare family farm of which theer are 52-hectares of hops, 10-hectares of vines, 2-hectares of plums and 2-hectares of cherries. There are various vineyard sites on the farm, some north- and north-west-facing and about 75-metres above sea level. The soil is mainly fine sandy loam over Wealden clay and all the vines are Guyot trained at 2 x 1.3 or 1.4-metres. There are 6-hectares at Hoads Farm and 4-hectares at Bourne Farm (see separate entry) which is on the other side of the village of Sandhurst.

Christopher Nicholas, who manages the farm together with his mother Anne and various other family members, became interested in vines a few years earlier and had a very small vineyard next door to his cottage at Bourne Farm which featured in the 1989 edition of this book. This small vineyard produced such great crops that Chris took the plunge and established a much larger area on the main farm. Many of the grapes produced at Sandhurst have been sold to either Lamberhurst Vineyards or latterly to Chapel Down and only a relatively small proportion of them have been turned into wine for the Nicholas family to sell. This seems to work well as production can be tied to sales, most of which take place from the farm-gate to visitors and bed-and-breakfast guests and at farmers' markets, agricultural shows and the like. Having made their wines myself for many years, I know that their excellent fruit can be turned into good wine and they have won several awards including an EWOTYC Gold for their 1991 oak-aged Bacchus and the Bernard Theobald Trophy for the Best Red for their 2004 Pinot noir. Owen Elias at Chapel Down has made their wines since 2000.

Having known the Nicholas family for almost three decades and followed the ups and downs of their farming activities, their experience of growing vines has always been of great interest to me. They do not grow them for any other reason than they can be grown profitably and had this not been the case, the vineyards would have been grubbed-up many years ago. Chris Nicholas is certainly one of the best viticulturalists in the UK and produces some of the best grapes that Chapel Down ever receives. In 2009, 4-hectares of Champagne varieties under contract for nearby Hush Heath Estate were planted and such is the demand for good English hops that a further 16 hectares of these were also put in. Their investment in a fully mechanised in-bin hop-drying system, in which only the hops are heated and not the building as well, together with a computerised hop-baling system, is saving them 40 per cent of their fuel costs and 50 per cent of their labour costs.

Nicholas has produced grapes for almost 30 years and maintains that in cultural terms, they are easier to manage than hops, apples or other fruit crops (and contrary to what many think require less spraying than these other crops) and they are no more fickle in terms of cropping and price, i.e. in total returns, than the other things he grows or has grown. One of the reasons he is able grow the vines efficiently is that as he grows such a large area of hops, he has labour available when he needs it for the vines and as he generally has two sprayers running more or less full time during the growing season, keeping mildews and *Botrytis* at bay is not a huge problem. Anyone wishing to grow large areas of vines in the UK and make money out of them could do not better than to take note of how they are managed at Sandhurst Vineyards.

Sandridge Barton Vineyard

Sandridge Barton, Stoke Gabriel,Totnes, Devon, TQ9 6RL
Contact: Christopher Smith, Knight Frank LLP, Crown House, 37-41 Prince St, Bristol, BS1 4PS
Telephone: 0117 945 2631   Mobile: 07836 275605
E-mail: christopher.smith@knightfrank.com
Website: www.knightfrank.co.uk
Vineyards: 1.6194 hectares
Grape varieties: Pinot noir, Bacchus, Pinot noir Précoce
Not open to the public.

Sandyford Vineyard

Salix Farm, Great Sampford, Saffron Walden, Essex CB10 2QE
Telephone: 01799 586586
E-mail: info@sandyfordvineyard.co.uk
Website: www.sandyfordvineyard.co.uk
Contact: Mike Lindsell
Vineyards: 0.8097 hectares
Grape varieties: Bacchus, Reichensteiner, Rondo, Regent, Triomphe
Open to the public. See website for details.

Sealwood Cottage Vineyard

Seal Wood Lane, Linton, Swadlincote, Derby, Derbyshire, DE12 6PA
Telephone: 01283 761371
Mobile: 07964 032387
E-mail: johngbotanybay@btinternet.com
Website:
Contact: John Goodall, Elizabeth Goodall
Vineyards: 1.5 hectares
Grape varieties: Ortega, Solaris, Rondo, Regent
Not open to the public.

Secret Valley Vineyard

Cobbs Cross Farm, Goathurst, Bridgwater, Somerset, TA5 2DN
Telephone: 01278 671945
Mobile: 07803 280551
E-mail: janhardwick@btconnect.com
Website: www.cobbscrossactivitycentre.co.uk
Contact: John and Jan Hardwick
Vineyards: 2 hectares
Grape varieties: Orion, Pinot noir, Solaris, Rondo, Reichensteiner, MA
Open to the public. Telephone for details.

Sedlescombe Organic Vineyard

Hawkhurst Road, Cripp's Corner, Sedlescombe, Robertsbridge, East Sussex, TN32 5SA
Telephone & Fax: 01580 830715
E-mail: enquiries@englishorganicwine.co.uk
E-mail: sales@englishorganicwine.co.uk
Website: www.englishorganicwine.co.uk
Contact: Irma Cook
Vineyards: 7.35 hectares. Spilsted (2.2267 ha) and Bodiam (1.8219 ha) vineyards are also rented
Grape varieties: Bacchus, Regent, Reichensteiner, MT, Seyval blanc, Johanniter, Pinot noir, Faberrebe, Regner, Kerner, Gewürztraminer, Auxerrois
Open to the public. See website for details.

Sedlescombe Organic Vineyard is the oldest organic vineyard in the UK and vines were first planted here in 1979. The site is mainly south-facing, between 60 and 120 metres above sea level and the soil a light sandy loam. Various training techniques are used, including double Guyot, Scott Henry and 'Sedlescombe Special'. Vineyard fertility is maintained using organically approved manures or compost and intercropping the alleyways with green manure crops such as clover. Disease control involves careful canopy management including shoot positioning and hand de-leafing around the bunches. Mineral sprays such as copper and sulphur are used against fungal diseases, and weeds are kept at bay by mechanical means and either straw or plastic mulches.All Sedlescombe wines, together with other products, apple juice, cider and fruit wines, bear the Soil Association organic symbol. Roy Cook is also a supporter of WWOOF or Worldwide Opportunities On Organic Farms, which aims to satisfy 'those who are interested in manual participation in the organic movement', and some of the work in the vineyard is carried out by this organisation. In 1987 a group of self-build students and WWOOF volunteers helped Cook and his wife, German-born Irma, build a house on the site. In the winery too, Cook sticks to his organic principles, and uses only techniques and materials approved by the Soil Association. The aim in the winery is to treat the grapes as gently as possible, avoid mechanical handling as much as possible so as to avoid unwanted astringent phenols and to keep sulphur dioxide levels low so as to meet the organic standards. He makes a range of wines, both still and sparkling, red and white.

Competitions used to be avoided, but in recent years the EWOTYC has been entered into and a few medals gained. Their 2008 Regent won Highly Commended at the 2009 EWOTYC. Cook also rents nearby Bodiam and Spilsted Vineyards.

Setley Ridge Vineyard

Lymington Road, Brockenhurst, Hampshire SO42 7UF
Telephone: 01590 622246
E-mail: enquiries@setleyridgevineyard.co.uk
Website: www.setleyridgevineyard.co.uk
Contact: Paul Girling
Vineyards: 2.48 hectares
Grape varieties: Seyval blanc, Pinot blanc, Schönburger, Regent, Rondo
Wine and farm shop open seven days a week, 9.30 am to 5.30 pm for sales and tastings. Tours by appointment only. See website for further details.

Shardeloes Vineyard

Shardeloes Farm, Cherry Lane, Amersham, Buckinghamshire, HP7 0QF
Telephone: 01494 433333
Fax: 01494 432344
Mobile: 07836 245555
E-mail: shardeloes@msn.com
Website: www.shardeloesfarm.com
Contact: Tony Williams, Cindy Williams
Vineyards: 4 hectares
Grape varieties: Triomphe, Reichensteiner, Dornfelder, Dunkelfelder, Léon Millot
Not open to the public.

Sharpham Vineyard

Sharpham Estate, Ashprington, Totnes, Devon TQ9 7UT
Telephone: 01803 732203 and 01803 732600
Fax: 01803 732122
E-mail: info@sharpham.com
E-mail: duncan@sharpham.com
Website: www.sharpham.com
Contact: Duncan Schwab
Vineyards: 3.4 hectares
Grape varieties: MA, Dornfelder, Pinot noir, Phoenix
Open to the public: 1 March until Christmas Eve, Mon to Sat, 10 am to 5 pm. Closed on Sundays, except June, July, August and September. See website for details, including tours for groups.

Situated a few miles from Totnes and overlooking the River Dart, Sharpham Vineyard is in one of the most beautiful parts of the country. The Sharpham Estate of 200-hectares comprises woodland, pasture and vineyards and has three distinct enterprises:

a 70-strong herd of Jersey cows, a creamery making an award-winning range of cheeses and the vineyard, also award-winning. The partnership that runs Sharpham, founded in 1981, prides itself on managing these enterprises on an environmentally sustainable basis.

The vineyards, planted between 1987 and 1993, produce wines of real quality and interest. The vineyards are planted with an interesting mix of varieties including Phoenix (the Geilweilerhof Bacchus x Villard blanc interspecific-cross which can now be made into Quality Wine) and over 1.7-hectares of genuine Madeleine x Angevine 7672 (grafted from wood from Robin Don's Elmham Park vineyard – now grubbed-up – the vines in which were known to have come from Ray Brock's Oxted vineyard). Winemaker Duncan Schwab reckons it is consistent and reliable and produces 'good flavoured wines on our soil types'. The vineyards are all trellised on the Scott Henry divided curtain system and Sharpham is one of the few UK vineyards to use this system.

The winery is well equipped with a Willmes UP 1800 pneumatic press, Seitz plate and membrane filters, Spadoni kieselguhr filter, refrigerated stainless steel tanks and a GAI eight-head filler. There are also oak *barriques* for the fermentation of the Madeleine Angevine which is lees stirred and goes through partial malolactic conversion. Reds, made from Pinot noir and Dornfelder grown at Sharpham and

Cabernet Sauvignon and Merlot grown (under polytunnels) at Beenleigh are cold macerated for two to three days and then fermented at 30°C, followed by a short period of oak-ageing.

Their wines have won a large number of awards and medals over the years in both regional and national competitions, including one Gold, five Silver and two Bronze medals at the 2006 EWOYC alone. The Gold was awarded to the 2005 Bacchus, which also received the Jack Ward Trophy for 'Best Wine' from the previous vintage. At International level they received two Bronze medals for the Beenleigh 2003 and Barrel Fermented 2004 and a Silver medal for the Barrel

Fermented 2005. At the Taste of the West awards they were awarded a Gold and two Silver medals, as well as *Best Drink Product*. Together, these add up to an impressive tally and underline the quality of the wines being produced here. They also produce a small, but excellent, range of delicious award-winning cheeses from their purpose-built creamery.

Shawsgate Vineyard

Badingham Road, Framlingham, Woodbridge, Suffolk IP13 9HZ
Telephone: 01728 724060
Fax: 01728 723232
E-mail: wines@shawsgate.co.uk
Website: www.shawsgate.co.uk
Contact: Thomas Jarrett
Vineyards: 5.5 hectares
Grape varieties: Acolon, Rondo, Bacchus, MT, Reichensteiner, Schönburger, Seyval blanc
Open to the public. See website for details.

The vineyards at Shawsgate were established in 1973, making it one of the oldest wine producers in East Anglia, and over the years it has seen a number of different owners, changing hands in 1985, 2000 and 2003. The current owner is Les Jarrett, a local agricultural merchant who specialises in alternative crops. The Shawsgate team is led by winemaker and vineyard manager Rob Capp whose high standards have resulted in productive vineyards and some good wines. The well-equipped winery provides a valuable winemaking service to a number of local vineyards, as it has done for many years.

The site at Shawsgate is flat, about 91 metres above sea level and the soil is a medium to heavy clay. The vines are grown on both 2.1 x 1.3-metre double Guyot and 4 x 2-metre GDC systems. The vineyards are beautifully kept, creating a haven for birds and wildlife as well as several species of rare orchids and wildflowers. There is no charge for visitors to explore the vineyards and many take advantage of such a beautiful spot to picnic and relax with friends. Recently the vineyard has expanded the facilities available for visitors with events and experience days throughout the summer months. The experience days allow guests to really get to know the vineyard, the wines and the people behind it all in the relaxed surroundings of their marquee and gardens. Over the years Shawsgate has won a number of awards regionally, nationally and internationally for its own wines, its Bacchus usually being its best wine.

Sheffield Park Walled Garden Vineyard

The Walled Garden, Sheffield Park, Uckfield, East Sussex, TN22 3QX
Telephone: 01825 790775
E-mail: via website
Website: www.sheffieldparkvineyard.co.uk

Contact: Harry Godwin
Vineyards: 1.2145 hectares
Grape varieties: Not known
Open to the public. See website for details.

Sheffield Park Walled Garden Vineyard

Sherborne Castle Vineyard

Sherborne Castle, Digby Estate Office, 9 Cheap Street, Sherborne, Dorset DT9 3PY
Telephone: 01935 813182
Mobile: 07966 417942
E-mail: paulc@sherbornecastle.com
Website: www.sherbornecastle.com
Contact: Paul Carter
Vineyards: 2.8 hectares
Grape varieties: Seyval Blanc, Schönburger, Bacchus, Regner, Reichensteiner, Pinot noir, Pinot noir
Précoce, Léon Millot
Open to the public. See website for details.

Shere Vineyard

Winterfold End, Hound House Road, Shere, Surrey GU5 9JJ
Telephone: 01483 203491
Mobile: 07768 172068
E-mail: john_knight@hotmail.com
Contact: John Knight
Vineyards: 0.8097 hectares
Grape varieties: Bacchus, Chardonnay, Pinot noir
Open by appointment.

Shotley Vineyard

c/o Wickham Vineyards, Botley Road, Shedfield, Southampton, Hampshire SO32 2HL
Location of vineyard: Frogs Alley, Shotley, Ipswich, Suffolk, IP9 1EP
Telephone: 01329 834042
Fax: 01329 834907
E-mail: info@wickhamvineyard.co.uk

Contact: Wilhelm Mead
Winemaker: William Biddulph
Vineyard Manager: Julien Miran 07809 674133
Vineyards: 7.5 hectares
Grape varieties: Pinot noir, Rondo, Bacchus, Reichensteiner, Chardonnay, Auxerrois, Ortega, Seyval Blanc
Not open to the public.

Somborne Valley Vineyard

Hoplands Estate, Kings Somborne, Stockbridge, Hampshire SO20 6QH
Telephone: 01794 388547
E-mail: bertmartyn@frobisherltd.com
Contact: Bert Martyn   07885 163159
Vineyards: 7.3752 hectares
Grape varieties: Pinot noir, Chardonnay, Pinot blanc, Pinot Meunier, Rondo
Not open to the public.

Somerby Vineyards

Manor House, Somerby Green, Somerby, Lincolnshire DN38 6EY
Telephone: 01652 629162
Fax: 01472 351438
Mobile: 07714 155057
E-mail: linda@somerbyvineyards.com
Website: www.somerbyvineyards.com
Contact: Bill Hobson, Linda Hobson
Vineyards: 6 hectares
Grape varieties: Rondo, Regent, Solaris, Phoenix, Orion, Ortega
Not open to the public.

Sour Grapes Vineyard

Oak Tree House, Michelmersh, Romsey, Hampshire SO51 0NQ
Telephone: 01794 367300
Mobile: 07867 524242
E-mail: sourgrapesvineyard@tiscali.co.uk
Website: www.sourgrapesvineyard.co.uk
Contact: Sharon Thomas, Iain Thomas
Vineyards: 0.4049 hectares
Grape varieties: Triomphe, Seyval blanc
Open to the public by arrangement.

South Pickenham Estate Vineyard

The Estate Office, South Pickenham, Norfolk, PE37 8DZ
Telephone: 01760 756376
Mobile: 07703 118042
E-mail: ian.george@specoffice.co.uk

Contact: Ian George
Vineyards: 2.03 hectares
Grape varieties: MT, Seyval blanc, Huxelrebe, Schönburger
Not open to the public.

Southcott Vineyard

Southcott, Pewsey, Wiltshire SN9 5JF
Telephone: 01672 569190
E-mail: tim@ingramhill.co.uk
Contact: Tim Ingram Hill
Vineyards: 0.6 hectares
Grape varieties: Chardonnay, Pinot noir, Pinot Meunier
Not open to the public.

Southcott Vineyard was originally established in 1972/3 by Dr Gerry Crabb when he planted 0.6-hectares of Müller-Thurgau, Ortega and Septimer but in 1982 these were grubbed up and replaced with Madeleine Angevine, Reichensteiner and Huxelrebe. In 1997, when in his 80s, Dr. Crabb pulled them all up. He had successfully produced some good wines, of medal standard in some years, and the current owners inherited 48 bottles of unknown vintage and a reputation for good lunches after the harvest.

On Dr. Crabb's death in 2003 the Ingram Hills purchased the property and planned to re-plant the vineyard on the adjacent ground to the south of the original site. The soil is Greensand on chalk. In 2005, on May 7 and 8, a total of 1,800 vines were planted on 0.6-hectares of which 60% are Chardonnay on SO4, 30% Pinot Noir and 10% Pinot Meunier. After planting the family helpers were toasted with the 1996 vintage. In 2006 a further 200 Chardonnay were planted. The summers of 2007 and 2008 were a disaster with a major attack of both Powdery and Downy Mildew which caused a loss of 150 vines but with careful management and spraying in 2009 it is hoped that a commercial crop can be produced.

Southcott is located in the Vale of Pewsey and is under the Pewsey White Horse. Mixed hedging has been planted around the boundary with alders to the west to break the strong prevailing south-westerly wind that blows off Salisbury Plain. If good

quality sparkling wines can be produced then the original 0.6 hectares of vineyard, that is currently resting, could be replanted. Tim and his wife Sarah are greatly assisted in the whole enterprise by Paul Langham from a'Beckett's Vineyard and Plumpton-trained local resident Mike Warren.

Southlands Valley Vineyard

c/o Mitchbourne Farm, Malthouse Lane, Ashington, West Sussex RH20 3EU
Location of vineyard: RH20 2JU
Telephone: 01903 892203
E-mail: john.gibert@btconnect.com
Contact: John Gibert
Vineyards: 1 hectare
Grape varieties: Chardonnay, Pinot noir, Pinot Meunier
Not open to the public.

South Shore Vineyard

c/o Abbey Vineyards Group, Irnham Grange, Irnham, Corby Glen, Grantham, Lincolnshire, NG33 4NE
Location of vineyard: Off Lyndon Road, Manton, Oakham, Rutland, LE15 8RN
Telephone: 01476 550191
Fax: 01476 550080
E-mail: info@abbeyvineyards.co.uk
Contact: Phil Kerry 07815 308838
Contact: Jonathan Kerry 07805 315763
Vineyards: 1.6194 hectares
Grape varieties: Bacchus, Reichensnteiner
Not open to the public.

Southwood Vineyard

St Andrew's Wood, Dulford, Cullompton, Devon EX15 2DF
Telephone: 01884 277945
E-mail: anthony.watkinson@rdeft.nhs.uk
Contact: Tony and Melanie Watkinson
Vineyards: 0.434 hectares
Grape varieties: Léon Millot, Dornfelder, Triomphe, Siegerrebe, Pinot gris, MA
Not open to the public.

Sparchall Vineyard

Sparchall Farm, Tarrington, Hereford, Herefordshire HR1 4EY
Telephone: 01432 850800
Mobile: 07977 589132
E-mail: edward@ewatkins.co.uk
Contact: Edward Watkins
Vineyards: 1.0089 hectares
Grape varieties: Bacchus, Pinot noir, Rondo, Regent, Seyval blanc
Open by appointment.

Spilsted Vineyard

Stream Lane, Sedlescombe, East Sussex TN33 0PB
Telephone: 01580 830715
E-mail: enquiries@englishorganicwine.co.uk
Contact: Roy Cook, Sedlescombe Organic
Vineyards: 2.2267 hectares
Grape varieties: Bacchus
Not open to the public. Rented by Sedlescombe Organic.

Spring Cottage Vineyard

c/o 6 Highfield Way, Walsall, West Midlands, WS9 8XF
Location of vineyard: Allotments, Green Lane, Walsall, West Midlands, WS4 1RT
Telephone & Fax: 01922 454447
E-mail: geoffcard@blueyonder.co.uk
Contact: Geoff Card
Vineyards: 0.25 hectares
Grape varieties: Rondo, Triomphe, Pinot noir, MA, Phoenix, Solaris, Seyval blanc
Not open to the public.

Springfield Vineyard

Springfield Farm, Howe Road, Watlington, Oxfordshire OX49 5EL
Telephone: 01491 612095
E-mail: ellydaniels@hotmail.com
Contact: Elly Daniels
Vineyards: 0.1349 hectares
Grape varieties: MA, Seyval blanc, Triomphe
Not open to the public.

Springfields Vineyard

Deerview Farm, Down Street, Piltdown, East Sussex TN22 3XX
Telephone: 01825 713421
E-mail: wickham.hippo@btinternet.com
Contact: Peter Wickham
Vineyards: 3 hectares
Grape varieties: Chardonnay, Pinot noir, Pinot Meunier
Not open to the public.

Squerryes Court Vineyard

c/o Squerryes Estate Office, 2 The Granary, Westerham, Kent TN16 1SL.
Location of vineyard: Gaysham Farm, Pilgrims Way, Westerham, Kent TN16 2DT
Telephone: 01959 562345   Fax: 01959 565949
Mobile: 07803 144489

E-mail: johnwarde@squerryes.co.uk
Website: www.squerryes.co.uk
Contact: John Warde
Vineyards: 11.5471 hectares
Grape varieties: Chardonnay, Pinot noir, Pinot Meunier
Open by appointment.

Squerryes Court Vineyard was planted following abortive negotiations with the Champagne house of Duval-Leroy who had investigated the possibility of establishing vineyards in the UK. Squerryes was selected because of its perfect chalk soils, the amount of suitable land available and – for the French an important factor – its proximity to both the Channel and London. Following the ending of talks with Duval-

Leroy, I was brought in as consultant and over two years, 2006 and 2007, 11.5-hectares of Champagne varieties were planted, all under contract to Chapel Down. The first harvest (26-tonnes) was taken in 2008 and as I write, the second harvest, which ought to total around 70-80-tonnes, is being harvested. A further 2-hectares will be planted in 2010.

Stalbridge Weston Vineyard

Stalbridge Weston, Sturminster Newton, Dorset, DT10 2LA
Telephone: 01963 362281
Contact: Tony Coggans
Vineyards: 0.2 hectares
Grape varieties: MA, MT
Not open to the public.

Standen Vineyard

Standen Farm, Standen, West Sussex RH19 4NE
Telephone: 01342 328835
Fax: 01342 317704
Mobile: 07803 755560
E-mail: jillsdevelin@aol.com
E-mail: islamredhill@aol.com
Contact: Jill Develin
Vineyards: 1 hectare
Grape varieties: Auxerrois, Seyval blanc, Reichensteiner
Open by appointment.

Stanford Bridge Vineyard

Stanford Bridge House, Pluckley, Ashford, Kent, TN27 0RU
Telephone: 01233 82232
Mobile: 07860 630952
E-mail: kevin.acott@ipc.com
Contact: Kevin Acott
Vineyards: 0.1 hectares
Grape varieties: Chardonnay and Pinot noir
Not open to the public.

Stanlake Park Wine Estate

Twyford, Reading, Berkshire RG10 0BN
Telephone: 01189 340176
Fax: 01189 320914
E-mail: peter@stanlakepark.com
E-mail: vince@stanlakepark.com
Website: www.stanlakepark.com
Contact: Peter Dart, Vince Gower
Vineyards: 10 hectares
Grape varieties: Pinot noir, Dornfelder, Triomphe, Rondo, Pinot gris, Bacchus, Ehrenfelser, Kerner, Optima, Pinot Meunier, Regner, Reichensteiner Scheurebe, Schönburger, Seyval, Siegerrebe, Würzer ... and one Merlot vine!
Open to the public. See website for details.

Stanlake Park Wine Estate was formerly known as Valley Vineyards and prior to that as Thames Valley Vineyards. It was originally planted and brought into prominence by one of the pioneer UK viticulturalists of the modern era, part-time Australian Jon Leighton and its reputation enhanced and embellished by his winemaker and full-time Australian, John Worontschak. Together these two forged a reputation for wine quality that in its time was unrivalled and without doubt it held the accolade of the UK's 'best vineyard'. In 2005 the estate was purchased by Peter and Annette Dart, professional marketers, who have spent the past few years investing in the property, re-branding it and laying the groundwork for a new golden era. But first some history.

The house at the heart of Stanlake Park dates from the fifteenth century and Charles II is reputed to have stayed there in order to be near Nell Gwynne with whom he had a rendezvous at the local pub – the Dog and Badger! The estate (once part of the Windsor Great Estate) had been in Leighton hands since 1952. Leighton, a one-time motor racing and rally driver, had his interest in English Wine awakened by a visit to the English Wine Festival held at Charleston Manor in September 1978. As the owner of the Stanlake Estate (although at the time the house and buildings were leased to tenants) he saw the possibility of putting some of his land under vines and in 1979 he planted a trial plot of 500 vines and a larger 1-hectare plot in 1980. He and his then vineyard manager, Patricia White, continued planting and developing the vineyards until by 1988, they extended to over 8-hectares and contained one of the largest collections of varieties and trellising and training systems in any UK vineyard. At one time he grew Chasselas rosé, Gewürztraminer and Scheurebe in winemaking quantities and was one of the first to grow and make good wine from Ortega, Regner and Siegerrebe. He was one of the pioneers of Pinot noir in the UK – the 'heartbreak' grape as he called it – and when others were struggling to make something interesting with the variety, Leighton occasionally succeeded. He also used Gamay Noir (sourced from the now-defunct Send Vineyard) in some very good sparkling wines.

The estate is in the heart of the Thames Valley, not far from where Westbury Vineyards used to be, where the bearded eccentric Bernard Theobald could often be heard claiming that *our climate is better than Bordeaux's for growing vines*! While Leighton held back from this claim, he did point out as a matter of fact that the natural sugar levels of many of the grape varieties grown by him were the highest recorded in the country and that de-acidification seldom had to be carried out. However, this is an area well away from the coast, and spring frosts can be a problem. Although born and brought up in England, Leighton spent some 20 years living in Australia and learnt much of his viticulture and winemaking there and with Antipodean enthusiasm he was not afraid of trying new varieties, new growing systems and new techniques. He spent some time at Riverina College in New South Wales where, with viticulturalist Max Loder, he studied the subject. He first questioned the notion, taken then (as now) by many as the gospel truth, that 'competition planting' – where a high density of vines competes for root space, water and nutrients – can actually control and reduce excess vigour. He decided that this was patently not the case and that one only has to look at UK vineyards planted at densities as high as 6,000 vines per hectare to know that this is not true. He felt that planting vines in rows between 3 and 3.5-metres wide gave just as much (or as little) vigour control, but offered serious savings on establishment costs (1,200 vines per hectare) and annual labour and management costs. While yields might not be as high, land costs are relatively low and with the proper pruning system, almost as many annual fruiting buds can still be laid down.[20]

In the mid-1980s, he and Pat White developed the 'Stanlake Bow', which was a Guyot or Pendlebogen system, where instead of the replacement arms starting from the middle of the trunk and going out away from the centre, a T-shaped trunk was created with the canes starting from the ends of the T and coming back towards the centre. This made for a clearer area in the centre of the vine which opened it up to light and air and in addition, gave each vine a larger volume of permanent wood in which to store its winter nutrients. This helped promote early bud-burst and lessened frost damage. This system was tried and for some years and worked well, but as the

---

20 I still think that closer planting does create root competition, but only once vines are sufficiently established. Having said that, once vines get to 15+ years old, their vigour usually declines anyway. However, what close planting definitely does is to help create a better vineyard microclimate, something wide-spacing can never achieve.

vines got older the starting point of the annual canes got further and further away from the centre point of the vines until they started to crowd their neighbours and fruiting area was being lost.

Today, many of the vines are trained on another unique system – the 'Stanlake Ballerina'. This is a variant of the Smart-Dyson Ballerina which viticulturalist Richard Smart helped develop and is in effect a mid-height Sylvoz system. This combines the benefits of short cane/long spur pruning (speed, simplicity and the ability to vary bud numbers on an annual basis) with those of having a large body of permanent wood (earlier bud-burst and some protection from spring frost). Added to these are the financial advantages of low density of planting, a lack of summer leaf work and the health benefits of an open growing system.

The vineyard management at Stanlake Park is of a fairly high standard (but always with an eye on the bank balance) with all-over grass and no herbicide strip under the vines, a low nitrogen, high potassium and phosphorous fertiliser regime and a little-and-often pest and disease control programme. Spray materials are switched as often as possible to break the build up of any resistant organisms. This gives a very low

disease incidence, leading to clean crops which can be allowed to hang and ripen to maturity. Sheep are often used under the vines to keep the grass down and Schönburger, Reichensteiner and Triomphe are grown as close to organically as possible.

Stanlake Park's winery, or at least the fermentation tanks and barrel department, is housed in a barn built in 1688 to commemorate the Glorious Revolution (when the Catholic King James II was overthrown and the Dutch Protestant King William III was installed) and which was once the headquarters of the Garth Hunt. It has a fine (listed) clocktower, complete with clock with the inscription 'Revolution 1688'. The modern equipment it contains aims to reduce mechanical damage to the grapes as much as possible and there are different pumps for different uses. A Demoisy crusher/de-stemmer and 4-tonne pneumatic Europress are at the start of the winemaking process, the tanks are all temperature-controlled stainless steel with a Pedia-Kreyer heat exchanger, there is a fully insulated and cooled wine store, fully automatic bottling/labelling line (installed in 2007) and capable of inserting natural corks, synthetic corks and sparkling wine corks, as well as screwcaps and crown-caps for the first stage of the sparkling wine process. There is also a semi-automatic sparkling wine disgorging line. Extensive use of French oak *barriques* is made and one-third of them are replaced each year. Both kieselguhr and sheet filtration are used.

Between 1983 – when the first small batches of experimental wine were made – and 1987, the cellar was in the hands of Leighton and an Australian winemaker, Andrew Hood, and together they made a tentative start on establishing a Thames Valley (as it then was) style. Success came early and in 1988 their 'Siegerwürzertraminer 1987' (Siegerrebe, Würzer and Gewürztraminer blend) won the UKVA's President's Trophy. In 1988, Hood left and John Worontschak arrived to take over the winery and – as they say in a certain type of cliché-ridden novel – things were never the same again. John arrived at a time when English and Welsh wine was already in a period of change. The old German style of UK-grown wine was, in the light of a rapid fall in sales of this type of wine in general, declining, and a new type of English wine was starting to appear. Wines were becoming softer and more approachable, reliance on imported *süss-reserve* was lessening and winemakers were blending varieties to achieve more consistency. Oak-ageing had been in use for several years (Karl-Heinz Johner at Lamberhurst and myself at Tenterden had been making *barrique*-aged wines since 1986) and there were even a few interesting sparkling, sweet and red wines being produced.

To this party, Worontschak was able to bring his considerable skills and experience. With the raw materials at his disposal from both Stanlake Park and from the other vineyards where he was either winemaker or consultant, he made, in the 14 or so years that he was active in English wine, some impressive wines. His wines were often gentler and fruitier than other English wines and many had more depth and character. Careful handling, the use of the right enzymes and yeasts, more malolactic fermentations than in most UK wineries, and better control of oxidation and phenolic content all helped. Judicious blending of varieties to adjust flavours was also a very important part of the Worontschak way. He also produced – or helped produce – some of the best of the sweet, red and sparkling wines produced in the UK at that time. Without wanting to swell his pride any more than would be good for his health, one has to acknowledge that he notched up an impressive and totally unrivalled tally of awards and medals. To list just the major ones says it all.

In the EWOTYC, Worontschak's wines have won: the Gore-Browne Trophy (five times) in 1992 with the 1991 Clocktower Selection Botrytis, in 1993 with the 1991 Valley Vineyards Fumé, in 1996 with the Heritage Brut, in 1997 with the 1995 Clocktower Selection Pinot Noir and in 1998 with the Heritage Brut Rosé; the President's Trophy (three times) in 1991 with the 1989 Botrytis, in 1995 with the 1994 Northbrook Springs Thames Valley Botrytis and in 1998 with the 1997 Clocktower Selection Pinot Noir; the Jack Ward Memorial Salver (four times) in 1990 with the 1989 Sweet Lee, in 1992 with the 1991 Clocktower Selection, in 1997 with the 1996 Hidden Springs Sunset Rosé and in 2000 with the Denbies 1999 Redlands; the Wine Guild of the UK Trophy (five times) in 1993 with the 1991 Fumé, in 1996 with both the Heritage Brut and the 1994 Mersea, in 1997 with the 1995 Clocktower

Selection Pinot Noir and in 1998 with the 1996 Hidden Spring Dark Fields; the Bernard Theobald Trophy (four times) in 1992 Pinot Noir, in 1995 with the 1993 Hidden Spring Dark Fields, in 1998 with the 1997 Clocktower Pinot Noir and in 2000 with the Denbies 1999 Redlands; and the Vintner's Trophy once with the Heritage Brut Rosé. In the Country Landowner's Association's English and Welsh Wine Competition the 1995 Regatta won Wine of the Year in 1997, the Ascot Sparkling was Sparkling Wine of the Year in 1998 and the Heritage Brut was Sparkling Wine of the Year in 1999. Added to this list are UKVA Gold, Silver and Bronze medals, together with awards and commendations in the IWSC, the Wine Challenge and the T&CVA regional competition.

In both the 1989 and the 2001 editions of this book, I was fulsome in my praise of Leighton and his vineyards. I said that it was usually the winemaker that got all the glory and the grapegrower that was often overlooked, but that Leighton had: *not only managed consistently to grow crops of good grapes, but also had both the foresight and the good fortune to employ a winemaker, John Worontschak, and an assistant winemaker, Vince Gower, who have been given the facilities and encouragement to produce top quality wines. The combination of a dedicated owner/grower and a talented winemaking team have put Valley Vineyards at the top of this industry.* I also said that Leighton had done as much to advance the cause of growing grapes and making wine in the UK as anyone and that the work he had carried out was a great bonus to the English and Welsh wine industry. I still stand by those comments.

In 2003, as Leighton approached retirement age, he decided that after 25 years creating what had become the most-decorated vineyard in the UK, he would sell. Worontschak had already started to lessen his involvement with the winemaking at Stanlake Park, leaving the day-to-day work in the hands of his very capable long-term assistant, Vince Gower. In 2005 the property and business were sold to the Darts.

Peter Dart is a professional marketer whose day job is at one of the world's largest advertising and marketing agencies, WPP. The Darts have spent the past three years giving the place – both physical and spiritual – a complete makeover with the aim to bring it back into the fold of the top wine producers in the UK. They changed the name from Valley Vineyards to Stanlake Park, which they felt was more authentic, could be registered as a trademark and had an available URL for a website. Peter feels that the quality of English Wine 'is now very good, but at the prices we charge we need to work on perception and presentation'. Since the Darts took over, substantial investments have been made in several areas. The main house has been substantially renovated; a new fully automatic bottling line has been installed; 2,000 new vines have been planted (Bacchus, Schönburger and Pinot noir) and a new sales outlet – the Stanlake Park Cellar Shop – has been opened. Vince, who has now been in the winery at Stanlake Park since 1989, continues as winemaker and in addition to making the estate's own wines, is winemaker to around 20 other UK vineyards who bring their grapes for him to process. He services are so sought after that there is even a waiting

list for contract-crush customers.

The selection of wines available under the Stanlake Park name is very wide and one of the best from any UK producer. It consists of four white varietals: Bacchus, Gewürztraminer, Ortega and Madeleine Angevine; four white and rosé blends: Regatta, Hinton Grove, King's Fumé and Pinot Blush; three reds: Ruscombe, The Reserve and Pinot Noir; and four sparkling wines: Stanlake Park, Stanlake Park Rosé, Heritage Brut and Hinton Brut; and two liqueurs: Blackcurrant and Whitecurrant.

Since the heady days of the 1990s, when wines from this vineyard appeared with regularity in the medal winner's lists, the tally of prizes and awards has slipped somewhat. However, under the new ownership, things seem to be improving with two Silvers in the 2006 EWOTYC, a Silver, three Bronzes and two Highly Commendeds in the 2007 EWOTYC, four Bronzes and three HCs in the 2008 EWOTYC and four Bronzes and one HC in the 2009 EWOTYC. Their 2006 King's Fumé was in Decanter Magazine's "Top Ten" English Wines of June 2009. Let's hope that they can soon get back to the point where they are winning Golds and Trophies as well.

Staplecombe Vineyard

Burlands Farm, Staplegrove, Somerset TA2 6SN
Telephone: 01823 451217
E-mail: curshams@supanet.com
Contact: Martin Cursham
Vineyards: 0.3675 hectares
Grape varieties: MA, Rondo, Huxelrebe, Reichensteiner
Open by appointment.

Staverton Vineyard

The Rookcry, Eyke, Woodbridge, Suffolk IP12 2RR
Telephone: 01394 460271
Fax: 01394 460818
E-mail: estate@sheepshanks.co.uk
Contact: Andrew Sheepshanks
Vineyards: 0.53 hectares
Grape varieties: Bacchus, MT, Ortega, Reichensteiner, Seyval blanc
Open by appointment.

Stopham Vineyard

Stopham, Pulborough, West Sussex RH20 1EG
Telephone: 01273 566826
Mobile: 07962 425625
E-mail: info@stophamvineyard.co.uk
Website: www.stophamvineyard.co.uk
Contact: Simon Woodhead
Vineyards: 6 hectares
Grape varieties: Pinot gris, Pinot blanc, Chardonnay, Bacchus, Pinot noir, Auxerrois, Dornfelder
Open by appointment. See website for details.

Stopham Vineyard is located in the beautiful hamlet of Stopham in the designated South Downs National Park and was planted in 2007. This area, not far from where Nyetimber has most of its vineyards, is rapidly becoming the biggest grapegrowing region in the UK. The soil is a sandy-loam and between 15 and 40 m above sea-level. The vines are spaced at 2.2 x 1.2-metres and both Single and Double Guyot pruned.

Simon Woodhead runs the vineyard, together with Tom Newham, who Simon met at Plumpton College. Still white and rosé will be the main focus of production from 2010, based on the Alsatian varieties of Pinot gris, Pinot blanc and Auxerrois. Additionally, small amounts of sparkling wine will also be made each year. A winery is planned for the first major production year in 2010 and will be located in the disused Victorian farm buildings. A second field of 5-hectares is planned for 2010, which would bring the annual production to around 60,000 bottles.

Stopham Vineyard

Storrington Priory Vineyard

Our Lady of England Priory, School Lane, Storrington, West Sussex RH20 4LN
Telephone: 01903 742150
E-mail: whitecanons.storrington@btinternet.com
Website: www.norbertines.co.uk
Contact: Paul MacMahon
Vineyards: 1.0396 hectares
Grape varieties: Pinot noir, Chardonnay
Open by appointment.

Strawberry Hill Vineyard

47 Orchard Road, Newent, Gloucestershire GL18 1DQ
Telephone: 01531 822669
E-mail: enquiries@strawberryhillvineyard.co.uk
Website: www.strawberryhillvineyard.co.uk
Contact: Tim Chance
Vineyards: 1.8 hectares
Grape varieties: Outdoors: Regent, Reichensteiner, Schönburger, Orion, Siegerrebe.
Under glass: Cabernet Sauvignon, Chardonnay, Merlot, Pinot noir
Open by appointment.

Struddicks Farm Vineyard

Deviock Wine Company, Looe Hill, St. Martin, Looe, Cornwall, PL13 1PA
Telephone: 01752 812178
Contact: Adrian Derx
E-mail: adrian_derx@hotmail.com
Mobile: 07815 196199
Contact: Alex Davidson
E-mail: larajo36@hotmail.com
Mobile: 07882 097339
Vineyards: 2.3 hectares
Grape varieties: Seyval blanc, Auxerrois, Pinot noir Précoce, Pinot noir, Rondo, Chardonnay
Not open to the public.

Sugar Loaf Vineyard

Dunmar Farm, Pentre Lane, Abergavenny, Monmouthshire NP7 7LA, Wales
Telephone: 01873 853066
E-mail: enquiries@sugarloafvineyard.co.uk
Website: www.sugarloafvineyards.co.uk
Contact: Louise Ryan
Vineyards: 2 hectares
Grape varieties: MA, Regent, Reichensteiner, Rondo, Seyval blanc, Siegerrebe, Triomphe
Open to visitors. See website for details.

Summerhouse Vineyard

New Close Lane, Skelbrooke, Doncaster, South Yorkshire DN6 8NB
Location of vineyard: DN6 8NB
Telephone: 01302 721688
E-mail: skellowmill@aol.com
Contact: Elizabeth Scott
Vineyards: 0.572 hectares
Grape varieties: Seyval blanc, Rondo, MA, Pinot noir, Phoenix
Open by appointment only.

Summerhouse Vineyard started in 2004 when ten experimental vines were planted. They did so well that in the following year, 500 Rondo and 500 Seyval blanc were planted on the south-facing limestone slope below the farmhouse. In 2006 MA and Pinot noir were planted and in 2007 some Phoenix to bring the vineyard up to 1-hectare.

Summermoor Vineyard

c/o Marsh Cottage, Mill Lane, Burrington, Umberleigh, Devon EX37 9JN
Location of vineyard: Hearson, Swimbridge, Barnstaple, Devon, EX32 0QH
Telephone: 01769 520776
Mobile: 07736 771790
E-mail: summermoor@tiscali.co.uk
Contact: Allan Petchey, Julia Petchey
Vineyards: 1.417 hectares
Grape varieties: MA, Chardonnay, Siegerrebe, Rondo, Phoenix
Open April to September, Tuesday to Thursday, 10 am to 4 pm. Saturday 10.30 am to 2.30 pm. At other times by appointment.

Summermoor Vineyard

Sunnybank Vineyard and Vine Nursery

Cwm Barn, Rowlestone, Herefordshire, HR2 0EE
Telephone: 01981 240256
E-mail: sarah@sunnybankvines.co.uk
Website: www.sunnybankvines.co.uk
Contact: Sarah Bell
Vineyards: 0.34 hectares
Grape varieties: nearly 500 varieties including seedless, dessert and wine varieties
Not open to the public.

Under the previous ownership of Brian Edwards, this vineyard was awarded the National Collection of Outdoor Vines (although I am not sure how, as there is a vineyard as part of the National Fruit Collection at Brogdale, Faversham, Kent – see entry) and is now in the process of applying for National Collection status. Where possible most vine varieties are available for purchase by mail order during the dormant period either as one-year old rooted cuttings on their own roots or as bare wood for propagation. (As a matter of interest, the National Collection of indoor grape varieties is at Reads Nursery, Hales Hall Loddon, Norfolk. NR14 6QW.)

Surrenden Vineyard

Walnut Tree Farm, Swan Lane, Little Chart, Ashford, Kent TN27 0ES
Telephone: 01233 840214
E-mail: martin@surrenden-vineyard.co.uk
Contact: Martin Oldaker
Vineyards: 1 hectare
Grape varieties: Chardonnay, Pinot noir, Pinot Meunier, Pinot noir Précoce
Not open to the public

Sustead Lane Vineyard

c/o Abbey Vineyards Group, Irnham Grange, Irnham, Corby Glen, Grantham, Lincolnshire, NG33 4NE
Location of vineyard: Sustead Lane, Gresham, Norfolk, NR11 8RR
Telephone: 01476 550191   Fax: 01476 550080
E-mail: info@abbeyvineyards.co.uk
Contact: Phil Kerry 07815 308838
Contact: Jonathan Kerry 07805 315763
Vineyards: 1.62 hectares
Grape varieties: Bacchus, Chardonnay, Pinot noir
Not open to the public.

Syndale Valley Vineyards

Parsonage Farm, Seed Road, Newnham, Sittingbourne, Kent ME9 0NA
Telephone: 01795 890693
E-mail: bacchus.vin@virgin.net
Contact: Jonathan Abbs, Paula Abbs
Vineyards: 4.052 hectares
Grape varieties: Pinot noir, Chardonnay, Pinot blanc, Pinot Meunier, Bacchus
Open by appointment.

Tarrington Court Vineyard

Tarrington Court, Tarrington, Hereford, Herefordshire HR1 4EX
Telephone: 01432 890632
E-mail: catherine@cirenergy.com
Website: www.simplesite.com/tarringtoncourt
Contact: Keith Jago, Catherine Jago
Vineyards: 0.25 hectares
Grape varieties: MA
Open by appointment.

Tas Valley Vineyard

c/o Abbey Vineyards Group, Irnham Grange, Irnham, Corby Glen, Grantham, Lincolnshire, NG33 4NE
Location of vineyard: Bunwell Road, Forncett St Peter, Norwich, Norfolk ,NR16 1LW
Telephone: 01476 550191
Fax: 01476 550080
E-mail: info@abbeyvineyardsgroup.co.uk
Contact: Phil Kerry 07815 308838
Contact: Jonathan Kerry 07805 315763
Vineyards: 1.2146 hectares
Grape varieties: Bacchus, Reichensteiner, MT
Open by appointment.

Tenterden Vineyard

Small Hythe, Tenterden, Kent TN30 7NG
For contact and opening details, see Chapel Down Wines
Vineyards: 8.33 hectares
Grape varieties: Pinot noir, Bacchus, Chardonnay, Pinot blanc, Rondo, Regent, Gutenborner, Siegerrebe
Open to the public. See Chapel Down Wine's website.

Terlingham Vineyard

Terlingham Manor Farm, Gibraltar Lane, Hawkinge, Kent CT18 7AE
Telephone: 01303 892743 Fax: 01303 892743
Mobile: 07771 601736
E-mail: info@terlinghammanor.com
Website: www.terlinghamvineyard.co.uk
Contact: Penny Riley, Steve Riley
Vineyards: 1.5 hectares
Grape varieties: Pinot noir, Chardonnay, Pinot Meunier, Seyval blanc, Bacchus, Rondo, Dornfelder
See Website for details of visiting arrangements.

Terlingham Vineyard was planted in 2006 on a chalky south facing site site at between 133 and 155-meters above sea level. The purpose built winery with underground cellar enabling a stable temperature to be maintained throughout the year for the benefit of the sparkling and still wines, was completed in 2008. Penny and Steve Riley are the winemakers and all aspects of the winemaking process are carried out in a traditional handmade way. Terlingham is the least mechanised winery, even hand riddling the sparkling wines in *pupitres*

and disgorging by hand. The vineyard has adopted a version the Kent white horse (Invicta) as it's logo as it appears on the hillside above the Channel Tunnel close to where the vineyard is situated. Terlingham Vineyard is also known as the White Horse Vineyard.

Tern Valley Vineyard

Hall Farm, Tern Hill, Market Drayton, Shropshire TF9 3PU
Telephone: 01630 639688
E-mail: info@ternvalleywine.com
E-mail: bob.obrien@bigfoot.com
Website: www.ternvalleywine.com
Contact: Bob O'Brien
Vineyards: 1.67 hectares
Grape varieties: Phoenix, Rondo, Regent, Dornfelder
Open by appointment.

Theale Vineyard

Laithwaites, New Aquitaine House, Exeter Way, Theale, Reading, Berkshire RG7 4PL
Telephone: 0118 903 0903
E-mail: anne.linder@directwines.com
Contact: Anne Linder
Vineyards: 0.14 hectares
Grape varieties: Chardonnay
Open by appointment.

Planted on the rubble the builders left behind, Theale Vineyard is one of those nice little oddities in the world of wine. The builders in question were putting up new offices for Tony and Barbara Laithwaite, owners of Laithwaites Wines, the UK's largest wine company (annual sales of £350m) and probably the most successful mail-order wine company in the world. They decided that rather than grass over the unsightly lump they would level it – slightly south-facing – add a bit of topsoil and in 1998, with advice from Mike Roberts at RidgeView, plant 704 Chardonnay spaced at 2.0 x 1.0-metres. The wines from this *très boutique* vineyard, which have all been made at RidgeView, have been highly impressive and their first vintage, the 2002, showed what was possible. Their *2003 Founder's Reserve* however, of

which there were only 756 bottles, did the Laithwaites proud and picked up a Silver in the 2007 IWC and, surprise, surprise, a Gold Medal and top ten position in the French sparkling wine competion *Effervescents du Monde* in 2007. I served a bottle of this wine (blind) at one of my MW student tastings and they ALL thought that it was a good vintage Champagne in the £40-60 level! It was certainly one of the most impressive English sparkling wines I have ever tasted.

The current release is the 2004, of which there were 1,274 bottles (which equates to 68 hl/ha, so around half the yield in Champagne, but about the same amount per vine) and is available from – you guessed – Laithwaites at £22.99 per bottle. Tony Laithwaite says: *"We don't really know why the sparkling wine from this vineyard has proved so successful. Perhaps it is due to the carefully built south-facing slope or the shelter and heat from the surrounding buildings? Certainly RidgeView's skills and the dedication of the team who keep the vineyard immaculate have lead to its success."*

Laithwaites also have another vineyard in their UK portfolio which is even smaller, just 160 vines at 1.5 x 1.0-metres of Merlot planted outside their shop in Virginia Water. What the wine is like from this holding I cannot say and to date I don't think they have shared any of it with the world. Barabara Laithwaite is also involved with a partner in Wyfold Vineyard in Oxfordshire (see separate entry).

Thelnetham Vineyard

Thelnetham House, High Street, Norfolk IP22 1JL
Telephone: 01379 890739
Mobile: 07973 481476
E-mail: neil.gillis@btinternet.com
Contact: Neil Gillis
Vineyards: 0.9 hectares
Grape varieties: MT, Bacchus
Open by appointment.

Thomas Walk Vineyard

Haven Hill, Summercove, Kinsale, Cork, Ireland
Telephone - Ireland: 00 353 21 477 2072
Telephone - Germany: 00 49 6021 23190
Fax-Germany: 00 49 6021 29000
E-mail: k.t.walk@walk-net.de
Contact: Thomas Walk

Vineyards: 0.98 hectares
Grape varieties: Rondo
Not open to the public.

The Thomas Walk Vineyard is owned by Thomas Walk who is a golf club expert (that's as in drivers, putters, wedges etc) from Ashaffenburg, Germany where he develops and sells innovative golf hardware. Google Earth shows what looks like three separate vineyards which together total just under 1-hectare.[21] They are planted with 'Amurensis Walk' – which is in fact Rondo – which were obtained from Geisenheim's Professor Helmut Becker, Rondo's creator. In my 2001 guide, the details I had were that the vines were planted between 1985 and 1996 and that there were 0.98 ha of vines at 1.7 x 1.2-metres and Double Guyot trained. I have read on an Irish website that the vineyards were "seven acres" in size (2.83 ha) but this is probably just a bit of Irish imagination at work. Walk is very secretive about his vineyard and said that vine numbers "are not to be released". He also says that the vines are pruned in a "special Irish way of pruning to allow for mixed weather during flowering" and that the vineyard is "100% organic, no sprays, no fertilisers". The wine, of which he makes two sorts, *Amurensis Walk Clairet* and *Amurensis Walk Ruby* is likewise "organic except for preservation" (by which I assume he means SO2) and is made in quantities "not to be released" (by which I assume he means that not much is made).

What I was told at Longueville House – Ireland's only other (almost) commercial vineyard – is that the Walk grapes go into the red wine they sell at the hotel which is

called Amurensis Walk and the current vintage is the 2006. I was also told that there was no crop in 2007 or 2008 as the weather had been so bad – which I can believe, knowing what it was like in the UK. The 2006 was fermented in oak and then aged after fermentation for 6 months in oak.

If you want to see a video clip of someone called Lar Veala, who runs a blog called 'Sour Grapes', tasting the 2006 Amurensis Walk go to www.sourgrapes.ie and search for 'amurensis' or go to: http://tinyurl.com/nagnn8. Another wine blogger, Michael Kane who is at www.curious wines.ie, also tasted it – chilled as suggested by O'Callaghan – and

---

21 To find the vineyards, go to the end of Haven Hill and before the first left-hand corner, two are to be found on the right, with a third a few fields over to the south-east.

reported that the wine was: *"I'm afraid, not the most drinkable. Powerful medicinal and vegetal flavours, with a punishing lack of acidity and fruit to carry it".*

Whatever the wine tastes like, it says something that Walk has managed to keep the vineyard going for almost 25 years and still manages to produce a crop in all but the very worst years. Rondo is not as hardy or weatherproof as Becker thought it would be in the UK/Irish climate and had Walk chosen a better variety he might have had more luck – although what that variety might have been is anyone's guess! [22]

Thornbury Castle Vineyard

Castle Street, Thornbury, South Gloucestershire BS35 1HH
Telephone: 01454 281182   Fax: 01454 416188
E-mail: info@thornburycastle.co.uk
E-mail: reception@thornburycastle.co.uk
Website: www.thornburycastle.co.uk
Contact: Brian Jarvis
Contact: Ingrid Bates 07779 085420 E-mail: ingridbates@mac.com
Vineyards: 0.2 hectares
Grape varieties: MT, Phoenix
Open by appointment.

Thorncroft Vineyard

Thorncroft Drive, Leatherhead, Surrey KT22 8JD
Telephone: 01372 372159 and 01642 791792
Mobile: 07970 818131
Fax: 01642 791793
E-mail: guy@thorncroftdrinks.co.uk
Contact: Guy Woodall
Vineyards: 0.4 hectares
Grape varieties: Pinot noir
Not open to the public.

Three Choirs Vineyard

Newent, Gloucestershire GL18 1LS
Telephone: 01531 890223
E-mail: ts@threechoirs.com
Website: www.three-choirs-vineyards.co.uk
Contact: Thomas Shaw
Vineyards: 30 hectares
Grape varieties: Bacchus, Huxelrebe, MA, MT, Orion, Phoenix, Pinot noir, Regent, Reichensteiner, Schönburger, Seyval blanc, Siegerrebe, Triomphe, Ehrenfelser, Faberrebe, Gamay, Maréchal Foch, Ortega, Pinot blanc, Rondo, Würzer, Zweigeltrebe
Open to the public. See website for details.

---

22 See Appendix IV for a brief history of vineyards in Ireland.

First planted in 1973, Three Choirs Vineyard was one of the first large commercial vineyards to be planted in the UK and for many years it was by far the largest and most important vineyard in the western half of the UK. The original owner was Alan McKechnie and his apple farm at Newent was then known as Fairfields Fruit Farm. Tom Day, his farm manager, took a keen interest in the vineyard side of the farm and it is really due to his, and wife Brenda's, endeavours that Three Choirs took shape and became what it is today[23]. In 1984, McKechnie wanted to sell up and Tom persuaded a consortium of local businessmen and vineyard owners to put up some funds and buy it. Under the new ownership, the vineyards expanded and Three Choirs developed in both size and complexity. To begin with, the winery, shop and offices were situated in the old apple packing buildings which were situated down a rather tortuous lane which coaches could not easily navigate. However, in 1990 the site they occupy today, which adjoined their existing land and which fronted on to the main road, came up for sale, was purchased and in 1991 a brand new winery – air conditioned, insulated and with a epoxy floor that cost an arm and a leg – was erected. An existing house was converted into offices and a restaurant and a new shop and café were built. Eight well appointed guest rooms were added in 2000.

For the first two vintages, 1976 and 1977, the grapes were sent to Nigel Godden at Pilton Manor, but for the 1976 vintage, a winery was installed and Tom Day took over as winemaker. He was soon joined by Dr. Kit Morris (who founded the Bottle Green Drinks Co.) who remained as winemaker from 1977 until 1988 when the present winemaker, Martin Fowke, succeeded him. As one would expect with a vineyard of this size, the winery today is well equipped with two Willmes UP 1800 pneumatic presses, the usual filtration and other winemaking equipment and a fully automatic GAI/Enos filling/labelling line. Tanks are a combination of both newer stainless steel and older glass fibre and there is a cold store for the cold stabilisation of their wines as well as for the production and storage of süss-reserve. They also make wine under contract for a considerable number of small vineyards. Without them, the lot of Welsh wine would be far less rosy. Although they have 30-hectares of vines, they also buy-in a considerable quantity of grapes from other vineyards.

---

23 Three Choirs winemaker Martin Fowke is married to Tom and Brenda's daughter and their son, Simon Day, who made wine at both Lamberhurst and Jersey's La Mare Vineyard, now runs Vine and Wine Ltd.

Over the years, Three Choirs have earned themselves a fair reputation for their wines and today have a wide range of whites, rosés and reds, both still and sparkling. In the 1980s and 1990s, the range tended to be varietally based, but today they have several different ranges of wines: blends with names such as Coleridge Hill, English House, May Hill, Willow Brook and Four Oaks which are for sale and distribution to the trade; and then three other ranges – Premium Selection, Cellar Door and Estate Reserve. Quite what the distinction between these ranges is I have no idea and their wesbite gives no clues! They also have a few varietals, Bacchus and Siegerrebe. Their prices are at the lower end of the English Wine spectrum – on Waitrose WineDirect, four of the first five English wines listed are from Three Choirs (£5.69 – £6.16 a bottle). They are the only UK-grown still wine to be sold by The Wine Society, who list three exclusive blends, again at very reasonable prices: a Rosé at £6.95, Stone Brook at £6.75 and Midsummer Hill at £6.25. Their *NV Classic Cuvée* sparkling wine (80% Seyval blanc and 20% Pinot noir), which they sell from their own website at £10.25 a bottle, must be the cheapest UK-grown sparkling wine available today. Whether this is a deliberate sales policy, related to the cost of production, or where they think it fits viz-a-viz other UK sparklers, I have no idea.

Despite their size and output, their tally of awards has never quite been as good as some of the other big vineyards. Since 1984 they have won the Gore-Browne Trophy once, five Gold medals and eleven other trophies. Compare this to Chapel Down (with roughly the same level of output) who have won three Gore-Brownes, sixteen Golds and nineteen other trophies. I put this down to the fact that their slightly more northerly location put them at a disadvantage in ripeness terms. However, with climate change this factor has probably now been eliminated and may explain why it took them until 2008 to get their first Gore-Browne which helped Fowke win the McAlpine Winemaker of the Year Trophy. Another factor is that they tended in the past to rely on a large amount of Huxelrebe – never a good variety in a less-than-perfect year, plus copious quantities of Seyval blanc – a good, but not always award-winning variety. Quite how they bill themselves on their website as *England's leading and most awarded, single estate vineyard* I have no idea! At one stage they made a successful 'New Release' which was fermented, clarified and bottled with an almost indecent haste and launched to coincide with the release of Beaujolais Nouveau in late November. This wine was – despite its youth – very drinkable and surprised people with its quality.

Today, Three Choirs tends to concentrate on their successful mini-hotel, together with the retail shop, the tours and tastings, their brewery and other periphal add-ons.

Despite asking on several occasions for information from Three Choirs to accompany their entry in the 2008 UK Vineyards Guide, nothing was forthcoming and their entry remained rather bare. For this 2010 update I again attempted to get someone to submit something interesting, but again, had no response. The above entry is all my own work and may therefore contain some innacuracies – but hey guys – I did try!

Three Sisters Vineyard

The Laurels, Mulberry Road, Claxby, Market Rasen, Lincolnshire LN8 3YS
Telephone: 0845 4735539 and 01673 828359
Mobile: 07703 146194
E-mail: david@three-sisters-vineyard.co.uk
E-mail: sales@three-sisters-vineyard.co.uk
Website: www.three-sisters-vineyard.co.uk
Contact: David Lofthouse
Vineyards: 0.6189 hectares
Grape varieties: Siegerrebe, Reichensteiner, Ortega, Regent, Pinot noir Précoce
Visitors are welcome between May and October but please ring first. Group visits weekdays, evenings and weekends can be arranged.

Three Sisters Vineyard is situated on a gentle south-facing slope on the western edge of the Lincolnshire Wolds Area of Outstanding Natural Beauty. It is protected from the cold northerly and easterly winds by the surrounding hills. The vineyard was planted in 2002 and 2003 and five varieties of vines were chosen: Siegerrebe, Reichensteiner and Ortega for white wine; Regent and Pinot noir Précoce for red. The 1,650 vines are grown as a single curtain system in rows approximately 2.5 metres wide with the vines 1.5 metres apart. A small stable block was converted into a winery and a range of dry wines is made: three whites, a couple of reds and a rosé.

Throwley Vineyard

The Old Rectory, Throwley, Faversham, Kent ME13 0PF
Telephone: 01795 890276
E-mail: duncanm.wilson@virgin.net
Website: www.throwleyvineyard.co.uk
Contact: Duncan Wilson
Vineyards: 1.38 hectares
Grape varieties: Chardonnay, Ortega, Pinot noir
Open to the public. See website for details.

Throwley Vineyard was planted in 1986 on a south-west facing slope of the North Downs close to the Kent coast on a light chalky soil. Throwley Vineyard has won international awards for its wines, both still and sparkling, including rare Gold Medals in the IWC and IWSC. In the 2008 EWOTYC it won a Bronze for its *2002 Throwley Reserve Brut Sparkling.*

Ticehurst Vineyard

c/o Burnt House Farm, Burwash Weald, Etchingham, East Sussex TN19 7LA
Location of vineyard: TN5 7HE
Telephone: 01424 441979
Mobile: 07836 655570
Contact: Peter Etherton
Vineyards: 1.0567 hectares
Grape varieties: Reichensteiner, MT, Kerner, Shönburger, Dornfelder, Dunkelfelder
Not open to the public.

Tiltridge Vineyard

Upper Hook Road, Upton-upon-Severn, Worcestershire WR8 0SA
Telephone: 01684 592906
Fax: 01684 594142
E-mail: sandy@tiltridge.com
Website: www.elgarwine.com
Contact: Sandy Barker, Anna Bailey
Vineyards: 0.74 hectares
Grape varieties: Huxelrebe, Schönburger, Phoenix, Seyval blanc
Open to the public, Monday to Friday, 9 am to 5 pm, exc. Bank Holidays. See website for full details.

Tiltridge Vineyard is situated on a low ridge between the attractive riverside town of Upton-upon-Severn and the Malvern Hills. The site is south-east-facing and around 38 metres above sea level and has a soil described as 'mudstones'. The land was once part of a County Council tenanted farm and when the last tenant died it was in such a poor state that the Council decided to sell and in 1982 the Barkers were able to buy the house, some buildings and land. Having liked the local Three Choirs wines, they thought that they would have a go themselves and in 1988 and 1989, 0.60 hectares of vines was planted. Originally four varieties were planted: Huxelrebe, Schönburger and Seyval Blanc with a small area of Triomphe following a few years later. However, the Triomphe did not perform well and has been replaced with Phoenix. The jury is still out on how these will perform but the signs are good. All vines are trained to GDC which seems to work well here and harvests have been taken every year since 1991. Annual production varies between 3,000 and 6,000 bottles of wine and the grapes have always been taken to the Three Choirs winery.

All Tiltridge wines are sold under the 'Elgar' and related labels (the composer Elgar lived nearby) which helps give them a Worcestershire flavour. Their 2006 'Cello' won a Bronze at the 2007 EWOTYC, a Bronze for their Dorabella 2007 in 2008 and two Bronzes for Elgar Dry 2008 and Elgar Medium Dry 2008 in 2009. Other wines include Variations, Enigma and Sonata, the last a Rosé made in conjunction with Three Choirs.

Timber Lane Vineyard

c/o 19 Barnes Way, Dorchester, Dorset, DT1 2DZ
Location of vineyard: Timber Lane, Dorchester, Dorset, DT2 9DS
Telephone: 01305 880069
Mobile: 07845 140589
Contact: Steve Barnard
Vineyards: 0.5 hectares
Grape varieties: Not known
Not open to the public.

Tinwood Vineyard

c/o Groves Farm Office, Colworth, Chichester, West Sussex PO20 2DX
Location of vineyard: Tinwood House, Tinwood Lane, Halnaker, Chichester, West Sussex, PO18 0NE
Telephone: 01243 788478
Mobile: 07968 340494
E-mail: art.tukker@tinwoodvineyard.com
E-mail: lisa.gough@goldenplain.co.uk
Contact: Art Tukker
Vineyards: 18.1764 hectares
Grape varieties: Chardonnay, Pinot noir, Pinot Meunier
Not open to the public.

Tinwood Vineyard is owned by the Tukker family, 25 per cent owners of RidgeView Estate. Further vineyards will be planted to bring the total up to 40-hectares.

Titchfield Vineyard

Misty Haze, Brownwich Lane, Hampshire PO14 4NZ
Telephone and Fax: 01489 895773
E-mail: sales@titchfieldvineyard.co.uk
Website: www.titchfieldvineyard.co.uk
Contact: Tracey Thurlow
Vineyards: 1.1 hectares
Grape varieties: Bacchus, Faberrebe, Pinot noir, Reichensteiner, Auxerrois, Seyval blanc, Rondo, Dukelfelder, MA, Pinot Meunier, Chardonnay
Open to booked groups only. Please enquire.

Tixover Vineyard

c/o The Knoll, 103 Main Street, Lyddington, Rutland LE15 9LS
Location of vineyard: Barrrowden Road, Tixover, Rutland PE9
Telephone: 01572 823912
Mobile: 07967 097486
E-mail: john.atkinson37@talktalk.net
Contact: John Atkinson MW
Vineyards: 1.5 hectares
Grape varieties: Pinot noir, Pinot gris, Pinot blanc, Acolon
Open by appointment.

Tixover Vineyard, owned by Master of Wine, John Atkinson, who is UK 'Brand Ambassador' for Champagne house, Billecart-Salmon, is planted at one of the highest vine densities in the UK. The initial plantings were at 1.85 x 1.1-metres, but later plantings have been at 1.7 x 0.6-metres, a density of 9,804/ha (3,969/acre). This definitely puts it on a par with Champagne vineyards – if only on density terms. Many of the vines are *selection massale* rather than clonal, although some of the Pinot noir are clones 777, 828 and Abel (the NZ 'gumboot' clone). Most are on rootstock 161-49, with a few on SO4. The following was written by John Atkinson on 13 Auhust 2009:

> *Strip away quarternary glaciation, and the Jurassic strata along the spine of England is identical to Burgundy. Our vineyard site has been fluvially eroded leaving undulating karst-type features, and it occupies stony slopes of bajocian limestone with a 25-45 cm of pebbly rendzina soil. It is the analogue of Chambolle and Morey. The UK is obviously deficient in warmth and light vis-a-vis Burgundy, but the general faulting of local geology means we are very sheltered, and at between 35-45 metres above sea level, relatively warm. Rainfall averages around 450-500 mm per year, considerably less than Burgundy, but mean temperatures through the growing season are 2°C down on Burgundy and irradience about 15% less.*

> *Burgundy's best soils stress Pinot noir in the pre-veraison period. Stress keeps berries small, and encourages bunches to veraise early, switching over from their preference for vegetative enlargement, to an accelerated reproductive cycle. Crucially xylem rupture at veraison breaks the link between soil mosisture and berry size, though evaporation late on in the season can similarly advantage ratio of solids to juice.*

> *Shallow Burgundian soils have relatively low water saturation and water storage capacities. Moreover Calcium Carbonate binds in nutrients, particularly nitrogen. The mix of clay and calcium carbonate also means soils tend towards hardness once they dry, and soil hardness and dessication together reinforce the stress stimulus for early veraison.*

> *The other interesting feature of Burgundy's viticuture are the small*

vines. Six 80 cm shoots are seen as the right productive unit and small crops per vine allow for translocation of carbohydrates from woody tissue during ripening, but close planting needs some sort of barrier to deep rooting.

Our latest plantings are at 0.6 x 1.7-metres [earlier ones were 1.85 x 1.1-metres]. *Soil depth is 40 cm. I want six moderately vigorous shoots per vine. The Burgundians maintain that in order to achieve the optimum level of hydric stress, shoot height has to be at least 70% of row width. Running with 1.35m shoots will give a value of about 80% of row width which should make up for our reduced evaporation values, and give us more leaf per bunch. One disdvantage of short shoots is they encourage verjus, keeping auxins high, and delay maturity. At 1.35* [leaf-wall height] *we only tip once, and never have second flower-sets. So far the low vigour across the site means we only have one leaf layer; in fact, I would prefer more vigour in laterals.*

The vineyard was planted in 2005, and our first two vintages [2007 and 2008] *have been difficult. Notwithstanding this, we have harvested Pinot noir at between 12.5 and 12.8 potential alcohol, and a pH of 3.3. I think Pinot moves quite quickly between 22-24°C, and slows rapidly above 28°C. Burgundy gets a lot of hot days, as does Central Otago* [in New Zealand], *and I wonder if these bring any benefit to the vines. 26°C good, 30°C bad? The other thing that interest me is the impetus lignification gets from shortening day length, and falling temperatures. Again, I am really pleased with the hardness we get with the seeds. Anyway, arguably the sample all this is based on is too small, but I am interested to see what this summer* [2009] *throws up. We already have some veraising* [sic] *berries.*

Torview Wines

Beara Farm, Sheepwash, Beaworthy, Devon, EX21 5PB
Telephone: 01409 895773
Mobile: 07977 408829
E-mail: wine@torviewwines.co.uk
Website: ww.torviewwines.co.uk
Contact: Tim Gowan
Vineyards: 1.67 hectares
Grape varieties: Dornfelder, Pinot noir Précoce, Pinot noir, Acolon
Not open to the public

Townsend Farm Vineyard

Brampton Abbotts, Ross-on-Wye, Herefordshire HR9 7JE
Telephone: 01989 563772
Mobile: 07710 814475
E-mail: ben@bdavies11.orangehome.co.uk
Contact: Ben Taylor-Davies

Vineyards: 0.514 hectares
Grape varieties: Regent, Rondo, Phoenix, Seyval blanc
Not open to the public.

Treago Vineyard

St Weonards, Hereford, Herefordshire HR2 8QB
Telephone: 01981 580208
E-mail: fiona.mynors@cmail.co.uk
Contact: Richard Mynors
Vineyards: 0.2 hectares
Grape varieties: Seyval blanc, Huxelrebe, Bacchus, Regent
In polytunnels: Cabernet Sauvignon, Syrah
Open by appointment.

Trevibban Mill Vineyard

St. Issey, Wadebridge, Cornwall, PL27 7SE
Telephone: 01841 532186
Mobile: 07876 332200
E-mail: liz_mumcuoglu@hotmail.com
Contact: Liz Mumcuoglu, Engin Mumcuoglu
Vineyards: 3 hectares
Grape varieties: Seyval blanc, Reichensteiner, Dornfelder, Pinot noir Précoce
Not open to the public.

Tullens Vineyard

Tullens Fruit Farm, Pickhurst Lane, Pulborough, West Sussex RH20 1DA
Telephone: 01798 872108 and 01798 873800
Mobile: 07967 110639
E-mail: ivorkiverstein@aol.com
Contact: Ivor Kiverstein
Vineyards: 7.5 hectares
Grape varieties: Pinot noir, Chardonnay, Pinot Meunier
Open by appointment.

Ty Croes Vineyard

Ty Croes Farm, Dwyran, Llanfairpwll, Anglesey LL61 6RP, Wales
Telephone: 01248 440358
E-mail: info@tycroesvineyard.co.uk
Website: www.tycroesvineyard.co.uk
Contact: Harry Dean
Vineyards: 1.6194 hectares
Grape varieties: Phoenix, Solaris, Rondo, Regent, Seyval blanc
Open to the public. See website for details.

Tyringham Hall Vineyard

Tyringham Hall, Tyringham, Newport Pagnell, Buckinghamshire, MK16 9EX
Telephone: Office 020 7235 0422
Contact: Anton Bilton
E-mail: abilton@theravengroup.co.uk
Contact: George Edwards 07776 126051
Vineyards: 0.651 hectares
Grape varieties: Chardonnay, Pinot noir, Pinot Meunier
Not open to the public.

Tytherley Vineyard

The Garden House, West Tytherley, Salisbury, Wiltshire, SP5 1NL
Telephone: 01794 340644
Contact: Garth Alexander
Vineyards: 0.66 hectares
Grape varieties: Bacchus, MT, Triomphe
Not open to the public.

Upperton Vineyard

Upperton Farm, Tillington, Petworth, West Sussex GU28 0RD
Telephone: 01798 343958
Mobile: 07976 620230
E-mail: uppertonvineyards@hotmail.co.uk
Contact: Andrew and James Rogers
Vineyards: 5.77 hectares
Grape varieties: Pinot noir, Chardonnay, Pinot Meunier
Not open to the public.

Upperton Vineyard (Nyetimber)

c/o Nyetimber Vineyard, Gay Street, West Chiltington, West Sussex RH20 2HH
Location of vineyard: New Road, Upperton, Petworth, West Sussex GU28 9BG
See entry for Nyetimber Vineyard for contact details
Vineyards: 8.0972 hectares
Grape varieties: Pinot noir, Chardonnay, Pinot Meunier
Not open to the public.

Valley Farm Vineyards

Valley Farm, Wissett, Halesworth, Suffolk IP19 0JJ
Telephone: 01986 785535
Mobile: 07763 941806
E-mail: valleyfarmvineyards@tiscali.co.uk
E-mail: jrcraft@btinternet.com
Website: www.wissettwines.com
Contact: Jonathan Craft
Vineyards: 3.2 hectares
Grape varieties: Pinot noir, Pinot gris, Pinot Meunier, Auxerrois, MA
Open 10 am to 6 pm daily, March to December, but please telephone in advance.

Valley Farm Vineyards – sometimes also confusingly known as Wissett Wines – was planted in 1987 on a (for the time) traditional 12' x 6' GDC system on a site 27 metres above sea level. Some of the original varieties – Huxelrebe and MT – have been grubbed, but Auxerrois, Pinot gris and Pinot Meunier have been retained and Pinot noir added. Later plantings are all on a 12' x 8 ' modified Scott Henry syatem. Their 2005 Wissett Brut Reserve was awarded the 'Wine of the Year' and 'Best Sparkling Wine' trophies at the 2009 EAWG Wine of the Year Competition, and their 2006 Wissett Pink won Best Rosé in the same competition. Both wines were awarded Silver medals.

Vernon Lodge Vineyard

Tiffield, Towcester, Northamptonshire NN12 8AB
Telephone: 01327 350077
Mobile: 07973 941984
Contact: Mike Dean
Vineyards: 0.09 hectares
Grape varieties: MA, Siegerrebe, Madeleine Sylvaner
Open by appointment.

Vernon Lodge is a private hobby vineyard that relies on village help for harvesting and pruning and helpers are rewarded in kind. The vineyard, conveniently situated at the top of Mike Dean's garden, is in the best traditions of small non-commercial vineyards: immaculately maintained with not a weed or a shoot out of place and able to produce useful crops which are turned into award winning wines. The vines were planted in 1980 at 1.52 x 1.22 metres on a double Guyot system. The south-east-facing site is 114 metres above sea level and the soil is a loam over heavy clay. Madeleine x Angevine 7672 and Siegerrebe are reckoned to be the best varieties – Madeleine for its consistency and Siegerrebe for its exceptionally aromatic fruity wine. The wines are made in a well-insulated building, built in 1983 for the first vintage, which houses a small basket press, stainless steel and PVC tanks and a three-head filler, as well as the usual equipment needed to make wine. Mike tries to ensure a long, slow fermentation using cold-tolerant strains of yeast and bottles in the spring following harvest. His efforts are well worth it as Vernon Lodge wines regularly win awards in the Mercian Vineyards competitions.

Virginia Water Vineyard

Laithwaites, Unit 1, London Road, Virginia Water, Surrey GU25 4QU
Telephone: 0118 903 0903
Telephone: 01344 849267
E-mail: annelinder@directwines.co.uk
Contact: Anne Linder
Vineyards: 0.024 hectares
Grape varieties: Merlot
Open to the public.

Walton Brook Vineyard

Horseleys Farm, Burton-on-the-Wolds, Loughborough, Leicestershire, LE12 5TQ
Mobile: 07779 622858
E-mail: ceri@waltonbrook.com
Website: www.waltonbrook.com
Contact: Ceri Griffiths
Vineyards: 0.65 hectares
Grape varieties: Seyval blanc, Solaris, Regent, MA
Not open to the public.

Warden Abbey Vineyard

Southill Park, Biggleswade, Bedfordshire SG18 9LJ
Telephone: 01462 816226
E-mail: sue@wardenwines.co.uk
Website: www.wardenwines.co.uk
Contact: Sue Parke
Vineyards: 1.6194 hectares
Grape varieties: Bacchus, Regner, Reichensteiner, MT, MA
The vineyard is not generally open to the public, except certain weekends. See website for details.

Wareside Wines

Findon, New Hall, Wareside, Hertfordshire, SG12 7SD
Telephone: 01920 468733
E-mail: David.Briscoe@btgplc.com, david.briscoe@protherics.com
Contact: David Briscoe
Vineyards: 0.33 hectares
Grape varieties: Pinot noir Précoce, Bacchus
Open by appointment. Please telephone.

Warnham Vale Vineyard

The Old Barn, Northlands Road, Warnham, West Sussex RH12 3SQ
Telephone: 01306 627603
Mobile: 07717 220035 and 07717 220036
E-mail: dkmacleod@onetel.com
Contact: Kay Macleod
Vineyards: 1 hectare
Grape varieties: Seyval blanc, Schönburger, Reichensteiner
Not open to the public.

Warren Farm Vineyard

Warren Farm House, Warren Road, Guildford, Surrey GU1 2HF
Telephone: 020 3116 2959
Mobile: 07787 554465
E-mail: pmhargreaves@reedsmith.com
Contact: Mark Hargreaves
Vineyards: 0.4 hectares
Grape varieties: Bacchus, Schönburger, Rondo, Pinot noir Précoce
Not open to the public.

Watchcombe Vineyard

c/o Lyme Bay Winery, Shute, Axminster, Devon, EX13 7PW
Location of vineyard: Watchcombe, Shute, Axminster, Devon, EX13 7QN

Telephone: 01297 551355
Fax: 01297 551366
Mobile: 07812 554861
E-mail: technical@lymebaywinery.co.uk
Website: www.lymebaywinery.co.uk
Contact: Nigel Howard, Rob Corbett
Vineyards: 1 hectare
Grape varieties: Seyval blanc, Pinot noir
Winery open to the public. See website for details.

Wayford Vineyard

Wayford West Country Wines, Dunsham Lane, Wayford, Crewkerne, Somerset TA18 8QN
Telephone: 01460 74321
Telephone: 01360 72783
E-mail: stueylefevre@aol.com
Contact: Peter Woodward
Vineyards: 1.7 hectares
Grape varieties: Pinot noir
Not open to the public.

Webb's Land Vineyard

Webb's Land Farm, Tanfield Lane, Wickham, Hampshire PO17 5NS
Telephone: 01329 833633
Mobile: 07802 269316
Fax: 01329 834800
E-mail: plpeters@webbsland.com
E-mail: info@webbsland.com
Website: www.webbsland.com
Contact: Philip Peters
Vineyards: 3.21 hectares
Grape varieties: Reichensteiner, Bacchus, Pinot noir
Open for tours and tastings by appointment.

Webb's Land Vineyard, situated on the outskirts of Wickham village, in the heart of the Hampshire countryside, was originally planted in 1993. Covering some 3.21 hectares, this south-facing site of chalky loam was chosen for its perfect microclimate for vinegrowing. Great care is taken to produce the best quality grapes possible, including yield reduction and selective picking. Wine by the case can be bought from the vineyard.

Weir Quay Vineyard

Cleave Farm, Weir Quay, Bere Alston, Devon PL20 7BS
Telephone: 01822 840480
Contact: Lysbeth Gallup

Vineyards: 0.1 hectares
Grape varieties: Kernling
Not open to the public.

Welcombe Hills Vineyard

Vine Cottage, Kings Lane, Snitterfield, Stratford-on-Avon, Warwickshire CV37 0QB
Telephone: 01789 731071
Mobile: 07770 533767
E-mail: chrisgallim@hotmail.com
E-mail: info@welcombehills.co.uk
Website: www.welcombehills.co.uk
Contact: Chris and Jane Gallimore
Vineyards: 0.71 hectares
Grape varieties: Pinot noir, Bacchus, Dornfelder, Auxerrois, Pinot noir Précoce, Chardonnay, Sauvignon blanc, Kerner
Open to the public by appointment. See website for details.

Welcombe Hills Vineyard was planted in 2001 on land once owned by the Shakespeare family. With spectacular views towards Stratford-on-Avon, facing south and relatively frost-free with a *terroir* of clay with good drainage, this is probably as ideal a microclimate for grapes as can be found in the English Midlands.

Its owners, Chris and Jane Gallimore, began planting in 2001. An initial area of 0.40 hectares was planted with Pinot noir, Dornfelder and Bacchus. This was subsequently extended in May 2003 with a second planting of 1,200 more vines (Auxerrois, Chardonnay, and Pinot noir Précoce) and a third area of Sauvignon blanc, Seyval blanc and Bacchus trellised – as an experiment – using GDC instead of the more usual Double Guyot. Although a very small crop was picked in 2002, the first full harvest, the 2003, was taken to Three Choirs winery for winemaking and bottling.

Since then Welcombe Hills Vineyard has established a reputation at both local and national levels for producing award-winning wines of high quality. The very first vintage, Welcombe Hills Pinot Noir 2003, won Highly Commended at EWOTYC, together with Silver and 'Best Red' at the MVA competition and since then, notable successes have included a Silver Medal at EWOTYC for the Bacchus 2006. The current range of wines includes Pinot noir, Pinot noir Précoce, *blanc de noir*, Bacchus, Sparkling Bacchus, a rosé made from

Dornfelder and Bacchus, and Hollow Meadow (a blend of Bacchus and Auxerrois). After the bumper harvest of 2006 a more specialised range of red wines was released, including a Special Reserve Pinot noir and a Grand Reserve Pinot noir (matured in French oak barrels with different levels of toast), and a *blanc de blancs* is due for release in 2010

Welland Valley Vineyard

Vine Lodge, Marston Trussell, Market Harborough, Northamptonshire LE16 9TX
Telephone: 01858 434591
Mobile: 07989 091721
E-mail: welland@tiscali.co.uk
Website: www.welland-vineyard.com
Contact: David Bates
Vineyards: 0.8 hectares
Grape varieties: Reichensteiner, Bacchus, MA, Seyval blanc, Rondo, Regent, Acolon, Phoenix, Solaris, Orion, Dornfelder
Open to the public. See website for details.

Wernddu Vineyard

Wernddu Farm, Pen-y-Clawdd, Monmouth, Monmouthshire NP25 4BW, Wales
Telephone: 01600 740104
E-mail: info@wernddu-wine.co.uk
Website: www.wernddu-wine.co.uk
Contact: Frank Strawford
Vineyards: 0.5 hectares
Grape varieties: Pinot noir, Reichensteiner, Seyval blanc, Phoenix, Schönburger, plus test plantings of Ortega, Faberrebe, Bacchus, Sauvignon blanc
Open to the public. Guided tours of the vineyard and talks on production are available by appointment. See website for details of opening dates and times.

Frank and Leigh Strawford moved to the beautiful and tranquil Wernddu Farm near Monmouth in South Wales with their children Lauren and Taylor in 1999. 'Since we moved here, the nature all around has led us to a different way of thinking and we decided to set up a vineyard producing a range of organic wines, and, from our cider apple and perry pear trees, cider and perry.'

They started planting vines in March 2002, just 200 Reichensteiner to begin with, but over the next four years an additional 4,000 vines were planted. In September 2004 they registered with the Soil Association so that their produce could be considered 'organic'.

Much of their produce is sold at farmers' markets, food festivals and local shows, although they also have a tasting room next to their winery where visitors can sample their wines and buy local produce and crafts. Wernddu wines have a distinctive label; a portrait of the Strawford's teenage daughter Lauren, sketched by a street artist in

Paris. A further venture in 2006 was to start breeding Alpacas. These are unusual and friendly animals that have a wonderful fleece and some of these are depicted on the labels of their cider and perry.

Westward House Vineyard

Silchester Road, Little London, Tadley, Hampshire RG26 5EX
Telephone: 01256 851599
E-mail: sarmitage@origsoft.com
Contact: Sue Armitage
Vineyards: 0.1 hectares
Grape varieties: Not known
Not open to the public.

Westwell Wines

c/o 2 Foley Hill Cottages, Lower Street, Kent ME17 1TL
Location of vineyard: Westwell Lane, Charing, Kent TN27 0DR
Telephone: 01622 862102
Mobile: 07879 430721
E-mail: rowe.ja@pg.com
Website: www.westwellwines.co.uk
Contact: John Rowe
Vineyards: 4.84 hectares
Grape varieties: Chardonnay, Pinot noir, Pinot Meunier, Ortega
Not open to the public.

John Rowe acquired this site, situated in an area of outstanding natural beauty between Charing and Ashford, on the edge of the historic Pilgrims' Way in Kent, in 2007. The search for the ideal site took three years using ground & aerial geological mapping and has resulted in a site with 6 differing soil geologies. A bowl-shaped SSW facing hillside with a chalk sub-layer and sand-loam screed mixed with a high proportion of flint makes an ideal palette for growing sparkling & still wines. All the soils are very free-draining with high heat retention. Rowe comes from a viticultural background, having Italian wine-making in his blood. His aims are twofold: to produce exceptional quality wine as well as share his passion for wine within the local community.

Over the last two years the site has been improved with the addition of trees, meadows and the reinstatement of hedges. To date 16,000 vines have been planted (some by hand) trained to Double Guyot with further plantings planned. Varieties include quality clones of Chardonnay, Pinot Noir and Pinot Meunier as well as a new clone of Ortega. Much care has been taken to site each variety and clone in the best position within the vineyard. With already much interest regionally, this vineyard will 'sparkle' in the next few years! Wines are planned to be released in 2012/13.

White Castle Vineyard

Crodt Farm, Llanvetherine, Abergavenny, Monmouthshire, NP7 8RA, Wales
Telephone: 01783 821443
Mobile: 07810 563084
E-mail: robb.merchant@btinternet.com
Website: www.whitecastlevineyard.com
Contact: Robb Merchant, Nicola Merchant
Vineyards: 1.75 hectares
Grape varieties: Pinot noir, Regent, Rondo, Phoenix, Seyval blanc
Open to the public on Saturdays and Sundays by appointment.

White Horse Vineyard

Please see entry under Terlingham Vineyard

Whitworth Hall Vineyard

Whitworth Hall Country Park, Stanner's Lane, Spennymoor, County Durham DL16 7QX
Telephone: 01388 813311
E-mail: jill@whitworthhall.co.uk
Contact: Jill Lax
Vineyards: 0.1 hectares approx.
Grape varieties: Not known.

Wickham Vineyards

Wickham Holdings, Botley Road, Shedfield, Southampton, Hampshire SO32 2HL
Telephone: 01329 834042
Fax: 01329 834907
E-mail: info@wickhamvineyard.co.uk
Website: www.wickhamvineyard.co.uk
Contact: Wilhelm Mead
Winemaker: William Biddulph
Vineyards: 6.2 hectares
Grape varieties: Bacchus, Dornfelder, Faberrebe, Kerner, Pinot noir, Reichensteiner, Rondo, Schönburger, Triomphe, Würzer
Open to the public. See website for details.

Wickham Vineyards was originally planted between 1984 and 1987 by John and Caroline Charnley, who got planning permission to build a house on-site. They also converted a magnificent oak-framed barn into the winery and established both a shop and resturarant on the premises. They achieved a number of awards for their wines, but in 2000, following large losses as a member of the Lloyds insurance market, John was forced to sell. The new owners were Angela Baart and Gordon Channon who sold it in 2006 to the current owners, Wickham Holdings. The vineyards are planted on gentle south and south-west facing slopes between 50 m and 60 m above sea level and on a clay-loam soil over gravel. The vines are planted at 3.66 x 2.44-metres (12' x 8') and 3.66 x 2-metres and are mainly GDC trained.

Wickham has always had a good reputation for its wines and they make a wide range from their many different varieties. They currently have ten wines on their list – white, red, rosé still wines, plus white and rosé sparkling – and have a clutch of national and international medals and awards to their name including Tesco Drinks Awards Still Wine Winner for their 2008 Celebration Rosé. Their 2008 Vintage Selection Dry White is the only still English wine to be stocked by Berry Brothers.

In recent years considerable investment has gone into new machinery and equipment in the winery to cope with demand and there are now 130,000 litres of temperature-controlled stainless steel tanks, a new Bucher-Vaslin XPF 5 tonne bag press, a complete Bucher-Vaslin Delta destemmer-crusher and a Bucher-Vaslin Flavy FX1 cross-flow filter. Barrel-aged wines have always been a feature at Wickham (I seem to recall making an oak-aged wine for them in 1991 whilst I was at Lamberhurst which won a silver medal) and they currently have 80 *barriques* and are planning to obtain more. 2009 should see 110 tonnes of grapes crushed, their largest tonnage to date. This will include fruit from both Wickham and their vineyard at Shotley in Suffolk (see separate entry), plus some bought-in fruit and contract wines.

Wickham also has a restaurant on-site which is now under the management of Michelin star chef Atul Kochhar and has been re named 'Vatika'. This fine dining restaurant specialises in ground-breaking British cuisine, with a unique Indian twist and has recently been recognised as one of the top restaurants in England. Wickham Holdings also owns WineShare (bought from Andrew Gordon in 2007) which operates a sophisticated rent-a-vine scheme with three vineyards in France, one in Italy, plus Wickham. See www.wineshare.co.uk for further details.

Willhayne Vineyard

Willhayne Cottage, Colyton, Devon EX24 6DT
Telephone: 01297 553463
Mobile: 07746 950793
Fax: 01297 553463
E-mail: david.baxendale@virgin.net
Contact: David Baxendale
Vineyards: 0.155 hectares
Grape varieties: Bacchus, Phoenix, Pinot noir, Seyval blanc
Open by appointment.

Willhayne Vineyard is situated 0.75 km north-west of Colyton in the heart of East Devon. Planted in 2002 and 2003, the vines enjoy an elevated position over-looking the River Coly, 4.5 km inland from the Jurassic Coast. Between 1,000 and 1,500

bottles of still white and rosé wines and a small quantity of bottle-fermented sparkling wine are produced each year. The wines, made by Juliet White at Yearlstone Vineyard, have regularly won awards in both local and national competitions.

Willow Grange Vineyard and Winery

Street Farm, Stone Street, Crowfield, Ipswich, Suffolk IP6 9SY
Telephone: 01449 760612
Contact: Peter Fowles
Vineyards: 0.4 hectares
Grape varieties: MT, Optima, Ortega
Open by appointment.

Winchester Vineyard

20 Arthur Road, Winchester, Hampshire SO23 7EA
Telephone: 01962 863492
E-mail: julian.roderick.chisholm@googlemail.com
Contact: Julian Chisholm
Vineyards: 0.01 hectares
Grape varieties: Pinot noir, Triomphe, Seyval blanc, Chardonnay, Rondo
Open by appointment.

Windmill Vineyard

Windmill Hill Farm, Hellidon, Daventry, Northamptonshire, NN11 6LG
Telephone: 01327 262023
Fax: 0181 891 8291
E-mail: dohill@fsmail.net
Contact; Tom and Doreen Hillier-Bird
Vineyards: 0.26 hectares

Windmill Vineyard was planted in the late '70s and sits on the southern slope of a 200 m hill. When the Hillier-Birds bought it in 1986, the vineyard had been neglected for several years and the only treatment was "vicious pruning". Both red and white wines are produced, together with country wines from fruits either grown on the holding or picked from the local hedgerows. There is also an orchard and cider and perry are produced. The vineyard is open to the public every weekend, from Easter until October, and for the whole of December and tours are given to parties of 10/20, but must be booked in advance. Entrance to the vineyard shop is free, but guided tours are £3.50 per person.

Winner Hill Vineyard

Winner Hill Farm, Alderley, Gloucestershire GL12 7QT
Telephone: 01453 844237
E-mail: malcolmsargent@lineone.net
E-mail: quantumltd@lineone.net
Contact: Malcolm Sargent
Vineyards: 0.27 hectares
Grape varieties: Bacchus, Seyval blanc, Reichensteiner, Regent
Open by appointment.

Wisley Vineyard at the RHS Garden

RHS Wisley Gardens, Wisley Lane, Wisley, Woking, Surrey GU23 6QB
Telephone: 01483 224234
Telephone: 01483 212430
Mobile: Jim Arbury 07515 224763
Mobile: Alessandra Valsecchi 07949 719710
Fax: 01483 212343
E-mail: jimarbury@rhs.org.uk
E-mail: alessandravalsecchi@rhs.org.uk
Website: www.rhs.org.uk
Contact: Jim Arbury, Alessandra Valsecchi
Vineyards: 0.24 hectares
Grape varieties: Phoenix, Orion, plus collection of 100 other varieties
Part of RHS Wisley Gardens. Open daily except for Christmas Day. See website for details.

Wiston Estate Vineyard

c/o North Farm, London Road, Washington, Pulborough, RH20 4BB
Location of vineyard: Findon, Worthing, West Sussex BN14 0RL
Telephone: 01903 812129 Fax: 01903 879902
E-mail: wtrinick@wistonestate.co.uk
E-mail: dermot@wistonestate.co.uk
Contact: William Trinick 07767 203402
Contact: Dermot Sugrue 07887 507216 or 07941 284134
Vineyards: 6.546 hectares
Grape varieties: Chardonnay, Pinot noir, Pinot Meunier
Open by appointment.

The Wiston Estate is undoubtedly one of the most exciting new sparkling wine enterprises in the UK today. The 2,550 hectare estate, situated on the South Downs just north of Worthing in West Sussex, has been in the Goring family since 1743. In

2004, Harry and Pip Goring were approached by the Champagne house of Duval-Leroy to find a UK site to establish a sparkling wine enterprise, but after negotiations lapsed, they decided to go it alone and establish vineyards themselves, and asked me to be their consultant.

The vineyard at Wiston was planted on a south-facing chalk bank, well sheltered from the prevailing winds, and was established with the three classic Champagne varieties: 55 per cent Chardonnay, 36 per cent Pinot noir and 9 per cent Pinot Meunier at an average density of 4,000 vines per hectare. The philosophy is one of sustainable viticulture and no herbicides are used, instead a Boisselet intervine cultivator from Burgundy is employed for weed control.

In October 2006, Dermot Sugrue, previously winemaker at Nyetimber (who, when looking for additional grape suppliers for Nyetimber, had already identified the Wiston site as exceptional) was brought in to manage the vineyards and, in a joint venture with the Gorings, establish a winery. This will be an innovative, gravity-fed, winery using a traditional Coquard Champagne press (the only one of its kind in the UK) and will also use a wide range of old Burgundian barrels for fermentation and *élevage* of selected musts. A temperature controlled lees-aging cellar is currently under construction in readiness for the first vintage in 2008. Sparkling wines will be

made under contract for several other vineyards, including Jenkyn Place at Alton in Hampshire and nearby Storrington Priory. The Wiston Estate wine growing enterprise promises much. With the quality chalk-soil site, together with Sugrue's experience in making exceptional sparkling wines, this vineyard is one to watch over the next few years.

Wodetone Vineyard

Spence Farm, Wootton Fitzpaine, Dorset DT6 6DF
Telephone: 01297 561364
Mobile: 07813 051697
E-mail: nigelriddle@hotmail.co.uk
Contact: Nigel Riddle
Vineyards: 10.92 hectares
Grape varieties: Chardonnay, Pinot noir, Pinot Meunier
Open by appointment.

Wodetone Vineyard was planted in 2007 and 2008 and consists of 40% Chardonnay, 40% Pinot noir and 20% Pinot Meunier and they are all Scott Henry trained. The soil is a sandy loam over greensand with a great deal of flint, which, by using a stone-burying rotovator, has been piled into rows under the vines to store heat and reflect light. The site is a south-facing slope, three kilometres inland from Charmouth, with spectacular views over Lyme Bay. A vineyard at Wootton Fitzpaine, belonging to Aiulf the Chamberlain, Sheriff of Dorset, was recorded in the 1086 Doomsday Book and is thought to have been planted on the same farm as the current vineyard. The name Wodetone is Saxon for 'a wooded place' and is the ancient name of the village. The grapes are grown under contract to the nearby Furleigh estate and the first small crop is expected in 2009.

Womack's Vineyard

25 Eastville Terrace, Harrogate, North Yorkshire HG1 3HJ
Telephone: 07802 358737
E-mail: jgwomack@hotmail.com
Contact: Jonathan Womack
Vineyards: 0.02 hectares
Grape varieties: Bacchus
Not open to the public.

Wooldings Vineyard

c/o Coates and Seely Ltd, Northington House, Overton, Hampshire, RG25 3DJ
Location of vineyard: Wooldings Farm, Whitchurch, Hampshire RG28 7QT
Telephone: 01256 771461
Mobile: 07799 478888
E-mail: nicholas.coates@northingtonhouse.com

Contact: Nicholas Coates
Vineyards: 10.4 hectares
Grape varieties: Chardonnay, Pinot noir, Pinot Meunier
Not open to the public.

Wooldings Vineyard was originally planted between 1989 and 1997 by Charles Cunningham on his family farm in a sheltered valley on the chalky Hampshire Downs. The site is between 90 and 120 metres above sea level and the orginal site is mainly south-west facing. The soil is a chalky clay-loam, free draining and well suited to vines. Cunningham sadly met an untimely death whilst on holiday on the Balinese island of Lombok in April 2002 and his mother, Daphne, was left to manage the vineyard (and the rest of the farm). For several years it was run by ex-Denbies viticulturalist Bert Martyn and the grapes were used by Somborne Valley Vineyards at nearby Kings Somborne. During Cunningham's time the Wooldings wines won several awards. The 1992 Schönburger was WVA 'Wine of the Year' in 1994 and the 1992 Wooldings Brut was T&CVA 'Wine of the Year' in 1995. A Wooldings wine was served by the Queen at a gala dinner in Paris in November 1998.

In early 2009, Daphne Cunningham formed a partnership with a new company, Coates and Seely Ltd, to run Wooldings Vineyard. The new company is a joint venture between Nicholas Coates, who was head of RBS High Yield Group and who resigned from the City in 2006 to pursue a life in the country, and Christian Seely, English-born managing director of *AXA Millésimes*, the wine arm of AXA, the French insurance company, whose properties include Châteaux Pichon-Longueville Baron, Suduiraut and Petit Village in Bordeaux, Belles Eaux in the Languedoc, top Port producer Quinta do Noval in the Douro Valley and Tokay producer Disznókő in Hungary. Seely is also a shareholder in Quinta da Romaneira, a Port estate which has been completely restored and where a luxury (€1,100 a night) boutique hotel has been built. Coates and Seely met whilst doing their MBAs at top French business school INSEAD.

The restoration of Wooldings started in October 2008 and progressed in May 2009 with the planting of 8-hectares of Champagne varieties (55% Pinot noir and 45% Chardonnay) on the south-east facing site opposite the original vines. Prior to planting, a soil sample was sent to a Bordeaux soil laboratory who, not knowing its provenance, declared it to be *"un sol très Champenoise"* – felt to be a good omen by Coates and Seely. Apart from the 1-ha of Chardonnay and Pinot noir which were planted by Cunningham, the remainder of the original 4-ha will be top-grafted in 2010 with Pinot noir and Chardonnay. The winery is being renovated and a new Bucher Vaslin Inertys controlled atmosphere press has been bought. The winemaker will be Seely's oenoligist wife Corinne Chevalier, previously winemaker at Domaine de Chevalier in Bordeaux. Other consultants will also be used.

Coates and Seely's aim is to produce a top English sparkling wine, or as they put it: "a sparkling wine that reflects the unique characteristics of the English chalk *terrior* with the established crafts and skills of the *Champenoise* wine-maker". With Seely's experience and expertise in all matters viti- and vini-cultural, Coates' business skills and their combined vision and enthusiasm, this is definitely a project to watch.

Wootton Vineyard

c/o Bagborough Winery, Pylle, Shepton Mallet, BA4 6SX
Location of vineyard: North Wootton, Shepton Mallet, Somerset, BA4 4AG
Telephone: 01749 831146
Fax: 01749 830832
Mobile: 07831 773737
E-mail: brooksbank@bagborough.freeserve.co.uk
Contact: Steve Brooksbank
Vineyards: 0.1 hectares
Grape varieties: Seyval blanc
Not open to the public.

Until March 1999, Wootton Vineyard was owned by Colin and Sue Gillespie, two pioneers of the revival of commercial viticulture in the UK and in their day, producers of some of the best English wines. Colin, who took early retirement from the Royal Engineers in the 1970s, became interested in viticulture after paying a visit to nearby Pilton Manor, then owned by Nigel Godden. In the week that he retired from the army, he started to plant the first of his vines: 4000 Müller-Thurgau and Seyval Blanc. At one time the vineyard, planted on a steep south facing site with rich red soil between 24 and 37-metres above sea level, extended to over 5-hectares.

Colin mastered the art of winemaking quickly and success in tastings and competitions soon came for Wootton. One of the wines from their first vintage (1973) came top in a blind tasting of English and Continental wines held by the South West Vinegrowers Association at Harveys of Bristol. In 1976, their Schönburger was awarded the Challenge Cup for the best wine from that vintage in the South West Vineyards Association's Competition, and went on to win joint second place at the English Wine of the Year Competition. The 1977 Müller-Thurgau won an EVA gold medal in 1979 and the 1981 Schönburger and 1985 Seyval blanc both won the Gore-Browne Trophy. Colin was also a noted contract winemaker and made wines for numerous local vineyards. He was a director of the EVA for many years and Chairman between 1981 and 1987. Colin was affectionately known as 'good lunch Gillespie' for his habit of starting reports on meetings that he had attended with one of the many organisations with which a Chairman has to deal by saying 'Well, we had a jolly good lunch ...'

The vineyard has been severely reduced in size since the Gillespie days and is now down to *a bare quarter of an* acre according to local winemaker, Steve Brooksbank, who looks after the vineyard and uses the grapes for his own wines.

Wootton Park Vineyard

The Gables, Wootton, Canterbury, Kent CT4 6RT
Telephone: 01303 844334
Contact: B. H. Prichard
Vineyards: 0.81 hectares
Grape varieties: Seyval blanc, MA, Chardonnay
Not open to the public.

Worthenbury Vineyard

The Old Rectory, Worthenbury, Wrexham LL13 0AW, Wales
Telephone: 01948 770257
E-mail: sales@worthenburywines.co.uk
Website: www.worthenburywines.com
Contact: Martin Seed
Vineyards: 0.25 hectares
Grape varieties: Sauvignon blanc, Pinot noir, Chardonnay
Open by appointment.

Wrangling Lane Vineyard

c/o 187 Wood Road, Heybridge, Maldon, Essex CM9 4AU
Location of vineyard: Great Buckland, Luddesdown, Gravesend, Kent ME13
Telephone: 07967 585632
E-mail: wranglinglane@tiscali.co.uk
Contact: Robin Smith
Vineyards: 0.0675 hectares
Grape varieties: Seyval blanc, Bacchus, Rondo, Pinot noir
Not open to the public.

Wraxall Vineyard

Wraxall, Shepton Mallet, Somerset BA4 6RQ
Telephone: 01749 860331
E-mail: jackybrayton@btconnect.com
Website: www.wraxallvineyard.co.uk
Contact: Jacky Brayton
Vineyards: 2.28 hectares
Grape varieties: MA, Bacchus, Seyval blanc, Pinot noir
Open by appointment. See website for details.

Wroxeter Roman Vineyard

Wroxeter, Shrewsbury, Shropshire SY5 6PQ
Telephone: 01743 761888
E-mail: wine@wroxetervineyard.co.uk
E-mail: wroxeterwine@btconnect.com

Website: www.wroxetervineyard.co.uk
Contact: David Millington
Vineyards: 2.685 hectares
Grape varieties: Dornfelder, Dunkelfelder, Regner, MA, Reichensteiner, Phoenix
Open to the public. See website for details.

Wychwood House Vineyard

Shermanbury, Horsham, West Sussex, RH13 8HE
Telephone: 01403 710328
E-mail: nic.packwood@wychwoodhouse.org
Contact: Nic Packwood
Vineyards: 0.012 hectares
Grape varieties: Huxelrebe, Schönburger, Faberrebe, Bacchus, Dornfelder
Not open to the public.

Wyfold Vineyard

Wyfold Lodge, Wyfold, Oxfordshire RG4 9HU
Telephone: 01491 680495 or 0118 9723683
E-mail: cherrythompson@mac.com or barbara.laithwaite@directwines.com
Contact: Cherry Postlethwaite or Barbara Laithwaite
Vineyards: 1.188 hectares
Grape varieties: Chardonnay, Pinot noir, Pinot Meunier
Not open to the public. Maiden Vintage 2006 to be released late 2009

Wyfold Vineyard originated from an idea of Cherry's late husband, the celebrated Formula One engineer Harvey Postlethwaite. Having embraced the Italian life at Ferrari, Harvey had often dreamed of a vineyard back home in England, so Cherry, formed a partnership with her friend Barbara Laithwaite (owner and director of Laithwaites, the largest privately owned wine retailers in the UK) to start the vineyard based in the Chilterns. The first 1,000 vines were planted in 2003 and the hectareage completed in 2006 with a fruitful harvest yielding a maiden wine for release in 2009.

This is an owner/worker vineyard, and help from family and friends, and enthusiastic Laithwaite wine teams, many of whom have trained at Plumpton, ensure a high standard of viticulture. The grapes are sent to RidgeView to be vinified by Michael and Simon Roberts who have also been great mentors in this project.

Recent additions to the Wyfold Vineyard partnership include Ben Postlethwaite

(Cherry's son) himself involved in motorsport and Henry Laithwaite (Barbara's son), an independent winemaker and Bordeaux viticulturist. The picture was taken in 2006 just as they had finished planting the last lot of vines.

Wyken Vineyard

Stanton, Bury St Edmunds, Suffolk IP31 2DW
Telephone: 01359 250287
Fax: 01359 253821
E-mail: vineyard@wykenvineyards.co.uk
Website: www.wykenvineyards.co.uk
Contact: Charles Macready
Vineyards: 2.76 hectares
Grape varieties: Bacchus, Triomphe, Pinot noir, Auxerrois, Kernling, MA, Léon Millot
Open to the public. See website for details.

Wylye Valley Vineyard

Sutton End, Crockerton, Warminster, Wiltshire BA12 8BB
Telephone: 01985 846767
Mobile: 07768 287064
Contact: Paul Dale
Vineyards: 3.6 hectares
Grape varieties: Regner, Kernling, Seyval blanc
Open to the public: Monday to Saturday, 10 am to 5.30 pm.

Yearlstone Vineyard

Bickleigh, Tiverton, Devon EX16 8RL
Telephone: 01884 855700
Mobile: 07963 800550
Fax: 01884 855726
E-mail: roger@yearlstone.co.uk
E-mail: juliet@yearlstone.co.uk
Website: www.yearlstone.co.uk
Contact: Roger White, Juliet White
Vineyards: 3 hectares
Grape varieties: Pinot noir, Pinot gris, MA, Bacchus, Seyval blanc, Dornfelder
Winery and café open to the public all year-round. See website for full details.

Yearlstone is Devon's oldest vineyard and belonged to viticultural pioneer Gillian Pearkes until her untimely death in 1993. Gillian was one of the best-known people involved in the revival of UK viticulture and was an author and lecturer and made a series of videos on winegrowing and winemaking in England. She was a founder member of the EVA and at that time had a small vineyard at Tillworth, near Axminster, which had been planted in 1963 when she was only 18. In 1969 she moved to Rhyll Manor, near Dulverton, taking her vineyard with her and then again, in 1976, moved once more, this time to more permanent surroundings at Yearlstone. In 1969, the first of her books on viticulture was published. *Growing Grapes in Britain*, published by the Amateur Winemaker magazine, helped lay the foundations of many early vineyards and was republished throughout the 1970s. Her second book on the subject, *Vinegrowing in Britain* was published in 1982 and revised in 1989. Gillian was never content to let sleeping dogs lie and was forever trialling new grape varieties and new ways of growing them. In 1976 she was awarded a Nuffield Farming Scholarship and toured Europe's vineyard regions (including a visit to Geisenheim in Germany where I first met her) and the report she wrote after her grand tour concluded that viticulture was a viable occupation in Great Britain. It is still worth reading and my copy is well thumbed.

In 1994 Yearlstone Vineyard was bought by Roger White, a journalist and BBC presenter, and his wife Juliet. The vineyard was expanded from 1 to 3 hectares and Seyval blanc and Reichensteiner were planted. While Gillian's preference was for very narrow double Guyot trained vines, the Whites prefer the wider-spaced Scott Henry training and the original vines have been converted. Juliet White, who had a background in interior design, took a course on viticulture and winemaking at Plumpton College to prepare for her new rôle as winemaker and now makes wine for around a dozen vineyards in Devon, Cornwall and Somerset. In 2007 she made eight out of just over 60 wines from the 2006 vintage awarded Highly Commended and above at the 2007 EWOTYC. She achieved seven commendations and above for 2005 wines at the previous year's competition – the first time Yearlstone wines had entered this event. In her first competition a rosé made for Pebblebed Vineyards won a Gold medal, one of only two Gold medals awarded for wines of that vintage. Yearlstone has invested heavily in its winery, first built in 2001, with a new 3-tonne membrane press, Speidel variable capacity stainless steel tanks, a cold stabilisation facility and a GAI-2500 filler with screwcapper, one of the few wineries to have this facility. The overall capacity of the winery is 100,000 litres. Yearlstone's wines have certainly come a long way since its early days when Gillian made some of the most uncompromising wines in the country (I still have a half-bottle of a Yearlstone Red that I bought in about 1982 which I am sure will still be too young when I eventually open it) and Juliet has proved herself a talented winemaker.

At one stage, Yearlstone did not have their wines classified as Regional or Quality

Wines, preferring the anonymity of UK Table Wine status which denied them the right to label their wines with a vintage or grape variety. Hence their wines were labelled 'Yearlstone No.1' through to 'Yearlstone No.6' – which sounded to me more like snuff mixture than wine! For the past two years however, their wines have been put in for, and achieved, Regional Wine status, a welcome change, although they still stick to their No.1 to No.6 labelling.

Yearlstone is a founder member of the Devon Wine Trail and organiser of the Devon Wine Weeks, so far the biggest regional celebration of English Wine Week. Yearlstone's first sparkling wine was its 2004 Vintage Brut which was recommended by Oz Clarke on BBC One in autumn 2007, and which gained equal marks with New Zealand's Montana sparkling wine at a Devon vs NZ wine competition held in 2007 at the wine school of Master of Wine Alastair Peebles. The small production run of 1,300 bottles sold out in less than six months. In the 2008 EWOTYC they won two Silver and four Bronze Medals, as well as two Highly Commendeds.

Group tours including talks on English wine, winemaking and full tastings are available, along with supper for groups of no more than 25. In 2009 Yearlstone revived its long tradition of holding wine education courses, opening a new purpose-built lecture and wine tasting room . The first course there was held there on July 9 - "How to Make a Living from a Vineyard". A second course was held later in July on "Practical Issues around building your own winery". Yearlstone's first exclusively contracted vineyard has been planted and other local growers are being encouraged to plant. In the 2009 EWOTYC, Yearlstone-made wines won nine awards, five for Yearlstone's own wines, and four for other vineyards who have their wine made by Juliet. (Portesham, Manstree, Avonleigh & Pebblebed).

Yorkshire Heart Vineyard

Kirk Hammerton Lane, Green Hammerton, York, North Yorkshire YO26 8BS
Telephone: 01423 330716   Fax: 01423 330716
E-mail: krisspak2@tiscali.co.uk
Contact: Chris Spakouskas
Vineyards: 1.8 hectares
Grape varieties: Ortega, Solaris, Rondo, Pinot noir, Dornfelder, Seyval blanc, Siegerrebe, Acolon, Chardonnay, Pinot gris, Gamay, Cabernet Franc
Open by appointment.

Did the British invent Champagne?

Although it's a nice thought, I don't think that the British can really claim to have invented a place in France, but there *is* evidence to suggest that they played a significant part in the development of a sparkling wine named after it. Intrigued?

The story starts, rather strangely, with the King, his navy and the need for oak. It took a large number of oak trees to find enough timber of the right size and shape (shape very important – all those ribs and curved bits and pieces) to build a large warship and King James I, or more especially one of his admirals, Sir Robert Mansel[1] (1573–1656), was worried that England was running out of them. The main problem was that charcoal burners, a pretty indiscriminate bunch of folk, were taking all the oaks before the King's shipbuilders and foresters could get to them. Charcoal was in big demand, especially where high temperatures were needed such as in metal working and – this is where we start getting on to wine – for glass production. On 23 May 1615 the King issued Royal Proclamation No 42 which banned the use of charcoal in both glassmaking and iron smelting, forcing the iron and glass-makers to start experimenting with other fuels, namely coal and oil shale. Mansel, who apparently was in league with the King when it came to selling oak to the Navy at double the usual price, then became interested in glass production himself and between 1618 and 1622, Mansell, in conjunction with fellow Welshman James Howell (1594-1666) sought out foreign glassmakers and experimented with two different fuels: oil shale at Kimmeridge, Dorset and coal in the Forest of Dean. In secret, Mansel and Howell perfected strong bottle glass and in 1623 Mansel was granted a hotly-contested Royal Patent giving him a monopoly over all coal-fired glassware.

Mansel, a man of many parts (Treasurer of the Navy, MP for King's Lynn, Carmarthen, Glamorgan and Lostwithiel, and industrialist), was instrumental in setting up glass-works in a number of places – London, the Isle of Purbeck, Milford Haven, the Trent Valley and Newcastle-on-Tyne) – which used coal instead of charcoal for heating the furnaces. This meant that the glass coming from these furnaces was significantly stronger due to the much higher combustion temperatures. Glassmakers also started adding iron and manganese ores to the raw materials which, although initially done for purely cosmetic purposes, also had the side effect of making the glass even stronger.

---

1   The name Mansel is sometimes spelt Mansell and even Maunsell.

What all this meant was that our glass bottles were in all respects better than those of the French; they were far stronger and more able to withstand the considerable forces generated by the secondary fermentation. One has to remember that in those days all wine was shipped to Britain in wooden casks and the actual bottling was carried out by vintners in the great wine-trade centres such as London, Bristol and Leith – a practice which lasted until relatively recently for many Clarets, Burgundies and Ports. Vintners, as well as inn-keepers who also did much of the bottling for their own establishments, would routinely bottle 'young wines' (wines from the previous vintage) which would have sometimes still contained unfermented sugars (winters were colder then and natural yeasts stopped working when wineries got too cold) and – more importantly – some viable yeast cells. As the spring turned to summer and the vintner's and inn-keeper's cellars warmed up, some of those bottles would have started re-fermenting and of course, given strong bottles and decent corks, the CO_2 produced would have added a little sparkle to the wine. Obviously some customers liked this and asked for more. It didn't take long for those involved to work out that if they added a little extra sugar to almost any wine, used strong bottles and tied the corks on with string, the sparkling effect could be achieved on demand!

James Crowden, author of *Ciderland* in a talk given at the Royal Society on 10 October 2008 entitled *Sparkling Cider and the Evolution of the Méthode Champenoise* said that spakling cider was a well known product in the 1600s and between 1628 and 1632, Lord Scudamore (later to be appointed Charles 1st's ambassador to France) experimented with *bottles, corks cordage etc and a new lock for the sydar* [sic] *house*

door. He was helped in his experiments by Sir Kenelm Digby (1603-1665) who was described as *a pirate and dilettante, Ornament of All England.* He was also a *keen experimenter with glass, oxygen and carbon dioxide* as well as *a swordsman and keen on duelling.* He – and his wife Venetia on her death-bed – were both painted by Van Dyke (picture on the left). Digby – whose father had been the first of the Gunpowder plotters to be executed – owned an estate in the Forest of Dean and was therefore well positioned to experiment with coal-fired glass production. He is also credited as the first person to use corks to seal bottles and preserve wine for longer periods than had hitherto been possible, as wines with dissolved carbon dioxide in them and sealed in strong bottles with leak-proof corks could last many months longer than wines kept at normal pressures. In 1662 he was credited with the invention of the modern wine bottle and his glass was known by the French as *verre Anglais.* Also in 1662, on 10 November, the Reverend John Beale (1608-1683) presented a paper at the recently founded Royal Society on cider and mentioned using *a walnut of sugar when bottling.* This idea had been contained in a book by Ralph Austen (1612-1676) who was the Parliamentarian Proctor of Oxford University and ran a cider works there between 1653 and 1657. The book, *The Treatise on Fruit Trees and Spiritual Use of an Orchard* told how cider might be kept *perfect for a good many years* by keeping the bottles *well stopt with corks, and hard wax melted thereon and boun down with a Packthread* [sic]. In the second edition, published in 1657, an extra quote was inserted into the margin which stated that cider makers should *put into each bottle a lump or two of hard sugar, or sugar bruised.*

Much of this came to light when Tom Stevenson, the well known expert on Champagne and sparkling wines, wrote in his book *Christie's World Encyclopaedia of Champagne and Sparkling Wine* (Absolute Press 2000) the he had discovered what he believed to be the first mention of a technique to make wine (that is wine made from garpes and not cider) sparkling *on purpose*. A paper, written by a Dr Christopher Merrett[2] (sometimes spelt Merret) was presented to the newly formed Royal Society on 17 December 1662 and stated that: *our wine coopers of recent times use vast quantities of sugar and molasses to all sorts of wine to make them brisk and sparkling*[3]. In July 1663 two other cider-makers, Sir Paul Neil and Captain Silas Taylor also presented papers to the Royal Society. Neil mentioning using *a nutmeg of sugar* and Taylor described bottling cider and keeping it in cool water which makes it *drink quick and lively, it comes into the glass not pale or troubled, but bright yellow, with a speedy vanishing nittiness*[4] *(as the vintners call it) which evaporates with a sparkling and whizzing noise.* All this was some 6 years before Dom Pérignon (widely touted as the 'inventor' of Champagne) arrived at the Abbey of Hautvillars and some 30 years before the French themselves even claim that Champagne was made by the process of secondary fermentation!

In *Vinetum Brittanicum, or a Treatise on Cider* by John Worlidge, published in 1676, there is extensive mention of bottles, corks and sugar and the first description of storing bottles horizontally with their necks down in a wooden rack – perhaps the precursor of today's *pupitre*? In *Vinetum Angliæ*, written by "D.S." and published in 1690 and sold by "G. Conyers, at the Gold Ring in Little Britain (Price One Shilling)", mention is made of adding *little lumps of Loaf-sugar* to cider so that *it may the better feed and keep.* "D.S." then continues when describing Perry making, by saying *work it as the Cyder, and put in a few lumps of Loaf Sugar for it to feed on; and being well fined, and drawn off, it will drink brisk, and exceeding pleasant.*

---

2   Dr. Merret came from the Gloucestershire village of Winchcombe where there is a street called Vineyard Street and one wonders if his interest in wine was in any way stimulated by this. The street is presumably named after a monastic vineyard maintained by the monks at Winchcombe Abbey, founded in 798 by Cenwulf, King of the Mercians, which survived until it was 'surrendered' on 23 December, 1539.

3   Brisk meant slightly effervescent.

4   The Oxford Dictionary decribes 'nittiness' as being: *full of small air bubbles (referring to wine).*

It would appear therefore, that cider makers and vintners in England were well versed and instructed in the art of making sparkling wines some while before Champagne was first decribed as effervescent – *le vin du diable* – by Madame de Sévigné, a well-known diarist and letter writer, in 1689.

Development of Champagne

The idea that Champagne (and for that matter all other bottle-fermented sparkling wines) were ever anything other than the product we know and love today is hard to believe, but a look back through some old wine books shows otherwise.

Sir Edward Barry, a Fellow of both the Royal College of Physicians and of the Royal Society, writing in 1775, over 100 years after Merrett, wrote: *for some years the French and English have been particularly fond of the sparkling, frothy Champaigns* [sic]. *The former have almost entirely quitted that depraved taste; nor does it now much prevail here.* Barry goes on to warn against drinking wines that have: *active gas, so powerfully injurious to the nervous system* and says that those: *that have indulged themselves too freely, in the use of these Wines, are particularly affected with a tremor in the nerves and spasmodic rheumatic pains.* Hardly the sort of ringing endorsement that the Champenois and their PR departments would like to see talked about today! Barry also quoted his friend Charles Hamilton, owner of the vineyard at Painshill Place, who said about his winemaking techniques: *the only art I ever used was putting three pounds of white sugar-candy to some of the hogsheads ... in order to conform to a rage that prevailed to drink none but very sweet Champaign.*

The French did not really start using bottles for wine until the mid-1700s and it took them a long while to perfect a bottle to take the pressures of Champagne. Cyrus Redding writes, in *A History and Description of Modern Wines,* published in 1833, about the problems associated with the bottles used in Champagne. He says that they: *are jingled together in pairs, one against the other, and those that break are carried in account against the maker.* This however, was by no means a foolproof test of a bottle's integrity and despite inspections for air bubbles and obvious cracks, many of the bottles broke while undergoing secondary fermentation and maturation. Redding writes at some length about the precautions the workers have to go to in order to protect themselves against flying glass and states that it is normal for between 4 per cent and 10 per cent of bottles to break in store, although: *sometimes, however, it amounts to thirty and forty percent.* During the spring and summer (when bottles were likely to explode) visitors to Champagne cellars were issued with metal masks!

Although Redding devotes a whole chapter to Champagne – some 24 pages – going into great detail about hectareages of vines, the amount of wine made in the region, the varieties used, the exact processes involved with the initial fermentation, the way the wines were bottled, had their corks inserted and wired on, etc. – he is genuinely perplexed by the way in which the sparkle is created! He says that it is a result of the: *carbonic acid gas produced in the process of fermentation* and that this is due to the: *saccharine* [becoming] *decomposed*. This shows that he was aware of the basic principle, but the idea that this could be controlled and provoked at will by the addition of extra sugar and yeast at bottling (one of the cornerstones of the modern *Méthode Champenoise*) seems to have escaped him.

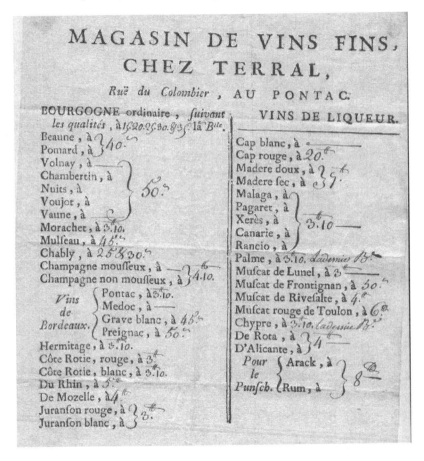

Wine list from 1760s, showing both 'mousseux' and 'non mousseux' Champagne

Was it that the French themselves did not appreciate this? I suspect so. Redding states with some authority that: *the effervescence of the Champagne wine, considered in all its bearings, is most uncertain and changeable, even in the hands of those best acquainted, through experience, with its management.* He continues and says that there are many factors that: *all have a varied and often inexplicable influence on the phenomena of effervescence.* One wonders who it was that first fully appreciated that an addition of 18 grams of sugar per bottle to a bone dry wine, plus some active yeast, gave the required degree of CO_2 pressure (5–6 bars), together with an increase of around 1.25 per cent alcohol? Certainly not Dom Pérignon!

Redding was not alone in his ignorance of the facts about the secondary fermentation. David Booth, who wrote a highly respected book called *The Art of Winemaking in all its Branches* published a year later in 1834, was equally in ignorance of why some wines sparkle and others do not. Indeed he states quite categorically that: *the theory of fermentation, as laid down by Chaptal, is of little value to practical men*! (In 1807 Chaptal had proposed that sugar was the necessary ingredient for fermentation to take place. In fact it wasn't until Louis Pasteur started on the problem in the 1860s and proposed that it was yeasts that were the real culprits, that fermentation was properly explained.)

This ignorance about the relationship between sugar, yeast and the sparkle in Champagnes continued to perplex wine writers. W. H. Roberts, writing in the 5th edition of his *British Wine-Maker and Domestic Brewer* in 1849 quotes a Dr Shannan (his name was actually Shannon) who says that: *for about twenty years last past, the gust* [taste] *of the French has been determined for a frothy wine* and goes on to wonder about how the *froth* gets into the wine. He writes: *some believe that it proceeds from the force of the drugs that they* [the French] *put in it, which makes it froth so strongly*. Later he dismisses this possibility and puts it down entirely to inexplicable natural circumstances which are all to do with the time of bottling. He states with some certainty that: *one may always be sure to have the wine perfectly frothy when it is bottled from the 10th to the 15th of the month of March* (in the year after the harvest).

Thudichum and Dupré's *Complete manual of viticulture and Œnology* of 1872 has a long section in it about the winemaking techniques used in Champagne, describing the bottling in some detail, but covering the question of how the sparkle gets into the bottle in a few lines. They state that: *as the Rhenish wines after their fermentation and ageing no longer contain any sugar, it is necessary to add an amount of sugar so that the whole of the sugar in the wine to be fermented is 2%. This presence of 2% of sugar, the manufacturer of Champagne mostly secures by mixing young wines only.*

Even though the authors of this book go into some detail about the exact amount of sugar required to provide the required amount of *mousse* (so called, they say, because when it foams from the bottle it resembles a little patch of moss) and advise the use of a *Schintz's Manometer* to test when fermenting bottles of champagne are nearing their breaking point due to excess pressures, it is clear that the system of Champagne manufacture was, until relatively recently, very haphazard and relied upon chance to a great degree.

The system seems to have been that the young wines i.e. those from the previous year, were allowed to ferment as slowly as possible so that some of them would stop fermenting and some of the original natural sugar, together with whatever was added at harvest time, remained in the wine when the weather turned cold. By March, when the weather might be expected to start warming up, these sweeter partially fermented wines were blended with dry wines, whether from the previous or even older vintages, so that at bottling, some residual sugar was retained in order for the secondary fermentation to take place. This ensured that the wines sparkled, although not as consistently, or probably as much, as they do today.

So, whether or not it was *our wine coopers* or not who first discovered that sugar was required in wine in order for the sparkle to appear, who knows? It does seem however, that only 100 years ago, the precise mechanism of this phenomenon was not fully understood or appreciated and was put down as much to magic as to science. It's a nice thought though, that perhaps the English had something to do with the development one of France's most famous wines and that the modern production of English and Welsh sparkling wines is actually a tradition that goes back at least as far as Dr Merrett's 1662 paper.

The author paying homage to Dom Perignon
(Photograph courtesy of Giles Fallowfield)

Jack Ward, Horam Manor and Merrydown

No history of the revival of viticulture in the British Isles would be complete without recognising the part played by Jack Ward, his vineyards at Horam in East Sussex and the company he co-founded, the Merrydown Wine Company.

Merrydown was founded in 1946 by two friends, Ian Howie and Jack Ward, to make cider and fruit wines from local Sussex produce. Jack, who had graduated from Trinity College, Cambridge with a degree in English, had become interested in wine while studying his first love, music, at the *Frankfurt Conservatorium*. In the early 1950s, he became interested in the revival of viticulture and in what Ray Brock, whom he visited, was doing at Oxted. In 1953 he planted six vines, obtained from Oxted, in the grounds of Horam Manor: two Riesling Sylvaner (Müller-Thurgau), two Madeleine Royale and two Gamay Hâtif des Vosges.

No sooner had these trial vines been planted than a property known as The Grange, a house with several acres of garden attached, came up for sale across the road from Horam Manor and was bought by the company to provide accommodation for some of its employees. Ward promptly claimed the gardens and in 1954 planted a 2-acre vineyard. This was at a time when Hambledon was the only other vineyard in the country, planted two years earlier in 1952 and yet to produce its first harvest. The varieties that Ward chose do not seem to be recorded, although one of them was certainly Müller-Thurgau, as a wine from this variety from the Grange vineyard was served to Prince Philip at a dinner held at The Vintners Hall in London. In 1962, however, with the vineyard only just reaching maturity, the company decided that the offer they had received from a local builder to develop the site was too tempting and it was sold.

Ward had perhaps foreseen this and had already thought about where else he might establish a vineyard. The company owned, in addition to the Horam Manor site, a property a mile up the road behind a row of houses known as Kingston Villas. This had been the site of an old brickworks and the heavy clay soil, although suitable for making bricks, could not be considered ideal for vines.

Unperturbed by this, Ward planted 800 grafted vines in the spring of 1963 but the heavy soil conditions were too much for them and not a single one survived! He reckoned that they had all been planted too deeply and had been killed by waterlogging. Not one to be put off easily, Ward planted further vines, this time using some rooted cuttings that had been raised on the site, as well as some others that had been grafted by Merrydown as an experiment. However, the latter were not a success and home-grafting was soon abandoned. At the Brickyard, as the vineyard came to be known, the vines slowly established themselves, not helped by the extreme winter frosts of 1967 that cut a lot of the vines back down to the ground. The main business of Merrydown, the making of cider, perry and fruit wines, produced a by-product in the form of vast heaps of pomace (fruit skins, pulp and pips) left over from the pressing process. Not knowing quite what to do with it, they experimented with feeding it to pigs but soon realised that even pigs could only eat so much of the stuff and looked for other outlets. They had the idea of using it as a compost and soil conditioner and contacted a recently opened broiler-chicken producer at nearby Buxted (Buxted Chickens) who were only too happy to supply chicken manure for nothing. This, when mixed and turned with the press waste and then thoroughly composted, was bagged and marketed as 'Pompost'. Initially it was a great success and although eventually forced off the market by an entirely unfounded *salmonella* scare, it was not before large quantities of it had been spread about the Brickyard vineyard. This greatly improved the clay soil and by 1969 1½ acres had been planted. Ward was constantly trying to improve the soil at the Brickyard by growing 'green manure' crops in the rows and I well remember seeing most of the vineyard down to sunflowers which, at the end of the summer, were cut down and then rotovated into the soil. The Brickyard vineyard was eventually expanded by cutting down a three acre coppice that adjoined it and grubbing-up all the tree roots that remained. A proper land drainage system was then installed before it was planted with vines.

In addition to the Brickyard, Ward had found a spare patch of ground at the Horam Manor site and in 1968 planted almost ¾ acre of vines. That year saw the first harvest from the Brickyard site, reported as: *12 cwt of grapes, which yielded 100 gallons of wine*. The next year was marginally better and a yield of *106 gallons* was recorded, together with the juice from some Baco noir vines on a wall at the Manor. 1970 was a real bumper year, and some 4½ tons were picked from both vineyards. In 1971 another five varieties were planted at Horam Manor: Reichensteiner, Ortega, Faberrebe, Kerner and Augusta Luise, the last an early table grape. The harvest that year was 1 ton 6½ cwt from the Horam vineyard and 1 ton 3½ cwt from Horam – a grand total of 2½ tons. Some plastic tunnels were put up at Horam and the crops under these helped improve the harvests. Somebody who shared the same enthusiasm for the vines as Ward was Reg Parsons who had been gardener at The Grange, the site of the first vineyard. Together, he and Ward managed both the Brickyard and the Horam Manor vineyards.

In 1979, Ward retired as Managing Director of Merrydown and his successor, Richard Purdey, was forced by commercial considerations to take a hard look at the future of the vineyard and (grape) winemaking operations. Reluctantly it was decided that both the vineyard and the Merrydown Co-operative Scheme (see below) would have to go as the company could no longer continue to subsidise it. The 1980 vintage had not been large and the vineyard would have to be sold.

By good fortune, Ward happened to share a railway compartment back from an English Vineyards Association Board Meeting with Kenneth McAlpine, owner of Lamberhurst Vineyards.[1] Ward explained the predicament that the vineyard was in and by the time they got to the end of the train journey, it was decided that the vineyard would be bought by McAlpine and become an outpost of the Lamberhurst operation. Reg Parsons had also been facing an uncertain future and although well past retirement age, he was asked to continue to help look after the vineyard. The vineyard at Horam Manor was needed for the expansion of storage tanks and bottling facilities and this was grubbed-up. Reg continued to live in a cottage overlooking the vineyard until he died in 1988.

Under Lamberhurst's management, the Brickyard vineyard was almost entirely replanted with new grafted stock. The original vines were planted on a 5-foot (1.52-metre) row width, far too narrow for the tractors and implements used by Lamberhurst, and the new vines were planted with 7-foot (2.13-metre) wide rows and 4 feet (1.22 metres) between the vines. Varieties planted were Kerner, Müller-Thurgau, Reichensteiner and Schönburger. During one stage of the replanting it was realised that parts of the soil consisted almost entirely of broken bricks, probably the waste heap from the brick kilns and the vines had to be pickaxed into their new homes. Despite this, they seem to grow happily and full production was resumed in 1986. The vineyard remained in McAlpine's ownership until October 1994 when it was bought by John Worontschak, the flying winemaker then based at Valley Vineyards (now called Stanlake Park), who had plans to build a winery, reduce the vineyard in size and graft the vines over to Pinot noir. Sadly these plans never came to fruition and John sold the vineyard to some travellers who parked their caravans on it (and eventually got planning permission to build a house on it). Curiously though, it still appears on the WSB's Vineyard Regsiter!

The establishment of the Merrydown Co-operative Scheme in 1969 was another important milestone in English viticulture. Ward had seen a growing number of small vineyards with owners who, having managed to grow a good crop of grapes, had problems turning them into commercially acceptable wine. Their vineyards were either far too small to warrant the equipment needed or they lacked the expertise required to make good wine: very often it was both. Ward's ambition was to see the revival of English winegrowing well established and anything that he or his company could do to help it would be done. It is interesting to read in one of the first contracts issued by Merrydown, the reason given for the scheme having been instituted: *Because it* [Merrydown] *considers that the enterprise* [that of growing grapes in the United Kingdom] *presents a unique challenge to the British people and is therefore worthy of such support as we are able to give.*

---

1 Ward was extremely lucky in this as Kenneth McAlpine told me that he never took the train having a car and driver at his disposal at all times (as well as flying his own helicopter for longer journeys).

The scheme was essentially one of contract winemaking whereby grapes would be individually processed for their owners and returned to them as finished wine. The difference between this and other contract winemakers was that the service could either be paid for in the normal way or a proportion of the wine made would be retained to cover all costs. The proportion of a grower's wine retained varied, depending on a number of factors, but to start with it was 70 per cent for the grower and 30 per cent for the co-op. As the years went by and the true costs or running and administering this scheme became apparent, the amount retained rose to 44 per cent. The scheme was run as a co-operative non-profit making enterprise and the charges were consequently very reasonable. The wine retained by the scheme was blended together and sold under the 'Anderida' label, either through the Merrydown wine-shop or through their trade sales division. A Merrydown wine list from 1974 shows that the 1971 Anderida was selling for £1.26 a bottle, while the Brede Riesling Sylvaner, which the year before had won the first Gore-Browne Trophy, was selling for £1.83!

In 1976, Christopher (known as Kit) Lindlar, who had recently returned from some practical winemaking experience on the Mosel in Germany, joined Greg Williams in the winery just before the harvest and together they handled the largest crop ever pressed at Horam – over 180 tons – which severely strained the facilities. In 1977, the whole of the English Wine interests of Merrydown were put into a new company 'Merrydown Vineyards Limited'. Over the 10 years that it was in existence, the Merrydown Co-operative Scheme made wines for almost all the vineyards then cropping. At a time when good equipment and technical knowledge were both in short supply, it had certainly enabled many vineyards to get a properly made and presented commercial product on the shelf. It also had Royal patronage. In *Merrydown, 40 Vintage Years* by Graeme Wright, it is recalled that Princess Margaret once sent some grapes that had been grown on a wall at Kensington Palace to be made into wine, although only enough for 6 bottles!

In one sense the co-op scheme was a victim of its own success. As vineyards sending grapes to Horam became bigger and as the vines became more mature, their owners gained in confidence and started to set up their own wineries, leaving only the smaller, newer vineyards to use the scheme. Eventually it became obvious that the costs of running the scheme were too high and in 1980 it was wound up. Lindlar and Williams decided that the time had come to find a new home and in August 1980 they both moved to Biddenden Vineyards, Lindlar to become a contract winemaker on his own account and Williams to concentrate on vine sales. Most of the old Merrydown customers moved with Lindlar to Biddenden. Lindlar later left Biddenden to set up his own winery, High Weald Wines and made the first few vintages of an experimental sparkling wine called – wait for it – Nyetimber. Lindlar eventually gave up winemaking, sold most of his winery equipment to RidgeView and took up the cloth, becoming a minister in the Church of England. Williams continued to sell vines for a number of years until tragically killed in an accident in 1988.

Apart from putting the services of Merrydown at the disposal of English winegrowers through the Co-operative Scheme, Ward was also very involved with the English Vineyards Association. He was its first Chairman from the initial Annual General Meeting on 18 January 1967 until April 1981. During his time as Chairman, the Customs and Excise were persuaded to grant growers their 'Domestic Use Allowance', an annual duty-free award of up to 1,100 litres of wine; the Wye College experimental vineyard was planted and produced some good data for growers; and the EVA Certification Trade Mark or Seal of Quality as it became to be known, was eventually agreed to by the Board of Trade and put into operation. He remained as a Director until 1983 but continued to attend Board Meetings until 1985. He was awarded the OBE in the 1979 New Year's Honours List for 'Services to English Wine' and was presented with his award by the Queen at Buckingham Palace on 27 March (and missed – for the first and last time – an EVA Board meeting). After the presentation he was given a celebration lunch at the Farmers Club by the whole Board together with Sir Guy and Lady Salisbury-Jones. Ward also wrote *The Complete Book of Vine Growing in the British Isles* (1984, Faber and Faber) and although now out of print, is remains the only book on viticulture written specifically for this climate.

Jack Ward died on 10 August 1986. He was responsible in no small way for the development of the industry at a time when few believed it had a future. He was a kind, sensitive man, who gave time to anyone who wanted to speak to him about growing vines or making wine and must be judged as one of the founding fathers of English wine.

The Wrotham Pinot story

The vine that Edward Hyams discovered in Wrotham was in all probability the variety known as 'Miller's Burgundy' which had been widely grown on walls and in gardens in Great Britain for many years. Archibald Barron writing in his book, *Vines and Vine Culture,* the standard Victorian work on grape growing, states that the variety was: *found by* [the famous horticulturalist] *Sir Joseph Banks in the remains of an ancient vineyard at Tortworth, Gloucestershire* – a county well known for its medieval vineyards. When compared to supplies of Meunier from France, Brock recorded that Wrotham Pinot: *had a higher natural sugar content and ripened two weeks earlier.* Hyams, ever the journalist in search of a good story, claimed that this vine had been left behind by the Romans although provided no evidence for this. Brock sold cuttings and the variety became quite popular in early vineyards, although it is unlikely that any vines from the cuttings supplied by Brock survive in any of today's UK vineyards. Despite the fact that today all plantings of Pinot Meunier in the UK stem from French and German nurseries, the name Wrotham Pinot is still a legally acceptable synonym for this variety, although not used at all in the UK.

In 2004, a well-known grower from California, Richard Peterson, (who was winemaker at Beaulieu Vineyards in Napa after the famous Andrè Tchelistcheff) announced that he had a vineyard in Napa planted with Wrotham Pinot, with vines propagated from cuttings taken from *original Wrotham Pinot vines* in 1980. Peterson was a judge at the time at the International Wine and Spirits Competition (IWSC) and had been told about a vine *growing wild against a stone wall in the village of Wrotham.* He then (apparently) inspected it and found that it had *tiny white hairs* on the upper surface of the leaves and was *unlike any vine he had ever seen.* Eventually he tasted a wine from the variety *made by local winemakers from the area and immediately recognised its potential* and decided to take some cuttings back to California with him (whether legally or illegally is not known!). These cuttings he had analysed by the University of California's Davis wine department who pronounced the vine's DNA to be identical to Pinot noir. Peterson now makes a wine from Wrotham Pinot, a bottle-fermented rosé sparkling, which now sells for $60 a bottle. Its quality is obviously excellent as the 2001 vintage recently won a Double Gold at the US National Women's Wine Competition. Peterson has a 2-acre Wrotham Pinot vineyard at Yountville in the heart of the Napa Valley and grows these vines without any need to spray them with sulphur against *Oidium.* The full story can be found at *www.richardgrantwine.com.*

Despite several attempts to contact Peterson, I have been unable to verify whether he personally visited the cottage in Wrotham or who the 'local winemakers' were that had made the wine he tasted. The Wrotham Historical Society publishes a booklet *Farming in Wrotham Through the Ages* which I purchased for £3 in the hope that it might provide some useful information. The booklet mentions that: *there is reputed to have been a Roman vineyard on the slopes of the North Downs above Wrotham* (funny how reports about Roman vineyards always start with 'reputed' or 'thought to have been') but about the location of the cottage it gives little help. The booklet merely says that the cottage wall was *on the main road in the village* which is hardly giving the game away. The text in the booklet is more or less the same as can be found on Richard Peterson's website. One day I must go to Wrotham on my way down to Kent and ask a few questions!

Alan Rook in his vineyard at Stragglethorpe Hall, near Lincoln in the mid-1960s, contemplating the typical summer weather

A short history of vineyards in Ireland

One of the first mentions of vines in Ireland must be in the writings of the Venerable Bede, already referred to in the historical section of this book. Writing in his *Ecclesiastical History of the English People* (completed in AD 731) he stated that: *Ireland abounds in milk and honey, nor is there any want of vines* although this was challenged by a twelfth-century writer, Giraldus Cambrensis, who stated that Bede was wrong and that Ireland has not, and never had, vines. Unlike England and Wales, where monastic viticulture, both pre- and post- the Norman conquest, was a recorded fact of life, I have not been able to unearth any details of grapes being grown for wine production in this – or indeed in any other – period until modern plantings. Table grapes in greenhouses were certainly grown and my copy of Speechley's *Treatise on the Culture of the Vine* was owned (and is signed by) Robert Gregory from Coole, near Gort in County Galway.

According to Dr. Billy Christopher, of whom more later, vines were planted in the 1960s by a gentleman who was in the army with Sir Guy Salisbury-Jones (who planted the first UK vineyard at Hambledon in 1952) in a small vineyard south of Wexford in the vicinity of the ferry port of Rosslare. Apparently, both Cabernet Sauvignon and Merlot were grown, outdoors, on terraces and against south-facing walls.

The next sign of viticultural activity seems to have been in 1972 when Michael O'Callaghan, then proprietor of Longueville House Hotel[1] at Mallow in the Blackwater Valley in County Cork, planted Müller-Thurgau and Reichensteiner. My late mentor, Professor Dr. Helmut Becker from Geisenheim, visited this vineyard in the mid-'70s (his daughter was studying in Dublin) and told me about his visit. He also told me that on the front of the hotel wine list it stated 'The River Blackwater – the Irish Rhine'! In the entry in my 1989 book I say that O'Callaghan is very proud of his vineyard which was then *Ireland's only producing vineyard* (this despite the fact that there was one a few miles down the road) and that *he won every competition for Irish wine hands down.* The vineyard at that time covered 1.1-acres (0.445-hectares), but now consists of six rows of vines and occupies about 630 m^2. It is in a sheltered part of the garden to the side of the hotel, with a vine-clad brick wall at the back of it. The vines are spaced at about 3.0 m apart which makes me think that probably originally they were much closer and that every other row has been removed at some

---

1   See entry under Longueville House for the full story of this vineyard.

stage. The vines are very low to the ground (almost touching in some places) and when I visited in the summer of 2009, the vines looked quite healthy with plenty of lush vegetation, but there was barely a crop to be seen, apart from on the wall-grown vines. O'Callaghan has a winery in a converted coach house at the back of the hotel where he also has a small still for the (entirely legal) production of spirit which is used for making liqueurs. The only Irish wine that the hotel sells is called *2006 Amurensis Walk* which is apparently made by O'Callaghan from grapes grown at the Thomas Walk Vineyard – of which more later – in Kinsale in County Cork. In September 1977, O'Callaghan and local Mallow GP, Dr. Billy Christopher went to Germany and visited Geisenheim and Dr. Becker. Christopher then decided to plant his own vineyard, not far away from Longueville House which he called Blackwater Valley Vineyard.

Christopher – known locally as Dr. Billy – planted his first vines in 1985 with further plantings in 1990. At its peak, the vineyard consisted of around 3.2-hectares (8-acres) of Madeleine Angevine, Reichensteiner & Seyval blanc planted on various trellising systems. The first plantings were on a narrow Guyot system, but advancing years and the desire not to bend down so much, meant that the later plantings were on a high wire single-curtain system (which I call the Blondin system) which was suggested by two passing New Zealanders. The first vintage from the vineyard was in 1989 and it produced wine until the vineyard was grubbed in 2006. Dr. Billy's best year was in 1990, but on average, only 150 bottles per acre were produced. Of the three varieties planted, Reichensteiner was the only variety to fruit and ripen with any regularity. The Seyval, although they cropped, were prone to low sugars and excess acidity. The Madeleine seldom performed at all, remaining small and unripe. Dr. Billy told me that he bought the vines from Lamberhurst Vineyards and I suspect that he was supplied with were the 'wrong' Madeleine Angevine i.e. the French table grape of that name. In 1990, some Schönburger were planted, but these never came to much and were grubbed. Dr. Billy told me that he'd had 'twenty years of fun' with the vineyard, but that with the level of yield he was able to achieve, the risk and reward ratio was too far out of balance. When I wrote the 1989 version of this guide, Dr. Billy said that 'the Excise people' had yet to catch up with his winemaking, but catch up they did (together with the winery at Longueville House) and duty was paid in the normal way. In his early years Dr. Billy was paid a visit by a 'Vineyard Inspector' from the Department of Agriculture, Fisheries and Food, who needed to create a Vineyard Register so that 'Irish Table Wine' could be legally labelled. On being told that the inspector was visiting all the vineyards in the Republic, Dr. Billy demanded to know where his phytosanitary protective suit was to safeguard against *Phylloxera* being brought into his vineyard. Sadly, the inspector explained, he did not have one. In that case, said Dr. Billy, you cannot inspect it. Retreat of DAFF inspector never to re-appear.

In my 2001 book, I had an entry for Derrynane Vineyard which was at Derrynane

Beg, Caherdaniel, County Kerry, but this small vineyard (0.07-hectares) of Bacchus seems to have disappeared. At the time I wrote that book, I also had details of another vineyard – whose name and location I cannot recall – who's wines, made from Schönburger, were found to have been adulterated with apple juice. I do seem to recall that there had been a prosecution and they had given up growing vines.

At around the same time as Dr. Billy was planting his vineyard, another pioneer, German Thomas Walk, was establishing his vineyards on the south-east coast near Kinsale in County Cork.[2] Again, with the help of Professor Becker, Walk planted what he calls *Amurensis Walk* but which he confirms are Rondo (known at the time as Gm 6494-5). Today, the vineyards – there appear to be three different sites – occupy around 0.98-hectares. The grapes from these vineyards appear to be taken to Longueville House where they are made into wine. The only wine currently on sale at the hotel is the *2006 Amurensis Walk* wine which gets very poor reviews on a couple of websites. Still, to keep the vineyards going for almost 25 years takes some doing and one has to acknowledge this, whatever the wine tastes like!

The next name in the Irish wine story is David Llewellyn whose story can be found under the entry for Lusca Vineyard. Llewellyn originally had a small experimental area of vines at Swords, just outside Dublin, planted in 2000, which acted as a test-bed for his current venture – Lusca Vineyard – where he makes and sells several different wines from vines grown both out-of-doors and under polytunnels. He is currently the only regular producer of Irish wine, albeit in very small quantities – he usually makes about 350-litres which he bottles in 75cl and 37.5cl bottles and sells for €40 and €25 respectively. Llewellyn may prove to be the pioneer that makes Irish viticulture possible and it will be interesting to see how he gets on. His wines certainly achieve high prices.

My only other experiences with Irish viticulture was in about 1995 when I was visited by a Californian grapegrower who had been asked by some investors to look into establishing a vineyard near Blarney Castle in County Cork, home of the Blarney Stone and a much-visited tourist attraction. After touring several UK vineyards with me and visiting Ireland, he concluded that it was far too cool and wet for profitable grapegrowing – something I could have told him before he left California!

Still – there is some viticultural activity in Ireland and who knows which way the weather is going? The main problem I suspect is low temperatures in May and June when inflorescences are being formed in the growing buds, and poor weather during flowering – late June, early July. These two factors determine crop level which equates to viability. Diseases – mildews and *Botrytis* – can probably be kept at bay with the better spray materials now available and the newer interspecific crosses, with their increased disease resistance, will help.

---

2   See entry under Thomas Walk for the full story of this vineyard. The vineyards can be seen on Google Earth to the north-west and south-east of the house at 51°42'01.42"N and 8°29'30.07"W.

UKVA English and Welsh Wine of the Year Competition

In 1974, the English Vineyards Association (EVA) established the English and Welsh Wine of the Year Competition. Whereas in the early years there was but one class and only one trophy, in later years, as the number of wines entered into the competition grew, so did the awards, medals and trophies. In 1985, the competition was spilt into two sections: Section A for wines bottled in quantities in excess of 1,500 litres (except for sweet wines – 45 g/l RS or more – which may be entered in section A with 500 litres or more) and Section B, for wines bottled in quantities of between 100 and 1,499 litres (sweet wines 100–499 litres). In 1999 Section C was added for wines bottled in quantities of 10,000 litres or more. Each section is today further subdivided into eleven classes, each class reflecting a different style, type, colour or vintage of wine. Gold, Silver and Bronze medals are awarded, together with Highly Commended certificates. Until recently, the competition was only open to EVA members, but since the formation of the United Kingdom Vineyards Association (UKVA) in 1996, it has been open to all who make wines from UK grown grapes. The competition rules are reviewed annually and changes are made to reflect the developing nature of English and Welsh wines.

The numbers of entries to the competition varies with the vintage. In 1991 there were 255 entries, a number which the judges found quite daunting in the single day then set aside for judging. In an attempt to make the judge's task somewhat easier and allow them to concentrate their efforts on fewer wines of better quality, entry fees were raised and all wines must now conform to the analysis requirements for Quality and/or Regional Wine (depending on the wine in question). Growers now tend to enter only their better wines and today the number of entries is seldom higher than 150. Since 1982, the awards ceremony has been held on the river terrace at the House of Lords by kind invitation of the UKVA President, Lord Montagu of Beaulieu.

The competition has, over the years, been a tremendous catalyst for the improvement in quality of English and Welsh wines and the prestige and publicity, together with the extra sales that go with winning one of the major prizes, spurs friendly rivalry between growers and winemakers.

The Chairman (or Chairwoman) of the judging panel has, since 1989, been an MW (although this is not part of the rules) and he or she selects a panel and a venue for the judging. The panel is usually chosen from a wide cross-section of the wine industry, including wine writers, wine merchants and winemakers and they are asked to judge the wines against an international standard; there are no allowances made because these wines are grown in a marginal climate. This ensures that medals gained in this competition are comparable to those awarded in other competitions open to wines from all over the world.

Chairmen of the competition

1974–1980	Michael Broadbent MW, Christies
1981–1983	Hugh Johnson, wine writer
1984–1985	Kenneth Christie MW, wine merchant
1986–1988	Christopher Fielden, wine writer
1989–1991	Dr Arabella Woodrow MW
1992–1994	Maggie McNie MW, wine writer
1995–1997	Margaret Harvey MW, wine merchant, Fine Wines of NZ
1998–2000	Rosemary George MW, wine writer
2001–2003	David Wrigley MW, Wine and Spirit Education Trust
2004–2006	Julian Brind MW, wine buyer, Waitrose
2007–2008	Patricia Stefanowicz MW
2009	

Trophies and awards

The Gore-Browne Trophy, a magnificent silver rose-bowl presented in 1974 by Mrs Margaret Gore-Browne in memory of her husband Robert, is awarded to the best wine in section A or C. The President's Trophy, presented by Lord Montagu of Beaulieu in 1985, is awarded to the best wine in section B.

The Jack Ward Memorial Salver, presented by Mrs Betty Ward in 1987 in memory of her husband who was Chairman of the EVA from 1976 to 1981, is awarded to the best still wine of the previous vintage in section A or C. The Wine Guild Trophy presented in 1990 by the Wine Guild of the United Kingdom (Chancellor, Lord Montagu of Beaulieu) is awarded to the best still wine of any other vintage in section A or C. The Vintner's Trophy for Sparkling Wine, presented by the Worshipful Company of Vintners in 1998, is awarded to the best sparkling wine in any section. Thus the winner of the Gore-Browne Trophy always wins either the Jack Ward Salver or the Wine Guild Trophy if a still wine, or the Vintner's Trophy if sparkling.

The Bernard Theobald Trophy, presented by the Thames and Chilterns Vineyards Association in 1992 in memory of Bernard Theobald, one of the most colourful characters from the modern history of winegrowing in the UK and a great pioneer of English red wines, is awarded to the best still red wine in any section. The McNie Trophy, presented by Maggie McNie MW competition Chairman 1992–1994, is awarded to the best oaked still white wine in any section. The Dudley Quirk Memorial Trophy, presented by English Wine Producers in memory of founder member Dudley Quirk of Chiddingstone Vineyards, is presented to the best still wine in section C. The

Montagu Trophy, presented by Lord Montagu in 2002, is given to the wine in any section with the best prestentation. Between 1999 and 2001 this award was known as the UKVA Trophy.

The Tom Day Trophy, presented by the Day family in memory of Tom who first planted vines in 1974 at what is today Three Choirs Vineyard and who died on 30 April 2001, is awarded to the best single variety still wine in any section. The Waitrose Rosé Trophy, presented by Waitrose Ltd, is awarded to the best still rosé wine in any section. The Berwick Trophy was presented by past-Chairman Ian Berwick and is awarded to the best unchaptalised still wine in sections A or C of the competition.

The McAlpine Winemaker of the Year Trophy, presented by Kenneth McAlpine MBE in 2001, is awarded to the winemaker with the highest average score from their top three wines, still and sparkling.

Note: Stanlake Park was called Thames Valley Vineyards until 1992 and Valley Vineyards until 2004. Tenterden Vineyards changed it name to Chapel Down in 1995.

Gore-Browne Trophy (Best large volume wine, still or sparkling)

1974	Brede	1972 Riesling Sylvaner
1975	Pilton Manor	1973 Riesling Sylvaner
1976	Pilton Manor	1975 Riesling Sylvaner
1977	Pulham	1976 Magdalen Rivaner
1978	Kelsale	1977 Müller-Thurgau & Seyval Blanc
1979	Adgestone	1978 Adgestone
1980	Pulham	1979 Magdalen Rivaner
1981	Tenterden	1980 Spots Farm Seyval Blanc
1982	Wootton	1981 Schönburger
1983	Lamberhurst	1982 Huxelrebe
1984	Barton Manor	1983 Barton Manor Dry
1985	Lamberhurst	1984 Schönburger
1986	Wootton	1985 Seyval Blanc
1987	Biddenden	1986 Ortega
1988	Chiltern Valley	1987 Old Luxters
1989	Carr Taylor	1988 Reichensteiner
1990	Lamberhurst	1988 Schönburger
1991	Tenterden	1989 Seyval Blanc Special Reserve
1992	Thames Valley	1991 Clocktower Selection Botrytis
1993	Valley	1991 Fumé
1994	Pilton Manor	1992 Westholme Late Harvest
1995	Wyken	1992 Bacchus
1996	Valley	NV Heritage Brut

1997	Valley	1995 Clocktower Selection Pinot Noir
1998	Valley	NV Heritage Brut Rosé
1999	Chapel Down	1998 Bacchus
2000	RidgeView	1996 Cuvée Merret Bloomsbury
2001	Nyetimber	1994 Aurora Cuvée Blanc de Blancs
2002	RidgeView	1996 Cuvée Merret Cavendish
2003	Nyetimber	1995 Première Cuvée Blanc de Blancs
2004	Nyetimber	1996 Première Cuvée Blanc de Blancs
2005	Nyetimber	1999 Classic Cuvée
2006	Nyetimber	1998 Prestige Cuvée Blanc de Blancs
2007	Camel Valley	2004 Cornwall Pinot Noir Rosé
2008	Three Choirs	2006 Estate Reserve Siegerrebe
2009	RidgeView	2006 Knightsbridge Blanc de Noir

President's Trophy *(Best small volume wine, still or sparkling)*

1985	Avalon	1984 Seyval Blanc
1986	Astley	1985 Madeleine Angevine
1987	Astley	1986 Kerner
1988	Stanlake Park	1987 Siegerwürzertraminer
1989	Chapel Down	1988 Rosé
1990	Chiltern Valley	1989 Noble Bacchus
1991	Thames Valley	1989 Clocktower Selection Botrytis
1992	Sharpham	1990 Beenleigh Red
1993	Partridge	1992 Bacchus Dry
1994	Scott's Hall	NV Traditional Method Rosé
1995	Northbrook Springs	1994 Noble Dessert
1996	Three Choirs	1995 Estate Bacchus Reserve
1997	Sharpham	1995 Beenleigh Red
1998	Valley	1997 Clocktower Selection Pinot Noir
1999	Camel Valley	1998 Seyval Blanc Dry
2000	Warden Abbey	1999 Warden Vineyard
2001	Sharpham	1999 Beenleigh Red
2002	Chiltern Valley	1999 Aluric de Norsehide
2003	Sharpham	2001 Beenleigh Red
2004	Three Choirs	2003 Reserve Noble Rot
2005	Sharpham	2003 Pinot Noir
2006	Three Choirs	2003 Reserve Noble Rot
2007	Ickworth	2005 Walled Garden White
2008	Camel Valley	2005 Cornwall White Pinot Noir (Batch 2)
2009	Three Choirs	2007 Siegerrebe

Jack Ward Trophy (Best large volume still wine previous vintage)

1987	Three Choirs	1984 Three Choirs Medium
1988	Carr Taylor	1986 Reichensteiner
1989	Carr Taylor	NV Non Vintage Sparkling
1990	Thames Valley	1989 Sweet Lee
1991	Chiltern Valley	1990 Noble Bacchus
1992	Stanlake Park	1991 Clocktower Selection Botrytis
1993	Monnow Valley	1992 Huxelrebe & Seyval Blanc
1994	Pilton Manor	1993 Pilton
1995	Pilton Manor	1994 Westholme Late Harvest
1996	Nutbourne	1995 Sussex Reserve
1997	Hidden Spring	1996 Sussex Sunset Rosé
1998	Chapel Down	1997 Bacchus
1999	Chapel Down	1998 Bacchus
2000	Denbies	1999 Redlands
2001	Shawsgate	2000 Bacchus
2002	Chapel Down	2001 Bacchus
2003	Chapel Down	2002 Schönburger
2004	Three Choirs	2003 Reserve Bacchus
2005	Camel Valley	2004 Bacchus
2006	Sharpham	2005 Bacchus
2007	Astley	2006 Severn Vale
2008	Denbies	2007 Rose Hill Rosé
2009	Biddenden	2008 Ortega

Wine Guild of the UK Trophy (Best large volume still wine any other vintage)

1990	Lamberhurst	1988 Schönburger
1991	Tenterden	1989 Seyval Blanc Special Reserve
1992	Elham Valley	1990 Müller-Thurgau
1993	Valley	1991 Fumé
1994	Pilton Manor	1992 Westholme Late Harvest
1995	Wyken	1992 Bacchus
1996	Mersea	1994 Mersea
1997	Valley	1995 Clocktower Selection Pinot Noir
1998	Hidden Spring	1998 Dark Fields
1999	Chapel Down	1997 Schönburger
2000	RidgeView	1996 Cuvée Merret Bloomsbury
2001	Nyetimber	1994 Aurora Cuvée Blanc de Blancs
2002	RidgeView	1996 Cuvée Merret Cavendish
2003	Nyetimber	1995 Première Cuvée Blanc de Blancs
2004	Nyetimber	1996 Première Cuvée Blanc de Blancs

2005	Nyetimber	1999 Classic Cuvée
2006	Chapel Down	2004 Tenterden Pinot Noir
2007	Chapel Down	2005 Bacchus Reserve
2008	Three Choirs	2006 Estate Reserve Siegerrebe
2009	Chapel Down	2006 Cinque Ports

Berwick Trophy *(Best large volume unchaptalised still wine)*

2006	Denbies	2003 Coopers Brook
2007	Wroxeter Roman	2005 Madeleine Angevine
2008	Bothy	2007 The Paradox
2009	Biddenden	2008 Ortega

Tom Day Trophy *(Best single varietal still wine)*

2002	Chapel Down	1999 Pinot Noir
2003	Chapel Down	2001 Pinot Blanc
2004	Chapel Down	2002 Pinot Noir
2005	Nyetimber	1999 Premiére Cuvée Blanc de Blancs
2006	Chapel Down	2004 Tenterden Pinot Noir
2007	Chapel Down	2005 Bacchus Reserve
2008	Three Choirs	2006 Siegerrebe
2009	Three Choirs	2007 Siegerrebe

EWP Dudley Quirk Trophy *(Best still wine Section C)*

1999	Chapel Down	1998 Bacchus
2000	Chapel Down	NV Downland Oak
2001	Camel Valley	1999 Cornwall Brut
2002	Nyetimber	1994 Premiére Cuvée Blanc de Blancs
2003	Nyetimber	1996 Classic Cuvée
2004	Nyetimber	1996 Premiére Cuvée Blanc de Blancs
2005	Nyetimber	1999 Classic Cuvée
2006	Three Choirs	2005 Willowbrook
2007	Denbies	2004 Redlands
2008	Camel Valley	2006 Bacchus
2009	Camel Valley	2007 Bacchus

McAlpine Winemaker of the Year Trophy *(Highest marks for three wins, any type)*

2001	Sandra Moss	Nyetimber
2002	Owen Elias	Chapel Down
2003	Owen Elias	Chapel Down
2004	Martin Fowke	Three Choirs
2005	Owen Elias	Chapel Down

2006	Owen Elias	Chapel Down
2007	Sam Lindo	Camel Valley
2008	Martin Fowke	Three Choirs
2009	Michael Roberts	RidgeView Wine Estate

McNie Trophy *(Best oaked still wine)*

1999	Chapel Down	NV Downland Oak
2000	Chapel Down	NV Downland Oak
2001	Valley	1998 Fumé
2002	Chapel Down	NV Lamberhurst Fumé
2003	Valley	1998 Fumé
2004	Valley	1999 Fumé
2005	Denbies	2003 Hillside Chardonnay
2006	Denbies	2003 Coopers Brook
2007	Wickham	2006 Special Release Fumé
2008	Wickham	2007 Special Release Fumé
2009	Sharpham	2007 Barrel Fermented

Montagu Trophy (UKVA Trophy 1999–2001) *(Best presentation)*

1999	Frome Valley	1998 Madeleine Angevine
2000	Breaky Bottom	1996 Seyval Blanc
2001	Denbies	1999 Limes Riesling
2002	Denbies	2000 Juniper Hill
2003	Denbies	2000 Coopers Brook
2004	Davenport	2002 Limney Estate
2005	Davenport	2000 Limney Estate (joint winner)
2005	Down St Mary	2004 Yeo Vale (joint winner)
2006	Camel Valley	2004 Cornwall Brut
2007	Polgoon	2006 Rosé
2008	Camel Valley	2006 Cornwall Brut
2009	Astley	2007 Veritas

Bernard Theobald Trophy *(Best still red wine)*

1993	Sharpham	1990 Beenleigh Red
1994	Valley	1992 Pinot Noir
1995	Hidden Spring	1993 Dark Fields
1996	Chapel Down	1994 Epoch Reserve
1997	Sharpham	1995 Beenleigh Red
1998	Valley	1997 Clocktower Pinot Noir
1999	Sharpham	1998 Beenleigh Red
2000	Denbies	1999 Redlands

2001	Sharpham	1999 Beenleigh Red
2002	Chapel Down	1999 Pinot Noir
2003	Chapel Down	2000 Pinot Noir
2004	Chapel Down	2002 Pinot Noir
2005	Sharpham	2003 Pinot Noir
2006	Chapel Down	2004 Tenterden Estate Pinot Noir
2007	Sandhurst	2004 Pinot Noir
2008	Titchfield	2006 Pinot Noir
2009	Mount	NV Recession Red

Vintner's Trophy *(Best sparkling wine)*

1998	Valley	NV Heritage Brut Rosé
1999	Bearsted	NV Brut
2000	RidgeView	1996 Cuvée Merret Bloomsbury
2001	Nyetimber	1994 Aurora Cuvée Blanc de Blancs
2002	RidgeView	1996 Cuvée Merret Cavendish
2003	Nyetimber	1995 Première Cuvée Blanc de Blancs
2004	Nyetimber	1996 Première Cuvée Blanc de Blancs
2005	Nyetimber	1999 Classic Cuvée
2006	Nyetimber	1998 Prestige Cuvée Blanc de Blancs
2007	Camel Valley	2004 Cornwall Pinot Noir Rosé
2008	Camel Valley	2005 Cornwall White Pinot Noir (Batch 2)
2009	RidgeView	2006 Knightsbridge Blanc de Noir

Waitrose Rosé Trophy *(Best still rosé wine)*

2005	Camel Valley	2004 Cornish Rosé
2006	Chapel Down	2005 English Rosé
2007	Polgoon	2006 Polgoon Rosé
2008	Denbies	2007 Rose Hill Rosé
2009	Camel Valley	2008 Rosé

Gold Medals

1978	Adgestone	1976 Adgestone
	Felsted	1977 Felstar Müller-Thurgau & Siegerrebe
1979	Wootton	1977 Müller-Thurgau
1980	None awarded	
1981	None awarded	
1982	Adgestone	1980 Adgestone
1983	Lamberhurst	1982 Huxelrebe
	Lamberhurst	1982 Schönburger
	Tenterden	1982 Spots Farm Seyval Blanc Med-Dry

	Tenterden	1982 Spots Farm Müller-Thurgau Dry
	Tenterden	1982 Spots Farm Gutenborner Dry
1984	Abbey Knight	1983 Pinot Noir Rosé
	Barton Manor	1983 Barton Manor Dry
	Barton Manor	1983 Barton Manor Sparkling Rosé
	Biddenden	1983 Ortega
	Westbury	1981 Müller-Thurgau
	Westbury	1982 Müller-Thurgau & Seyval Blanc
1985	Avalon	1984 Seyval Blanc
	Biddenden	1983 Ortega
	Carr Taylor	1984 Reichensteiner
	Chalk Hill	1983 Müller-Thurgau
	Lamberhurst	1984 Schönburger
	Lamberhurst	1982 Schönburger
	Wootton	1983 Seyval Blanc
1986	Astley	1985 Madeleine Angevine
	Kents Green	1985 Kents Green
	Three Choirs	1984 Seyval Blanc & Reichensteiner
	Wootton	1985 Seyval Blanc
1987	Biddenden	1986 Ortega
	Chiltern Valley	1987 Old Luxters
	Three Choirs	1984 Three Choirs Medium
1988	Carr Taylor	1986 Reichensteiner
	Carr Taylor	Vintage Sparkling
1989	Carr Taylor	1988 Reichensteiner
1990	Chiltern Valley	1989 Noble Bacchus
	Lamberhurst	1988 Schönburger
	Penshurst	1985 Ehrenfelser
1991	None awarded	
1992	None awarded	
1993	Valley	1991 Fumé
	Wyken	1991 Bacchus
1994	Pilton Manor	1992 Westholme Late Harvest
	Sandhurst	1991 Oak Aged Bacchus
1995	Northbrook Springs 1994 Noble Dessert	
1996	None awarded	
1997	Breaky Bottom	1992 Seyval Blanc
	Great Stocks	1995 Symphony
	Hidden Spring	1996 Sussex Sunset Rosé
	Kents Green	1995 Müller-Thurgau & Huxelrebe
	Sharpham	1995 Beenleigh Red

	Valley	1995 Clocktower Selection Pinot Noir
1998	Chapel Down	1997 Bacchus
	Hidden Spring	1996 Dark Fields
	Valley	NV Heritage Brut Rosé
	Valley	1997 Clocktower Pinot Noir
1999	None awarded	
2000	RidgeView	1996 Cuvée Merret Bloomsbury
2001	Denbies	1999 Brokes Noble Harvest
	Nyetimber	1994 Aurora Cuvée Blanc de Blancs
	Nyetimber	1993 Première Cuvée Blanc de Blancs
	Sharpham	1999 Beenleigh Red
2002	Chapel Down	NV Chapel Down Brut Magnum
	Nyetimber	1995 Première Cuvée Blanc de Blancs
	RidgeView	1998 Cuvée Merret Cavendish
2003	Chapel Down	2001 Pinot Blanc
	Chapel Down	2001 Rosé
	Nyetimber	1995 Premiére Cuvée Blanc de Blancs
	Nyetimber	1996 Classic Cuvée
	RidgeView	1999 Cuvée Merret Knightsbridge
	Sharpham	2001 Dart Valley Reserve
2004	Chapel Down	2002 Pinot Noir
	Nyetimber	1996 Première Cuvée Blanc de Blancs
	Nyetimber	1995 Classic Cuvée
	Nyetimber	1995 Première Cuvée Blanc de Blancs
	RidgeView	2000 Cuvée Merret Bloomsbury
2005	Chapel Down	2003 Nectar
	Chapel Down	2002 Pinot Noir
	Chapel Down	2000 Pinot Reserve Sparkling
	Chapel Down	2001 Pinot Reserve Sparkling
	Denbies	2003 Hillside Chardonnay
	Denbies	1999 Greenfields Sparkling
	Nyetimber	1999 Classic Cuvée
	Nyetimber	1999 Première Cuvée Blanc de Blancs
	Nyetimber	1997 Classic Cuvée
	Pebblebed	2004 Rosé
	Sharpham	2003 Pinot Noir
	Sharpham	2003 Beenleigh Red
2006	Chapel Down	2005 English Rosé
	Chapel Down	2004 Tenterden Pinot Noir
	Chapel Down	2004 Bacchus Reserve
	Nyetimber	1998 Première Cuvée Blanc de Blancs

	Nyetimber	1998 Classic Cuvée
	Nyetimber	2000 Classic Cuvée
	Nyetimber	2003 Blanc de Noirs Pinot Meunier
	Sharpham	2005 Bacchus
	Three Choirs	2003 Noble Rot
2007	Camel Valley	2004 Pinot Noir Rosé Sparkling
	Camel Valley	2005 Pinot Noir
	Camel Valley	2005 Pinot Noir Rosé Sparkling
	Chapel Down	2005 Bacchus Reserve
	Ickworth	2005 Walled Garden White
	RidgeView	2004 Cuvée Merret Bloomsbury
	RidgeView	2004 Cuvée Merret Fitzrovia Rosé
2008	Camel Valley	2005 Cornwall Pinot Noir Rosé
	Camel Valley	2005 Cornwall White Pinot Noir (Batch 2)
	Camel Valley	2006 Bacchus
2008	Denbies	2007 Rose Hill Rosé
	Eglantine	2004 North Star
	Nyetimber	2001 Première Cuvée Blanc de Blancs
	Nyetimber	2001 Classic Cuvée
	RidgeView	2005 Cuvée Merret Bloomsbury
	RidgeView	2005 Cuvée Merret Cavendish
	Three Choirs	2006 Estate Reserve Siegerrebe
	Warden Abbey	2006 Warden Bacchus
2009	Biddenden	2008 Ortega
	Biddenden	2008 Gribble Bridge Ortega Dry
	Camel Valley	2006 Cornwall Pinot Rosé
	Camel Valley	2007 Cornwall White Pinot
	Chapel Down	2004 Pinot Reserve
	Davenport	2005 Limney Estate Sparkling
	Mount	NV Recession Red
	RidgeView	2006 Cavendish
	RidgeView	2006 Grosvenor Blanc de Blanc
	RidgeView	2006 Knightsbridge Blanc de Noir
	Three Choirs	2007 Siegerrebe

International Wine and Spirit Competition

The International Wine and Spirit Competition (IWSC) has had a section for UK-grown wines since 1983 and between 1983 and 2000 awarded an English Wine Trophy to the best wine in that section. Since 2001 the producer of the best wine in this section has been awarded the UK Wine Producer Trophy. Sparkling English Wines are also eligible for the Bottle Fermented Sparkling Wine Trophy for the best (non-Champagne) bottle-fermented sparkling wine, and this was won in 1998 by the *1993 Nyetimber Classic Cuvée*, in 2006 by the *1998 Nyetimber Classic Cuvée* and again in 2009 by the *1992 Nyetimber Première Cuvée Blanc de Blancs* – the same wine that won them the English Wine Trophy twelve years earlier.

1983	Pilton Manor	1982 Pilton Manor Müller-Thurgau
1984	Hambledon	1982 Hambledon
1985	Wickenden	1982 Wickenden Green Cap
1986	Wickenden	1984 Wickenden Green Cap
1987	Chiltern Valley	1986 Old Luxters Reserve
1988	Bruisyard	1987 Bruisyard St Peter Müller-Thurgau
1989	Pilton Manor	1982 Pilton Manor Müller-Thurgau
1990	Shawsgate	1986 Shawsgate Müller-Thurgau
1991	Rock Lodge	1989 Rock Lodge Impresario Sparkling
1992	Throwley	1989 Throwley Chardonnay Sparkling
1993	Carr Taylor	1987 Carr Taylor Vintage Sparkling
1994	Shawsgate	1991 Shawsgate Bacchus
1995	Chapel Down	1993 Chapel Down Epoch I Red
1996	Denbies	1995 Denbies Late Harvest Dessert
1997	Nyetimber	1992 Première Cuvée Blanc de Blancs
1998	Nyetimber	1993 Classic Cuvée
1999	Nyetimber	1993 Première Cuvée Blanc de Blancs
2000	RidgeView	1996 Cuvée Merret Bloomsbury
2001	Nyetimber	1994 Classic Cuvée
2002	RidgeView	1998 Cuvée Merret Bloomsbury
2003	Nyetimber	1995 Classic Cuvée
2004	Nyetimber	1996 Classic Cuvée
2005	RidgeView	2002 Cuvée Merret Bloomsbury
2006	Nyetimber	1998 Classic Cuvée

2007	Denbies	2003 Greenfields (Sparkling)
2008	Nyetimber	2001 Classic Cuvée
2009	Nyetimber	1992 Première Cuvée Blanc de Blancs

International Wine Challenge

The International Wine Challenge (IWC) started in 1984 when David Carr Taylor – of Carr Taylor Vineyards – challenged Robert Joseph and Charles Metcalfe (who at that time ran Wine Magazine) to a vinous duel, pitching English Wines against a selection of foreign wines. English and Welsh wines have always been entered into the IWC, albeit in quite small numbers, and occasionally Gold Medals (as well as Silver, Bronze and Highly Commended awards) have been given. In addition, an English Wine Trophy has been awarded to the top scoring UK-grown wine.

Below is a list of the Gold Medal and Trophy winning wines from 1993. Unfortunately the records prior to 1993 have been lost. In years where no wine is listed, no Gold medals were awarded to UK-grown wines. In 1993 the Trophy was jointly shared.

1993	Breaky Bottom	1990 Seyval blanc
	Throwley	1991 Ortega
2004	Chapel Down	NV Pinot Reserve Sparkling
2005	Camel Valley	2001 Brut Sparkling
2007	Denbies	2003 Greenfields Sparkling
2008	Hush Heath	2004 Balfour Brut Rosé Sparkling
2009	Camel Valley	2007 Bacchus

Decanter World Wine Awards

The Decanter World Wine Awards (DWWA) started in 2004 and are now, in their sixth year, the largest of the three major UK wine competitions. In 2009 a total of 10,285 wines were judged, making it larger than either the IWC or IWSC, although these other two competitions taste spirits, sakes and other alcoholic beverages which the DWWA do not. In the first five years, 2004-2008, English and Welsh wines were lumped together with 'Eastern and Middle Europe' under the chairmanship of Angela Muir MW. For 2009, it was felt that with over 60 entries, the category deserved to have its own dedicated panel. I chaired it, together with John Atkinson MW, owner of Tixover Vineyard and UK sales representative for Champagne Billecart-Salmon, Oz Clarke and Justin Howard-Sneyd MW, head of wines at Waitrose. Also in 2009, it was decided to instigate a trophy for the best UK wine.

The wines shown below are those gaining the highest scores in the year concerned. i.e. in 2004 and 2007, no Silvers or Golds were awarded, in 2005, 2006 and 2008, no Golds were awarded.

2004	RidgeView	Bloomsbury 2000	Bronze
	RidgeView	Cavendish 2000	Bronze
2005	Eglantine	North Star 2002	Silver
2006	Camel Valley	Bacchus Dry 2005	Silver
2007	Brightwell	Oxford Flint 2004	Bronze
	Camel Valley	Brut 2005	Bronze
	Camel Valley	Bacchus Dry 2006	Bronze
	RidgeView	Bloomsbury 2004	Bronze
	RidgeView	Grosvenor Blanc de Blancs 2004	Bronze
2008	Denbies	Hillside Chardonnay 2006	Silver
	Nyetimber	Première Cuvée Blanc de Blancs 2001	Silver
2009	Camel Valley	Cornwall White Pinot Noir 2005	Gold
	Hush Heath	Balfour Brut Rosé Sparkling 2004	Gold + Trophy

Some useful addresses

Associations

United Kingdom Vineyards Association (UKVA)
PO Box 354, Abingdon, Oxfordshire OX14 9BZ
Tel: 01865 390188
E-mail: sian@ukva.org.uk
Website: www.englishwineproducers.com/ukva.htm
UKVA General Secretary: Sian Liwicki
Chairman: Bob Lindo, Camel Valley Vineyard

English Wine Producers (EWP)
PO Box 5729, Market Harborough, Leicestershire LE16 8WX
Tel: 01536 772264   Fax: 01563 772263
E-mail: info@englishwineproducers.com
Website: www.englishwineproducers.com
Marketing Manager: Julia Trustram Eve Tel: 07775 760451

East Anglian Winegrowers' Association
New Hall Vineyards, Purleigh, Chelmsford, Essex CM3 6PN
Tel: 01621 828343   E-mail: piers@newhallwines.co.uk
Website: www.eastanglianwines.co.uk
Chairman: Piers Greenwood

Mercian Vineyards Association
Wroxeter Roman Vineyard, Wroxeter, Shrewsbury, Shropshire SY5 6PQ
Tel: 01743 761888   E-mail: wine@wroxetervineyard.co.uk
Website: www.ukvines.co.uk/mercia/index.htm
Chairman: David Millington

South East Vineyards Association
Plumpton College, Ditchling Road, Lewes, East Sussex BN7 3AE
Tel: 01273 890454   E-mail: chris.foss@plumpton.ac.uk
Website: http://seva.uk.com/moodle
Chairman: Chris Foss

South West Vineyards Association
Vine and Wine Ltd, 1 Putley Green, Putley, Ledbury, Herefordshire HR8 2QN
Tel: 01531 660668   E-mail: simon@vineandwine.co.uk
Website: www.swva.info
Chairman: Simon Day

Thames and Chilterns Vineyards Associations
Brightwell Vineyard, Rush Court, Wallingford, Oxfordshire OX10 8LJ
Tel: 01491 836586   E-mail: wines@brightvines.freeserve.co.uk
Website: www.thameschilternsvineyards.org.uk
Chairman: Bob Nielsen

Wessex Vineyards Association
Furleigh Estate, Salway Ash, Bridport, Dorset DT6 5JF
Tel: 01308 488991   E-mail: iemail@btinternet.com
Chairman: Ian Edwards

Larger Growers and Producers Group
c/o English Wine Producers
Chairman: Mike Roberts, RidgeView

Vine suppliers

Stephen Skelton MW
1B Lettice Street, London SW6 4EH
Tel: 07768 583700   E-mail: spskelton@btinternet.com
Website: www.englishwine.com

Three Choirs Vineyards Ltd
Newent, Gloucestershire GL18 1LS
Tel: 01531 890555   E-mail: kevin@threechoirs.com
Contact: Kevin Shayle

Vigo Ltd
Dunkeswell, Honiton, Devon EX14 4LF
Tel: 01404 892100   E-mail: sales@vigoltd.com
Website: www.vigoltd.com

The Vine House
Farfield Farm, Westow, York, North Yorkshire YO60 7LS
Tel: 01653 658507   E-mail: stuart@thevinehouse.fsnet.co.uk
Website: www.thevinehouse.co.uk   Contact: Stuart Smith

Vine & Wine Ltd
1 Putley Green, Putley, Ledbury, Herefordshire HR8 2QN
Tel: 01531 660668   E-mail: simon@vineandwine.co.uk
Website: www.vineandwine.co.uk
Contact: Simon Day

Late July, the House of Lords Terrace
UKVA Annual tasting and prize giving

Bibliography

Barron, A. F. *Vines and Vine Culture,* published by the *Journal of Horticulture*, London, 1883, 1812.

Barry, Sir Edward, *Observations on the Wines of the Ancients*, T. Caddel, London, 1775.

Barty-King, Hugh, *A Tradition of English Wine*, Oxford Illustrated Press, 1977. *A Taste of English Wine*, London, Pelham Books/Stephen Greene Press, 1989.

Basserman-Jordan Dr von, *Belgian Vineyards*, London, The Wine and Food Society, No.86, 1955.

Brock, Raymond Barrington, *Report No.1 – Outdoor Grapes in Cold Climates*, Oxted, Surrey, The Viticultural Research Station, 1949. *Report No.2 – More Outdoor Grapes* 1950. *Some Aspects of Viticulture in Southern England*, 1951. Ph.D thesis. *Report No.3 – Progress with Vines and Wines*, 1961. *Report No.4 – Starting a Vineyard*, 1964.

Bush, Raymond, *Fruit Growing Outdoors*, London, Faber and Faber, 1935, 1942, 1946.

Castella, François de, *Handbook on Viticulture for Victoria*, Melbourne, Royal Commission on Vegetable Products, Board of Viticulture, 1891.

Coombe, B. G., and Dry, P. R., (eds), *Viticulture Volume 1, Resources*, Adelaide, Winetitles, 1992 and 2nd edition, 2005. *Viticulture, Volume 2, Practices.* 1995.

Crowden, James, *Ciderland*, Edinburgh, Birlinn Ltd, 2008

D.S. *Vinteum Angliae: Or a New and Easy Way to make Wine of English Grapes,* London, G. Conyers at the Gold Ring in Little Britain, ca 1690.

English Vineyards Association Ltd, newsletters, journals and the *Grape Press*, London, EVA Ltd, 1967–1996.

Fielden, Christopher, *Is this the Wine you Ordered Sir?*, London, Christopher Helm, 1989.

Gabler, James M., *Wine into Words – a History and Bibliography of Wine Books in the English Language*, Baltimore, Bacchus Press, 1985, 2004.

Galet, Pierre, *A Practical Ampelography – Grapevine Indentification*, translated by Lucie T. Morton, London, Cornell University Press, 1979.

Gore-Browne, Margaret, *Let's Plant a Vineyard*, London, Mills and Boon, 1967.

Hamner, Sir Thomas, *The Garden Book of Sir Thomas Hamner 1659*, reprinted by Gerald Howe Ltd, London, 1933.

Hooke, Dr Della, 'A Note on the Evidence of Vineyards and Orchards in Anglo-Saxon England', *The Journal of Wine Research*, Vol. 1, No.1, London, The Institute of Masters of Wine, 1990, pp. 77–80.

Hughes, W., *The Compleat* [sic] *Vineyard*, London, Will Crook, 1670.

Hyams, Edward, *The Grape Vine in England*, London, John Lane, The Bodley Head, 1949 *From the Waste Land*, London, Turnstile Press, 1950. *Grapes Under Cloches*, London, Faber and Faber, 1952.

Vineyards in England (ed.), London, Faber and Faber, 1953.

The Speaking Garden, London, Longmans Green and Co, 1957.

Vin – The Wine Country of France, London, George Newnes Ltd, 1959.

Dionysus – A Soacial History of the Wine Vine, London, Thames and Hudson, 1965.

An Englishman's Garden, London, Thames and Hudson, 1967.

Jackson, David, *Monographs in Cool Climate Viticulure – No.1. Pruning and Training*, Christchurch, New Zealand, Lincoln University Press, 1997.

Monographs in Cool Climate Viticulure – No.2. Climate Wellington, New Zealand, Daphne Brazell Associates Ltd with Gypsum Press, 2001.

Jackson, David, Schuster, Danny and Skelton, Stephen, *The Production of Grapes and Wine in Cool Climates*, UK edition, Christchurch, New Zealand, Gypsum Press, 1994.

Lee, Roland, *Growing Grapes in the Open*, Birkenhead, Roland Lee Vineyards, 1939.

Lott, Heinz and Pfaff, Franz, *Taschenbuch der Rebsorten*, 13th edition, Mainz, Germany, Fachverlag Dr Fraund GmbH, 2003.

Louden J. C., *Encyclopaedia of Gardening*, London, 1834.

Lytle, S. E., *Vines Under Glass and in the Open*, Liverpool, Horticultural Utilities Ltd, ca 1951.

Successful Growing of Grape Vines, ca 1954.

Martin, Claude, *David Geneste – a Huguenot Vine Grower at Cobham*, Guildford, Surrey, The Surrey Archaeological Society, Collections Volume LXVIII, 1971.

Ministry of Agriculture, Fisheries and Food, *Soils and Manures for Fruit,* London, Ministry of Agriculture, Fisheries and Food 1975.

Outdoor Grape Production, 1978.

Grapes for Wine, 1980.

Morton, Lucie T., *Winegrowing in Eastern America*, New York and London, Cornell University Press, 1985.

Ordish, George, *Wine Growing in England*, London, Rupert Hart-Davis, 1953.

The Great Wine Blight, London, J. M. Dent and Sons Ltd, 1972, 1986.

Vineyards in England and Wales, London, Faber and Faber, 1977.

Pearkes, Gillian, *Vinegrowing in Britain,* London, J. M. Dent and Sons Ltd, 1982, 1989.

Robinson, Jancis, *Vines, Grapes and Wine*, London, Mitchell Beazley, 1986.

Oxford Companion to Wine (ed.), Oxford University Press, 1994, 1999, 2006.

Rook, Alan, *The Diary of an English Vineyard*, London, Wine and Spirit Publications Ltd, 1971.

Rose, John, *The English Vineyard Vindicated*, London, B. Teuke, 1672.

Royal Horticultural Society, *Journals,* Wisley, Surrey, Royal Horticultural Society, 1898, 1985.

Salisbury-Jones, Sir Guy, *The Compleat Imbiber No.2*, (Ray, Cyril, ed.). 'Hampshire Vigneron', London, Putnam Ltd, 1958, pp. 89–95.

Salway, Peter. *Roman Britain,* The Oxford History of England, Oxford University Press, Oxford, 1991.

Selley, Richard C., *The Winelands of Britain: Past Present and Prospective*, Dorking, Surrey, Petravin, 2004.

Seward, Desmond, *Monks and Wine*, London, Mitchell Beazley, 1979.

Simon, André J., *Bibliotheca Vinaria*, London, The Holland Press Ltd, 1979.

The History of Champagne, London, Ebury Press, 1962.

'S. J.' – A Gentleman in his Travels, *The Vineyard*, London, W. Mears, 1727.

Skelton, Stephen P., *The Vineyards of England*, Ashford, Kent, S. P. and L. Skelton, 1989.

The Wines of Britain and Ireland, London, Faber and Faber, 2001.

Smart, Richard and Robinson, Mike, *Sunlight into Wine – A Handbook for Winegrape Canaopy Management*, Adelaide, Winetitles, 1991.

Smith, Joanna, *The New English Vineyard*, London, Sidgwick & Jackson, 1979.

Sneesby, Norman, *A Vineyard in England*, London, Robert Hale Ltd, 1977.

Speechley, William, *A Treatise on the Culture of the Vine*, 1790.

Tod, H. M., *Vine-Growing in England*, London, Chatto & Windus, 1911.

Tritton, S. M., *Grape Growing and Wine Making*, Almondsbury, Gloucestershire, Grey Owl Research Laboratories, ca 1955.

Turner, Ben and Roycroft, Roy, *The Winemaker's Encyclopedia*, London, Faber and Faber, 1980.

United Kingdom Vineyards Association Ltd, newsletters, journals and the *Grape Press*, London, UKVA Ltd, 1996–2008.

Unwin, Dr Tim, 'Saxon and Early Norman Viticulture in England', *The Journal of Wine Research*, Vol. 1, No.1, London, The Institute of Masters of Wine, 1990, pp. 61–75.

Wine and the Vine – An Historical Geography of Viticulture and the Wine Trade, London, Routledge, 1991.

Ward H. W., *The Book of the Grape*, London, John Lane, The Bodley Head, 1901.

Ward, Jack, *The Complete book of Vine Growing in the British Isles*, London, Faber and Faber, 1984.

Webster, D. and H., Petch, D.F. *A possible Vineyard of the Romano-British period at North Thoresby, Lincolnshire.* Lincolnshire History and Archaeology No.2, 1967.

Williams, G., *A Consideration of the Sub-Fossil Remains of Vitis vinifera L. as Evidence for Viticulture in Roman Britain*, Britannia Vol 8, pp. 327–34, 1977.

Wright, Graeme, *Merrydown, Forty Vintage Years*, Horam, East Sussex, Merrydown Wine Company plc, 1988.

Wrotham Historical Society, *Farming in Wrotham Through the Ages – The Wrotham Grape*, Wrotham Historical Society, 2004, pp. 56–8.

The author – biographical details

Stephen Skelton beside some 100-year-old vines in the Barossa Valley

Stephen Skelton has been involved with growing vines and making wine since 1975. He spent two years in Germany, working at Schloss Schönborn in the Rheingau and studying at Geisenheim, the world-renowned college of winegrowing and wine-making, with the late Professor Helmut Becker. In 1977 he returned to the UK to establish the vineyards at Tenterden in Kent (now the home of the UK's largest wine producer, Chapel Down Wines), and made wine there for 22 consecutive vintages. From 1988 to 1991 he was also winemaker and general manager at Lamberhurst Vineyards, at that time the largest winery in the UK. He now works as a consultant to vineyards and wineries in the UK and is currently setting up vineyards for the production of sparkling wine.

In 1986 Stephen started writing and lecturing about wine and has contributed articles to many different publications. In 1989 he wrote (and published) his first book, *The Vineyards of England* and in 2001 his second, *The Wines of Britain and Ireland* (Faber and Faber) which won the André Simon Award for Drinks Book of the Year. He is the English and Welsh vineyards contributor for the annual wine guides written by Hugh Johnson, Oz Clarke and Tom Stevenson and wrote the section on English and Welsh wine in the 3rd edition of Jancis Robinson's *Oxford Companion to Wine*. He has also written *"Viticulture – A guide to commercial grape growing for wine production"* (see below) which is aimed at MW and Diploma students.

Stephen was a director of the English Vineyards Association (EVA) from 1982–1995 and of its successor organisation, the United Kingdom Vineyards Association

(UKVA) from 1995–2003. He was Chairman of the UKVA from 1999–2003. He was also at various times between 1982 and 1986 Treasurer, Secretary and Chairman of the South East Vineyards Association, Secretary of the Circle of Wine Writers between 1990 and 1997 and has served on various EU committees in Brussels representing UK winegrowers. In 1999 he took three years off from the wine business to do a BSc in Multimedia Technology and Design at Brunel University. While at Brunel, Stephen was awarded the Ede and Ravenscroft Prize.

In 2003 Stephen became a Master of Wine, winning the prestigious Robert Mondavi Trophy for gaining the highest marks in the Theory section of the examination. He was a member of the MW Education Committee from 2003-6 and was course wine co-ordinator. In 2005 he won the AXA Millésimes Communicator of the Year Award for services to the MW education programme. In 2009 he was elected to the Council of the Institute of Masters of Wine.

Stephen now runs tastings and tutors MW candidates in the intricacies of passing the notoriously difficult tasting examination. He has also judged or still judges on: the Decanter World Wine Awards, the International Wine Challenge, the International Wine and Spirit Competition, the Japan Wine Challenge and the Veritas Wine Awards.

Viticulture – An introduction to commercial grape growing for wine production
Available from: www.lulu.com Reference: 688007

Index

Grape varieties are listed in bold type (eg **Acolon**). Page references in **bold** identify the location of main entries in the 'Vine variety descriptions A-Z' and the 'Vineyards A-Z' sections. Page references in *italics* refer to illustrations. Information in footnotes is indicated by 'n' (eg 148n).

Wessex
  Vineyards Association
Regional Wine Scheme, x, 101–5, 122–
3, 149, 451
  see also Protected Geographical
Indication
Regner, 43, 132, 134, 137, 138, 139,
145, 147, 148, 154, **178**
Regner, Ferdinand, 166
Reichensteiner, 70, 85, 86, 122n, 123–
4, 127, 129, 139, 154, 165, **178–9**, 185
  area planted, 76, 133, 134, 137,
138, 144, 145, 178, 179
  as permitted variety, 130, 146–7,
148
  yields, 134, 150, 178–9
Reine Olga, 34
Renishaw Hall Vineyard, Derbyshire,
71, 191, **368–9**
residual sugar levels, 46, 50, 71, 86,
118, 119, 123–4, 240
retailers, x, 76, 77, 78, 81, 144, 244,
320
  see also supermarkets; wine
merchants
Retsina, 11
Rheingau, 56, 114, 240
Rheinpfalz *see* Pfalz
Rhenish-wine, 17, 126
RHS *see* Royal Horticultural Society
Rhyll Manor, Somerset, 432
Riddiford, Richard, 267n
Ridge Farm, Kent, 311, 315
RidgeView Wine Estate, East Sussex,
369–72, 444
  planting of, 116, 143, 369
  'RidgeView effect', 143
  size, vii, x, 190, 192, 200
  sparkling wines, ix, 79–80, 85,
122, 140, 158, 370–71
  trophies and awards, 79–80, 370,

454, 455, 457, 458, 460, 461, 462, 465
  vineyards under contract, 80, 200,
370
  wine styles, 158, 370–71
  winery, 119, 238, 286, 294, 369–
70, 402, 430
Riesling, 36, 39, 62, 64, 89, 134, 137,
138, 139, 148, 154, 163, 165n, 166,
167, 170
Riesling Sylvaner *see* **Müller-
Thurgau**
Riley, Penny and Steve, 400
Rivaner *see* **Müller-Thurgau**
River Walk Vineyard, Nottinghamshire,
195, 200, **372**
Robert Fleming Wines, Essex, 80, 192,
200, 339, **372**
Roberts, Christine, 369
Roberts, Mardi, 370
Roberts, Michael, 369, 370–71, 401,
430, 457, 467
Roberts, Simon, 370, 371, 430
Roberts, Tamara, 370
Roberts, W.H., *British Wine-Maker and
Domestic Brewer*, 439
Robinson, Jancis, 109, 234, 240, 321,
361
Robinson, Mike, 114
Robson, Liz and Matthew, 309
Rock Lodge Vineyard, West Sussex,
71, 85, 197, 200, 242, 362, **372**, 462
Rock Moors Vineyard, Devon, 191,
372–3
Roland's Muscatel, 34
Roman Villa Vineyard, West Sussex,
197, **373**
Romans, 1–7, 11, 125, 238, 340, 446
Rondo, 45, 82, 98, 121, 123, 141–2,
148, 154, 169n, 177, **179–80**, 303, 404
  area planted, 137, 138, 140, 141,
142, 144, 145, 179, 180